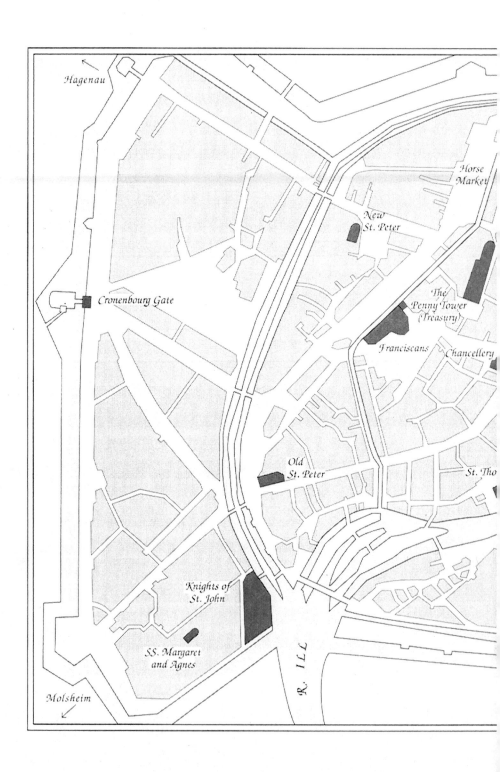

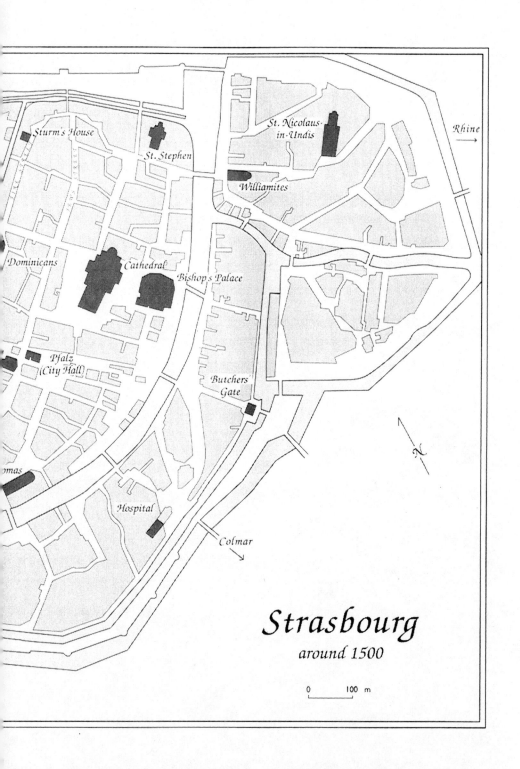

Sturm's House

St. Stephen

St. Nicolaus-in-Undis

Williamites

Rhine

Dominicans

Cathedral

Bishop's Palace

Pfalz
(City Hall)

Butchers
Gate

...mas

Hospital

Colmar

N

Strasbourg

around 1500

0   100 m

Protestant Politics:
Jacob Sturm (1489–1553)
and the German Reformation

STUDIES IN GERMAN HISTORIES

Series Editors: Roger Chickering and Thomas A. Brady, Jr.

PUBLISHED

Communal Reformation
Peter Blickle

Protestant Politics:
Jacob Sturm (1489–1553)
and the German Reformation
Thomas A. Brady, Jr.

Karl Lamprecht
A German Academic Life (1856–1915)
Roger Chickering

German Encounters with Modernity
Katherine Roper

Communities and Conflict in
Early Modern Colmar: 1575–1730
Peter G. Wallace

Protestant Politics: Jacob Sturm (1489–1553) and the German Reformation

Thomas A. Brady, Jr.

HUMANITIES PRESS
NEW JERSEY

First published 1995 by Humanities Press International, Inc.,
Atlantic Highlands, New Jersey 07716.

© Thomas A. Brady, Jr., 1995

Library of Congress Cataloging-in-Publication Data
Brady, Thomas A.
    Protestant politics : Jacob Sturm (1489–1553) and the German
Reformation / by Thomas A. Brady, Jr.
        p.   cm. — (Studies in German histories)
    Includes bibliographical references (p.   ) and indexes.
    ISBN 0-391-03823-0
    1. Sturm, Jacob, 1489–1553. 2. Reformation—France—Strasbourg—
Biography. 3. Reformation—Germany. 4. Germany—Church
history—16th century. 5. Strasbourg (France)—Biography.
6. Strasbourg (France)—Church history. I. Title. II. Series.
BR350.S78B73 1993
944'.38353028'092—dc20
[B]   93–3015
                                                                      CIP

A catalog record for this book is available from the British Library.

Printed in the United States of America

This book is dedicated to teachers:

Miriam Usher Chrisman
François-Joseph Fuchs
† John Patrick Dolan
† Eric Cochrane
† Hans Baron
Jean Rott

Contents

List of Illustrations

Maps

Illustrations

Tables

Note on Money

Most sums of money are given in Rheingulden or Rhenish florins, abbreviated "fl." First minted in 1348, this gold coin was the chief monetary standard for South Germany. Its relationship to the local money of account, the Strasbourg pound, fluctuated around 11 shillings, so that conventionally a pound was worth a half-florin. The value of the florin may be suggested by the fact that 15 fl. per year was considered the absolute minimum for survival for one person. A master artisan who worked for wages received about 45–50 fl. per year. 200 fl. was considered quite a lot of money; 500 made one well off; and 5,000 fl. made one the equivalent of a modern millionaire.

FIGURE 1 Jacob Sturm (1489–1553), stettmeister of Strasbourg, age 56.
Woodcut by Bernhard Jobin from a (lost) oil portrait by Hans Baldung Grien.

Preface

A quarter of a century has passed since Jacob Sturm eased his way into my life by way of a compromise, a path he would have heartily appreciated. My undergraduate teachers, especially John Patrick Dolan, had awakened in me a strong taste for philosophy and for German history, especially of the medieval and Reformation eras. My graduate teachers, however, were mostly Italianists, and because I was determined to be just as stubborn as Eric Cochrane was, I resisted his pressure to devote myself to Italian history, just then becoming one of American historiography's glories. It was the late Hans Baron who eased my dilemma, torn between two loves, with a suggestion that I could unite my interests in cities and in the German Reformation through a study of Jacob Sturm of Strasbourg. I began with no formal study of German history in general or Reformation history in particular.

Having chosen Strasbourg in the Reformation era, I plunged into the history of politics, which, I knew from my populist upbringing, was about public values, public actions, and the confrontation between private interests and the common good. The times, too—it was the latter half of the 1960s—opened my eyes to many aspects of the political and social world about which my formal education had been silent. And when I submitted my dissertation on Jacob Sturm's political career down to 1532, I knew that I had made little more than a beginning.

The odyssey I then began has taken me through two earlier volumes to my goal in this one. What was I searching for? At first, for the *context* of political action, those forces and facts that set the conditions of, though, as Marx truly said, they do not determine, human action in history. This led me to study the *local* social and political context, including the social places of Sturm and his fellow magistrates, in *Ruling Class, Regime, and Reformation at Strasbourg, 1520–1550*. Next, I turned to the regional level to examine the South German cities, their political culture, and their political options before and during the age of the Reformation. Out of this came a second volume, *Turning Swiss: Cities and Empire, 1450–1550*, in which I tried to map the cities' social and political affinities with the Swiss and to chart their turn away from the Confederacy and toward the Empire. There remained the need to escalate the story to the Imperial level, while retaining the integrity of the other, smaller stories in the larger narrative.

Contrary to my early expectations, my main task was not to challenge Leopold von Ranke's once canonical picture, which had been based on the identity of confessional and national destinies. That story lay in ruins since 1945, probably since 1918, but nothing had taken its place. The subject required a new kind of story, which would take into account both the modern view of the Reformation as a social movement and the modern understanding of the Holy Roman Empire as a vast, multilayered, and variegated structure with a head but no center.

What held the entire project together was the strand of biography, Jacob Sturm's biography, around which could be braided the stories of the conjuncture of Imperial structure and Reformation movement. I hope that the haunting resonance between the grand story and the small one is the work of history rather than of art alone. For the two stories display a common rhythm, moving from languid fragmentation to a quickened pace and greater integration toward crisis and slump back into the earlier pattern and tempo. Except that the defeat of Protestant politics' defeat on the Imperial level corresponds to Sturm's greatest political triumph on the local one. Protestant politics was an Imperial failure, but a local success.

This project was feasible only because the political correspondence of Strasbourg, including almost all of Jacob Sturm's surviving papers, is so accessible. It forms—after the acts of the Imperial Diets—the second largest mass of printed sources for the political history of the German Reformation. Six huge volumes of the *Politische Correspondenz der Stadt Straßburg im Zeitalter der Reformation*, which appeared between 1883 and 1933, contain texts, summaries, and citations of many thousands of documents. The early volumes were fairly heavily used in the years before 1914, but volumes 4 and 5, which appeared after 1918, have never been properly exploited by historians of the German Reformation. Not only are they much fuller than the earlier volumes, the consequence of both denser surviving documentation and more generous (and abler) editing, they also illuminate the German Reformation's second great crisis in the years 1545–52.

Rarely does this mass of documentation allow a peek behind the mask of Sturm's public persona into his private thoughts or his familiar surroundings. If the sources for these aspects of his life ever existed, they disappeared in the tragic losses suffered by Strasbourg's libraries and archives during the eighteenth and nineteenth centuries. The degree to which Sturm's private self remains in shadow is best suggested, I think, by the fact that I could not even discover his wife's Christian name. This book is not, therefore, and could never have become, a "biography" in the sense this term is understood today. Every utterance by Sturm about religion, for example, is touched or tinged by the logic of policy, by his role as a magistrate and a public man.

This book, to anticipate some criticism, is not about religion as such, except as religion touched, as it constantly did, all aspects of social life, including politics. I have taken my chief cue from the great fourteenth-century Muslim philosopher, Ibn Khaldûn, who wrote: "Only by God's help in establishing His religion do individual desires come together in agreement to press their claims, and hearts become united." This uniting of hearts—Sturm himself called it "the proper sort of love for one another"—is central to my study of Protestant politics.

One further point needs to be made. The German Reformation continues to fascinate historians, not least because at this moment the common people broke through history's recorded surface on a scale and with an effect unprecedented in European history. The movement that culminated in the great Peasants' War of 1525 became the benchmark of the symbiosis of religion and politics for the entire Reformation generation. In this great upheaval, which framed the beginnings of Jacob Sturm's political career, the common people came onto the stage of Imperial history, where they remained, often silent but always present.

Some peculiarities of usage in this book need to be explained. I have treated personal names as seemed best, giving the rulers English forms and leaving most of the others alone. I call the other Sturm "Jean," rather than "Johann" or "Johannes," because he was one of the most highly Gallicized Germans of his day, but more particularly because from that day to this he has been confused with his (unrelated) patron, the subject of this book. As for place names, I have used English forms where they are truly standard and unconfusing, such as *Brunswick* for *Braunschweig* and *Hanover* for *Hannover*, but not where they are peculiar to British English, such as *Bale* or *Basle* for *Basel*. I have avoided some anglicized Gallicisms, such as *Mayence* for *Mainz* and *Ratisbon* for *Regensburg*, and accepted others, such as *Munich* for *München*. My rule of thumb has been to choose the form that sounds best to me, so long as the choice introduces no confusion. I have also tried to avoid studding the text with untranslated terms by rendering as many of them as possible into English, such as Imperial Governing Council (*Reichsregiment*), Imperial Chamber Court (*Reichskammergericht*), Imperial Diet (*Reichstag*), and Senate & XXI (*Rat und XXI*). Sometimes, as with Ammeister, Stettmeister, and Reichsmoderationstag, I simply gave up. One other usage may seem somewhat odd. I have tried to use for Germany's Protestants the name they used for themselves, *Evangelicals*, and to reserve *Protestant* for the rulers and urban regimes that adhered to this cause, a practice that also follows their usage. All Protestants were Evangelicals, but not all Evangelicals were Protestants.

My use of capitalization, too, needs some explanation. I capitalize *Empire* and *Imperial* when they refer to the Holy Roman Empire, and *Reformation* when it refers to the whole Protestant Reformation as a single process, but not when it refers to reformations in particular places.

If some readers find the geography of this study more detailed than they might wish, I ask their indulgence. Social and political geography lie at the conceptual heart of this book, and the distinctions among provinces—Alsace, Swabia, Bavaria—and regions, south and north, are vital to the understanding of Imperial politics it tries to convey. This emphasis on locality and concreteness reflects my understanding of the political structures of the Holy Roman Empire, in which locality, province, and region claimed weights that had no exact counterparts in the more highly centralized kingdoms of Europe's western tier. This local, provincial, and regional weighed-downness reflected the particularism of life in the Empire, which may be illustrated by the fact that a middling German free city, such as Colmar or Reutlingen, had more self-governance and more of the apparatus of sovereignty than contemporary London or Paris. There were also pockets of free peasants in South Germany who were "freer," in the sense of having more extensive rights of self-government, than all but the greatest nobles of England or France. At this great distance we may forgive our predecessors, who oversimplified the Empire in their desire to yoke its history to national tasks and a national future, but we must not repeat their mistakes.

Every writer incurs debts, but "debts" cannot be the proper term for obligations that can never be discharged. This book is dedicated to six persons who helped to put, or keep, me on the path that led to its completion. There are three teachers, all dead now: John Patrick Dolan, Eric W. Cochrane, and Hans Baron. There are the two Alsatians who initiated me, as one of a whole generation of North American novices, into the mysteries of archival research: François-Joseph Fuchs and Jean Rott. The sixth person is my mentor and dear friend, Miriam Usher Chrisman, who has suffered Jacob Sturm longer than I have, and whose immortal words, that Jacob Sturm looked like "a bourgeois Henry VIII," have often lightened my spirits. She and James J. Sheehan, to whom also my thanks, read the entire manuscript. My thanks go, too, to the many librarians and archivists who supported my work with materials, advice, and patience. Chief among these are the directors—Philippe Dollinger, François-Joseph Fuchs, and Jean-Yves Mariotte—and staff of the Archives Municipales de Strasbourg for countless acts of help and kindness over the past quarter of a century. After them come their colleagues in the Stadtarchiv Augsburg, the Staatsarchiv Basel, The Newberry Library at Chicago, the Stadtarchiv Konstanz, the Royal Danish Library at Copenhagen, the Hessisches Staatsarchiv Darmstadt, the Niedersächsische Staats- und Universitätsbibliothek at Göttingen, the Generallandesarchiv at Karlsruhe, the Stadtarchiv Lindau, the Württembergisches Staatsarchiv Ludwigsburg, the Hessisches Staatsarchiv Marburg, the Bibliothèque de la Société de l'Histoire du Protestantisme Français at Paris, the Archives Départementales du Bas-Rhin at Strasbourg, the Bibliothèque Universitaire et Nationale at Strasbourg, the Bibliothèque Municipale at Strasbourg, the Hauptstaatsarchiv Stuttgart, the University Library at Uppsala, the Staatsarchiv Weimar, and the Herzog August-Bibliothek at Wolfenbüttel.

I owe a special kind of debt to the students, staff, faculty, and other friends at the University of Oregon in Eugene, where I taught for twenty-three years, and where many parts of this book first saw the light. Their cooperation and respect, which I shall never forget, have eased my passage into a new setting at Berkeley.

My last word is to Kathy, to whom I owe most.

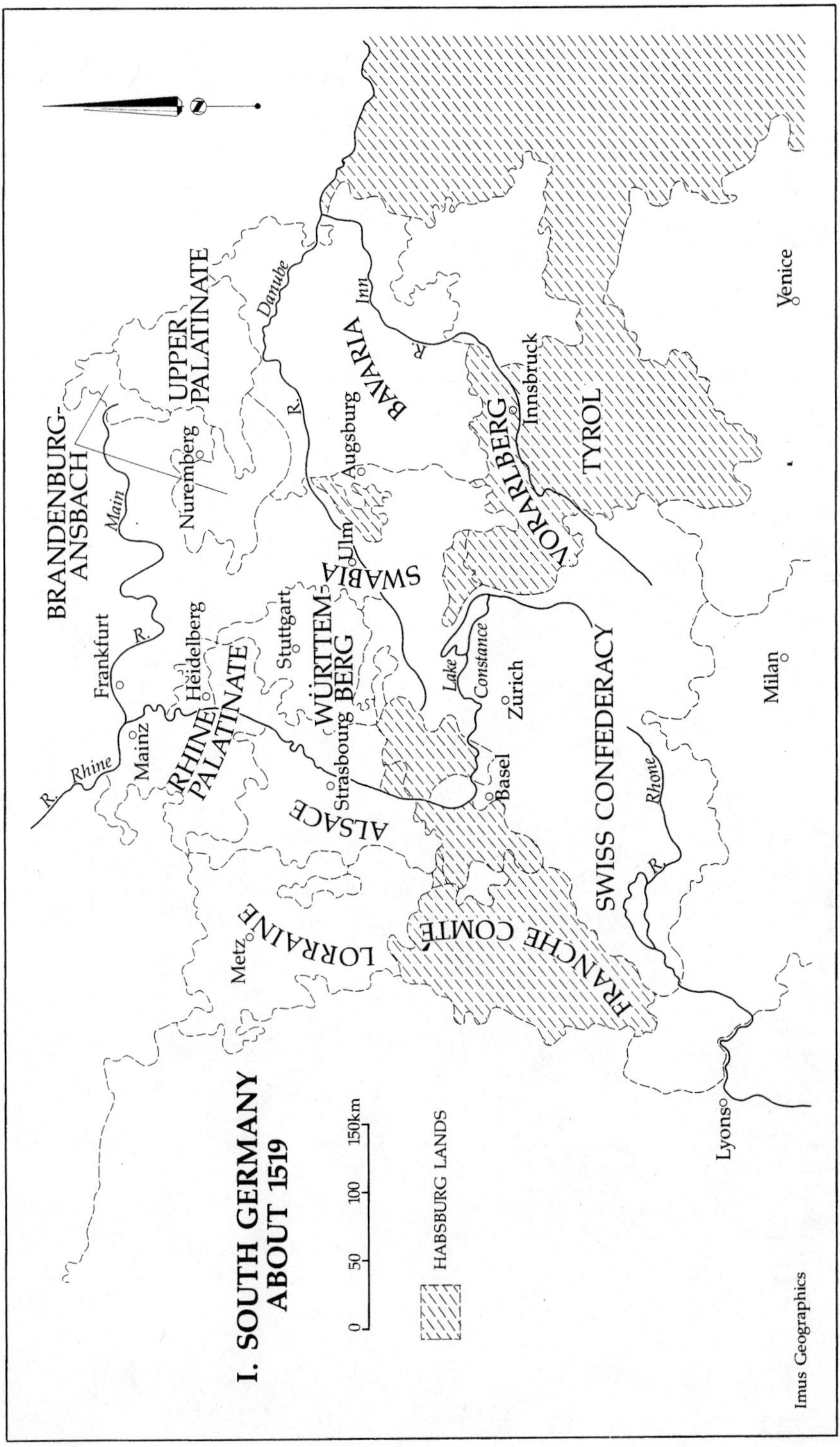

I. SOUTH GERMANY ABOUT 1519

HABSBURG LANDS

0   50   100   150km

BRANDENBURG-
ANSBACH

UPPER PALATINATE

Nuremberg

Main R.

Frankfurt

Rhine R.

Mainz

Heidelberg

RHINE PALATINATE

Stuttgart

WÜRTTEM-
BERG

Strasbourg

ALSACE

SWABIA

Ulm

Augsburg

Danube R.

BAVARIA

Inn R.

VORARLBERG

Lake Constance

Zürich

Basel

Innsbruck

TYROL

SWISS CONFEDERACY

Rhone R.

Milan

Venice

LORRAINE

Metz

FRANCHE COMTÉ

Lyons

Imus Geographics

MAP 1

xvii

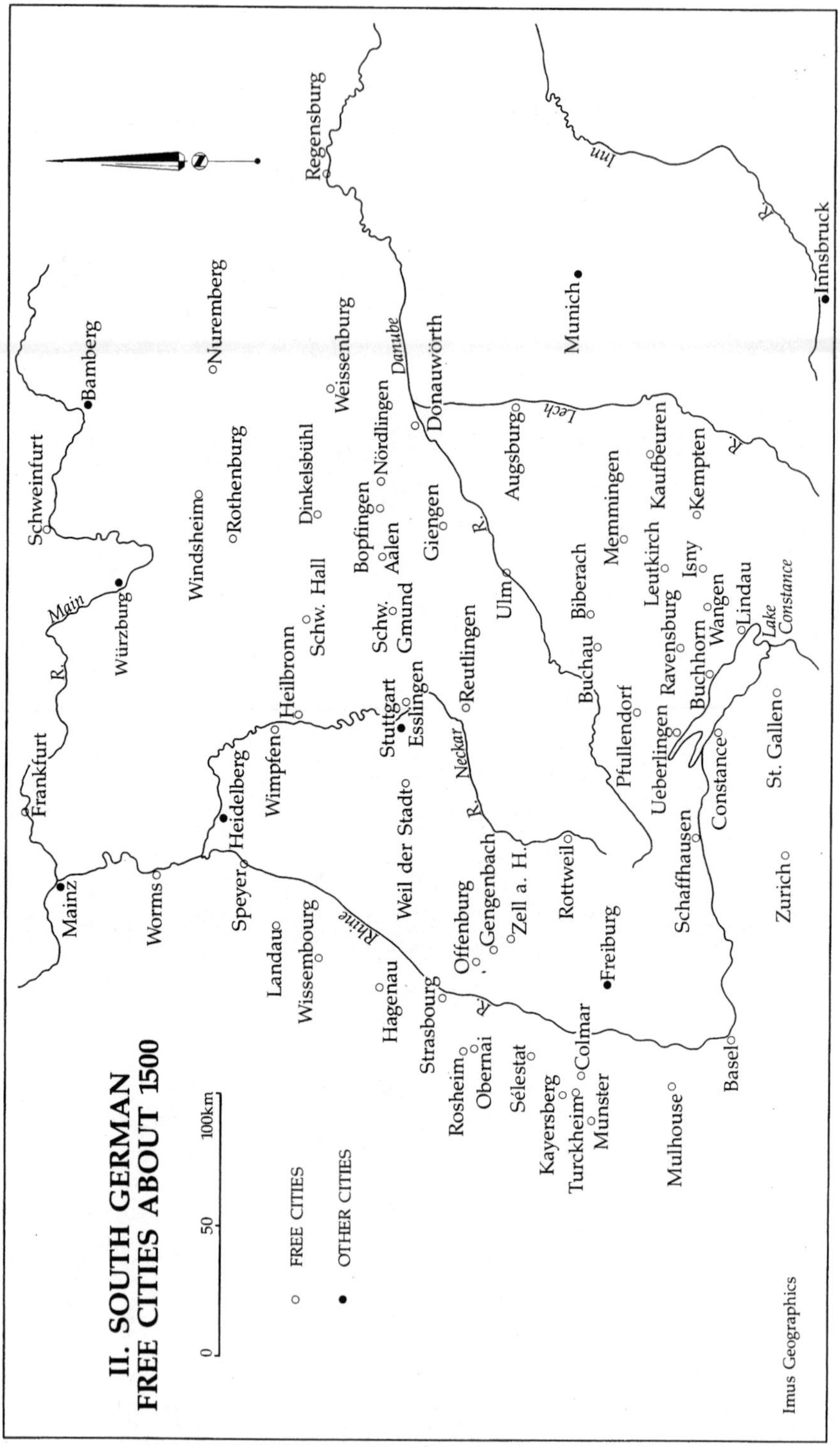

II. SOUTH GERMAN
FREE CITIES ABOUT 1500

○ FREE CITIES

● OTHER CITIES

0   50   100km

Frankfurt

●Mainz

Main R.

●Würzburg

Schweinfurt

●Bamberg

Windsheim

○Rothenburg

Nuremberg

Regensburg

Weissenburg

Danube

Dinkelsbühl

○Nördlingen

Donauwörth

Munich●

Inn

●Innsbruck

Worms

Speyer○

Heidelberg●

Wimpfen○

Heilbronn○

Schw. Hall

Bopfingen○

Aalen○

Schw.
Gmund

Giengen○

Augsburg○

Lech

Landau○

Wissembourg○

Hagenau○

Strasbourg○

Stuttgart
Esslingen●

Weil der Stadt○

Neckar R.

Reutlingen○

Ulm○

Buchau○

Pfullendorf○

Biberach○

Memmingen○

Leutkirch Kaufbeuren○

Isny○

Kempten○

Lindau○

Lake
Constance

Roshein○
Oberai○

Sélestat○

Kayersberg

Turckheim○ Colmar○

Münster○

Mulhouse○

Offenburg○
Gengenbach○
Zell a. H.○

Rottweil○

●Freiburg

Schaffhausen○

Ueberlingen○
Ravensburg○

Buchhorn○
Wangen○

Constance○

St. Gallen○

Zurich○

Basel○

Rhine

MAP 2

Imus Geographics

xviii

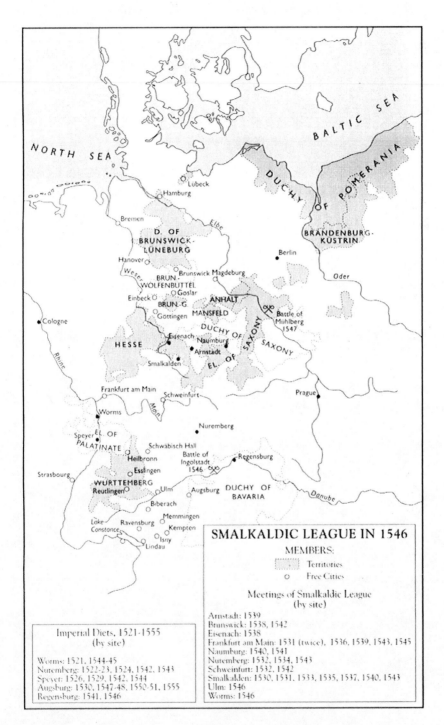

NORTH SEA

BALTIC SEA

DUCHY OF POMERANIA

Lübeck

Hamburg

Bremen

Elbe

BRANDENBURG-KÜSTRIN

D. OF BRUNSWICK-LÜNEBURG

Hanover

Weser

Brunswick   Magdeburg   Berlin

BRUN-WOLFENBÜTTEL

Goslar   Oder

Einbeck

BRUN-G.   ANHALT

Gottingen   MANSFELD

DUCHY OF SAXONY   Battle of Mühlberg 1547

Cologne   SAXONY

HESSE   Eisenach   Naumburg

Arnstadt   EL. OF SAXONY

Smalkalden

Rhine   Frankfurt am Main   Schweinfurt   Prague

Worms   Main

Nuremberg

Speyer   EL. OF PALATINATE

Schwäbisch Hall

Heilbronn   Battle of Ingolstadt 1546   Regensburg

Strasbourg   Esslingen

WÜRTTEMBERG   Ulm   Augsburg   DUCHY OF BAVARIA   Danube

Reutlingen

Biberach

Lake Constance   Ravensburg   Memmingen   Kempten

Isny

Lindau

SMALKALDIC LEAGUE IN 1546

MEMBERS:

Territories

○   Free Cities

Meetings of Smalkaldic League
(by site)

Arnstadt: 1539
Brunswick: 1538, 1542
Eisenach: 1538
Frankfurt am Main: 1531 (twice), 1536, 1539, 1543, 1545
Naumburg: 1540, 1541
Nuremberg: 1532, 1534, 1543
Schweinfurt: 1532, 1542
Smalkalden: 1530, 1531, 1533, 1535, 1537, 1540, 1543
Ulm: 1546
Worms: 1546

Imperial Diets, 1521-1555
(by site)

Worms: 1521, 1544-45
Nuremberg: 1522-23, 1524, 1542, 1543
Speyer: 1526, 1529, 1542, 1544
Augsburg: 1530, 1547-48, 1550-51, 1555
Regensburg: 1541, 1546

MAP 3

Part I

1

The German Reformation
as Political Event

The recent political fortunes of Central Europe's peoples encourage a re-thinking of their pasts. Political identity is largely composed of historical memory, and the Central Europeans, like other peoples, map their pasts by means of meaning-laden events. For the German-speaking peoples, one of the most controversial of such landmark events has been the Protestant Reformation, which occupied "a position analogous in some ways to that of the Civil War in American historiography, as the crucial and (in a quite literal sense of the term) epoch-making event by which the nature of an entire national community and of its history has been defined."[1] For nearly a century, the Reformation held a privileged position—at least for German-speaking Protestants—as the birth hour of the German nation. The mid- and later twentieth century has dealt nearly as cruelly with this conviction as the early part of the century did with its political embodiment, the Second Empire, and the large narratives of German history written in recent decades claim a much shorter genealogy, generally beginning in the eighteenth century, for modern Germany. They, too, have been cruelly served, for the tumultuous events of 1989–90 have unhinged these refabricated, modernized narratives by casting doubt on any thesis about continuity and identity in German histories.[2] The present moment, therefore, when all accounts of the Central European past are fraught with uncertainty, seems a good time to think about the place of the German Reformation in the histories of the German-speaking peoples. It is the central task of this book to contribute to this rethinking and to suggest how the German Reformation might be integrated into a narrative of political history. The building blocks for such a task lie at hand, strewn through the rich post-1950 literature, but they require a sense of appropriate temporal and spatial scale. This starting point cannot be grasped without a sense of what happened to the traditional narrative of the Reformation and German history, which was Protestant in sentiment and national in intent.

Simply stated, during the era when the Reformation was a landmark event in German national history, roughly from the early nineteenth to the mid-twentieth century, its place depended on the identification of the German nation with Protestant Christianity. The origins of this idea, which was central to the dominant political culture of the New Germany created in 1871, lay in the resistance to Napoleonic imperialism that gave rise to the German national movement. To many educated Germans of that era, the Reformation had little or nothing to say. Goethe, for example, thought that "the only interesting thing in the whole affair [of the Reformation] is Luther's character . . . All the rest is a confused hodge-podge [*ein verworrener Quark*] that is still our daily burden."[3] To others, however, Luther's reformation supplied the key to a new conception of what it meant to be German. Most important of these, perhaps, was a Prussian theologian, Friedrich Daniel Ernst Schleiermacher, who in 1809, three years after Napoleon crushed Prussia, announced the need to overcome the Germans' religious division, which "arose from Rome alone and was forced upon Luther," through the evangelization of the Catholic Germans. It was well enough, he said, "to allow the continued existence of Catholicism for the Latin peoples," so long as the Protestants strove "with good conscience to spread the reformation among the Germanic peoples as the form of Christianity most properly suited to them."[4]

The man who formed Schleiermacher's idea into a history, at once a picture of the past and a vision of the future, was Leopold von Ranke. Born the son of a Thuringian pastor in 1795, one year after the fall of Robespierre, the young Ranke chose for his first great theme the history of the papacy, which he considered to have been the embodiment of the universalizing force of Christianity and a central power in European history down to the Reformation, though not beyond.[5] This work led him, as he acknowledged, to look at the particularizing counterpoint in European history, the nation, in his *German History in the Age of the Reformation*, which he wrote during the 1840s.[6] Its task was to show "the other aspect of the [historical] process—the way in which individual nations appropriated this universal [Christian] spirit."[7] Although purely religious in origin, he believed, Luther's reformation had addressed the German "nation's need to consolidate itself into a certain unity" by defining itself against Rome in terms of a rejuvenated Christian religion.[8] Ranke, to be sure, did not deny the German Reformation the more universal mission of leading "the Latin-Germanic peoples" in the movement "to restore the purity of the revealed truth."[9] His chief interest, however, attached to its other task, the national regeneration of the Germans, which posed itself quite apart from, perhaps contrary to, Luther's own starting point, which was not "the nation's needs" but "religious convictions, . . . without which he could have accomplished nothing," and the pursuit of which "led him to go further than was necessary or even beneficial to the political struggles."[10] The essence of the German national renaissance between approximately 1480 and 1524/1525 thus lay in the fact that "the spirit of Christianity, deeply rooted in the Germanic character, had gradually matured to a consciousness of its own autonomy, beyond all contingent forms, and had turned back to its origins, to that document which directly transmitted the eternal Godhead's covenant with the human race."[11] Never before, Ranke rhapsodized, "had there been a more favorable prospect for the unity of the nation and its continuation on the chosen way," as there was during the years just after Luther's defiance of his emperor in 1521 at the Diet of Worms.[12]

If Ranke's Reformation began as romance, it ended as tragedy, for no sooner had the conjuncture between the national movement and Luther's reformation been effected than the whole process began to jump the track. By 1524, he thought, the forces of Catholicism began to recover their nerve, and "before any sort of state formation in a Protestant sense was even conceivable, we meet a contrary organization, dedicated to the maintenance of the Catholic principle. For the fate of our fatherland, this organization was to be of the greatest possible importance."[13] In the Catholic resistance to Luther, his reformation, and the national cause lay "the origin of the split, which since those days has never been settled, ever renewed by that same foreign influence which had produced it. It is truly remarkable, that already in those days appeared all the tendencies which later endured for centuries."[14] Indeed, for three hundred years the mysterious survival of German Catholicism, nurtured by an alien Roman system, had blocked the political renovation of the German nation. For Ranke, this conundrum robbed German history in the age of Reformation of its intelligibility and forced his account of it to dribble away into pure narrative.[15]

The essential lesson of Ranke's history nonetheless stood out with the starkest possible clarity: Rome, and Rome alone, bore the responsibility for the three-hundred-year slumber of the German nation, which, by implication, only a liberation from that alien influence could end. In effect, Schleiermacher's message. Ranke's vision was as deeply confessional as it was national. He was not blindly confessional, and in the *History of the Popes* he had risen above a purely confessional view of the papacy, but he also believed that Protestant Christianity represented a higher, more spiritual, though less universal, form of religion.[16] Modern Protestantism he identified with cultural progress and with the national aspirations of all Germans, Catholicism with spiritual superficiality and political alienation. "Apart from any doctrinal preference," he wrote,

> from the purely historical point of view, it seems to me that [the triumph of the Protestant system in all Germany] would have been the best thing for the national development of Germany. . . . The fundamental strivings which now characterized the lives of the German Protestants gave a fulfilling context to the national consciousness.[17]

To be Protestant, in Ranke's eyes, was to be truly and fully German, for the Reformation was a product of the distinctive German genius that entered creatively into the realms of the self-conscious spirit for the first time ... [It] expanded the vital elements of the traditional culture by breathing into it a fresh spirit which strove for real knowledge and thereby itself became an essential part of the universal-historical process which connects centuries and nations with one another.[18]

Such was the spirit of Ranke's vision in the 1840s, when he wrote his masterpiece on the age of the Reformation.[19] He saw no way to overcome the situation, not until the European revolutions of 1848 revealed to him the solution to the German Reformation's conundrum: a state made "national" by historical events rather than by popular sentiment or medievalizing nostalgia. As Meinecke wrote, in Ranke's view "a nation is not based on self-determination but on predetermination."[20] The predetermined form of the German nation was the Prussian state. Later, when the events of 1870–71 converted Ranke's intuition into political reality, the stage was set for his disciples and admirers to articulate his vision in a myth that recapitulated "the whole of German history under the heading 'From Luther to Bismarck.'"[21]

The Rankean vision of the Reformation and the German nation shared in the wreck of 1918 and, like the monarchy, has never been restored. No work reveals its wreckage more poignantly than the 1926 biography of Luther by Gerhard Ritter, himself a neo-Rankean heart and soul, who crowned his work with a hysterical and utterly un-Rankean comment on Luther: "He is ourselves—the eternal German."[22] The shock of 1945 then precipitated a flight from both Luther and the history of his reformation, so that by the early 1960s Bernd Moeller could complain that Reformation history was becoming "an antiquarian exercise."[23] This evolution is not difficult to comprehend, for the Rankean vision always saw the Reformation in terms at once confessional and national, which hardly suited the politics of the postwar German Federal Republic. It had a longer life in the German Democratic Republic, where the prevailing interpretation of the Reformation as an "early bourgeois revolution" actually recapitulated, though in Marxist language, the Rankean notion of a progressive Protestant-national movement. Indeed, developing the insights of Friedrich Engels (1820–95), the Leipzig historian Max Steinmetz (d. 1990) characterized the entire process as a "first attempt of the popular masses to create a unified national state from below."[24] Curious echoes of this Whiggish sort of neo-Rankean interpretation have appeared from time to time abroad, chiefly in England, but on the whole the events of 1933, 1945, and 1989 have simply reconfirmed the obsolescence of Ranke's confessional-national interpretation of German history in the age of the Reformation.

There are two reasons why the present moment is favorable to the reconstruction of a political narrative of the German Reformation. First, both terms of the Rankean teleology—confessional and national—have lost their grip on Reformation history.[25] The questions they addressed—the superiority of Protestant Christianity, the development of the German nation—no longer animate much research, and their disappearance has cleared the ground for another kind of narrative, inspired by a different experience. This book attempts to form such a narrative by seeking how we might reintegrate the story of the religious Reformation and the history of the German-speaking peoples. It offers one way of looking at the Reformation, a vision quite different from, but not necessarily contradicting, the view of the Reformation in the context of Christian thought.[26] Though the book's scope is Rankean, Germany in the age of the Reformation, its Germany is not a nation in the process of self-fashioning but a vast, complicated, and regionally and locally articulated system of law and politics.

FOUNDATIONS OF A NEW APPROACH

Current research offers three keys to a new conception of the politics of the German Reformation: the urban reform, the rural reform, and the structure of the Empire.[27] First, since the early 1960s, the Imperial free cities and their burghers have come out of the twilight to demonstrate how the interplay between popular agendas and oligarchic policies shaped the Reformation at the local level. Secondly, since the Peasants' War jubilee of 1975, the country people have emerged out of the shadows to display the close connection between political communalism and the decisive first wave of religious reform. Thirdly, the Holy Roman Empire, long despised as a political monstrosity, has arisen from its sickbed to display new vitality and effectiveness, so that "Germany's position in central Europe makes the political solution which the old empire [das Alte Reich] comprised appear far from inappropriate."[28] Taken together, these three lines produce a picture of the Holy Roman Empire radically different from the one imagined by Leopold von Ranke.

These three lines of research share the general approach of "social history," which places at center stage not the state but other social institutions, chiefly class, household, and gender. The category covers both Marxist history and structuralism, which in the German-speaking world is often associated with the name of the Austrian medievalist Otto Brunner (1898–1982) and more remotely with that of Karl Lamprecht (1856–1915).[29] The hallmark of structuralist social history is its opposition to the projection of modern historical forces—whether Ranke's state or Marx's class struggle—into premodern history. It tends to ignore or even deny the rootedness of people's mental worlds in their ways of life, in the conditions—constraints and opportunities—for survival and endurance that they inherit and that, within limits, they reshape. On the other hand, this approach deals easily with multicentered and multilayered structures of authority and power. It is as though the approach had been invented to study the Holy Roman Empire, where the complex and variegated institutions of the early modern era—for example, the regional structures known as "circles" (Reichskreise)[30]—defy explanation in terms of either medieval kingship and vassalage or the modern state.

The ability to shift from level to level and region to region allows us to study movements that can only be grasped on regional scales, such as the "communal reformation" in the Empire's southern tier.[31] In this region, our vision has moved from A. G. Dickens's remark that "the Reformation was an urban event," to Hans-Christoph Rublack's comment that "the Reformation . . . was also much more than an urban event," to Peter Blickle's unification of the urban and rural movements for religious reform under the rubric of the "communal reformation."[32] This development has yielded a picture of the movement of both burghers and peasants for a locally responsible "communal" church in the 1520s as the religious culmination of their late medieval striving for communal governance. Viewed on an Imperial or a "national" scale, the common, communal character of this movement hardly becomes visible, and the concept's explanatory power is largely restricted to the South and to the movement's early phase. This forms a particularly clear case of the possible conceptual benefit to be had from abandoning the notion of a Reformation that was "unitary" in either a political or a religious sense. The religious qualities of the various reformations may have been shaped by their respective theologies—Lutheran, Zwinglian, Anabaptist—but they were also influenced by different experiences of authority, and authority in the Empire cannot be understood on one level alone. Indeed, the unparalleled progress of particularism, local self-government, in the Empire's southern tier had created structures of authority so uncentralized that the voices of quite ordinary people in specific places could rise into the audible layers of the Reformation's history. This did not happen elsewhere to anything like the same degree of audibility, and even in the South the surface of authority cracked sufficiently to allow deeply buried voices to speak on a supralocal scale only for a few years between 1521 and 1526. Here, however, what was once a mysterious, imponderable event—to Ranke a "natural event [*Naturereignis*]"—has become the culmination of a fairly well understood historical process, the "communal reformation." In it the vague and ghostly "German nation" has yielded place to real people, whose real lives in real places were framed by real institutions, techniques, beliefs, and dreams, which cannot be grasped, much less understood, except on the local and regional scales on which such people lived.

Once this level of understanding is appropriated, the narrative of the German Reformation becomes a cluster of interrelated stories, played out by different sorts of actors on different stages, connected at some levels, but not all, by a common religious tradition, common traditions of governance, and at least some elements of a common language. The most common possession, of course, was religion, which is why the Reformation is the most important event in the history of the age. The different stories are related, too, in a chronological way, for it was the ordinary people who gave the movement its initial thrust. The German Reformation—reversing Maximilien

Robespierre's dictum about the French Revolution—was begun by the common people and finished by the uncommon people, the rich and the mighty.

Our response to the loss of the national narrative, therefore, need not be to speak of "all coherence gone." There is coherence, intelligibility, in the larger story of the German Reformation, but it cannot be grasped in developmental terms, either confessional or national—largely interchangeable terms, I have suggested, in Ranke's vocabulary. Once we lay aside the idea that the German-speaking peoples ought to have formed a nation-state between 1490 and 1550, we can begin to build a new framework for the story of the German Reformation on the basis of the Empire's layered structure—village, city, province, region, and Empire. This accomplished, we can envisage the Reformation as a challenge to and regrouping of authority at every level and between levels. Actions, prompted by the gospel's legitimation of popular grievance, disrupted the prestige of long-established and well-understood arrangements, such as the boundaries between temporal and ecclesiastical authority, the security of ancient forms of property, and the sacramental validity of marriage. A new political history of the German Reformation must therefore unite political structures with social movements, and it must operate simultaneously on several levels—local, provincial, regional, and Imperial—if it is to marshal the various experiences into a common narrative.

POLITICAL STRUCTURES

In the fashioning of a new narrative, much depends on the starting point, the political situation of the pre-Reformation Empire. Currently, two competing perspectives frame the possibilities: one sees the fifteenth century as a time of social and political crisis, the other as an era of intensification of governance. The first perspective's most important statement is the thesis of "the early bourgeois revolution in Germany," which was advanced chiefly, though not exclusively, by Marxist historians in the former German Democratic Republic.[33] It holds that the Reformation is part of the final stage of a revolutionary situation, which arose from the disintegration of the feudal mode of production. The thesis forces us to recognize the existence of a long-term crisis in agrarian life, which was unleashed by the agricultural depression of the fourteenth century and exacerbated by the breakup of the manors; the resulting disruptions of social relations and governance found connection to a growing dissatisfaction with conditions in the church to form a chronic state of crisis.[34] Despite adjustments in the relations of governance and power, by the 1470s the pressure for change broke through institutional containments and fueled the movements that from the 1510s climbed toward their peak in the great convulsion of 1524–26. The Reformation, in this view, "is a constituent part of what is understood by Marxist historiography of the German Democratic Republic as Early Bourgeois Revolution, without being fully identical with it."[35]

Whatever its limitations, the thesis of the early bourgeois revolution forces us to take constant account of the Reformation as part of a movement for real change, based on real grievances. The movement's climax in the Peasants' War of 1525 created a memory shared by the Reformation's chief actors, which acted as a powerful mortgage on decisive action for change and encouraged prudence and political sobriety on all sides. In the form of this memory, which encouraged the Empire's divided ruling classes to settle the schism by negotiation rather than by force, the sign of the Peasants' War stood over the politics of the entire Reformation generation.

Another current picture of the late medieval Empire portrays it in terms of an intensification (*Verdichtung*) of institutions of governance at all levels. This picture, which emphasizes the era's political creativity, is a welcome antidote to an older view of this age as "a pitiful tale of dissension, debility and disintegration."[36] To a very great degree, this insight rests on Karl Lamprecht's lesson that medieval (i.e., premodern) German history is chiefly regional history.[37] Once considered the age of the territorial state's creation, the late medieval era is now seen as an epoch of institutional intensification on *all* levels of governance. It was par excellence, for example, the age of communes, which arose in the towns beginning in the thirteenth century and on the land a little later, and which often formed themselves into regionally potent leagues and federations.[38] The most successful, the Swiss Confederacy, endured until 1798.

Elsewhere, the process of intensification eventually favored the territorial states, as the great dynasts, supported by lawyers, churchmen, judges, clerks, and financiers, transformed loosely ruled patrimonial domains into distinct states. The centrality of this process justifies a recent comment that "in Central Europe the modern state developed in the territory, in the regional dominion."[39] However much the cities feared these princes, the communal and the territorial states nonetheless shared many elements of intensification, such as representative assemblies, civil bureaucracies, chancelleries, courts, written judicial procedure, treasuries, bureaus of accounts and audits, and militias.

By the later fifteenth century, the process of intensification gripped the monarchy, as a movement toward consolidation began under King Sigismund (r. 1410–37) and continued, though fitfully, through the reigns of Emperor Frederick III (r. 1440–93) and his son, Maximilian I (r. 1493–1519).[40] Monarchs, princes, burghers, and peasants alike wanted law and order, that is, more effective government, but the movement to realize this agenda on the Imperial level stalled about 1500, because of the stalemate between Emperor Maximilian's demands for money and men to fuel his enterprises in the Netherlands, Italy, and Hungary and the Imperial princes' determination not to allow "Latin tyranny" a foothold in the Empire.[41] The great loser of this struggle was an exhausted Austria, for "Maximilian conducted grand policy on credit, and Austria had to pay the bill." The only workable outcome, given this constellation of forces, was a compromise between particularism and centralism, which were not alternatives but complementary parts of the reformed Imperial system. Many innovations, to be sure, evoked strong popular resistance, notably taxes, Roman law, and learned lawyers.[42] Yet the fundamental need for stronger governance was widely accepted. During the Peasants' War, for example, not even the most radical programs attacked the Imperial monarchy, and where viable territorial states already existed, the rebels tried to reform them in a popular sense rather than to abolish them.[43] The Empire was too large, its regions too diverse, and its governance too thoroughly devolved to local and provincial levels to support anything more centralized than the dualistic system, called "emperor and Empire" (Kaiser und Reich), which the reform era from 1495 to 1512 produced.[44] This outcome reflected the immense changes that so distinguished the polycentric Holy Roman Empire of the Reformation era from the Empire of around 1250, which had possessed only one highly developed political center, the Lower Rhenish region.[45]

Another characteristic of this vast structure is suggested by its new (since the 1440s) name, the "Holy Roman Empire of the German Nation." While this curious formula expressed the growing weight of the Empire's German-speaking heartlands vis-à-vis its Romance- and Slavic-speaking margins, it nonetheless reflected the consciousness more of belonging to a single state than of speaking a single language.[46] There was, to be sure, a sentiment of solidarity based roughly on similarity or mutual intelligibility of language, but its political meaning is usually difficult to determine. When Margrave Albert Achilles of Brandenburg, for example, objected in 1468 to the Hungarian king as a candidate for the Imperial dignity, did "non-German [undeutsch]" mean that the king did not speak German or than he was not an Imperial prince?[47] Was Charles of Ghent, who was an Imperial prince, open to the same objection of being a "non-German" in 1519? And what did Jacob Sturm mean when he referred to Imperial Chancellor Nicolas Perrenot de Granvelle, a Franche-Comtois who spoke no German, as "by heritage a German"?[48] Two generations of wars against France, Venice, and the papacy, no doubt, intensified German-speakers' prejudices against the "Latins," but the main struggle was not "national" or "ethnic," and the destruction of the French kingdom, the chief objective of Maximilian's "great plan of war" in 1496, remained that of his French-speaking grandson, Charles V, to the end.[49] The French king's reputation for "Latin tyranny" in the Empire also rested less on cultural considerations than on the notorious royal power to tax that made France a byword for tyranny among the German nobles. Emperor Maximilian once joked that whereas he was a "king of kings," whose vassals could do as they pleased, the French monarch was a "king of animals," whose subjects had to obey.[50]

None of this recommends an analysis of Imperial politics of the Reformation era in terms of national interest or national development. The aims of Maximilian I and Charles V were not "foreign," because Austrian and dynastic, and those of the princes "national," any more than German Protestantism was more or less "national" than German Catholicism. The political actors of the German Reformation era were confronted not with a choice, centralism *or* particularism, but with a fact, centralism *and* particularism. The critical point was *whose* centralism and *whose* particularism.

These perspectives supply two principles for a post-Rankean history of the German Reformation. First, the sites of this history were at once Imperial, regional, provincial, and local, whereby *Imperial* means the Holy Roman Empire as a state or country, *regional* the broad sections of south and north (dividing roughly at the Main basin), *provincial* such parts of regions as Bavaria, Swabia, Alsace, Saxony, and the Lower Rhine, and *local* a town and its environs in which people could know one another. None of these levels is more or less "German" or "national" than any other.

The second principle is the common people's constant presence. The German Reformation's peculiar character and fate, as contrasted with other Reformation movements, was determined largely by the very high level of popular involvement in political life, higher than in any other large country of Europe in this or in any earlier age. This condition derived from the late medieval Empire's devolution of governance in communal form into the hands of quite ordinary people, and it was enhanced by mobilization of opinion by means of printing. These factors gave political voice in one or another forum to some of the Empire's common people, who in the figure of "the Common Man"—those (mostly men) who lacked power and status—claimed a right to political voice under certain circumstances.[51] They posed this claim often at the local and provincial levels, but only once (in 1524–26) to the entire Empire.[52]

Based on the connectedness of these two principles—multilayered politics and popular presence—we can begin to see in sharper outline how that era's politics worked. The structural relationships between the layers—dominion, subordination, cooperation—possessed both inertia against sudden change and the ability to respond to social movements. The central act of the Reformation drama, variously called "the Peasants' War" or the "Revolution of the Common Man," could neither capture nor unhinge these structures, but neither could its voice be silenced by them. More than any previous event in European history, the German Reformation came "from below," both in the sense that it survived and flourished only because of the commitment and dedication of quite ordinary men and women and in the sense that the movement was local before it became regional or Imperial.[53] For a generation it altered the relationships among the levels of Imperial political life, but it could not change them permanently. The unsettlement was nonetheless sufficient, under these conditions, to permit the Reformation movement to create lasting centers within an Imperial system it could not conquer. Probably, if a centralized monarchy of the Western type had formed in the Empire before 1519, the German Reformation's fate would have resembled that of the French, a hopeless challenge to the Crown by an alliance of reforming clergy and nobles. For, as the following chapters will show, German Protestantism lacked the mobilizing power to create a new type of political community, which might have transformed the Empire into a new kind of state.

These are the principles of a book that seeks to contribute to a new political history of the German Reformation. Its perspective is that of an inverted pyramid, which rests its point at Strasbourg and mounts in ever larger layers—Lower Alsace, the Upper Rhine, South Germany, the Smalkaldic League—to the Empire. The point is more solidly fixed than the other layers, for the documents on Strasbourg's political relations in this era are accessible to a unique degree. While much of the Smalkaldic League's history remains in darkness, that of the Imperial diets has entered a new age, as the edition of their acts approaches the great Augsburg Diet of 1530 and will soon push into the terra incognita between 1530 and 1555.[54] The history of another institution central to this story, the Imperial Chamber Court (*Reichskammergericht*), which had long languished because of the dispersal of its archives, has become the object of intensive study by both social and legal historians.[55] These advances have made the completion of this book a less daunting task than it seemed twenty years ago. Meanwhile, the work has grown into a story of the Empire, a vast, regionally divided and multi-layered structure of law, authority, and power, and the Reformation as a movement for religious reform. It tells of how the movement altered, if only briefly, the communications and interactions among the structure's levels and parts, and how it was, in turn, domesticated and absorbed by them. The deepest concern of this book has become, in a sense, identical with Ranke's concern to discover why the Reformation failed to attempt, much less to accomplish, a political revolution in the Empire. Its answer, however, is utterly unlike Ranke's, for the explanation is found in the great process of political devolution during the preceding era. The book thus frames the large question in local terms. It begins inside the walls of Strasbourg and ends just outside them.

Notes

1. Pelikan, "Leopold von Ranke as Historian of the Reformation," 90.
2. The "historians' dispute [*Historikerstreit*]" of the 1980s in West Germany was essentially about this issue.
3. Goethe to Knebel, 22 August 1817, quoted in Bornkamm, ed., *Luther im Spiegel*, 216, and also in Schuffenhauer and Steiner, eds., *Martin Luther*, 252.
4. Schuffenhauer and Steiner, eds., *Martin Luther*, 364.
5. Prodi, *Papal Prince*, 2, who also notes (184) that after the First Vatican Council, Ranke revised his view that the papacy no longer exercised any important role.
6. Not, as is so often assumed, a history of the German Reformation. An orientation

to this subject is supplied by Pelikan, "Leopold von Ranke as Historian of the Reformation," but the best guide is Krieger, *Ranke*, who has corrected the tendency of modern interpreters of Ranke, such as White, *Metahistory*, and Iggers, *German Conception of History*, to make far too much of Ranke's programmatic writings and too little of his practice.

7. Krieger, *Ranke*, 159.
8. Ranke, *Deutsche Geschichte* 1:142.
9. Ibid.
10. Ibid., 218.
11. Ibid., 288.
12. Ibid., 289.
13. Ibid., 292.
14. Ibid., 303.
15. This is why the second book of the *German History* degenerates into a pure narrative and closes without a trace of the grand speculation which enlivens its noble beginning. It may also explain why Sarah Austin, Ranke's English translator, left the task unfinished.
16. Prodi, *Papal Prince*, 182–83: Ranke saw the papacy "beyond the confessional arguments, as an indispensable element in our understanding of the development of the West in its entirety."
17. Quoted by Krieger, *Ranke*, 167.
18. Quoted in ibid., 168.
19. Krieger speaks modestly of Ranke's "sporadic partiality," and "exceptional partiality," and "apparent discrepancies, both partisan and moralistic, from Ranke's own scholarly prescriptions," which form in Krieger's view one of the "special puzzles" in Ranke's *History of the Popes*. Krieger, *Ranke*, 153–56.
20. Meinecke, *Cosmopolitanism*, 205.
21. Mommsen, "Ranke and the neo-Rankean School," 136–37; and see Faulenbach, *Ideologie*, 125–31. On the Rankean succession in the universities, see Weber, *Priester der Clio*, 208–9.
22. Quoted by Bornkamm, ed., *Luther und der deutsche Geist*, 20. See my comments in "Continuity in Gerhard Ritter."
23. Moeller, "Problems of Reformation Research," 3–4.
24. Quoted by Brady, "The Common Man and the Lost Austria," 143. See Dickens and Tonkin, *The Reformation in Historical Thought*, 237–43.
25. See, Ozment, *Protestants*, which pursues the confessional argument, but not the national one—a traditional American approach, for which see Brady, "The Reformation's Fate in America."
26. Ranke's *Deutsche Geschichte im Zeitalter der Reformation* became, in Sarah Austin's partial translation of 1845–47, a *History of the Reformation in Germany*. Curiously enough, a similar change had occurred, many years earlier, in the title of the first history of the Reformation. Johann Sleidan's *De Statu religionis* became in Edmund Bohun's translation *The General History of the Reformation of the Church* (London, 1689).
27. See Brady, "From the Sacral Community," 229–45, which updates and modifies my "Social History," in Ozment, ed., *Reformation Europe*, 161–81.
28. Press, "The Holy Roman Empire in German History," 51. For orientation, see Strauss, "The Holy Roman Empire Revisited," 290–301; Moraw, "Fragen der deutschen Verfassungsgeschichte," 59–101; Moraw and Press, "Probleme der Sozial- und Verfassungsgeschichte."
29. Melton, "Otto Brunner," and now the translators' preface to Brunner, *Land and Lordship*, xiii–lxi; Chickering, *Karl Lamprecht*. For the rise of structuralist history in Germany, see Lehmann and Melton, eds., *Continuity and Change*.

30. See, for examples, Blaich, *Wirtschaftspolitik*; Diestelkamp, *Reichskammergericht* and *Forschungen*; Dotzauer, *Reichskreise*; and for an overview, see Duchhardt, *Deutsche Verfassungsgeschichte*.

31. Blickle, *Gemeindereformation*, now in English as *Communal Reformation*. For critical reactions, see Schilling, "Die deutsche Gemeindereformation," 325–32; Scott, *Freiburg and the Breisgau*, 229–35. For a perspective on the urban reformation very similar to Blickle's on the countryside, see Brady, "In Search of the Godly City," 14–32.

32. Rublack, "Is There a 'New History' of the Urban Reformation?" 122; and see Greyerz, "Stadt und Reformation"; Rublack, "Forschungsbericht Stadt und Reformation." Dickens's comment comes from his *German Nation and Martin Luther*, 182. This shift makes useful the term, "people's reformation," on which see Peter Blickle's introduction to *Zugänge zur bäuerlichen Reformation*, 11–18.

33. For the present state of the discussion, see Steinmetz, "Reformation und Bauernkrieg—die deutsche frühbügerliche Revolution."

34. See Engel and Töpfer, eds., *Deutsche Geschichte* 2:278–373.

35. Laube, "Radicalism as a Research Problem," 14.

36. Barraclough, *Origins of Modern Germany*, 355, quite in the gloomy spirit of Tout, "Germany and the Empire," 288–328.

37. Gerlich, *Geschichtliche Landeskunde*, 71–76.

38. Blickle, *Gemeindereformation*, 167–82; Brady, *Turning Swiss*, 28–34; Dollinger, *The German Hansa*.

39. Moraw, *Von offener Verfassung*, 183; and see Du Boulay, *Germany in the Later Middle Ages*. The details may be studied in Jeserich, Pol, and Unruh, eds., *Deutsche Verwaltungsgeschichte* 1:21–214; and for the cities, Isenmann, *Die deutsche Stadt*, 131–244.

40. See Angermeier, *Reichsreform*, 63–70, 215–29, who argues that the Imperial reform did not proceed essentially from practical motives; and Du Boulay, *Germany in the Later Middle Ages*, 61, who argues that it did.

41. Wiesflecker, *Kaiser Maximilian I*. 5:410–47, 566–76, and the following quote is at 204.

42. Strauss, *Law, Resistance, and the State*, 127–35.

43. Buszello, "The Common Man's View," 117; Blickle, *Revolution of 1525*, 125–45.

44. Unruh, "Die Wirksamkeit von Kaiser und Reich," 270.

45. Moraw, *Von offener Verfassung*, 19.

46. On the whole subject of center and margins, of "Germany" and the Empire in the later Middle Ages, Moraw, *Von offener Verfassung*, 17–25, and the ethnohistorical treatment on 31–55. I follow Guénée, *States and Rulers*, 216–21, and my own views on states and nations in the early modern era are expressed in Brady, "Rise of Merchant Empires."

47. Minutoli, ed., *Das kaiserliche Buch*, 330.

48. Lenz, ed., *Briefwechsel* 1:156 n. 8; and there, too, the following quote.

49. There is a good picture of how this happened in Wiesflecker, *Kaiser Maximilian I*. 5:410–47; and another of how it ended in Rodríguez-Salgado, *Changing Face of Empire*.

50. Wiesflecker, *Kaiser Maximilian I*. 5:5.

51. Strauss, *Law, Resistance, and the State*, 129–30.

52. Blickle, *Revolution of 1525*, 165–69; Vogler, "Der deutsche Bauernkrieg."

53. Schulze, "Soziale Bewegungen"; Scribner, "The Reformation as Social Movement."

54. Brady, "Phases and Strategies"; H. Grundmann, "Deutsche Reichstagsakten, Jüngere Reihe"; Lutz, "Zur Einführung"; Kohler, "Der Augsburger Reichstag."

55. Diestelkamp, "Stand der Arbeiten."

2

A Man of the City

May the Empire be happy and free from woes,
May no free city fall to its foes,
Help, Immaculate Mary, this is our prayer,
And guard the Common Man from every care.*

Between the grim horrors of the fourteenth-century "age of crisis" and the tumults of the sixteenth-century age of Reformation, the fifteenth century sits in our picture of Central European history like a lumpy grab bag from which we occasionally pull odd things: now a medieval remnant, now a portent of modernity.[1] We owe this picture almost entirely to the old national narrative of German history. If we shift our vision down to the localities and regions, quite a different picture of the fifteenth-century Empire comes into view. It is a world of immense political creativity, in which small powers, singly and in their federations, manifest the varieties of particularism like a political coat of many colors. In later centuries, German particularism proved volatile and, except for the Swiss Confederacy, vulnerable to the war-making and state-building powers of the territorial states during the sixteenth and seventeenth centuries. For a little while, however, the late medieval intensification of local and regional political formations lent a remarkable solidity and security to regions that seem, in the deceptive retrospect of historical cartography, to have been fragmented into irreparable impotence. Swabia and Franconia were such regions, and so was the Upper Rhine, where the political hierarchy keyed on one leading city, the proud commune of Strasbourg.

The Upper Rhine Valley at the end of the fifteenth century sheltered a brilliant rainbow of highly successful small states, ranging from tiny free communes, such as Zell am Harmersbach with its eighty-five burghers, to regional metropolises, such as Strasbourg and Basel; from clusters of free Imperial knights in Lower Alsace and the Ortenau region of Middle Baden to middling nobles, such as the counts of Hanau-Lichtenberg, to second-rank princes, such as the margraves of Baden and the prince-bishops of Strasbourg, Speyer, and Basel. They all shared space in the great trench of the Upper Rhine Valley, an immense graben through which the proud Rhine flows down from Basel, where it breaks through the ancient Jura Mountains, to Mainz, where it slams against the Johannisberg and swings to the west. From the great conifer-clad walls of the Black Forest on the east and the Vosges Mountains on the west, the land swept down through vineyards and orchards to the alluvial plain, strewn thickly with rich, densely populated villages and small cities, to the Rhine. The river was a highway, along which goods and people moved downstream to the Lower Rhine and the Netherlands or upstream to Basel, the Alpine passes, and Italy. A fruitful land, this valley, warmer and richer than the higher plateaus on its flanks, Lorraine to the west and Swabia to the east, which is doubtless why young ambitious folk, especially clergymen, flocked down to find good livings there. Two aspects of its social development lent a special immediacy to the region's bonds of authority. In the first place, the relations between town and countryside were particularly close, for the Upper Rhine had neither large numbers of servile farmers nor any cities dominated by export industries, and every city sheltered considerable numbers of burghers who lived in town and worked on the land, as well as nobles who lived in town and drew their substance from the land. In the second place, this rich region had managed to avoid incorporation into a major state. The Valois dukes of Burgundy had tried, but their armies had been shattered by Swiss and Upper Rhenish troops and guns during the 1470s, and the House of Austria, which fell heir to the Burgundians on the Upper Rhine, hardly gave notice to this most distant corner of Austria. It remained a land of small liberties, where the communes customarily attacked predatory nobles with fire and sword, and where farmers were among the earliest to raise the standard of revolt in the 1490s. Nowhere in the Holy Roman Empire, except for the neighboring Swiss Confederacy, had the late medieval devolution of governance and the local intensification of authority reached such extremes as in this fortunate land.

On the river's left bank, where the River Ill starts its last run toward the Rhine, sat the region's jewel, the proud free city of Strasbourg, in about 1500 home to some 20,000 souls. Strasbourg sat behind its mighty walls in the shape of a football, oriented along a southwest-to-northeast axis, and from its walls and many spires the vista swept up to the mountain walls on both sides of the Rhine, the foothills of which were studded with the fortresses of the landed nobility. The city's eastern quarter lay on the site of the ancient Roman city, clustered around the tremendous bulk and soaring spire of its cathedral, then the tallest in Europe. Unlike Cologne, Metz, and Regensburg, which had blossomed during the twelfth and thirteenth centuries, Strasbourg was essentially a late medieval creation. Its very large number of convents, monasteries, and churches, of course, betrayed its high medieval prosperity, but the power and number of its guilds embodied the late medieval devolution of power from the old noble patriciate to the merchants and craftsmen. By the 1480s, after the Burgundian Wars, 150 years of social strife had taught leisured patrician, rich merchant, busy shop-keeper, and skilled artisan master how to live together, sharing the magistracies that collectively ruled the common house. Since the 1440s, when the "Armagnacs" had spilled into Alsace from war-torn France, no one had dared test the strength of this great commune, and up and down the length of the Upper Rhine from Basel to Mainz, Strasbourg had no enemies and few rivals. Around 1489, when Jacob Sturm was born, the city enjoyed a security surpassed by no other German-speaking city outside the Swiss Confederacy.

A CIVIC HERITAGE

Few burghers of his epoch came into a more secure world than did Jacob Sturm, who was born at Strasbourg on 10 August 1489, the second son among the eight or more children of Ottilia von Köllen and Martin Sturm.[2] Their marriage represented the fifteenth-century harmony between the two fractions of Strasbourg's ruling class, for the Sturms were nobles and the Schotts, Ottilia's mother's people—the von Köllens were noble nobodies—were not.

The Sturms were deeply rooted in the city, on the land, and in the church. Their forebears had migrated about 1250 from the free city of Offenburg across the Rhine to Strasbourg, where they had become a principal lineage of the civic nobility and served the commune with "word and deed [mit rat und that]" all through the later Middle Ages. Martin Sturm and his brothers maintained the lineage's tradition in the civic magistracy, as Martin served for fifteen years (1506–21) in the privy council of the XV, Uncle Ludwig for five years as a patrician senator, and Uncle Ott as stettmeister, the highest noble office, for twenty annual terms between 1484 and 1512. For all their prominence in the urban world, the Sturms also maintained their status among the rural nobility of Lower Alsace. They not only held fiefs of the Holy Roman emperor, the Elector Palatine, the bishop of Strasbourg, and a number of lesser Alsatian lords, they were also seigniors, notably in the village of Breuschwickersheim, a few miles southwest of the city, where Martin and Ludwig Sturm had bought the chateau and seigniorial rights from the Winterthur family.[3] Like most of their kinsmen, all male Sturms were eligible for knighthood, though none seems to have sought it since Uncle Ott won his spurs in 1476 against the Burgundians on the glorious field of Murten.[4]

The Sturms also entered the church. Jacob's Uncle Leonhard was a monk of Alpirsbach, a Benedictine abbey at the head of the Kinzig Valley, high in the central Black Forest, and his cousins Ott and Stephan, Uncle Ott's boys, both got good benefices in local collegiate chapters around 1508.[5] The family's special affection, however, attached to the local Dominicans, especially the women's houses, which enjoyed the favor of many local families of the better sort.[6] Margarethe Sturm, Martin's sister and Jacob's aunt, joined the convent of St. Nicolaus in Undis in the suburb called "the

Krutenau"; Jacob's sister Clara was placed in 1508 in the convent of SS. Margaret and Agnes; and his cousin Magdalene, Uncle Ott's daughter, joined the same house. In the male house of the same order, Uncles Ludwig and Ott and their wives were laid to rest.

As befitted an old lineage of high status, the Sturms were rich. No wills survive from this family before 1562 and no death inventories before 1579, but the fragmentary evidence provides plenty of suggestions of Sturm prosperity.[7] Martin Sturm owned property in the city, allodial lands at Düttelnheim and Achenheim, and, with his brother Ludwig, since around 1508 the allodial seigniory of Breuschwickersheim, a few miles southwest of Strasbourg, the buildings and incomes from which were estimated later in the century to be worth about 4,800 fl.[8] The Sturms do not seem to have acquired urban properties much beyond the lineage's needs, and the bulk of their wealth lay not in real property but in interest-bearing debts. True, they do not appear among either the big lenders to the commune or the city's most notorious usurers, but, like most other wealthy families, much of their income came in many small sums from little people, mostly peasants.[9] Martin Sturm was a sharp businessman who invested his money in the accumulation of small debts and incomes.[10] He did not invest, however, in trade, though he and his brothers were closely related to families that did, such as the Wurmsers and the Miegs.[11] All in all, the Sturms seem to have stuck to the traditional investments of the Strasbourg nobles, land and usury.

Jacob Sturm's mother came from a quite different kind of family. The von Köllens were a relatively insignificant patrician family, but Ottilia von Köllen's mother was a Schott, and her grandparents, Peter Schott and Susanna von Köllen were easily the most remarkable personalities in Jacob Sturm's immediate lineage. The Schotts were as new a family as the Sturms were old. Old Peter Schott had come to Strasbourg in 1449, acquired citizenship through marriage, entered the government in 1465, and became fifteenth-century Strasbourg's greatest statesman. His tireless leadership brought the city both external security and internal peace.[12] Externally, Old Peter became the soul of the Alsatian-Swiss federation that smashed the Burgundian power on the Upper Rhine during the 1470s. Not only did he take part in the 1473 trial and execution of the hated Burgundian governor, Peter von Hagenbach, but his fiery oratory stirred the Bernese and the Solothurners to make war on Burgundy in the summer of 1475. When he campaigned with them that year in Upper Burgundy, the Bernese confessed that "they had come on campaign out of respect and love for the Strasbourgeois, their best friends and allies, and so they will stick by them and the others, for good or for ill."[13] Together they killed Duke Charles the Bold and wrecked his armies, and when peace came in 1478, Old Peter Schott helped to make it.[14] He was the architect of Strasbourg's traditional foreign policy, which aimed at safety through a strong provincial alliance (the Lower Union), anchored upstream by the friendly Swiss and downstream by the friendly Elector Palatine.[15]

Internally, Old Peter Schott presided in 1482 over the formal end of the guild revolts and the last revision of Strasbourg's constitution (*Schwörbrief*) before 1789. He thereby cemented the alliance between nobles and merchant commoners, on which the city's political stability depended.[16] In the 1480s and 1490s, Peter Schott was the grand old man of Strasbourg's commune, and the youthful Jacob Sturm basked in the afterglow of respect and deference his great-grandfather had won.[17]

To the Sturms' rank, wealth, and ancient lineage, the guildsman Schotts brought political eminence, learning, and piety.[18] Three of Susanna's and Peter's daughters made good matches with noblemen or rich merchants; Anna, who could write German and Latin, lived as a nun at SS. Margaret and Agnes; and Young Peter became a priest, a lawyer, and a humanist.[19] These children were nurtured in a domestic atmosphere of learning and fervent piety, to which Susanna gave the tone, and which reached beyond the home into the convents of Dominican women, to whom the Schotts, like the Sturms, "had a special love."[20] The ammeister, who shared his wife's fervency, took this piety out of the home and into the commune.[21] Angered at the low quality of preaching in the cathedral parish, the story goes, at the beginning of the 1480s Old Peter Schott waylaid Johann Geiler of Kaysersberg, the great Alsatian preacher, on his way to a new preaching post at Würzburg and persuaded him to come to Strasbourg instead.[22] The Schotts endowed Geiler's preachership with the large sum of 2,230 fl., and Old Peter, who was a curator (*Pfleger*) of the cathedral, had built the magnificent stone pulpit, adorned with nearly fifty saints, from which Geiler censored Strasbourg's morals for the next thirty years.[23] In the years around Jacob Sturm's birth, therefore, the Schotts took a more prominent place in civic affairs than the Sturms did, though the two families combined to provide him with a heritage that was, with very few exceptions, firmly bounded by city and region, for the men and women who shaped it had lived, worked, and died within sight of waters that flowed down to form the Upper Rhine.

BOYHOOD YEARS

When Jacob Sturm was born in the late summer of 1489, his parents had been married for about five years. Despite her chronic ill health, Ottilia von Köllen bore at least three more children and lived for another twenty years.[24] The Sturm children probably grew up in a house in Peacock Street, near St. Martin's Church and near Uncle Ott's mansion called "the Large Camel."[25] From infancy, Jacob was special, for his birth came just before a family tragedy, the sudden death of his great-uncle, Young Peter Schott, whose promising career as a scholarly priest had stirred great hopes in the doting elder Schotts, who had managed their son's life "with over-much indulgence and affection."[26] The shadow of his nearly prominent kinsman was to hang over Jacob Sturm's life for nearly thirty-five years, for from a very young age he was shepherded toward the priesthood and scholarship to be the surrogate for his lamented kinsman. One shepherd was Peter's sister, Anna, a Dominican nun, who in 1499 had the ten-year-old Jacob copy out a letter in which her late brother had once sent her some religious counsels.[27] Another was doubtless Johann Geiler, a familiar of the Schott household and, perhaps, friendly with the Sturms as well.

Just after the turn of the century, another learned Alsatian priest appeared on the scene to accelerate the fashioning of Jacob Sturm into a clergyman. Jacob Wimpheling, a native of Sélestat in central Alsace, arrived at Strasbourg in 1501 from Heidelberg, where he had been a university professor. He settled in the Williamite monks' convent and began to lobby the magistrates for his plan to establish a civic Latin school, and when this failed, he earned his keep by preparing boys of good family for the university.[28] Among them were Jacob Sturm and his younger brother Peter, to whose kinfolk Wimpheling had ties through his late protegé, Young Peter Schott, and through Geiler. Wimpheling had known of these boys before he arrived at Strasbourg. He had been a principal patron of Young Peter Schott, whose writings he prepared for a posthumous edition and whose life and learning he commended to the youth of Strasbourg.[29] Even before he left Heidelberg, Wimpheling, who was encouraging Jacob Sturm to study classical rhetoric, tried to drive home to the young Sturms the model of their dead kinsman.[30] He directed this message, for example, through his presentation to Jacob Sturm in 1499 of a composite volume of ancient and modern (mostly Italian) texts on education, which he inscribed "to Jacob Sturm, son of Martin Sturm." The boy added below, in his own hand, the first lines that survive in his hand: "This volume belongs to the grand-nephew of the most venerable gentleman, Peter Schott, citizen of Strasbourg 1499."[31] At the age of ten, therefore, Jacob Sturm had begun to assume the identity toward which his whole familiar world was nudging him, the imitation of that "most venerable gentleman," Great-Uncle Peter. Once established at Strasbourg, Wimpheling began actively to shape Jacob for the church, which aim, he attested, coincided with both parents' wishes. Later, when Jacob was studying at Freiburg, Wimpheling moved into the Sturm household, and he took his leisure during these years at the Sturms' country seat at Breuschwickersheim.[32]

Wimpheling's chief role in Jacob Sturm's formation was to supply content and reinforcement through repetition to Sturm's model, the idealized figure of Young Peter Schott. Among his tools were dedicatory letters to his books, such as one dated 17 November 1501, which reminded the boy of his future. "You know," the teacher wrote,

> that I prefer you to study theology and that both God and serious men hold the study and practice of law in low esteem. Remember that Francesco Petrarca abandoned the study of law, not because laws are bad in themselves, but because humanity is corrupted by their abuse. I therefore urge and exhort you, a lover of true integrity, to prefer the love of God, the

friendship of those around you, good reputation, the honor of your entire family, and the health of your own soul, to all of which the study of theology conduces.[33]

"Consider," Wimpheling mused, "that Peter Schott, the brother of your maternal grandmother, regretted that he did not dedicate himself at an earlier age to the study of true learning [i.e., theology]."

Four years later, when the sixteen-year-old Sturm was a theology student at Freiburg, Wimpheling reminisced that "you said that your ultimate wish is to begin the study of sacred things." "Since," he wrote,

> you have brothers, who *deo volente* can continue your lineage, you can aspire to the priesthood and celibacy. And you have been openly display-ing your intention of following the example of Peter Schott, your grand-mother's brother, for chastity and modesty.

"What could be more pleasing," the teacher continued, "what could be dearer to me than to see you imitate in manly way the noble conduct and great learning of Peter Schott?"[34] The decision for the priesthood was also "your father's fondest wish" and "your mother's strongest desire."[35] Wimpheling's words aimed to stiffen the young Jacob Sturm's resolve to become what everyone seemed determined that he become, a learned priest in the mold of his late kinsman.

University Days

Besides excellent connections, the surest path to ecclesiastical preferment lay through the university, and in Jacob Sturm's youth the Alsatian clergy's univer-sities of choice were Basel, Freiburg, and Heidelberg.[36] On Wimpheling's advice, he was sent in 1501 at the age of twelve to Heidelberg in the Rhine Palatinate, a land to which his mother's people had family ties. Here he was registered in the arts faculty on 29 September.[37] The curriculum at Heidelberg, a daughter of Paris, was divided between the two scholastic traditions, *via antiqua* and *via moderna*, and although Geiler and Wimpheling were *moderni*, Jacob Sturm enrolled as a Scotist (i.e., follower of Duns Scotus) in the *via antiqua*.[38] It was all one to Wimpheling, who had once lectured the Heidelberg faculty that "we have one faith, one baptism, the same rules and laws, the same privileges and libraries, one head, one Lord, and the same path to salvation."[39]

All the more was Wimpheling concerned about the threats to young stu-dents' morals that lurked in and around Heidelberg, and he bombarded his pupils with exhortations to industry and virtue. "Some people want great riches," he wrote them during Sturm's first semester in Heidelberg, "they would gaze on gold, drink out of silver, don bright silks, take delight in spectacles, rage after love, . . . languish from the pleasures of the flesh, waste time in gambling, reek of wine, rush to Rome, look around that city, and accumulate benefices." He trusted, however, that Sturm and his fellows would rather embrace philosophy out of desire to have time for the study of wisdom, to pursue virtue, to become involved in humane studies, to learn agreeable habits and detest vices, to become accustomed to morality in all things, never admiring vain or ephemeral things, . . . to persevere in good letters and virtues, to bear all things with equanimity, to restrain passions and motions of the soul, to quarrel with no one, to love chastity, to fear God, to love parents and friends, to reflect on the immortality of the soul, to dread the inextinguishable fire of hell, and never to lose sight of the hour of death, . . . so that God, our Creator and Redeemer, Who brings you many things from nature and for fortune, may receive you at last into His eternal kingdom among the blessed.[40]

His exhortation, possibly, kept the boys from catching songbirds, going about in disguise, poaching in the elector's fishponds, and other forbidden pleasures. Jacob Sturm's Heidelberg days ended abruptly in the summer of 1504, when a Hessian army appeared before the city's gates. "At that time," Wimpheling recalled "Sir Martin Sturm and Matthias Pawel . . ., my very good friends, asked me what would happen to their sons, whom at my advice they had sent to Heidelberg three years before. They then recalled the boys, who had become expert neither in sloth nor in licentiousness."[41] The two teenagers—Jacob Sturm was now fifteen—were sent to continue their studies at Freiburg im Breisgau, where they were matriculated on 27 July 1504.[42] At Strasbourg they just missed King Maximilian and Queen Bianca Maria, who entered the city by torchlight on 9 August 1504, and they missed, too, Geiler's sermon to the crowned heads a week later, in which he warned that one day God would raise up a prophet "who will restore our fallen religion."[43]

Wimpheling visited Jacob at Freiburg and brought Peter Sturm there to study in 1506, though the choice of Freiburg for Jacob still sat poorly with Martin Sturm's Dominican relatives, who wanted him sent to the Dominican theological faculty at Cologne. "But I said," Wimpheling commented, "that whatever Jacob could learn at Cologne, he can also learn at Freiburg."[44] The young university in the Austrian town of Freiburg was just beginning to attain real distinction. Sturm enrolled not in law, where the great Ulrich Zasius held sway,[45] but in theology in the *cursus biblicus*, the five-year preliminary course for theologians. He lectured simultaneously as a Scotist in the arts faculty, giving Aristotle's *De generatione animalium* in 1505 and the *Nicomachean Ethics* in 1506–7 and 1508. He probably received minor orders by 6 May 1507, when he preached a Latin sermon to the theological faculty assembled in the Dominican church.[46] Among his fellow students were several men who were headed for distinguished clerical careers, such as the Swabian Johann Eck, three years Sturm's senior and also a Wimpheling protegé, and two Alsatians, Mathis Zell from Kaysersberg and Wolfgang Capito (Köpfel) from Hagenau, both future Protestant reformers at Strasbourg.[47]

In 1509, for reasons unknown, Peter Sturm shifted to Heidelberg and the law, and Jacob left the university for good. He returned without a degree in theology, though in later years he was considered an adept student of the Bible.[48] Jacob was then twenty years old, time to begin a career, and perhaps he came home from Freiburg in the hope of getting a good benefice, as two of his cousins, Uncle Ott's sons, recently had: Ott, Jr., at New St. Peter's and Stephan at St. Thomas.[49] The world he had known as a boy was changing, most notably through Johann Geiler's death. On 10 March 1510, shortly after his return to Strasbourg, Jacob stood at Geiler's deathbed, and next day he looked on, as magistrates and burghers packed the cathedral to bid farewell to the man who had worn himself out for reform, the hope of which went into the grave with him.[50] Geiler left ominous words ringing in the burghers' ears: "You laymen, you hate us priests!"

HUMANISM'S "MEDIOCRE PROGRAM"

The eight years between his return to Strasbourg in 1509 and his employment as secretary to Count Palatine Henry in 1517 are Jacob Sturm's "lost years," a period of his life so poorly documented that it was once customary to fill them with further studies in Liège and Paris.[51] Nonetheless, enough is known to show that Jacob Sturm spent most of this third decade of his life at Strasbourg, where he lived, just as Great-Uncle Peter had lived, the leisured life of a gentleman-clergyman.

In his survivors' wistful memory, Young Peter Schott had been the great local hope of the new humanist learning, cut down in his prime, or perhaps, as malicious rumor whispered, poisoned by "the priests."[52] The truth was both more prosaic and more characteristic of both his times and his class. After the best education money could buy—private tuition, the Latin school at Sélestat, philosophy at Paris, and law at Bologna[53]—Schott had returned to Strasbourg in 1481. An only son, he refused to follow in his father's political footsteps, he said, because of the endless traveling and the burghers' ingratitude, and decided instead for the church. Nourished by a prebend in the collegiate church of New St. Peter's, he received Holy Orders and said his first mass in December 1482—an occasion for luncheons and parties, to hear him tell it.[54] Then he settled down to prepare some texts, including some of Jean Gerson's writings, for publication and to write legal opinions for friends and relations.[55] To achieve his true heart's desire, he announced, "as soon as I have satisfied the mandatory year of residence for my canonry at New St. Peter's, God willing, I shall study theology" at Paris.[56] Somehow, the right time for Paris and theology never came, as Schott settled into a gentleman's life in his parents' home, toured the spas of the Black Forest, and visited his sister Ottilia in her chateau at Wasselonne.[57] Unlike the figure of posthumous legend, the real Young Peter Schott was the pampered only son of a doting family. He lived out his life under the thumbs of his parents and siblings, whose management evoked many complaints but no resistance.[58] He rejected the active life of service in any form, whether to church or to commune, and devoted his brief career not to religious reform, as legend later had it, but to family, friends, parties, and humanist learning (the *bonae litterae*), fortified by a good benefice. Such was the life, the memory of which dominated Jacob Sturm's youth and young adulthood, prompted and reinforced by his great-grandparents' and parents' desires, Wimpheling's pedagogy, and his own ambitions.

Sturm came home in 1509 to his family and to a cultural milieu to which Wimpheling gave the tone. The old priest, whose vanity made him a natural patron and former of coteries, drew an assortment of ambitious young men to himself and to what has been called the "mediocre program" of humanism at Strasbourg.[59] Himself the quintessential climber—a successful burgher's son who had become tutor to princes and councilor to an emperor—Wimpheling in his later years made a living from showing others that the way to success led through education and self-discipline to preferment in the church and thence to a life devoted to the *bonae litterae*.

About education, his strongest suit, Wimpheling was a practical man.[60] Although in his pedagogical writings he extoled to Jacob Sturm and others the Italianate learning of which he was an important salesman in South Germany, he also knew that the road to success lay not in neoclassical scholarship but in more traditional learning, as witness his project for a civic Latin school at Strasbourg. As a former professor, Wimpheling knew that the universities offered a training that was truly practical and useful, and that, at least in his own diocese of Strasbourg, a good education readily brought preferment.[61]

Self-discipline formed the second element in Wimpheling's "mediocre program." For years he drummed into his pupils the need for discipline in daily life, beginning with the simple precepts he composed for Peter Sturm in 1499: "Love God. Honor your parents. Get up at dawn. Make the sign of the cross. Put on your clothes. Wash your hands and dry them. Wash your mouth, but not with water that is too cold, which will damage your teeth."[62] To older boys, such as the twelve-year-old Jacob Sturm in 1501, Wimpheling offered cautions against three vices to which students might be especially vulnerable—drunkenness, gambling, and fornication—and illustrated their dire consequences with stories drawn from the boys' native milieu.[63] Wimpheling's pupils learned that the world of the active life was filled with vices, to guard against which he taught them solid burgher and Christian values, such as frugality, constancy, perseverance in learning and virtue, equanimity, self-control, modesty, love of God, parents, and friends, and concern for one's immortal soul.[64] He aimed to form each pupil into a *vir probus atque perfectus* or *homo christianus*, to adopt the expressions favored by his beloved Italian humanists.[65]

Fortified by education and self-discipline, the way to success led through ecclesiastical preferment. Wimpheling's own quest for preferment went back at least to 1487, when he had sought expectancies on several benefices,

and continued into his Strasbourg period. His long effort, however, to secure a benefice at St. Thomas came to nought in 1504, when the patron
on whose support he relied, Johann Burckhart—master of ceremonies in
the papal palace at Rome and the most spectacular Alsatian pluralist of his
age—chose another man instead.[66] Wimpheling bitterly attacked current
methods of distributing benefices, not because they drained resources away
from pastoral work but because benefices gravitated to the well-born or the
merely greedy rather than to the learned.[67] In a sense, Wimpheling—and
the same was generally true of the German humanists—attacked existing
conditions not to reform the church in a pastoral sense but to make its
resources more available to the support of the *bonae litterae* and, not inci-
dentally, themselves.

The relevance of Wimpheling's program to the contemporary church can
best be grasped by comparing it to that of the other major influence on
the young Jacob Sturm, Johann Geiler. In the Strasbourg of Jacob Sturm's
youth, Geiler embodied the tradition of reform thinking that descended
from writers such as Jean Gerson, Nicholas of Cusa, and the anonymous
author of *The Reformation of Emperor Sigismund*. Their common aim was to
produce a more devout laity through a better formed and disciplined clergy
more devoted to pastoral service, and they saw the key to this goal in the
reform or even abolition of the benefice system. Wimpheling owed something to this tradition, although his own criticism of the clergy and the
benefice system aimed to free the church's resources for the support of learning.
Geiler, by contrast, conceived of the clergy as servants of the commune.
"The Son of Man," he once preached,

> is not come to be ministered to but to minister. All rulers, temporal and
> spiritual, should hear this and should believe not that the commune belongs
> to them, but they to the commune. The communes exist not for their
> sake, but they for the commune's sake. They are the commune's servants.[68]

Through his emphasis on the material and spiritual interdependence of laity
and clergy, Geiler tried to hold at bay the specter of anticlericalism that
haunted his last years at Strasbourg. The wine and corn, he preached, which
"is packed into our cellars, is all given to us so that we might celebrate the
mass and do our other duties, not so that we can collect three or four
whores apiece, as the proud college boys at the bishop's court do."

Sturm's two mentors, Wimpheling and Geiler, thus presented two different but related images of the clerical life. In Wimpheling's way, one became a clergyman in order to be free for personal improvement and learning;
in Geiler's way, a clergyman was called to minister to the laity. The benefice
system, which suited Wimpheling so long as the nobles were not allowed to
hog it, formed a formidable barrier to Geiler's idea of reform. This contrast
found political expression as well. Wimpheling was the familiar of princes
and kings; during the 1470s he had tutored young Wittelsbach princes at

Heidelberg and joined the hue and cry against Burgundy;[69] in later years he praised the House of Austria and vilified its foes, the French and the Swiss.[70] His mockery of the Swiss as upstarts contrasted with Geiler's view that the Swiss were common folk who had quite justifiably revolted against their oppressors.[71]

These differences help to explain why Wimpheling's program, which may have helped his pupils get ahead in the church and opened their eyes to the new Italian learning, bore little direct relevance to what may be called the church's "pastoral deficit." The inability to meet demands for better pastoral service by the clergy arose, at least in the diocese of Strasbourg— the only Imperial diocese that has been studied—from the clergy's dependence on the benefice system, usury, and the market in foodstuffs to maintain its economic position at the expense of the peasantry. Reform thus meant to turn the clergy and the church's patrimony from the exploitation of the laity to their service, an enterprise to which Wimpheling's "mediocre program" was relevant only in a very remote sense.[72]

Wimpheling's guidance nonetheless did convey to young men a love of the new humanist learning, more suited than the old, perhaps, to the burghers' world, and a sense of how to get ahead in the church. Ambitious young clergymen clustered around him during his Strasbourg period between about 1505 and 1517, many of them beneficed canons in the local collegiate churches, others active in the schools or the printshops.[73] Into their ranks Jacob Sturm moved when he returned from the university in 1508.

A GENTLEMAN OF THE CLOTH

The activities of Wimpheling and his circle framed Jacob Sturm's life at Strasbourg from 1508 to about 1517. The old mentor strove to bring the new learning to a city that one humanist described in these sneering words: "Strasbourg is like a mother to the illiterate, while she treats the learned and virtuous like a stepmother."[74] Wimpheling was above all a skilled cultivator of networks, and, already in Jacob Sturm's Freiburg days, he took his pupil on his travels, to Basel to see the publisher Johannes Amerbach and to Pforzheim to the great Johannes Reuchlin, who could tell the young man stories about Young Peter Schott.[75] Back at Strasbourg, Sturm developed under the watchful eye of Wimpheling, who continued to give him books, such as a large volume containing both scholastic and humanist writings, plus twenty-eight of his own letters, a collection which typifies both Wimpheling and the Upper Rhenish humanism of this era.[76] And Sturm reciprocated by helping Sebastian Brant to see one of Wimpheling's books through the press. He also began to establish his own persona as a scholar. When, for example, a Swabian scholar wrote to ask about an Augsburg woman who allegedly lived without eating, Sturm replied—based on the opinion of Gianfrancesco Pico della Mirandola, who had visited Strasbourg in 1505—that the phenomenon was natural rather than miraculous.[77]

Sturm also participated in the circle's social gatherings. It may be doubted that Strasbourg was ever home to a formal literary club (*sodalitas*) with regular meetings, but beginning about 1505, Wimpheling and the other friends of the *bonae litterae* gathered occasionally to dine, drink, declaim, and discuss. The custom may have begun at Martin Sturm's chateau at Breuschwickersheim, where Wimpheling and some friends were visiting in the summer of 1505 or 1506, when a local farmer dug up a Roman cult object. The group amused themselves by identifying the figures on it: Venus by her nudity, Minerva by her shield and helmet, and Juno by her peacock.[78]

Wimpheling's circle at Strasbourg contained some genuine scholars, such as the Lorraine schoolteacher Matthias Ringmann, called "Philesius," who in 1507 helped to prepare the great Waldseemüller map for the press.[79] It also included some clerical thugs, such as the notorious Wolf clan. Their chief was Thomas Wolf, Sr., the son of a rich Eckbolsheim farmer and a Strasbourgeoise, who became a gentleman-clergyman and pluralist at Strasbourg.[80] Of the four nephews who followed his lead as clerical idlers, two, Cosmas and Johann Andreas, ranked among the most notorious clerical seducers of young women at Strasbourg.[81] Wimpheling, a strong critic of concubinage and sexual impropriety in others, corrected the Wolfs privately but maintained their friendship. The fourth Wolf brother, Amandus, died young, and the memorial volume the circle produced for him offers an insight into its mentality. The volume contained a treatise entitled *De miseria humana* by the Bolognese humanist Giovanni Garzoni, a teacher of Peter Schott's, who managed to discuss the human condition at length with only one Christian allusion.[82] Jacob Sturm contributed to this volume a Latin couplet, the only lines he ever published.

The remainder of Wimpheling's Strasbourg circle, which Othmar Nachtigall once called "the learned and virtuous," was perhaps more respectable but not much more distinguished. A list composed about 1514 of a "literary sodality of the city of Strasbourg" mentions "the four noble Sturms," presumably Jacob, Peter, their elder brother Friedrich, and either their youngest brother, Stephan, or their father, plus other men, mostly Wimpheling protegés who never attained distinction.[83] Other contemporary lists confirm that the circle consisted mostly of beneficed Alsatian clergymen born between 1470 and 1490, few of whom acquired more than minor literary reputations.[84] They mostly fit the Wimpheling mold: ambitious, well-educated men from modest backgrounds in provincial towns, who sought financial security through the church and fame through letters.[85] Jacob Sturm and a couple of other rich boys departed from this pattern only by virtue of their social rank.[86]

Into this milieu in the mid-1510s, Erasmus of Rotterdam shot like a meteor across the heavens. The great Dutch humanist was everything Wimpheling advocated but could not become. His program taught "the reform of education by a return to the classics, the reform of piety by a return to the original meaning of Scripture, and the moral amelioration of society by means of these reforms in piety and education."[87] Perhaps the most important initial sign of Erasmian influence was that the young men at Strasbourg began to push beyond Wimpheling's program of morals and learning into the direct study of pagan antiquity, classical Latinity, and Greek. These studies brought them through the gateway into a new world, the international republic of letters, another great step away from the needs of the everyday, local world in which they lived, where an ignorant laity superstitiously, in the Erasmian view, clung to its ritual religion, blind to the edifying wonders of ancient philosophy.[88]

The central moment in the Erasmian conquest of Wimpheling's circle came in August 1514, when the great man stopped on his way upstream to Basel.[89] The Strasbourgeois laid on a splendid dinner—Wimpheling and Brant presiding—in the house of the Knights Hospitaler, called "St. John's on the Green Island," which the Netherlander repaid in effusive praise, his best coin. At Strasbourg, he wrote, he had discovered "the virtues of all the most celebrated city-states: Roman severity, Athenian wisdom, and Spartan self-restraint."[90] The twenty-five-year-old Jacob Sturm stood out in this group, for he caught Erasmus's eye and held it. In his letter of thanks, Erasmus sent greetings "particularly to that incomparable young man, Jacob Sturm, who adds luster to his distinguished family by his own high character and crowns his youth with a seriousness worthy of riper years, and whose incredible modesty lends great charm to his uncommon learning."[91] Fifteen years later, his opinion had not changed: "First . . . among the nobles now for doctrine, sincerity, candor, and prudence is the most noble Jacob Sturm, to whose counsels not only the illustrious city of Strasbourg is indebted, but nearly all of Germany as well."[92] Erasmus's praise, in turn, evoked lifelong devotion from Jacob Sturm, who sprang to defend him against detractors, such as the a Strasbourg Dominican who ridiculed Erasmus's edition of the New Testament. Sturm asked the friar if he read it, and when he replied he had not, Sturm responded: "How then can you say so much about a book you have not read nor even seen?"[93] Erasmus repeated this story with relish and called Sturm "a young man of excellent wit and good judgment, unusually learned and a very great supporter of mine."[94] In fact, the banquet at Strasbourg in 1514 was probably the only occasion on which the two men ever met.

The value of Erasmianism to Jacob Sturm and his like is difficult to overestimate, for it led them from Wimpheling's cluttered eclecticism into the international neoclassical world of the *bonae litterae*. One mark of belonging to this world was a knowledge of Greek, and in 1515, one year after Erasmus's visit, the Sélestat humanist Beatus Rhenanus reported that the friends at Strasbourg were busy learning Greek.[95] Sturm's horizons widened with the others'. He studied Greek with the others, and he cultivated Rhenanus, whom he presented with a collection of poems by Hungary's leading Latin poet, János Csezmiczei, bishop of Pécs.[96] Gradually, even though he published nothing, Sturm's reputation for learning was getting around.

Jacob Sturm's reputation first spread beyond his native city because of the literary battles of the 1510s. Polemics in print belonged to Wimpheling's style and did much to cement his circle's self-consciousness. One chose an opponent, preferably a mendicant friar, and published a volume of polemics against him, suitably adorned with admiring verses and letters contributed by friends. The issues could be trivial—whether St. Anne had been married, whether St. Augustine had been a monk, whether the Swiss or the Alsatians were the true "Helvetians," or whether Alsace had ever been ruled by a French monarch—the combat itself was everything. Such ritualized combats enabled Wimpheling's circle, and later the German humanists as a whole, to become "a self-conscious group with a heightened sense of common interests and solidarity," whose wit, levity, and irreverence contributed to the intellectual atmosphere in which Luther later emerged into public life.[97] During the 1510s, the Wimpheling circle merged into the larger party of the *bonae litterae*, which under the titular presidency of Erasmus pressed the causes of rhetoric against that of logic and the ancient writers against the scholastics, hoping, at least at their most socially conscious, that unprejudiced study of the biblical and other texts could afford that wisdom that would both bring to light the genuine truth and revivify once more both church and society. This party's battles, mainly against real or alleged advocates of traditional, scholastic learning, shared a style of combat with the earlier feuds of Wimpheling and his circle.[98] Their scale, however, was immensely greater, and in the 1510s broke out the monster literary battle of the era, the Reuchlin affair, which from that day to this has shaped the reputation of German humanism. Its most important literary monument, the *Letters of Obscure Men* (1515–17), defended Reuchlin against the Dominicans of Cologne by means of ridicule, hyperbole, and "clever mockeries" and extolled the ranks of Reuchlin's real and alleged partisans, including "Jacob Sturm, a nobleman, who is said to be a good Latinist."[99]

Was Jacob Sturm a "humanist" in this sense, an advocate of the *bonae litterae*? He certainly was, for his opinions are documented by a memorial he wrote in 1522 for Florenz von Venningen, chancellor of the Palatinate, on the reform of studies at Heidelberg.[100] The document opens with a critique of the education Sturm obtained at Heidelberg. "Eighteen years ago, at the age of twelve," he wrote, "I learned grammar and logic there, which have partly been wiped from my memory and partly improved in the interim." The method of instruction then, he complained,

> was most pedestrian, traditional, and poor, and contrived assignments were intentionally given to squander talents and misuse the precious hours. Indeed, the books of Aristotle were read then . . ., but by a most unfortunate teacher, who was nearly ignorant of both Greek and Latin. So neither he who read nor any of his hearers understood it—a great waste of money, time, and ability, and devoid of benefit to the students.[101]

Logic and rhetoric, Sturm thought, should be learned not from the old writers but from "George of Trebizond or Rudolph Agricola (whose ashes rest here in Heidelberg at the Franciscans' house) or others of the rhetoricians," and Aristotle in "the translations by [Johannes] Argyropoulos or Leonardo Bruni Aretino" and in "Jacques Lefèvre d'Étaples's paraphrases." A professor of classics should be hired, who "should know both Latin and Greek and be able to teach his students the rudiments of the Greek language."

Sturm also had some ideas about theological studies, "albeit I never heard theology at Heidelberg, I fear that things there are much as in other German universities." "In my experience [at Freiburg]," he wrote,

> nothing was taught but those scholastics, called "doctors," who wrote after the Gothic and Vandalic invasions had destroyed all good letters. Their books neglect the New and Old Testaments, esteem none but one Master of Sentences [Peter Lombard], and contain many curious things which are not conducive to Christian piety.

The mendicants might continue to teach "their Thomas and Scotus to the students who want to study them," but two theologians should give daily lectures on the Bible, one on each testament, "taking also as seems good from the older Greek and Latin theologians—Origen, Basil, Gregory of Nazianzus, Chrysostom, Jerome, Hilary, and Augustine."

To contrast Sturm's program with that of Wimpheling, who also wrote for Venningen, is to measure the change Erasmianism had effected. For although the mentor admitted that much modern (i.e., scholastic) theology was conducive neither "to the honor of God, to the salvation of souls, nor to the progress of Christian states," and though he lamented the backwardness of Latin speech and style and condemned "neglect of the Bible and the Fathers," Wimpheling did not want to abandon scholastic textbooks for neoclassical ones.[102] Sturm, by contrast, promoted a typically Erasmian combination of ancient and humanist authors, based on classical Latin and Greek, against most of what had been thought and written between the Germanic invasions and the fourteenth century.

A Young Clergyman

In 1517, after a decade of *dolce far niente*, Jacob Sturm embarked on a career. By July of that year he had become secretary to Count Palatine Henry, sixth son of the late Elector Palatine Philip and brother of the current elector.[103] Only two years Sturm's elder, Henry already held benefices as provost of two cathedral chapters, Aachen and Strasbourg, the beginnings of a brilliant career as one of the greatest pluralist prelates of his age.[104] When he got the post as Henry's secretary, probably on Wimpheling's recommendation, Sturm began to style himself "clergyman [*clericus*]," a sign of his embarkation on a career.[105] Indeed, he had hitched his wagon to a mighty horse, for as provost of Strasbourg, Count Henry administered the wealth of the cathedral chapter, a body so aristocratic, Erasmus once joked, that Jesus Christ could not have joined it for lack of sufficiently noble ancestors.[106] For more than six years, from July 1517 to November 1523, Sturm served as secretary and looked after the prince's far-flung properties, incomes, and interests. He traveled a good deal in Henry's service, to Aachen, for example, for several months at the beginning of his service, and when the prince moved to Ellwangen in 1521 or 1522, Sturm acted as his agent at Strasbourg.[107]

The times were hardening, as Jacob Sturm began his new career. Following two bad harvests in Alsace, vines froze during the winter of 1516–17. Around Obernai, Joss Fritz tried to breathe new life into the insurrectionary movement, known as "the *Bundschuh*," in the villages, including Martin Sturm's Düppigheim.[108] Wimpheling, who in 1517 took up residence in his parish at Sulz in Lower Alsace, expressed the somber mood of the later 1510s in a remarkable "Prayer of the Common Man to God," which voiced the just complaints of the peasants, "who nourish the whole of society and in return have only their poverty."[109]

Jacob Sturm's new post gave him his first taste of the world of high politics, in which the great German dynasties strove to hold and increase what they had. That his political initiation occurred in this world, not in the communal-federal world his great-grandfather had known, was a sign of how times had changed. Sturm's most important charge was to act for Count Henry in the struggle to gain the prince-provostship of Ellwangen in the Jagst Valley of Lower Swabia.[110] Vacated in 1519, when the Swabian League ousted Duke Ulrich from his state of Württemberg, Ellwangen became the object of a three-way contest among Count Henry, a Hohenzollern claimant, and the league's candidate. Henry possessed the emperor's support and played on the Lutheran danger to secure backing in Rome and on the local townsfolk's sentiment to bully Ellwangen's stubborn chapter.[111] His victory, aided by "the power of his brothers, kinsmen, and friends [*fratrum consanguineorum et amicorum potestas*]," made a powerful impression on his young Alsatian secretary.

Good patrons reward faithful servants, and Count Henry, as befitted such a powerful young prince, tried to reward Sturm with a good benefice. A rich store of benefices flowed from the rights an emperor acquired at his election, and Count Henry got control of some of the appointments that the new emperor, Charles V, bargained away during his electoral negotiations.[112] One of them, the next vacant canonry at St. Stephan's, Strasbourg, the count intended for his secretary. Alas, Sturm's old friend Othmar Nachtigall, then living at Augsburg, had been promised the same benefice, and the ensuing fight between two benefice-hunting disciples of Wimpheling lasted into 1523 and went all the way to Rome. It became so bitter that Nachtigall spread the charge that Sturm would not reside and intended, in any case, to leave the clergy.[113] This may well have been so, for Sturm had earlier been frustrated in his efforts to secure a benefice at Mainz through Wolfgang Capito, a Hagenauer whom he had known at Freiburg. Now a councillor of the elector of Mainz, Capito had stood for the provostship of St. Thomas, Strasbourg, and in June 1520 Sturm sought his aid in getting a canon at Mainz to resign in Sturm's favor.[114] When Capito in 1521 claimed the provostship at St. Thomas in absentia, "Master Jacob Sturm, clergyman of the diocese of Strasbourg," was one of his procurators.[115]

By 1522, fourteen years after he left the university, Jacob Sturm still had no benefice. It must have been maddening to go empty handed while all around him young clergymen of ignoble birth raked in fat livings. The Wolfs, for example, literally wallowed in them. The elder Thomas Wolf, who was a rich peasants' son, held many benefices at his death in 1511; his nephew, Thomas, Jr., was beneficed well before he died at Bologna in 1509; and another nephew, Cosmas, was already a canon when he arrived to study at Freiburg in 1504, three months after Jacob Sturm arrived.[116] What was their secret, these base-born, high-living Wolfs? Jacob Sturm, by contrast, was now a thirty-three-year-old unbeneficed clergyman, despite his honorable ancestry, influential family, powerful patron, and reputation as a friend of the *bonae litterae*. Twice, when a benefice appeared within his grasp, he reached for it, and twice he failed. He had already lived longer, but made much less of a mark, than his kinsman and model, Young Peter Schott. Indeed, since his departure from Freiburg, fourteen years before, he had done nothing to distinguish himself from the hundreds of other young clergymen who pursued clerical livings in the region. Meanwhile, time went flying, and death carried off much of his family: Uncle Ludwig and his wife, Anna von Endingen, in 1516, his mother and maternal grandmother in 1519, his father in October 1521, Uncle Ott in 1522, and his brother Stephan shortly thereafter.[117] That left six Sturm siblings: Anna a married woman, Clara a Dominican nun, and Veronica; and Friedrich, Jacob, and Peter—all unmarried.

The Reformation movement thus broke in on Jacob Sturm's life after a long period of idleness, frustrated hopes of preferment, and losses of kinsmen and -women to death. The early 1520s, of course, was a time of testing for clergymen in the Empire, especially in the south, as Luther's movement began to challenge the very reasons for their existence. What had begun with isolated preaching and pamphleteering in 1520–21 had burst out into the streets, shops, taverns, homes, and guildhalls.

By early 1523, when the South German Reformation movement was "shaking the townsmen to their depths," Jacob Sturm was confronted on all sides by a world in religious flux.[118] The movement challenged him directly in two ways, through the conversions of friends and acquaintances and through books. All around him by 1523, important people were embracing the new movement, such as Hans Bock von Gerstheim, Sturm's future father-in-law, a university-educated nobleman, prominent stettmeister, and familiar of

Wimpheling's.[119] At the Diet of Worms in 1521, Bock had begged Luther, "Dear Sir Doctor, please don't burden your own heart and those of other Christians"—to which Luther had replied, "No, the pope has burdened my heart and those of others, and I want only to relieve the burden through God's Word and the truth."[120] Although during Lent 1522 Bock still thought that Luther would end up at the stake, in 1523 he came over to Luther's side. Jacob Sturm knew from the best sources—Friedrich, his brother, had entered the Senate in 1520—that the movement was steadily gaining ground among the magistrates and their relations. One of their Mieg cousins, Daniel, who became ruling ammeister in 1524, became an Evangelical, though his rich kinsman, Andreas, did not.[121] By 1523 hot words were flying in the Senate's chambers at city hall, as the new movement gained powerful advocacy in the persons of two young altammeisters, fiery Martin Herlin from the Furriers' Guild and Claus Kniebis, a tough lawyer from the Smiths' Guild.[122]

Clergymen, too, were taking sides in 1523. Mathis Zell, Sturm's acquaintance from Freiburg days and now the cathedral parish's pastor, had been since 1522 the movement's most effective local voice.[123] Then, in 1523, the movement won a truly important clerical leader. Wolfgang Capito of Hagenau, another former Freiburg student and former professor at Basel, had come from Mainz to Strasbourg as provost of St. Thomas in February 1523.[124] Although he strove for months to remain uninvolved, by autumn the pressure on him was mounting, as the priests began to marry in public defiance of their bishop and the canon law. Jacob Sturm's decision to abandon his own clerical career coincided with these first clerical marriages and with Capito's growing partisanship.[125]

The written word, too, pressed Sturm toward decision, as the Evangelical movement gathered strength from the tremendous torrent of books and pamphlets about religion, which poured from the Empire's presses during the first half of the 1520s. Strasbourg, a chief center of the printing industry, was also a major fount of Reformation agitation through the printed word. Between 1518 and 1524 the number of new editions from the city's presses nearly tripled, and Evangelical literature formed most of the increase.[126] The printed word's role in his own conversion was attested by Sturm in a 1540 conversation at Worms with Johann Eck, another acquaintance from Freiburg days. In response to an ill-tempered jibe from Eck, Sturm said that in those days, "I read the writings of both sides and was persuaded by those of our side."[127] This testimony asserts, nearly two decades after the fact, that in 1523 Sturm made a deliberate choice, an act of conversion. This is substantiated by an unexpected source, his old teacher, Wimpheling. In 1523 the seventy-year-old teacher and priest was living in retirement at his native Sélestat. To him the new Evangelical movement seemed a revival of Hussitism, the "Wycliffism" that the Bohemians had spread more than a century before. The old man heard that Capito was preaching at Strasbourg that one might as well "pray to a dog" as to the Mother of God, the city's patroness. "O, how horrible," he wrote to Capito, whom he begged not to desert the Fathers and the scholastic theologians for "the foul-mouthed Wycliffites."[128] Even worse, in early November he wrote to a Strasbourg friend to lament that his favorite lamb, Jacob Sturm, "is patently infected with the Wycliffite poison."[129] When Wimpheling asked Sturm whether this rumor were true, the reply went straight to the old man's heart: "If I am a heretic, you made me one."

By his own testimony, therefore, Jacob Sturm's conversion to Evangelical religion around the end of October 1523 depended in some way on his formation at Wimpheling's hands. How is this to be understood? Did Luther's influence hatch the egg planted by Wimpheling and incubated by Erasmus? Sturm's formation, after all, followed a pattern familiar to us from the careers of other young clergymen of his generation, many of whom moved from typical university formations through Erasmianism to the Evangelical religion.[130] Clearly, Wimpheling's own pedagogy contained criticisms of the contemporary church that, as he admitted to Capito, could become explosively anticlerical in the hands of persons not loyal to the Roman church.[131] Just as clearly, however, Sturm moved with much of his generation beyond the loyal criticism of tradition and of abuses to a sharp rejection of much of the theology that legitimized the old church. This is already clear in his opinion on university reform of 1522, in which his sharply Erasmian critique went well beyond anything Wimpheling could tolerate.[132] Sturm's religious views, too, reflect the more advanced spiritualism of Erasmus, whose influence intensified Wimpheling's moralism and emphasis on self-discipline.[133] There is no trace in Sturm's record, on the other hand, of a movement from this line of intensifying spiritual religion to a direct engagement with the core of Luther's theology.

Another clue to Sturm's conversion, perhaps, is provided by its consequences. Most of the young clergymen who became Evangelicals at this time simply shifted their lives toward preaching, teaching, and other pastoral work. Their demonstrative marriages and their willing assumption of citizenship advertised their desire to close the gap between clerical and lay ways of living, but they remained clergymen. Jacob Sturm did not. Instead, within a couple of months of his conversion, he entered the Senate and embarked on a political career. Sturm's fall away from the old toward the new in religion, therefore, pushed him back into his heritage, the world shaped by both sides of his lineage. The Reformation made Sturm not a better man of the church, something he had never truly been, but a true man of the city. This movement contained, too, a minor element of homecoming. Jacob Sturm had moved from a world shaped by the sternly pastoral moralism of Johann Geiler into the eclectic, personalist piety of Wimpheling, and thence through the learned, eloquent elitism of Erasmus. Each transition took him further from his ancestors' religious world, which combined personal devotion with public observance in a communal setting.

Sturm's laicization, therefore, brought his humanist-spiritualist formation back into a communal setting. Here, in contrast to Count Henry's service, he found a common good worthy of his service and a platform adequate to his talents.

A BURGHER'S WORLD

When Jacob Sturm took his first oath of office on Schwörtag (7 January 1524), the day on which new magistrates were invested and the burghers renewed their oath of citizenship, he entered a world defined by rank, gender, and wealth. The burghers filed through the cold streets toward Cathedral Square by corporations, the patricians from their social clubs (*constoffeln*) and the commoners from their guildhalls, and took their customary places around three sides of the wooden scaffold that stood before the cathedral's stupendous west portal. After a reading of the constitution of 1482, Old Peter Schott's *Schwörbrief*, the burghers swore to uphold the commune's liberties and obey its laws.[134] This year, 1524, Jacob and Peter Sturm joined their brother Friedrich on the scaffold for this most solemn of the commune's rituals.

Active burghers were by definition adult males, and the traditional conception of the commune as a pyramid of male authority—a corporation of corporate guilds and societies made up of corporate households—drew new force from the Reformation's pressure on the clergy to marry and conform to this pattern.[135] Jacob Sturm also married, as befitted his new station. Not long after his conversion he married a daughter—her name is unknown—of Hans Bock von Gerstheim and Ursula von Fleckenstein, who were as well connected among the nobilities of southwestern Germany as any citizen could be.[136] Jacob Sturm's wife soon died, however, and in 1529 he and Peter bought a mansion in Fire Street (*Brandgasse*), a quarter favored by Strasbourg's leading families. There Jacob Sturm lived for the rest of his life, together with Friedrich, Peter, and their sister Veronica, none of whom ever married.[137]

Nothing more is known about Sturm's marriage, which was so fleeting that many who later knew him believed he had never been married.[138] Nor is anything known about why he did not remarry, or why so many of his siblings did not marry at all. Whether his sister Clara, whom Jacob and his brother in 1524 removed from the Dominican convent of SS. Margaret and Agnes, ever married, is unknown.[139] Their sister Anna did marry an ultrarespectable Zorn von Plobsheim, but Jacob and his unmarried brothers left the male line of the Sturms in a precarious state: of at least eight male Sturms of their generation, sons of Martin and his brothers, only one of Uncle Ott's boys, Cousin Stephan, produced male heirs. The Sturms' reluctance to marry took its revenge several generations later, when the entire lineage came to an end in 1640, four centuries after they had come across the Rhine from Offenburg.[140]

To their bachelorhood and the leisure it afforded, the three Sturm brothers brought another prime asset for magisterial careers, substantial incomes. No matter how broadly based, the inner regimes of the South German and Swiss cities were composed of full-time, unpaid offices for life, which only the well-to-do could afford to fill.[141] The Sturm brothers could very well afford their long magisterial careers. Their household, among the city's best, was amply supplied by rents in kind—wheat, rye, barley, beans, peas, and wine—from their holdings around Breuschwickersheim, and the feudal dues— the tallage (*Bede*) of 60 fl. plus about forty chickens (*Fastnachtshennen*)— supplemented their long roll of peasant rents and debts from the same district.[142] What they didn't use for their own household, they sold, for example, to local bakers.[143] They also continued the practice of their father— and most other wealthy Strasbourgeois—of usury, that is, lending money at interest to humble folk.[144] Other sums came in from scattered holdings, some allodial and some feudal, in other parts of the region. The siblings had inherited many properties, rentes, and fiefs, the allodial portions of which passed to Cousin Stephan, Uncle Ott's son, and to Anna Sturm, and through her to the Bocks von Gerstheim, while the feudal tenures passed in 1559 from Friedrich, who held them for himself and his childless brothers, to Cousin Stephan and his male heirs.[145] The administration of the lands demanded time and energy, for charters of enfiefment had to be renewed each time the family's fiefholder or the enfiefing lord died,[146] and allodial lands were subject, like the city's own rural lands, to civic regulations and taxes.[147] Peter Sturm undertook most of this work for himself and his brothers, as we find him in 1530 mediating a dispute over a fee between the Sturms' village of Düttelnheim and a surgeon of the Great Hospital, and somewhat later lodging a complaint to Bishop William that the Sturms' co-tenants of the wine tithe at Northeim were collecting more than their share of it.[148]

The Sturm siblings in Fire Street seem to have maintained both personal and communal property. Jacob Sturm appears alone, for example, in a list of 1533–34 as a leading creditor of the city.[149] Although his testament has not survived, that of his brother, Friedrich, has.[150] It lists a large debt of 1,500 fl. owed him by Duke Christoph of Württemberg, which yielded 75 fl. a year, plus considerable wealth in plate ("*meyn silberen geschierlin*") and gold chains, which he divided among his nephews. He also left his sister, Veronica, some plate and 200 fl. "in interest or in peasants' money," plus a gold chain. She possessed, of course, no claim on the feudal revenues. These data, plus the testament of the siblings' cousin and heir, Stephan Sturm, bolster the general impression of secure wealth and comfortable living, an image enhanced by their possession of a fine library, the core of which came from Young Peter Schott, supplemented by Jacob Sturm's many purchases.[151]

All in all, Jacob Sturm fit perfectly into his new social place. If he had abandoned the path of Young Peter Schott, he had done so to follow that of Old Peter. Much had changed, of course, during the forty years since

Old Peter had laid down his offices. The Burgundian power was gone, the comradely Swiss had become estranged neighbors, the Palatine power had been humbled, the House of Austria had risen in the west, and the insurrectionary movement of the *Bundschuh* smoldered in the Upper Rhenish villages. And although civic power, based on the guilds and the societies, remained much as Old Peter had left it, the magistrates of 1524 faced a domestic conflict over religion and religious reform, the likes of which no previous generations of magistrates could have imagined.

A MAGISTRATE'S WORLD

When Jacob Sturm donned his long, fur-trimmed coat and mounted the scaffold on Schwörtag in 1524, he entered an oligarchic world ruled by age and experience. On certain occasions, true, the magistrates consulted the three hundred ruling officials (Schöffen) of the twenty guilds, but everyday management rested with the Senate & XXI, a body shaped by cooptation and lifetime magistracies.[152] At the bottom was the Large Senate, or simply Senate, in which six (plus the four stettmeisters) patrician and twenty guildsman senators sat for two-year terms, half replaced annually. They combined with the XXI to form the commune's ordinary deliberative body, the Senate & XXI. The XXI comprised the privy councils of the XV for domestic affairs and the XIII for diplomacy and war, plus a few others. The four patrician stettmeisters, ceremonial heads of the government, rotated quarterly in office, whereas the de facto head of the government, the ammeister, was a guildsman who served for one year in office and the following five years as "old ammeister" and member of the XIII. The XIII, called "the old men [*die alten herren*]," was always composed of the city's most experienced magistrates, the innermost core of its regime. The Senate & XXI referred current business to them and received advice from them; the whole body then acted or, occasionally, consulted the assembly of the Schöffen.

Jacob Sturm, a gentleman descended from many generations of nobles, entered this hierarchy in 1524 as a patrician senator, and as he rose, more rapidly than others, in the system, he constantly worked alongside men, such as Ammeister Claus Kniebis, whose families and money came from God alone knew where, and whose behavior at the Reformation—Kniebis enriched himself from the dissolution of the convents—was hardly up to a gentleman's standards.[153] Although in many things—business skills, management of their fellows in the guilds, and foreign languages—Sturm's colleagues were fit to rule, they hadn't much advanced education. A handful (5 of 102 privy councillors in Sturm's time) had attended university, and only one—Sturm himself—had any theological training.[154] Then, too, the political changes of the Reformation era took Strasbourg's magistrates far beyond the familiar world of the Upper Rhine, Swabia, and Switzerland and into the company of men from Hesse, Thuringia, Saxony, the Rhineland, and even the Hanseatic towns, regions whose languages and traditions were more poorly comprehended at Strasbourg than were those of Lyon or Venice.

In such a world, Jacob Sturm's connections, manners, and skills were valuable assets, and he rose very swiftly through the government's ranks. He entered the Senate in January 1524, the XV in 1525, the XIII in October 1526, and the stettmeistership, the highest patrician office, on 31 December 1526.[155] He climbed to the summit in three years and remained there for the next twenty-seven, always in the highest seats of power. A privy councilor's regimen was backbreaking: six mornings a week, except when he was on mission, which was often, Sturm walked to the city hall for sessions of the Senate & XXI or one of the privy councils, and between sessions he and his fellows did their very heavy committee work. Sturm's passage upward during the mid-1520s was marked by appointments to important permanent commissions, those dozens of supervisory bodies through which the government's ears, eyes, and hands reached out into the city's shops, taverns, guild-halls, and homes. In 1524 Sturm, for example, joined the Welfare Commission (*Almosenherren*), charged with supervising the city's new poor law, an office that passed to Peter (1531–37) and then to Cousin Stephan (1537–48).[156] Besides the permanent commissions, there were the ad hoc committees that drafted diplomatic correspondence, dealt with petitions, framed new laws and revised old ones, and investigated rumors. The value of Sturm's connections in troubled times is illustrated by an incident from his first year in office. During the summer fair, he reported on 13 July 1524, he talked with the dean of St. Thomas—one of his Wurmser cousins—who avowed that he was no longer willing to play "the bishop's squire."[157] This was a useful tidbit at a time when the regime was trying to break the bishop's hold on the city's clergy.

A vigorous, well-born, well-educated, and well-spoken man of leisure was even more valuable outside the city walls than within, and it was inevitable that, given German urban regimes' chronic shortage of men able to pass in the world of princes and bishops, Jacob Sturm would find his special metier in the city's external affairs. The Reformation movement brought external and internal policy into an especially close connection. The magistrates, for example, hoped that some external power—the emperor, Imperial Diet, or a general council of the church—might provide relief from the mounting pressure for change inside the walls.[158] Hope for the emperor's intervention was especially strong during Jacob Sturm's first months in office, for in 1523 the southern urban regimes had sent envoys—one was Cousin Bernhard Wurmser von Vendenheim—to Charles V in Spain. They sought his protection for their merchants and trade from the princes in return for their financial support. Parallel to this policy—urban solidarity and loyalty to the Crown—ran the demand to refer the religious question to a general council, of which Hans Bock was the chief spokesman at Strasbourg.[159] Both of these hopes were dashed in 1524, when the emperor forbade the calling of a council. By the end of Sturm's first year in office, therefore, the magistrates confronted mounting popular pressure for change within the city and saw no hope of relief from without. All signs pointed to the need for a new foreign policy, as the storm broke over South Germany: in the city, ordinary burghers were disrupting services and demanding new pastors; in the countryside, militant artisans were evangelizing the villagers; and at city hall, reports streamed in about the spread of rebellion out of the Black Forest into the lowlands on both sides of the Rhine.[160]

IN THE EYE OF REVOLUTION

Jacob Sturm's formation in the broader world of Imperial politics occurred during the German Peasants' War of 1525, the greatest popular insurrection in European history before 1789. Just as the revolution's main phase gathered steam, he was sent on mission, his first, to the Imperial Governing Council (*Reichsregiment*), a committee of estates founded in 1521 at Nuremberg to govern the Empire during the emperor's absence.[161] Cousin Bernhard Wurmser von Vendenheim had held this seat in 1522, though in the meantime the council had moved to Esslingen. When Sturm arrived at this middling free city on the Middle Neckar River in late winter 1525, he found the insurrection even more advanced in Swabia than in his native Alsace.[162] The council sent him and Simon Pistoris, a Saxon jurist, across the mountain to Upper Swabia to investigate the situation and to mediate between the rebels and the Swabian League. They came to Ulm, where the league, a very large regional peace-keeping federation, was trying to decide what to do, and from 30 March until about 14 April they moved as arbitrators back and forth between Ulm and the rebels' capital at Memmingen.[163] While the league's army was away in Württemberg, the envoys of its urban members, who desperately pressed for a negotiated peace, were being mocked by the Bavarian chancellor, Leonhard von Eck: "Those who pretended to rule the whole world through their guns, their power, and their learning, are now afraid of their own peasants."[164] Under the leadership of Eck and others of like mind, Sturm and Pistoris were told at Ulm that "the league intends to punish the rebels and will not tolerate a truce."[165] The envoys nonetheless rode on Sunday, 2 April, to Memmingen, and as they started back, one of the rebel armies, the Baltringers, was marching out to meet its doom (on 4 April) at the hands of the league's oncoming army. That left two Upper Swabian armies, which, Sturm and Pistoris reported to Esslingen on the seventh, "will in no way [*gar nicht wollten*] allow themselves to be separated from one another."[166] They rode to the two armies' camps and back to Ulm to negotiate "generously and fairly" for the peasants with the lords, because, the rebels told them, if "we can't get assurance that we, as poor folk, may hold to what is good and just . . . we must rely on divine justice through self-help. Our miserable condition and the whole land's people drive us to this."[167] On 13 April, Sturm and Pistoris made a final appeal to the league's general, Georg Truchsess von Waldburg, whose army next day—

it was Good Friday—crushed one peasant army at Wurzach, and when the third army accepted terms on 24 April, the Upper Swabian revolution was over.[168]

By this time Jacob Sturm was en route to another theater of the revolution.[169] Under orders from the council "to work for a truce and to learn the reasons why [the peasants] rebelled," he came to Heilbronn in the Neckar Valley, where he discovered "all sorts of strange and incredible things."[170] The city and the district lay in the hands of two armies, Jäcklein Rohrbach's Neckar Valley men, fresh from the Weinsberg massacre, and Jörg Metzler's Odenwalders.[171] When the armies appeared before Heilbronn, Sturm reported, the city's senate, under

> pressure from the Common Man, especially the women, had to open the city to them on Easter Tuesday [April 18]. Today [April 22] their commander, Jörg Metzler of Ballenberg, came with many other captains into the city and moved into a special chamber in the city hall. They hold their deliberations there, having posted their own men at the gates, and do what they please. They've occupied all the convents and clerical establishments and plundered them. . . . The Heilbronners have to put up with all this.

Many of the burghers made common cause with the rebels, just as Sturm had seen at Memmingen. "Just as I write this here at Heilbronn," he wrote,

> a placard has been posted ordering all citizens and journeymen who want to join the army to assemble at one of the gates. The senate has to let depart anyone who will. The talk here is that Würzburg has surrendered to the peasants, but I know nothing certain about it.

Heilbronn's helpless mayor stood at the gate and wept, as his people streamed out to join the rebels.[172]

At Heilbronn the rebels' treatment of nobles especially impressed Sturm. The count of Helfenstein's widow, he wrote,

> was brought here in a wagon and robbed of everything she had. . . . Each day many noblemen and captains come to seek terms from the army, and they are given safe-conducts. The counts of Leonstein have made peace, also the city of Wimpfen and everyone else in the neighborhood.

In this world turned upside down, where lords sued their subjects for peace, what could the envoys accomplish? It was another case for the generals and the hangmen, and the envoys prudently rode back upriver, while the Swabian League's army made ready to invade Franconia.

Sturm's term on the council was over, and after brief trips to Esslingen and Ulm, he started for home, arriving sometime after 4 May.[173] Around the city he found the revolution in full swing, fired by a powerful insurrectionary tradition and inflammatory preaching in the villages.[174] One army, commanded by the remarkable Erasmus Gerber of Molsheim, had organized its villages into a federation by means of a constitution.[175] Gerber then moved his men northward, and on 13 May they entered Saverne, the bishop's seat and administrative capital of Lower Alsace.[176] Meanwhile, the citizenry of Strasbourg resonated to the shocks on the land, as burghers crept out to join the rebels, and one rebel army, the Neuenburgers, even asked the Butchers' Guild for powder, guns, and pikes.[177] The whole countryside was out, including the tenants of the Sturms and the Bocks, while a flood of refugees—priests, lords, ladies, and others—streamed into the city for protection.[178] Although the city's mood became volatile between mid-April and mid-May, Strasbourg's commons did not rise, and the guilds' Schöffen stood by the magistrates in votes taken on 11 and 14 May.[179]

At this moment, just as Jacob Sturm arrived from Swabia, the magistrates turned to the task of averting a Swabian-style catastrophe on the Upper Rhine. They resolved "to aid in everything that will be conducive to peace and to the dispersal of the [peasants'] army." It was the policy of the Governing Council and the Swabian League's free cities: a negotiated truce followed by arbitration of grievances and damages.[180] The situation on the Upper Rhine was made especially dangerous by the lack of strong powers in the region, which both presented the rebels with time to organize and tempted neighboring princes to intervene. The prince-bishop's absence at Mainz and the Baden margraves' paralysis created a power vacuum on the right bank and permitted rebel cooperation across the river.[181] No power stood against the rebels, until Duke Antoine of Lorraine's army invaded from the west and Elector Palatine Louis's from the north. Their presence settled the revolution on the river's left bank, but there was still hope for negotiations on the opposite side.

The magistrates' mediation efforts began on 25 April, before Jacob Sturm's return, and for the next three weeks mission upon mission followed, especially to Gerber's forces, who lay twelve to fifteen thousand strong at Saverne.[182] Mediation was fruitless, for Duke Antoine's tough mercenaries came over the mountains in the night of the fifteenth, crushed Gerber's men at Saverne in a tremendous mêlée on the seventeenth, and smashed the peasant army of central Alsace at Schwerwiller on the twentieth.

> What a terrible price to pay,
> Thirteen thousand on a single day.[183]

The Strasbourgeois had no better success in northern Alsace, where Sturm and Mathis Pfarrer joined envoys from five other free cities to ask the Elector Palatine for mercy for the tiny free city of Wissembourg—to no avail. Strasbourg's policy of mediation proved a total failure on the left bank.[184]

The policy of conciliation met with better success on the Rhine's right bank, where by 25 April peasants in the highly parceled Ortenau had united with those of the Acher and Rench valleys to form the eight-thousand-man Oberkirch army. Strasbourg's envoys persuaded this army to sign a truce, but not the Ortenauers farther south, who plundered the monasteries and moved southward to join with the Breisgauers. The first week of May saw a convergence of rebel armies on Freiburg.[185]

On 21 May, four days after the Battle of Saverne, the Senate & XXI of Strasbourg sent Jacob Sturm and Conrad Joham, a wealthy young banker and silk merchant, upriver to mediate between the rebel armies and the city of Freiburg, which opened its gates after an eight-day siege. With the revolution victorious east of the river, Sturm and Joham crossed from Breisach to Sélestat to wait for a reply to their offer of truce from the rebel commander, the redoubtable Hans Müller of Bulgenbach.[186] Meanwhile, in the northern Ortenau, Cousin Bernhard Wurmser was helping to negotiate the Treaty of Renchen, which became a model for the right-bank settlements.[187]

Prospects for a comparable settlement in the south were threatened by the rebel triumph at Freiburg and by Margrave Ernest of Baden's attempts to lure Duke Antoine and his army over the Rhine.[188] The Strasbourgeois, now joined by Baselers and backed by the Austrian regime at Ensisheim and other powers, redoubled their meditating efforts at Offenburg.[189] When some Breisgau commanders moved troops northward to Lahr, eighteen kilometers south of Offenburg, in an obvious attempt to influence the negotiations, Sturm, Joham, and the Baselers rode out to the camp, where fifteen thousand men lay in arms, to persuade those who had not been summoned to Offenburg to move back southward. Most of them did so.[190] It was Sturm's fourth visit to a rebel camp or a rebel-held city. Then, on 13 June, Margrave Ernest and his subjects signed the Treaty of Offenburg, which set interim conditions until a peace conference at Basel on 18 July, which extended the Treaty of Renchen's provisions to Margrave Ernest's subjects, restored the status quo ante, and forbade the further use of force by either side.[191] At a final meeting on 27 August at Basel, Sturm and the Baselers secured general assent to forty articles, plus a fine of five florins per peasant household. "The settlement for the Markgräflerland," writes the revolution's modern historian, "thus fulfilled what the Twelve Articles demanded and, in so doing, removed the causes of the rebellion.[192]

Jacob Sturm spent five months in four major theaters of the revolution of 1525: Upper Swabia, the Swabian-Franconian borderlands in the Neckar Valley, Lower Alsace, and central and southern Baden. As a noble and seignior, his interests lay with those who crushed the revolution; as a burgher and magistrate, he represented a policy of negotiation. He rode into cities brimming with tension, through rural landscapes racked by revolt, and into rebel camps and rebel-held towns; he negotiated with frightened burghers, proud peasants, and vengeful princes. The revolution taught him three lessons. First, farmers—men and women just like his own tenants—would fight "to become their own lords," and many burghers would join them, if they could. Second, the Imperial government was too feeble to influence, much less to control, the course of events. Third, the force of decision lay with the princes, whose power—credit and mercenaries—the rebels could neither match, appropriate, nor neutralize. Such were Jacob Sturm's three lessons from the great revolution: the Common Man's courage, the Empire's weakness, and the princes' might. He experienced the revolution at closer hand and in more places, probably, than any other politician of his generation. At Ulm, Memmingen, Heilbronn, Wissembourg, Breisach, and Offenburg, this master of men saw masterless men and women who strove for justice and a better law, armed with pike, gun, and the "pure gospel" that would set them free. An immense moral distance separated these months from his life, only eighteen months ago, as a gentlemanly clergyman and secretary. Yet the theater of his political baptism worked within familiar bounds—Strasbourg, Alsace, the Upper Rhine, and southwestern Germany. This boundedness of the political landscape, essentially the fifteenth-century world of Sturm's ancestors, was now about to dissolve, for the revolution of 1525 and the Reformation animated and integrated the Empire in a new way, stitching together its regions as had no other events within memory. Together, revolution and Reformation burst the old bounds and opened Jacob Sturm's way into the new political world of the Protestant era.

Notes

* "Ich wünsche dem reich gelück und alles hail,/daß kainer von steten werd seim feind zu tail/das hilf uns, muter Maria one mail,/und hab die arme gmain in deiner pflicht!" Liliencron, ed., *Historische Volkslieder* 1:416, no. 89, stanza 9.

1. The quoted phrase is from Graus, *Pest—Geissler—Judenmorde*, 555. My picture of the fifteenth century and the success of local and regional formations owes a great deal to Moraw, *Von offener Verfassung*.

2. See Brady, *Ruling Class*, 78, 83, 87, 90–91, 311–12, 350–55; Brady, "La famille Sturm," 29–44; Mathis, "Les origines de Jacques Sturm." For the city's topography, I rely on Seyboth, *Das alte Straßburg*.

3. Out of this sale came a long, bitter quarrel over the chateau and other properties between the Sturms and the Rebstocks, the kinsfolk of the last male Winterthur's widow. The details are contained in an agreement of 24 October 1525, in AMS, KS 20, fol. 53r–54v.

4. Some Strasbourgeois were knighted after the Battle of Nancy in 1477, but the larger number became knights after Murten. They were named by the lost Duntzenheim Chronicle, notices from which are preserved in BNUS, MS. 1223, fols. 35v, 36r.

5. Rapp, *Réformes*, 101, 253, 356 n. 68; Santifaller, "Die preces primariae Maximilians I.," 645, no. 517.

6. Rapp, *Réformes*, 101–2, 284–87.

7. HStAD, F 26, nos. 18 and 49. Some nobles did participate in commercial firms, which local law forbade, but the Sturms were not among them. See Fuchs, "Noblesse et grand commerce."

8. HStAD, F 26, no. 18, fol. 15r.

9. Brady, *Ruling Class*, 147–62. In the death inventory of Stephan Sturm, the chief heir of Jacob Sturm and his brothers, Breuschwickersheim comprised only a tenth of his assets. HStAD, F 26, no. 18. There is no comparative material, as no one has yet studied the wealth of Lower Alsatian noble families of this era, but Stephan Sturm was worth more than 47,000 fl. at his death in 1579.

10. See, for example, AMS, KS 14, fol. 23r (7 May 1520), where Martin Sturm buys a third of an inheritance, of which he already had the other two-thirds, consisting of incomes in cash, chickens, wine, and grain, from a butcher ["carnifex"] and his wife.

11. See Fuchs, "Les foires," 318.

12. Wittmer-Meyer, eds., *Livre de Bourgeoisie* 1:68, no. 658; BNUS, MS. 1058, fol. 166v; Schott, *Works* 1:131, no. 111, and 136, no. 116; Wimpheling, *Epithoma* (1505), fol. 36r; Straub, "Notes généalogiques," 91–93; *Ann. Brant*, no. 3350; Mathis, "Les origines de Jacques Sturm," 87–88.

13. Schilling, *Berner Chronik* 1:251. See Brady, *Turning Swiss*, 50–51.

14. Matzinger, *Vereinigung*, 80–81, 268 n. 5; Schilling, *Berner Chronik* 2:167, 169.

15. It was he who proposed to admit Elector Louis to the Lower Union, in which Schott was long a commanding figure. Matzinger, *Vereinigung*, 91, 109, 119, 221; EA, vol. 3, pt. 1:6n.

16. Dollinger, "La ville libre," 110. All earlier accounts of late medieval Strasbourg's regime must be revised in the light of Alioth, *Gruppen an der Macht*.

17. Janssen, ed., *Frankfurts Reichscorrespondenz*, vol. 2, pt. 1:429, no. 608; Schott, *Works* 1:141, no. 34.

18. It is unknown whether these Schotts were related to the prominent Strasbourg printers of that name. See Rott, "Note sur l'imprimerie alsacienne," 69 and the table between 72 and 73; Chrisman, *Lay Culture*, 4, 6–7, 9–10, 14–15.

19. BNUS, MS. 1058, fol. 166v; Wencker, *Collecta archivi*, 428; Schmidt, *Histoire littéraire* 2:1–35, esp. 9 n. 20, 29, 29 n. 78; Dacheux, *Un réformateur catholique*, 426–27.

20. Schott, *Works* 1:31, no. 22, 74, no. 66, 131, no. 111; Schmidt, *Histoire littéraire* 2:3 n. 5; Dacheux, ed., *Fragments*, no. 4235. On the Schotts' charities, see Geiler, *Pater noster*, F. iii.

21. Old Peter, for example, took his son on pilgrimage in 1482 to see Nicholas of Flüe (1417–87), the hermit of Obwalden. Schott, *Works* 1:117–18, no. 107.

22. Ibid., 30, no. 21 (1481); 2:542–43, no. 955.

23. Jacob Wimpheling, *Apologia pro republica christiana*, chap. 34; Berler, "Chronik," 112–13.

24. Schott, *Works* 1:60, no. 54 (1484).

25. Seyboth, *Das alte Straßburg*, 125, 131, 247. The Martinsplatz is long gone; its space is now part of the Place Gutenberg. For the city's social topography, I rely on Kintz, *La société strasbourgeoise*, 94–102, and on my own researches.

26. Wimpheling, *De integritate*, chap. 24; Schott, *Works* 1:80, no. 73; 2:392 n. 87.

27. Schmidt, *Histoire littéraire* 2:29 n. 78. She had pasted the letter in a book, a gift from her brother, which contained some sermons by St. Vincent Ferrer and Geiler's great reform sermon to the diocesan synod of April 1482. Rapp, *Réformes*, 348, calls the sermon "parmi les plus beaux morceaux d'éloquence que Geiler nous a laissés." The volume was destroyed in 1870.

28. Knepper, *Jakob Wimpfeling*, 133–35.

29. Schott, *Works* 1:323–24; JWOS 3:290–91, no. 84.

30. Jacob Wimpheling to Jacob Sturm and Franz Pawel, Heidelberg, 13 September 1499, in JWOS 3:330–31, no. 99.

31. Ibid. 1:31–32; and see ibid. 3:330–31, no. 99. Later, perhaps after he settled at Strasbourg, Wimpheling added a dedication "to Jacob Sturm and his brothers." On Wimpheling's *Adolescentia*, see Herding, in JWOS 1:8. For other aspects of this project, including the parents' approval, see Wimpheling, *De integritate*, E.1; Wimpheling, *Adolescentia*, in JWOS 1:128, 128 n. 351, 130–31; Wimpheling, *Apologia*, chap. 44.

32. Matthias Ringmann Philesius to Jacob Sturm, n.d., in Wimpheling, *Epistola excusatoria ad Suevos*, A.6. Ludwig Sturm's wife did receive several dedications, for which see Schmidt, *Histoire littéraire* 1:212, 263 n. 61.
33. Wimpheling, *Declamatio Philippi Beroaldi*, A.iv–A.iir, now in *JWOS* 3:372–73, no. 119; and there, too, the following quote (but see ibid. 1:130–31). Young Peter had heard Beroaldo at Bologna.
34. Wimpheling, *De integritate libellus*, chap. 1.
35. Ibid., chap. 29. In the second edition (1506), Wimpheling made the reference specific by adding "quoad Jacob Sturm."
36. Rapp, "Préréformes," 193–94.
37. Toepke, ed., *Matrikel Heidelberg* 1:442. On the other pupil, Franz Pawel, see Winterberg, *Schüler*, 56. For the von Köllen–Adelsheim connection, see Brady, *Ruling Class*, 83–84.
38. E. Winckelmann, ed., *Urkundenbuch* 1:161–66, nos. 109–10; Toepke, ed., *Matrikel Heidelberg* 2:615. On the university, see Ritter, *Universität Heidelberg* 1:387–89, 418–19; and on the two schools of philosophy, see Oberman, *Masters*, 3–14.
39. Knepper, *Jakob Wimpfeling*, 102 n. 1; and see 101–2.
40. Riegger, *Amoenitates*, 210.
41. Ibid., 424.
42. Mayer, ed., *Matrikel Freiburg* 1:157 n. 26.
43. Specklin, *Collectanées*, no. 2190. See Douglass, *Justification*, 9, 9 n. 3; Schmidt, *Histoire littéraire* 1:369.
44. *JWOS* 1:364; Riegger, *Amoenitates*, 204–5; Mayer, ed., *Matrikel Freiburg* 1:172. See Knepper, *Jakob Wimpfeling*, 180–81. Wimpheling visited Jacob Sturm at Freiburg in July 1508. *JWOS* 3:636–37, no. 244. The boys grandly styled themselves "Sturm von Sturmeck," an appellative used by other Sturms, though never by the adult Jacob Sturm. It referred to a mill they owned on the Ill River. Hatt, *Une ville du XVe siècle*, 250. For the opposition of Martin Sturm's relatives, see Riegger, *Amoenitates*, 172. Cologne enjoyed some favor among Alsatians, though not as much as Freiburg, Basel, and Heidelberg. Rapp, "Les strasbourgeois et les universités rhénanes," 11–22.
45. There is a very long, erroneous tradition that Jacob Sturm studied law at Freiburg. See, for a recent example, K. Fuchs, "Zur Politik," 170: "Der Straßburger Jurist und Ratsherr Jacob Sturm." It may be laid to rest by this passage from a letter by Jacob Sturm to Landgrave Philip of Hesse, Strasbourg, 29 June 1534: "Eurer fürstlichen gnaden schreyben sampt den vberschickten Artickeln hab ich empfangen. Vnd nach dem ich der sachen fur min person zu klein verstendig, der rechten auch vnerfaren vnd nitt gelert, vnd dan wenig der rechten gelerten hie, so mit diser sachen zuuertrawen, hab ich sollich artickel doctor [Franz] Froschen euerer fürstenlichen gnaden begern noch zugestölt." HStA Marburg, PA 2915, fol. 310r.
46. Riegger, *Amoenitates*, 163n.
47. Mayer, ed., *Matrikel Freiburg* 1:146, no. 11; Oberman, *Masters*, 128–57; Bauer, *Fakultät*, 187–88; Schaub, "Elsässische Studenten," 279–82; Ziegelbauer, *Johannes Eck*, 11–12, 81.
48. Herminjard, ed., *Correspondances* 5:401–2, no. 182a; Wimpheling, "Das Leben des Johannes Geiler von Kaysersberg," in *JWOS* 2:84n.
49. Santifaller, "Die preces primariae Maximilians I.," 645, nos. 515, 517.
50. *JWOS* 2:18, 84 lines 837–48; Riegger, *Amoenitates*, 124–25. The funeral is described by Matern Berler, "Chronik," 115.
51. These details and others were transferred from the biography of Jean Sturm,

Strasbourg's humanist schoolmaster, an error which arose in the late sixteenth century and, alas, continues to this day. See Lehr, "Jacques Sturm de Sturmeck," 162–63, one of many examples.

52. Specklin, *Collectanées*, no. 2163, with the wrong year of death.

53. Schott, *Works* 1:xxi–xxxi; Schmidt, *Histoire littéraire* 2:2–35.

54. Schott, *Works* 1:38, no. 30; 43, no. 36; 45, no. 39; 46, no. 40; 208–9, no. 190.

55. Ibid. 1:226–35, 255–56, nos. 213–15, 228.

56. Ibid. 1:143, no. 36. On his desire to return to Paris, see ibid. 1:65–66, no. 60; 2:405 n. 121.

57. Ibid. 1:202–4, nos. 184–85, and 2:700; Schmidt, *Histoire littéraire* 2:32–33.

58. Schott, *Works* 2:391–92 and n. 87, gathers the sources.

59. The phrase "mediocre program" comes from Rapp, *Réformes*, 162–65, who provides the first realistic assessment of humanism at Strasbourg.

60. See, in general, Overfield, *Humanism*, 81–88.

61. Rapp, "Préréformes," 167; Rapp, *Réformes*, 164, 298; Oberman, *Masters*, 4–10; Oberman, "University," 19–41.

62. Wimpheling, *Adolescentia*, in *JWOS* 1:365–67.

63. Wimpheling, *Declamatio*, A.iv, in *JWOS* 3:409–14, no. 135. Hans von Kageneck, the subject of one story, had campaigned with Uncle Ott Sturm in the 1470s. Wimpheling's warnings against fornication took force from the appearance of syphilis ("*mala Frantzosen*") at Strasbourg only five years before. "Strassb. Archiv-Chronik," in *Code historique*, vol. 1, pt. 2:216.

64. See, e.g., *JWOS* 3:377–78, no. 121. See Schmidt, *Histoire littéraire* 1:314 and n. 168.

65. Müller, *Bildung und Erziehung*, 321.

66. The story is told rather sheepishly by Knod, *Jakob Wimpfeling*, 176–77. On Burckhart, see Oliger, "Der päpstliche Zeremonienmeister," 100–232; Rapp, *Réformes*, 229–30, 291 n. 60.

67. *JWOS* 3:629–30, no. 242; 682–85, no. 277; 696, no. 282a; 704–5, no. 287. He had nonetheless attacked papal reservations on the ground that they deprived German princes of German benefices. See his reply to Enea Silvio Piccolomini, excerpted by Strauss, ed., *Manifestations of Discontent*, 46; and more generally, see Rapp, *Réformes*, 164.

68. Geiler, *Die Emeis*, 8v–9v, and there, too, the following quote. See Brady, "'You Hate Us Priests,'" 181–82.

69. "Germania," ed. von Borries, 110, 118. See Knepper, *Jakob Wimpfeling*, 108–31; Singer, *Fürstenspiegel*, 176–212.

70. Newald, *Probleme*, 349–50; Strauss, *Sixteenth-Century Germany*, 69–72; Mertens, "Reich und Elsass," 271–72; Marchal, "Bellum justum," 114–37. Wimpheling even claimed that the Alsatians had better claim than the Swiss did to the name Helvecii. *JWOS* 3:392, no. 127. On Wimpheling's social ideas in general, see Brady, "The Themes of Social Structure."

71. Geiler, *Evangelia mit Ussleg*, 63, quoted by Dacheux, *Un réformateur catholique*, 527 n. 1. See Brady, "'You Hate Us Priests,'" 178–80.

72. I follow the findings and argument of Rapp, *Réformes*, and "Préréformes."

73. See *JWOS* 3:101–13, where the editors reconstruct Wimpheling's chronology.

74. Gumbel, "Humanismus," 8.

75. Hartmann, ed., *Amerbachkorrespondenz* 1:233, no. 248; and see ibid., 351, no. 385, and 403–5, no. 437; Reuchlin, *Briefwechsel*, nos. 45, 71; Specklin, *Collectanées*, no. 2202; Dacheux, ed., *Fragments*, no. 3967; Hedio, *Chronik*, 701–2; Schott, *Works* 1:311, no. 290.

76. This is the collection now in Uppsala, University Library, C 687, on which see *JWOS* 3:70–72, 89–93.

77. Varrentrapp, "Zwei Briefe," 292; Horawitz, *Hummelberger*, 32. On Pico's visit, see Schmidt, *Histoire littéraire* 2:76.
78. Wimpheling, *Epistola excusatoria ad Suevos*, A.vi. See Schmidt, *Histoire littéraire* 2:80. Martin Sturm bought it and gave it to Thomas Wolf, Sr., even though his wife's brother-in-law, Florenz Mieg, was also an avid collector.
79. Ibid., 87–132; Livet, "Géographes et cartographes," 183–201.
80. Schmidt, *Histoire littéraire* 2:74; Chrisman, *Lay Culture*, 61, 82; Rott, "Library," 33–58.
81. *JWOS* 1:144–45. See Jacob Wimpheling to Thomas Wolf, junior, 16 September 1507, in ibid. 3:607–10, no. 234, which concerns Wolf's relapse into concubinage. See Spitz, *Renaissance*, 53–54; Rapp, *Réformes*, 165–66, 299, 302–4; Rapp, "Préréformes," 191–93, for this subject. On the Wolf brothers, see Rapp, "Préréformes," 192–93, who calls them "sombres brutes"; Schmidt, *Histoire littéraire* 2:212 n. 5; Rott, "Pfaffenfehde."
82. Garzoni, *De miseria humana* (unpaginated), on which see Schmidt, *Histoire littéraire* 2:74–75, whose estimate of its tone is accurate. Jacob Sturm's contribution reads: "Distichon Iacobi Sturmi artium doctoris./Hunc superauit Amandus Amatus Amabilis orbem./Immundum reptens atria munda poli."
83. Riegger, *Amoenitates*, 427; Schmidt, *Répertoire* 7:45, no. 148.
84. Allen and Allen, eds., *Opus epistolarum Erasmi* 2:7–9, no. 302, lines 11–16 (1 September 1514); Rhenanus, *Briefwechsel*, no. 54 (31 December 1515). Schmidt, *Histoire littéraire* 1:xvii, collates the two lists.
85. Rapp, "Gesellschaft," 87–107. The group contained no pastors but a number of pluralists and absentees.
86. Among them were Lorenz von Duntzenheim and Jörg Ingold, on whose families, see Fuchs, "Les foires," 315–17; Brady, *Ruling Class*, 104–10.
87. Tracy, *Erasmus*, 10.
88. Ibid., 11.
89. *JWOS* 3:757, no. 309; Van Seggelen, "Erasme à Strasbourg."
90. Allen and Allen, eds., *Opus epistolarum Erasmi* 2:19, no. 305, lines 85–87 (English: *CWE* 3:26, no. 305 lines 92–94); *JWOS* 3:773–77, no. 314. See also Wimpheling's account of the event in Allen and Allen, eds., *Opus epistolarum Erasmi*, 2:7–10, no. 302; *JWOS* 3:766, no. 312. On Erasmus and Strasbourg, see Schmidt, *Histoire littéraire* 1:xvii; van Seggelen, "Erasme à Strasbourg," 21–24; Rapp, "Préréformes," 234–36.
91. *CWE* 3:27, no. 305, lines 132–37.
92. Erasmus to Johann Vlatten, Basel, 24 January 1529, in Allen and Allen, eds., *Opus epistolarum Erasmi* 9:19, no. 2088, lines 87–90. See also, ibid. 3:56, no. 633, lines 9–11 (24 August 1517); 3:420, no. 883, lines 7–10 (20 October 1518); 9:285, no. 2509, line 34 (summer 1531?); 9:285–86, no. 2510 (6 July 1531); 11:239–40, no. 3065 (23 October 1535).
93. Allen and Allen, eds., *Opus epistolarum Erasmi* 3:888, no. 948 (English: *CWE* 6:310–18, no. 948, here at 315, lines 158–59). On Erasmus's relations with the Strasbourg reformers, see Rott, "Erasme," 49–56.
94. Allen and Allen, eds., *Opus epistolarum Erasmi* 3:545, lines 45–46, no. 948 (English: *CWE* 6:315, lines 154–55).
95. Rhenanus, *Briefwechsel*, no. 54. He does not mention Sturm, but Sturm could certainly read Greek, and he probably learned it at this time. See *JWOS* 3:71, which notes that the volume now in Uppsala, which Wimpheling presented to Sturm, has Sturm's name in Greek on the inside rear cover. See also Adam, *L'humanisme à Sélestat*, 61–62.
96. Beatus Rhenanus to Jacob Sturm, 15 July 1518, in *Jani Pannonii Quinquecclesiensis Episcopi Sylua Panegyrica* (1518), 3–4; and there is a modern edition by Robert

Walter, ed., *Beatus Rhenanus*, 151–61. Rhenanus thanks Sturm for the gift of a collection of János's epigrams and offers this oration in return. On this Hungarian poet, a pupil of the famous Guarino da Verona, see Birnbaum, "Humanism in Hungary," 296–98, 303–5.

97. Nauert, "Clash," 7–9. On the most celebrated of Wimpheling's battles, the Jacob Locher affair, see Overfield, *Humanism*, 202–7.

98. Nauert, "Clash," 1–2; Borchardt, *German Antiquity*, 99–100.

99. Stokes, ed., *Letters of Obscure Men*, 266, 269. On the Reuchlin affair, see Overfield, *Humanism*, 247–97, from whom "clever mockeries" comes (247). His is the soundest general treatment.

100. Press, *Calvinismus*, 29; Knod, "Wimpheling und die Universität Heidelberg," 331 n. 1; Burger, *Renaissance*, 61 n. 12. Venningen married a Bock from Strasbourg, sister to Jacob Sturm's future wife. Brady, *Ruling Class*, 89–90. On the context, see Overfield, *Humanism*, 314–16, who, alas, repeats the old confusion of the two Sturms, Jacob and Johannes/Jean. As Overfield points out (315), the reformed statutes of December 1522 disappeared in the late seventeenth century, so their connection with the opinions written for Venningen by Sturm, Wimpheling, and Jacob Spiegel (Wimpheling's nephew) is unknown.

101. This and the two following quotes are from Winckelmann, *Urkundenbuch* 1:214–16, no. 162 (22 July 1522).

102. Ibid., 216–17, no. 163, on which see Knepper, *Jakob Wimpfeling*, 306–8.

103. Press, *Calvinismus*, 168–71. On his benefices, see Eubel, *Hierarchia catholica* 3:198, 223, 315; Toepke, ed., *Matrikel Heidelberg* 1:475; Grandidier, *Nouvelles oeuvres inédites* 3:42. Henry's predecessor died in 1515, he was in Strasbourg by 1516, and the pope confirmed his appointment as provost of Strasbourg's chapter on 10 March 1518. Bernays, "Jakob Sturm als Geistlicher," 30; Riegger, *Amoenitates*, 460, 463; Levresse, "Prosopographie," 30.

104. Henry became prince-provost of Ellwangen and administrator of Worms (1523), bishop of Utrecht (1524) and coadjutor of Freising (1540), though he merely kept pace with his uncles and brothers, who included some of the Empire's greatest pluralists. Isenburg, *Stammtafeln* 1:table 31; Raab, "Hochstifter," 69–80; Duggan, "Church as an Institution," 154–55.

105. Riegger, *Amoenitates*, 460, 463; Bernays, "Jakob Sturm als Geistlicher," 352–53.

106. Decker-Hauff and Seigel, eds., *Chronik der Grafen von Zimmern* 3:72, lines 37–38: "Christus het [in] das collegium, da sie nit dispensirt, nit angenomen werden megen." Among the cathedral chapters, Strasbourg enjoyed a reputation for being the most aristocratic, which was well deserved. See Levresse, "Prosopographie."

107. The first mention of Sturm in Henry's service is by Matthias Schürer to Erasmus, Strasbourg, 21 July 1517, in Allen and Allen, eds., *Opus epistolarum Erasmi* 3:29, no. 612. The last direct mention is in a letter of the cellarmaster (*Keller*) at Weinheim in the Palatinate, 16 May 1522, who notes that Sturm had told him to send his accounts to Heidelberg. StA Ludwigsburg, Bestand 396 aus Büschel 171, a document in the acts of the chapter at Ellwangen. Sturm's service can be traced in Count Henry to Jacob Sturm, 11 July 1522 (ibid., Bestand 387 aus Band 14, no. 194); Jacob Sturm and Bernhard Freyder to Count Henry, Strasbourg, 20 July 1523 (ibid., Bestand 396 aus Büschel 172, no. 2); Count Henry to the Dean and Cathedral Chapter of Strasbourg, Ellwangen, 25 September 1522 (ibid., Bestand 387 aus Band 14, no. 216); Count Henry to the Dean and Chapter of Strasbourg, Ellwangen, 27 November 1523 (ibid., no. 217).

108. Franz, *Der deutsche Bauernkrieg*, 77; Rapp, *Réformes*, 437–38. On Martin Sturm

and Düppigheim, see AMS, AA 1552; Rosenkranz, *Bundschuh* 2:275 note.

109. Knepper, *Jakob Wimpfeling*, 247 n. 1, 303–4; *JWOS* 3:112.

110. On this affair, see Giefel, "Streit," 171–76, 241–53; Pfeiffer, *Fürstpropstei Ellwangen*, 198, 227; Reinhart, "Untersuchungen," 318–21; Tüchle, "Reformation und Gegenreformation," 225–26.

111. Giefel, "Streit," 173, for Sturm's role, and 171 n. 2 for the following quote.

112. Several of Sturm's kinsmen got benefices from this source under Emperor Maximilian, including two Sturm cousins and, much earlier, an Adelsheim. Santifaller, "Die preces primariae Maximilians I.," 623, 645; Schmidt, *Histoire littéraire* 2:32; Schott, *Works* 2:700.

113. Othmar Nachtigall to Sixt Hermann, Augsburg, 7 April [1523], printed by Bernays, "Jakob Sturm als Geistlicher," 356–58, in which (357) Nachtigall charges that Sturm "ambit canonicatum predictum et precibus piscabitur illum si liceat." Nachtigall's charges are in the dedicatory letter to his Greek grammar, *Progymnasmata Grecae literaturae* (1521). See Bernays, "Jakob Sturm als Geistlicher," 351 n. 2.

114. Jacob Sturm to Wolfgang Capito, Strasbourg, 29 June 1520, in Paris, Bibliothèque de la Société de l'Histoire du Protestantisme Français, Collection Labouchère. On Capito at Strasbourg, see Kittelson, *Wolfgang Capito*, 54; Rott, "Clercs et laïques," 39.

115. AST 19/37: "Magister Jacobus Sturmius, clericus Argentinensis." Rapp, *Réformes*, 160, notes that this title probably means that the man who used it was not a priest.

116. Knod, *Deutsche Studenten*, 641–43, nos. 4274, 4277–78; Mayer, ed., *Matrikel Freiburg* 1:158, no. 57.

117. AMS, KS 11, fol. 283v; Straub, "Notes généalogiques," 84; Brady, *Ruling Class*, 351–52; Grandidier, *Nouvelles oeuvres inédites* 5:366–67. This Stephan Sturm died before 11 May 1526, for his name is stricken from a confirmation by Charles V of the Sturms' Imperial fief at Offenburg. ADBR 12 J 2006/1.

118. The quote is from Moeller, *Imperial Cities*, 118.

119. See Brady, *Ruling Class*, 302–3; Jakob Wimpheling, *Das Leben des Johannes Geilers von Kaysersberg*, in *JWOS* 2:21; Schmidt, *Histoire littéraire* 2:326.

120. Specklin, *Collectanées*, no. 2222; Förstemann, *Neues Urkundenbuch* 1:81, no. 33; Brady, *Turning Swiss*, 120.

121. Brady, *Ruling Class*, 334–35.

122. Ibid., 205–6, 317–18, 326–27, 350. The city hall, long since razed, stood on St. Martin's Square (the modern Place Gutenberg). Seyboth, *Das alte Straßburg*, 128.

123. Chrisman, *Lay Culture*, 156–63, with figures of production; Lienhard, "Strasbourg et la guerre des pamphlets," 128–29. On preaching, see Lienhard and Rott, "Anfänge der evangelischen Predigt."

124. Kittelson, *Wolfgang Capito*, 102.

125. Anton Firn announced on 18 October his intention to marry his housekeeper; Mathis Zell married a local woman, Katharine Schütz, on 3 December. Stafford, *Domesticating the Clergy*, 151–65.

126. Chrisman, *Lay Culture*, 155–65, 287 (fig. 2), 289 (fig. 5).

127. Johannes Timannus to the Preachers at Bremen, 18 November 1540, in Spiegel, "Johannes Timannus Amsterodamus," 42–44. See this volume, chap. 6.

128. Jakob Wimpheling to Wolfgang Capito, Sélestat, 6 September 1523, in *JWOS* 3:871–72, no. 353.

129. Jakob Wimpheling to Sixt Hermann, Sélestat, 2 November 1524, in ibid., 879–84, here at 882, no. 357; also in Ficker-Winckelmann 2:48. See Rapp, *Réformes*, 479.

130. Moeller, "German Humanists."
131. Jakob Wimpheling to Wolfgang Capito, Sélestat, between 6 September and 25 October 1523, in *JWOS* 3:873–74, no. 354: "Verbi gracia Mathei 23 Ecclesia (vel Romana) emendanda est, sed non delenda et eradicanda, ut Huttenus et vos Wickleffiste institutis. Musca a fronte claudi abigenda est, sed non cum securi."
132. See, for example, in ibid., 872, the authorities on whom Wimpheling calls against Capito's "Wyclifism": Augustine, Albertus Magnus, William of Auvergne, Jean Gerson, Bernard of Clairvaux, Gabriel Biel, Conrad Summenhart, and Georg Northofer, Capito's own theology professor at Freiburg.
133. Sturm's religious views are examined in this volume, chap. 3.
134. See Brady, "Rites of Autonomy," 16–18; and for such ceremonies in general, see Isenmann, *Die deutsche Stadt*, 90–92; Isenmann, "Die städtische Gemeinde," 195–97.
135. See Roper, *Holy Household*, 206; Brady, "'The common man,' 'the common good,' 'common women.'" For the Strasbourg context, see Brady, "'You hate us priests.'"
136. Sturm, *Quarti Antipappi*, 9, followed by Röhrich, *Geschichte* 1:172 n. 8; Jung, *Geschichte der Reformation*, 189. The evidence is collected by Bernays, "Jakob Sturm als Geistlicher," 355. She died (probably long) before 1 July 1540. On Jacob Sturm's in-laws, see Brady, *Ruling Class*, 88–90, 227, 302–4.
137. Seyboth, *Das alte Straßburg*, 22; *Ann. Brant*, nos. 3535, 4807. On Veronica Sturm, see the funeral sermon by Pappus, *Christliche Leichpredig*; AST 198, fol. 102r; Winckelmann, *Fürsorgewesen* 2:641, 254–55, 262; and Büheler, *Chronique*, no. 533, who wrongly calls her "Margareth."
138. Jean Sturm to Conrad Hubert in AMS, MS. 85 (J. Wencker, "Argentoratensia historico-politica," I), no. 98; Büheler, *Chronique*, no. 347: "Und er ... hat auch sein leben lang, wie wol er uff die 63 jar oder mehr worden, nie kein eheweib gehabt."
139. Baum, *Magistrat und Reformation*, 124 n. 4; Brady, *Ruling Class*, 352; Rapp, *Réformes*, 520. See in general Chrisman, "Women of the Reformation," 164–66. For Jacob Sturm's part in the dissolution of the houses of Franciscan and Dominican men, see *Ann. Brant*, nos. 4584, 4768; Winckelmann, *Fürsorgewesen* 2:131, no. 92.
140. Testament of Friedrich Sturm, Strasbourg, 31 December 1562, in HStAD, F 26, no. 49, fols. 2r–8r; death inventory of Stephan Sturm, Strasbourg, 21 January 1579, in ibid., F 26, no. 18, fols. 1r–18v; testament of Hugo Sturm von Sturmeck, Strasbourg, 13 January 1617, in ibid., F 26, no. 19, fols. 1r–148v.
141. Brady, *Ruling Class*, ch. 4.
142. The mayor (*Schultheiß*) collected the *Bede* in semiannual installments. HStAD, F 26, no. 18, fol. 7r–v.
143. See, for example, AMS, KS 27/I, fol. 63v (2 May 1530), where Weindling Emmerich the baker ["der brotbecker"] acknowledges a debt for grain he bought from the Sturm brothers, to secure which he pledges his share of a house, which his brother left him, behind the civic slaughterhouse.
144. See, for example, AMS, KS 23/I, fols. 77r–79r (3 November 1528), where Jacob Sturm and his brothers possess an annual income of one pound (1/2 fl.) ["ein Zinsbrief"] from Happer Hans, a gardener.
145. GLAK, 67/1023, fols. 190r–91v, 382r–83r. Stephan went to the Imperial Diet of 1559 to be enfiefed in Friedrich's place, apparently for the Sturm's Imperial fief-rente at Offenburg. AMS, XXI 1559, fols. 55v–56r.
146. GLAK, 67/1007, fols. 30v–31r; 67/1011, fols. 215r–v, 323r–v; 67/1013, fol. 243r–v; 67/1016, fols. 485r–v; 67/1023, fols. 190r–91v, 382v–83r; 67/1057, fols. 257r–58r; 67/1058, fols. 297r–v.

147. Brant, "Waal und einritt," 278. He had the same assessment in 1516, for which see Wunder, "Verzeichnis," 63, 63 n. 60. The Sturms had also been assessed on their allods in 1490. AMS, IV 86/17.
148. AMS, H 590, fols. 27r (5 November 1530) and 37r (15 April 1531); AMS, XXI 1546, fols. 547v–48r. The customary (Weistum) of Breuschwickersheim from 1533 is preserved in HStAD, F 26, no. 133.
149. Brady, Ruling Class, 374.
150. Testament of Friedrich Sturm, Strasbourg, 31 December 1562, in HStAD, F 26, no. 49, fols. 2r–8r.
151. AMS, KS 27/I, fols. 63v; Brady, Ruling Class, 148–49. See Ann. Brant, no. 3599, where Peter Sturm is said to have looked up something "üss einer alten cronica, so h. Peter Schotten gewesen und sie daheim haben."
152. Hatt, Une ville, 199–201. On Strasbourg's constitution in general, see Crämer, Die Verfassung und Verwaltung Straßburgs.
153. Brady, Ruling Class, 326–27.
154. Ibid., 189–93.
155. Ibid., 351.
156. Winckelmann, Fürsorgewesen 1:88.
157. PC 1:93 n. 2. This was Dr. Nikolaus Wurmser, on whom see Ficker-Winckelmann 2:53.
158. This picture of Strasbourg's situation rests on my Turning Swiss, 119–33, 138–50, 166–74, 178.
159. Chrisman, Strasbourg, 114–16, 138–40, 144; Brady, Ruling Class, 166–68; Bornert, La réforme, 133–34. For the Reformation's impact on urban cooperation, see Brecht, "Die gemeinsame Politik der Reichsstädte"; M. Meyer, "Die Haltung der Freien und Reichsstädte."
160. AMS, AA 396 (October 1524–December 1525), for which my thanks are due Jean Rott. See Rott, "Artisanat," 144; Conrad, Bäuerliche Gesellschaft, 86–116. For the larger setting, see Blickle, Revolution of 1525, 122–24; Blickle, Untertanen, 56–57; Brady, Turning Swiss, 32, 151–83.
161. Specklin, Collectanées, no. 2240 (wrongly dated to 1523); Ann. Brant, no. 4584; Wolfgang Capito to Huldrych Zwingli (Strasbourg), 6 February (1525), in ZW 8:no. 362, lines 6–7: "Nobilis iuvenis Iacobus Sturmius designatur est pro assessore, ut vocant, pius iuxta ac erudita."
162. Angermeier, "Reichsregiment in der deutschen Geschichte," 46. On the council's organization, see Arndt, "Organisation," 51–54; Neuhaus, "Wandlungen," 139. On Stettmeister Bernhard Wurmser von Vendenheim and his service in the council, see Brady, Ruling Class, 356–57; Winckelmann, "Straßburger Frauenbriefe," 173, 177–81. He was the brother of Dr. Nikolaus Wurmser.
163. Volk, "Frage," 63–64. On Pistoris, see Wartenberg, Landesherrschaft und Reformation, 76–83.
164. Quoted in Brady, Turning Swiss, 188.
165. W. Vogt, "Correspondenz Arzt," 1:300, no. 22; 2:122–3, no. 170. On the situation, see Franz, Bauernkrieg, 132; and this account of the mediation effort rests on Volk, "Frage," 75–89. The attitude of the league's cities is detailed by Sea, "Imperial Cities," 26–27; Greiner, "Politik," 55 n. 241 (references).
166. Volk, "Frage," 77. This contradicts the assertion by Max Steinmetz that after Leipheim Waldburg could pursue the Baltringers at will, "weil ihnen die Allgäuer und die Seebauern jede Unterstützung versagten." Steinmetz, "Die dritte Etappe," 672.
167. Volk, "Frage," 79 n. 26, 82.
168. Baumann, Akten, nos. 211, 216.
169. Sturm was supposed to have been relieved in the council by a Goslarer on

1 April; the other urban seat during Sturm's term was supposed to have been filled by Lübeck, but no one was sent. Arndt, "Organisation," 51–57; Neuhaus, "Wandlungen," 139.

170. Jacob Sturm to Strasbourg, Heilbronn, 22 April 1525, in PC 1:196, no. 344; also in Rauch, ed., Urkundenbuch 4:71–72. My account is based on Sturm's report.

171. Franz, Bauernkrieg, 187–201; Blickle, Revolution of 1525, 130–33.

172. Rauch, ed., Urkundenbuch 4:70–71, no. 2381; Franz, Bauernkrieg, 192.

173. More precisely, between 4 and 16 May. PC 1:210–11, no. 363, and 216 n. 1.

174. Rapp, "Vorgeschichte," 29–45 (English: "Prehistory," 52–62).

175. Blickle, "Alternativen," 10. See PC 1:127–28, no. 230, and 152–55, no. 289; Franz, ed., Quellen, 244–45, no. 76; Franz, Bauernkrieg, 142; Rapp, "Dorlisheim," 51–60.

176. Wollbrett, "Saverne-Lupstein," 56–58.

177. PC 1:122–23, no. 215.

178. Ibid., 126, no. 224 (27 April 1525), 122, no. 214 (23 April 1525); Chrisman, Strasbourg, 151; Deppermann, Melchior Hoffman, 143.

179. See Rott, "Artisanat," 148–52; Chrisman, Strasbourg, 151–52. See PC 1:150, no. 274 (11 and 14 May 1525); Lienhard, "La Réforme à Strasbourg, I," 385–87.

180. Rott, "La Guerre des Paysans," 25. The quote is from Daniel Mieg and Reimbolt Spender to the Bailiff (Landvogt) of Hagenau, 29 April 1525, in PC 1:128, no. 232. See Burg, "Hagenau," 49–54.

181. Brady, "'Sind zu beiden theilen Christen,'" 70; Klein, "Bauernkrieg in der Ortenau," 130.

182. PC 1:nos. 232–33, 235, 238, 245, 258, 262–63, 266, 271, 291, 294, 303–5, 308–10, 312.

183. Wollbrett, "Notes sur le Duc Antoine de Lorraine," 108; Wollbrett, "Scherwiller-Châtenois et le Valle de Villé," 90 (verse).

184. PC 1:184 n. 3. See Hartfelder, Südwestdeutschland, 168.

185. Scott, Freiburg and the Breisgau, 199–223, the best account of events on the right bank; and see Klein, "Bauernkrieg in der Ortenau," 130–31.

186. PC 1:216, no. 376; Schreiber, Der deutsche Bauernkrieg 1:no. 241 (24 May 1525). On Joham, see Brady, Ruling Class, 322–23.

187. PC 1:nos. 342, 349, 351–52, 355–56, 359, 363, 367, 372. The treaty is printed by Franz, ed., Quellen, 563–69; it is summarized by Franz, Bauernkrieg, 139–40. See Klein, "Bauernkrieg in der Ortenau," 131. Blickle, Revolution of 1525, 111, 123, 175, calls it the most important effort to translate the "Twelve Articles" into practice.

188. Hartfelder, Südwestdeutschland, 333–44.

189. PC 1:nos. 383–88; Hartfelder, Südwestdeutschland, 335; Bischoff, "La Haute-Alsace et la Guerre des Paysans," 116.

190. Dacheux, ed., Fragments, no. 3993; Supplément à la chronique de Wencker, no. 3237e. See Hartfelder, Südwestdeutschland, 337 n. 1.

191. Printed by Schreiber, Der deutsche Bauernkrieg 1:no. 332. See Hartfelder, Südwestdeutschland, 337–40; Scott, Freiburg and the Breisgau, 216–17.

192. Blickle, Revolution of 1525, 175.

3

The Formation of
German Protestantism

You've [i.e., the free cities] done them so
  much damage
The nobles and princes, too,
And they'll repay you fully
And give you your full due.
When you think they're sleeping,
That's when they'll make their play
With all their trusty weapons.
The nobles will surely awaken
To attack you in their manly way.*

Just as Jacob Sturm moved toward the new faith, Strasbourg's magistrates were searching for a new foreign policy. From its traditional policy, amity with the Swiss and the Elector Palatine, the city had moved during the early 1520s to one of urban solidarity and loyalty to the monarchy.[1] The magistrates kept a weather eye open, however, and the rumor heard in August 1523, that "the Strasbourgeois are intriguing with the Swiss," was true.[2] When Sturm entered the regime, his colleagues were looking for an escape hatch, in case neither emperor, diet, nor general council produced a general settlement on religion.

THE MIDDLE WAY

Initially, the Peasants' War strengthened urban solidarity.[3] The cities had recently resumed their periodic assemblies, called "urban diets [Städtetage]," in which they discussed common problems and framed common policies on regional and Imperial issues. Their situation was vexed, for although the princes' aggressiveness about taxes and against the commercial firms ("monopolies") drove cities and emperor together, the Reformation's advance was driving them apart.[4] The matter came to a head in 1524, when Charles V ordered the enforcement of the Edict of Worms against Luther and Lutheranism (18 April) and rejected (September) the Imperial Diet's plea for a

53

national church council to settle the religious question.[5] At this point, the revolution's storm broke over South Germany.

Jacob Sturm's political debut at the urban diet of Speyer in September 1525 brought him fresh from the revolution's front lines.[6] He knew, better than others, "what danger to the soul's salvation, apostasy, and destruction of authority and social discipline [*policyen menschlichen geschöpf*] have arisen from the fact that the preachers proclaim and explain the holy gospel to the common people in the cities in contradictory ways [*mit onglichem verstant*]."[7] This concern prompted the diet to send Sturm and Conrad Peutinger, Augsburg's city secretary, to ask Archduke Ferdinand to work for a uniform "policy for the usages of the Christian churches, conforming to the Word of God, ... so that the cities and others in the Holy Roman Empire can restore law and order, and so that the cities and lands will be guarded from rebellion and ruin."[8] This policy of a middle way between Evangelical militancy and resistance to all reforms, waiting for a solution from above, was precisely Peutinger's line at Augsburg.[9] It was also more or less the policy of the Strasbourgeois, who, in a curious mirror image of the two cities' subsequent roles, backed moderation against Nuremberg's Evangelical militancy.[10] This policy also corresponded to Jacob Sturm's view, for in August 1525 he opposed the preachers' demand for abolition of the Catholic mass, "because to alter or abolish it would awaken a great deal of ill will both outside and inside the city, and because the whole matter requires further thought and deliberation by the Senate. ... Both sides are Christians, however, may God have mercy!"[11]

The one great triumph of the middle way came at the Imperial Diet of 1526 at Speyer, where Jacob Sturm first trod the stage of Imperial politics.[12] As Strasbourg's noble envoy, the neophyte became ex officio one of the cities' house's two speakers, which was just as well, because his companion, Ammeister Martin Herlin of the Furriers' Guild, was a typical guild politician— competent enough in any aspect of business at home, where he was a big man, but lacking the manners, experience, languages, and oratorical ability to carry much weight elsewhere.[13] Their instruction ordered Sturm and Herlin to maintain urban solidarity and to work for a permanent religious settlement through a general council of the church, because "no one, no matter to what party he belongs, should have to fear attack because of his faith, which in any case is, and should be, a matter of free choice."[14] This was a realistic policy, for the Diet of Speyer met in an atmosphere of chastened reasonableness, sandwiched between the shock of the revolution and the sultan's impending invasion of Hungary.[15] The times thus counseled moderation, and Sturm soon discovered that on both "the Evangelical matter [*der evangelische handel*]" and the defense of urban rights in the diet, Strasbourg held the middle position between neutralist Augsburg and militant Nuremberg.[16]

Archduke Ferdinand, desperate to help his brother-in-law, King Louis II of Hungary, agreed to refer the religious question to a twenty-person committee, in which Sturm and Nuremberg's Christoph Kress sat for the cities.[17] Sturm warned the committee that to enforce the Edict of Worms "would affect many estates, and especially the cities, by weakening and even destroying peace, order, and unity," and urged the calling of a general or national council.[18] The archduke promised a council within eighteen months, even though Duke George the Bearded of Saxony groused that "if the cities will not obey the council and give it decisive authority, then it must be judged that they want to separate themselves from the Christian Church."[19] The committee's majority nonetheless framed a policy, which the diet adopted, that until the council met, each ruler and urban government would act "in such a way as he will be responsible for to God and the emperor."[20] The spirit that led to this ambiguous formula was explained by the diet's letter to Charles V:

> During the month of March last year, there occurred a general rebellion and revolt of the Common Man in all parts of the Upper German nation against many [the first draft reads "all"] rulers and lords, clerical and lay. The common people very quickly came together and formed bands in many places, each thousands strong, and attacked clerical and lay rulers, perpetrating arson and murder.[21]

Fearing "a new, larger revolt," the Diet of Speyer begged Charles to stay execution of the Edict of Worms, to come to Germany in person, and to call a church council, national or general. The diet chose Jacob Sturm to join the embassy, later canceled as too costly, which would carry this message to the emperor in Spain.[22]

The policy of the middle way triumphed at Speyer, and Jacob Sturm came home to a hero's welcome. To honor their new star, the Senate & XXI ordered a medal struck in his honor, an act of gratitude without parallel in this era.[23] It bears Sturm's portrait and name: IACOBVS STVRM. ANNO AETA[TIS] SVE XXXVI. The portrait, though not fine, is the only extant likeness of him from this stage of his life. It shows a young man of strong facial features, including a prominent nose, and less stout than he would later become. The hair is curly and close cropped, and he bears a short, full beard in the style of his father's generation. The medal's obverse bears trophies, the Sturm arms, and an inscription: VICTRIX FORTVNE PATIENTIA. MDXXVI. Patience, not arms or learning, conquers fortune. It was the lesson of the revolution of 1525: negotiation, not force, wins the day for law and order. Only one event of these days hinted at a different future. At one point, when the free cities had been hard pressed at Speyer, Sturm and Kress consulted two apparently friendly princes: Elector John of Saxony and Landgrave Philip of Hesse, the future chiefs of the Smalkaldic League.

TOWARD A PROTESTANT ALLIANCE

Ambitious and headstrong, intelligent but poorly educated, the twenty-two-year-old Landgrave Philip of Hesse was becoming the pile driver of German Protestantism.[24] His Hesse sat astride the Central Highlands, facing both north and south, though for the moment his gaze was drawn southward to the tempting string of prince-bishoprics along the Main River's "priests' alley [*Pfaffengasse*]" and beyond to the occupied duchy of Württemberg, at once the northernmost bastion of Austrian power and a center of Catholic resistance to the Reformation in southwestern Germany.[25] For the restoration of Württemberg's Duke Ulrich, his cousin, client, and long-term guest, Landgrave Philip needed allies, and the political changes encouraged by the Reformation seemed to answer his need. He did not share the Saxon fear of the south as the fount of heresy and rebellion, for, as he told his father-in-law, Duke George the Bearded, "the gospel, which is now called 'Luther's doctrine,' brings forth not peasants' revolts but every form of peace and obedience."[26]

On Hesse's eastern flank lay the domains of the other Evangelical chief, the Saxon Elector John, called "the Constant" or "the Steadfast." Though not intelligent, John was pious, loyal, and a convinced Lutheran.[27] Despite the partition of Saxony in 1485, which had badly weakened the House of Wettin's power, John's lands still stretched from Coburg in present-day Bavaria to the environs of Berlin, and the mines of the Erzgebirge along the Bohemian border gorged his treasury with silver.[28] John's other inheritance from his brother, Elector Frederick the Wise, a bitter rivalry with their Albertine cousins at Dresden, formed a permanent mortgage on his freedom of action.[29]

In 1526 these two princes, Philip and John, formed the League of Torgau-Gotha to defend what Duke George called "the Lutheran sect," though their different ruling styles made them an ill-matched team.[30] Philip, his own prime minister, recruited councillors from his own burghers and nobles and ruled the Hessian clergy with an iron hand; John swayed between the activists at his court, led by Count Albert of Mansfeld, and the devout faction around Gregor Brück, of whom the landgrave said that "the old chancellor listens too much to the preachers."[31] Hessian and Saxon policies also reflected the deeper social differences between their respective lands. Philip, a prince of the old Empire, felt comfortable with burghers, banking, and credit, and he understood the boisterous political life of southwestern Germany and Switzerland. Elector John's more recently settled lands, by contrast, lacked deeply rooted traditions and rights of local self-rule, and he and his advisers harbored strong reservations about the infinitely fragmented, urbanized world of the south, home of heresy and rebellion.

This background helps to explain why it was the Hessian prince who pressed for a broad alliance with the southern Evangelical powers. Not only had he a specific project in mind, restoration in Württemberg, but Philip saw in Evangelical religion the best specific against another rebellion.[32] "Nothing," he instructed his envoys to Speyer in 1526, "will help hold all subjects in peace, unity, and obedience [more than] to have the holy gospel preached to the people, clearly and purely, and to provide the subjects with pious, godfearing, learned preachers."[33] "If any ruler," he wrote in 1526, "attacks another on account of the Word of God, . . . we can aid one another and help protect his lands and subjects. And a special union and league should be established for this purpose." His sponsorship of this project made Landgrave Philip of Hesse the true father of the Smalkaldic League.

In 1526 the southern Evangelicals were not yet ready to speak of "a special union and league." At the Diet of Speyer the landgrave talked with Kress of Nuremberg on 16 July about "a broad alliance [*weitläufig Bündnis*]," and next day he hosted the envoys of Nuremberg, Augsburg, Strasbourg, Frankfurt, and Ulm and told them of his new alliance with Elector John for the defense of religion.[34] Jacob Sturm probably met Landgrave Philip for the first time on this occasion. Impressed, he asked the Senate & XXI for permission to explore the two princes' offer of alliance but was told not to discuss it further, except in the presence of the other urban envoys.[35] Both sides agreed to continue speaking of the matter at Frankfurt during the Spring Fair, and there the matter rested.

This initial rebuff of the Hessian prince's overtures is not difficult to understand. He had need of the southern cities, but they had no need of him. Not only had the leading cities few economic ties to Hesse, but the landgrave's pious declaration to Sturm and Kress at Nuremberg, that he and the elector would exclude the emperor from the prospective foes of the league they proposed, was hardly to be taken seriously. What the burghers almost certainly did not know was that already at this time, Philip was intriguing with the Bavarian dukes against the election of Archduke Ferdinand as Charles's successor on the Imperial throne.[36] At Strasbourg all such motives remained secondary to the hope that the Imperial estates would unite behind a policy of reform as a remedy for revolution. "The desire of men to hear the gospel's truth for the salvation of their souls," a Strasbourg instruction asserted in 1527, "was the source of the peasant rebels' desire to be free from obedience to His Imperial Majesty."[37] When their man brought home from Frankfurt a draft of an alliance with the Evangelical princes, the Senate & XXI failed to take any action, and they sent Sturm and Herlin to the Diet of Regensburg in May 1527 with instructions to give the princes "a friendly refusal," on the grounds that the move was not "useful or beneficial" while the emperor and pope were at war.[38] The same temporizing policy, Sturm discovered, held sway at Nuremberg, where he and Herlin were entertained on 29 May 1527 by eighteen patrician senators, the artist Albrecht Dürer, and Lazarus Spengler, the city secretary.[39] Spengler opposed the middle way and urged his masters that "this is the time to decide! Either we are and remain Christians, or we deny Christ. There is no middle ground."[40] The magistrates, however, took the middle ground and joined hands with the Strasbourgeois to rebuff the Protestant princes' overtures. Well into the following year Sturm received instructions that "if you are approached again concerning an alliance with Saxony and Hesse, simply repeat what we told them last time."[41]

Their common stance on the middle way gave the magistrates of the leading southern cities reason to hope that a purely urban league would suffice to protect them. They declined to form a general urban league, such as the mighty federations of old, because, as an Augsburg document said, it "would lead in time to their ruin, for they would have to be perpetually ready to aid the other, smaller cities."[42] The Augsburgers dreamed of reforming the Swabian League, and the Strasbourgeois resumed their talks with the leading Swiss cities, but the sense of urgency was missing. Then, in 1528 the landgrave threw a grenade into this atmosphere of drift and uncertainty. One of Duke George's advisers fed him some (forged) documents about a (mythical) Catholic League of Breslau, which was preparing to attack the Evangelical powers.[43] Philip mobilized to strike at the Franconian bishoprics, and he and Elector John of Saxony appealed to the principal southern free cities for aid.[44] Jacob Sturm had a small part in this script, for about a month earlier he had been sent to Hesse to discuss Strasbourg's help in recruiting infantry and gunners for the Hessian forces.[45] Though the Senate & XXI refused this aid, soon Claus Kniebis wrote home from Speyer to warn about Catholic intrigues.[46] Then, in late June 1528, Balthasar Merklin of Waldkirch, vice-chancellor of the Empire, arrived at Strasbourg to demand that the magistrates revoke recent religious innovations and supply military aid to the emperor.[47]

This situation—the alarms of war and Merklin's visit—prompted Jacob Sturm in June 1528 to begin thinking about a new alliance based on reformed religion. In his own instruction to the urban diet at Esslingen, Sturm noted that although ideally "all of the honorable free and Imperial cities would meet and formulate a common policy concerning what should be done," even if time allowed, "nothing appropriate could result from such a meeting, because the cities are divided over the matter from which all the present troubles arise, and they do not trust one another very much."[48] Therefore, he thought,

> it might be more useful to consult with those who are favorable or favorably inclined to the cause [dem handel] and stand in the same danger or under the same threats. Thus, each of the four cities should consult its neighbors and friends and learn from them how we should aid and support one another in these dangerous times.

By "neighbors and friends" Sturm did not mean only the free cities, for among Strasbourg's neighbors and friends he numbered Zurich, Bern, Basel, other Swiss towns, Metz, and the margraves of Baden. The crucial point, however, was "the cause," religion, that united these "neighbors and friends," for Sturm proposed an alliance based on that cause, namely, Evangelical religion. Although he perhaps did not yet see the other changes this policy would require, such as the elimination of the Swabian League, Sturm had nonetheless taken his first large step toward the Protestant alliance.[49]

The second step quickly followed. In a new instruction for the urban diet at Esslingen in late July 1528, Sturm proposed a league of four cities—Strasbourg, Ulm, Augsburg, and Nuremberg—for mutual defense against attacks on grounds of religion.[50] He omitted the customary exceptions of the emperor and Swabian League and added that "the Swabian League must be blocked."[51] Here Sturm grasped the logic of the Reformation movement's collision with the political landscape of South Germany. And his colleagues soon grasped his point, for they told the Ulmers they would refuse any alliance that did not oppose the Swabian League.[52] At this point, in the autumn of 1528, Jacob Sturm had formed the policy he would maintain until Charles V defeated the Smalkaldic League, nearly two decades later: a common defense of the common religion against the Swabian League and the House of Austria. To the three lessons of the revolution of 1525—the Common Man's courage, the Empire's weakness, and the princes' might—he added a fourth, the cities' inability to act alone.

At year's end, when the Imperial Governing Council issued a new order not to suppress the mass, Sturm was closeted with Landgrave Philip at Worms.[53] No one recorded this first private conversation between them, but when Sturm brought home a fine stallion as the landgrave's gift to the magistrates, they expressed their pleasure by presenting it to Sturm.[54] Now, five years after his conversion, Jacob Sturm took the wheel and steered his city in an entirely new direction. To complement the new, Evangelical faith, he fashioned a new, Protestant politics.

A POLITICIAN'S FAITH

Religions are distinguished most definitely not by their doctrines but by their forms of worship, and when one religion's leaders hold other rites to be idolatrous or blasphemous, as the Evangelical reformers did the Catholic mass, it is impossible that old and new should long coexist. The Evangelical clergy could not feel safe, so long as the mass continued to be enacted in Strasbourg.[55] Because they could not advocate its suppression by force, especially not during or after 1525, they had to persuade the magistrates that abolition of the mass, though illegal, was necessary to uphold God's honor and to preserve the civic common good. The campaign against the mass, which began during the Peasants' War, thus legitimized centralized magisterial authority over the church and dashed all hope of the city's parishes governing themselves.[56] There was, however, a second, hidden cost to the assault on the mass, which the preachers held to be "nothing but worthless human inventions and fantasies."[57] The campaign highlighted an issue, the proper form of the sacrament, over which the Evangelical theologians themselves were disunited, and it fed the split between Luther and Zwingli over this issue. In this Evangelical "eucharistic dispute," which erupted in 1526, Strasbourg's preachers enthusiastically defended Zwingli's "spiritual" view of the sacrament in explicit opposition to Luther's more "realistic" one.

Cultural, social, and religious affinities between the South German and the Swiss cities doubtless contributed to placing the Strasbourgeois squarely on the Zwinglian side of this fateful dispute.[58]

No expression of religious opinion by Jacob Sturm can be evaluated outside of this dual framework of Catholic vs. Protestant and Zwinglian vs. Lutheran. To begin with, he opposed the preachers' attack on the mass.[59] The magistrates' position on this question varied with the situation. On 31 October 1524 the Senate & XXI had forbidden further liturgical innovations; three months later (2 February 1525) they suppressed daily mass, except in the four collegiate churches; on 1 May they decided "to abolish the masses, so that the common man does not intervene"; and they relented as soon as the situation eased.[60] This latter step angered the preachers, who on 10 August petitioned the regime, claiming that "the common citizenry is convinced that Christian communities may not tolerate the mass." The council of the XV referred the petition to a committee, for which Jacob Sturm prepared his memorial on public worship.[61]

Sturm defended the mass as not unbiblical, because "it is certain and proved by Scripture that God may be praised in every tongue, so Latin singing cannot be considered improper or blasphemous, providing that the abuses which have crept in are eliminated."[62] Besides, "because to alter or abolish it would awaken a great deal of ill will both inside and outside the city," and because the whole subject needs the magistrates' further attention, "for the time being the collegiate churches should be allowed to sing high mass [Fronmesse]."[63] As for the preachers, they ought to be told

> to teach the people what Christ's purpose was in instituting the sacrament, namely, that we should be reminded that He saves us and that through Him we have a common Father in heaven, if only we will believe in and trust Him. And that we, who eat one bread and drink from one cup, are members of one body, and that we should therefore display love for one another.

If Christians quarrel about the externals of worship, "we will lose sight of the intention and purpose for which the sacrament was established—brotherly love." Sturm saw in worship less a personal access to God's saving Word than a reinforcement of the bonds of community. At the present time, he wrote,

> each condemns the other, as if his mass, his way, were better than the other's. Some Christians call themselves "Evangelicals" and the others "papists" and "hypocrites," while the others consider themselves the true, old Christians and the others "Hussites" and the like. Both sides are Christians, however, may God have mercy![64]

Weighed down by his fresh experience of revolution, Sturm recommended that "because such misunderstanding exists between rulers and subjects now, many things should be tolerated and overlooked for the time being, until the Lord God grants better wisdom." The preachers, he thought, throw caution to the winds and "think that they can abolish in one year the consequences of a hundred years' decline."[65]

Sturm's policy of the middle way—tolerate both sides and wait for more favorable times or for action from above—pitted him directly against the city's Evangelical preachers, who, though no revolutionaries, understood that their party was stronger outside city hall than inside, where the moderately Evangelical "politiques," such as Sturm, had the upper hand.[66] And in the middle he stayed, for in the following year, when the Senate & XXI narrowly decided that "the mass should be preserved until the envoys to His Majesty return and we hear what His Majesty thinks," rumor held that Jacob Sturm "had cast the deciding vote for the mass."[67] He spoke for those magistrates "who would close their ears to any gospel that did not promote peace, harmony, and the *bonum commune*."[68]

Was Sturm's antipathy for religious militancy a policy of the post-revolutionary moment, or did it express a deeper conviction? The spotty evidence speaks for the latter. Sturm, who always tried to avoid arguing about theology, once confessed himself "not sufficiently competent" to treat "points concerning religion" in a public setting, despite his theological training at Freiburg.[69] He came to hate the Protestants' own dispute about the sacrament so deeply that in latter days he would not attend the Lord's Supper.[70] Like most of those touched by Erasmianism, he held that practice must lead principle. "If all the evil abuses of the clergy were first abolished and reformed," he wrote in 1530, "doctrine would later follow of itself."[71] Yet if Sturm sometimes acted the trimmer, he nevertheless possessed theological opinions, and they were decidedly Evangelical of the South German–Swiss type. He held, for example, the "spiritualist" interpretation of the Lord's Supper, and in 1530 he wrote that "we do not teach that the Christians who with true faith receive the sacrament, receive mere bread and wine, but they receive the true body and blood of Christ—a position delineated, though not very openly, by Schwenckfeld."[72] The reference to Schwenckfeld—a red flag to Wittenberg—aside, Sturm's comment conforms to what Strasbourg's reformers put in their "Tetrapolitan Confession" at the Diet of Augsburg in 1530: believers receive in the sacrament the true body and blood of Christ, unbelievers do not. The same position lies behind Sturm's glosses on the Schwabach Articles, which Elector John of Saxony in summer 1529 set as a precondition for the Protestant alliance.[73] Based on his view that "biblical truth cannot be translated into articles of faith," Sturm commented on Article 1, about the Trinity, that "the terms 'person' and 'trinity' are not in the Bible, and their use emphasizes a [false] separation. But since they are in common use, we do not object to them here." To Article 2, on the person and natures of Christ, Sturm asked why the names of ancient heresies were used, "if not to arouse suspicion that our people are guilty of such views, which we deny?" "We see clearly why this was put in," he said, "as though someone wanted to separate Christ from God—as Zwingli is accused of doing." On the chief issue, the eucharist, Sturm argued the sacramentarian position that

> faith and the Spirit are given, and must be had, before the sacrament and not first through the sacrament, for the sacrament is but a witness to faith [testimonium fidei] and a confirmation and sign [sigillum] of faith.[74]

He admitted that on this issue, there was no agreement, "as can readily be seen from the writings. The issue is whether the presence [of Christ] is corporeal [praesentia corporalis] or exists only through faith [praesentia fidei]. They hold the former, the others the latter." Jacob Sturm's profession of the South German–Swiss theology thus included an Erasmian unwillingness to go beyond the biblical language, plus a very strong animus against the papacy, a defense of infant baptism, and an insistence on the individual's inner disposition—itself a product of God's election—as a condition of the sacrament's effectiveness. Sturm was a genuine "sacramentarian," one of those who thought that the Lutherans had not sufficiently rid themselves of the Catholic error of making the divine presence in the world concrete, objective, and material.

Sturm nonetheless differed markedly in his ecclesiology, his idea of the church, from Zwingli and his followers, who cinched together worldly justice and divine justice, communal freedom and Christian freedom.[75] Sturm's view of the church, to judge by his rare statements about it, resembled more the typical "spiritualist" attitude. In 1526, angered by Wolfgang Capito's provocation of the Swiss Catholics, Sturm wrote,

> It seems to me that one who undertakes to preach the gospel of Christ should freely cast body, life, honor, and property to the winds. For it is certain that the world, which never tolerated Christ while He was here on earth, will also not tolerate him to the very end of time and will consider all who sincerely and openly confess Him, to be knaves and rascals and will persecute them.[76]

Whoever, he continued, "preaches the true, genuine Christ should be resigned to never pleasing the world and to being rejected by the world, except for a little band [ein kleins hüfle] of the elect [usserwelten]." For this reason,

> the preachers . . . shouldn't rely much on [the power of] large, strong cities, . . . as though they trusted more to the power of this world [uf ein fleischlichen arme] than to Christ alone. God . . . has promised us Christians no temporal happiness here, as He did the Jews in the Old Testament, but only suffering and persecution.

God does not, in other words, transform the world through the gospel into the kingdom of Christ.

Sturm repeated this spiritual view of the church twenty years later, on the eve of the Smalkaldic War.[77] "Just as in the time of Jesus, the apostles, and the martyrs," he wrote to Landgrave Philip, "religion spread against the will and consent of the Jewish and pagan authorities, so today a household, tomorrow another, then a village, and finally a whole land receives the faith, which gradually comes to prevail despite all persecution." As it did of old, the faith will grow through persecution, until "the civil authority accepts it out of desire for peace and from necessity."

Though separated by two decades, Sturm's two statements express a common image of the Reformation as a renewal of the early church, when the apostles and martyrs went out to preach the gospel without protection and without fear. The true faith has always been the possession "of the little band of the elect . . . in whose hearts the true Christ rules and is confessed." Sturm altogether lacked the urban reformers' Zwinglian political theology, which trusted the actions of the Spirit to fuse divine with worldly justice, political with Christian freedom, and the righteousness of faith with the common good. That is to say, he did not share Zwingli's view that "a Christian man is nothing more than a good and loyal citizen," and "a Christian city is nothing more than the Christian Church."[78] On the contrary, Sturm combined a highly spiritual view of the true, invisible church as a persecuted minority with a belief that the visible church is a necessary structure of authority in this world. This position might be called "Marsiglian," after the fourteenth-century Italian writer, Marsiglio of Padua, or "Erastian," after the Swiss physician of the later sixteenth century, both of whom subjected the church to lay authority, but it also conformed more or less to Luther's teaching. The government could not promote salvation—"laws make hypocrites," was Sturm's view[79]—but the commune needed the prayers and the unity of opinion fostered by an established church. "You know from experience," he once wrote, "that in our times scarcely anything else so unites people's minds or drives them apart as unity or disunity in religion does."[80] For this reason, Sturm led the campaign against the sects at Strasbourg in 1534; for the same reason, he broke with Martin Bucer in 1548.[81] Probably, the wild scenes he witnessed in 1525 taught Sturm by means of an indelible fear that "variety [in preaching] will lead astray the popular mind, which is not used to such matters, and through some preachers' loud cries the people might be divided into unwholesome factions."[82]

The printed word, too, lent itself to the promotion of "unwholesome factions." During the Capito affair in the summer of 1526, he remarked about clandestine printing by Wolfgang Köpfel, Capito's nephew, that

> I have told Köpfel more than once, how damaging the printers can be through their clandestine printing. Dear God, their poverty drives them to it, though that is no excuse. I believe now that if the printshops are not reformed [*reformiert*] and the violators severely punished, the printers will one day bring our city into great danger.[83]

"Unwholesome factions" and "danger to our city" justified official regulation of preaching and printing, the gospel's chief channels, in the name of the common good. If, at the same time, the people's salvation required "that the voice of the Holy Spirit alone should be heard," then the magistrates, and they alone, though with the clergy's advice, had to determine what could be preached, and by whom.[84]

Jacob Sturm's religious position can thus be characterized as a union of an Erasmian-spiritualist view of the Bible and the sacraments with a Marsiglian-Lutheran ecclesiology. The resemblance to Marsiglio's teaching may reflect less the Italian's direct influence, though from 1522 his *Defensor pacis* could be bought and read at Strasbourg, than the general predilection of urban ruling classes for a gospel of otherworldliness proclaimed by clergymen without power.[85] Nothing in Jacob Sturm's career suggests that he ever deviated from this position.

Sturm's opposition did not stem the movement against the mass at Strasbourg. As the campaign approached its peak in 1527, Caspar Hedio sneered from Geiler's pulpit that "the nursemaid who washes the diapers and wipes the baby's butt does more good than a thousand priests reading three masses each."[86] The demand for abolition, once voiced by the gardeners and other guildsmen of the poorer sort, by 1528 was heard in the rich guilds, such as Zum Freiburg and Zum Spiegel. Ammeister Daniel Mieg, Sturm's cousin, favored abolition, and so did others of his sort.[87] There were opponents, such as Martin Betscholt, member of the XV from the Butchers' Guild, who thought that the preachers railed against the mass because their own movement could not stand to be judged by its own fruits.[88] His point was admitted by some moderate Evangelicals, such as Peter Butz, the city secretary, who conceded that

> [although] the Word of God has been preached clearly and purely in this city for quite a while [*ein gute zit lang*] and has been heard by many people, it has produced—God have mercy!—little enough Christian fruit. It has not lessened the arrogance of the poor against their betters [*die forigen*], and adultery, fornication, blasphemy, usury, and forestalling, along with other forbidden misdeeds, are committed openly and blatantly [*ungeschuht*], and are, alas, a daily occurrence, committed without punishment.[89]

Men of such moderate views, including Jacob Sturm, held a majority in the Senate & XXI, but they realized that they could not decide this divisive issue alone, and a committee, including Sturm, recommended that "the Schöffen should be assembled to hear and asked their opinion as to whether the mass should continue to be said or not."[90] The Schöffen were assembled in their respective halls on 10 January 1529 to hear the question, though no vote was taken at this time, possibly because Sturm and others were absent. Sturm, who was then meeting with Landgrave Philip at Worms, wrote to warn against any provocative action on the eve of an Imperial Diet. Returned home, he drafted the ammeister's address to the Schöffen, when they were reassembled on 20 February.[91] In Sturm's words, the Schöffen were told that after discussion [*gehabter underred*] a majority of us [Senate & XXI] has decided that it would be more useful and better for the entire city and the citizenry, also for the Evangelical cause [*gescheffde*], to delay the suppression and abolition of the mass until the end of the coming Diet, and thus to have patience [*gedult*] for this short space of time. Perhaps the Lord God will grant His grace that at this Diet the estates of the German Nation will find and pursue some means or way to further and establish God's honor and the peace and security of the entire nation.

If the Diet did not act, the Schöffen were promised, "we will undertake with your advice and consent whatever will promote God's honor and be useful and honorable for the entire city and the citizens." It was not to be, for the Schöffen voted overwhelmingly—184 to 94—against the regime's request and for immediate abolition, and when the Senate & XXI took a final vote, Sturm's side lost by one vote.[92] With this vote, the magistrates following the elite of their guilds, the ancient Catholic mass was suppressed in Strasbourg's collegiate churches.

TURNING SWISS: THREE LESSONS

In abolishing the mass, the Strasbourg magistrates sailed in Zurich's wake. This Swiss city had for some years set the pace for the South German–Swiss urban reform, the unity of which fed from a common Swabian-Alemannic language, a common social situation, and a dense network of correspondence and acquaintance among the Evangelical clergymen.[93]Strasbourg's magistrates turned in this comfortable direction in mid-1527, when the Schöffen gave them permission "to look for an alliance [*umb ein rücken zu besehen*]." The XIII, prodded in April 1528 "to take the matter in hand," began sending secret missions to Zurich.[94] These contacts led to the formation on 5 January 1530 of an alliance among Strasbourg and Constance allied with Zurich, Basel, and Bern, called a "Christian Federation [*christliches Burgrecht*]."[95]

The magistrates "turned Swiss" slowly and against growing reservations on the part of Jacob Sturm.[96] In a period of eight months between November 1528 and June 1529, Sturm witnessed Swiss conflicts over the Reformation in three different settings. First, in November 1528 he mediated between the Bernese magistrates and some of their subjects in uplands (the "Oberland"), who had ejected their Evangelical preachers, reinstalled their priests, restored the mass, refused to pay tithes, and declared their will "not to be driven from the old faith and their liberties."[97] As the Catholic cantons began to mobilize support, the Bernese struck with speed and decision, and on 4 November the rebels had to surrender "unconditionally [*uf gnad und ungnad*]." About ten days later, Jacob Sturm rode into Bern at the head of a mediating party from Strasbourg, and in the ensuing negotiations, "they handled the matter as best they could, so that the subjects might be forgiven."[98] The valley folk of Hasle reminded the Bernese of their promise not to force changes, but the magistrates replied that the Haslers must "uproot the mass, burn and destroy the images, break up and destroy the altars, and drive out the priests immediately, [or we will] do it with might and main and acts of force, and by no means will we tolerate such disobedience."[99] Two months later, Sturm—puzzled, perhaps, by his experience of common people who struggled *for* the mass and *for* their priests—advised his colleagues at Strasbourg not to suppress the mass with force. Forcing consciences created discord.

Sturm saw the same forces at work at Basel toward the end of 1528. He came with other mediators "to see if they couldn't help plant a goodly peace and unity among us [Baslers], so that we should come to an agreement about God's Word."[100] He found the city on the brink of insurrection, as he told Landgrave Philip.

> The two parties had assembled in arms on Christmas Eve, but the senate was able to persuade them to go home, with the proviso that both parties might address their concerns to the senate through their respective committees. Then, around two thousand citizens petitioned for preachers to be appointed who agreed on preaching the pure, clear Word of God. From the other side, four to five hundred citizens desired to remain with the old preachers, ceremonies, and masses. By dint of much trouble and work, the senate at last achieved through [our] mediation the consent of both parties, that from now on nothing but the pure Word of God should be preached, grounded in Holy Scripture, both Old Testament and New. Whoever preaches otherwise will be sacked.[101]

On Sunday after Trinity (30 May), he continued, there would be a public disputation between "those who want to maintain the mass, to justify it from the Bible, and the other party, which claims that the mass is a blasphemy and abomination." Then the citizens "will be asked to judge by their consciences whether the mass should remain or be abolished, and what the majority decides, the city will stick to." The Evangelicals, whom Sturm thought the probable winners, did not wait, for three weeks later they brought forth "quite revolutionary" proposals for both religious and political reform, whereupon the magistrates drew the correct lesson and abolished the mass.[102]

Sturm's third experience of Swiss-style conflict over religion unfolded on a much larger and more dangerous scale. In June 1529 he went to mediate between the Catholic and Evangelical powers in the First Kappel War, which had been provoked by Zwingli's determination to push his doctrines into the jointly ruled lands called "common lordships." Sturm and Conrad Joham arrived at Basel on 14 June, where they heard the city secretary, a Strasbourg man named Caspar Schaller, moan that "if it comes to blows, it will be the worst war in a hundred years."[103] Sturm's judgment, that "Bern and Basel would rather negotiate than let it come to war," proved correct at Kappel, where Bernese diffidence and rain, which delayed the Austrians' arrival, cooled the two sides' ardor for battle.[104] Tradition says that Sturm rode between the battle lines at Kappel, and Basel reports gave the

Strasbourgeois the lion's share of credit for the peace signed on 25 June.[105] According to a tradition reported by Heinrich Bullinger, Sturm expressed his wonder at how quickly the parties' mood turned from war to peace. "You Confederates," he said, "are wondrous folk. When you are at logger-heads, you are really united, for even then you don't forget the old friend-ship."[106] As the mediators rode off next day toward Zurich, Sturm expressed a cautious hope that "through God's grace this business is thus settled this time [*uf dis mol*], and may He grant that it endure and remain for a long time."[107] After a gigantic banquet at Zurich, at which 726 guildsmen feted them as heroes, Sturm and Joham rode off to Basel and then home.[108] In the Confederacy as whole, as earlier in the Bernese highlands and in the city of Basel, civil war over religion had been averted "this time."

In some respects, Jacob Sturm's three journeys to Switzerland in 1528–29 confronted him with his own city's past and possible future. The Swiss Reformation had re-empowered the fractious and stubborn particularism, which, lying ever just below the Confederacy's political surface, had nour-ished all the late medieval struggles of small communities and groups to protect themselves from larger or alien dominations. The same spirit had fed the urban "guild revolts" at Strasbourg and elsewhere, and had also animated the great alliance of Swiss and Alsatians against the Burgundian power. Since the seedtime of the Alsatian *Bundschuh* in the 1490s, how-ever, the urban elites had begun to regard this spirit with caution, even fear, emotions which the revolution in 1525 confirmed in full. This change lay between the era of Jacob Sturm and that of Old Peter Schott, who had come in 1474 to preach war at Bern, where his great-grandson arrived in 1528 as a messenger of peace. Old Peter and Uncle Ott Sturm, who had led Strasbourgeois into battle shoulder to shoulder with Swiss comrades, had understood and approved a world in which armed burghers and armed peasants combined to defend their liberties. But the world had changed since then, and their young kinsman had witnessed the terrifying simulacrum of that old world—the common people for local liberty with pike and gun—in the campfires of rebel armies in 1525. His crucial political experience occurred at Memmingen, Heilbronn, and Lahr, as their's had taken place on the battlefields of Héricourt and Nancy. Sturm's Swiss travels in 1528–29 thus confirmed the lessons of 1525, and they explain why he rejected the policy of "turning Swiss" in favor of alliance with the Lutheran princes. The princes, at least—unlike the revolutionaries of 1525, the Hasle folk, Basel's gardeners, and Huldrych Zwingli—did not yoke the gospel as godly law to people's freedom to be their own lords. Princely power, as dangerous as it might be, posed no threat to the peace of great urban communes. Some of Sturm's colleagues agreed, or at least enough to decide in August 1529 to work simultaneously in both directions, to pursue both "a neighborly alliance with the Swiss" and "at the same time [*similiter*] . . . the Christian alliance [*die christliche verständnüs*]" with the Lutheran princes.[109]

BIRTH AND DEATH OF THE PROTESTANT ALLIANCE, 1529

The pursuit of an alliance with the Lutheran princes proved a deeply humiliating experience for Sturm and Strasbourg. The project began well, better than they could have imagined, with the attainment of full unity in April 1529 at the Imperial Diet of Speyer; it collapsed eight months later at the small Thuringian town of Smalkalden. The project failed, because the Saxon elector lent himself to a ferocious Lutheran campaign against the "sacramentarians" of the south and demanded their subscription to a doctrinal formula, the "Schwabach Articles," which the cities, Strasbourg in the van, were not willing to sign.

Sturm and Ammeister Mathis Pfarrer came to Speyer in early March 1529 with instructions to maintain Evangelical—not, as in 1526, urban—solidarity. When the diet's committee recommended enforcement of the Edict of Worms against Luther and his teachings, Sturm wrote home in disgust, "Christ is handed over to Caiphas and Pilate."[110] In reply the XIII at home gave the envoys a relatively free hand to negotiate with "electors and princes, also lords and cities," especially those "who adhere to the gospel," though not to strike an alliance.[111] Although he responded eagerly to the Lutheran princes' invitation to join a formal protest against the diet's recess, Sturm balked at their policy of refusing to pay taxes, for "we should approve this recess in temporal matters, so that others are shown that in our protest we seek no material thing."[112] The logic of polarization, however, favored the princes' more radical stance, as Sturm shortly discovered, when his kinsman, Ammeister Daniel Mieg, was barred from taking Strasbourg's seat in the Imperial Governing Council, because his city had abolished the mass.[113] "Even the Jews are looked on with more favor here than are the cities who adhere to the gospel," wrote Mieg, and Sturm angrily told the diet in plenary session that "if Strasbourg is to be deprived of its rights for having worked for the greater glory of God and dethroning idolatry, then the city can no longer take any regard for the Empire in its affairs." When asked sarcastically where his city would find support, Sturm retorted that

> for some time the king of France has wanted to treat with us and has offered us an annual subsidy of several thousands crowns. Our Swiss neighbors will be equally willing to admit us to their Confederacy, just as they took in Basel twenty-nine years ago. We certainly do not lack friends.[114]

France and the Swiss were far away, however, and the Lutheran princes were not, and by 12 April Sturm came over to their policy of tax refusal.[115] Then, against his colleagues' order not to sign an alliance, on 22 April Sturm signed a mutual defense pact with the Saxon elector, the Hessian landgrave, and Nuremberg and Ulm.[116] This forerunner of the Smalkaldic League provided for mutual aid against attacks made "on account of religion [Glaubenssachen]" for the next six years.[117] The Evangelical alliance was achieved.

History calls the new alliance "Protestant" after its religious basis, the solemn protest against the Diet of Speyer's recess by the Evangelical powers on 22 April 1529. The same process, however, that created a Protestant party and a league also began to fracture them, for as the Evangelicals clarified their identity against Catholicism, they also sharpened the identities of their own parties. The canny Hessian landgrave, who sensed this thorn on the rose at Speyer before anyone else did, brought Sturm together with Luther's Wittenberg colleague, Philip Melanchthon, to plan a meeting for unity among theologians from both Evangelical parties.[118]

Sturm did not yet see the danger the definition of Evangelical belief posed to the Protestant alliance. His permission to sign the Speyer accord, which defined the party simply as those who adhered to "the divine Word [*das göttliche Wort*]," had rested on a written statement of what the Strasbourgeois preached on the main issue, the Lord's Supper, which Sturm presented to the Saxons on 21 or 22 April.[119] This document—"error clothed in such finely ornamented and chosen words," Nuremberg's preachers later called it—denied Christ's real presence in the sacrament and insisted that each side should be permitted to hold its own opinion, so long as it confessed belief in God through Jesus Christ.[120] Sturm thought it adequate, and so did the landgrave, who reported that the Evangelicals found themselves "in agreement on the chief doctrine, though differing in their understandings of it."[121]

Only for the moment did the protest and alliance framed at Speyer mask the seething conflict between "Lutheran" and "Zwinglian" factions among the Evangelical clergy, which broke into the open as soon as the alliance offered it a concrete political target.[122] The Lutheran theologians in Saxony, at Nuremberg, and elsewhere believed that "sacramentarianism"—Zwingli's doctrine of the Lord's Supper—opened the door to religious and political rebellion à la Müntzer and 1525. "They teach that the Holy Spirit is not given through the Word or the Sacrament but is given without the Word and the Sacrament," Melanchthon wrote, and "Müntzer taught the same thing and thereby lapsed into his own opinions."[123] The other side believed, as Strasbourg's Martin Bucer wrote, that it was wrong to infer "from those [Zwinglian] teachings the repudiation of Christ, the abolition of the pulpit, the abandonment of Holy Writ, and the destruction of all good discipline and obedience—as though the spirit of Müntzer reigned there, the most intolerable and terrible that can be imagined."[124] The apparently gross mismatch between such dire language and the points at issue is easily explained, for over the entire sacramentarian quarrel hung the image of the old and the specter of a new Peasants' War. Those who spiritualized theology, the Lutherans argued, would also use force, "from which is to be feared not only a terrible and great butchery but also great disputes in all ecclesiastical affairs and the erosion of government, which could not be repaired in a hundred years—nay, not for the rest of time."[125] This was denied by the landgrave, who told Melanchthon that the Zwinglians were not revolutionaries, "as I am told."[126]

Naïvely innocent of their peril, Sturm and his colleagues steamed ahead on their chosen course. They pledged to aid Philip against attack with all the city's might and began to tailor their Swiss connections to Hessian specifications. At Basel on 26 June, Sturm and Conrad Joham told their Swiss friends that Strasbourg wanted a bilateral alliance of Strasbourg and Hesse with the Swiss cities, not a Swiss-style "Christian federation [ein christliches Burgrecht]."[127] The landgrave, meanwhile, moved ahead with preparations for a meeting of Evangelical theologians at Marburg in the fall.[128]

Just at this moment, the Lutheran storm was breaking at Nuremberg and Wittenberg. Once the bellwether of Evangelical militancy, Nuremberg's regime had begun its flight into neutrality, though Lazarus Spengler, the city secretary, disguised the turn by giving soft words to the Strasbourgeois' faces and calumnies to their backs.[129] Soon the heavier calibers from Wittenberg began to register along the same front.[130] The Strasbourgeois' first clue to the new situation came in early June, when Mathis Pfarrer brought home from Rodach, a small Franconian town, a new set of Saxon conditions for alliance; the second clue appeared in August, when Sturm and Pfarrer arrived for a meeting at Schwabach, also in Franconia, only to learn of its cancellation by the elector.[131] Puzzling developments, though nothing to halt preparations for the Marburg Colloquy in late September, where, as Sturm told the Baslers, "perhaps there would be discussion not only about the [doctrinal] concord but also about highly important matters concerning the welfare of the German nation."[132] In fact, the landgrave planned to use the Marburg Colloquy to solidify the whole southern wing of the Protestant alliance, and he notified Sturm that "for pressing reasons, we want you especially to be present" and to bring "two judicious, unquarrelsome ones [preachers], who are inclined to peace and unity" and specified that one of them should be Martin Bucer.[133] The landgrave was steaming ahead. In July he told the elector of his firm support for "Strasbourg, Ulm, and others, who are suspect concerning the Sacrament," and when he heard of the Schwabach Articles, he announced that

> we have discussed, considered and finally decided, . . . if any power adhering to the gospel [dem Evangelio anhengig] is attacked or invaded, we, in order to protect ourselves, will not fail to give his counsel, support, and aid.[134]

The Marburg Colloquy in September 1529 marked the formal beginning of the landgrave's long collaboration with Jacob Sturm and of his patronage of Martin Bucer, whose presence at Marburg he specifically requested.[135] The Swiss participants, including Zwingli, Oecolampadius of Basel, and magistrates from Zurich and Basel, assembled in mid-September at Strasbourg, where they were received "with great honor," and thence came under Sturm's care via friendly stations to Marburg in Hesse.[136]

The theatrical confrontation of Luther and Zwingli at Marburg enacted and proclaimed the Protestant split. On Sunday, 3 October, sensing a debacle in the making, Sturm begged the landgrave to admit Martin Bucer to the talks. "Gracious lord," he said,

> you have arranged this meeting in order to achieve, with God's help, unity about the disputed article on the Sacrament. I was sent by my masters at Strasbourg to help attain this same end. Then, however, Doctor Martin Luther at the start of these talks charged that the doctrine taught at Strasbourg contains errors not only about the Sacrament, but about other points as well. I find it intolerable, having been sent to reach concord on a single point, to have to go home and report disunity on four or five different ones. I therefore humbly request that Your Grace allow one of our preachers, Martin Bucer, to be heard on behalf of my masters concerning the doctrine in question, and that, if we are in error, it be explained to us just where we err.[137]

It did not work. Bucer, a neophyte on this stage, achieved nothing, and neither did the articles of agreement, called the Marburg Articles, which suited no one except those—Strasbourg and the landgrave—for whom the main object was the alliance.[138]

The landgrave used the setting of Marburg Castle to reveal his scheme for a grand southern alliance against the Habsburgs. Flanked by Sturm and Duke Ulrich of Württemberg, he told the Swiss politicians about how the Habsburg menace could be countered by a union of "all or the majority of the governments that have, up to this time, encouraged the proclamation of God's Word in their lands," not to oppose "the Imperial Majesty or any estate of the Holy Empire"—a point unlikely to trouble the Swiss—but only to defend divine truth and the public peace.[139] If the Swiss cities entered the alliance, Philip would ride to their aid with two thousand horse, artillery, and provisions, backed by his friends and allies among the northern princes. This unveiling of the "Hessian matter [*Hassiacum negotium*]" formed the real business of the Marburg Colloquy, for the Swiss politicians took the proposal home, and ten months later the short-lived Hessian-Strasbourg-Swiss axis came into being.[140]

Meanwhile, the full weight of the Lutheran retrenchment arrived on stage, as Luther's performance at Marburg was followed, one month later, by the presentation to the Strasbourgeois of a doctrinal statement, the Schwabach Articles, subscription to which was the Saxon price of alliance.[141] Months earlier, the elector had secretly pledged himself not to ally with those "who do not share a common faith with the members of [our] league nor practice one baptism and one eucharist."[142] The landgrave fumed and sputtered, warning John that, for the sake of one doctrinal point, he was throwing away the cities' might, which he reckoned at fifty- to sixty-thousand foot.

In this rage at the Saxon betrayal, Landgrave Philip opened his heart to Jacob Sturm for the first time.[143] "Dear Jacob Sturm," he wrote, dispensing with the usual formal greeting, "it is time. If we sleep and let the lamps burn out, the Bridegroom will not let us in"—perhaps he knew the magnificent wise and foolish virgins on the façade of Strasbourg's cathedral. The crisis, he went on, admitted of three solutions: submission to the emperor and revocation of the reforms, passive resistance and resignation to persecution, or active defense. "In the latter choice lie fortune and hope, in the others absolutely nothing."

At Strasbourg, the XIII thought that a purely southern Evangelical league would be "too small," but neither would they submit to the Schwabach Articles.[144] "We are agreed on the chief points of our true Christian faith," ran the instruction Sturm took to the Thuringian town of Smalkalden in December 1529, "[namely,] that Almighty God, out of love for the human race, sent His only-begotten Son into this world, Who in His true, assumed human nature, died for us and for our justification arose from the dead."[145] If the Saxons would not yield, Sturm should propose a double league of Strasbourg with the Swiss and the Lutheran princes among themselves, "and then the two leagues should ally with one another."[146] Sturm and Pfarrer came on 28 November 1529 to Smalkalden, and when the cities' envoys were asked for their views, Sturm replied that "the [Schwabach] articles are excessive and argumentative [witleufig und disputierlich], and it is to be feared that if the preachers have or develop divergent opinions about them, it will help our enemies and lead to divisions."[147] On 2 December, Ulm's Bernhard Besserer at his side, Sturm told the princes that "our masters will also agree to no league in any form, except one that protects and guards their faith, such as they have held it for some time [ain zit her] and, with the Almighty's help, intend to hold in the future."[148] This message delivered, he and Mathis Pfarrer rode home. There he laid the situation before the Senate & XXI on 15 December in the landgrave's exact words: "In summary, the matter rests on three alternatives: we await God's pleasure; we try to placate the emperor; or we prepare to expect his wrath."[149] The Senate & XXI responded by stepping through the only open door: three days after Sturm's report, the XIII sent envoys "up to the [Swiss] Confederacy to treat of all manner of business, about which you [Landgrave Philip] know from us, finally to agree upon it, and if possible to conclude it [so vil moglich zu beschliessen]."[150] The treaty's text was ready by 20 December, and Strasbourg's Schöffen voted on it on the twenty-ninth: 184 for the treaty, 30 for delay, and only 4 against. On 9 January 1530, the Senate & XXI approved the treaty—38 votes to 11—and eight days later the ammeister announced to the guilds that "it is done and approved."[151] Strasbourg had turned Swiss. At Nidau in Bernese territory, a householder marked the moment by having carved on his sandstone fireplace the allied arms of Nidau, Mulhouse, Basel, Strasbourg, Bern, Zurich, Constance, Schaffhausen, St. Gallen, and Biel.[152]

The treaty broke Ammeister Conrad von Duntzenheim's heart. The old man, one of whose sons had gone with Jacob Sturm in 1501 to study at

Heidelberg, had ridden in 1521 with Hans Bock to Worms, where Luther challenged Charles V. Although his surviving sons followed Bock into the Evangelical religion, their father never conformed.[153] In his last act of his last term as ammeister, Duntzenheim tried to head off the treaty. If the emperor should move against the Upper Swabian towns, he told his colleagues, "then, though I wish those cities well and hope they prosper, I am my own best friend. I would rather other cities were harmed and Strasbourg left alone."[154] Only ten others, a mere one-fifth of the Senate & XXI, voted with him, and on 7 January 1530 he and Stettmeister Egenolf Röder von Diersburg swore the oath of alliance on Strasbourg's behalf. Completely out of step with Strasbourg's policy, Duntzenheim then laid down his offices and died two years later at Venice.

Duntzenheim's was the last public voice raised against Strasbourg's new Reformation foreign policy. In its place he could only recommend a policy of isolation, which is precisely what his colleagues feared, for, having rebuffed the southern sacramentarians, the Saxon elector was preparing for concord with the emperor. It was a propitious moment on all sides. Charles V now stood at the peak of his reign.[155] His imminent arrival in the Empire, many expected, would begin a healing of the schism, for although Charles's antipathy for the Lutheran heresy had not abated since 1521, he intended to deal with the German dissidents not with force, as his Spanish confessor advised, but with the instruments of negotiation, pressure, and promises.[156] On the other hand, Elector John of Saxony, who wanted Habsburg backing against his Wettin cousin at Dresden, thought the surrender of his quondam sacramentarian allies a fair price for it. Then, too, King Ferdinand needed the Saxon's vote to become king of the Romans and his brother's successor.[157] Against this convergence of interests for reconciliation in the early months of 1530 huddled the "Christian alliance [*christliches Verständnis*]" among Zurich, Bern, Basel, Strasbourg, and, prospectively, the landgrave of Hesse.[158] Some in this camp, such as Landgrave Philip and Zwingli, dreamed of a grand anti-Habsburg front; others, such as Jacob Sturm, merely wanted to get the Protestant alliance back on track.

Why had this happened? Why, after the grand act of Protestant solidarity at Speyer in April 1529, did the new-found friendship crumble away? Did it happen because prominent Lutherans, such as Philip Melanchthon and Lazarus Spengler, truly believed that a respectable gentleman such as Strasbourg's Jacob Sturm was a Müntzerite plotter of a new Peasants' War? Probably not, for the hardening of the Lutheran reaction during the autumn of 1529 seems to have been inspired not by the fear of a new revolution of the Common Man but by apprehension over Charles V and his imminent return to the Empire. The chief sign of this was the emergence of a new political position, the doctrine of nonresistance to authority.

Tradition to the contrary, Martin Luther did not forge the Lutheran doctrine of nonresistance.[159] It emerged, rather, in the autumn of 1529 among urban Lutherans in South Germany, who felt trapped between the sacramentarian associations of the free cities and the impending return of Charles V to settle the schism. As late as October 1529, a common Saxon-Brandenburg instruction held that if the emperor attacked on religious grounds, he ceased to be a legitimate ruler and became no better than the Turk.[160] The contrary position, nonresistance, seems to have been voiced first by Nuremberg's Lazarus Spengler in November 1529. Although, he wrote, according to reason a Christian *can* "resist with all his power anyone who wants to drive him with force away from Christ's kingdom and into the realm of the Antichrist, it is not a question of what a person, but of what a Christian, should do, and not according to natural or human law but properly in obedience to God's command, law, and order."[161] What, after all, "has the darkness in common with the light, or what reason or natural, carnal wisdom with the Spirit of God?" Here Spengler merely translated into the Imperial context what the Nuremberg preachers had taught in a local context since the revolution of 1525: every act of disobedience violates divine law. That Spengler's advocacy of nonresistance flowed directly from his fear of the Swiss is clear from his condemnation of Strasbourg's alliance with Zurich, Bern, and Basel, which ends with a categorical statement: "He is otherwise of the opinion that for the sake of the gospel no Imperial estate . . . may protect itself with force or resist force with force against the emperor as his legitimate overlord."[162]

From Nuremberg the doctrine of nonresistance spread to other southern urban Lutherans, such as Johannes Brenz of Schwäbisch Hall and Heilbronn's Johannes Lachmann.[163] Brenz's formulation of it reveals the targets of nonresistance to have been the southwestern sacramentarian powers, especially the Swiss, whom Brenz condemned in late November 1529—the very moment of the turn to nonresistance—as "a people without a head, which they lack both in heaven and on earth, [who have] left the unity of the Christian church and have lost the head, Jesus Christ, and [have] exterminated their own lords."[164] Philip Melanchthon, by origin also a southern burgher, recoined the same formula—sacramentarians = rebels—for Saxon consumption. It horrified and frightened the Strasbourgeois, of course, to be tarred as Müntzerites bent on revolution—"as though Müntzer's spirit reigned there, the worst and most horrible one could imagine."[165] Taken literally, the charge was patent nonsense, but the polemic's subtext was true enough: whereas the Lutheran powers aimed to help Charles V heal the schism, the sacramentarians were plotting war against Austria in the south. The Nurembergers, who understood this, accordingly broke off cooperation with Strasbourg.[166] The chief plotter, the Hessian landgrave, as much as admitted the plot, when he begged Elector John to declare "if Your Grace will fight the emperor, . . . [and] tell me, what I can expect from you . . . if I am attacked."[167] Philip also turned his guns on Margrave George of Brandenburg-Ansbach, through whose court Spengler's doctrine of nonresistance flowed toward Saxony, and blasted him for saying that "he will defend against the ruler in temporal matters, [but] not for the sake of the eternal salvation of ours and our poor subjects' souls."[168] Temporal or spiritual, Philip stormed, "it seems to me, a German fifer who is innocent of Latin and learning, that if it is all right to resist in one case, it is all right in the other." "Oh, dear God," he went on, "we have such a narrow conscience concerning damage to our subjects and to the truth, but when our property is at stake, we take a much broader view. One could well say to us, as Christ said to those pompous scholars: 'you swallow a camel and gag at a gnat [Matt. 23:24].'" His rage came all too late, for in early March 1530, as the emperor moved toward Augsburg, the Wittenberg theologians went over to nonresistance.[169]

PROTESTANT POLITICS AT THE CROSSROADS

The landgrave's plans fully justified the Lutheran theologians' reaction, for during the winter of 1529–30 he and Zwingli were plotting a grand assault on the Habsburg power in South Germany. Zwingli had thought small—a league of Swiss and Swabian cities—but then the landgrave opened his eyes to the possibility of a triple strike by an anti-Habsburg front, backed by France, to split the western from the eastern Habsburg lands.[170] Jacob Sturm learned of this design when Zwingli wrote to him at the end of February 1530 to complain about the "faithlessness and betrayal" of Ulm's Bernhard Besserer. Then, at Basel in mid-March, Sturm learned of Zwingli's *Consilium*, "which has also been sent to the landgrave,"[171] and of preparations for an invasion of Württemberg—the landgrave's true object.

Making war on the House of Austria was the last thing on Jacob Sturm's mind in early 1530, when he was frantically preparing for the impending Diet of Augsburg.[172] His great goal was to retrieve the lost solidarity with the Lutherans, for whom he prepared an argument that the dispute was largely verbal, and "no one should be forced to surrender his opinion on this point, and that each should be permitted his view, so long as he believes in God through Christ and in the love of neighbor through faith."[173] This document expressed Strasbourg's official line: "The two opinions on the Sacrament are nothing more than a verbal dispute [*wortzank*] . . . from which each draws his own understanding and meaning."[174] Just in case, Sturm also prepared an apology [*entschuldigung*] for Strasbourg to the emperor, the tone of which demonstrated his desire to conciliate, not provoke.[175]

Sturm and Mathis Pfarrer left on 22 May 1530 for Augsburg, which they found a cauldron of preaching so inflammatory that "we fear this split on the article concerning the Sacrament will bring little good."[176] Sturm saw that for his main task, convincing the Saxons that the Strasbourgeois were not heretics, the XIII would have to send him "some of your preachers . . . to give a reckoning and reply concerning their doctrine and beliefs."[177] Although he could not expect to influence the course of negotiations between the emperor and John of Saxony, he had to be prepared to play

Strasbourg's card, should the negotiations falter or even fail. This daring policy banked on the calculation that just as the hope of reunion had split the Protestants, the failure of reunion would bring them back together.

The show opened splendidly enough on 15 June, when Charles and Ferdinand arrived at Augsburg, accompanied by the papal legate, courtiers and clergy—Spaniards, Italians, Netherlanders, Germans, Hungarians, and Bohemians—guarded by a thousand mercenary infantry and the three-hundred-man Imperial bodyguard, and trailed by the Imperial cooks, druggists, falconers, and two hundred Spanish dogs.[178] Into the city they came, escorted by the electors and other princes and their entourages, the envoys of sixty-one free cities, and the mayors of Augsburg at the head of a thousand guild militia and two hundred armored horse. It was the most glittering assembly of the Reformation era, a dramatization of the Empire itself, though in this show the burghers played a very minor role, both socially, for they were mostly excluded from the grand whirl of parties, balls, dinners, and hunts, and politically, for the diet's main business consisted of negotiations on religion between the emperor and the princes.[179]

At the outset, the Strasbourgeois felt like pariahs, for the Saxon clergy preached "in a very unfriendly manner against our theologians' opinions," as though the Zwinglians "were hatching marvelous plots to ally with foreign nations, to divide up the bishoprics among ourselves, and all in all to arouse tremendous rebellion and war."[180] Worse yet, when the emperor commanded that "everyone [ein jeder]" should submit his "opinion and view [opinion und meinong]," Sturm was refused permission to sign the Saxon confession—called the Confession of Augsburg—because, "since they do not agree with our theologians on the doctrine of the Lord's Supper, they will not permit us to join them in this matter."[181] What to do? Well, for one thing, Strasbourg needed a distinct voice, not an echo of Zwingli's, for which purpose Sturm called Bucer and Capito to Augsburg and hid them in his quarters while they produced the Tetrapolitan Confession. The name spoke for itself: only three other free cities would sign it—Constance, Memmingen, and Lindau— and even the loyal Constancers found it "excessive or disputatious [weitloeffig oder disputierlich]."[182] This pitiful showing got the respect it deserved. The Lutheran princes and cities had their Confession of Augsburg solemnly read to the monarchs and two hundred notables on 25 June; Sturm delivered the Tetrapolitan Confession to the Imperial chancellery without ceremony on 9 July. The Lutheran confession received a reply in four weeks; Sturm and his little band had to wait more than fourteen. Then, on 25 October, they stood for three hours before Charles, Ferdinand, and all the Catholic princes, prelates, and envoys, while a secretary read a reply [confutatio] in which "we are so much and so often called heretics, worse than the people of Capharnum, worse than the Jews, and it is said that we are more unbelieving than the Devil."[183] Sturm then rose to respond. The document, he said, "is filled with the sharpest and most provocative words, such as 'heretical,' 'blasphemous,' 'impious,' 'wanton,' and the like," and it "contains all sorts of matters and tales quite unknown to us, especially concerning the most worthy sacrament of the body and blood of Christ, which are not preached in our cities. Even if they were, our governments would punish those who preached them."[184] "It was a tough, difficult thing," Hans Ehinger proudly wrote home to Memmingen, "for five good men and burghers to speak up and give reply to the Roman emperor, electors, princes, and so many estates as supported them." [185] A brave act, but a fruitless one.

It was not for the emperor and the Catholic bishops, however, that Sturm intended Strasbourg's distinctive voice, but for the Lutherans. To set it off, he needed an authentic Zwinglian voice, preferably Zwingli's own. He therefore set afoot a cunning, even ruthless, scheme to exploit Zwingli's radicalism to show how little Zwinglian Strasbourg was. Sturm sent Zwingli a copy of the Lutheran Schwabach Articles, and suggested that "if *you and your people* meanwhile compose apologies to the emperor and the princes, in which you give an account of *your* faith [*fidei vestre rationem redderetis*], I do not believe *your* effort will be fruitless."[186] Zwingli took the bait and sent to Augsburg his defiant *Fidei ratio*, which just happened to fall into Lutheran hands and made their theologians howl with rage—at Zwingli.[187]

All this was but Sturm's scene setting for the moment when the emperor's policy of reunion might begin to falter.[188] On 24 August, nearly a month before the negotiations finally failed, came the first good news: Bucer and Melanchthon had talked, and the landgrave was trying to get Sturm "a secret interview" with the elector's men.[189] As the talks with the emperor's theologians soured, Melanchthon discovered that Bucer's views were "not so bad as they were made out to be and were comparable to Luther's view," and by mid-September Sturm, seeing light at the end of the tunnel, dispatched Bucer to Wittenberg and Capito to Switzerland.[190] Now Sturm had to deal directly with the Saxons, for the Hessian landgrave had left the Diet early, having accomplished nothing. The Saxon elector, just before he left Augsburg, said to Sturm, "God grant His grace that all of us Protestant princes and Imperial cities will shortly come together again in a united alliance."[191] Sturm nodded wisely and, according to Gregor Brück, softly replied that Strasbourg had "been forced to yield a bit only on account of the Common Man, who had taken up the new opinion, so that there would be no tumult."[192] With everything clicking into place for a Protestant accord, on 12–13 October Sturm and Pfarrer talked with Count Albert of Mansfeld, the leading militant in the elector's council.[193] Speaking as though nothing now stood between them and an alliance, Sturm told Count Albert that he should ask the elector

> not to separate from or reject the city of Strasbourg, but rather to unite with it, since in faith, so far as concerns the Holy Sacrament, there is no difference between His Electoral Grace and his allies and Strasbourg. And though there had been a certain verbal dispute between their preachers,

there is no real dispute about the presence of the true body and blood. If this union and alliance is established between His Electoral Grace and Strasbourg, it will be useful and encouraging to both parties for resistance and other purposes.[194]

Albert, who was no fool, asked whether Strasbourg would sign the Confession of Augsburg. Sturm stalled. He said that Albert could be confident that "there would be no problem there," because Bucer had said of the confession that "he saw nothing wanting in it nor anything that needed changing."[195] Next day Sturm and Albert made plans for canvassing the Evangelical powers for bilateral talks "to agree upon a common defense and mutual aid. And since the matter cannot be long delayed, as firm a commitment as possible should be made at that meeting."[196] During these two days in October 1530 at Augsburg, the Protestant alliance arose from the dead.

Elector John of Saxony, as anxious as Sturm to maintain appearances, informed Strasbourg in early November that "the councilors we left at Augsburg have reported the statement your envoys made to them concerning the most worthy sacrament of the body and blood of Christ. Now that there is no disagreement between us, we receive that report with special favor and enthusiasm."[197] Sturm fully realized the fragility of the moment, and on his way home he stopped at Ulm to confer with Besserer and the other Ulmers, who were Strasbourg's most faithful allies in the alliance matter.[198] "Everything depends," he told them, "on whether we have the proper love for one another. If we are allied, and this love is not present, then the alliance will have been made in vain. At the first sign of trouble, members will offer trivial excuses and begin to withdraw from the league."[199] "The proper love for one another" was Sturm's phrase for the friendships that, in the burghers' political culture, could alone transform self-interest into firm, traditional bonds and lasting federations. "If we attend yet another meeting," he told the Ulmers, "only to learn that the elector will ally with none but those who share his beliefs, then all this effort will be for nothing. He cannot expect that my government and others will permit him to dictate the norms of faith." This was precisely what the Strasbourgeois, in the end, did permit.

When he rode in the evening of 22 December 1530 into Smalkalden, the scene of his humiliation one year before, Sturm had not slept in his own bed for seven months.[200] His saddlebags contained full powers to represent Constance, Lindau, and Memmingen, limited powers for Zurich and Bern, and instruction from Strasbourg to bring the treaty home, for "we must confer and decide with the commune and not as an individual person."[201] The negotiations ran for nine days until, on the old year's final day, the allies formed "a Christian association for defense and protection against violent assault" and agreed to send Charles an appeal "for the amelioration of the intolerable recess" of Augsburg.[202] Sweeping aside all nice formulations about resistance, they proclaimed solidarity against "the Imperial fiscal [the Chamber Court's enforcement office], the Swabian League, the emperor's commissioners, or any other agency."[203] Count Albert told Sturm on 31 December that "it would be good if the league could be expanded, and the elector and the princes desire that we treat with Zurich, Bern, and Basel to the extent that they will also subscribe to our [Tetrapolitan] confession."[204] Sturm, though reluctant to drop the Swiss, feared that "the proper love for one another" was not fervent enough to stretch from Zurich to Wittenberg. He discussed the problem with the landgrave in person on New Year's Day and again by letter in early February.[205] "Though I know full well how loyally and graciously Your Grace has treated us and will continue to treat us," Sturm wrote, "yet I fear not a little that there are those who would like to scotch our concord for the sole purpose of putting an end to the Christian alliance founded at Smalkalden, which they can prevent in no other way."[206] "If one has the desire, will, and love for unity," he continued,

> such a concord can begin with the confession that the body and blood of Christ are truly present in the eucharist, truly offered, eaten, and drunk. The rest—whether He is actually eaten and drunk through the physical mouth and by the unbelievers and the godless—will work itself out in time and perhaps to degree better than we can now conceive.

Sturm here touched on the Smalkaldic League's central nerve, the definition of its solidarity—Sturm's "proper love for one another"—as a common subscription to an elaborate formulation of Christian doctrine. Although Sturm and Strasbourg might lead Ulm and the other South German cities into the fellowship of that common faith, doubtless the Swiss cities would not follow. "God Almighty knows that we here mean the whole thing good and honestly," he wrote, "and in this effort we do not seek carnal support or aid, which we could expect from our Swiss co-citizens more than from others, but only to prevent scandal to men of good will and to further the advance of truth." The Swiss towns, as Sturm knew from his own family's traditions, formed Strasbourg's most effective allies against a threat of war in their own region. Against the present danger, however, which was Imperial in scope and political and legal in nature, Swiss aid was useless, and if the co-citizens had to be thrown over for more effective friends, then Sturm, for one, would throw over these good, old neighbors and adopt a new basis of solidarity—doctrinal agreement—for the old—cultural and social affinity and geographical proximity. The Reformation, Evangelical religion, had altered Sturm's inherited concept of political community and enabled him to imagine and work for an alliance that could act effectively within the structures of Imperial governance.

This change must have seemed right in the heady days just after Smalkalden, when John of Saxony wrote to commend Sturm, "whom we now recognize as one who knows best how to further the cause and who understands, better than others do, the grace of the Almighty. We graciously ask that you exert every possible effort to see that your preachers . . . adhere to the articles upon which we agree."[207] The elector had reason to be concerned, for one of his agents, Matthis Reinboldt, stopped at Strasbourg on his way to Paris in late winter 1531 and reported that the city "is divided into three groups. Many are Zwinglian, many Lutheran, and also many papist, and there is no sign that the preachers are backing away from the Zwinglian teachings."[208] Even bigger trouble loomed on Strasbourg's southern flank, where the Swiss regimes' attitude was expressed pithily by Zwingli's retort that if the Lutherans believed in Christ "in one place, in the bread, and in the wine," he wrote to Bucer on 12 February 1531, "then they are simply papists."[209] Sturm and the Hessian prince wanted the Swiss in the new alliance, and the landgrave invented interesting excuses about why Basel, Zurich, and Bern failed to send their assents to the articles of alliance and the doctrinal statement on the eucharist, which was appended to it.[210] It was not to be, and the dream of a grand Evangelical alliance, from the foot of the Alps to the northern seas, gradually faded away.

Another effect of the new politics was to thrust Strasbourg into the role of leader of the Evangelical free cities of Swabia, which were by no means its traditional allies or clients. When Ulm, Constance, Memmingen, Biberach, and Isny signed the treaty of Smalkalden in February 1531, they sealed the doom of South German Zwinglianism. In the following autumn, when the Swiss highlanders again boiled out of their valleys to battle Zurich and its allies, the XIII of Strasbourg turned a deaf ear to pleas from Landgrave Philip and Basel for aid to their Swiss allies.[211] That was the end of the Christian Federation and of "turning Swiss" at Strasbourg. The world had changed since the days of Old Peter Schott, and his great-grandson's ability to see how it changed made Jacob Sturm by 1531 the political leader of the urban reformation in the German Southwest.

Signs of hard times hung over Strasbourg's entry into the Smalkaldic League. The scourge of famine haunted the land since 1529, and during the year ending in June 1531, 23,548 refugees and other poor were fed from the civic welfare fund.[212] Taxes had to be raised, of course, though the additional two pence on the shilling "astonished the citizens, for in this year there was a great famine."[213] On the road to Eckbolsheim were found the corpses of a woman and two children, dead of hunger, and one day, when the civic granary opened to sell flour, the crowd surged forward and crushed a young girl to death. There were portents, too, and on Pentecost Sunday at nine o'clock in the morning, a star appeared in the heavens, "which was regarded as a remarkable thing."

FORGING PROTESTANT UNITY

Born in hard times, the Smalkaldic League nonetheless ushered in the halcyon days of the South German reformation. The freshly made alliance progressed from its foundation in early 1531 to a doctrinal concord at

Schweinfurt in April 1532 to the Truce of Nuremberg in the same year. Then, after the Swabian League dissolved in 1534, Landgrave Philip of Hesse with Jacob Sturm's support restored Duke Ulrich in Württemberg. Finally, in 1536 the league approved its own constitution, and the Wittenberg Concord ended the controversy over doctrine. These years of success with hardly a setback made the Smalkaldic League a powerful force in Imperial politics and guaranteed the security and prosperity of the Reformation's cause.

The league's first fruit, the Truce of Nuremberg in 1532, aimed to give the Protestant powers relief from suits before the Imperial Chamber Court (*Reichskammergericht*) at Speyer for the restoration of Catholic ceremonies and clerical incomes and properties.[214] Prompted by the Diet of Augsburg's decisions, these suits, rather than an immediate threat of war, drove a number of South German free cities into the Smalkaldic League for protection.[215] Charles V was willing to deal with Protestants about the suits, because he needed their support for his brother's royal election and against the Turks and France. His policy gained strength from the formation about this time of a Catholic party of mediation, electors and princes who, whatever their views on religion, stayed neutral between the confessional blocs.[216] Charles, who sat, in Luther's German phrase, "in the midst of many snakes," could hardly refuse to meet the Protestant princes, in Ferdinand's Spanish phrase, "beard to beard."[217] On 8 July 1531 he suspended the restitution suits until the next diet and instructed two Catholic electors, Louis of the Palatinate and Albert of Mainz, to treat with "the duke of Saxony, his son [John Frederick], the landgrave of Hesse, and their supporters concerning the articles of faith."[218] The mediators and the allies met at Schweinfurt in April 1532, while Charles was hurrying from the Netherlands to stage an Imperial diet at Regensburg.

Although he pleaded "ill health [*leibsblödigkeit*]," Jacob Sturm agreed to go to Schweinfurt, so Claus Kniebis, who was not an experienced diplomat, had to make the even longer ride to Regensburg.[219] The two assemblies were closely linked, for Charles V had already stipulated that the truce should cover only those who accepted "the opinion and assertion of said duke, landgrave, and allies as presented in the said Confession of Augsburg," to which the southern cities had not yet subscribed.[220] Sturm had persuaded Bucer and the other preachers to state, with a few face-saving qualifications, their opinion that the Confession of Augsburg "is in agreement with our faith and understanding of the Bible, and it all agrees with our [Tetrapolitan] confession."[221] This was already a step beyond the understanding of 1530, which had regarded Lutheran and Zwinglian as equivalent, but it did not suffice, for when negotiations opened at Schweinfurt on Easter Monday (1 April) 1532, Margrave George and the Nurembergers, who were not members of the league, immediately charged that Strasbourg, contrary to Sturm's assurances, seethed with heresy. Sturm pleaded with Chancellor Brück of Saxony that if they would only stick to the Bible's language, "namely, that one receives in the eucharist the true body and true blood of Christ," and leave out all the irritating words—"symbolic," "figurative," "bodily," "essentially," "spiritually," and the like—there would be neither a quarrel nor grounds for one.[222] All in vain, for the Saxons insisted on the exclusive validity of their Confession of Augsburg, and in mid-April Sturm had to fetch Bucer to Schweinfurt to sign that document and commit Strasbourg formally and fully to the Lutheran confession.[223] It was a bitter moment for Bucer, who had to follow the lead of Sturm's policy, and for Sturm himself, and Cardinal Albert of Mainz's taunt made it no sweeter. "How will your preachers explain," Albert said to Sturm, "that you now subscribe to the Saxon confession, though they used to teach quite differently?" "If our preachers were here," Sturm responded with mock gravity,

> they would be able to answer you. To the extent that they were in error and now reject what they formerly taught—mind you, they were accused of teaching much they never taught—they should be praised rather than blamed. I imagine that if we abandoned our faith for Your Grace's, Your Grace would lay that to our credit.[224]

"Let's speak of it no more," the prelate replied.

Meanwhile, at Regensburg the Diet awaited the outcome of the mediating electors' negotiations with the Protestants at Schweinfurt. Until these negotiations were concluded, the Protestant estates would not take their seats at Regensburg, although some of them—Sturm named Ulm—were so unsettled by the grim news from Hungary that they were prepared to vote the taxes anyway. Frightened by the same terrible news, Strasbourg's XIII decided that Strasbourg should "offer its share of the tax with good will" in order not to endanger the peace.[225] Finally, on 23 July 1532, Charles suspended the suits for restitution until a general council could be held. He thereby conceded de facto toleration to the Lutheran powers, who agreed to keep the public peace and support the defense of Hungary.[226] All sides regarded the agreement as temporary: the moderate Catholic princes, because they hoped to replace it with a political settlement of the schism; the militant Catholic powers, because they held it to be an unacceptable, purely personal arrangement by the emperor; Charles himself, because he expected it to be superseded by a general council; and the Protestants, because their boundless optimism about the convincing power of their own faith dispelled all doubts about its ultimate victory throughout the Empire, to which the establishment of legal parity with Catholicism was a mere transitional phase.[227] In the event, however, the Truce of Nuremberg's recognition of the Empire as one country with two religions contained the first legal step toward the peaces of Augsburg in 1555 and Westphalia in 1648.

Renewed in 1534 and again in 1539, the Truce of Nuremberg provided the Protestant powers with the time and the security to bring their churches under control and deal with religious radicalism. It also ushered in the halcyon days of the South German reformation, though at a price. Bucer, who had once more trimmed his convictions to Strasbourg's policy, groused about the concessions and called for a resumption of religious war in Switzerland.[228] Sturm and the XIII, however, did not flinch from the deal they had struck: on 29 July 1532, 388 infantry marched out of Strasbourg—the cavalry followed on 12 August—under the command of Bernhard Wurmser von Vendenheim, with his cousin Friedrich Sturm, Jacob's older brother, as paymaster. Off they went to Vienna, living proof of their masters' good faith and belief "that such aid [should] be given willingly and without compulsion."[229] The Smalkaldic League had proved its worth, though at a price.

The Truce of Nuremberg provided the new Protestant alliance with breathing space and new horizons. When Charles V returned to Spain in April 1533, his mind no longer on the German question, Landgrave Philip of Hesse turned his attention once more to the Württemberg problem. His restoration of Duke Ulrich in Stuttgart in the summer of 1534, aided by good luck, daring, Jacob Sturm's support, Bavarian ambition, and French gold, proved to be one of the few opportunities the Protestants fully recognized and truly exploited. More than any other event, it ensured the survival of Protestantism in South Germany.[230] The success of this strike depended on King Ferdinand's neglect and on the revival of Duke Ulrich's cause. Ferdinand grasped too late that Württemberg, as one observer had written, was "practically the heart of Germany [*gleichsam das Herz Deutschlands*]," a natural bridge between the Austrian Upper Rhine and Austrian Upper Swabia.[231] As for Ulrich, though his past criminal behavior warranted no regrets, a lingering resentment of foreign officials gradually combined with the spread of Evangelical religion to fan enthusiasm for the Württembergers' natural prince, who sat waiting up north in Hesse.[232] Although it may have been an exaggeration to say that "the majority of the land of Württemberg is strongly Evangelical and cries for its old Duke Ulrich," it was true that the Reformation transformed this "prince of thieves [*princeps latronum*]" into a champion of the gospel.[233]

The Truce of Nuremberg unleashed Landgrave Philip, who was heart and soul for his kinsman's restoration. By March 1533 he was agitating for the formation of a new "temporal alliance [*usserliches verstendnus*]" to rival and disrupt the Swabian League, which was due to expire in the following year.[234] The landgrave also argued to the Bavarian dukes and other potential allies that "the Württemberger's ten-year punishment and penance were, measuring the consequences against his offense, more than enough."[235] A lucky conjunction of events created an opportunity to rectify the situation in 1534: the Bavarian dukes joined the landgrave in opposing Ferdinand's election as king of the Romans and Charles's successor; the expiration of the Swabian League weakened Austrian Württemberg's defenses; and a treaty with King Francis at Bar-le-Duc on 28 January 1534 supplied French gold to pay for the enterprise.[236] The Smalkaldic League could not be used, because, as

Philip told Chancellor Eck of Bavaria, the young Saxon elector, John Frederick (r. 1532–47),

> is no warrior and is not inclined to war. He will gladly help the young Württemberger [Duke Christoph, Ulrich's son] as best he can with words, but he cannot be brought to follow them with deeds. He will remain hard for the alliance against the [Ferdinand's] election, but he cannot be moved to make war for that cause.[237]

As if to confirm the Hessian's judgment, John Frederick wrote on the eve of the campaign that "we cannot understand how, after our numerous pleas, warnings, and advices, Your Grace could allow himself to be moved to such an action in the Württemberg affair."[238] He begged the landgrave to cease operations, "so that peace and order can everywhere be preserved in the Empire, rebellion and uproar be prevented, and God's honor not be blasphemed either by Your Grace or by our opponents."[239] The Saxon's views were echoed by the other Protestant powers, with one exception.

Of all the Smalkaldic League's leaders, only Jacob Sturm supported the Württemberg project and saw that his regime backed it with money, men, and propaganda.[240] Sturm appreciated what Württemberg, with its strategic position and its size—80,000 square kilometers and 250,000 people—would mean to the league's military position in South Germany, and he doubtless expected that a restoration there would ease pressures on the Evangelical free cities of Swabia.[241] In the future, he later told Ulrich, "the landgrave would supply the cavalry, you the infantry, and the southern cities the artillery."[242] The coarse, unbridled duke himself was another story, and the landgrave had to remind Sturm that "you know perfectly well what Duke Ulrich's religion is, and that he has a special feeling for the city of Strasbourg. If he regains his land, he will act tolerably toward the Ulmers and all the other Protestant cities in the south."[243] Sturm had other reservations—he mistrusted the Bavarians and felt that the royal election was none of the burghers' business—but he decided to support the enterprise. In April 1534 the Strasbourgeois permitted Hessian agents to borrow forty-six thousand florins, a tenth of the campaign's total costs, to recruit in the vicinity, to buy pikes from the civic arsenal, and to hire local gunners.[244] This aid helped the landgrave to rout the Austrian governor's troops near Lauffen on 12–13 May and enter Stuttgart three days later.

The fall of Württemberg evoked enthusiasm and joy from Strasbourg's preachers, who immediately sent the princes a program for reforming the conquered duchy in the South German manner.[245] They declined to yield to the Saxons here, on their own doorstep, as they had at Schweinfurt, and the "impartial [unpartheiisch]" men they nominated to lead Württemberg's reformation—one was Ambrosius Blarer of Constance—were in fact hardcore Zwinglians.[246] They thus prepared for precisely the test of strength that Jacob Sturm longed to avoid.

Sturm feared the Treaty of Kaaden, which Elector John Frederick had mediated between King Ferdinand and Duke Ulrich, and which conceded the right to reform the duchy's church under the Truce of Nuremberg, "except that the sacramentarians, Anabaptist sects, and also other new, unchristian sects, which may subsequently arise, are expressly excluded."[247] When Sturm strongly objected to this language, the landgrave tried to soothe him: "We also noticed in your last letter that you are quite dissatisfied with the word 'sacramentarian' in the treaty, on the suspicion that it might work to Strasbourg's disadvantage."[248] "We have to be concerned," Sturm shot back, "that the king and the mediators mean us with this word—please God, no one else will say the same—and will seize the opportunity to drag us under this name, whether we wish it or no." This was no idle fear, not in the summer of 1534, when the Anabaptist kingdom at Münster was the scandal of the Empire. No one in South Germany knew that better than did Jacob Sturm, whose regime had the Münsterites' spiritual leader, the prophet Melchior Hoffman, locked up in their jail.[249] The Treaty of Kaaden had nonetheless to be signed, and Sturm swallowed his anger, "though at the same time I did not refrain from pointing out the dangers to His Grace [Ulrich], if he did not ratify the treaty."[250] And truly, no sooner was the duchy in Ulrich's hands than the old sacramentarian controversy flared anew, as Erhard Schnepf, Philip's Lutheran chaplain, began calling Ambrosius Blarer and his Strasbourg sponsors "fanatics [*schwermer*]," with the consequence, Sturm told the landgrave, that "the papists take his charge as an indication of who the sacramentarians are, who are excluded from the peace [of Kaaden]."[251] "Sir Jacob Sturm has done his best," Bucer wrote, "to persuade Duke Ulrich to take the matter in hand, so that Schnepf doesn't have it entirely his own way."[252] The strife between Blarer and Schnepf—a "knothead, whom I knew years ago at Heidelberg," Bucer called him—undid all of Sturm's labors.[253] "By God's grace it has happened," he wrote to the landgrave in August 1534, "that peace has reigned for quite a while among the southern cities. Now we hoped that should My Gracious Lord, Duke Ulrich, get his land back, . . . things would get even better. Perhaps God wills it otherwise, so that the victories and good fortune don't make us haughty."[254]

Sturm was often in Stuttgart during these months—the landgrave wanted him to stay and even to join Ulrich's court as chamberlain (*Hofmeister*)[255]— and he advised Ulrich to enforce the Confession of Augsburg as the norm for preaching in Württemberg. Sturm also asked the landgrave to announce that "as Your Princely Grace and the other electors and princes have accepted us into the [Smalkaldic] League as being in doctrinal agreement with them, therefore, so long as preaching accords with the Saxon confession, no one should be pressed beyond the words of Scripture into other words."[256] In his zeal to keep the peace, Jacob Sturm became a promoter of the Lutherans' Confession of Augsburg, and doubtless strengthened Ulrich's mind against the Zwinglians' plans for reforming the duchy. The Zwinglian project in

Württemberg was doomed, however, not because of Sturm's desire to keep the peace, nor yet because of Duke Ulrich's prejudice against the Zwinglians' congregationalism, but mostly because the central issue had already been settled by the Zwinglians' submission at Schweinfurt. Schnepf had this in mind when he taunted Blarer, "If you don't agree with me on the sacramental question, one of us will have to leave the land." In fact, although the two men did hammer out yet another union formula, which made Duke Ulrich "jump for joy" and fire off a copy to Jacob Sturm, it was all a charade.[257] The decision had fallen at Schweinfurt, and Jacob Sturm was going to live by it.[258]

The taking of Württemberg was that rarest of political gains, a cheap and permanent victory, which was sealed by Duke Ulrich's entry into the Smalkaldic League in 1536. Yet the enterprise taught Jacob Sturm a lesson about thorns and roses. On the one hand, it awakened the landgrave's appetite for a general war against the House of Austria—the old plan with Zwingli—and he complained bitterly of Sturm's lack of stomach for this project. "I wish that Jacob Sturm and the cities," he later wrote to Ulrich, "had given the needed money and had argued as strongly *for* an attack on the king as they in fact argued *against* it—then would have been the right time. But they gave Your Grace nothing free."[259]

The Württemberg affair taught Jacob Sturm a lesson about the fragility of Protestant solidarity. Although Sturm himself always professed to believe that the quarrel was a mere "quarrel over words [*wortzanck*]," he was well aware that others saw it in a very different light. "I am not a little concerned," he had written to Landgrave Philip in February 1531,

> that there are people who want to prevent this agreement [*verglichung*] solely in order that the Christian alliance founded at Smalkalden will not continue. For they see no other way to do this than through this dispute. I have always thought that if we had the desire for and love of unity, it would be enough at the beginning for such an agreement that we mutually confess that the body and blood of Christ are truly present in the eucharist and are truly eaten and drunk. The rest, whether it happens through the corporeal mouth, or whether the unbelievers or the godless truly eat and drink them—that could all be agreed upon in time, and perhaps more completely than we can now imagine. There are many who cannot now understand one another, because of the heated quarrel that has raged between the two parties for some time, but who later, when heads become cooler and the dispute has died down, will understand one another perfectly and will come to agreement.[260]

Time and patience, Sturm hoped, would overcome the—in purely worldly terms—unnatural character of this alliance. "God Almighty knows," he sighed,

> that we have always meant it well and truly, and that in this matter we seek not earthly power or aid—which we could, in any case, expect more from our co-citizens, the Swiss, than from others—but we seek only to

avoid scandal to good-hearted folk and would gladly see the progress of truth fostered.

The quarrel over Württemberg's reformation demonstrated that the Zwinglians' submission at Schweinfurt in 1532 had dampened the quarrel but not scotched it.

Sturm's fears were confirmed in late 1534, when Elector John Frederick proposed that league members send their theologians to a meeting "to reach agreement [*vergleichong*] on this dispute." Sturm told the landgrave "confidentially [*geheim*]" about his misgivings. "I fear," he wrote,

> some [*ettliche*] who proposed this assembly of scholars to the elector did so not because they seek agreement [*vergleichong*] but because they expect, knowing how some of the scholars think, there will be no agreement. Then they can wrest the elector away from us [*von disem teil gar abreissen*] and more easily lead him into other schemes they have in mind.[261]

Philip, he thought, ought to persuade his kinsman not to bring a whole flock of preachers together, including the worst stormcrows, "but only some few from both side's scholars—ones who are not stubborn and self-centered but reasonable and pacific—should be called together."[262] Every new application to join the league, Sturm realized, might reopen the quarrel, and he thought it perhaps better "if we did not consider any further expansion and admission of other powers but let the league stand as it is and form another, so that it would be thought that we did it not because of doctrinal disagreements but because of the great distances."[263]

If Sturm truly believed that the "quarrel of words" could be settled by words alone, he was building castles in Spain, for from Wittenberg the largest calibers in the Protestant world were now taking southern cities under fire, one after another. "At Augsburg," Luther had raged in August 1531, "Satan himself reigns through the enemies of the sacrament . . ., and the same is true at Ulm."[264] Over the next few years, he blasted the Zwinglians at Kempten, Augsburg, and Frankfurt, always sensing behind them "the double-tongued gang" at Strasbourg, who clung to the old error "that the sacrament is mere wine and bread" and were fit only to serve a church "built in a pigsty."[265] Ulm, where the Zwinglian clergy had nearly revolted against the Schweinfurt agreement, was no better, and Augsburg's church remained in the hands of obdurate Zwinglian splitters.[266] Among the large towns, only Strasbourg and Ulm belonged to the Smalkaldic League at this time, but the probable applications of Frankfurt and Augsburg promised to touch off fresh explosions.

And yet, the Protestant success in Württemberg also turned Luther's mind toward concord, not least because of the nightmarish prospect of the Zwinglian Blarer rampaging through the duchy's southern half.[267] "I have always wished most devoutly for unity," he wrote to the landgrave on 17 October 1534, "because the papists' high-handed spite, which pains me and damages Christ's kingdom, is strengthened through this disunity, without which they [the Catholics] would long ago have become more manageable."[268] If Philip would sound out Bucer and his followers, whom Luther believed to be very few, "I would gladly be prepared to do whatever I could in good conscience do. Dear God, it is hard for me, this affair, which was begun not by me but by others." This letter passed via Hesse and Sturm to Bucer, who rode off to Augsburg to cool down the Zwinglians there, while Sturm worked to the same end among the urban regimes.[269] "So far as I know," he wrote to Ulm's privy council (*Geheimen*) at the end of November 1534, "relying on what Sir Martin Bucer told me ... your preachers share and are in agreement with Bucer's opinion and the moderation that he represents in this mediation."[270] The two Strasbourgeois jumped at the landgrave's offer to host a meeting at Kassel between Bucer and Melanchthon at the end of 1534. Sturm, though "not a little pleased with the accord [*Vergleichong*]," had to tell the landgrave on 1 May 1535 that "it grieves me now [*mit ganz beschwertem gemüt*] to hear that some on the other side don't want to accept it."[271]

Sturm was grieved, because the Lutherans were presenting one final price of the doctrinal concord: Augsburg. In no other free city did the struggle between the two Evangelical factions rage so long or with such intensity as in the great Swabian metropolis on the Lech.[272] Tortured by strife between Catholics and Evangelicals and between Lutherans and Zwinglians, plus the magistrates' inaction, the city stood on the brink of revolution, according to Gereon Sailer, Augsburg's city physician and Bucer's confidant. "Terrible things, pregnant with revolt, are happening here," he wrote in June 1533, "and every day come new complications.... The magistrates believe that the people will rise against them.... I play merely the role of spectator in what, I fear, is not a comedy but a tragedy."[273] The magistrates' inaction reflected both their own divisions about religion and the Habsburg-Wittelsbach stalemate in South Germany. The coincidence in 1534 of new Evangelical burgomasters and the restoration in Württemberg broke the logjam and triggered the regime's decision in favor of the Evangelical religion.[274] On the one hand, this change brought to a head and intensified the need for a general Evangelical concord, because of Augsburg's size, wealth, and political stature, but, on the other hand, it also opened the way for Jacob Sturm and Martin Bucer to influence the outcome in the Lutheran sense. They were aided by the local situation, for Wolfgang Rehlinger, a strong Lutheran who was a burgomaster in 1534, was also Sturm's kinsman.[275] When Augsburg's magistrates, coached by Bucer, announced their desire to receive a Lutheran preacher, plans for a theologians' meeting to bring doctrinal concord could move forward. Zwinglian resistance continued, of course, and when Johann Forster, a preacher sent from Wittenberg, suggested that the Augsburgers model their religious practices on those of Wittenberg, the local preachers—southerners all—replied that such "children's games [*puppenwerk*]" might do for "the Saxons, a crude, stupid people," but not for the "wise, intelligent Augsburgers."[276] Resistance spoke, too, from Constance, South Germany's most stalwartly Zwinglian city, whose magistrates retorted that it would be better to tolerate differences in doctrine "than to burden the churches with newly prescribed rules and requirements [*satzungen und bedingungen*]."[277] All in vain, for nothing could stop the progress toward concord, not even continuing strife over the reformation in Württemberg, where, as Sturm sighed, "some preachers act as though they want to ruin the land and would like to expel [*usbeissen*] those installed by Blarer. That would make the whole matter bitter and set it back again."[278] Bucer, too, saw that they must strike while the iron was hot, so that "Our Heavenly Father [might] relieve us at last of this painful quarrel [*des leidigen zanks*] and the burden of this dispute over the Holy Sacrament, which has done so much and such widespread harm."[279]

The theologians' meeting at Wittenberg, moved from Eisenach on account of Luther's health, approved on 29 May 1536 the Wittenberg Concord, a document no one could stretch in a non-Lutheran direction.[280] The Swiss, whose preachers had refused to come to Eisenach, would never accept it, but their military paralysis since 1531 made their exclusion all the more sufferable. The others all accepted it—Strasbourg, Duke Ulrich, Frankfurt, Augsburg, Kempten, Esslingen, and, after much wrangling, Ulm—thus closing the book on South German Zwinglianism.[281] Only the stubborn Constancers grumbled that clerical assemblies "have from the beginning of Christianity always caused more trouble and damage than benefit to the true faith, correct ceremonies, and Christian reform [*besserung*]."[282] Sturm warned them that the concord bound all members of the league, and that "it is not true that Sir Martin Bucer wanted to establish a new agreement, or whatever else might have seemed good to him, but he was to treat for a full and common peace on behalf of the alliances' cities and their churches."[283]

The Wittenberg Concord healed the decade-old rift in the Protestant camp. Its price was a surrender of the South German–Swiss heritage of communal reformation, its profit the final consolidation of the Smalkaldic League. Lasting concord made the league a stable force in Imperial political life and an effective shield to German Protestantism. It also made Jacob Sturm and Landgrave Philip, who had held north and south together, the undisputed leaders of this political force.

Notes

* "Dem adel und den fürsten/habt ir verdruß gethan/die werden euch erst birsten/ und geben den rechten lon;/wann ir mainen, sie schlafen,/hert werden sie euch strafen/mit iren guten wafen;/wachen wirt der adel schon,/manlich euch greufen an." Liliencron, ed., *Historische Volkslieder* 3:446, no. 375, stanza 12.
1. See Brady, *Turning Swiss*, for this entire subject.
2. Baumgarten, *Geschichte Karls V.* 2:313n.

3. For orientation, see G. Schmidt, *Städtetag*, 476–525; H. R. Schmidt, *Reichsstädte*, 298–325.
4. G. Schmidt, *Städtetag*, 147–52, 173–77, 352–62, 428–39, 441–49, 451–54, 461–64, 469; H. R. Schmidt, *Reichsstädte*, 75–81, 130–220. These two works supersede my account in *Turning Swiss*, 151–83.
5. H. R. Schmidt, *Reichsstädte*, 227–34; G. Schmidt, *Städtetag*, 487–90. They agree that the turning point came at the urban diet of Ulm in December 1524.
6. Naujoks, *Obrigkeitsgedanke*, 64–65.
7. Quoted by G. Schmidt, *Städtetag*, 490; and the following quote is at 491.
8. PC 1:100, no. 188; H. Lutz, *Conrad Peutinger*, 251–52.
9. G. Schmidt, *Städtetag*, 491–92. On the background to this policy at Augsburg, see Sieh-Burens, *Oligarchie*, 151–53.
10. Quoted by G. Schmidt, *Städtetag*, 491. Strasbourg's position appears in its instruction to the Imperial Diet of Speyer 1526, in PC 1:no. 456.
11. Brady, "'Sind also zu beiden theilen Christen,'" 75–76.
12. He had just finished a second term on the regency council at Esslingen. Wolfgang Capito dedicated on 14 March 1526 a book to "nobili ac erudito Iacobo Sturmio, Ciui et Senatori Argentinen. Caesarei Senatus hoc temporis consiliario," and on 29 March Sturm wrote to Peter Butz from Esslingen. Capito, *In Habakuk prophetam . . . enarrationes*, A.iir; Jacob Sturm to Peter Butz, Esslingen, 29 March 1526, in AST 176, fol. 511r. The Imperial Diet's customary procedures are described by Oestreich, "Zur parlamentarischen Arbeitsweise"; Schlaich, "Die Mehrheitsabstimmung im Reichstag."
13. Brady, *Ruling Class*, 317–18. Herlin was no furrier but a merchant and a well-to-do interloper from the Merchants' Guild.
14. *Ann. Brant*, no. 4682; PC 1:255–56, no. 450, and the following quote is at 255.
15. The quote is from Blickle, *Revolution of 1525*, 165; and see Friedensburg, *Reichstag*, 507–8, and Ludolphy, *Friedrich der Weise*, 313–14.
16. PC 1:256–58, nos. 451–52. See Baron, "Religion and Politics," 410; and Brady, *Turning Swiss*, 197. On urban rights (*stimm und session*), see Wendelin von St. Johann to Caspar Hedio, Speyer, 24 June 1526, in AMS, AA 407a/7, fol. 1v; Friedensburg, *Reichstag*, 244, 248, 255–56, 256 n. 1, 285 n. 2, 322, 355; G. Schmidt, *Städtetag*, 247–89.
17. PC 1:266, no. 468; Friedensburg, *Reichstag*, 334–39; Neuhaus, "Wandlungen," 138. On Kress, see Zophy, *Christoph Kress*.
18. PC 1:259, no. 453 (26 June 1526). The letter does not say that Sturm gave the speech, but this is probable. See Friedensburg, *Reichstag*, 244 n. 2, and PC 1:258 n. 6. For Charles V's agenda for this Diet, see ibid., 217–18, 523–24.
19. Friedensburg, *Reichstag*, 348. On the committee, see ibid., 228–38, 257, 272–74, 344–47, 538–40, 543–51; and on the Turkish problem, see Fischer-Galati, *Ottoman Imperialism*, 25–28.
20. Schmauss, ed., *Reichs-Abschiede* 2:274. On the origin of this formula, see Friedensburg, *Reichstag*, 279–82, 481–82.
21. Friedensburg, *Reichstag*, 558–67, here at 560.
22. Ibid., 417–18, 418 n. 1, an appointment Sturm may have owed to his old employer, Count Palatine Henry, now bishop of Utrecht. On the embassy's cancellation, see ibid., 418–19, 473–75; PC 1:275–76, no. 484.
23. Reproduced by Ficker, *Bildnisse*, table 1.
24. On the landgrave, see Dueck, "Religion and Politics in the Reformation"; Heinemeyer, "Weg in die Politik," 176–92; Demandt, *Hessen*, 169–74.
25. Brady, *Turning Swiss*, 102–15; Oberman, *Masters*, 240–59.
26. Landgrave Philip to Duke George, Sababurg, 10 July 1528, in Dülfer, *Packsche*

Handel 2:131–39, no. 106, here at 134. Also printed by Rommel, *Philipp der Grossmüthige* 3:17–26.

27. This was Luther's view, for which see Ludolphy, *Friedrich der Weise*, 27. His cousin, Duke George, was an exception to the general mediocrity of the Wettin princes. See Blaschke, *Sachsen*, 26–27.

28. Ludolphy, *Friedrich der Weise*, 65–73, 281–89; Blaschke, *Sachsen*, 19–23, 33–48; Laube, *Studien*, 77–81, who shows that Frederick got more from the mines than from any other source.

29. Fabian, *Entstehung*, 304–7; Ludolphy, *Friedrich der Weise*, 239–81.

30. Fabian, *Entstehung*, 21, 25, 27, 33, 332–38, with the quote at 25.

31. Ibid., 23, 308–9, 334; Demandt, *Hessen*, 179; Fabian, *Dr. Gregor Brück*, 14–16.

32. See Landgrave Philip to Margrave George of Brandenburg-Ansbach (14 January 1526), in Friedensburg, *Reichstag*, 497–500. He was already writing in this sense in 1525, in Stoy, *Bündnisbestrebungen*, 25–26.

33. Friedensburg, *Reichstag*, 497–98, for this and the remaining quotes in this paragraph.

34. *PC* 1:265, no. 467; Friedensburg, *Reichstag*, 309–13.

35. Herlin and Sturm to the Senate of Strasbourg, Speyer, 16 August 1526, in *PC* 1:268, no. 472; Senate & XXI to Sturm and Herlin, undated but later than 1 August, in ibid., 269, no. 473. A note on the latter document lists the drafting committee: Claus Kniebis, Mathis Pfarrer, and Ludwig (?) Böcklin. AMS, AA 427, fol. 93r. The Nurembergers received similar orders on 20 August, for which see Friedensburg, *Reichstag*, 458 n. 1.

36. *PC* 1:268, no. 472; Friedensburg, *Reichstag*, 517–19. For orientation, see Kohler, *Politik*, 92–97.

37. *PC* 1:278–80, no. 490, here at 279. On Meyer, see Brady, *Ruling Class*, 331. His instruction tells him "doch sollichs unvergriffen vnd uf hindersichpringen und nichts besliessen ze handlen oder fürzenemen."

38. His reports are in *PC* 1:280–83, nos. 491–92, 494, and see Dülfer, *Packsche Handel* 1:36–42, on the Frankfurt negotiations with the princes.

39. On the Diet, see *RTA, jR* 7:55, 57–59, 62–65, 68–69, 71, 73–77, 999–1105; Schmauss, ed., *Reichs-Abschiede* 2:284–89. On the visit to Nuremberg, see *PC* 1:282 n. 2; Schnelbögl, "Ratsmahl," 446–51; Pfeiffer, "Albrecht Dürer und Lazarus Spengler," 392. On Nuremberg's policy in general, see E. Franz, *Nürnberg, Kaiser und Reich*.

40. This and the following quote are from a letter of Spengler to Peter Butz, in *PC* 1:256, no. 451.

41. Ibid., 285–86, no. 501. Very soon thereafter, Nuremberg began its retreat into isolation. See G. Schmidt, "Die Haltung des Städtecorpus zur Reformation." The shift was connected with the city's rapprochement with the new ruling margrave of Brandenburg-Ansbach, George, called "the Pious," on whose policies see Schornbaum, *Zur Politik des Markgrafen Georg*.

42. Quoted in Brady, *Turning Swiss*, 195. On the situation at this time, see ibid., 193–202; H. R. Schmidt, *Reichsstädte*, 237–43.

43. See Fabian, *Entstehung*, 340–42.

44. Dülfer, *Packsche Handel* 1:84–107. See the appeals in *PC* 1:290–91, 290 n. 1.

45. *PC* 1:288–89, nos. 507, 509. Sturm met a Hessian official, Jakob von Taubenheim, at Butzbach; he complained that Taubenheim's instructions called him "Caspar Storben, burgher zu Straszburg."

46. Ibid., 292–95, 298–99, nos. 515, 517–20, 523–24, 526, 527.

47. Ibid., 299–300, no. 530. On Merklin, see Brady, *Turning Swiss*, 39–43. In *PC* 1:303, the last three names should read: Hans Erhart von Rotweil, Franz Bertsch, and Sifrid von Bietenheim.

48. PC 1:296–98, no. 525. This is the first recorded instance of Sturm drafting his own instruction. There, too, are the other quotes in this paragraph.
49. Ibid., 297. On the landgrave's hostility to the Swabian League, see Dülfer, Packsche Handel 1:30–31, 52–53; Fabian, Entstehung, 307. See Oberman, Masters, 240–59; and Naujoks, Obrigkeitsgedanke, 67, on the Swabian League's defense of Catholicism.
50. RTA, jR 7:331–32, 335–36, 1061–64 (recess, ca. 30 July 1528); Ann. Brant, no. 4746; PC 1:503–4, nos. 533–34; G. Schmidt, Städtetag, 159–61; H. R. Schmidt, Reichsstädte, 300.
51. See Sea, "The Swabian League and Government," for the league's role in governing South Germany.
52. PC 1:310, no. 543, to the Geheimen of Ulm.
53. Ibid., 312–14, nos. 548–49; Schelp, Reformationsprozesse, 45.
54. HStA Marburg, PA 2915, fol. 23 (PC 1:311, no. 546).
55. Scribner, "Ritual and Reformation," 141–44.
56. H. R. Schmidt, Reichsstädte, 333, 337.
57. Andreas Keller, ca. 1523–24, quoted in Oberman, Masters, 293 n. 10.
58. Rott, "Bucer et les débuts"; and see now the study by Kaufmann, Abendmahls-theologie. That the quarrel had political implications from the beginning, is argued by H. R. Schmidt, Reichsstädte, 335–36.
59. This section expands on my comments in Brady, "Architect of Persecution," 264–67.
60. Ann. Brant, no. 4604; BDS 2:461. See the precise chronology by H. R. Schmidt, Reichsstädte, 195–98. Chrisman, Strasbourg, 155–76; and Barton, "Abschaffung der Messe," 141–57. Some sources are published in BDS 2:423–555; others are noted by Brady, "'Sind also zu beiden theilen Christen,'" 79 n. 21.
61. BDS 2:462–65, here at 462, lines 8–9; and the Senate's action in ibid., 466–67. See Brady, Ruling Class, 208–15. The committee's report of 15 August 1525 is printed in BDS 2:468–69, but beware of Ernst-Wilhelm Kohls' annotation. The Sebott on this committee, for example, is not Lamprecht (d. 1519) but his son Diebold. Brady, Ruling Class, 328, 347–48, 358.
62. Sturm's memorial is published in Brady, "'Sind also zu beiden theilen Christen,'" 69–75, whence the quotes in this paragraph.
63. Ibid., 75, lines 68–73.
64. Ibid., 75–76, lines 76–99.
65. Ibid., 76, lines 109–19.
66. See Gérard Roussel to Nicolas Le Sueur, (Strasbourg), (December 1525), in Herminjard, Correspondances 1:413, no. 168. Deppermann, Melchior Hoffman, 150, repeats the oversimple notion of only two parties (for his "Conrad von Gottesheim" read "Conrad von Duntzenheim"). On the preachers and revolution, see Conrad, Bäuerliche Gesellschaft, 49–85; Maurer, Prediger im Bauernkrieg, 351–55.
67. Ann. Brant, no. 4701 (24 September 1526).
68. Oberman, Masters, 187–209, esp. 187–89, 293.
69. PC 4:857, no. 729.
70. Sturm, Quarti Antipappi, 166.
71. Specklin, Collectanées, no. 2316. On the restoration of doctrine as the reformers' goal, see Ozment, "Humanism, Scholasticism," 146–49.
72. Ficker, "Jakob Sturms Entwurf," 152. Locher, Zwinglische Reformation, 454–59, summarizes the evidence.
73. Sturm's comments, recorded at Smalkalden in December 1529 by Chancellor Georg Vogler of Brandenburg-Ansbach, are printed by Schubert, Bekenntnis-bildung, 167–82, from which the quotes in this paragraph are taken.

74. Ibid., 177.
75. Hamm, *Zwinglis Reformation der Freiheit*, 117.
76. Jacob Sturm to Peter Butz, Speyer, 15 July 1526, in PC 1:263–64, no. 464; and there, too, the remaining quotes in this paragraph.
77. Quoted by Baumgarten, *Jacob Sturm*, 32 n. 23, and extracted by Lenz, ed., *Briefwechsel* 2:450 n. 2. The passage is omitted from PC 4:103, no. 76.
78. ZW 14:424, lines 19–22. See Oberman, *Masters*, 274, 292; Locher, *Zwinglische Reformation*, 167–71. Sturm's views resemble those of Nuremberg's patricians, for which see Strauss, "Protestant Dogma," 38–58.
79. *TAE* 2:354 n. 2, line 41.
80. PC 2:237, no. 259 (15 December 1534).
81. See Oberman, *Masters*, 238 n. 127. The phrase "between sect and city" comes from Hammann, *Entre la secte et la cité*.
82. Wolfgang Capito to Jacob Sturm, Strasbourg, 4 March 1526, in *In Habakuk prophetam . . . enarrationes*, A.iir. The following quote is from the same source.
83. PC 1:264, no. 464. See EA, vol. 4, pt. 1a:964 s, for Köpfel's punishment.
84. Capito relates that after this conversation with Sturm, the preachers began to meet in the old Dominican convent to study the Bible and develop a preaching program. Capito, *In Habakuk prophetam . . . enarrationes*, A.iiv–A.iiir.
85. Reeves, "Marsiglio of Padua and Dante Alighieri," 86–89, 101–4; Skinner, *Foundations* 1:18–22. On the publication of Marsiglio's *Defensor pacis*, see Stähelin, "L'édition de 1522 du Defensor Pacis," 209–22.
86. Gottesheim, "Les éphémérides," 272.
87. A. Baum, *Magistrat*, 170–71, from AST, Varia ecclesiastica Ia, fol. 127v; Martin Bucer to Ambrosius Blarer, Strasbourg, 13 September 1528, in Schiess, ed., *Briefwechsel* 1:165, no. 124.
88. A. Baum, *Magistrat*, 179. On Betscholt, see Brady, *Ruling Class*, 300–301.
89. BDS 2:427 n. 18.
90. *Ann. Brant*, nos. 4735, 4741; and ZW, 9:593–94, no. 773, for the preachers' recognition that the moderates held the upper hand in the Senate & XXI.
91. "Vorhalt bej den Schöffen der Meß halb," in AST Supplement 45 (in Sturm's hand), from which the following quotes are taken.
92. One Schöffe voted that the mass should never be abolished (the undervote was only 21). See A. Baum, *Magistrat*, 188; Chrisman, *Strasbourg*, 172, for the Schöffen's vote; and Büheler, *Chronique*, no. 239, for the division in the Senate & XXI, where Egenolf Röder von Diersburg cast the deciding vote.
93. See Brady, *Turning Swiss*, 157–59; Brady, "In Search of the Godly City," 21–22; Oberman, *Masters*, 284–89; Rott, "Bucer et les débuts."
94. *Ann. Brant*, no. 4734.
95. Hauswirth, *Landgraf Philipp*, 87–95, 157–60; Bender, *Reformationsbündnisse*, 11–52; Rublack, "Die Aussenpolitik der Reichsstadt Konstanz." A *Burgrecht* was a traditional Swiss form of federation that involved an exchange of citizenship.
96. The first contact involved a stettmeister of Strasbourg. AGBR 3:106, no. 112. On Basel's policy, see F. Meyer, *Beziehungen*, 130, 155.
97. Dellsperger, "Zehn Jahre," 42–48 (the quote at 47); Walder, "Reformation und moderner Staat," 512–30.
98. AGBR 3:185, no. 263; Ryff, *Chronik* 1:67. *Ann. Brant*, no. 4753, is dated 16 November 1528, which is too late, for the envoys were in Bern on 15 November, for which see Arbenz, ed., *Vadianische Briefsammlung* 4:141; Stähelin, ed., *Briefe und Akten* 2:256, no. 617.
99. Quoted by Dellsperger, "Zehn Jahre," 45.

100. Ryff, *Chronik*, 73. See Wackernagel, *Geschichte der Stadt Basel* 3:502–8; Füglister, *Handwerksregiment*, 257–92.
101. Jacob Sturm to Landgrave Philip, Strasbourg, 15 January 1529, in *AGBR* 3:238–39, no. 348; and there, too, the remaining quotes in this paragraph.
102. Guggisberg, *Basel*, 29.
103. Haas, *Kappelerkrieg*, 85–86, 95–97.
104. *PC* 1:374, no. 620; *AGBR* 3:568, no. 644. See *PC* 1:373–74, 376, nos. 615–19, 624; *AGBR* 3:562, 574, nos. 634, 653; *EA*, vol. 4, pt. 1b:229. On the whole situation, see Haas, *Kappelerkrieg*, 158–64, 166–78.
105. Ryff, *Chronik*, 101–2. The tradition about Sturm is related by Jung, *Reformation in Straßburg*, 191 n. 16.
106. Bullinger, *Reformationsgeschichte* 2:183, who in 182–93 gives a good account of the mediation.
107. *PC* 1:380, no. 630. The Catholic Swiss saw the Strasbourgeois as hand in glove with the Swiss Evangelicals, a point expressed by the secretary (*Landschreiber*) of Obwalden, who decorated the walls of his house with the arms of Zurich, Bern, Basel, and Strasbourg hanging on a gallows. Haas, *Kappelerkrieg*, 120 n. 418.
108. Bullinger, *Reformationsgeschichte* 2:193. At Zurich there were also talks among the members of the Christian Federation, for which see Schiess, *Briefwechsel* 1:192–93, no. 148; *AGBR* 4:8, no. 5.
109. *Ann. Brant*, no. 4794.
110. *PC* 1:321, no. 559; and see *RTA, jR* 7:576, 606, for reactions of other urban envoys, and 547–50, 1128–36, for the Diet's agenda. Sturm and Christoph Tetzel of Nuremberg represented the cities in this committee. Neuhaus, "Wandlungen," 138. The lost Strasbourg instruction can be reconstructed from *PC* 1:326–27, nos. 566–67. They consulted the landgrave, who blamed the Catholic bishops. See *PC* 1:324–25, no. 565; *RTA, jR* 7:624 n. 1. On this Diet, see Kühn, *Die Geschichte des Speyerer Reichstages 1529*.
111. *Ann. Brant*, no. 4779; *PC* 1:326.
112. *RTA, jR* 7:607 n. 1; *PC* 1:336, no. 581; *Ann. Brant*, no. 4011; and there, too the following quote. On the policy of tax refusal, first broached at this time, see Fischer-Galati, *Ottoman Imperialism*, 13–37.
113. *PC* 1:nos. 578, 583–85, 593. Mieg arrived at Speyer on 10 April. This incident was garbled by tradition into the exclusions of both Mieg and Sturm. See Bullinger, *Reformationsgeschichte* 2:47.
114. Specklin, *Collectanées*, no. 2302; Trausch, "Straßburgische Chronik," no. 2682. The story may rest on Sturm's report to the Senate & XXI; and see *PC* 1:347, no. 593, and see nos. 578, 584, 586, 591.
115. *PC* 1:338–39, no. 584; *Ann. Brant*, no. 4011; Trausch, "Straßburgische Chronik," no. 2682; Specklin, *Collectanées*, no. 2302. This put him in advance of opinion at home, for the XIII ordered its envoys to vote for an emergency tax (*eilende Hilfe*) but against a long-term tax (*beharrliche Hilfe*) against the Turks.
116. *RTA, jR* 7:1321–24; Fabian, *Entstehung*, 20–21, 43–44.
117. The treaty's detailed financial and military provisions suggest a considerable gestation period, perhaps since 10 or 11 April, though Sturm's reports after 15 April are silent on the subject. See Schubert, *Bündnis und Bekenntnis*, 2; *RTA, jR* 8:4; *PC* 1:nos. 581, 589.
118. *RTA, jR* 7:621–22, 621 n. 1; Köhler, *Zwingli und Luther* 2:20–26. Melanchthon had studied at Heidelberg with Peter Sturm.
119. "Artikel vom Sacrament des Altars, der Zwinglianer meinung, etc.," StA Weimar, Reg. H, no. 42, fol. 85r. It is printed from this (unique?) version in *PC* 1:349 n. 1. There is a reference to it in StA Weimar, Ernestinisches

Gesamtarchiv, Reg. H, no. 42, fol. 109r: "Dabej der von Straspurg meinung vnd lehr vom Sacrament." Sturm had requested the document, which was drafted by Hedio, not by Bucer (as Pollet, *Correspondance* 1:20).

120. Riederer, *Nachrichten* 2:218. See Köhler, *Zwingli und Luther* 2:32.

121. *RTA, jR* 7:820–21. The doctrinal vagueness in the Evangelical camp at this time is suggested by a recommendation of Strasbourg's XIII that Sturm should sign a condemnation of sacramentarianism, if it would preserve solidarity with the Lutherans. They did not yet grasp that they themselves were "sacramentarians." *PC* 1:356, no. 599; Köhler, *Zwingli und Luther* 2:26–27. The Saxon theologians knew from their Strasbourg informant, the lawyer Nicolaus Gerbel, what was being preached there. *Melanchthons Briefwechsel* 1:208, 220, nos. 447, 478. For the evolution of Bucer's position, see Greschat, *Martin Bucer*, 83–89, 103.

122. H. R. Schmidt, "Häretisierung"; Brady, *Turning Swiss*, 29–43, 202–11.

123. *CR* 1:1101, no. 637.

124. *BDS* 3:355.

125. *CR* 2:93, no. 718, by Melanchthon and Johannes Brenz. See also ibid., nos. 664, 666, 677, 711, 718; Oberman, *Masters*, 284–88; H. R. Schmidt, "Häretisierung."

126. *CR* 2:no. 719, and there, too, the following quote.

127. AMS, AA 1808/10, fol. 26; *PC* 1:366 n. 1, and 394, no. 651; AGBR 4:8–9, 12–17, nos. 5, 7, 12–13; Schiess, ed., *Briefwechsel* 1:192–93, no. 148; Schubert, *Bündnis und Bekenntnis*, 21; Hauswirth, *Landgraf Philipp*, 143–46.

128. *Ann. Brant*, no. 4806. See Lenz, ed., *Briefwechsel* 1:2, no. 1.

129. The preachers' opinion of 19 June 1529, sent to Saxony on 22 June, is printed in Riederer, *Nachrichten* 2:215–26. Spengler's precisely contemporary (21 June) words are in *PC* 1:377–79, no. 628. See Schornbaum, "Nürnberg," 181.

130. *WA B* 5:75–78, no. 1424; *RTA, jR* 8:77, no. 60. See also *WA B* 5:78–81, Beilage to no. 1424; extracts in *RTA, jR* 8:78, no. 61; Schubert, *Bündnis und Bekenntnis*, 8–9; Köhler, *Zwingli und Luther* 2:32–37.

131. The note and the recess of Rodach are printed in *RTA, jR* 8:97–114; Pfarrer's instruction (but see Steglich, "Stellung," 87 n. 5) and report are in ibid. 7:87–89, 93–97; *PC* 1:367–73, nos. 613–14. For Schwabach, see ibid., 387–88, 390, nos. 640, 646; *RTA, jR* 8:211–12, 215; Steglich, "Stellung," 161–91.

132. *ZW* 10:no. 910. See also ibid., no. 905; Staehelin, ed., *Briefe und Akten* 2:no. 681.

133. *PC* 1:382, no. 632; Lenz, ed., *Briefwechsel* 1:8. This explains why Sturm took Hedio and not Capito to Marburg. The landgrave's request for Martin Bucer by name began his rise to prominence outside Strasbourg.

134. Landgrave Philip to Elector John, Kassel, 18 July and 24 August 1529, in StA Weimar, Reg. H, no. 12, fols. 2r–4v, here at 2r; fols. 29r–30v, here at 29v–30r.

135. There is some evidence of familiarity between the two men before this time. See, for example, Bucer's letter to Guillaume Farel, Strasbourg, 26 September 1527, in Herminjard, *Correspondances* 2:52, no. 205.

136. Bullinger, *Reformationsgeschichte* 2:224; *Ann. Brant*, no. 4804; Köhler, *Zwingli und Luther* 2:60–61; Hauswirth, *Landgraf Philipp*, 147–52.

137. Köhler, *Marburger Religionsgespräch*, 127–28.

138. *PC* 1:113, no. 139; *Ann. Brant*, no. 4812; Köhler, *Zwingli und Luther* 2:116, 116 n. 4, 158; Greschat, *Martin Bucer*, 104.

139. *EA*, vol. 4, pt. 1b:484, no. 196 zu "b."

140. Hauswirth, *Landgraf Philipp*, 221–28. In the lore about Marburg, the Luther-Zwingli confrontation held the stage, and the political discussions were forgotten.

See Bullinger, *Reformationsgeschichte* 2:232–36.

141. The articles were probably ready by sometime in July, certainly by early August. Steglich, "Stellung," 182 n. 81. The discussion of the Schwabach Articles and the alliance policy by Grimm, *Lazarus Spengler*, 137–41, ignores discoveries made by Karl Schornbaum and Hans von Schubert many years ago and is therefore based on false assumptions.

142. *RTA, jR* 8:245–68 (with the quote at 255), 268–72, 313–14, 317; *PC* 1:406–8, no. 674; Schubert, *Bündnis und Bekenntnis*, 16–19; Köhler, *Zwingli und Luther* 2:164–66.

143. *PC* 1:408, no. 675.

144. Ibid., 410–11, no. 678, and 417, no. 682.

145. Ibid., 412–18, no. 682; also in *RTA, jR* 8:389–94, no. 1214.

146. *PC* 1:418. This double structure had been used in 1474 by the League of Constance between the Swiss Confederacy and the Lower Union.

147. Ibid., 419.

148. Köhler, *Zwingli und Luther* 2:170, from Conrad Zwick's report to Constance.

149. *Ann. Brant*, no. 4828.

150. Jacob Sturm to Landgrave Philip, Strasbourg, 19 December 1529, in *PC* 1:425, no. 689; *RTA, jR* 8:521.

151. *AST* 47/I, no. 18; *Ann. Brant*, no. 4836, 4843. Four others demanded—a step unheard of at Strasbourg—that the treaty be put to the whole commune, and one man thought it should be laid aside until Charles V came to Germany.

152. It is now in the Bernisches Historisches Museum, object no. 1750.

153. Brady, *Ruling Class*, 308–9; *JWOS* 3:415, no. 136 n. 1, on him and his son, Conrad, junior, who died in 1502. The letters of Conrad, senior, from Worms are headed "Jesus, Maria, Johannes." AMS, AA 374a, noted in *PC* 1:31 n. 3.

154. AMS, AA 1808/11, fols. 27r–28v, here at fol. 28r-v.

155. Not *the* highpoint, for that came, as Ferdinand Seibt has noted, in 1548. Seibt, *Karl V.*, 8–9.

156. Brandi, *Kaiser Karl V.* 1:253. On Charles's situation in early 1530, see ibid., 235–42, 252–54; Reinhard, "Die kirchenpolitischen Vorstellungen"; Seibt, *Karl V.*, 110–13; Rabe, "Befunde und Überlegungen zur Religionspolitik."

157. *RTA, jR* 8:581–693; Steglich, "Stellung," 161–91; Fichtner, *Ferdinand*, 53–56.

158. Long in the making, but not made final until 18 November 1530. Hauswirth, *Landgraf Philipp*, 160–228.

159. On this topic, see Wolgast, *Wittenberger Theologie*; Dueck, "Religion and Temporal Authority"; Schoenberger, "The Development of the Lutheran Theory of Resistance"; Schoenberger, "Luther and the Justifiability of Resistance." On the broader context of Luther's ideas, see Skinner, *Foundations* 2:194–206; Cargill Thompson, *Political Thought of Martin Luther*.

160. Wolgast, *Wittenberger Theologie*, 148, and see 125–48 on the earlier discussion. *Brandenburg* here means Margrave George of Brandenburg-Ansbach.

161. *RTA, jR* 8:470, lines 5–18; and there, too, the remaining quotes in this paragraph. Hamm, "Stadt und Kirche," 710–29, is the best study of Spengler's theology; and see Wolgast, *Die Wittenberger Theologie*, 149–51. Andreas Osiander had preached (on Matt. 17) nonresistance to authority on 26 March 1525, and Nuremberg's regime formally adopted it in January 1530. Jegel, "Gutachten Andreas Osianders," 64; Schornbaum, "Nürnberg," 198.

162. Lazarus Spengler to Peter Butz, Nuremberg, 28 January 1530, in Rott, "La Réforme à Nuremberg et à Strasbourg," 141–42.

163. *RTA, jR* 8:483–84 (Brenz) and 219, 448–51 (Lachmann). See Wolgast, *Wittenberger Theologie*, 148 n. 9, correcting Hauswirth, *Landgraf Philipp*, 20–21.

164. *RTA, jR* 8:1058, lines 7–15. See Luther (1526), quoted by Hauswirth, *Landgraf*

Philipp, 102. Brenz ascribed Swiss success less to their mountainous homeland than to their unity and social solidarity [*ainigkait und gesellschaft*]," qualities he also attributed to the Swabian League. *RTA, jR* 8:1056, lines 9–13.

165. Martin Bucer, in *BDS* 3:335, lines 8–16.
166. Ann. *Brant,* no. 4828; *RTA, jR* 8:390; *PC* 1:431–33; *CR* 2:34; Schornbaum, "Nürnberg," 199.
167. *RTA, jR* 8:242, lines 2–17; and there, too, the following quote. See Skinner, *Foundations* 2:195–96.
168. *RTA, jR* 8:569; and there (572–73) too, the remaining quotes in this paragraph. Margrave George, who seems to have been the prime mover behind the Saxon turn against resistance, had sent Spengler's views to the landgrave. Grimm, *Lazarus Spengler,* 143.
169. Wolgast, *Wittenberger Theologie,* 154–65; and the crucial text is printed by Scheible, ed., *Widerstandsrecht,* 60–63, from *WA B* 5:250–61, from which comes the following quote.
170. Hauswirth, *Landgraf Philipp,* 129–37, 187; Brady, *Turning Swiss,* 205–6.
171. *ZW* 10:474–75, 505, 511, nos. 986, 995, 997. See Hauswirth, *Landgraf Philipp,* 191, 197–202, 202–8 for Philip's military preparations.
172. See, for what follows, Brady, "Jacob Sturm and the Lutherans," 183–202. Two of the four documents prepared for this Diet are in *BDS* 3:421–92.
173. Ficker, ed., "Jakob Sturms Entwurf," 152. The XIII accepted this strategy. *PC* 1:439, no. 718. So did Bucer, who took a major role in preparations for this Diet. See *BDS* 3:325, lines 1–11, 327, lines 7–12, and 337, lines 19–20. What Bucer really thought of the Lutherans, he wrote to Zwingli on 14 May 1530, in *ZW* 10:575, no. 1023. At Augsburg, the Memminger Hans Ehinger supported the same line of argument. Dobel, *Memmingen* 4:41–42.
174. *PC* 1:486–87, no. 782.
175. *BDS* 3:390, line 23–391, line 8. In ibid., 342–92, are the two versions with Sturm's revisions. Bernd Moeller correctly notes that Sturm's changes betray "immer wieder seine Bemühung um die Milderung übergrosser Schärfen." Ibid., 190 n. 13; and see, for example, Sturm in Ficker, ed., "Jakob Sturms Entwurf," 152, lines 58–66.
176. *PC* 1:446, no. 726 (28 May 1530). See ibid., 447, 450, nos. 728, 732; and Schirrmacher, ed., *Briefe und Acten,* 45–47, for the landgrave's similar impression.
177. *PC* 1:446, no. 728. He mentioned Bucer and Capito.
178. Sender, "Chronik," 199. See Roth, *Augsburgs Reformationsgeschichte* 1:328–34; Aulinger, *Bild,* 193–200, 329–39; Brady, "Rites of Autonomy."
179. Aulinger, *Bild,* 264–87.
180. *PC* 1:455–56, no. 741. The passage follows Melanchthon's words so closely that he was almost certainly the source of these charges. *CR* 2:no. 725.
181. *PC* 1:459, no. 746. This happened after Sturm and Pfarrer had sent for theologians from Strasbourg. Ibid., 453, no. 737; Greschat, *Martin Bucer,* 106. The emperor's call of 20 June is in Förstemann, ed., *Urkundenbuch* 1:309.
182. According to Hans Ehinger, in Dobel, *Memmingen* 4:37–39; and see Schirrmacher, ed., *Briefe und Acten,* 407. Ehinger admitted that the article on the eucharist "closely depends on Zwingli's opinion." Johannes Brenz's comment, however, that it was "sly and foxy," suggests that the Lutherans found it less Zwinglian than they had expected. *CR* 2:220; and see Bernd Moeller, in *BDS* 3:21 n. 38, 22. The text is now in *BDS* 3:13–185, superbly edited by Bernd Moeller in Latin and German. It was very clearly modelled on the Lutheran confession. See *PC* 1:no. 751.
183. Dobel, *Memmingen* 4:88–89; and see the report of Sturm's reply to the document called the "Confutation," in *PC* 1:529–30. The text of the "Confutation"

is edited by Immenkötter, *Confutatio der Confessio Augustana.*
184. From two versions in *PC* 1:529–30, by Sturm, who doesn't mention that he made the speech, and in Dobel, *Memmingen* 4:88–90, no. 38, by Ehinger. See also Johannes Aurifaber's remarks in Schirrmacher, ed., *Briefe und Acten*, 322–23, with the wrong date. Sturm's role is mentioned by the Nurembergers in their report of 27 Oct. in *CR* 2:423, no. 931.
185. Dobel, *Memmingen* 4:96–97.
186. *ZW* 10:599–604, no. 1035, with emphases added. The identifications are confirmed in a letter from the government of Zurich to that of Bern, 25 June 1530, in *EA*, vol. 4, pt. 1b:677–78. The reasons for the precaution of ciphers Sturm explained to Zwingli (*ZW* 10:603, line 5): "Scis, quam teneras quidam aures habeant."
187. See Locher, *Zwinglische Reformation*, 513; Lienhard, "Evangelische Alternativen." For reactions, see Dobel, *Memmingen* 4:38, 39; Blanke, "Zwinglis 'Fidei ratio' (1530)," 100–101; Arbenz, ed., *Vadianische Briefsammlung* 4:217, no. 608.
188. On the very extensive religious negotiations at Augsburg, see Immenkötter, "Reichstag und Konzil"; and G. Müller, "Zwischen Konflit und Verständigung." They are based on documentation assembled for King Ferdinand in 1532 by Hieronymus Vehus, chancellor of Baden, and edited by Honée, *Der Libell*, who prints the recess on religion at 347–52; it is also in Förstemann, ed., *Urkundenbuch* 2:473–48.
189. *PC* 1:489. On the landgrave's attempts to mediate, see Fabian, *Entstehung*, 106–8.
190. The remark is attributed to Melanchthon by a Strasbourg source, Specklin, *Collectanées*, no. 2316. On this rapprochement, see *PC* 1:nos. 785, 794, 799, 807; Brecht, "Luthers Beziehungen," 498–99.
191. *PC* 1:499–500, no. 794; Specklin, *Collectanées*, no. 2318; Dobel, *Memmingen* 4:64. On the landgrave's poor performance at Augsburg, see H. Grundmann, *Landgraf Philipp von Hessen.*
192. Printed by Bucholtz, *Geschichte* 9:23–24, referred by Brück to something Sturm wrote after the Diet of Augsburg.
193. *PC* 1:507, no. 802. The three extant accounts of these talks are in ibid., 517–18, no. 810 (Sturm), Förstemann, ed., *Urkundenbuch* 2:726–29, no. 250 (Mansfeld), and StA Constance, Reformations-Akten 4, fols. 274r–76r (Zwick), summarized in *EA*, vol. 4, pt. 1b:813–16. Zwick's report is based on information from Sturm, and his remark that Albert proposed the talks is contradicted by Sturm (*PC* 1:517). See Köhler, *Zwingli und Luther* 2:235–36.
194. Förstemann, ed., *Urkundenbuch* 2:727.
195. Ibid., 728. Mathis Pfarrer played so little part in these talks that Count Albert calls him "Jacob Pfaff." Ibid., 726.
196. *PC* 1:517–18. Neither man had powers to commit his principal(s), though Albert went further than his instructions allowed: "Dann durch graff Albrechten von Mansfelden, wiewol durch sich selbs on bevelch der fursten, verschiner tagen mitt ettlicher bottschafft jetz zu Ougspurg were, was zu Schmalkalden . . . nit mocht ain furgang haben." StA Constance, Reformations-Akten 4, fol. 275r-v.
197. *PC* 1:535–36, no. 830.
198. See in general Brecht, "Ulm und die deutsche Reformation."
199. *BOSS* 1:57. There, too, is the following quote.
200. *PC* 1:567, no. 861, which contains Sturm's notes on this meeting.
201. Ibid., 541, no. 838. For the views of the Swiss allies, see the recess of the allies' meeting at Basel, 18 November 1530, in Fabian, ed., *Quellen zur Geschichte der Reformationsbündnisse*, 68–69.

202. *SBA* 1:12.
203. Ibid., 14.
204. *PC* 1:569; Köhler, *Zwingli und Luther* 2:236–76; Fabian, *Entstehung*, 165–66.
205. *SBA* 1:17; Winckelmann, *Der Schmalkaldische Bund*, 273 n. 137, and another copy in HStA Marburg, PA 269, fol. 66. See Fabian, *Entstehung*, 181.
206. *PC* 2:7–8, no. 10. There, too, the two following quotes.
207. Ibid., 16, no. 19.
208. "Mattis Reinboldts bericht, wie sich die sachen haben zugetragen vff den reissen . . . pariss, 1531," in StA Weimar, Reg. H, no. 51, fol. 16r.
209. *ZW* 11:no. 1168. Bern to the XIII of Strasbourg, 24 February 1531, in AMS, AA 425a/5, fols. 45, 48; Zurich to the XIII of Strasbourg, 9 March 1531, in ibid., fols. 43, 46–47; *PC* 2:21, 28–30, 57–58, nos. 24, 31, 64; Lenz, ed., *Briefwechsel* 1:27–31, no. 8. See, in general, Köhler, *Zwingli und Luther* 2:261–65, 265–73. For the third Smalkalden meeting, see BOSS 1:151; *PC* 2:32–33, 49–51; Winckelmann, *Der Schmalkaldische Bund*, 107–8, 121–22; Fabian, *Entstehung*, 231; Pollet, ed., *Correspondance* 1:65–66.
210. Landgrave Philip to Elector John, Kassel, 7 April 1531, in StA Weimar, Reg. H, no. 59, fols. 27r–31r, at 27r, where he blames the failure on "deren von Bassel vorsaumbung."
211. *AGBR* 5:576, 589–90, 593–94, nos. 675, 681, 687, 690, 694; *PC* 2:868–67, nos. 117–18. When Caspar Schaller came in November 1531 to borrow money for Basel, Mathis Pfarrer, his brother-in-law, told him that Basel could have money but Bern and Zurich could not. On the Second Kappel War of 1531, see Hauswirth, *Landgraf Philipp*, 236–44; Meyer, *Der Zweite Kappeler Krieg*, 23–33.
212. Caspar Hedio's sermon "an ein ersamen rat und frumme bugerschaft zu Straßburg," of 6 January 1533 is printed by Winckelmann, *Fürsorgewesen* 2:167–72, no. 118, here at 168. There is a very good documentation of this famine, and the measures taken against it, in ibid., 120–79.
213. "Straßburgische Archiv-Chronik," 218–19, for this and the rest of the paragraph.
214. Cardinal Loyasa's remark is in Brandi, *Kaiser Karl V.* 2:218–19. On the Chamber Court, see Smend, *Reichskammergericht* 1:138–44.
215. Buck, *Anfänge*, 249–444, 511.
216. Brandi, *Kaiser Karl V.* 1:263–69, 270–71; Luttenberger, *Glaubenseinheit*, 32–92, 164–83; Aulinger, "Verhandlungen."
217. Brandi, *Kaiser Karl V.* 2:225 (Luther); Fichtner, *Ferdinand*, 89 (Ferdinand).
218. Bucholtz, *Geschichte* 9:28–29; Luttenberger, *Glaubenseinheit*, 181–83. On the origins of the mediation policy, see Aulinger, "Verhandlungen," 198–99.
219. *Ann. Brant*, no. 4962 (4 March 1532); *PC* 2:104, no. 130. Their instructions, in ibid., 105–7, nos. 134–35, conform to the league's policy: no peace, no taxes.
220. Bucholtz, *Geschichte* 9:29.
221. *PC* 2:108, no. 136. See Köhler, *Zwingli und Luther* 2:288. Bucer's own statement, "pure Bucer," spoke "now with a Zwinglian voice, now with a Lutheran one." Ibid., 2:289. Greschat, *Martin Bucer*, 109–10, essentially agrees, though his tone is gentler.
222. *PC* 2:113, no. 139; Schiess, ed., *Briefwechsel* 1:337, no. 27. On the course of this meeting, see Winckelmann, *Der Schmalkaldische Bund*, 187–209, 298–313; and Köhler, *Zwingli und Luther* 2:289–91.
223. See *PC* 2:144–45, no. 141; Pollet, ed., *Correspondance* 1:116 n. 8.
224. *PC* 2:117–18, no. 140; and from the same source come the remaining quotes in this paragraph. The archbishop asked about books by Schwenckfeld and Michael Servetus, which, he had heard, had been printed and sold at Strasbourg. This was true of Schwenckfeld's writings (see Chrisman, *Bibliography*,

337–38), though Servetus's book had been printed at Hagenau.
225. PC 2:150–53, 158–59. Since the Protestants refused to take their seats, the cities had to be represented in the Diet's committee on taxes by men from Catholic cities, Cologne and Überlingen. Neuhaus, "Wandlungen," 138.
226. Winckelmann, Bund, 242–51; Fischer-Galati, Ottoman Imperialism, 51–55; Engelhardt, "Der Nürnberger Religionsfriede."
227. So it is put by Luttenberger, Glaubenseinheit, 174.
228. PC 2:177–78, no. 171, which is printed in full by Strickler, ed., Actensammlung 4: no. 2019 (26 October 1532). See Müller, Kurie, 228–29.
229. PC 2:159, no. 155. See Hunyadi, "Participation de Strasbourg," 195–98. Hunyadi's figures (see the table on 237) indicate that Strasbourg paid about 12,050 fl., about three-quarters of its levy and its largest tax payment under Charles V.
230. Rückert, "Bedeutung," 269. The best characterization of Habsburg policy and the Württemberg affair is by Kohler, Politik, 337–70.
231. Quoted by Feine, "Territorialbildung," 294.
232. Puchta, Die habsburgische Herrschaft; Grube, Landtag, 108–74; Press, "Herzog Ulrich"; Deetjen, Studien, 13–19; Brady, Turning Swiss, 112–14. The Austrian government at Stuttgart was nonetheless a great improvement on Duke Ulrich's regime.
233. Förstemann, ed., Neues Urkundenbuch 1:197, no. 75. Wolfgang Capito wrote on 6 February from Strasbourg that "favor ducis W[irttembergensis] hic magnus est." ZW 8:299, line 4, no. 362. The phrase "princeps latronum" is Johann Reuchlin's, in Reuchlin, Briefwechsel, 319, no. 285. On the Reformation's spread in Württemberg, see Oberman, Masters, 256–57; and on the situation there in 1534, see Deetjen, Studien, 78–89, though his view of Ulrich is more sanguine than the one expressed here.
234. Landgrave Philip to Elector John Frederick, Kassel, 16 March 1533, in StA Weimar, Reg. H, no. 89, fol. 3r.
235. RTA, jR 8:738, lines 18–20. See ibid., 738–39, for this unsuccessful effort.
236. Metzger, Leonhard von Eck, 188–202; Press, "Bundespläne," 66–67. For the background and development of this strategy, see Kohler, Politik, 63, 126–27, 298–303, 378–82; Hauswirth, Landgraf Philipp, 73–76; Lauchs, Bayern, 22. For Bavarian attitudes toward Ulrich, see Wille, Philipp der Großmüthige, 234, 238.
237. Quoted by Wille, Philipp der Großmüthige, 101 n. 5.
238. Instruction of Elector John Frederick for Anarch von Wildenfels to Landgrave Philip of Hesse, 28 April 1534, StA Weimar, Reg. C, 644–46, no. 1069, fols. 40r–49r, here at fol. 40v.
239. Wille, Philipp der Großmüthige, 178–79; and see the warning in Mentz, Johann Friedrich 2:27–28, and 3:349–51, here at 351, para. 5.
240. This account is based on Brady, "Princes' Reformation." For the reactions of other Protestant powers, see ibid., 281 n. 92a; Ludewig, Die Politik Nürnbergs, 150–51.
241. Stettmeister and Council of Strasbourg to Landgrave Philip of Hesse, 9 October 1532, in StA Weimar, Reg. H, no. 80, fol. 33r: "Vnnd also ye ainer nach dem andern angerennt wurdet."
242. Brady, "Princes' Reformation," 262–63, no. 287. On Württemberg's size and situation, see Deetjen, Studien, 27–33.
243. PC 2:199–200, no. 204 (3 October 1533). For Sturm's reservations and his encouragement of the Ulmers, see ibid., nos. 200 n. 3, 251, 253, 257, 259; Kohler, Politik, 130–31.
244. Brady, "Princes' Reformation," 273–77, 279–81. On Strasbourg's economic ties to Swabia, see Fuchs, "Les foires," 259–305.
245. Lenz, ed., Briefwechsel 1:36–37, no. 10 (18 May 1534), which contrasts dra-

matically with Bucer's panic on the eve of the invasion. When Zurich's Heinrich Bullinger sent the landgrave his congratulations on 4 July 1534, he was already worried about further trouble with the Lutherans: "Bitt . . ., sy [the landgrave] wölle iro die erbreyterung deß euangelii Christi lassen angelägen sin und nitt achten, unsere mißgünstigen verklagen, die unß für schwermer, uffrurer und verachter der heyligen sacramente ußruffend, . . ." Fabian, ed., *Quellen zur Geschichte der Reformationsbündnisse*, 112–13.

246. Oberman, *Masters*, 276. The Strasbourgeois proposed Ambrosius Blarer of Constance and Simon Grynaeus, formerly professor of Greek at Heidelberg, then teacher at Basel and Strasbourg (he did not come to Württemberg).

247. The text is in Schneider, ed., *Ausgewählte Urkunden*, 95–106, no. 27 (29 June 1534), with the quote at 97, lines 35–98, line 4. For commentary, see Bofinger, "Kirche und werdender Territorialstaat," 75–149; Oberman, *Masters*, 269, 271; Deetjen, *Studien*, 34–37. The price of this concession was that Württemberg became an Austrian fief.

248. PC 2:218, no. 236. The following quote is from ibid., 219, no. 237. Sturm first had the treaty's text from the landgrave on 13 July 1534, for which see ibid., 216–17, no. 324.

249. Stayer, *Anabaptists*, 255–57; Deppermann, *Melchior Hoffman*, 253–70.

250. PC 2:219, no. 237.

251. Ibid., 221, no. 239. Compare Bucer's letter in Lenz, ed., *Briefwechsel* 1:42–43, no. 12, written on the day of Sturm's return from Stuttgart.

252. Lenz, ed., *Briefwechsel* 1:4.

253. Schnepf, Bucer told Bullinger, "est . . . facundissimus, sed duri simul capitis. Ita a multis annis eium novi. Egimus simul Heydelbergae." Bullinger, *Briefwechsel* 4:311, no. 436, lines 16–17.

254. PC 2:221, no. 239. The best account of the Reformation in Württemberg is by Brecht and Ehmer, *Südwestdeutsche Reformationsgeschichte*, 195–266, on which the following paragraphs rest.

255. PC 2:216, no. 234 (13 July 1534). Sturm was distantly related through his maternal grandmother to Hans Konrad Thumb von Neuburg, marshal of Württemberg and, until his ouster in 1543, the most powerful man at court. Bernhardt, *Zentralbehörden*, 674–75; Deetjen, *Studien*, 286–87.

256. PC 1:222.

257. Köhler, *Zwingli und Luther* 2:335–53, with the quote at 339. See Oberman, *Werden und Wertung*, 342 n. 35 (mostly missing from *Masters*, 270 n. 35); Bullinger, *Briefwechsel* 4:342 n. 21, 379 n. 25.

258. Württemberg's dual Reformation continued until Blarer's dismissal in 1538, which was taken as a sign of defeat by, among others, John Calvin and Guillaume Farel. Herminjard, ed., *Correspondances* 5:30–32, no. 718.

259. Wille, *Philipp der Großmüthige*, 225.

260. Kolde, ed., *Analecta Lutherana*, 160–61. The following quote is from the same source.

261. PC 2:244.

262. Ibid., 245.

263. Ibid., 244, no. 265.

264. Quoted by Brecht, "Luthers Beziehungen," 500. For other attacks, see ibid., 500–502; Jahns, *Frankfurt*, 222.

265. Jahns, *Frankfurt*, 223. On Bucer's union formula, which provoked Luther's wrath, see Köhler, *Zwingli und Luther* 2:302, who calls it a "pseudo-synthesis (*Scheinsynthese*)."

266. Hoffmann, "Konrad Sam (1483–1555)," 263; Deetjen, "Licentiat Martin Frecht," 299; Brecht, "Luthers Beziehungen," 502.

267. WA B 7:130, no. 2156, lines 10–12: "Et scribitur mihi, Ducem Wirtembergensem habere in deliciis Blaurerum. Quodsi verum est, quid speres de tota illa superiore Germania?" On 19 August 1535 the Strasbourg preachers wrote to Luther (ibid., 236, no. 2224, lines 55–59), "Cupimus Ecclesias, non nos tantum, non unum et alterum, in plenum veritatis consensum adducere."
268. WA B 7:110, no. 2142; and there, too, the following quote.
269. Brecht, "Luthers Beziehungen," 503.
270. PC 2:234, no. 254.
271. Ibid., 228, 232, 268 (from which the quote), nos. 249, 252, 293; Lenz, ed., Briefwechsel 1:43–44, no. 13; BDS 6, pt. 1:21–25; Brecht, "Luthers Beziehungen," 503–4.
272. Seebaß, "Die Augsburger Kirchenordnung," 37. The Strasbourg preachers' submission is in a letter to Luther, WA B 7:234. On the struggle at Augsburg, see PC 2:675–97, which contains a very full account from Strasbourg's point of view; BDS, vol. 6, pt. 1:25–27; Seebaß, "Die Augsburger Kirchenordnung"; Brecht, "Luthers Beziehungen," 505–6; Köhler, Zwingli und Luther 2:385–89.
273. Gereon Sailer to Martin Bucer, Augsburg, 22 June 1533, in AST 157, fol. 385, quoted by de Kroon, "Die Augsburger Reformation," 63 n. 15.
274. Sieh-Burens, Oligarchie, 134–55; Immenkötter, "Die katholische Kirche in Augsburg," 20–21.
275. de Kroon, "Die Augsburger Reformation," 60; Sieh-Burens, Oligarchie, 134–39; Brady, Ruling Class, 85 n. 111.
276. Quoted by Seebaß, "Die Augsburger Kirchenordnung," 39.
277. Quoted in PC, 2:679. Bucer's role as broker in the events leading up to the Wittenberg Concord has been judged both negatively by Walter Köhler (Zwingli und Luther 2:330) and positively by Robert Stupperich (BDS, vol. 6, pt. 1:20).
278. PC 2:296, no. 322.
279. AMS, AA 462, fols. 45–46, quoted in PC 2:681.
280. Köhler, Zwingli und Luther 2:432–55; BDS, vol. 6, pt. 1:30–34; Brecht, "Luthers Beziehungen," 507–9.
281. Pollet, ed., Correspondance 1:167–70; PC 2:687; BDS, vol. 6, pt. 1:34–40; Brecht, "Luthers Beziehungen," 510–11. The trouble at Ulm came from the clergy, although the regime had accepted the need for unity on the basis of the Confession of Augsburg. See BOSS 3:311–12. On the Swiss refusal to attend, see BDS, vol. 6, pt. 1:29–30.
282. BOSS 3:306–10, here at 306.
283. Ibid., 696–97. The Constancers persisted in resisting what they called "der fürsten confession [i.e., the Confession of Augsburg]" long after the Wittenberg Concord. See the Constance instruction for the league's diet at Smalkalden, 25 January 1537, in Fabian, ed., Quellen zur Geschichte der Reformationsbündnisse, 124–26.

Part II

4

Strasbourg as Godly City

Listen up, while I tell
How the miracle came to pass:
Baptism first came into being
At John the Baptist's hands.
And then the cry began
Just on the very same day,
Of how to destroy true baptism,
But the Word of God abides.*

If religion, as Ibn Khaldûn wrote, brought individual desires together and united hearts, it was also, alas, true that, as Jacob Sturm wrote in 1534, "in our times scarcely anything else so unites people's minds or drives them apart as unity or disunity in religion does."[1] For this reason, the Smalkaldic League, which lacked any powerful bonds of economic interest or geographical proximity and cohered only because of a common religion, was a truly remarkable institution. Within a year of its formation, the league bargained an edict of toleration from the emperor; three years later it constituted itself as a powerful military federation. Its early history displays the power of a common religion to sustain solidarities, though it also nearly foundered on the split between the Lutherans and the Zwinglians. The interplay of unity and strife in the league replicated the Reformation's effects in the free cities, where the perceived need for religious unity led to forced uniformities, which led to new dissent and exclusions. The special volatility of Evangelical religion derived from its pursuit of unity through words rather than acts, that is, through common doctrine rather than through common ritual. Whereas Catholic religious community displayed itself chiefly in actions or rites—*lex orandi, lex credendi*—Protestant unity required conformity in belief—*lex docendi, lex orandi.*[2] Although Protestant communities could form very rapidly, because words move swiftly, they were especially vulnerable to challenge and disruption, because verbal protest, unlike ritual action, can be potent even when made by small groups or individuals. The city, whether conceived as a community of coordinated hearts or as a class-ordered system of production and exchange, could not tolerate very much dissent, and it is hardly surprising that

104

the civic magistrates moved to coerce dissenters sooner and more decisively than did, say, the Imperial authorities. Coercion became especially urgent where, as at Strasbourg, a reputation for tolerating heresy affected a city's external security. Responding to this connection, Jacob Sturm and his colleagues suppressed dissent at Strasbourg in 1534, two years before the Wittenberg Concord performed the same service to the Smalkaldic League.

A variegated, shifting stream of popular dissent had arisen in South Germany in the wake of the failed revolution of 1525. Wherever the dissenters settled, their proselytizing seemed to endanger civic religious unity, and the mark of 1525 upon them meant that to tolerate them was to tarnish a regime's reputation for law and order.[3] By the end of the 1520s the most active center of dissent, and therefore the city with the most threatened reputation, was Strasbourg. In this "New Jerusalem," as local dissenters named it, converged South German and Swiss rivulets of migrant radicals, whose activities soon provoked repressive action from the magistrates. Measures against the sects began in 1527, quickened about 1531, and culminated in the synod of 1533–34 and the new church ordinance of 1534.

Jacob Sturm took the lead in the suppression of dissent at Strasbourg. It may seem a surprising undertaking for an Erasmian who believed, as Sturm did, in the individual human heart as the secret seat of true religion. Sturm, however, unlike the cosmopolitan, rootless Erasmus, was also a man of his city, a thoroughly rooted aristocrat of unqualified loyalty to Strasbourg and its established order. The Spirit might move the human heart, but the body must obey, and the magistrates' ability to command obedience must be unchallenged—by pope, preachers, prophets, or dissenters. Jacob Sturm was a true Marsiglian, for whom the dissolution of clerical authority meant both greater spiritual liberty and enhanced magisterial control of the church. For him, the proper forum for the free play of ideas was not the church but the schools, which under his leadership became Reformation Strasbourg's crowning creation. While the church became regimented, rigid, and local, the schools flourished and brought international distinction to the city and enlivened its cultural life. Although the schools themselves operated safely in Latin, they fertilized "a brief cultural revolution" in vernacular literature.[4] The church's regimentation and the schools' liberty formed two sides of a single process, and both sides, Reformation church and Reformation school, bore the marks of Sturm's authoritative hand.

STRASBOURG AS NEW JERUSALEM

If Strasbourg were truly a New Jerusalem, its holiness was not palpable. Dr. Caspar Hedio painted a somber portrait of reformed Strasbourg in his Schwörtag sermon for 1534. "Many have thrown off the papacy," he said,

> and slipped out from under its heavy human yoke. But they do not now want to take up the gospel and place themselves under the light yoke of Christ. . . . One no longer hears mass, but then one also does not hear

the gospel. Before there were many holidays, but now one doesn't even observe Sunday. With what terrible laziness the priests, monks, and nuns used to devour the income and goods of the church, . . . but now it is the workers and youth who run wild, and many have no respect for God, worship, good works, or any honorable thing. The same is true of the peasantry on the land.[5]

Once the Strasbourgeois abandoned the papal yoke, at least in Hedio's eyes, they also rejected their preachers' demands for continuing reformation.

Strasbourg's magistrates reconstructed the civic church in four stages. First, they renewed earlier laws against blasphemy, gambling, fornication, adultery, drunkenness, and other moral offenses (25 August 1529).[6] Second, they established a marriage court (*Ehegericht*) to replace episcopal jurisdiction (16 December 1529).[7] Third, they created a system of parish churchwardens (*Kirchenpfleger*), three laymen in each parish "whose task was to supervise the doctrine, morals, and work of the parish clergy and to discipline the laity" (30 October 1531).[8] The fourth and most important step came in 1534, when the Senate & XXI enacted into law the recommendations of an ecclesiastical assembly, or synod, on doctrine and discipline.[9] The magistrates defended this church settlement—sometimes against the clergy themselves, constantly against other critics—until long after Jacob Sturm's death.

Sturm's hand is visible at every stage of this ecclesiastical reconstruction, beginning with the edict on churchwardens, which he drafted.[10] He also presided over the church settlement of 1533–34 as member of the planning committee, as senior president of the synod, as reporter to the Senate & XXI on the synod's progress, and as framer of the church constitution of 1534.[11] Sturm was the chief persecutor of Strasbourg's numerous dissenting sects, and he helped to supply the civic church with a new statement of doctrine, a new church governance, and a new police of morals.[12]

Strasbourg's Protestant magistrates did not crush dissent because they possessed an abstract desire for uniformity or a general will to persecute. The beaten Catholics, for example, were discriminated against but not often persecuted, even though there were plenty of them in the city and not just, as Katharine Schütz (Zell) alleged, "lost souls and a few bad old women."[13] Reformed Strasbourg did persecute the dissenters, called Anabaptists [*wieddertouffer*] or Baptists [*touffer*], who converged on Strasbourg in the years 1526–29 from the Zurich region, Franconia, and Swabia.[14] In the van came the Swiss Brethren, whose mixture of biblicism and pacifism attracted some Strasbourgeois, among them Wolfgang Capito; next came the Augsburg dissenters, who bore the chiliastic and communistic heritage of Thomas Müntzer's Central German revolution of 1525;[15] and lastly came the spiritualist stream of the Bavarian Hans Denck, who taught the universality of grace, free will, good works, and the inner word. These groups recruited not only among Strasbourg's artisans and shopkeepers—the sects' normal milieus—but also among more substantial folk, such as the rich merchant Friedrich Ingold and Fridolin Meyger, an episcopal notary from Säckingen.[16] On the margins of the movement hovered a good many clergymen and former clergymen of the sort whom the preachers called Epicureans, men who believed the Reformation had been stopped short of its goal, and who branded the new police of religion and morals a "new papacy."[17]

Into this bubbling spiritual stew came in May and June 1529 two more pilgrims to the New Jerusalem. One was the elegant Silesian nobleman, Caspar Schwenckfeld, who moved in with Capito and began mocking the concept of "Christian government [*christliche Obrigkeit*]."[18] Although he did well with the upper classes at Strasbourg as elsewhere—Sturm's distant relation at the court of Württemberg, Hans Konrad Thumb von Neuburg, admired him—Luther hated him enough for Strasbourg's regime to decide that Schwenckfeld "must go."[19] The other new arrival was Melchior Hoffman, a Swabian furrier and chiliast, who planted at Strasbourg an apocalyptic tradition that went straight back to Thomas Müntzer himself.[20] Strasbourg was to be Hoffman's New Jerusalem—just as Rome was the New Babylon—from which 144,000 saints would pour forth to preach the true gospel, the Müntzerite gospel that made Hoffman such an albatross around the regime's neck. Sturm understood perfectly the danger Hoffman posed, for, as he reported on 11 November 1533, people in North Germany were saying that "Melchior Hoffman has triumphed here, and the whole city follows his opinion."[21] Sturm here broached the most compelling reason for Strasbourg's regime to end the city's "rare policy of consistent religious tolerance."[22] Policy, the wish to avoid the Müntzer-Münster stain, and not some vague desire to persecute, made the Erasmian Sturm an architect of persecution.[23]

ARCHITECT OF PERSECUTION

Jacob Sturm disliked compulsion in religion, and he sometimes scolded the preachers for relying on temporal power. "God promised us Christians," he once wrote, "not happiness in this life (as He did to the Jews in the Old Testament) but only suffering and persecution."[24] He nonetheless masterminded the suppression of dissent at Strasbourg from the first law against the Anabaptists (27 July 1527), which appeared over his name.[25] The situation grew graver in 1528, when the Augsburg refugees brought to Strasbourg a far more radical tradition, which was alleged to hold that "whoever owns property, may not take the Lord's Supper," and "within two years, the Lord will come from heaven, . . . the godly and the elect will rule the earth with the Lord."[26] Sturm and his colleagues decided to allow no public disputations, and they proceeded with arrests, hearings, and banishments to break up the meetings, get rid of the leaders, and cow the followers.[27] Undeterred, Anabaptists streamed into their New Jerusalem between 1529 and 1531, and soon the Tyrolean engineer Pilgram Marpeck was asking the regime to turn over a parish church to the Anabaptists.[28] This led to a remarkable disputation before the Senate and XXI, which was held behind closed doors on 9 December 1531. The scene unfolded like nothing ever before seen at Strasbourg, as Marpeck declared that "between the papists and the Lutherans the dispute is largely a temporal quarrel," for Bucer and his like preached "either in the absence of the common man or in the presence of princes and urban magistrates, instead of preaching freely before the cross of Christ." Sturm had said much the same about Capito in 1526.

The local preachers closed ranks against the dissenters and told the regime that "on account of the Common Man they should consider the matter and also restore order and punish sins, and as the citizenry alleges that there is a division within the senate, they must do away with dissension and foster unity."[29] The preachers' well-grounded worry arose from the fact, as they admitted, that

> everyday, pious burghers here tell us how so many people in this city, in the inns and shops, in the squares, on the boats, and in the streets, blaspheme and dishonor most terribly the same Christian doctrine that our lords have confessed before His Christian Majesty and we have taught most faithfully.[30]

It is a terrible thing, they chided the senators, "that such a great number of people have become totally godless, alienated from the whole community of Christ and His church," and all Christian rulers "are obliged to help us all they can" to fight this blasphemy, to the end "that Strasbourg, too, will at last have one doctrine and religion."[31] *Lex docendi, lex orandi.*

It was a short step from hearing dissent to persecuting it. The magistrates expelled Marpeck in December 1531, arrested Hoffman, warned the Spanish antitrinitarian Michael Servetus "to stay out of Strasbourg, or he will be punished," and began to crack down on clandestine printing.[32] They made little or no distinction between heresy and sedition. A complaint was registered, for example, against the *Chronica, zeytbuch vnd geschychtsbibel* by the Swabian writer Sebastian Franck. As Sturm discovered when the book was shown to him by his father-in-law, Stettmeister Hans Bock, Franck's book "insults the Roman Empire, and he also mentions Erasmus at several places, once calling him a 'heretic.'" The Senate & XXI arrested Franck, who was then in Strasbourg, questioned and expelled him, and banned the local printing or sale of his book.[33] News of it nonetheless reached Cardinal Albert of Mainz, who baited Sturm about it during the Schweinfurt talks.[34]

Bucer and the other preachers, as much as they welcomed actions against the most obnoxious individual dissenters, longed for a general suppression of the sects.[35] "Every ruler," they affirmed, "should oblige its subjects [*die ihrenn*] to refrain from blaspheming the true faith, to hear the truth, and to encourage their dependents [*die seinen*] to do the same," for otherwise, God "will cast the ruler down entirely and hand the entire people over to the Devil."[36] The turning point may well have been Ammeister Kniebis's report that on Schwörtag 1532 some burghers had refused to raise their fingers to swear the oath.[37] By late November 1532 the synod's agenda was ready: religious education of children; attendance at preaching services; discipline of former priests, monks, and nuns; hearing and disposition of the Anabaptists; church life in the villages; care of the sick and the needy; and excess in dress and other things. The synod's goal, it was noted, was "not at all, as some allege, to compel anyone to belief, but to suppress public offenses, which is the obligation of every ruler according to divine and Imperial law."[38]

Jacob Sturm agreed that the time had come "to combat the sects, hold a disputation, and hold to one [i.e., infant] baptism."[39] And though he thought young people should be made to attend sermons, he drew the line at compelling adults to go to church. "How can they be ordered to do it?" he asked himself, "who should and would determine this? . . . It is good that they be gathered in to listen, but I don't know how. And how should transgressors be found out and punished? Yet, if they are not punished and warned, gradually the order will be greeted with contempt."[40] So, the Senate & XXI placed the synod in the hands of Jacob Sturm, Ammeister Martin Herlin, Sturm's kinsman Andreas Mieg, and the good-hearted Bastian Erb.[41] With these appointments at the end of November 1532, the regime set a course for the suppression of dissent and reconstruction of ecclesiastical discipline.

THE FALL OF THE SECTS

Although Strasbourg's synod in 1533 has sometimes been plotted as a straight fight between preachers and dissenters, Jacob Sturm's hands held the reins from opening day, 3 June 1533.[42] Behind closed doors, he announced the synod's purpose: "As much disagreement over the faith and doctrine has arisen, the senate's commissioners are to deliberate with the churchwardens, preachers, pastors, and curates about how we can achieve unity in doctrine.[43] If the clergy accepted the proposed statement of doctrine—Sixteen Articles prepared by Bucer—"that will be good; if not, then the senate's commissioners and the churchwardens will deliberate on the majority and minority views and bring them before the Senate & XXI, who will determine what may be pleasing to God."[44] In this assembly, "everyone should speak his mind freely, and it will be listened to in a friendly spirit, for otherwise, if there is a dispute later, it will serve the church little and God even less."[45] *Lex docendi, lex orandi*—unity in belief would bring unity in practice.

Sturm might as well have tried to harness the wind, for around him howled a gale of grumbling, recriminations, accusations, and objections, so that he felt obliged to admonish the clergymen that "this assembly was arranged solely to further the honor of God and the welfare of this city," and to "ask them to have regard for this end and stick to it, and to lay aside whatever one may have against another."[46] The clergy, after all—Sturm bared his teeth—"have opponents on all sides among the Catholics and the sects, who might say that their disunity is proof of their false teachings. They ought to reflect on this." After Sturm reported to the Senate & XXI on

4 June that "the matter is more serious and bigger than my lords had realized,"[47] the magistrates decided to bring representatives of the guilds into the synod, though still behind closed doors. They took this step, they said, "so that during the synod no disorder arises from the press of the common folk, and so that some from the people can nonetheless be present."[48] This clever move packed the synod's meeting hall with laymen, presumably chosen for their loyalty and good sense. The clergy must have been further sobered by the scrutiny held on 10 June 1533, in which Sturm and the other presidents reviewed the clergy's behavior and performance. This was followed by hearings of dissenters, in which Sturm took a leading role, for example, in the hearing of Claus Frey, a furrier from Rottenberg who had had the poor judgment to marry a baron's sister without divorcing his own wife.[49]

When he opened the synod's final session on 23 October 1533, Sturm said that "the senate does not intend to force anyone in matters of faith, but only to suppress conspiracies [rottungen] that might lead to division of the common weal."[50] The ensuing doctrinal debate centered, naturally enough, on the article "concerning government [obrigkeit]."[51] "The entire matter must rest on the fourth article," Sturm declared, and the Senate & XXI must now decide "which of the doctrines we have heard is to be held as God's Word, for it would be fruitless to take up the other points before we have decided which one we hold to be God's Word."[52] Knowing how unsuited his colleagues were to this task, Sturm had printed copies of the Tetrapolitan Confession distributed, because many magistrates would not sit still long enough for it to be read.[53] Nevertheless, on 4 March 1534 the senators voted "unanimously [einhelliglich] . . . to remain with the oft-mentioned [Tetrapolitan] confession and the [Sixteen] articles read to the synod, and to have them preached here as the correct Christian doctrine and enforced as such," and they charged the four presidents to recommend action against the sects.[54] At this moment, when the Senate & XXI moved like general councils, popes, and Christian Roman emperors "to determine what may be pleasing to God"[55]—Sturm's words—the fate of Strasbourg's sects was decided.

Sturm's role in the church settlement of 1533–34 reveals a good deal about his reasoning. The most difficult problem, he thought, was how to instill godly discipline in the burghers, many of whom looked on the official clergy "as scoundrels, ass-kissers, etc., who had never preached God's Word," for they "are hated by many people, and many nasty things are said of them."[56] "It would be a good thing," Sturm wrote, "if we could find a way to get the people to come to church and hear the Word of God." This could not be achieved through laws, however, "for in matters of faith, which is a voluntary act and gift of God, little can be gained through laws. Then, too, the hearing of sermons is an external thing,[57] not an act of faith itself." He feared the scandal that would arise "if the law were not obeyed and the violators were not punished, it would only diminish the government's authority . . . and prompt people to say that 'a new papacy has been established.'"[58] This is a typically Sturmian line of reasoning, in which the public character of religion is a matter more of policy than of doctrine. "Laws," he wrote, "make hypocrites."[59] The magistrates should not resort to compulsion but themselves set a good example for their fellow citizens, and "on Sunday every member of the government should hear at least one sermon and, since the common people look up to them, they shouldn't go strolling about the city during the sermon."[60] Here, indeed, was the crux, for if the Catholic clergy had discredited their faith through their behavior, the church's new governors had brought no improvement.

Sturm wanted to suppress dissent without creating more dissent by imposing compulsion on loyal burghers. It was on this point that he would one day reach a parting of the ways with Martin Bucer, who saw in persecution of dissent merely a prologue to the establishment of Christian discipline and the transformation of Strasbourg into a godly city. Sturm's reluctance, however, meant no reprieve for the sects. He announced that "since we have already decided to hold to the [Tetrapolitan] confession submitted at Augsburg and the synod's [Sixteen] articles, it follows that all other sects, who oppose this doctrine, are not to be tolerated, and their supporters should be dealt with."[61] Dissenters could renounce their errors and conform, or they could leave Strasbourg within two weeks.[62] Sturm drafted the speech with which Ammeister Mattheus Geiger presented on 7 February 1535 to the three hundred Schöffen the church ordinance that was to endure for half a century.[63] He reviewed the past decade's events and his hearers' co-responsibility with the magistrates for the course Strasbourg had taken. "Years ago," he wrote, "it was asserted and decided by the stettmeister and Senate & XXI and also by the Schöffen and ammeister, that in this city of Strasbourg the holy gospel was to be preached purely and clearly, and also that all sorts of anti-Scriptural abuses should be abolished." Later, when it seemed that force might be used against the city on account of these actions, "our lords, with the knowledge and approval of Schöffen and ammeister, entered into a Christian alliance with some electors, princes, counts, and cities who agree with us on faith. This happened so that we might more peacefully hold to the confessed truth and the biblical doctrine." Now, however, there have arisen

> all sorts of heretical sects, unnecessary argument, and contentious opinions about the faith in this city, which caused many to fall away from the confessed truth and to have contempt for the doctrine and preaching of the holy gospel and its preachers alike, leading in turn through many harmful splits and divisions to considerable scandal and provocation of many Christians and to the destruction of civic peace and unity.

This unfortunate development justified, even compelled, the magistrates to act against "the seducers, most of whom first came here from foreign parts." With this clever introduction, designed to rally support, the regime brought before the Schöffen the new church ordinance, which was designed "to forestall such evils, prevent divisions, and avert the ruin, physical and spiritual, of the whole city and its citizens."

Sturm's speech presents his most detailed explanation of these events, in which he had played a major, even the leading, role. As notable as his explanation, however, is what he did not say: the gospel, which he and the landgrave had named a specific against disorder and division, had proved a source of new disorders and divisions. His only explanation for this apparent conflict between the gospel and the common good was an oblique reference to sectarians who came from "foreign parts." He did confirm, on the other hand, the perceived need for unity in belief as the foundation of community—*lex docendi, lex orandi*, the constitutive principle of the Evangelical movement. He had learned this lesson from the Lutherans, and he never forgot it. By now it had fully superseded his policy of "the middle way," which had led him to argue that "both sides are Christians, may God have mercy!" The dissenters in his Strasbourg would be given no chance to serve the Evangelicals as, only ten years before, the Evangelicals had served the Catholics. This parallel was exact, and a Tyrolean soap maker, Leupold Scharnschlager, drove it home to Sturm and his colleagues. "My dear lords," his Tyrolean accent grated on the ears of Alemannic-speakers,

> You assert and press us to abandon our faith and accept yours. That is just the same as when the emperor said to you, you should abandon your faith and accept his. Now I speak to your consciences: Do you think it right to obey the emperor in such things? Ah, well, then you might also say that we ought to obey you in such things. Then you would be obliged to reinstate all the idolatry and papist convents, also the mass and other things. If, however, you find that before God it is not right to obey the emperor in such matters, so I, a poor Christian, ask and admonish you for the love of God and the salvation of your own souls, that you leave our consciences alone in the matter and have mercy on and protect us poor folk.[64]

Strasbourg's magistrates were not used to such tones from anyone, much less foreigners, and Scharnschlager, too, had to leave town.

Scharnschlager's brave words stripped the garb of policy from the contradiction between the Reformation as renewal of the Christian gospel and the Reformation as promotion of the common good conceived as law and order.[65] One or the other, gospel or common good, must rule the common house, and, in the absence of a clear distinction between temporal and spiritual authority, the dream of their partnership—the fundamental ideal of Zwinglianism—had to dissolve into either a Marsiglian rule of the church by the lay magistrates as "new popes" or a revolutionary transformation of the city as a New Jerusalem. Jacob Sturm's was the first way, the Marsiglian way; the Anabaptists favored the second way, the way of the New Jerusalem; whereas Martin Bucer, typically, swung back and forth between the two ways until exile made choice irrelevant. It was John Calvin whose clear-headed diagnosis of the dilemma, which he made in situ at Strasbourg in 1537–41, gave rise to a new solution, which revitalized Protestantism as an international movement for religious reform.

The Marsiglian way adopted at Strasbourg proved intolerant of organized dissent, and its need to persecute expressed a tension between religion's two tasks, the fundamentally religious task of "the redemption of the laity" and the fundamentally political one of "the reformation of the world."[66] It also served the far more mundane desire to preserve the Protestant alliance by ridding Strasbourg of its unsavory reputation for radicalism and heresy. These motives forged a strong link between the onset of persecution at Strasbourg and two other events of 1534: the restoration in Württemberg, which opened the way to doctrinal concord with the Lutherans, and the rise and fall of the Anabaptist kingdom at Münster.

During 1533 the influence of Melchiorite (i.e., Hoffmanite) Anabaptists spread among the common people of the Westphalian city of Münster.[67] In the following year, the city came under the charismatic leadership of Jan Beukelszoon, one of Hoffman's Netherlandish disciples, and in the summer of that year, two failed assaults on the city by the prince-bishop's army, plus news of the scandalous introduction of polygamy there, made Münster a matter of general Imperial concern.[68]

Events at Münster warranted careful attention at Strasbourg, where Melchior Hoffman languished in the Hangman's Tower.[69] Jacob Sturm relayed on 11 November 1533 a request from Münster's town attorney, Johann van der Wyck, that the magistrates scotch the rumor that "Melchior Hoffman has won out there, and the whole city [of Strasbourg] holds his opinion."[70] Melchiorite lore did indeed link Strasbourg with Münster, where the leaders "told the common folk in the city of Münster that they had a vision of three cities in the night. . . . One was the city of Münster, the second Strasbourg, and the third was Deventer. These same cities . . . God has chosen as the places where he will raise up a holy people."[71] News from Münster flowed via Hesse to Strasbourg and on to Switzerland, where magistrates were curious to know, as the Baslers asked, "if there are Anabaptists involved, also if they are practicing polygamy."[72] Reports from Westphalia rolled into Strasbourg all through the weeks when Jacob Sturm was laboring over the church settlement.

Sturm's colleagues did not initially see Münster as their business, and when the Empire moved in December to take action through its system of Circles, the Strasbourgeois—along with most other southern cities—pleaded their "remoteness."[73] Both King Ferdinand and Landgrave Philip reminded Strasbourg's magistrates that in their case refusal to pay the assessment against Münster—3,660 fl.—would surely be taken as a sign of sympathy for the Anabaptists.[74] This argument the Senate & XXI could not refuse, and they sent Sturm and Pfarrer to an assembly of the Circles at Worms on 4 April

1535, which voted an aid against Münster and called for the persecution of Anabaptists throughout the Empire. Strasbourg punctually paid its share of this tax, 975 fl., and on 25 June 1535 arrived news of the fall of the Anabaptist kingdom at Münster to Imperial troops.[75]

The fall of Anabaptism at Münster and at Strasbourg in 1534–35 preserved the Strasbourg magistrates' two chief gains from the Reformation, magisterial control of civic religious life and the formation of the Smalkaldic League. The sects rekindled memories of 1525, the legacy of which Anabaptists were held to cherish, and confirmed the belief of both Lutheran and Catholic authorities in the connections between radical religion and radical politics. The participation of Jacob Sturm and his regime in persecution, both at home and abroad, settled accounts with the urban reformation's sacramentarian heritage, the broader communal reformation, and the revolution of 1525.

The church settlement of 1534 at Strasbourg also closed the process through which the civic magistrates acquired "a control over the church and religious life that would have been unthinkable a generation earlier."[76] In Jacob Sturm's boyhood, when his great-grandfather was still the town's leading politician, religion had been arbitrated by popes, councils, and bishops, and political security had been supplied by regional federations. The Reformation era had altered both of these patterns, bringing religious affairs and political security to depend on both local control and political associations much wider than the old regional ones. By the mid-1530s the tensions created by this shift had largely been mastered, so that guarded by the Smalkaldic League, the city could domesticate control of its religious life in relative peace.

During the decade that followed the settlement of 1534, civic religious life at Strasbourg settled into routine patterns, as clerical institutions were fleshed out, regional bonds renewed, and the slow processes of religious pedagogy given an opportunity to work undisturbed in the city's parishes. It all went on under the vigilant eye of the Church Assembly, which grew out of informal meetings of the Evangelical clergy in the 1520s and received official recognition in 1531.[77] Although the parish churchwardens, who were laymen appointed by the Senate & XXI, were supposed to attend its meetings, the assembly remained a clerical body, which met weekly to discuss the assignment of duties, lay discipline, education, and additional reforms of the church.[78] This body gradually acquired the authority to discipline the clergy and the power to mediate government oversight, both of which gave the clergy a measure of independence in practice they lacked in principle and relieved the magistrates of the routine supervision of religious life. One more synod met during Jacob Sturm's lifetime. On 26–28 May 1539 in an altogether calmer atmosphere than in 1533, it addressed the problem of "conformity [gleichförmicheit]" in preaching and in the administration of the sacraments, and its liturgical reforms made public worship more uniform and more solemn. This happened, however, at a pace that reflected the changed circumstances, for the Senate & XXI took nearly five years to publish the second synod's recommendations.[79]

The regime's firmer grip on the civic church after 1534 also led to efforts to reestablish contact with the bishop, William von Honstein, the Thuringian nobleman who had been elected in 1506. He had resisted the Reformation movement as well as he could, and despite the total collapse of his authority at Strasbourg, he continued to supervise his diocese and rule his principality.[80] In 1538 the Strasbourg preachers began to approach William about resuming his ecclesiastical jurisdiction in the city, if he would accept a minimal reform agenda of the German mass and a married clergy.[81] Perhaps they were merely looking for a source of leverage against the Senate & XXI and for stricter religious discipline in the city. William's successor, Erasmus of Limburg, was "a mild and tractable man with a conciliatory disposition."[82] His election in 1541 dramatized the many changes since William's in 1506, for Hedio preached and no mass was sung; the new bishop made no solemn entry, nor did he return to Strasbourg for eleven years thereafter. Shortly after his election, however, the Senate & XXI—it was the era of the Imperial colloquies—asked for a conversation with the bishop and his councilors. On 18 October 1541, Peter Sturm, Martin Herlin, Mathis Pfarrer, and Caspar Hedio went to Molsheim to meet with Bishop Erasmus, who so nonplused them with his call for a unified theology—they had expected him to accept theirs—that the meeting broke up without results. These efforts led to nothing, but they illustrate the desire of the magistrates and preachers to re-root, or to appear to re-root, their reformation in the religious life of the city's own region. Unfortunately, this shrewd policy failed, and religious strife within the diocese was to cause the city and its magistrates untold troubles during the next generation.[83]

A third change in civic religious life after 1534, subtler but ultimately more significant, was the slow inculcation of the burghers with Evangelical piety in its specifically Lutheran form. The advance of Lutheran practice at Strasbourg fit very precisely Jacob Sturm's foreign policy, the submission at Schweinfurt, and the growth of the Smalkaldic League. More and more, local clergymen were prepared at the local Latin school and trained in theology at Wittenberg or Tübingen, both Lutheran universities. Richard Hillis, an English cloth merchant resident at Strasbourg since 1540, wrote in 1546 that "[Johann] Marbach is altogether a Lutheran: but this is nothing among us, because almost all the preachers here are chiefly imbibing and inculcating Lutheranism."[84] This slow process matured earlier in practice than in principle, for although Martin Bucer, now undisputed leader of Strasbourg's church, accommodated his eucharistic doctrine somewhat to Luther's in the wake of the Wittenberg Concord of 1536, the convergence remained incomplete. Bucer's position "became frozen, and between the Wittenberg Concord and the Interim, from 1536 to 1549, the Strasbourg theology remained stagnant, on this point as on others."[85]

At humbler, ultimately more important levels, however, official religion at Strasbourg began to take on a definitively Lutheran flavor. In the 1540s Strasbourg children began to learn their Christian doctrine with a decidedly Lutheran flavor, and in raising their voices to praise God, the Strasbourgeois used the new hymnal of 1541, which replaced most of the familiar hymns of Strasbourg and Constance provenance with Luther's compositions.[86] At this level—catechetical instruction, hymn singing, and daily sermons—the Wittenberg reformer maintained at Strasbourg his stature as a religious leader and guide, which no other Evangelical clergyman, not even local ones, could ever rival. He never lost entirely the wonder-working aura that had surrounded his image in the early days, and the power of his liturgical creations—the German mass and the hymns—assured that all German Protestants would be, in some sense, "Lutherans." At Strasbourg, as elsewhere, the routine of everyday religious practice, not doctrinal statements, gradually made the city predominantly Protestant in religion, and on this ground Luther's double legacy of charisma and liturgy overcame all the competing local tradition.[87]

Strasbourg's church from the mid-1530s, therefore, developed a life of religious routine based on three events—the Schweinfurt submission (1532), the Wittenberg Concord (1536), and the church constitution (1534)—becoming Marsiglian in constitution and Lutheran in doctrine and practice. This rhythm needs to be emphasized in the face of the long historiographical tradition that swallows whole the legend invented by Jean Sturm, rector of the Latin school, that "Marbach abandoned Bucer's [and Jacob Sturm's] ideals and sought to impose foreign values and his own tyranny on the local church."[88] During the doctrinal quarrels that racked Strasbourg in the 1560s and 1570s, both parties—the orthodox Lutherans represented by Johann Marbach and Johann Pappus, and the Calvinists headed by Jean Sturm—could claim with some legitimacy the legacy of Jacob Sturm. For the Latin school, which became the center of resistance to orthodox Lutheranism in those decades, was also his personal creation, which gave institutional form, financial resources, and social prestige to the culture, including religious culture, which his Erasmian heritage made dear to him.

THE SCHOLARCH

"Void of learning is Mother Strasbourg," wrote someone, perhaps Othmar Nachtigall, around 1520, and in Jacob Sturm's youth the city was, indeed, infamous for the poor quality of its schools.[89] Thomas Platter of Zurich, who visited Strasbourg in 1517, the year Sturm began to work for Count Palatine Henry, complained that "when we came to Strasbourg, we found lots of poor students but not a single good school; but at Sélestat, there was a good school. So we went there."[90] It had been the same in the time of Great-Uncle Peter Schott, who had also studied at Sélestat. Nothing had changed by century's end, and in 1501 Jacob Wimpheling had asked the Senate & XXI to found a Latin school, arguing that a knowledge of correct

Latin was indispensable for sound civic government. The school would prepare young Strasbourgeois for the universities by means of three to five years of a curriculum based on ancient and modern (Italian) writers.[91] Wimpheling's project of 1501 represents more or less what Jacob Sturm, his most famous pupil, achieved.

The Reformation movement's emphasis on preaching the gospel increased concern for good schools, and the Evangelical clergy seized the initiative in a petition of 1525, in which they urged the magistrates to take over education much as they had taken over the supervision of poor relief, marriage law, the religious houses, and public worship.[92] The School Board was established on 9 February 1526 as a permanent commission of the Senate & XXI.[93] All three members of the School Board, called variously "Schulherren," "Scholarchs," or "praefecti scholarum," were privy councillors serving for life according to the Strasbourg formula, one noble and two commoners.

Jacob Sturm, who had served on the ad hoc committee of 1525 on schools, public worship, and other matters, became the first noble member of the School Board, a post he held until his death.[94] His two colleagues were the Ammeister Claus Kniebis, a man of leisure who had studied at Freiburg, and Jacob Meyer, president (*Oberherr*) of the Masons' Guild, who, though a man of substance, probably had no Latin.[95] Jacob Sturm, the best educated magistrate of his, or any previous, generation, presided over the School Board and became its dominant figure, as over the next twelve years the board transformed the educational establishment of Strasbourg, obliterating once and for all its reputation for indifference to learning.[96] The board assumed control over the existing schools; it established a library; it created a school treasury out of the properties and incomes of the former convents of the Dominicans, Franciscans, and Augustinians; and it managed to get the benefices at St. Thomas, the second most important collegiate church, assigned to the support of teachers. This record, in which one could justly take pride, grew directly out of the civic reformation, as the magistrates noted in 1530:

> So that none of the priests will lack for better instruction, we have on our own provided for the two schools, where boys are taught Latin and Greek, that experienced and learned scholars shall give instruction in the Dominican convent in Hebrew, Greek, rhetoric, poetry, mathematics, and civil laws; the Holy Bible is taught at St. Thomas.[97]

All this was but groundwork for the achievements of the 1530s, the great decade of consolidation in reformed Strasbourg. First to be put in order were the grammar schools, for which Jacob Sturm drafted the ordinance approved on 19 November 1531.[98] It set the tone for the board's future: "First, that no one should hold school or teach publicly here at Strasbourg, unless he has first come before the scholarchs and gained their permission." Two and a half years later, in March 1534, Jacob Sturm drafted a

comprehensive ordinance for the city's grammar schools—the most centralized for any German-speaking city of the time.[99]

From grammar schools the scholarchs turned to a new institution, a college for training preachers, preparations for which date to early 1534 between the synod and the church constitution. In the first months of 1534,
Bucer and Ambrosius Blarer of Constance discussed the plan for a college—
"a nursery for sacred studies," in Bucer's words—to train clergymen for Strasbourg, Constance, Lindau, Biberach, and Isny.[100] Three of these five cities,
of course, had signed the Zwinglian Tetrapolitan Confession at the Diet of
Augsburg in 1530, and the plan for a college shows that this community
did not die after the political collapse of South German Zwinglianism. Though
relatively distant from Upper Swabia, the other cities' region, Strasbourg
formed their political and intellectual center, now that Zurich had become
politically quiescent.

The preachers' college got underway in short order. Two wealthy patricians of Isny, the Bufflers, endowed the school, and Joachim Maler,
Constance's city attorney, brought the first eight Swabian boys on 10 June
1534 to Strasbourg, where the school was being organized in the Dominican convent.[101] This preachers' college for the Zwinglian cities, therefore,
was getting underway just as Landgrave Philip was mobilizing to invade
Württemberg. Indeed, the restoration in Württemberg briefly formed the
capstone on this grander conception for tying together the Protestant churches
of South Germany, for not only would Württemberg have provided a large
territorial base, but Tübingen would have provided the Zwinglian party
with a university.

The situation in the spring of 1534 comes to light in a discussion of a
proposal to found a full university at Strasbourg. The idea came from Bucer,
who at the end of March 1534 planted it in a memorial to the Senate &
XXI about housing and instruction for the preaching college's students.[102]
Noting that "outside of Wittenberg and Marburg, there is no university to
which the youth can be sent with benefit both to their learning and to
their sanctity," Bucer recommended instruction in languages, dialectic, philosophy, rhetoric, mathematics, and civil law, "so that the foundations may
be laid for all faculties."[103] At least one member of the School Board, Kniebis,
understood that Bucer aimed for a full university at Strasbourg, a scheme
he thought far too grandiose for the city's needs.[104] Kniebis believed that
"we [i.e., the School Board] are not charged with providing instruction in
all faculties and disciplines, nor is the schools' income large enough to make
it feasible." Instead, instruction should be provided only in the disciplines
"which foster our common good [so vnserm gemeynen nütz zu erhalten]," such
as grammar, theology, moral philosophy, natural philosophy, and the Bible.
Kniebis, who held a licentiate in civil law, thought that "civil law is needed
for dealings with other peoples, and we must accept it to the degree that it
is not expressly against God. Otherwise, God's own law provides a sufficient

standard of justice." A university, he estimated, "would cost about 3,000 fl. per year, which we don't have." Kniebis's comments are sober, practical, and attuned to the local common good rather than to the wider political and clerical networks managed by Jacob Sturm and Martin Bucer. The localism of his views on education also informed his politics, for Kniebis became the main critic of Sturm's grand policy and advocated a return to the Swiss alliance.[105] Above all, Kniebis's position was more practical, more parochial, and more strictly civic, and it lacked any sense of connection between the local schools and the building of Protestantism in South Germany.

Jacob Sturm's strong support for the preachers' college shows in his careful supervision of its everyday life: instruction, teaching staff, and living conditions. Each year he presided over the audit of the college accounts, noting the outlays for firewood, meat, wine, and wages.[106] Occasionally, there were other, less pleasant, duties, such as his investigation into charges that the cook was stealing wine and preserved meat from the college stores.[107] The college housed an average of thirty students of theology from Strasbourg and other cities, and its reputation for nonpartisanship drew students from Zwinglian Bern as well as from Lutheran Esslingen.[108] The preachers' college began as and remained an institution closely tied to the chief motive of the preachers' original petition of 1525, the training of clergymen for civic service, and though its scope widened to serve other cities in Strasbourg's orbit of influence, the college never grew beyond this original purpose and scope.

Four years later was born an institution that differed from the preachers' college in every way. Since 1538 Strasbourg's Latin school acquired, under its founding rector, Jean Sturm (1509–81), an international reputation for general, not professional, education of a superior kind, and its aims and clientele expanded far beyond Strasbourg's province, region, or political orbit to make it a model of humanist pedagogy for much of the German-speaking world.

Tradition, though unconfirmed by a contemporary source, attributes the idea of founding a Strasbourg gymnasium, an advanced Latin school with a humanist curriculum, to Jacob Sturm.[109] His education, his close acquaintance with humanist studies, and his broad perspective on the world make Sturm's premier role likely, though the other scholarchs, Bucer, and others took part in drafting the plan of January 1538.[110] The new professor of dialectic, Jean Sturm, a native of Schleiden in the Eifel who had long studied at Paris, drafted a detailed plan of studies, and the new institution could open at Easter 1539 in the Dominican convent. The Latin school became the city's central educational institution, as all of the previously established lectureships were incorporated into it, and its ten teachers and eleven or twelve professors were combined into the corps of "school employees [*Schuldiener*]."[111] The school represented in education the same process of consolidation, centralization, and control that the synod and church constitution had produced in the church.

With the founding of the gymnasium in 1538, the School Board took on the final, fixed form, toward which it had been moving for a dozen years.[112] Since 1535 its warden (*Schaffner, oeconomicus*) had kept a record of the board's decisions and the presiding scholarch had kept minutes of their meetings, which occurred frequently but at irregular intervals. Four times a year, the board held a scrutiny of the schools, at which time every teacher in the German elementary schools and in the Latin school had to report problems and receive criticism. The routine work of supervision and criticism belonged to two, after 1538, three, visitors, who conducted regular visitations of the schools and reported on their progress. In Jacob Sturm's time, however, as the account books show, the scholarchs nonetheless maintained an extraordinarily close supervision of the schools. By 1538 they boasted that their system worked so well "that the schools, thank God, improve from day to day, and it has come to pass that many honorable folk in other towns send their children to our schools."[113]

This hierarchy of scholarchs and visitors embodied the fundamental character of the urban reformation: the rededication of resources and institutions, originally religious but long privatized and laicized, to religious purposes but under lay control. The authority of Strasbourg's scholarchs over the schools knew no bounds except for the superior authority of the Senate & XXI, and after the appointment of a third visitor in 1538—Christman Herlin, Martin's nephew[114]—the visitors included one clergyman, Dr. Caspar Hedio, and two schoolteachers (the other was the Greek master, Jacob Bedrotus). Only one of the top six school officials at Strasbourg, therefore, was a clergyman, which assured that the schools remained under strict lay control through a structure parallel to, but separate from, the hierarchy of the civic church.

Direct and exclusive lay control of the schools was guaranteed not only by the School Board's status as a permanent commission of the Senate & XXI, but also by the scholarchs' exclusive control of school finances and personnel matters, and it was never challenged in Jacob Sturm's time. Finance lay well within the capabilities of the average privy councilor, but personnel matters, especially as the Latin school rose to eminence, posed cultural burdens on scholarchs to which Jacob Sturm alone was equal.[115] He set standards his successors simply could not maintain, not even his brother Peter, who succeeded him, for within a month of Jacob's death the scholarchs referred for the first time the hiring of a schoolteacher to the full Senate & XXI. It was the theologian Peter Martyr Vermigli, a former Augustinian canon from Florence, whose orthodoxy lay in doubt. The Senate & XXI appointed two more magistrates, men no better qualified than were the non-noble scholarchs to judge such matters, and Vermigli, who later became a leading dissenter, was appointed, probably because Peter Sturm supported him.[116] Peter Sturm's successor as noble scholarch, his cousin Heinrich von Mülnheim, accepted the office only under protest and exercised it unwillingly and desultorily, so that by the early 1570s, the Senate & XXI regularly had to deal with matters that had formerly been managed by the scholarchs alone.[117] This was but one sign of the system's deterioration after Jacob Sturm's death. Others were the poorer quality of record keeping and the inability of the scholarchs to maintain an independent, decisive role in the selection of teachers. The deterioration of direct lay control forms the most important background to the great struggles between preachers and teachers that rocked Strasbourg in the decades after Jacob Sturm's death. For if the immediate consequence of faltering lay control was to strengthen Jean Sturm's grip over the Latin school, whose corps of teachers, together with the French parish, formed the major network of resistance to Lutheranism's advance at Strasbourg, at longer range the slippage encouraged the preachers under Marbach to try to capture the schools.[118] The ensuing struggles, which culminated in the dismissal of Jean Sturm in 1580 and in the final Lutheran settlement of the 1590s, ended the system of church and school in two separate, parallel structures under direct lay control, of which Jacob Sturm was the chief architect.

THE STRASBOURG PEDAGOGY

To historians, Jacob Sturm's roles in the consolidation of church and school in Strasbourg pose a dilemma: he was the formative figure in both the church settlement, which set Strasbourg on the path to confessional Lutheranism, and the establishment of the Latin school, which became the center of Zwinglian-Calvinist, Francophile dissent. The dilemma mirrors the tension in Sturm's own career as a Protestant civic politician. He belonged by heritage and policy to those who favored law and order, civic harmony and unity, and an official religion tailored to the needs of both the burghers and his own grand policy. On each of these counts, Jacob Sturm was at least the godfather, if not the father, of Strasbourg's passage into orthodox Lutheranism. On the other hand, Sturm belonged by education to those humanists whose horizons swept over the entire range of Christendom, past and present. Despite the grinding pace of official business, Sturm maintained to the end his taste for, and his belief in the great value of, the studies he had first savored during his years as a gentleman-clergyman. Only one book survives from the large collection with which he endowed the school's library, a Clement of Alexandria in Greek, printed at Florence in 1550, which he purchased as a gift to the school sometime in the last three years of his life.[119] Here, as elsewhere in his career, Jacob Sturm reveals his characteristic union of late medieval politics, Reformation religion, and Renaissance culture.

The place of the Latin school in Jacob Sturm's designs can be inferred not so much from what he said about the school as from what the school became under his care. In the first place, the Latin school realized in broad terms Jacob Wimpheling's plan of 1501: the institutionalization of a useful humanist pedagogy at Strasbourg. This was the "type of education which served at least potentially almost all European elites, and which maintained its integrative power down to the turn of the twentieth century," and which, with its emphasis on moral virtue, practicality, and the common good, made Latin schools "typically bourgeois institutions."[120] Jean Sturm's own conception of his school's political utility shows how far horizons had widened since Wimpheling's plan, which had been narrowly civic in scope. Sturm, by contrast, saw the influence of the gymnasium and the city radiating into the whole world of Imperial politics through the activities of former pupils. "After my death," he urged the scholarchs in 1566, they should not alter

> this establishment, which for more than twenty-eight years has brought such benefits to the churches, the schools, the assemblies of cities, royal courts, diplomatic missions, and Imperial Diets in all those matters which engage the wise and experienced men who were trained in our gymnasium.[121]

In this thoroughly elite institution mingled sons of wealthy burghers, future clergymen and jurists, and young nobles who came from great distances to partake of the school's combination of neo-Latinity and sound Christian piety.[122] This suprabourgeois, supralocal character of humanist pedagogy in the Strasbourg mold is illustrated by the great diversity of pupils attracted to the school under Jean Sturm's rectorate and by the school's paradigmatic influence across southwestern Germany.[123]

As its reputation grew, the Latin school formed and sustained connections between Strasbourg and the outside world that sometimes reinforced and sometimes diverged from the ties Jacob Sturm's foreign policy had fostered since 1528. The reinforcement is visible especially in the *objects*, the receiving side, of the Strasbourg pedagogy. Whereas Wimpheling's plan had envisaged education for civic service in the name of the civic common good, Jean Sturm's thoroughly aristocratic pedagogy aimed to "win the ruling princes and the nobility for his humanist program" by "propagating his doctrine of eloquence as a kind of 'professional course' for the political elites, especially the nobles."[124] His school drew noble students—academic orations customarily began by addressing "counts and barons"—especially from Hungary, Bohemia, Poland, and Prussia, though also from the nobilities of West Central Germany, such as the Wetterau and the Kraichgau. This pattern to some degree reflects the growing political dependence of the free cities on princes and of southern Protestantism on the Central and East Central German powers. If we compare what Wimpheling wanted to what Jacob Sturm and Jean Sturm achieved, we can see how the Strasbourg pedagogy reinforced Jacob Sturm's foreign policy.

A look at the *sources* of the Strasbourg pedagogy, however, gives an entirely different impression. They were far more classical, more international, and less Italian than the sources of Wimpheling's pedagogy had been. Jean Sturm had studied at Liège and Paris, and he based his plan of studies for Strasbourg's school on that of his own school of the Brethren of the Common Life at Liège.[125] Strasbourg's school thus belonged to a stage of humanist culture, the Erasmian stage, that had been planted at Strasbourg in Jacob Sturm's youth. Since those days, humanism had grown from an exotic, Italianate learning into an international cultural movement in northern Europe, as it radiated across the German-speaking world from centers in Italy, the Netherlands, and France.

The consequences of this change can be seen in the development of the gymnasium under Jean Sturm's leadership into a potential pole of tension with the civic clergy. The Evangelical clergy who worked at Strasbourg in Jacob Sturm's time were all South Germans: twelve from the lands west of the Rhine (Alsace, Lorraine, the Palatinate), three from the right-bank lands (Breisgau, Baden), five from Swabia, and one each from Franconia and the Tyrol.[126] The Protestant schoolteachers at Strasbourg before the founding of the gymnasium were also South Germans.[127] After Jean Sturm was installed as rector of the Latin school, the scholarchs hired a number of non-German-speakers to teach there, such as Paolo Lazise of Verona, Peter Martyr Vermigli, Emanuele Tremellio of Florence, and Francisco de Enzinas (called "Dryander") of Burgos. When Bucer sponsored Justus Velsius of The Hague for a teaching post in 1545, the mathematician Christman Herlin, whose uncle was an ammeister, blamed Bucer for recruiting North Germans and Netherlanders, beginning with Jean Sturm, instead of South Germans.[128] Though Jacob Sturm and the other scholarchs hesitated at first, they appointed the arrogant Hollander to the Latin school, and Bucer secured him a prebend at St. Thomas. They all lived to regret it, for in 1549 Velsius defended the emperor's religious policy and had to be dismissed.[129]

Later on, when the scholarchs' control weakened following Jacob Sturm's death, Jean Sturm's influence on appointments strengthened. The rector liked to promote and protect scholars whose talents he admired, even when their behavior left something to be desired. One such was the South Tyroler Michael Toxites, whose drinking and indiscipline repeatedly got him into hot water at Strasbourg.[130] Later on, Sturm urged the hiring of figures whose refusal to conform to the Lutheran doctrine provided an easy target for the guardians of orthodoxy. Those guardians were mostly pastors of South German origins, as their predecessors had been—Johann Marbach and his successor, Johann Pappus, were both Lindauers[131]—whereas the gymnasium's staff numbered many foreigners, such as Peter Martyr Vermigli and Girolamo Zanchi from near Bergamo, François Baudoin of Arras, François Hotman of Paris, and Hubert Giphanius of Buren in Gelderland.[132] Vermigli and Zanchi became special targets of the Lutheran clergy during the great doctrinal quarrels that shook Strasbourg's church and school after Jacob Sturm's death.

The immediate local effects of this divergence between church and school can be examined by means of the lists of the clergy and teachers who signed the Strasbourg Concord of 18 March 1563.[133] The twenty clergymen came from the regions covered by Jacob Sturm's policy of the Protestant alliance:

seven from the Upper Rhine (of whom four Strasbourgeois and two other Alsatians), four Swabians, three Franconians, and six from Thuringia and Saxony. At least eight had studied at Strasbourg and at least nine at the University of Wittenberg. The fourteen schoolteachers who signed the Strasbourg Concord came from quite different parts of Europe: ten from German-speaking lands west of the Rhine (of whom six Strasbourgeois and one [Jean Sturm] educated in the Netherlands and France), two Italians, one from the Graubünden, and one unknown. Nine of the teachers had studied at Strasbourg, but none at Wittenberg. The recruitment of clergy thus continued to reflect Jacob Sturm's foreign policy, whereas the recruitment of teachers drew from the international world of humanism centered in Italy, France, and the Netherlands, in the lands, therefore, where international Calvinism was coming onto the scene. Later on, during the 1570s, Strasbourg would be rocked by struggles over apparently conflicting demands to accept the Lutheran Formula of Concord or to tolerate the Calvinists and their campaign to draw German Protestantism into the French religious wars. The struggles pitted clergy against schoolteachers and magistrate against magistrate, and they disturbed the city's peace long after Jean Sturm's dismissal in 1580.[134]

The Latin school under Jean Sturm formed from the beginning a port of entry for ideas, influences, and interests from the world to the west. Another such port was the French parish, to which Gallicized German speakers, such as Jean Sturm and the historian Johannes Sleidan, also belonged. Founded in 1538, the birth year of the Latin school, by 1553 the French parish numbered 135 heads of household, of whom fully 100 were citizens of Strasbourg.[135] As the persecutions in France swelled their numbers, even Sleidan, a French-educated German from Jean Sturm's native town and an elder of the French parish, complained of the violence of the "Latin trash [welsch gesindlin]" then flooding into Strasbourg.[136] This large, unassimilable minority was thoroughly unpopular, not least because it formed a standing cover for French espionage and intrigue.

The man who stood at the point of convergence of these lines of influence from the west was Jean Sturm. Not only did he gather talented foreign scholars around him at the Latin school, he was an important person in the French parish and in the Chapter of St. Thomas—the three centers of the party that tried to claim the Strasbourg's reformation for what was to become "Reformed" Protestantism rather than for Lutheranism. The details of this process, by which Strasbourg began to be tugged into involvement in the Reformation's fate in France, are by no means yet clear. It is nonetheless quite certain that at the center of these forces stood Jean Sturm, Jacob Sturm's protégé.

Jacob Sturm hitched Strasbourg's church to the Lutheran party in the Empire;[137] he also nurtured institutions that opened Strasbourg to international humanist culture in his day and later to international Calvinism.

In the religious struggles that came to a head in the 1570s, the leaders of both sides, Johann Marbach for the church and orthodox Lutheranism, Jean Sturm for the school and Calvinism, claimed with justice the mantle of Jacob Sturm, Martin Bucer, and the early Strasbourg reformation.[138] Jacob Sturm's divided legacy was neatly symbolized at his death. Marbach, the Lindauer who was later to become the hammer of Calvinism at Strasbourg, attended Sturm's deathbed. "For myself," he wrote in his diary, "I have lost my best friend, yes, my father, in this city." The next day (31 October 1553) he preached Sturm's funeral sermon.[139] The civil eulogy, which followed before the Senate & XXI, was delivered by Jean Sturm, who used the occasion to mark off his claim to the legacy of Jacob Sturm.[140] Marbach and Jean Sturm, one day to be bitter foes, laid to rest the man to whom they both owed their places in the vineyard in which they labored.

Notes

* "Hab acht und merkt mich eben,/wie das mirakel ist:/die tauf hat sich erhaben/ zu erst am heiligen baptist,/da ist der schimpf zerspalten/recht auf den selben tag,/die widertauf muß erkalten,/das wort gottes bleibet noch." Liliencron, ed., *Historische Volkslieder* 4:120–21, no. 458, stanza 10.

1. PC 2:237, no. 259 (15 December 1534).
2. I take this formula from Bornert, *La Réforme Protestante du culte*, 596.
3. Stayer, *German Peasants' War*, 19–92, supplies nearly the last word on the connections between the revolution of 1525 and the rise of Anabaptism.
4. Chrisman, *Lay Culture*, 230, who makes a radical separation between vernacular culture and the schools.
5. Hedio, *Radts Predigt*, C.4v–D.1r, quoted by Ozment, *Reformation in the Cities*, 154, with a few minor alterations. See on this point, Abray, *People's Reformation*, 44.
6. Abray, *People's Reformation*, 189. There was a printed Low German translation of this edict, of which a copy survives in HAB Wolfenbüttel, MS. 181.16 Theol. 4to.
7. Abray, *People's Reformation*, 188–89.
8. Ibid., 47–48, 71–72.
9. Lienhard, "La Réforme à Strasbourg, I," 399–400. The fundamental work is Wendel, *L'Église de Strasbourg*.
10. Text in Roehrich, ed., *Mittheilungen* 1:257–60.
11. TAE 2:3, 15–16, 35, 39, 43, 70, 77–79, 204–6, 271–73, 279–80, 294, 355–61, 398–99. His hand is everywhere evident in the manuscripts, e.g., at ibid. 1:101, 180 n. 13, 193, 201, 361, 401, 421–31, 478–79.
12. Much of what follows is based on my "Architect of Persecution," which contains references and details omitted here. For different views on this subject, see Dollinger, "La tolérance à Strasbourg aux XVIe siècle"; Lienhard, *Religiöse Toleranz in Straßburg*.
13. Fuchs, "Les catholiques," 142–69; Levresse, "La survie du catholicisme"; Abray, *People's Reformation*, 118–19.
14. Stayer, *German Peasants' War*, 19–44; Stayer, *Anabaptists*, xxi, xxiii–xxiv, on the historiography of this issue. On the sect's establishment at Strasbourg,

see Williams, *Radical Reformation*, 149–65, 241–54; Deppermann, *Melchior Hoffman*, 158–78; Kittelson, *Wolfgang Capito*, 171–97; Lienhard, "La Réforme à Strasbourg, I," 392–93; Clasen, *Anabaptism*, 17.

15. Stayer, *German Peasants' War*, 107–22.
16. On Ingold and his family, see Brady, *Ruling Class*, 133, 214n, 321; *TAE* 1:60, lines 16–19, no. 64; Fuchs, "Les foires," 315–17. On Meyger, see Brady, "Architect of Persecution," 269–70; BNUS, MS. 1058, fol. 129r; Wittmer and Meyer, *Livre de Bourgeoisie* 2:692, no. 7369.
17. Bellardi, "Anton Engelbrecht (1485–1558)"; Bellardi, *Wolfgang Schultheiss*; Lienhard, "Les épicuriens," 17–45, plus the contributions to the same volume by Jean Rott, François-Joseph Fuchs, Steven Nelson, Cornelis H. W. Van den Berg, François Georges Pariset, and Jean Wirth.
18. McLaughlin, *Caspar Schwenckfeld*, 123–28; Husser, "Caspar Schwenckfeld," 510–35.
19. *TAE* 2:363, 368, lines 10–11. On Thumb and Schwenckfeld, see Clasen, *Wiedertäufer*, 30–31, 162 n. 58.
20. See Deppermann, "Melchior Hoffman à Strasbourg," 501–10; Stayer, *Anabaptists*, 203–328, on the Melchiorite tradition.
21. *TAE* 2:204, no. 452; *Ann. Brant*, no. 5022; and there, too, the following quote.
22. McLaughlin, *Caspar Schwenckfeld*, 126.
23. Stayer's work, especially his *German Peasants' War*, makes the policy seem quite realistic.
24. These lines are from his letter to Peter Butz, in *PC* 1:263–64, no. 464.
25. *TAE* 1:122, lines 13–15, 18–21, with the entire text on 122–23, no. 92 (republished in 1535, 1598, 1601, and 1670). See Lienhard, "Les autorités civiles," 196–215. Sturm was ruling stettmeister during the third quarter of 1527. Hatt, *Liste*, 197.
26. *TAE*, 1:238, lines 25–27; 239, lines 6–16; 140, lines 27–36. See, in general, Clasen, *Anabaptism*, 152–209; Stayer, *Anabaptists*, xi–xix, 1–23.
27. *TAE* 1:188, lines 26–28, no. 155; 189, lines 3–5, no. 155; 200, no. 170; 233–34, no. 178; 278, no. 225; 326, no. 243.
28. On the Marpeck affair, see ibid., 252–54, 273–76, from which the quotes in this paragraph are taken; and Yoder, "'Les frères suisses,'" 491–99.
29. *TAE* 1:356, lines 33–36, no. 283.
30. Ibid., 357, lines 17–21, no. 285.
31. Ibid., 358, lines 6–7.
32. Ibid., 355, no. 280; 358–59, no. 286, plus the relevant passages from Franck's book on 342–44, no. 262; Chrisman, *Lay Culture*, 30, 157, on the book's printer, Balthasar Beck.
33. *TAE* 1:395, no. 294. See Williams, *Radical Reformation*, 264–67.
34. Allen and Allen, eds., *Opus epistolarum Erasmi*, no. 2615; *TAE* 1:537, no. 315a (Erasmus's report); ibid., 541–43, nos. 323–25, 327, from *PC* 2:nos. 138, 141, 145 (Sturm and Cardinal Albert). For Strasbourg's reputation, see *TAE* 1:543, no. 326; 546, no. 321; and 2:293, no. 521.
35. See their declaration of August 1532, *TAE*, 1:548–51, no. 332a.
36. Ibid., 549, lines 3–9.
37. Ibid., 299, no. 238, reported by Capito in Jan. 1531. See Rott, "Exposition de documents," 225, no. 31.
38. Ibid., 575–78, no. 348, here at 575, lines 20–23.
39. Ibid., 1:577 n. 1, line 40.
40. Ibid., lines 30–34.
41. Brady, *Ruling Class*, 312, 317–18, 332.

42. See Wendel, *L'Église de Strasbourg;* Williams, *Radical Reformation,* 278–98; Chrisman, *Strasbourg,* 201–24.
43. *TAE* 2:36, lines 7–10.
44. Ibid., 36, lines 13–15.
45. Ibid., lines 15–20.
46. Ibid., 43, line 34, 44, line 10; and there, too, the following quote.
47. Ibid., 63, lines 17–18.
48. Ibid., 65, no. 376, lines 15–20.
49. Ibid., 121, no. 410; 345, no. 573 n. 1; Williams, *Radical Reformation,* 286–89, 292. Frey was executed for bigamy. Sturm also presided over the hearings of Clement Ziegler and Melchior Hoffman, though he was absent for Schwenckfeld's hearing. *TAE* 2:79, no. 27.
50. *TAE* 2:178, lines 26–31.
51. Ibid., 205, lines 8–34, no. 453; this was art. 4 of the "Sixteen Articles."
52. Ibid., 272, lines 14–15, 23–26.
53. Ibid., 272. See Brady, *Ruling Class,* 192.
54. *TAE* 2:294, no. 523. See Brady, *Ruling Class,* 192–93; Abray, *People's Reformation,* 180.
55. *TAE* 2:36, lines 13–15.
56. Ibid., 354, lines 2–3. This is from Sturm's report (see 361, lines 6–29, on his role) in 353–61, no. 557. His colleagues excised the second part of this quote.
57. The senators deleted from Sturm's draft the words, "which might have either good or bad results."
58. Ibid., 354, lines 10–23.
59. Ibid., 354, line 41. The question, whether the mentality of the urban elite was in principle "epicurean," that is, opposed to rigor in religion, is examined by Fuchs, "Les marchands strasbourgeois."
60. *TAE* 2:354, lines 25–31.
61. Ibid., 355, lines 19–24.
62. Ibid., 356–57, 396–99, nos. 620–21. The new Sabbath law was also Sturm's handiwork (ibid., 401, no. 624).
63. Ibid., 421–31, no. 637, from which the remaining quotes in this paragraph are taken. On Sturm's role in its preparation, see ibid., 430, lines 17–25.
64. Ibid., 348, line 2–349, line 11. See Williams, *Radical Reformation,* 295–96, who unaccountably calls him "Leonard." The same point was made in the poignant testimony of Catharina Seid, in *TAE* 2:309, lines 20–28.
65. See Blickle, *Communal Reformation,* 111–52.
66. Berman, *Law and Revolution,* 520.
67. Brendler, *Täuferreich;* van Dülmen, *Reformation als Revolution,* 229–360; G. Vogler, "Anabaptist Kingdom of Münster."
68. Brendler, *Täuferreich,* 132, 143, 155–56.
69. See Williams, *Radical Reformation,* 292–95. Hoffman was arrested on 20 May 1533, the consequence of his having twice returned to Strasbourg. Deppermann, *Melchior Hoffman,* 255; and see ibid., 278–301, for his influence on the Westphalian and Netherlandish Melchiorites.
70. *TAE* 2:204, lines 8–9. Van der Wyck, who became spokesman for the Lutherans at Münster, fled in February 1534 and was taken and killed by the bishop's men. Stupperich, "Johann von der Wycks Leben"; Brendler, *Täuferreich,* 115; Pollet, ed., *Relations,* 1:237–44. Sturm had met him as Bremen's envoy to the Smalkaldic League, but in March 1533 he had become city attorney of his native Münster.
71. Gresbeck, "Bericht von der Wiedertaufe in Münster," 22–23.

72. *TAE* 2:239, no. 260; and for the landgrave's news, ibid., nos. 247, 262, 267. See also Bucer's comment to Bullinger on 30 November 1533: "Monasterium tumultuatur misere. Cui consulimus magno labore." Bullinger, *Briefwechsel* 3:236, no. 290, lines 11–12.

73. This account is based on *PC* 2:323–29, here at 323–24. See G. Schmidt, *Städtetag*, 321–24; Neuhaus, *Reichsständische Repräsentationsformen*, 36–144, for the Imperial mobilization against Münster.

74. *PC* 2:248–52, nos. 269–71. For the landgrave's efforts, see G. Schmidt, *Städtetag*, 322; van Dülmen, *Reformation als Revolution*, 342–43; and there are notices of loans from the landgrave to Bishop Franz of Münster in HStA Marburg, K 29, fols. 31r–33r, 33v–35v, 61r–63v.

75. *PC* 2:326–29.

76. Abray, *People's Reformation*, 43.

77. Ibid., 68–71.

78. Ibid., 69; and see the analysis of the clergy's petitions on 245–46.

79. *BDS*, vol. 6, pt. 2:193–200; Bornert, *La Réforme protestante du culte*, 175–76; Lienhard, "La Réforme à Strasbourg, I," 412.

80. Chrisman, *Strasbourg*, 147. See Rapp, *Le diocèse de Strasbourg*, 81–82.

81. Chrisman, *Strasbourg*, 251–56, who gives these efforts proper prominence.

82. Ibid., 256, who quotes the passage from Büheler, *Chronique*, 85, on which the rest of this sentence is based.

83. Abray, *People's Reformation*, 96–103, on the Bishop's War of the early 1590s.

84. Quoted by ibid., 77, from Robinson, ed., *Original Letters* 1:no. 115.

85. Bornert, *La Réforme protestante du culte*, 332; and see 163 on Bucer's dominant position in theology. I agree with Johann Adam (*Kirchengeschichte der Stadt Straßburg*, 315) and Lorna Jane Abray (*People's Reformation*, 77–78), that the "Lutheranization" began in the mid-1530s under Bucer's leadership, not after his departure in 1549.

86. *BDS*, vol. 6, pt. 3:19–41; Ficker, "Prachtwerk," 214–16; Bornert, *La Réforme du culte*, 181–82. See *BDS* 7:176–82, for the preface.

87. This point is forcefully made by Abray, *People's Reformation*, 163–85, who notes the laity's "distaste for theology" and writes that "what the magistrates wanted from Lutheranism was not confessional precision but peace and salvation." Ibid., 180.

88. This must be emphasized against a long tradition that holds that "Lutheran orthodoxy" subverted the Bucerian reformation and ended the liberal, tolerant period of Jacob Sturm. See ibid., 76–77, with the quote from 77. The legend is reborn again and again, as witness Denis, *L'églises d'étrangers*, 51, 82, 109.

89. The entire couplet goes, "Doctrina vacuis est urbs Strasburgia mater,/Doctis atque bonis esse noverca solet." It has often been quoted, here from Kohls, *Die Schule*, 40.

90. Quoted from Platter's autobiography by ibid., 40. The fullest account of schools at Strasbourg is still Knepper, *Schul- und Unterrichtswesen*, esp. 173–89; and see also Kohls, *Die Schule*, 23–33; Schindling, *Hochschule*, 21–22.

91. The text is presented in both Latin and German by Borries, *Wimpfeling und Murner*. His views and those of Kohls (*Die Schule*, 33–39) are criticized by Schindling, *Hochschule*, 24 n. 11; and for good characterizations, see ibid., 24–26; Rapp, *Réformes*, 163–64.

92. The preachers' aims were not civic in Wimpheling's sense, a point made by Schindling, *Hochschule*, 27–28. The school question was first broached in a petition of 31 August 1524 (quoted by Kohls, *Die Schule*, 50, now edited in *BDS* 1:376, lines 10–22), but the idea of a school board first appears in the preachers' petition of 8 February 1525. Schindling, *Hochschule*, 28, 78–79.

93. *Ann. Brant,* no. 4659; Rott, "Jacques Sturm, scolarque," 462. Schindling, *Hochschule,* 80 n. 7, believes that the board was not created until 1528, but this is incorrect. Notices of other actions of the School Board in 1526 are in *Ann. Brant,* nos. 4674, 4699, 4703.

94. The members are listed in Sebiz, "Appendix chronologica," 210–20; and by Oseas Schad, "Kirchengeschichte," in AST 70/1, fols. 52r–53r. Jacob Sturm was succeeded by his brother, Peter (d. 1563). AMS, XXI 1553, at 4 November 1553. The noble seat was later held in succession by two of their kinsmen, Heinrich von Mülnheim (resigned 1573, d. 1578) and Wolf Sigismund Wurmser (d. 1574). Peter Sturm does not appear in Sebiz's list, but there is plenty of evidence of his work as a scholarch. See, for example, NSUB Göttingen, MS. Theol. 184, fols. 164–65, 176, an eighteenth-century transcription of a collection made by Martin Malleolus (1523–81), of which the original is in the Stadtbibliothek Hamburg.

95. Brady, *Ruling Class,* 326–27, 331.

96. Such is the judgment of the most knowledgeable student of the schools, Jean Rott. Rott, "Jacques Sturm, scolarque," 462; and see his introduction to Sturm, *Classicae epistolae,* viii.

97. BDS 3:354–55. This is a different document from the one cited by Schindling, *Hochschule,* 28 n. 19. See ibid., 28–29, on these reforms.

98. Kohls, *Die Schule,* 74–75; and the following quote is at 216 n. 17, based on the protocol in AST 324, fol. 1r.

99. Printed in BDS 7:512–16; and Kohls, the editor, refers to Sturm's notes of 1533 in TAE 1:577 n. 1. See Kohls, *Die Schule,* 74–75, who sees Sturm as the guiding hand behind this entire development. The text is also in Engel, *Schulwesen,* 63–64.

100. BDS 7:536–39, summarizing the literature on this foundation. Bucer's comment is from a letter to Blarer in Schieß, ed., *Briefwechsel* 1:424, no. 363.

101. The endowment's charter of 14 April 1534 is edited in BDS 7:539–46; the college's statutes of 1535 are in ibid., 547–50.

102. Bucer's opinion for the Senate & XXI, composed at the end of March 1534, is printed in BDS 7:522–32.

103. Ibid., 525.

104. Ibid., 533–35, from which come the following quotes.

105. See this volume, chap. 7.

106. The following audit records are in Jacob Sturm's hand: AST Supplement 41/I, fols. 16, 18 (1534–35); AST Supplement 41/II (1535–36); AST Supplement 41/VI, fols. 49r–52v (1537–38); AST Supplement 41/IV (1539–40); AST 1351, Coll. Praed., fasc. 3 (1544); AST Supplement 42, no. XXV (1546–47); AST 1351 Coll. Praed. 1548/9 (1548–49); AST 1352 Coll. Praed. 1551/52 (1551–52).

107. AST Supplement 42/XV: "Klag puncten der kuchen betreffen, von den Schulhern zusamen gezogen." The text is in Sturm's hand.

108. In 1537–38 it enrolled students from Strasbourg, Constance, Isny, Lindau, Biberach, Ulm, Esslingen, and Bern. AST Supplement 41/VI, fol. 54r. On the numbers for 1536/37–1545/46, see ibid., 42, no. XXIV.

109. Schindling, *Hochschule,* 29, who cites a report by Jean Sturm of 1567 that Jacob Sturm had proposed to the Protestant princes and cities that they support a common university. Also worth consulting on this school is Sohm, *Die Schule Johann Sturms.*

110. The older literature attributed the plan to Jean Sturm, but this has been effectively contradicted by Kohls, *Die Schule,* 83–88, and in his edition of the plan in BDS 7:553–68. Kohls attributes the plan to Jacob Sturm (88),

working from a visitation report by Bedrotus and Bucer's notes on it. He also shows that it was composed before 24 February 1538, when Jean Sturm presented his detailed plan of studies to the scholarchs. The latter document is printed by Fournier and Engel, *Statuts*, no. 1977, from the original in AST 324/7. It should be compared with the curriculum of the gymnasium of 1538/39, in Fournier and Engel, *Statuts*, no. 1988, from AST 319/42, fols. 97–99.

111. Schindling, *Hochschule*, 30.

112. Ibid., 80–97, is by far the best account of school administration at Strasbourg, and I rely on it and on Rott, "Jacques Sturm, scolarque."

113. Engel, *Schulwesen*, 73–75, here at 72. The minutes from these quarterly scrutinies in Jacob Sturm's time are in AST 372. Jacob Sturm's close attention can be seen in the account book now in AST Supplement 35, which contains the scholarchs' disbursements, 1526–1623.

114. Brady, *Ruling Class*, 317–18; id., "Social Place," 304.

115. I follow Schindling, *Hochschule*, 85–88.

116. AST 372, vol. VI, 18b; Ficker-Winckelmann, vol. 1:8. See Peter Martyr Vermigli to Peter Sturm, Zurich, 24 May 1562, cited by Marvin Anderson in *SCJ* 8, no. 3 (October 1977): 128. This probability is heightened by Peter Sturm's defense of Girolamo Zanchi against Johann Marbach, for which see Robinson, ed., *Zurich Letters*, 2d ser. 99, no. 43.

117. Schindling, *Hochschule*, 85–86.

118. See Abray, *People's Reformation*, 142–50.

119. Clement of Alexandria, *Opera* [in Greek] (Florence: Lorenzo Torrentino, 1550), dedicated to Piero Vittorio Marcello Cervino, Cardinal of Santa Croce. The bookplate bears Sturm's arms in color and the inscription "In usum studiosorum scholae Argentinensis Iacobus Sturm donabat." I am grateful to the late Rodolphe Peter, who showed me this volume, which is now in the library at St. Thomas, Strasbourg, and gave me a slide of the bookplate. See Rott, "Sources et grandes lignes," in Rott, *IH* 2:662. The rest of Sturm's books perished in 1870, during the German siege of Strasbourg, when the Dominican church, which contained both of the cities' libraries, was burned. His papers, which were in the municipal library, burned in the same fire, except for one group of letters, which is now in the Danish Royal Library, Copenhagen, MS. Thott 497, 2°. See BMS, MS. 435, fol. 37r; Rathgeber, *Schätze*, 57–58; Baumgarten, *Jacob Sturm*, 26 n. 4; Rott, "Jean Sleidan," 560 (on MS. Thott 497, 2°); Rott, "Bibliothèque," in Rott, *IH* 2:616, 620; Rott, "Sources et grandes lignes," in ibid., 633–34, 662.

120. Schindling, *Hochschule*, 6–7, a very cogent discussion of this theme; there, too, at 25, the following quote. See also Strauss, *Luther's House of Learning*, 44.

121. Rott, "Une lettre de Jean Sturm," 178; and on his pedagogy in general, see Mesnard, "La 'pietas litterata' de Jean Sturm." Jean Sturm hardly differed from Wimpheling on the political utility of humanism. The systematic neglect of this aspect of German humanism may be illustrated by Noel Brann's bland comment that "the primary urge of Renaissance humanism, in Germany as elsewhere, was a grammatical and rhetorical one, though it eventually moved beyond this point." Brann, "Humanism in Germany," 131.

122. This point, the supraclass appeal of humanism, is emphasized by Schindling, *Hochschule*, 386–88, 391–95. Jacob Sturm acknowledged from the first that the Latin school would be an elite institution; his plan of early 1538 notes that "dan vss den vorstetten werden wenig knaben zu den lateinischen schulen gethan." BDS 7:560–61.

123. Schindling, *Hochschule*, 36–44, who shows that both Jean Sturm and Johann Marbach were concerned to make Strasbourg the major center of Protestant

education in southwestern Germany. The gymnasium's matriculation lists for this period are lost.

124. Ibid., 382–83.

125. Kohls, *Die Schule*, 89, mentions the Latin schools at Zwolle, Deventer, and Leiden, but Schindling, *Hochschule*, 31, 98, 172, notes that Jean Sturm named the Hieronymite school at Liège as his curricular and organizational model. See also Post, *Modern Devotion*, 558–60.

126. Based on Ficker-Winckelmann 2:71, 78–87; Bopp, *Die evangelischen Geistlichen.* See B. Vogler, "Recruitement."

127. The most exotic was Simon Lithonius (d. 1545) from the Valais. Ficker-Winckelmann 2:67, 77–80.

128. "Videt vocari ex inferiori Germania, primo Sturmium, esse mirabili capite. Jlle curauit ut vocaretur Seuenus [a Saxon], quia praelatus est Dasipodio cotiori, et hoc miris practicis factum. Jam tertio vocari Velsium ex eodem loco [actually a Hollander]. Jta futur sicut in Monasterijs, ut tota scola pulsis Superioris Germaniae hominibus totat ex Niderlandis constet. Jta conspiratio erit quaedam illorum." Report of the gymnasium's professors on Justus Velsius, Strasbourg, 19 June 1544, in Pollet, ed., *Relations*, 2:206, no. 53, lines 78–83. See ibid. 1:320–41, 2:199–212; Ficker-Winckelmann 2:82–84.

129. Jacob Sturm's note on him begins, "Rebellionis, seditionis, non solum illum, sed Bucerum et alios pradedicatores. Nec illud in eos tantum redundare, sedet in senatum et nos. Ille a religione Caesaris ad nos venit approbauit nostram; in examine iurauit, communicauit. Iam damnat et minitatur de Caesare, quem prius fugit. Desertor, bis transfuga." AST 324/14, now printed by Pollet, ed., *Relations* 2:219, no. 61, whose text I quote. See ibid. 1:325–26, 2:207, no. 54.

130. Ficker-Winckelmann 2:81.

131. Ibid., 88–90. Of the clergymen who signed the Strasbourg Concord of 1563, I count five Alsatians, four Swabians, four Saxons and Thuringians, three Franconians, and four unknown; about half of them had studied at Wittenberg.

132. Ficker-Winckelmann 2:91–92; Thomann, "Humanisme et droit en Alsace," 274–76.

133. This paragraph is based on Ficker-Winckelmann 2:88–89; Bopp, *Die evangelischen Geistlichen*; id., *Die evangelischen Gemeinden.* On the occasion, see Abray, *People's Reformation*, 143; Lienhard, "La Réforme à Strasbourg, I," 424–25.

134. See Abray, *People's Reformation*, 142–62, which should form an agenda for the next generation of research on Strasbourg; Kittelson, "Landesherrliche-kirchenregiment."

135. I rely here on Rott, "L'église des refugiés," 525–50, (reprinted in Rott, *IH* 2:17–42).

136. Johann Sleidan to Johann von Nidbruck (Strasbourg), 29 December (1550), in Baumgarten, ed., *Sleidans Briefwechsel*, 155. Denis, *L'églises d'étrangers*, 82–83, 109, connects the restrictive measures against the French, the first of which was issued in October 1553, to "xenophobia" inflamed by the French invasion of Alsace in 1552, conveniently forgetting the complaints about the refugees' behavior at that time.

137. See Kittelson, "Landesherrlichekirchenregiment," 140, who agrees that the doctrinal settlements at Strasbourg were "a question of public policy and of foreign policy in particular."

138. Abray, *People's Reformation*, 142–50.

139. AST 198, fols. 99v–101v. Two weeks later, he reports, Sturm's sister, Veronica, sent over a basket of apples, money to buy a book in memory of Jacob, and a printed version of the Sturm arms. Ibid., fol. 102r.

140. See Brady, "Contemporary German Version," 680–81.

FIGURE 2   City Hall (Pfalz) of Strasbourg, constructed 1382, razed 1780–81.
Courtesy of the Archives Municipales de la Ville de Strasbourg.

FIGURE 3 Schwörtag at Strasbourg. Staedel Chronicle (early seventeenth century). Courtesy of the Archives Municipales de Strasbourg.

134

FIGURE 4   Claus Kniebis (1479–1552), ammeister of Strasbourg, age 66.
Silverpoint portrait by Hans Baldung Grien.

FIGURE 5   Mathis Pfarrer (1489–1568), ammeister of Strasbourg, age 79.
Woodcut by Bernhard Jobin, 1568.

136

Abcontrafactur des Ehr=
würdigen und hochgelehrten Herren/ Mar=
tin Butzer/Diener des Euangelions Jhesu
Christi zu Straßburg.

Ich weyß nichts dann Christum den gecreutzigten/ 1.Cor.2.

Diser from und gelehrte Mann/
Hat viel güts der Kirch gethon/
Mit dem Bapst ein harten streit/
Gehalten hat ein lange zeit/
Zületst hat er gesiget schon/
Helffen stellen die Confession.

Zületst das Interim kam zu handt/
Schifft er hinweg in Engellandt:
Darinn die Lehr gerichtet an/
Mit im Fagius der gelehrte Mann.
Darinn ist er in Gott entschlaffen/
Der ist sein Burg/Wehr und Waassen.

Getruckt zu Straßburg/
Anno 1586.

FIGURE 6 Martin Bucer (1491–1551). Woodcut, 1568.

PLVS·OVLTRE

FIGURE 7   Emperor Charles V (1500–1558), age 32. Woodcut by
Christoph Amberger, around 1532. Courtesy, The Bancroft Library,
University of California, Berkeley.

138

FIGURE 8   Philip, landgrave of Hesse (1504–1567), age 31. Woodcut by
Hans Brosamer, around 1535. Courtesy, The Bancroft Library,
University of California, Berkeley.

FIGURE 9 John Frederick, elector of Saxony (1503–1554), age 30. Woodcut
by Lucas Cranach the Elder, around 1533. Courtesy, The Bancroft Library,
University of California, Berkeley.

FIGURE 10   Ulrich, duke of Württemberg (1487–1550), age 46. Woodcut
by Hans Brosamer, ca. 1535. Courtesy, The Bancroft Library,
University of California, Berkeley.

FIGURE 11   King Ferdinand (1503–1564), age 45. Woodcut by
Lucas Cranach the Younger, 1548. Courtesy, The Bancroft Library,
University of California, Berkeley.

5

The Smalkaldic League as Earthly Republic

Then Frondsberg began to name
The nobles princes who were there,
Also the brave free cities
Who hold to the Word of God,
And how the pope opposes them
And sicks on them both emperor and king
To persecute with word and deed
The Word of God from morning to night.
And how at all the Diets
The pope charges them as heretics.
And how they reply in protest
And appeal to a general council
For they want to live under the Bible's rule.*

Jacob Sturm emerged from Strasbourg's past into the German Reformation as promoter, architect, agent, and undertaker of the Smalkaldic League, German Protestantism's foremost political creation.[1] "It does not seem exaggerated," a modern historian writes,

> to conclude that Landgrave Philip and Jacob Sturm for many years ruled the Smalkaldic League. Just as the emperor or king did in the Empire, these two men managed the conflicts that developed inside the league, and they assured that league did not founder on decisions about particular matters.[2]

What was a notable achievement for an Imperial prince was little short of astounding for an urban politician. Together they made the league both a shield for Protestant and would-be Protestant rulers, even for some who would not join it, and an occasional player in European diplomacy.[3] The league also exhibited occasional statelike tendencies and for a time promised to become, if not a godly polity, at least a kind of "earthly republic."[4]

The Smalkaldic League differed from the Empire's late medieval federations (*Einungen*) in two respects, its geographical extent and its ideological basis. Whereas all earlier federations had possessed a limited, regional extent, the league ranged up and down the Empire from Strasbourg to Pomerania and from Augsburg to Bremen. Spreading out from its Central German core in Saxony and Hesse, it became more "national" in a sense than even the southern-centered Imperial government was. Its combination of Central German rulers with affluent free cities possessed much military potential, despite an initial size so small that "it seemed evident," in Ranke's words, "that the evangelical party, . . . if once involved in a serious contest with the large majority of the States, the puissant emperor, and the whole of Latin Christendom united, must be instantly and hopelessly overwhelmed."[5]

The league's second peculiarity, its religious basis, had no precedent in Imperial history. The explicit principle of a common and exclusive faith, though unsupported by common economic interests or geographical proximity, allowed the league to draw strength from the accumulated sentiment for religious reform in many parts of the Empire. Its faith also lent the league a new kind of potential for political innovation, which it never fully realized, because it tended to make the traditional bases of governance less sacral and, therefore, more vulnerable to change. The limits, however, of realizing this potential were reached well before the Protestants went to war against the emperor. During its brief life, on the one hand, the league created a structure of governance, established ties to other European rulers, and crippled the machinery of Imperial justice. The league failed, on the other hand, to handle the problem of ecclesiastical property, it did not create a common church order to complement its common doctrine, and it refused to transform itself from an alliance of Protestant rulers into a community of German-speaking, reformed Christians.

STRUCTURES OF THE LEAGUE

The Smalkaldic League's diet approved its constitution at Smalkalden on 23 December 1535, six years after its birth.[6] Although it descended roughly from the Swabian League, the demise of which in 1534 brought several southern free cities over,[7] the Smalkaldic League divided itself not into estates, as the older league had done, but into a northern or "Saxon district [*sächsischer kreis*]" under the elector and a "southern district [*oberlendischer kreis*]" under the Hessian landgrave.[8] The constitution of 1535 allotted nine votes: two for Saxony, two for Hesse, one for the other northern princes and nobles, and two each for the southern and the northern free cities.[9] The league's war council, organized at Saxon initiative at Veste Coburg in 1537 and approved at Brunswick in April 1538, replicated this structure under the joint command of the Saxon elector and Landgrave Philip.[10] The league, anticipating expansion with the gospel's progress, resolved

> that those who in the future wish to join our Christian alliance and take part in the constitution we have framed [*angeczaigte vorfassung*] shall be

admitted, yet with caution [*beschaidenlich*], making sure that they adhere to God's holy word and the gospel, and that they cause to be taught and preached in their lands and territories solely according to the gospel and the pure doctrine of the confession we submitted at Augsburg [in 1530] to His Imperial Majesty and all estates of the Empire.[11]

Only a few new members joined between 1531 and 1535, and then the flood of 1536 from both south and north forced changes in the league's voting structure.[12] The diet agreed to allot one new vote each to Duke Ulrich, the Pomeranian dukes, and the southern and the northern cities, bringing the total to thirteen.[13] Although this measure magnified the cities' collective weight more than in comparable federations, it also overvalued the less powerful princes.

The league justified its existence through an appeal to its common religion and the members' obligations

> to give praise and due honor to Almighty God, to foster and spread his holy Word and the gospel, and, while remaining obedient members of the Holy Empire, to guide and keep our subjects in a Christian manner to all that is good, Christian, honorable, just, and conducive to their salvation, and to prevent by God's grace unjust, illegal violence and damages.[14]

Officially, the league's nature was purely defensive, for

> this alliance has, and wants to have, no other reason, cause, or intent than to defend and afford protection for ourselves and our subjects and dependents [*verwanten*], in case we are invaded, attacked, or in any other manner, as stipulated, interfered with, because of the Christian, just, and righteous cause for which our Christian alliance has been formed.[15]

In principle, at least, the league never wavered from this position.

The league arose as a military alliance organized for the conduct of war, and the command of its forces alternated between the Saxon elector and the Hessian landgrave, at whose call met the league's diet or the war council.[16] The operational command of forces belonged to the Saxon elector in North Germany, to Landgrave Philip in South Germany, and to a troika of these two plus Duke Ernest of Brunswick-Lüneburg in case of a general war. Following Imperial practice, the league in 1535 defined its military taxes in two ways: an "emergency force [*eilende Hilfe*]" of cash but no troops to aid a threatened individual member, and a "long-term force [*beharrliche Hilfe*]" of troops and guns for a general campaign.[17] The basic unit, called a "month" as in the Empire and the Swabian League, consisted of two thousand horse and ten thousand foot, or their financial equivalent, divided nearly equally between the northern and the southern districts. In 1535 the main levy (*Hauptanlage*), figured in "double-months," was reckoned at 70,000 fl. per "month," but two years later it had climbed to nearly 105,000 fl., and by the eve of the Smalkaldic War in 1546 it stood at nearly 200,000 fl.[18] Table 5.1 shows the assessments at that time.

TABLE 5.1

Assessments (*grosse Anlage*) of the
Smalkaldic League, 1546

SOUTHERN DISTRICT

Member	1 Double-Month (fl.)
Hesse	28,000
Württemberg	18,180
Tecklenburg	800
Strasbourg	10,000
Augsburg	10,000
Ulm	10,000
Frankfurt	6,000
Memmingen	2,900
Constance	2,600
Esslingen	2,900
Schwäbisch Hall	2,400
Biberach	2,200
Heilbronn	2,000
Lindau	1,800
Reutlingen	1,800
Kempten	1,400
Isny	1,200
Ravensburg	800
Subtotal	104,980

NORTHERN DISTRICT

Member	1 Double-Month (fl.)
Saxony	28,000
Other princes	19,000
Hamburg	7,260
Brunswick	7,120
Magdeburg	7,120
Bremen	6,400
Goslar	3,760
Göttingen	1,940
Einbeck	1,400
Hannover	1,280
Hildesheim	1,000
Minden	800
Subtotal	85,080
Total	190,060

Source: Gerber, "Die Kriegsrechnungen," ARG 32 (1935):
56 n. 1; 33 (1936): 247 n. 1.

The figures in table 5.1 show the southern free cities' relatively large contribution to the Smalkaldic League's costs: the cities paid 55.2 percent and 44.7 percent, respectively, of the southern and northern districts' levies, or just over one-half (50.5 percent) of the entire levy. This was much larger than the free cities' share of Imperial tax assessments according to the matricular system. Table 5.2 shows the aggregate assessments by class of estates for the Diet's general assessment in 1521 and its levy for support of the Chamber Court (*Kammerzieler*) in 1542.[19]

TABLE 5.2

Imperial Assessments of General Levy (1521)
and for the Imperial Chamber Court (1542)
by Class of Estate

Class of Estate	1521 (%)	1542 (%)
Electors	7.0	7.0
Ecclesiastical princes	13.3	13.3
Lay princes	20.0	22.2
Abbots and prelates	16.3	16.6
Counts and barons	12.9	11.5
Free cities	30.4	29.4

Sources: RTA, jR 2:no. 56; Kaul, "Kleine Beiträge," 208–12.

In the old Swabian League, too, the free cities had paid a much smaller share than they did in the Smalkaldic League: 37 percent in 1488, 28.6 percent in 1500, and 21 percent in 1530.[20] The cities' formal voting strength in the Smalkaldic League's diet reflected their relatively large financial contribution: four of nine votes in the constitution of 1535, six of thirteen votes in the revised constitution of 1536—a larger share than they held in the Swabian League through most of its forty-six-year existence.[21]

Based on finance and voting strength, then, the free cities might have played a greater role in the Smalkaldic League's diet or assembly than they had in the Swabian League. In some ways, perhaps, they did, for Jacob Sturm enjoyed greater influence than any urban politician, even old Ulrich Arzt of Augsburg, had ever exerted in the councils of the Swabian League. The Smalkaldic chiefs, indeed, often liked to deal with the southern cities through him.[22] Yet the Smalkaldic free cities rarely acted as a block, not only because of the league's great distances—what the southerners called "*weitleufigkeit*"—but also because the northern free cities lacked the southern cities' tradition of consultation and solidarity.[23] This tradition, which reached far back into the histories of the urban diet, the Swabian League, and the cities' house of the Imperial Diet, surfaced once more in the Smalkaldic League. From the beginning, Ulm and Strasbourg set the tone. In February 1531, for example, when Bernhard Besserer brought home the treaty founding the league, the Ulmers called the regimes of Memmingen, Lindau, Biberach, Kempten, and Isny to come and hear the terms, which they did, and then they sent their joint approval to Elector John of Saxony.[24] This began a pattern of consultation that lasted through much of the league's history, with Ulm and Strasbourg always in the lead. These patterns of hierarchy and consultation sat easily on the southern burghers, because of their political traditions.

The northern Smalkaldic cities possessed no similar tradition of hierarchy and consultation. The northern urban members, a much more heterogeneous lot, included both free cities, such as Lübeck and Goslar, which regularly participated in the Imperial and urban diets, and territorial cities of uncertain legal status, such as Göttingen, Einbeck, Magdeburg, Bremen, and Brunswick.[25] Their attendance at the league's meetings and payment of its taxes were both desultory, and the southern urban members came to regard them as habitual tax dodgers.[26] These "Saxon cities," a Strasbourg document of 1538 charged, "enjoy the peace and the protection of Christendom and of the German nation, though they pay nothing toward the Imperial assessments."[27] The northern cities' remoteness from the centers of Imperial governance and Habsburg dynastic power gave them a sense of security that southern Protestants could never share. The same was true of the northern princes. Dukes Barnim IX and Philip I of Pomerania, for example, joined the Smalkaldic League in 1536, but they performed their duties desultorily, habitually neglected to send envoys to the league's diets, and protested all league taxes.[28]

The absence of a common political culture made a genuine cooperation among the Smalkaldic League's southern and northern cities impossible. The southerners' habits rested on mutual understanding about circumstances and abilities to pay, whereas what did the Strasbourgeois know about conditions in Hamburg, or the Lübeckers of Constance's ability to pay? Jacob Sturm might show off his knowledge of northern history, as he did to the Stralsunders at Augsburg in 1548, but the average southern politician could hardly have cared less about those remote northern lands.[29]

Squarely between the two groups of cities, both geographically and as centers of news and organization, sat the two Smalkaldic chiefs. The Saxons were extremely sensitive to urban pretensions, and even before the league was founded, they opposed parity of votes on the grounds that it "would give the cities the deciding votes in all matters. What that would mean, is clear enough. The princes who sit in the Swabian League know only too well what usually happens in such matters."[30] The first year of the league's history witnessed a struggle between the Saxons, who wanted the cities to have only two of six votes, and Strasbourg, which wanted—and nearly got—parity.[31] It was the Saxons, too, who barred the cities from the league's commandership, though Landgrave Philip, ever more cordial to the cities, took a softer line and suggested in 1539 to Sturm that the command might rotate among the princes and even go occasionally "to someone from the cities. We ought to discuss this idea or some other good arrangement, such as the one the Swabian League had."[32]

The disproportion between the cities' financial contribution and their political power encouraged the urban politicians to believe, with much justification, that the princes thought that it was their part to command and the burghers' to pay. The disparity had dogged them since the beginning, at Speyer in 1529, when the Protestants shared out the costs of their embassy to the emperor, 37.6 percent to the princes and nobles and 62.4 percent to the free cities, on the grounds, as the Saxons and Brandenburgers pleaded, that the princes of Brunswick-Lüneburg and Anhalt "are poor and cannot pay much."[33] The Saxon elector did not evade his financial obligations to the league, for which his estates produced much more than he paid in taxes to the Empire.[34] His complaints about poverty, however, rang falsely in burghers' ears, especially when they saw what he spent on display and entertainments—his estates in 1542 voted the huge sum of forty thousand florins to support his entourage during the Imperial Diet.[35]

Given this disparity between contribution and power, the burghers' also feared that their chiefs might well employ urban money to serve "German liberty," that is, the liberties of princes and their dynastic wars. The Smalkaldic League's history shows that this fear was fully justified, a fact to which the Smalkaldic chiefs were not insensitive. Landgrave Philip, for example, had employed the league's connections, but not the league itself, to restore Duke Ulrich in 1534, and he and John Frederick showed a comparable sensitivity in 1540, when they wanted to aid the Catholic duke of Cleves-Jülich, who happened to be the Saxon elector's brother-in-law.[36] They planned a Protestant force of twenty-two hundred horse and ten thousand foot to aid the duke and counted on the possibility that the free cities—only four were included—might refuse to pay at all.[37] On the Lower Rhine in 1540, even more than in Württemberg in 1534, the Smalkaldic League planned to back a princely military operation of a quite traditional kind.

At the bottom of the dissension and misunderstanding lay the confrontation of two different political cultures, the burghers' and the princes'. Burghers customarily enforced policy by managing money, and during the first half of the 1540s the southern urban politicians charged wasteful management and unfair taxation in both diets, league and Empire, and advocated a direct tax, the Common Penny, in place of the matricular system. Jacob Sturm spoke for them in both assemblies, and they made some progress in the Imperial Diet, but none in the league.

The burghers also pioneered in administration, but the Smalkaldic League lagged well behind its model, the Swabian League—much less any contemporary royal or princely state—in the development of a central administration. Although a chancellor, Sebastian Aitinger of Ulm, was hired in 1540, he had only two secretaries to assist him, and the league's main business continued to flow through the chancelleries of Landgrave Philip and Elector John Frederick.[38] For this purpose the league's diet levied a separate "small assessment [*kleine Anlage*]" to reimburse the two commanders for officers' retainers and administrative costs of league business. The first such assessment, voted at Arnstadt in March 1540 for the year 1539, was not collected until 1542. The southerners sent money and the northerners excuses, as usual, and by 1543 the Northern District's arrears for this tax reached nearly thirteen thousand florins.[39]

"The league possessed greater financial strength than any of its opponents," one historian has written, "and it would also have possessed military superiority, had it not lacked the necessary unity."[40] Greater unity would have meant a greater degree of permanent administration, which would have strengthened urban influence, as it had in the old Swabian League.[41] Jacob Sturm grasped this point in his elaborate proposal for reform of the league's constitution, which he presented to the league's diet at Frankfurt in the winter of 1545–46, namely, that a more centralized and less "personal" regime would bring fairer government to the league.[42] One thing he wanted was a regular site for the diet's meetings. The diet met twenty-six times during its fifteen years: seven times at Smalkalden, six at Frankfurt am Main, three at Worms, twice each at Schweinfurt, Brunswick, and Nuremberg, and once each at Ulm (during the Danube campaign of 1546), Naumburg, Arnstadt, and Eisenach.[43] This pattern suited the league's two commanders, through whose chancelleries the federation's business flowed, but it did not suit the southerners. In 1545 Jacob Sturm urged that the league's diet make its permanent home at Frankfurt.[44] Many of the other sites were hard for the southerners to get to and uncomfortable when they got there.

The Smalkaldic League's weak central development is also visible in its failure to evolve a judicial structure for the settlement of disputes between members. The Swabian League had developed a very active court—"one of the most progressive of its age"[45]—complete with university trained judges, a permanent seat, and a marked receptivity to canon and Roman law. The Smalkaldic League developed nothing comparable, even though its crippling of the Imperial Chamber Court heightened the need for such machinery. The most important intraleague quarrel pitted Duke Ulrich of Württemberg against the free city of Esslingen. Ulrich was a proverbial scourge of the cities, who believed that "he plans to conquer and possess all the free cities in his lands, of which there are four or five, and . . . that Ulm would also surrender to him."[46] Bullying free cities had lost him his duchy in 1519, and the common reformed faith neither sweetened his temper nor allayed their fears. Although a few cities renounced their old claims against him in 1537, the Reutlingers set their hearts on getting him to pay at least 100,000 fl. in damages.[47] Ulrich's memory was just as long as the burghers', and he started harassing Esslingen in 1538 and in 1541 mounted a blockade of the city.[48] When the Esslingers took their cause to the urban diet and to the league, Chancellor Johann Feige of Hesse wrote to the landgrave that "there is a great rumble among the free cities, most of whom are unwilling to treat, for they believe that there is no other choice but to attack him again [dan si müssen sich noch einmal an ime versuchen]."[49] If he didn't mend his ways, Feige thought, "it is to be feared that he will suffer another hard blow [noch einmal ein herter anstoss], from which even greater griefs will follow." Indeed, Esslingen proposed that the cities refuse all taxes to the league, which brought Jacob Sturm and some colleagues to Swabia in 1542 to arbitrate the dispute.[50] When they met the fierce old man at Urach on 9 August, he flatly refused to lift the blockade. The Esslingers stood firm, Ulrich's men insulted the burghers at meetings of the league, and by 1545 Strasbourg was demanding that the league take sides for Esslingen, because the Protestants had blocked the Imperial judicial machinery.[51] Had Ulrich been a Catholic rather than a Protestant, the artful Esslingers pointed out in 1542, they would have gotten the league's aid against him readily enough.[52]

These weaknesses cast doubt on the attribution of any statelike qualities to the Smalkaldic League and suggest that its capture of political initiative between 1532 and 1541 owed more to Habsburg vacillation than to Protestant solidarity and strength.[53] There is, however, another side to the matter, namely, the expectations that Protestants placed on the Smalkaldic League. For some, even many, it formed the vanguard and to some degree a model of a more Christian and more just Empire, which might arise from, in Jacob Sturm's phrase, "the proper sort of love for one another." Such hopes did not lack foundation. The league won respect for the gospel abroad through its dealings with foreign kings, and it defended the gospel at home against the machinery of Imperial justice.

THE LEAGUE'S POWER: FOREIGN RELATIONS

Foreign rulers commonly dealt with emperors, Imperial diets, and individual Imperial princes. The kings of France and Hungary often sent envoys to the diet, and the French and English kings had stood as more or less serious candidates for the Imperial crown in 1519. After the pope, by far the most important foreign ruler for the Empire was the king of France, the resilience of whose military power each Habsburg emperor had in turn to learn.[54] Not only had French kings taken or interfered with the Empire's westernmost provinces—Provence, Burgundy, and Lorraine—but they were always the ally of choice for leaders of the German princely opposition to the monarchy. Never did the French card prove its trumping value so splendidly as in 1534, when French gold paid for Duke Ulrich's restoration in Württemberg.

The French card lay face up, the English one was a hole card, the value of which was debatable. Its continental holdings gone, England's chief stake in central Europe lay in the trade and politics of the northern seas: the Netherlandish-Hanseatic trade rivalry, the Swedish secession, and the Danish succession. Since 1527, however, English policy increasingly responded to the weight of "the king's great matter," the problem of the royal succession that led to Henry's divorce from the emperor's aunt and his break with Rome.

All other foreign relations of the Smalkaldic League, with one possible exception, pale into insignificance beside those with France and England. The exception was Denmark, where the king was an Imperial vassal, and where the struggle over the Reformation presented the Smalkaldeners with a combination of pro-Reformation and anti-Habsburg motives they easily understood. Other powers, such as King Sigismund of Poland and Jan Zápolya of Transylvania, naturally came under discussion whenever the Smalkaldeners dreamed of a grand anti-Habsburg league, but such schemes remained the idle dreams they had been in Huldrych Zwingli's day.[55]

The Smalkaldic League's relations with the two kings, France and England, ran very similar courses. An initial stage, lasting from 1531 to about 1535–36, saw the hope of permanent alliances based on religious affinity or even agreement; then came disillusionment in 1535–36, followed by nearly ten years of desultory contacts; finally, in 1545–46 the Smalkaldeners tried to mediate peace between the kings and secure their military aid against the emperor.[56]

The peak in French relations came in 1534–35. After the successful invasion of Württemberg with French financial backing, in June 1535 King Francis invited the Smalkaldic chiefs to send their theologians—Philip Melanchthon was named—to Paris for doctrinal discussions.[57] In between, of course, fell the turning point in France, as the sudden posting of Protestant placards one Sunday morning at Paris provoked a "shattering" effect in the form of a "savage and prolonged" persecution of French Protestants.[58] However avidly these events were followed at Strasbourg, at the Saxon court other considerations weighed against allowing Melanchthon to accept the French king's invitation to Paris. The problem, Elector John Frederick admitted, was not just the risk to Melanchthon's person but also that just now, when a new (the third under Charles V) Franco-Imperial War was abrewing, he did not wish to damage his reputation with King Ferdinand. Quite possibly, if Melanchthon should go to Paris, the emperor, the king, and others might suspect that he was sent to pursue "other, secret business."[59] Thus, the decision against a French alliance had in all probability already fallen, when the Sieur de Langey, Cardinal du Bellay's brother, came to the league's assembly at Smalkalden in December 1535 with the king's formal tender of alliance. Such, at least, seems the elector's message in his speech at Smalkalden on Christmas Day, in which he emphasized the league's Christian nature and its abhorrence of rebellion; and he declared that every new member must be "dedicated to the word of God, and shall permit the sincere doctrine of the gospel, conformable to our confession, exhibited to the emperor's majesty . . . at Augsburg, freely to be preached, taught, and kept."[60] The French alliance was dead, and although relations between the German Protestants and the French king improved somewhat during the peaceful years between 1538 and 1542, the coming of yet another (fourth) Franco-Imperial war in 1544 shattered all possibilities for collaboration. The league's frantic missions to France in 1545 and 1546 were acts of desperation, no more.[61] From first to last, the persecution of the French Evangelicals mortgaged all attempts to bring the undeniably common interest between French monarchy and German Protestants to an effective military combination.

The Smalkaldeners' English relations followed a similar rhythm, though with different accents.[62] Serious contacts began in 1533, when Henry VIII's chief minister, Thomas Cromwell, sent envoys to recruit German Protestant support for the king's divorce on the grounds of common antipapalism. At the same time, the king intervened in the northern seas, striking a brief alliance with Lübeck during the revolutionary rule of Jürgen Wullenwever. Cromwell's wooing of the German Protestants reached its peak in the last months of 1535, when King Henry, imitating his French cousin, asked John Frederick of Saxony to send Melanchthon to England for talks on doctrine. This overture, too, was followed by a formal embassy to the league's diet at Smalkalden in December 1535.

The speeches, which the two royal ambassadors made to the Smalkaldeners in December 1535, display the two kings' respective approaches to the German Protestants.[63] On 19 December Guillaume du Bellay arose to defend King Francis's punishment of French rebels, who, disguised as religious dissenters, hardly differed from the Anabaptists who had so recently fallen at Münster. Langey emphasized the long French tradition of support for German liberty and urged the Smalkaldeners to admit his monarch, the English king, and the duke of Gelderland to the league. When the English ambassador, Bishop Edward Fox of Hereford, rose on 24 December, he took a very different tack. The English king's friendship for the Germans, he said, was based on his zeal for religion, for he had abolished the power of the bishop of Rome in England, just as the allies had done in their lands. Henry exhorted them to unity in doctrine and in opposition to the papal general council—which the French king favored. Thus, whereas the French king promoted a grand anti-Habsburg union without much regard for a common basis in religion, the English king offered a grand antipapal union without much regard for German problems. The Smalkaldeners' dilemma was that although the French king's persecutions of French Evangelicals made the English alliance more welcome, his proven record of supporting the German opposition made the French alliance more practical.

The Smalkaldeners nonetheless opted to pursue the English alliance but not the French one, and the ensuing doctrinal negotiations actually made some progress, although the Wittenberg theologians took the English theological measure quite accurately and found it wanting.[64] Thereafter, though the Smalkaldeners talked a lot about an embassy to England, and at Frankfurt in the summer of 1536 they even appointed a substantial one, including Jacob Sturm and Martin Bucer, the envoys never departed.[65] Or only in legend, for later a tradition at Strasbourg told how Jacob Sturm, Bucer, Melanchthon, and a Hessian had indeed gone to England and returned "with great honors from the king."[66]

It was fortunate that this embassy never left home, for though Thomas Cromwell believed in the German alliance, the king believed only in his own "great matter." With Queen Catherine dead (January 1536), Queen Anne executed (19 May 1536), and his foreign position neatly clarified by the outbreak of the Third Franco-Imperial War, Henry had no need of the Germans. His new pronouncement on doctrine, Ten Articles (approved on 9 June 1536), struck "a compromise between the old and the new" that disgusted the Protestants.[67] In truth, the struggle over whether Henry's antipapal church was also to be Protestant was not even fairly joined until 1538. When the Protestants gained a first, brief ascendancy in 1538, true, the Smalkaldeners were invited to come to England for negotiations, which lasted five months. Next year, the English were back in Germany, but after the Smalkaldeners sent a rather low-level delegation to England in return, King Henry put an end to the matter with the Act of Six Articles, which "embodied fully catholic doctrine" and "effectively terminated the Smalkaldic League's collaboration with Henry VIII."[68] Or, not quite, for though the king was reluctant to commit himself to an alliance or his country to the Protestant faith, Cromwell, the soul of the German policy, still had one card to play—the German marriage. The marriage between King Henry and Duchess Anne of Cleves-Jülich, sister-in-law to John Frederick of Saxony, was contracted on 27 December 1539, solemnized on 6 June 1540, and nullified by Parliament on 16 July. Twelve days later, Thomas Cromwell took his turn on the scaffold.[69]

Thus, during the critical years of Smalkaldic activism in North Germany, the first half of the 1540s, neither the French nor the English king was a credible potential ally. King Henry persecuted Protestants after the fall of Cromwell in 1540, just as King Francis had done since the "affair of the placards" in 1534. Eventually, when English policy again veered toward Protestant religion in the mid-1540s, the Smalkaldeners recognized that their religion had a better chance to succeed in England than it did in France. "One can hardly deny," Jacob Sturm wrote to Landgrave Philip of Hesse in March 1546, "that England stands somewhat closer to our religion than France does." Still, the difference was not so great that Sturm was willing to forbid the French to recruit in the Smalkaldic cities but allow the English to do so. Even though the English king opposed the Council of Trent, and the French king supported it, Sturm thought that "we should not put much trust in either, for we have always found that they support not our interests but only their own, and they are as changeable as the weather."[70]

"As changeable as the weather"—the phrase sums up perfectly the faces the French and English kings presented to the German Protestants, not because the French and the English were more duplicitous or fickle than the Germans, but because the basis of common political interest, weak enough within the league, barely existed between the Smalkaldeners and their royal suitors. In the league, a common religion cushioned the clash of interests enough to allow it to act in concert on a number of occasions, most notably in the war of 1546. This compensatory sympathy, the basis of Sturm's "proper sort of love for one another," was lacking between the German Protestants and either the French or the English crowns. The Smalkaldeners, in turn, were as changeable as the kings, blowing hot and cold as their relations with the emperor and the threat of a general council waxed and waned.[71] Hot or cold, they nonetheless never forgot how the French king's gold gleamed or how wealthy his English cousin was reputed to be.[72]

Many German Protestants nonetheless did believe in a coming reformation in England. This was especially true in the south, for although the early English contacts had concentrated on Luther and Saxony, from the mid-1530s onward the English Protestant leaders began to draw more hope and inspiration from their ties to the southerners.[73] Thomas Cranmer and Edward Fox, for example, began exchanging letters with Martin Bucer and Wolfgang Capito.[74] The Strasbourgeois followed the twists and turns of English foreign policy with great attention. In 1536, for example, Sturm and his colleagues rallied the southern Smalkaldic cities to support the embassy to England,

> for duty obliges us to promote and spread the true, correct, godly, and Christian religion, . . . and especially among those who seek us out and request it from us. Since the English king's request concerns chiefly this matter, for which he asks us to send an embassy to discuss and come to an agreement on religion with him and his theologians, in what way could God's Word and Christ's gospel be better promoted and encouraged in England, God's honor be increased, and His name be praised?[75]

It was a good thing, probably, that Sturm had not heard Dr. Robert Barnes recently tell Martin Luther that "our king is not the guardian of our religion, he is religion."[76] Time, however, brought out the truth, and by 1539 Jacob Sturm realized "that the king of England has become a papist once more and reopened all the monasteries; . . . and though I've not yet heard that he recognizes the pope as supreme bishop, this is all a preparation, since he accepts and intends to hold strictly to [the pope's] doctrine."[77] This is an exaggerated view, of course, of the Six Articles, though in the right direction. The Strasbourgeois even responded to the English Protestant leaders' plea for an embassy on their behalf to the king, though the landgrave thought the situation too dangerous to send Melanchthon.[78] It is nonetheless easy to overestimate the familiarity between the leading English

Protestants and even the preachers at Strasbourg, especially looking backward from Cranmer's offer in 1549 to Martin Bucer of refuge in England.

Attention to English affairs waxed and waned, but the Strasbourgeois could never put France and its king out of their minds, for their city served, as a historian once remarked, as "the political observation post of German Protestantism" to the west.[79] Not that Strasbourg had any emotional basis for sympathy with France, things French, or the French king. Jacob Wimpheling had taken, as usual, a very safe road in his anti-Latin agitations at Strasbourg, and when King Francis sent soft words and promises to Strasbourg in the 1520s, hoping to woo them from support for his enemy, Charles V, the magistrates did not respond.[80] It was also generally recognized, at Strasbourg and elsewhere, how much the French king wanted to expand his military recruiting operations out of Switzerland into the cities of southwestern Germany.[81]

There was a reason, however, why the Strasbourgeois simply could not ignore France, and that reason was trade. Although the Strasbourgeois shared the trading privileges, which King Francis granted to certain South German cities at Lyon in 1516, down to the 1550s they rarely made use of their rights there.[82] Their trade into France, especially toward the Rhone Valley, was nonetheless growing during the 1530s and 1540s, which is why Strasbourg's regime faced the Third Franco-Imperial War (1536–38) with great trepidation.[83] On 2 August 1537 the XIII drafted a memorial on whether the city should participate in a regional defense force (*Landesrettung*) for Lower Alsace. They found it "inadvisable [*nit thunlich*]" to cooperate with the Austrian regime at Ensisheim for this purpose,

> by means of which the city of Strasbourg would become party to this quarrel and war [*veid und krieg*], which would be inadvisable for Strasbourg in view of the French king's power. Further, that the city is not obliged to participate and that, in view of the citizens' extensive trade and property [*grosze kaufmanschaft und hantierung*], which are still safe and secure in France, participation would be against the city's interest.[84]

The other Alsatian powers were to be reminded

> how and in what manner this province relates to the kingdom of France, and how the inhabitants and merchants have constant [*teglichs*] business over there and have until now been safe. It would be a disservice to become an enemy of and have to fight so mighty a foe, whom this province could not withstand, and who has done nothing hostile against the entire land of Alsace.[85]

The same reasoning came into play in the Fourth Franco-Imperial War (1542–44), for although Sturm and his colleagues wanted to refuse taxes voted by the Diet of 1544, Sturm warned that "you can imagine how it would fuel the charges of those who are already crying that we are good Frenchmen."[86] Sturm tried to arrange for Strasbourg to pay secretly, "but without the damages to Strasbourg and the land of Alsace, which will surely follow from our consent [to the taxes]" or even to pay taxes against the Turks but not against France.[87] This war, he thought, "would be most burdensome and damaging to Strasbourg and to Alsace; for because they lie so close to France, on which they nearly border, they not only trade in France but gain a good part of their livelihood from Lorraine." Indeed, there is evidence that by the 1530s and 1540s the growth of Strasbourg's trade in Lorraine and France had become an important consideration in the city's foreign policy, not least because a number of weighty men in local government were among those engaged in France.[88]

Sturm's comments reflected Strasbourg's strategic importance, a combination of strength and position, which formed a constant thread in calculations about the city, by its own magistrates or by others. Perhaps Jacob Sturm was incautious in 1529, when his cousin, Daniel Mieg, was excluded from the Governing Council, and Sturm told a plenary session of the Imperial Diet that "for some time the king of France has wanted to treat with us and has offered us an annual subsidy of several thousand crowns."[89] He may have said that, and he may also have said at Nuremberg in 1543, as Duke Henry of Brunswick-Wolfenbüttel charged, that "the French king is a good lord and chief to me."[90] It may have been, too, as Jacob Sturm complained, that his reputation for Francophilia arose from the widespread confusion, based on the common surname, of him with the elegant, well-connected rector of the Latin school, Jean Sturm. "Yes," Jacob Sturm once sighed, "I, too, am suspected by many, because of my name, as though I were the other Sturm. Even Lord Granvelle said to me privately that the emperor himself suspected me until he was informed that there are two Sturms at Strasbourg."[91] There was plenty of confusion about that, for even Landgrave Philip sometimes confused the two Sturms.[92] Jean Sturm and Johann Sleidan, both natives of the northern Eifel region, had studied at Liège, Louvain, and Paris, where they joined the entourage of Cardinal Jean du Bellay, who headed the anti-Habsburg party at the French court, and whose brother, Guillaume, was long the chief French agent in the Empire.[93] Jean Sturm admired the French monarchy more than any other political institution of his time, he worked long and hard to keep Cardinal du Bellay informed about German affairs and the Smalkaldeners about French affairs, and he labored doggedly to get French backing for the allies during the Smalkaldic War in 1546. He was not a fanatic Francophile, however, and in 1555, believing that the king of France had become "too powerful a neighbor" to Strasbourg, he changed sides and became an Imperial agent.[94] During Jacob Sturm's lifetime, however, Jean Sturm received a French pension and performed a vital brokerage role that made Strasbourg the Smalkaldeners' vital window on the West, the one place where French-speaking diplomats, interpreters, and scholars could always be recruited.[95]

It is easy, because of the very real confusion that reigned about the two

Sturms, to dismiss Jacob Sturm's notoriety for holding the French card in Imperial politics. After all, even Charles V admitted his error and praised Sturm for his "obstinacy against the French."[96] The truth is rather more complex. Jacob Sturm did not speak French, nor does there exist any evidence of his sympathy for the king, the country, or its culture.[97] What is certain, however, is that by the mid-1530s Sturm recognized that the king of France could play an important role in the future of German Protestantism, the Smalkaldic League, and Strasbourg. The building of the entire network at Strasbourg, which gave the Smalkaldeners access to intelligence about France, the French court, and French policy, was his construction. He began to build by 1536, for on 4 June of that year, Guillaume du Bellay wrote from Chalons to his brother, the cardinal, that he could be contacted either at Metz or "at Strasbourg at Sturm's place [*ou à Strasbourg chez Sturmius*]."[98] This can only be Jacob Sturm, of course, for Jean Sturm, who is mentioned earlier in the letter, did not come to Strasbourg until 1538, and it means that the chief French agent in the Empire at least collected his post, and perhaps lodged, at Jacob Sturm's home in Strasbourg's Fire Street. From this it is not hard to understand how Jacob Sturm brought two of the cardinal's young German agents, Jean Sturm and Johann Sleidan, to Strasbourg, where they became two of the Smalkaldic League's chief agents in French affairs.[99] The other two were also strangers, and they were both physicians: the Pforzheimer Ulrich Geiger and the Messin Johann Niedbruck, whose daughter married Sleidan.[100]

Why did Jacob Sturm build this group during the second half of the 1530s? Several years earlier, the French king had sought to build a permanent alliance system in the Empire, based on reconciliation of the Protestants with the Catholics. This policy ended at the league's diet at Smalkalden in 1535, when the allies rebuffed Guillaume du Bellay's overtures, largely because of the king's persecution of the French Evangelicals.[101] The Strasbourg preachers, hoping for a great future for their religion in France, collaborated with du Bellay's policy.[102] This collaboration did not cease until the end of 1535, after the league's diet rebuffed Langey, but by then the decisive event, the "affair of placards," was already a year in the past. The royal persecution of Evangelicals in France let loose a flood of anti-German feeling and indiscriminate lumping together of all shades of dissent.[103] An unfortunate Flemish merchant was lynched by a Parisian crowd with the cry, "He is a German! His death will gain us indulgences!"[104] Langey and the king's other agents, naturally, tried to soothe the German Protestants with assurances that only rebels were being suppressed, and if Bucer accepted this explanation, as he said he did in an opinion for the king, others did not.[105] The first religious exiles from France arrived at Strasbourg in 1535, and by 1538 there were so many that the Senate & XXI decided to give them a church, to which John Calvin was called as pastor.[106]

Sturm and his colleagues were well informed about events in France, initially via Basel, as the Swiss had very good intelligence there, later through their own agents and the French exiles at Strasbourg. Jacob Sturm, for example, knew by February 1535 that the Evangelicals were being persecuted in France and that despite Langey's excuses, "we nonetheless see what his king intends."[107] The persecutions in France destroyed any possibility of a meeting of minds on religion and fixed a permanent mortgage of mistrust on the league's relations with France. The Ulmers summed up this feeling vividly in 1538:

> The allies, and especially the cities, ought to remember why we made the alliance [in 1531] . . .; it was for God's Word and honor and our souls' salvation, and not for anything worldly [zeitlichs]. Should we now include worldly matters and ally with this king, who martyrs, persecutes, and expropriates his own people and subjects on account of godly doctrine, the same that we Christian powers hold to be right and true? What is more terrible, he has made himself the common foe [of Christendom] by allying with the Turk. His troops and galleys aid the Sultan, . . . who this year alone has carried off 100,000 Christians to be murdered, brutally slain, and killed.[108]

The Ulm politicians may well have expressed the common view of German Protestants about the French king, but Ulm was far from the French border, and Strasbourg was not. Yet as important as French policy was to Strasbourg, there was never any hope of a real understanding. When, for example, a new French embassy came to Worms in November 1540 to resume the cardinal's courtship of the German Protestants, Jacob Sturm told the Saxons that although the new envoy was a relative of the deceased Langey, he was also a Catholic who should not be trusted. The Saxons were really in the dark, as Chancellor Franz Burckhardt wrote to his master, the elector, that "we have no way of knowing whether Cardinal du Bellay actually regards religion and the honor, welfare, and good of the German nation so, as this envoy alleges." Sturm, their informant, assured them that the cardinal "is well disposed to the gospel," but he did not cease to spread word among the Smalkaldeners of the plight of the French Evangelicals.[109] These events illustrate both Sturm's role in the links between the league and the anti-Imperial faction in Paris, and also the ambivalent place that the French king held in his political thinking.

His French sources also kept Sturm well informed during these years about the factional infighting at the French court. Sturm drew his crew of agents from the familiars of Jean Cardinal du Bellay, the chief of the party at court that favored an anti-Habsburg foreign policy and religious reform—if not necessarily Lutheranism—for France. Against them stood a middling party headed by the constable, Anne de Montmorency, who "believed in a strong monarchy and was a conservative in religion," and another group even more strongly opposed to du Bellay.[110] One of the great differences between the French and English courts at this time is revealed by two events in the years 1540–41: Anne de Montmorency was brought down by the failure of the Franco-Imperial entente, but he lived to return to power in the palace revolution that followed the king's death; when Thomas Cromwell was brought down by the king's rejection of his religious policy and the failure of the German marriage, he paid with his life. At the French court, nothing ever seemed to be settled irrevocably, not least because the driving forces of French policy—the Franco-Imperial rivalry and the problem of a general council—lay outside the kingdom. There was always hope that the right word or the right pressure at the right place and time might alleviate, if not nullify, a bad policy.

The bad policy, from the point of view of the Smalkaldeners in general and Strasbourg in particular, was the French king's refusal to tolerate the Evangelicals, their worship, and the preaching of their gospel. No other motive explains the intense interest the Strasbourgeois took in French policy during the late 1530s, when relations between France and the Smalkaldic League stood at an ebb. In September 1539, for example, the XIII suggested to Landgrave Philip that the league send Dr. Niedbruck to Paris to plead for the persecuted brethren there, but neither the landgrave nor Elector John Frederick had any enthusiasm for such a move.[111] The most hopeful period in the last dozen years of King Francis's reign (1515–47) began in the summer of 1540, when the Franco-Imperial entente broke down and Montmorency fell from power, and ended when the league broke off negotiations in June 1541. The overtures this time came from Paris, and the common interest was the Cleves-Jülich affair, in which Duke William, the elector's brother-in-law, intended to secure his claim to the duchy of Gelderland against Habsburg resistance, and although William was not a Protestant, the Smalkaldic chiefs wanted to back his play.[112] The elector took the lead in the negotiations, hoping to draw the league after him, but Landgrave Philip proved difficult, for the new overtures from Paris coincided with the crisis over his bigamy.

At Strasbourg the new departure of 1540–41 found Jacob Sturm and his French experts ready. Already in January Sturm had prepared letters to be sent by the Smalkaldic chiefs to urge King Francis and Constable Montmorency not to renew the entente with the emperor except under conditions favorable to the German Protestants.[113] As Franco-Imperial relations cooled, Franco-Smalkaldic relations began to recover, and the Strasbourgeois were ready. On 19 May 1540, Langey wrote to Strasbourg that the king regretted his entente with the emperor.[114] Now began months of feverish work by Jacob Sturm, the preachers, and, above all, Cardinal du Bellay's former German secretary, Jean Sturm, and his current one, Johann Sleidan. Sleidan and his master sent no fewer than nine letters to Strasbourg within a month in the autumn of 1540, and in midsummer Sleidan himself—who was already passing news to the Strasbourgeois—came to the religious colloquy at Hagenau to talk to the Strasbourgeois.[115] Just at this time, however, appeared the first cloud on the horizon in the form of the initial rumors about the Hessian bigamy.[116] By autumn the cardinal was pressing through Sleidan, the two Sturms, and Bucer for an embassy from the league, for which Jacob Sturm recommended Dr. Ulrich Geiger, another of the cardinal's German clients, "who is known to the cardinal and friendly with Sleidan [*den Schledanum an der hand hett*], through whom, since Geiger does not speak French, he can discuss and handle things in Latin."[117]

Sturm continued to press for a Smalkaldic embassy to France at year's end and thought to flank the allies' resistance by means of a proposal to send envoys on behalf of the French Evangelicals.[118] Sturm's draft of the petition to King Francis contained a well-informed account of the Evangelicals' sufferings and an eloquent plea for ending them. This was as far as the matter got, for although John Frederick wanted the alliance, although the Strasbourgeois longed for an end to the persecutions, and although all German Protestants could take some hope from worsening Franco-Imperial relations, no one could move Landgrave Philip of Hesse away from his new and cozy relationship with Charles V. The landgrave was a bigamist, and for the sake of the emperor's favor, he scuttled the French alliance. "France," the Hessian prince groused, "has never given us anything, except for Duke Ulrich."[119] The new departure of 1540–41 was to be the last under King Francis. Soon, the Protestant princes rallied to the Fourth Franco-Imperial War, which terrified the Strasbourgeois.

From the league's standpoint, the most impressive part of this story is the operation of Jacob Sturm's team for French affairs. For about a decade, most of the threads of communications between the German Protestants and France ran through Strasbourg, mainly through his hands. Here the translating of documents was done, here the news was collected to be sent both ways, to the cardinal and to the Smalkaldic chiefs. To be sure, the specialization in French affairs did nothing good for Strasbourg's reputation at the Imperial court. Then, too, sometimes the team got out of hand, and the bullying treatment he received during the Imperial Diet of Speyer in 1544 broke Jacob Sturm's temper. "Both Jean Sturm and Dr. Ulrich Geiger are learned and loyal men, and both are dear to me," he wrote to his colleagues, "but I really think that they are doing things which I not only cannot praise, but which I think may damage themselves and our city."[120] Sturm told them of "the great hue and cry at the Imperial court" about how these two were always writing to France, "and that every Frenchman [who comes] comes to their houses, especially Jean Sturm's, and even lodges there." Sturm said that he was being warned every day about them, "for they are simply notorious and will have to pay for it." He had warned Jean Sturm and Geiger "enough times [*genugsam*]," and especially Jean Sturm, "that they must stop doing this—to little effect, I see or fear." He urged his colleagues to warn the two men formally, reminding them of their citizens' oath to obey, for if they would stop intriguing, the damage could be repaired. Jacob Sturm was afraid that an admonition might drive away Jean Sturm, "who has done our schools a lot of good and made them famous," and recommended that he be treated gently and be reminded that "since the French king allies with the Turks, it is not seemly that he or any other Christian should take the king's part." Should he respond that he acts "to promote the common liberty of the German nation and the true religion," he should be told that "the Lord God can accomplish this through other means rather than the king, who lives a godless life and supports the infidels, and who has caused all these wars." This letter reveals clearly enough the instrumental character of Jacob Sturm's engagement in the French enterprise, his distaste for the French king, whom he knew only by reputation, and his fear of the damage his French team was doing to the city's reputation and his own.

And yet, the French team showed its worth during the Smalkaldic War, when Jean Sturm and Johann Niedbruck traveled back and forth between France and England and the Empire, seeking to forge alliances and, in Sturm's case, to secure loans.[121] All to little avail, and when news came at the end of 1546 of the king's refusal to aid the Protestants, Jacob Sturm gave up, even though he made one last, desperate bid for French aid against, as he believed, the oncoming Imperial army.[122] It was far too late for that. The king's failing health, his ministers' disbelief in the emperor's will to make war and their overestimates of the league's military strength, and the corrosive effects of the king's Turkish alliance on his credibility, all played their parts.[123] But so, too, did the Smalkaldeners' rebuff to French overtures in 1541. One can speculate about how the Smalkaldic War would have gone, had Francis I sent an army toward the Rhine as his son did in 1552; one can just as well speculate, however, about what might have happened had the Smalkaldeners allied with France in 1541 to protect Cleves-Jülich in the Fourth Franco-Imperial War.

These are speculations. What is certain is the superb functioning of Jacob Sturm's French team during the Smalkaldic War. It was by far the best political network the Smalkaldeners ever possessed, and it was entirely built by Jacob Sturm. One has only to compare the management of the Smalkaldeners' French relations with their English relations, which, at least before 1545, operated out of the Saxon elector's regime, in order to appreciate Sturm's achievement. The elector's theologians were far superior to anyone the English could produce, but their diplomats were hardly up to the English level, which was not high, much less to that of the French. The one mission the Saxons sent to England, in 1538, was headed by Chancellor Burckhardt, and it contained no one who could speak English or knew much about English affairs. Sturm's French team, by contrast, mostly read, wrote, and spoke French, they enjoyed first-class connections at court, and Jean Sturm ran an intelligence-gathering operation second to none. Its operations were one of the Smalkaldic League's true successes.

THE LEAGUE'S POWER: IMPERIAL JUSTICE

The German Reformation was a struggle for faith; it was also a struggle for property. To a very great degree, the clergy lost the laity's respect—the precondition of the Reformation—through its accumulation of vast amounts of property, much of which was not turned to legitimate ecclesiastical purposes, such as supplying sacraments to the laity, supporting those who prayed for the whole church, and providing the poor with food, clothing, and shelter. This gave rise to the question, expressed by Johann Geiler from his pulpit at Strasbourg, "Why should [the clergy] have so much property? They have too much." Yes, Geiler sighed,

> many priests do have too much, but you shouldn't for that reason take it away. I don't know where it will end, if you start taking away from all who have too much. It would injure many people. If you took the priests' property, God knows, what would happen then.[124]

Within a few years of the moment when Jacob Sturm stood at Geiler's deathbed in 1510, there arose a movement to uncouple property and property relations from access to sacral power. This change not only helped to fuel the great movement of 1524–26 but also threatened the very foundations of governance in the Empire.

Ecclesiastical property, "the Achilles heel of the Evangelical free cities," drove them into the Smalkaldic League for protection against suits for restitution of clerical properties and rights.[125] The suits, called "reformation suits [Reformationsprozesse]," charged urban regimes and other rulers with expropriation of beneficed individuals and religious corporations, chiefly before the Imperial Chamber Court (Reichskammergericht). From very wobbly beginnings before 1500, this court had grown into a relatively effective capstone on the generally backward machinery of Imperial justice, and the Protestants could never ignore the writs and sentences pronounced by the presiding judge (Kammerrichter) and his fellow judges (Beisitzer) from the court's seat at Speyer.[126] When the court published the first such judgments against Constance and Ulm in 1531, it began a struggle that would end only at the emperor's suspension of the court in 1544. Among the suits, a fairly long list of which accumulated by 1532, when the Truce of Nuremberg first promised to suspend them, "it is pointless to distinguish secular from ecclesiastical or financial and political from theological points of view." Indeed, the very definition of "religious matters" lay at the heart of the struggle.[127]

Property lay at the heart of the politics of the German Reformation, because governance, the maintenance of law and order, rested on property, as did the possibility of reform, and resistance to reform, of the church since long before the Reformation era. To a far greater degree than in the free cities, the process of consolidation of authority and power in the territories during the late medieval era had thrust the princes more or less willingly into the regulation of the clergy and their property in consequence of the princes' assumption of the custody of their subjects religious common good.[128] The process proceeded on two levels. On the one hand, by extending and strengthening their protectorates over the abbeys, the princes also brought rural parishes, in many of which the pastorates were controlled by the abbeys, under their own custody. On the other hand, the desires to rationalize frag-mented ecclesiastical authority in their territories and to absorb the wealth of bishoprics prompted the princes to bring the nearest prince-bishoprics, a creation now five hundred years old, under their own control. The Evan-gelical movement massively accelerated this process by creating a new im-perative for weakening the clergy's authority and by substantially reducing its legitimacy. Everything conspired, therefore, to quicken the process of secularization, already well underway before the Reformation, into a torrent—until the Peasants' War. The rebels of 1525 widened the issue of property right, in a feudal society the foundation of all governance, to *all* property rights, lay as well as clerical. This situation created the Protestants' di-lemma about ecclesiastical property, for to the problem of secularization's illegality, which the Reformation movement merely inherited, it added the need for a standard of discrimination between property rights which the gospel protected and those from which it removed legitimacy. This standard was precisely the boundary between "religious" and "secular," and it was precisely the matter most in dispute. The civil courts, including the Impe-rial Chamber Court, claimed no authority to define such a distinction, and once the Protestants rejected the papal and episcopal jurisdictions, there was no court in the land, the authority of which all parties accepted, which could adjudicate disputes over ecclesiastical property.

This situation meant two things. On the one hand, it made the issue, incapable of resolution in law, an object of purely political negotiations among the emperor and the very confessional groupings of Imperial estates. On the other hand, it made secularization the subject of rough-and-ready solutions at the local level. Here, too, ownership was disputed. The par-ishes, for example, wanted the tithes repatriated, but how to decide to whom the property rights truly belonged? One answer was to apply a religious test based on the common good, although the advocacy of divine vs. human law by the rebels of 1525 lent such arguments a new and menacing po-tency. How this could work in practice may be illustrated by the following story from Württemberg.[129] The nobleman Hans Conrad von Tierberg had granted an annuity of forty florins a year from the parish of Ebingen, whose lay patron he was, to his brother, the former pastor. When challenged by the duke in 1535, Hans Conrad offered to sell the duke his rights "as inher-ited and purchased property." The Constance reformer Ambrosius Blarer, then active in the duchy's reformation, opined that the patron's property rights were secure, "so long as the holder installs in the benefice a man who is willing and able to accept the religion established by His Grace [Duke Ulrich]." Because the patron's brother was a Catholic, he had no right to the benefice, "since the subjects do not exist for the pastor's sake, but the pastor is appointed for their sake." The potentially revolutionary thrust of Blarer's opinion, which submits property rights to the test of true or false religion, lays bare the entire conflict created by the Evangelicals' need to redefine the relationship of property to religion. Whether called "godly law," "Christian common good," or simply "the gospel," the idea that God's will supersedes and breaks all human law contained the popular reformation's greatest energy. Luther tried to disable this energy by means of his doctrine of the "two kingdoms," which taught the division of life into two aspects, ruled by radically distinct, even incompatible, standards of divine and human justice. He ran headlong, however, against one of the age's deepest beliefs, that God, through the Bible, had established binding norms of social life. The Catholics, in their way, believed it, but so did, with greater energy, Zwingli, the Anabaptists, and almost all of the other radicals from Karlstadt to Melchior Hoffman. How to use this religious idea to justify expropriation of the Catholic clergy without empowering others to reject human law in the name of godly law?

This dilemma was not as difficult as it seemed. In the first place, no solution in principle was required where the rulers, as was often the case, had by tradition governed ecclesiastical property relations by virtue of their assumed custody of religious life, for the general Christian belief, that the properties were not "owned" by their possessors but were held justly so long as they were properly used, had legitimized such actions since long before the Protestant Reformation.[130] The massive appropriations of the Reformation era did, however, require legitimation in law, which the Protestant rulers expected to secure through direct negotiation with the emperor, who in return for their support in other matters was asked to suspend the suits against Protestant rulers before the Chamber Court. Such thinking led the Smalkaldic powers on 23 July 1532 to the Truce of Nuremberg, which gave them the emperor's secret promise to stay all suits "concerning the faith [den glauben belangend]."[131]

The bottomless ambiguity of this phrase, "concerning the faith [den glauben belangend]," nurtured the quarrel over suits for restitution that embittered confessional relations and constantly threatened the confessional peace between the Truce of Nuremberg in 1532 and the eventual disruption of the Chamber Court in 1543. A long historiographical tradition holds that the suits were skirmishes in a "legal war [rechtlicher Krieg]" against the Protestant powers after the Diet of Augsburg, and that the Chamber Court's failure to suspend all such suits after 1532 validated the Protestants' charge that the court's Catholic majority, acting out of pure religious prejudice, was responsible for the court's fate. The modern literature entirely undermines this tradition. The private records, which survive from three of the court's judges during the 1530s, lend no credence to the charges of systematic subordination of justice to religious prejudice against the Protestant powers.[132]

The judges tended to be more or less hard on alleged violators of clerical rights, it is true, according to their religious loyalties, but even more influential on their voting behavior—verdicts were handed down collegially—were the interests of those who nominated them to the court, including the emperor, the electors, and the princes who dominated the various Imperial Circles. Their argumentation rested on the Roman law, the *ius commune*, with its many points of interface with the canon law—the judges were mostly doctors of "both laws [*utriusque iure*]"—and it recognized that strictly religious matters, such as changes in liturgy and preaching, doubtfully fell under the purview of the Chamber Court and its strictly civil competence.[133] The court heard, among many other kinds of cases, however, suits against alleged violations of clerical property rights, and not just against Protestant defendants. The tempo of such cases quickened, naturally, after 1530, and although the Chamber Court asserted jurisdiction in most of them, no fixed factions, on religious or any other grounds, formed in the court during this decade.[134] In such cases, at least during the 1530s, the judges proceeded much as they had done before the Diet of Augsburg and the Truce of Nuremberg, and left most purely ecclesiastical matters to the territorial rulers.

What, then, was the basis of the long Protestant campaign against the Chamber Court that led to its suspension in 1543? Was it conjured out of thin air? By no means, for the Protestants believed that a higher law, God's law, permitted them to do what was clearly illegal and punishable by human law, and in order to escape the predictable punishments for such acts, they had to widen the scope of "the faith" as much as possible. The desire to escape penalties for their illegal actions drove them to interpret the Christian faith in their understanding as a kind of higher law, a step that smacked of radicalism in the generation of Müntzer and Münster. That they did it at all shows how clearly they understood the necessity of their illegality to the survival of their faith. Their campaign against the old legality, embodied in and administered by the Chamber Court, developed in two stages. In the first they claimed that matters "concerning the faith" covered all rights and properties of all clergy, while later on, frustrated by the court's obstinate rejection of this innovation, they claimed that Catholic judges could not judge Protestant defendants in any kind of case. The mere existence of a difference in religion, in this more extreme argument, made all suits into matters "concerning religion."

The initial impulse in this campaign to alter the existing legal distinction between religious and secular affairs came from the city of Strasbourg, which had been cited before the Chamber Court by the bishop of Strasbourg for the illegal razing of a monastery and alienation of clerical incomes.[135] The suit came up for hearing just at the time when the emperor forwarded the Truce of Nuremberg to the court, and Strasbourg's magistrates, who had already in September 1532 proposed that the Protestants hire a common solicitor at Speyer, began to discuss the radical idea of recusing—declaring incompetent because of religious bias—some of the Chamber Court's judges.[136] It took two years of argument, and a good many more suits, to bring the Smalkaldeners around to Strasbourg's point of view. At Smalkalden in June 1533, the League's members divided over whether, given the permissibility of recusation, it was advisable.[137]

Already, bolder voices were sounding, and Landgrave Philip led the general attack on the Chamber Court "in all matters and not just in religious ones."[138] It was impossible, he thought, for the court and the league to agree on a definition of a "religious matter." He also wanted to recuse the entire judicial bench, not just the judges suspected of partisanship. The Strasbourgeois, pioneers of recusation, now pulled back and advocated the recusation of individual judges, not of the entire court, and in religious matters alone.[139] The other urban members supported limited recusation, which held the day against the wishes of the two Smalkaldic chiefs.

The act of recusation (Rekusationslibell), which the league's agents submitted at Speyer on 30 January 1534, marked an important stage in the Smalkaldeners' campaign against the Imperial Chamber Court.[140] In 1529 the Protestants had opposed the handling of religion by the Imperial Diet; now they opposed its treatment by the Imperial courts. Although they still claimed in principle to recognize the jurisdiction of "a general, free, Christian council" over "faith, ceremonies, and all that pertains to them," in practice they could only delegate that jurisdiction to the league—an unlikely step—or confirm it in the hands of the Protestant rulers and magistrates. At Strasbourg in 1534, when the Senate & XXI crushed the sects, the government had already assumed the authority to define doctrine and regulate the church in every respect.

Jacob Sturm had played an important role in the organization of the Protestants' legal representation before the Chamber Court, and he participated in all stages of the league's campaign against the court.[141] He was not above retailing useful gossip. At the end of 1541, for example, he sent Landgrave Philip an account of the judges and their behavior and asked that it be forwarded to the Saxon elector as well.[142] This was very likely the long, juicy tract by one "Theophilus," who described the Chamber Court as groaning in the grip of a "Swabian conspiracy," mostly refugees from the fallen Habsburg regime at Stuttgart.[143]

Of the several reasons for Sturm's and Strasbourg's antipathy for the Chamber Court during the late 1530s, the most pressing was a suit brought by Count Philip IV of Hanau-Lichtenberg against the city. Its subject was the sort of quarrel that frequently occurred when cities admitted the subjects of neighboring lords to citizenship. This case began in 1526, when Jörg Harder of Eckbrechtsweiler ran off to Strasbourg and became a citizen.[144] Home on a visit, he was picked up and incarcerated in Castle Willstätt by the count's bailiff, whereupon Strasbourg's magistrates sent the militia to liberate him. Over the Rhine Bridge they came, eighty horse, six hundred foot, and eight cannon under the command of Daniel Mieg, Bernhard Ottfriedrich, and Jacob Meyer. At Willstätt they found Harder already at liberty, and after shooting up the count's dovecote and liberating some wine, they took him back to Strasbourg. This afternoon's tramp, the last campaign ever for Strasbourg's guild militia, infuriated the count, who launched a suit that lasted for nearly twenty years, until 1545. Its high point came on 26 September 1537, when the Chamber Court condemned Strasbourg to a fine of fifty gold marks, whereupon the Senate & XXI tried to get the Smalkaldic League to recognize it as a "religious matter." They spread around a good bit of money for legal consultations and took the unusual step of sending printed versions of the suit's acts to the princely chancelleries as a form of propaganda for their case.[145] The reasoning, that any suit decided by a Catholic majority of judges was ipso facto a "religious matter," fooled no one, for, as a Hamburg jurist said in his opinion for the Smalkaldic League,

> the Strasbourg case in not a religious matter and belongs to the civil jurisdiction. . . . Should it be accepted without grounds as a religious matter, that would be more harmful than helpful and would also violate conscience. It would also give the impression that we want to intermingle temporal matters with religion.[146]

The duke of Württemberg's jurists went even further and denied Strasbourg's allegation of a right to recuse the court on the basis of "common law," that is, Roman law, or out of fear of future prejudicial treatment, for otherwise, any judge might be recused for any cause, and the Chamber Court would be destroyed.[147] Strasbourg's magistrates were now hoisted by their own petard, for in 1534 they had argued, against the landgrave, for partial instead of general recusation, whereas now, faced by the Hanau-Lichtenberg suit, they veered to general recusation.[148] Indeed, how reckless the Strasbourgeois had become is illustrated by another case they brought to the league as a prospective "religious matter." This was a quite standard dispute with Bishop William of Strasbourg over his subject, one Martins Hans Steffan of Molsheim, who secured citizenship at Strasbourg and claimed, on this basis, exemption from episcopal taxes on his properties at Molsheim.[149] This case confirms that magistrates at this time took the radical position that difference of religion invalidated all judicial acts across confessional lines.

The Smalkaldic League, though it was moving toward general recusation, did not recognize the Hanau-Lichtenberg case as a "religious matter" in 1538. It rejected, too, other suits brought forward for recognition, but the difficulty of deciding for or against recognition doubtless increased the pressure for general recusation. On the other hand, the Truce of Frankfurt (1539), the colloquies on religion, and the landgrave's bigamy slowed the league's movement toward this policy, even though the list of restitution suits and judgments continued to mount year by year.[150] The Reformation's advance in North Germany nonetheless kept the league and court at loggerheads.

The first sentence of outlawry, against Minden on 9 October 1539, might have brought war but instead led to the Truce of Frankfurt.[151] Similar processes against Goslar and Bremen, however, split the allies into two camps, Strasbourg and the commanders for recognition and the majority against.[152]

Strasbourg's militancy against the court was fanned by a new suit on behalf of the local Carthusian monastery.[153] Its origins closely resembled those of the suits on behalf of St. Arbogast's, a house of Augustinian canons, which the Senate & XXI had destroyed with ruthless force in December 1530.[154] Despite the Carthusians' reputation for discipline and charity, the custodians (*Pfleger*) installed in 1525, Daniel Mieg and Egenolf Röder von Diersburg, drove out most of the monks and suppressed the house's worship. When the prior died in 1540, the zealous Mieg drove the remaining monks from their cells, seized their convent's properties, and proposed on military grounds that it be razed.[155] While the Senate & XXI vacillated— the two earlier cases had made them wise, or at least wary—the Chamber Court issued a writ forbidding them to interfere further in the Carthusians' affairs on pain of outlawry (*Acht*). There remained the Hanau-Lichtenberg case, which continued to stir up wrath at Strasbourg, where the regime printed and distributed its case against the court and its judgment in this case.[156] Now was the time for action, and in early summer 1539 the regime printed and distributed its protest against the Chamber Court. During the Imperial Diet of Regensburg in 1541, Jacob Sturm and Batt von Duntzenheim petitioned Charles V to nullify the whole case under the terms of the Truces of Nuremberg and Frankfurt.[157] As the Smalkaldeners were threatening to boycott the Diet over the same issue, Charles gave in and ordered suspension of this and other suits, including the one against Strasbourg on behalf of St. Stephan's. Political pressure, plus Bishop William's death in 1541, also neutralized the Carthusian order's resistance, and soon the community was dissolved and its buildings razed. The whole affair proved the effectiveness of political pressure and negotiations against the judicial system the Protestants could not conquer. The lesson was especially welcome to the Strasbourgeois, who had always displayed indifference to the legal issues, perhaps because their own reformation had involved so much illegality.[158] The Smalkaldic League, not the law, made Strasbourg in 1541 a "de facto victor over its plaintiffs and also over the Chamber Court itself."[159]

Although the emperor's Regensburg Declaration of 28 January 1541, which suspended the suits, dampened the southern cities' eagerness for further action against the Chamber Court, events in the North kept the kettle aboil. The Chamber Court's outlawry of Goslar on 25 October 1540 brought the fateful issue—what was a "religious matter"?—once more on the league's agenda, and Strasbourg initially supported the southern allies against the northerners, who wanted a commitment to defend the city.[160] But then the Carthusian case weighed in, and Strasbourg sent Michel Han to Esslingen to urge the southern Smalkaldic cities to support Goslar, "for although in principle and origin the matters, on which the judgment and decree of outlawry are based, are neither religious matters nor do they derive from such matters, it is nevertheless clear to any honorable person of intelligence," that the severity of Goslar's punishment arose solely from the Chamber Court's hatred for Evangelical religion.[161] The league's vote on 18 July 1541 to recognize Goslar's case as a "religious matter," though it patently was no such thing, proved to be just what the southerners' had feared, an enabling act for the Smalkaldic chiefs' strike against Goslar's main enemy, Duke Henry of Brunswick-Wolfenbüttel.[162]

The invasion of Brunswick-Wolfenbüttel in September 1542 gave the final impulse toward the league's general recusation of the Chamber Court. When the league's diet assembled at Schweinfurt in early November, the connection between the invasion and total recusation was clear to all, for only general recusation could block the invasion's legal consequences. The southerners gave way under pressure from Strasbourg, Hesse, and Saxony, and the league decided to declare why, in Gregor Brück's words, "we do not recognize the Chamber Court, in its present constitution, as a valid judicial instance."[163] Speaking on behalf of all Protestant powers, the league thus withdrew recognition from the Empire's highest judicial body until it should be "reformed," that is, until its Catholic complexion should be altered through replacement of judges.[164] This completed the political disruption of the court and led to its suspension from 1543 until 1548, when the emperor's victory over the Protestants allowed its reinstatement.[165] Now came the final fruit of the Protestants' victory: at the Imperial Diet of Speyer in 1544, they received recognition, initially temporary, of all their property claims in Imperial law.[166]

The suspension of the Empire's highest court of justice, the German Protestants' deepest impact on the structure of the Holy Roman Empire, has no parallel in the reformations of other European lands. Neither in England nor in France, nor in any other country, did the Protestants secure toleration by their own efforts, without or in opposition to the monarchy. The successful Protestant recusation of the Chamber Court in 1543 formed a kind of de facto recognition of their right to exist, and of the Empire as a kingdom with two religions, twelve years before the Peace of Augsburg wrote this principle into Imperial law in 1555. On the other hand, the recusation also offered the Protestants an opportunity, which they did not take, to develop their own administration of justice, based on their understanding of the gospel and its implications for the deployment of church property, and, ultimately, to reconstruct together the form of the church itself. Had they taken this step, the Smalkaldic League would truly have become the vanguard and model for a reformed Empire based on reformed religion. Their unwillingness to seize this opportunity reveals with utmost clarity the limits of German Protestantism's power to transform the Empire. Among the reasons for this unwillingness, the debate over ecclesiastical property took a prominent place.

THE LEAGUE'S LIMITS: ECCLESIASTICAL PROPERTY

In a world in which governance rested directly on property rights, the successful transfer of ecclesiastical properties to Protestant rulers preempted discussion of how the church should be reorganized. The foundations of the Protestant solution, the territorial (or magisterial) control of the church, had been laid by orthodox Catholics long before Martin Luther's entry onto the Imperial stage. Emperor Frederick III had only voiced what most rulers believed, when he said of the Austrian clergy, "What the priests have, belongs to us."[167] This development took a great lurch forward with the Protestant rulers' massive invasion of clerical property rights, redeployment of many benefices to pastoral, educational, and caritative purposes under governmental control, and secularization of whole bishoprics. They benefitted from the feeling, shared by many Catholics and nearly all Protestants, that the benefice system had to be reformed, because, in Geiler's words, "the priests have too much." It was unclear at the start, however, in what directions this great redeployment of property would flow, toward the service of the people or the profit of the rulers, but the question was practically settled by the emergence of civic regimes and princes as the chief guardians of Evangelical religion and agents of its advance. This is why the question of a common Protestant church ordinance, in principle a natural counterpart to the common confession of faith, never underwent a serious debate. It did come on the agenda very early at Smalkalden in December 1530, where the new allies discussed the formulation of a common order of worship and decided that theologians should meet to draft a common church constitution for the Protestant lands. This never happened. The theologians thought the time inappropriate, other impediments appeared, and only the Nurembergers and Margrave George of Brandenburg-Ansbach raised the call for a general Protestant synod.[168] These two powers practiced what they preached, for not only did they stay out of the Smalkaldic League, in 1533 they issued a common ecclesiastical constitution—a unique example of what they espoused for all of Protestant Germany.[169]

The Smalkaldeners took another route toward territorial and civic churches, and the wave of new reformations and church organizations in the mid-1530s sparked a debate, beginning in 1537–38, about how the old church's patrimony should serve the new.[170] Some free cities, notably Constance and Strasbourg, had taken control of convents and expropriated foreign benefice holders in the 1520s, and they paid for their boldness with restitution suits. In the main, however, the urban regimes began to invade clerical property rights during the mid-1530s, and in the main their behavior was correct if not legal, that is, ecclesiastical assets were turned to pastoral, caritative, and educational tasks.[171] This is not to say that individuals did not enrich themselves out of the urban reformation. In the 1520s at Strasbourg, for example, later the purest of the pure in these matters, at least one powerful politician, Ammeister Claus Kniebis, had done very well for himself and his dependents during the suppression of the mendicant women's houses.[172] Some civic regimes did use ecclesiastical assets to cover current expenses, but in the main the Protestant urban magistrates were fastidious about property matters, at least compared to the Protestant princes.

Partly from their feudal rights of patronage and protection (*Schutz und Schirm*) over religious establishments, sometimes from a sincere concern for monastic reform, the territorial princes had long become accustomed to managing the church's assets. The Reformation gave them a much freer hand, and probably they profited far more from the Reformation than used to be thought. Landgrave Philip, for example, early laid hands on the great Hessian abbeys' lands and revenues, so that "overall the lion's share of the church lands probably passed through [his] hands."[173] In the lands of the other Smalkaldic chief, Ernestine Saxony, some lands were sold for the elector's benefit or incorporated into his domain, others were sold to nobles and officials on favorable terms, and more went to cover the electoral debt than to support the clergy, schools, university, or the poor. In Württemberg, where the clergy's possession of about one-third of the duchy's land brought them incomes twice those of the duke, expropriation was irresistible, especially to someone of Ulrich's temperament, and the Reformation brought "the most extensive seizure anywhere of all forms of church property." Ulrich was nothing if not direct, and he "did more openly and on a grander scale what other Protestant rulers often practised while claiming greater disinterestedness." The story was much the same in the Protestant territories of North Germany, though here the process took longer, and the absorption of even greater prizes—the dozen or so bishoprics of the Northeast—mostly occurred after 1555.[174]

The broad divergences between the cities' and the princes' handling of the old church's patrimony reflected deep incompatibilities between burghers' and princes' attitudes toward government and property. To the burghers, the issue turned on the proper use of the clergy's property, which the Reformation rescued from mismanagement and made available for pastoral care, training the clergy, and feeding the poor. Greed there was aplenty in the town halls, but the burghers had long struggled to establish a civic ethic based on the idea of the common good, whereby magistrates served the community rather than themselves, their kinsmen, and their friends. To the princes, by contrast, dynastic welfare *defined* the common good, and property rights had to be seen accordingly. The point is illustrated very neatly by a Saxon official's reply in 1546 to a question from the Magdeburgers about how they should treat the Catholic clergy. "Dear sirs," he replied, "you burghers are too punctilious, and you should take your examples from other towns. Don't ask, for it is better to act than to ask. Indisputably, the priests are all our enemies, so just grab. If you get something, you have it and can keep it."[175] This advice reflected, perhaps, the experience in Brunswick-

Wolfenbüttel, where the Protestant occupiers plundered the church so mercilessly that Luther, who had greeted the invasion as "a truly godly victory," later moaned "that our people's will to plunder is so great that the inhabitants will soon long to have their old duke back."[176]

The property issue began to loom larger in June 1536, when Pope Paul III called a general council to Mantua for May 1537, but it became pressing during the league's diet at Smalkalden in February 1537, where Imperial Vice-Chancellor Matthias Held appeared to warn the Protestants to attend the council and to stop their depredations on the church's substance. Although the league rejected the papal council, from which, in the words of Strasbourg, "nothing could be hoped for the church's improvement," some members felt compelled to reply to Held's charges that they were "church robbers."[177] The Protestant theologians, now given their first opportunity to discuss the issue, painted a dark picture of Protestant practice, though they named no names. Based on their opinions, the league named five legitimate uses of ecclesiastical property: pastors and other parish officials, superintendents and other church officers, schools, impoverished students of theology, and hospitals. From this point forward, the property question occupied a place on the diet's agenda for five sessions between February 1537 and April 1540.[178]

From Strasbourg came both the instigation to debate the property issue and the strongest voice for the burghers' view that the church's property must serve the church's purposes. The main discussion occurred in the summer of 1538 at Eisenach, whither came Jacob Sturm and Batt von Duntzenheim with powers to conclude "as may seem appropriate [nach gelegenheit der sachen]" on this issue.[179] This important assembly—more than twenty cities and most of the princes sent envoys—met as the Empire approached the gravest internal crisis of the decade, and although little was done about the property question, Sturm did submit Martin Bucer's lengthy memorial on the subject, which was to play an important role in the subsequent debate.[180] Bucer presented the case that the church's properties must remain with the church, so that "no emperor, king, bishop, pope, or any human can transfer them or alienate them from the church, except to give them to other churches, to monasteries, or to civil uses."[181] Beyond the three legitimate uses—the clergy, the churches, and the poor—he held any other use to be "the worst sort of robbery of the church." The lay rulers might administer the church's property, but they had no right to any part of it, though Bucer allowed that in some cases surpluses might be used to protect the land against the Turks and other pious purposes. The document's cool reception by Johann Feige, the Hessian chancellor, with whom Sturm discussed it at Eisenach, suggested how the princes were going to receive it. The cities had even worse in store for them, for Augsburg's preachers condemned all non-ecclesiastical use of ecclesiastical property.[182]

The fronts formed on the property issue in 1539, after the Truce of Frankfurt eased the political crisis. On the one side, for the princes' right, positions ranged from the extreme view of Duke Ulrich to the moderate one of the Hessian landgrave, with Elector John Frederick in the middle.[183] On the other side, for the church's right, stood the southern Smalkaldic cities, whose regimes more or less supported Bucer. The test of strength came not at Arnstadt in the autumn of 1539, "for the reason," Duntzenheim reported, "that not all the allies have supplied powers to make a binding decision this time," but at Smalkalden the following March.[184] The discussion opened on 13 March with declarations on behalf of the most avid secularizers, Duke Ulrich and the Pomeranians. In reply Sturm declared that his government "took nothing for its own treasury but solely to support the ministers, the schools, and all with the consent of the convents' inmates." Many evil tongues, he warned, were whispering that the Protestants "only assumed this faith for the sake of the clerical properties, and once those are in hand, we'll believe what we please. Therefore, in order to still this charge, there should be a Christian investigation of the distribution of church properties." The other southern burghers provided a refrain to Sturm's song. Then the Hessian and Saxon envoys declared that their chiefs "would tolerate everything that is Christian, fair, and honorable" and proposed that a committee be formed. This discussion faded away after 29 March when many princes arrived in person at Smalkalden, but the theologians did produce a statement—a moderate one by Philip Melanchthon, which Bucer signed—and it was incorporated into the diet's recess.[185] The statement approved the rulers' seizures of the properties and declared—against Bucer's and the Augsburgers' view—that once the churches and schools were provided for, the rulers as "patrons [*patroni*]" might turn the surplus to their own needs. The princes had their way, Sturm said nothing.[186]

The recess of Smalkalden in April 1540 ended the league's continuous debate on property. After the Regensburg Declaration of January 1541 accepted the seizures and secularizations to date but forbade any further changes before the general council, the Protestant princes began to push the issue aside. This angered the league's urban members, for at the same time that Landgrave Philip and the others took this stance, the Saxon elector was laying hands on a whole bishopric, Naumburg.[187] This development put Martin Bucer in a peculiar position, for he had foreseen as early as 1539 that the property question, which had begun with convents, tithes, and rents, would culminate in a struggle for the biggest prizes of all, the prince-bishoprics. In a pamphlet he published pseudonymously in the winter of 1539–40, Bucer advocated the laicization of the ecclesiastical states, but not their secularization by the lay princes. Instead, the bishop would be a lay ruler elected by the lay nobles of a reformed cathedral chapter. Not only would succulent states be turned to Protestantism without being swallowed up by the Protestant dynasties, but the conversion of the three clerical electorates would guarantee a Protestant on the Imperial throne.[188] This scheme illustrates Martin

Bucer's abiding naïveté, for he both urged the Protestant rulers to take the old church's substance and denied them the right to keep what they took. Firm in his faith in ultimate Protestant triumph, he thought there would be a general settlement on property for the entire Empire, Catholic as well as Protestant.[189] In 1543 Bucer even went so far as to argue that the Protestants must openly confess their abuses before the Imperial Diet, so as to cease giving refuge to "church robbers."[190] Jacob Sturm advanced the same view at Frankfurt in the winter of 1545–46, where he noted that many were angry "that the ecclesiastical properties are handled so selfishly and against the rules [canones] of the Holy Scripture," and he proposed that the league withhold military aid from any member who had committed such acts.[191] Once again a burgher tilted at princely windmills, and with predictable results, for the league decided to let each ruler decide for himself how much and to what purposes the "surplus" ecclesiastical assets might be used. It was the urban reformation's final defeat in the Smalkaldic League.

The history of the Smalkaldic League's treatment of ecclesiastical property lays bare its limits as a political organization. The league's decision to allow each ruler to decide for himself replicated the Imperial Diet's decision at Speyer in 1526, that each ruler should treat religion as his—not his subjects'—conscience dictated, but it contradicted the league's spiritual basis, conformity to the Confession of Augsburg. The Smalkaldeners' decision assured that the church could be reconstructed only as a mirror image of governance on a civic or territorial basis, for the issues of property and religion were inseparable.[192] That the Smalkaldeners' decision with respect to property— against a central and for a territorial/civic solution—was no accident is confirmed by its decision on another question, the case of the Evangelicals of Metz.

THE LEAGUE'S LIMITS: THE CASE OF METZ

When the Evangelicals of Metz applied for admission to the Smalkaldic League in 1542, they confronted the alliance once again with the conflict between its two political cultures, that of the burghers, among whom those who ruled at one time could be subjects at another, and that of the princes, among whom they could not. Was the league to remain an alliance of Imperial estates, or was it to become a community of German Protestants?

Although the Imperial free city of Metz had drifted from its Imperial ties during the later Middle Ages, after the accession of Charles V in 1519, this French-speaking city moved back toward the Empire, though always with a weather eye cocked toward the duke of Lorraine and the king of France.[193] Unlike Strasbourg, whose region lacked powerful rulers, Metz sat among great powers—Lorraine, France, and the Habsburg Netherlands. Also unlike Strasbourg, the city was ruled by patrician rentiers, and the ordinary Messins were not directly represented in the ruling council (Schöffenrat, conseil des échevins). The annually elected mayor (Schöffenmeister, maître-échevin) held more power than other free cities' mayors, including exclusive responsibility for external affairs. The city's politics were dominated by aristocratic factionalism, much like Strasbourg about 1400, and the clergy were numerous, wealthy, and powerful.

Although the Reformation movement of the 1520s touched Metz, the patricians turned against it after 1525.[194] Still, the regime kept in close touch with Imperial affairs, mainly through Strasbourg, and Jacob Sturm thought for a moment in 1528 that Metz could be recruited for a league of Evangelical cities.[195] The following year Sturm met at the urban Diet of Speyer a Messin with whom he would be involved for the rest of his life. This was Dr. Johann Niedbruck, known at home as Jean Bruno du Pont de Nied, a university-educated physician whom rumor held to be a bastard son of Count Johann Ludwig of Nassau-Saarbrücken.[196] From the autumn of 1538, Sturm had regular contact with Niedbruck, who was the closest thing to a free professional diplomat. He had represented Metz abroad since 1520, but when he came to Strasbourg in 1538, he was also serving Count William of Fürstenberg, and he subsequently accepted a retainer from Strasbourg, served the Imperial governor at Thionville/Diedenhofen, and received an appointment as agent for the Smalkaldic League in France. He continued all the while to serve Metz.[197]

The revival of Evangelical religion at Metz in the early 1540s brought the city to the Smalkaldeners' attention. When Charles V passed through the city in 1541 on his way to the Diet of Regensburg, Mayor Robert de Heu maintained the city in peace.[198] A local Dominican, Pierre Brully, however, trailed the emperor to Regensburg to ask the Smalkaldic League to press Metz's regime for freedom to preach the gospel there. And though the Smalkaldeners' letter to this effect had no success, the religious calm at Metz broke in the summer of 1542, as clouds gathered for another war against France, the fourth under Charles V. The new mayor of Metz, Gaspard de Heu, was both more militant and more vigorous than his predecessor and older brother, Robert.[199] He decided to force the issue of toleration for his religion, and in August 1542 he sent Johann Niedbruck and Jean Karchien, an Evangelical member of the XIII, to Strasbourg to ask for the Smalkaldeners' official aid for the Evangelicals at Metz and to ask how Metz might join the league.[200] From here they went to Kassel to seek, with the blessing of Strasbourg and Bucer, the landgrave's backing.[201] The landgrave, hot for action, proposed to Strasbourg that they send an embassy—he wanted Jacob Sturm to head it—to Metz to negotiate on behalf of the Evangelicals. He also wanted to cooperate with Count William of Fürstenberg, the mercenary general who had custody of the abbey of Gorze in the neighborhood of Metz, with whose Catholic magistrates he had a bitter feud.[202] Strasbourg's regime readily fell in with the plan and made preparations for the embassy.[203] The Smalkaldeners' embassy to Metz, which took shape at Strasbourg on 24 September 1542, consisted of Jacob Sturm, the Frankfurt attorney Hieronymus zum Lamm, and a Hessian official named Johann Kendel, whom the landgrave instructed to "support you [i.e., Sturm] in all decisions about what is to be done, since you know best the situation at Metz and how best to improve it."[204] Sturm, just returned from the Diet at Regensburg, did not want to go. But when Martin Betscholt, "who knows French," begged off on account of his gout, Sturm yielded to the entreaties of his colleagues and of Dr. Niedbruck.[205]

The situation Sturm found at Metz fully justified his reluctance.[206] A plague raged in the city, so that when the envoys arrived on 28 September, they lodged in a suburban inn and asked that their servants alone be allowed in the city. When this was allowed only after Mayor Heu's intervention, they must have known how things stood, and next day a group of Catholic notables accused Heu of having forced a way into the city for the Germans.[207] When the magistrates, having tried excuses, sent someone out to the envoys, Sturm said that they had come as friendly arbiters to ease Metz's dangerous division and as advocates to plead for the freedom of preaching and worship.[208] Fortunately, the Messins did not ask if the Strasbourgeois allowed freedom in such matters at home. Instead, they referred to the bishop's authority and the emperor's policy and warned that Smalkaldic pressure would only push Metz toward France.

When Sturm and his colleagues returned to Strasbourg with empty hands— they had never even set foot in Metz—they left behind a breaking storm.[209] Mayor Heu, emboldened by the foreign support, marched his party out of the city, the reformer Guillaume Farel at his side, to worship at his brother's castle at Montigny. Back at Metz, after an altercation at the gates, Heu confronted his enemies in the presence of envoys from Queen Mary, regent of the Netherlands. An opponent named Androuin Roussel pointed at Heu and exclaimed, "There is the man who wants to ruin this city with the new Lutheran sect!" "Liar," shouted Heu, "I would love to make Metz Evangelical, but you and your gang want to wrest Metz from the Empire and bring it into alien [i.e., French] hands."[210] Heu could not win this contest, for most of the Messins backed the Catholic magistrates, who were now supported by Queen Mary and Duke Antoine of Lorraine.

Just after Sturm's report on 9 October, Strasbourg's Senate & XXI wrote to warn Metz's regime against continued suppression of Evangelical religion and to plead that at least one church be made over to that party; on the same day Duke Antoine wrote to warn the Catholic Messins to hold firm.[211] A fresh plea to the Protestant powers by Heu and Niedbruck availed nothing, for the magistrates forbade Messins to attend Farel's sermons at Montigny and then, in mid-January, deposed Heu and banished him and the other Evangelical leaders. Foreign pressure against foreign pressure, Netherlands regime against Smalkaldic League, the Protestants had failed. The Evangelical Messins' great hope, admission to the Smalkaldic League, was all in vain, for as soon as the Saxon elector learned the lay of the land at Metz, he began to build the case against a direct Smalkaldic involvement there:

"In the city of Metz there are two parties, and they are not united but divided over doctrine. . . . Further, the other, papist, party in Metz is larger than the Schöffenmeister's party."[212]

Why did Strasbourg's regime intervene at Metz and advocate the admission of its Evangelicals to the league? The policy was not Jacob Sturm's, for it was formulated just after Dr. Niedbruck came to Strasbourg in August 1542, when Sturm was still attending the Imperial Diet at Nuremberg.[213] The interventionist policy, rather, bears the mark of Martin Bucer, whom the XIII may well have consulted, for their arguments show a common concern that intervention might be construed as connivance with subjects against their rightful rulers. The XIII, for example, admitted that the request for admission to the league was problematical, "because it comes not from the whole council [*rath*] or the whole commune [*gemain*], but perhaps only from a minority [*der geringer theil*]." Against this they alleged that Mayor Heu, an Evangelical, was "the city's true chief [*das recht haupt der stadt*]" and that "important, prestigious, honorable, and honest persons from the nobility and the commons" among the Evangelicals may be compared with their opponents "in substance [*gelegenhait*] if not in numbers." Bucer defined the latter point as the principle of the "sounder part [*sanior pars*]," which should prevail over the numerically larger but socially inferior part.[214] He was apparently less sensitive to the charge of sedition than were the XIII, who argued that they were not counselling disobedience, for the Evangelicals of Metz would "be obedient in all temporal and civil matters [*zeitlich und burgerliche gehorsame sie anbieten*]." Otherwise, they thought, "if the Devil, as is usually the case with clandestine preaching, should establish himself in the form of an Anabaptist or other seductive sect, Good Lord, how troublesome that would be!" Who should have known better than they, who had crushed the sects at home?

One does not have to associate the hard-fisted rulers of Strasbourg with the likes of Müntzer or the Münsterites to understand what they were about. Heu's request, as they realized, involved the admission of private persons, other rulers' subjects, to a federation of rulers—something they would never have tolerated at Strasbourg. Bucer tried to blunt this objection by pointing to the mayor's right "to represent the city of Metz in such matters" and by inventing the fiction that the league would admit not subjects but "the city of Metz in its better part [*in ihrem bessern theil*]." They made this argument not because they were revolutionaries, but because they unwisely believed Gaspard de Heu's assurance that once the Evangelicals got a free hand, Metz would turn Evangelical "within a month or two [*in einem monat oder zweien*]," as the XIII told the landgrave.[215] If, on the other hand, the Smalkaldeners failed to act, they would "violate the rule of love [*nachteil der lieb*] and cause the Catholics to rejoice and Metz perhaps to leave the Empire."[216] The Smalkaldic chiefs, as "some of the highest members of the Empire [*als von den hechsten glidern des reichs*]," could intervene at Metz and help keep it in the Empire. Then, once Metz was safely in the Protestant camp, "a large part of France, Brabant, Flanders, Luxembourg, and also Lorraine and Burgundy could be brought over by means of the common language [der sprachen halber]."

It was all a pipe dream, of course, for it rested on the highly colored picture of the situation at Metz, which Dr. Niedbruck conveyed to the Strasbourgeois, combined with a certain amount of wishful thinking. One can imagine the effect on the excitable Bucer of the news that

> it is clear that the free city of Metz, a very large commune of many thousand souls, who have been baptized in Christ's name, is oppressed by the other part of the regime and their gang in a most dangerous and unbearable way and against God and the right. And those are especially and most grievously aggrieved in their consciences, who already in part recognize Christ's gospel and thirst to know it fully.[217]

Thousands of souls who thirsted for the gospel were being oppressed by a tiny clique in city hall—perhaps Bucer projected on Metz his memory of events at Strasbourg in the 1520s. It did not fit Metz in 1542, as Jacob Sturm may have learned during his few days there late September.

At Wittenberg they clearly understood the recklessness of Strasbourg's policy of admitting Metz's Evangelicals to the league. Luther's immediate reply to the elector's request for an opinion was that he "doesn't know what to say about this business [Stuckwerk], for it is so peculiar [seltsam]."[218] To ally with part of a commune rather than with its regime, he and Melanchthon thought, was "strange and unusual." Passing over Strasbourg's argument about Heu being the head of the regime and Bucer's argument about the "sounder part," they denied that the Christian possessed, as the Strasbourgeois alleged, an unlimited obligation to assist his neighbor. As for the Christian's duty to risk things for the gospel's sake, that was up to "the rulers, as those who through God's grace understand these matters better and have more to do with them than we do."[219]

Whatever the Strasbourgeois and the landgrave wanted, without Elector John Frederick's backing, the case of Metz's admission to the Smalkaldic League was doomed, though its failure may perhaps be laid more to the political situation than to the dangerous principles behind Strasbourg's policy.[220] Once the Messins could not wait, their cause was doomed. When Mayor Heu came in January 1543 as a refugee to Nuremberg, where the Imperial Diet and the league were sitting, he bore a letter of recommendation to Jacob Sturm from Strasbourg. Here the Messins made their plea to be admitted to the Smalkaldic League.[221] The leaguers having heard Heu's desperate plea to protect his party by admitting them to the league, they referred the matter to a committee headed by Sturm. He drafted the committee's report, which sealed the Evangelical Messins' doom by recommending against their admission.[222] Sturm's report announced the league's support for the

gospel at Metz but also the Smalkaldeners' "weighty reasons and consideration [*treffennliche vrsachenn vnnd bedencken*]" why the Messins could not be
admitted to the league. For if the league intervened, the consequences would
be renewed persecution and an attempt by the Catholics to take Metz out
of the Empire. "It is to be hoped," Sturm wrote,

> that with Christian patience the matter will yield to Almighty God's
> daily strengthening and spread of His Word, so that proper worship will
> be established in the same form as is evident in many other places—
> more than can be grasped by human reason.[223]

This was the only hope, for

> it is not the practice of this Christian alliance to protect private persons
> [*sonndere personen*] for religious reasons against their rulers. It should also
> not be done in this case, for if the estates should do it, the Catholic
> party would doubtless also regard as legitimate to protect those of our
> subjects who adhere to the papist teachings and to defend their attach-
> ment to this same seductive doctrine against their own rulers. One dis-
> ruption would therefore cause another.[224]

Besides, Sturm pointed out, to accede to Heu's request would violate the
emperor's declaration made at Regensburg in 1541, which forbade any power
to aid the subjects of another ruler on religious grounds. That was all. The
Messins went away empty handed, assured of a future as exiles, to eat the
cold comfort of Sturm's counsel of patience—"patience conquers fortune."

More curious than Jacob Sturm's stance on the opposite side of the Metz
question from his regime is his own silence about it. His diary from the
Diet of Nuremberg does not mention the affair at all, but it is filled with
the burning question of what to do with Brunswick-Wolfenbüttel.[225] Back
home, however, the magistrates did what they could for the Evangelical
Messins: they sent two stettmeisters, Peter Sturm and Philips von Kageneck,
and Dr. Heinrich Kopp, a French-speaking attorney, to mediate the conflict. In vain, for their compromise, which would have permitted the
Evangelicals the use of one chapel at Metz, was scuttled by a bloody raid by
Lorraine troops on Gorze, where they had taken refuge with Count William
of Fürstenberg.[226] Seething with rage, William threw over his French royal
master and swore an oath of loyalty to the emperor—thereby depriving the
Evangelical Messins of their only local protector. He begged the landgrave
and Strasbourg for troops and artillery to attack Metz, but here the
Strasbourgeois drew the line.[227] Instead, they staged talks between the count
and Metz's regime in mid-May 1543 at Strasbourg, while the Messin refugees watched hungrily for a settlement.[228] It was not to be. The Smalkaldic
chiefs petitioned the French king, who denied any complicity in the violence at Gorze but sided with Metz's regime.[229] That was the end of it, for
the Smalkaldic princes had much larger fish to fry. With Cleves-Jülich
defeated, war against France imminent, and the league in turmoil over

Brunswick-Wolfenbüttel, a handful of Messins on the run was a very small affair. Most of them settled permanently at Strasbourg, and their chiefs, Gaspard de Heu, Jean Karchien, and Dr. Johann Niedbruck, took service with the Smalkaldic powers. By the end of 1543, the Metz affair was over.

What did the Metz affair mean to the Smalkaldic League? It presented the Smalkaldeners with a profound question about their league's very nature, for from the Messins' petition, one historian has written,

> arose the possibility to expand the league from a federation of Imperial estates into a political organization of all Protestants in the Empire. From it, too, arose the danger of intervening in the existing relations between rulers and ruled.[230]

The Strasbourgeois, even Sturm on occasion, tended to be reckless with arguments about legality—for example, when they blithely assumed the right of active resistance to the emperor or when they argued that all legal suits against Protestants were "religious" matters—but the other Smalkaldeners feared the principle of intervention, even for the gospel's sake, between ruler and subject. How, in that case, would the Smalkaldeners' actions differ from those of Müntzer and the other rebels of 1525?

The Metz affair thus illustrates how the revolution of 1525 had mortgaged the German Protestants' power to break old political relations and forge new ones. It offered the Smalkaldeners a clear opportunity to overstep the bounds of political association in the Empire by creating a political community based on a common faith. The advocates of admission—Strasbourg's XIII, Bucer, and Landgrave Philip—recognized the danger this principle posed in theory, but they also believed—falsely, as it happened—that intervention would produce a swift Evangelical triumph at Metz. There is no evidence that Jacob Sturm shared this illusion and circumstantial evidence that he did not. He surely mistrusted the role of Count William of Fürstenberg, whom he held to be

> a choleric [zorniger] lord, who is ever intent on his own advantage. He cares not for what anyone says to him and will tolerate anything, so long as he sees a way out. He doesn't care, so long as he gains his own advantage. Sir Jacob [Sturm] doesn't like to deal with him, for he can never get rid of him [konde sein nicht los werden], and he knows that the only way to be rid of the count is to say, "let me be!"[231]

Probably, too, Sturm recognized that his government's policy on behalf of Gaspard de Heu and the Evangelical Messins differed not a whit from what the Anabaptists had demanded in the early 1530s at Strasbourg. He surely had not forgotten Leupold Scharnschlager's mocking Tyrolean drawl.

There is another reason for Sturm's silence in the Metz affair: his growing conviction during the early 1540s that the Smalkaldic League required not greater willingness to take risks, but more regular and more centralized governance. His belief crystallized in response not so much to the Metz

affair as to the league's quarrel about Brunswick-Wolfenbüttel, but his reform program nonetheless reflects his entire experience of the league after
the Truce of Frankfurt.

STURM AS REFORMER OF THE LEAGUE

Periodically, over the years, Jacob Sturm drafted recommendations on how
the Smalkaldic League's affairs could be better and more efficiently conducted. In one of them, he suggested that the Protestant cause would benefit
if the princes would attend the Imperial Diet in person.[232] Sturm's concern
for reform of the league matured in 1545, when the fifteen-year-old league's
constitution was coming up for renewal.[233] He tried to guide the debate in
the league's diet that began at Frankfurt in the winter of 1545–46 and
continued at Worms in the spring. The league's failure to take action for
Cleves-Jülich, Metz, and Cologne, the landgrave's flirtation with the emperor, the princes' support for the Imperial wars and higher taxes for the
free cities, and the strident quarrel over Brunswick-Wolfenbüttel had sapped
much of the original sense of solidarity. It was a moment ripe for a new
concept, and Jacob Sturm, well aware that his entire grand policy lay in
the balance, agreed to go to Frankfurt, because "on the issues which will be
treated now depend our city's prosperity or ruin."[234]

Sturm was almost certainly the author of Strasbourg's plan to promote
the league's statelike qualities and greater fairness in its conduct of business.[235] Beginning with the administration of justice, Sturm wrote that members
must settle their conflicts not "with the deed" but through arbitration,
mandatory in religious cases and facultative in temporal ones, because Imperial justice no longer functioned. To this end, the league must decide
what constituted "religious matters," which in the Strasbourg view embraced
the usual matters—churches, schools, and hospitals—but also, and more
controversially, invasions of any ruler's or regime's rights of governance and
property "on account of religion." This would have thrust the league into
every dispute between parties of different religions, and it would presumably have given the Protestant rulers carte blanche with respect to ecclesiastical properties. In order to block such a construction, Sturm advocated
that any ruler who employed such properties for any but sanctioned ends
be denied the league's protection. "Many believe," he confessed, "that the
church properties have been handled selfishly and against what Biblical
principles ordain or allow, which could incur God's wrath and easily cause
much dissent and grievances among the allies, and dissuade others from
joining us on grounds of conscience."[236] It was a simple, impossible solution
to the league's most bedeviling issue.

Sturm next turned to the conduct of the league's affairs. He wanted to
establish a permanent executive commission, as in the old Swabian League,
or at least to have the diet meet regularly at Frankfurt, with its plentiful
inns, doctors, and druggists, instead of in provincial nests in remote Thuringia.

Smalkalden, which could be reached from Franconia, was bad enough, but small Arnstadt and Naumburg lay much farther eastward. None of them suited the southerners. "Food is very expensive in this land," Sturm once wrote from Arnstadt, "and the wine is very sour, so that our servants have fallen ill, and the meals are not cooked in our fashion."[237] The wine must have tasted like vinegar to an Alsatian palate, and perhaps Sturm had heard the Thuringian joke about the "three-man wine," which was so sour that two had to hold down the third man while he drank it.

Sturm proposed to redistribute the diet's votes on the basis of parity between cities and princes, with ties to be decided by lot, instead of by the six-to-seven minority position the cities currently held. He also wanted the power to decide for peace or war transferred to the diet from the war council, whose members were "such folk as think more of war than of peace, and who know least of all [am wenigsten] about the League's affairs."[238] A glance at Strasbourg's war councillor, Cousin Ulman Böcklin, amply confirmed this statement.

Government by burghers turned mostly on the management of money, and Sturm's reform proposals made much of the league's finance and taxation.[239] In the league, as in all mixed political federations, the urban envoys always complained that they were assessed too heavily and the princes and nobles too lightly. A fair share for Strasbourg, Sturm thought, would be about a quarter—instead of more than a third (36 percent)—of what the Saxon elector paid, or about as much as the larger northern cities "whose wealth is greater than Strasbourg's."[240] Although he would preserve the present, inequitable tax structure "rather than allow the league to be destroyed," Sturm nonetheless championed the Common Penny against the matricular system for the league, as he had for the Empire.[241] The Imperial Diet had voted in the Common Penny at Speyer in 1544, and Sturm hit on the ingenious idea of paying the Smalkaldeners' undisbursed collections for the Imperial Common Penny into the league's treasury. This perfectly illegal act would at one stroke have relieved the league's financial straits, reformed its tax structure, provided the money to aid Elector Herman of Cologne, and sapped the Imperial treasury of funds.[242] At Frankfurt just after Christmas 1545, he and Sebastian Aitinger drafted a proposal to aid Cologne through "a common tax and contribution," for no one can long defray the costs of war "from his cameral revenues or any other kind of income."[243] It should be a general, direct property tax "from which kind of levy other nations finance their wars and other large expenses." The Protestants—this point is pure Sturm—should regard their lands as "one body [ein corpus]" and levy a tax of 0.5 percent, and the yield could be taken from the unused Imperial Common Penny granted recently at Speyer.

At Frankfurt Sturm also outlined the reasons, "on the basis of which the Common Penny may be collected from the subjects."[244] After sketching in dark tones the impending attack by pope and emperor, financed by the

Imperial Common Penny, Sturm proposed a Common Penny of the league, for if "no more equitable mode of taxation is found—and despite long debates and studious searching, we have found none—nothing can prevent the dissolution of this alliance." Upon that tragedy would follow disasters: restoration of the old faith and properties, confiscations of the allies' lands, severe punishments, and permanent bad conscience. Even a barely rational person, Sturm chided, can judge which alternative is preferable, whether

> to pay this tax or levy of 0.5–1.0 percent on wealth and to keep one's own property, the true religion, life, limb, and ancient liberty, or to lose all and suffer the penalties I have mentioned. If the subjects, rich or poor, are well informed of the reasons, they will pay willingly and without complaint.

Further—Sturm now pulled out all stops—"if this religion and its partisans are suppressed in the German lands, almost all German liberties would also be lost," for which reason even the Protestant princes' Catholic subjects ought "all the more willingly to pay their taxes and maintain their other livelihoods and the liberties and freedom of the German nation." Sturm also thought that the introduction of the Common Penny would strengthen the league by stilling the poorer members' complaints against the rich ones and by offering fair treatment to new members. Additionally, "through God's grace by this means we would not only save the taxes already paid but also maintain the peace and order of the Empire, while the pure doctrine of the holy gospel would spread and flourish in the German lands." The Common Penny thus would become the key to "a thoroughgoing, complete, and Christian reform of all Christendom."

Sturm's arguments show very clearly how, in his view, the Smalkaldic League ought to develop into a permanent, well-financed, and flexible political federation, the font of a reformed Empire with a reformed church. He never conceived it narrowly and legalistically as merely a league to defend only its members, but as a political force that represented all Protestant powers in the Empire. He took this position in 1539, for example, when he insisted that the Smalkaldic League must defend the count of Hoya, a Protestant but not a member.[245] For Sturm and his colleagues at Strasbourg, the common religion and not subscription to the constitution defined the community whose interests the Smalkaldic League represented—though Sturm drew the line between rulers and subjects—and which in the long run, as their religion spread across the land, would become identical with the Empire itself. Sturm hammered away at this theme, the centrality of a common religion, at the league's diet at Worms in April 1546. "If his masters look only to themselves," Sturm wrote, "they could well dispense with this league. But when they regard the common cause [*den gemainen handel*] and the dangerous state of current affairs, they believe that this league can best be preserved through loyal cooperation."[246] Sturm was well aware that the absence of common temporal interests—German liberty aside—gravely endangered the league's future, and, as he had argued at Frankfurt, this made a fair and equitable system of taxation all the more urgent. "On this account," he told the allies, "rather than indulging so much mistrust in the league and its business, it should be enough that we are dealing with honorable and Christian persons, who rest the matter on trust and faith, . . . for then God will make the cause flourish."[247] Perhaps, after all, he regretted his silence about the Evangelicals of Metz.

The central principle of Jacob Sturm's reform program was that justice in the form of equitable taxation would produce a commitment to the common good—Sturm's "proper sort of love for one another"—and make the league's political bond strong and durable. This is a burghers' idea, born of a political life based on association for a common purpose rather than on dynastic and feudal bonds of personal loyalty. The urban reformation's teaming of the gospel with the common good had intensified the fusion between Christian social ideals and burghers' culture in a way that made the urban Protestant politicians place expectations on the common faith very different from those of the princes. Just as Protestant burghers remained burghers, Protestant princes remained princes and retained their devotion to their own political culture, which valued military prowess, magnificence, dynastic right, feudal hierarchy, and, above all, personal loyalty and honor. Even Landgrave Philip, so comfortable with burgher ways, did not share Sturm's insistence that fairness in government is the fundament of fiscal efficiency and military strength. Sturm's reform was a burgher's reform, which held that taxation was "surely the chief point, which, once we are agreed, will allow the others to be settled all the more readily."[248] All of its subsidiary points, such as fines on tax delinquents and swearing the diet's members to the league rather than to their masters, served this central one.[249] The differences between his burghers' political culture and that of the princes is illustrated by the contrasting lessons he and the landgrave drew from the affair of Brunswick-Wolfenbüttel: Sturm the need for greater fiscal fairness and centralized control, the landgrave the need for greater military freedom for the commanders.[250] Each, in his characteristic way, wanted a stronger Smalkaldic League.

This difference of opinion mirrored the discord about taxation between cities and princes in the Imperial Diet, and behind it lurked the even more incendiary issue of ecclesiastical property, on which the two political cultures' differences became extreme.[251] Sturm touched this most sensitive of Smalkaldic nerves with his proposal to withhold protection from abusers of the church's patrimony. Ironically, he did so at a time when the Smalkaldic chiefs were contemplating their chances to despoil that patrimony of its crown jewels, the great prince-bishoprics.[252]

Sturm's reform program of 1545–46 came to nothing, because, in the absence of war and revolution, the league had reached the limits of political development based on traditional principles and practices. He projected his vision, a burghers' vision, onto an aristocratic world, when he proposed that the Smalkaldic League become an association of equals bound together by justice, law and order, and devotion to God's honor and the common good.[253] In Sturm's political values, which he tried his best to press on the Smalkaldic League, resided a tendency that, had history been kinder to it, would have made the German-speaking world a great burgher's federation, a giant Protestant version of "turning Swiss."

"JUST AS EACH THING HAPPENED": JOHANNES SLEIDAN

It was Sturm, fittingly enough, who arranged that the Smalkaldic League's memory should be preserved in a form adequate to the humanist standards of the age, namely, a history. Johann Sleidan's *Commentaries on the Condition of Religion and Politics under the Emperor Charles V* appeared at Strasbourg in 1555, two years after Sturm's death, and remained the standard history of the German Reformation until Ranke.[254] In some ways, this most successful history written by a German speaker in the early modern era is a monument to Jacob Sturm's vision of the Reformation and the Smalkaldic League, for it was Sturm who in 1545 gained for Sleidan a post as official historiographer to the league. With this commission, the tall, comely, highly Gallicized German, who was blind in his left eye, "set out to be the Polybius of the Reformation."[255]

Jacob Sturm's sponsorship of Sleidan is difficult to reconstruct.[256] He first met Sleidan, of whom he knew through Jean Sturm, at the colloquy at Hagenau in 1540 and then again at Worms in the following year. Already in these years, Sleidan was thinking of returning to the Empire. He wrote two speeches on German affairs, one in 1541 against the papacy, which he addressed to the German princes, and one in 1542—first published in 1544—on the restoration of the Empire, which he addressed to the emperor. Both were published under a pseudonym.[257] Finally, after much discussion with the Cardinal du Bellay, Sleidan came to settle at Strasbourg in 1544. He was and remained both a French agent and a German Evangelical, a situation that, as he admitted, caused him much difficulty. "Although I am the king's servant," he once told Christopher Mundt, Henry VIII's German agent, "I do not forget my where my fatherland is."[258]

The project for a history of the German Reformation and the Smalkaldic League took shape in conversations among Sleidan, Jacob Sturm, and Martin Bucer in the summer of 1544.[259] According to Bucer, he and Sturm had been looking for a suitable historian and found him in the person of Sleidan. Months later, in January 1545, Sleidan sent Jacob Sturm part of his Latin translation of the French historian Philippe de Commynes—artfully dedicated to the Smalkaldic chiefs—and asked Sturm to press his cause with the chiefs.[260] He renewed his pressures during the following months until Sturm, who was then at Worms, reported on 2 May 1545 that a group of leading Smalkaldic powers, including the two chiefs, had agreed to Sleidan's appointment as historiographer to the league at an annual salary of 250 fl.[261] "You cannot believe," Sleidan wrote to Sturm, "with what joy I regard my work," and he urged Sturm to make sure that the Hessian and Saxon princes would open their archives to him.[262] As a matter of fact, before he could fairly get started, Sleidan was put to diplomatic work for the league. It may be doubted that Elector John Frederick ever understood the appointment, for he noted in June 1545 that Sleidan had been hired "in place of [Ulrich] Varnbühler," one of the league's attorneys, and asked that he translate the text of the Treaty of Crépy from French into German.[263] Soon, Sleidan was again on the road, this time to England on a fruitless embassy to mediate between the English and French kings as the prelude to an alliance of both with the league.[264] When he returned to Strasbourg in late January 1546, he settled down in a double sense. He married Iola, daughter to the exiled Messin Dr. Johann Niedbruck, and began to write his history of "religious and political affairs under Charles V." In fact, the upheavals of 1546–47 and several missions on behalf of the league and the city meant that most of the history was written during the first half of the 1550s: by April 1554 he had reached the present, and in the following year the work was finally printed.

To a far greater degree than is commonly assumed, Sleidan's history, though commissioned by the league, reflects the perseverance and commitment of Jacob Sturm and the regime of Strasbourg. For despite his brave intention of scouring the archives, Sleidan in fact received next to nothing from abroad: nothing at all from Saxony, and only a few self-justifying pieces after the war from Landgrave Philip of Hesse.[265] For the rest, he exploited the archives of Strasbourg's regime, which opened to him "all documents and everything about what was done at all meetings, so that the events would be described as they really happened."[266] Jacob Sturm's role in the progress of the history was very great. Sleidan himself acknowledged that he asked Sturm "many times [allezeit] for explanation, as often as I needed it," and reported that on his deathbed Sturm read the manuscript of the history's first sixteen (of twenty-five) books and "made corrections, where they were needed."[267] It was Sturm, too, who decided that "the time was not yet ripe for translating it into German, which task required an excellent man with a special gift for rendering into German."[268]

Some passages in Sleidan's history reflect Sturm's own experiences. Several examples will suffice. In Sleidan's account of the Peasants' War of 1525, he gives details of the missions of Sturm on behalf of the Imperial Governing Council, including the name of his fellow diplomat, which are to be found in none of the extant correspondence.[269] Again, in his account of the Imperial Diet of 1547–48, Sleidan includes information not in the correspondence, such as the nickname—"armored Diet"—which the Protestants gave the Diet, and which Sleidan was apparently the first to use in print.[270] Sleidan also relates an otherwise undocumented explanation of how at the end of this diet Sturm evaded the emperor's demand that he accept the diet's recess and the interim. At length, he tells, Sturm and the other Protestant townsmen

> found a way both to satisfy the emperor, and to secure themselves. . . . They . . . presented a paper to him, declaring the conditions upon which they were willing to approve the Council. The emperor, having heard their speech, made them an answer through [Imperial Vice-Chancellor Georg Sigismund] Seld, that he was very well satisfied, that after the example of others, they referred the matter to him, and gave their consent with the rest. So that he attributed more unto them, than they were desirous of; for they had not consented with the rest.[271]

Some details, too, of the climactic interview between Sturm and Imperial Chancellor Granvelle at this diet have the ring of eyewitness reporting.[272] There is no need here to undertake a detailed analysis of Sleidan's portrayal of the Smalkaldic League and its fate. Some points, however, bear on Sturm's role in its genesis and execution. For this important task, Sturm chose another Gallicized German, as he had to lead the Latin school, whose experience of the world suited him to place local experience in a universal setting. Sleidan, indeed, raised the story of the German Reformation out of its parochial setting into a European framework, based on his realization, sharpened by long years in France, that the Reformation had introduced unprecedented changes into the life of Christendom. "Has there ever been a century," he once asked,

> in which such varied and wonderful occurrences have been compressed into the shortest space of time? What mighty changes have we experienced, as well in political as in ecclesiastical affairs![273]

The obverse of his Europeanization of the German Reformation, however, is the cool detachment with which he told the story. Following his ancient and modern humanist models—his favorite was Julius Caesar, the self-praising slayer of Celts—Sleidan adopted a lofty and detached tone, hiding his stout Evangelical hatred of popery behind a veil of cool Latinity.[274] This control reflects his models and especially the sense, which he gained from them, of the proper tone of historical writing, but it fits just as well the calm, patient fortitude of Sturm, whose reliance on negotiation suited his situation and his temperament—"patience conquers fortune." What in the end is impressive about Jacob Sturm's role in the project of Sleidan's *Commentaries* is his labor, right to the moment of death, to bring the story of the Reformation and the Smalkaldic League to the light of day in a dress worthy of the Erasmian age.

FROM "EARTHLY REPUBLIC" TO "GODLY POLITY"?

Sleidan's *Commentaries* built a monument to a movement that had succeeded in religion and failed in politics. It also provided evident examples of how the Smalkaldic League had foundered on its own centrifugal forces.

Some of the league's most effective moves, such as its attack on the Imperial courts, remain in the shadows, however, and Sleidan missed the issues—
ecclesiastical property and the Metz affair—that revealed the inherent limits
of the league's ability to build political community based on religious unity.

Sleidan's history, of course, could not subject the Smalkaldic League to a
critical analysis. He could not trace the tension between the community of
Evangelical religion and the Protestants' inability to legitimize on religious
grounds the breaches of legality that would have been necessary had they
built a common church to house their common faith. To the Lutheran faith, it
may be argued, such a house was neither necessary nor desirable, nor could it
countenance a transformation of existing relations of property and governance
in a godly sense.[275] Perhaps, though, many German-speaking Evangelicals at
that time still had a different sense of how gospel and law were related. Nor
could Sleidan, who had not spent his adult life riding up and down the
Empire, mingling with everyone from rebellious peasants to electors and
monarchs, measure how the Smalkaldic League's immense extent and social
diversity, and above all its lack of density, more than neutralized its potential
for change. The league, a modern observer might say, had no core, and the
modest wealth and meager urbanization of Saxony and Hesse made this central
belt unsuited to become the core of a large state. True, but the same could be
said of fifteenth-century Austria or seventeenth-century Brandenburg.

In the end, Jacob Sturm knew a lot more about the reasons for the league's
failure than he ever told Johann Sleidan. He knew, for example, that the
tendencies, which revealed themselves in the 1520s, to translate the new
sense of religious community into demands for new forms of political cooperation and legitimacy had through their violence and threat of revolution
mortgaged the possibilities for political change coupled with the religious
reformation. From that moment Protestant politics became defensive, and
in that guise it had no chance to transform the Empire from an "earthly
republic" into a "godly polity."

The ideal of the "godly polity" or "godly republic" was a burghers' ideal,
the moral heart of the urban reformation.[276] The burghers' political culture
centered on the local autonomy and liberties of late medieval German
particularism, but it conveyed such expansible ideals as the Christian common good, the community as "one body," and equity and "the proper sort
of love for one another" as the basis for government based on consent.
Under the right conditions, such notions might be translated to levels far
greater than the urban and rural communities in which they were at home.
But only under the right conditions, for the imbalance of power meant that
the burghers' ideal of a "godly polity" could never prevail against the aristocratic idea of "German liberty." Burghers and princes had different notions of what constituted a proper polity, and in the league, as in the Empire
generally, "German liberty" simply wore down the solidarities that had promised
political change.

Notes

* "Darnach Frondsperg erzelt mit namen/die werden fürsten all zusamen,/ desgleichen auch von den reichstedten,/die gottes wort bei inen hetten,/wie der babst sich darwider setzet,/könig und keiser auf sie hetzet,/die gottes wort mit rath und that/verfolgen beide frü und spat,/und der babst auf allen reichstagen/sie als ketzer of thet verklagen/und wie sie hetten protestirt,/auf ein concili appellirt,/da wolten sie die schrift lon walten." Liliencron, ed., *Historische Volkslieder* 4:307, no. 521, lines 387–99.

1. For an overview of the Smalkaldic League's history, see Brady, "Phases and Strategies," 162–81. There is no modern history of the league, though for the early period there is Winckelmann's *Der Schmalkaldische Bund.*

2. G. Schmidt, *Der Städtetag,* 194.

3. This point is indicted by the fact that Protestant powers that did not join the league, such as Margrave George of Brandenburg-Ansbach, continued to send envoys to the league's diets and to cooperate with the league in some political ventures, such as the campaign against the *Reichskammergericht.* See, e.g., *SBA* 2:18–22, 37–45.

4. Bucer's phrase comes from the title of his last major writing, *De regno Christi,* ed. François Wendel, in *BOL,* vol. 15. I adopt the phrase *earthly republic* to suggest the attitude toward politics of the Italian humanists, who, "while by no means denying that man had a destiny beyond the heavens, . . . provided assurances that man was at the same time a citizen of an earthly republic to which he owed duties and from which he derived legitimate satisfactions." Kohl and Witt, "General Introduction," 9.

5. Ranke, *Reformation in Germany,* 630.

6. The text is in Fabian, *Entstehung,* 357–76, and for its background and composition, see ibid., 269–315. It should be read together with the diet's recess, in *SBA* 2:66–74. The constitution went back to a draft presented on 2 July 1533, which was blocked by the objections of several northern cities. Ibid., 22–28, 67 n. 5.

7. On the Swabian League as model for the Smalkaldic, see Fabian, *Entstehung,* 254, 293–94; Laufs, *Der Schwäbische Kreis,* 62–63. On the southern cities' relationships to the two leagues, see *BOSS* 3:29–30; Nirrnheim, "Aktenstücke," 29. The connection is illuminated by two letters from Landgrave Philip to Elector John Frederick, from Kassel on 16 March 1533, and from Essdorf on 13 May 1533. StA Weimar, Reg. H, No. 89, fols. 3r, 13r. The former letter relates "das ettlich de[r] trefflichsten Oberlenndischen Stett verschiner zeit bei vnns durch mittel personen ansuchong thun lassen, das nicht vngeneigt weren, sich vs dem schwäbischen bund darjn sie itzt stunden vnnd in sachen leib vnd gut berurend zu e. l., vnns vnnd andern fursten zuthunde, dass haben wir nicht mogen vnderlassen, an e. l. zu pringen, damit disse stett vs dem bunde vnnd von konig Ferdinando mit fugen pracht wurden."

8. Sturm sometimes called them "benches," which was the usage of the Swabian League and the Imperial Diet. *PC* 4:86, no. 63 n. 13.

9. Fabian, *Entstehung,* 360, line 24–361, line 12.

10. Ibid., 363, line 23–364, line 5; *PC* 2:439–40, no. 459, 480, no. 496. The organizational meeting took place at Coburg in August 1537 (ibid., 444–45, 445 n. 1, no. 465). There are extracts from the Smalkaldic military ordinance (*Kriegsordnung*) of 1537 in Rommel, *Philipp der Grossmüthige* 2:375–78, which lists the war councillors of that time (Ulman Böcklin for Strasbourg), contains stipulations about the commanders and their staffs, and establishes regulations for the three arms, cavalry, infantry, and artillery.

11. SBA 2:69, from the recess of Smalkalden, 24 December 1535.
12. Esslingen, Brunswick, Goslar, Einbeck, and Göttingen joined between 1531 and 1535. In 1536 were admitted Dukes Philip and Barnim of Pomerania-Stettin, Duke Ulrich of Württemberg, and Count Rupert of Pfalz-Zweibrücken, Princes Hans-Georg and Joachim of Anhalt-Dessau, and the cities of Augsburg, Frankfurt am Main, Kempten, Hamburg, and Hanover. Fabian, *Entstehung*, 180–81, 201 n. 1350, 356; and SBA 2:70, 86–103.
13. Recess of Frankfurt am Main, 10 May 1536, in SBA 2:90. The war council was also expanded in the same way.
14. Fabian, *Entstehung*, 358, line 17–359, line 6.
15. Constitution of 23 December 1535, in ibid., 359, lines 22–29.
16. The best analysis of the structures is in ibid., 294–98.
17. Winckelmann, *Der Schmalkaldische Bund*, 154–56; Paetel, *Organisation*, 107–8; Fabian, *Entstehung*, 302.
18. Fabian, *Entstehung*, 302.
19. See G. Schmidt, *Städtetage*, 412–16; Schmid, "Reichssteuern," 157–58. I have used this tax rather than the much larger military taxes, because its apportionment was much less controversial. The total sums assessed for the *Kammerzieler* were not large. Strasbourg, for example, paid between 1522 and 1548 a total of 1,964 fl. AMS, I, 3.
20. Hesslinger, *Die Anfänge des Schwäbischen Bundes*, 201; Laufs, *Der Schwäbische Kreis*, 133–35, 144–45; RTA, jR 8:814–15.
21. Bock, *Der Schwäbische Bund*, 34–116.
22. See Elector John Frederick to his envoys at Worms, Zerbst, 27 November 1541, in StA Weimar, Reg. H, pagg. 329–34, no. 133, vol. 1, fols. 228r–232v, here at 230v, where he wants Sturm "bey den oberlendischen stendenn vnd stedtenn der Christenlichenn vorainigung, berurtte sachenn [i.e., the French alliance] vndterbauenn vnd dohin furdernn . . ., souil jme thunich vnd muglich."
23. The point is made by G. Schmidt, "Die Freien und Reichsstädte," 185, who describes the southern Smalkaldic urban diet on 182–88. See, for example, Lucke, *Bremen im Schmalkaldischen Bund*; Richter, *Bremen im Schmalkaldischen Bund*.
24. StA Weimar, Reg. H, no. 47, fols. 23r, 28r–30v. Reutlingen joined in the reply, whereas Kempten said it would join only if all the others did.
25. G. Schmidt, "Die Freien und Reichsstädte," 185. It remains to be investigated why the political culture of the Hansa did not nourish the northern cities' role in the Smalkaldic League.
26. G. Schmidt, *Städtetage*, 403–23, who analyzes the patterns of tax paying and shows that the large cities assumed most of the burden. Landgrave Philip of Hesse wrote to Elector John Frederick, Kassel, 11 January 1546, that "the Saxon cities are petty and mean-spirited [*clein vnnd enghertzig*], when it comes to paying out money." StA Weimar, Reg. H, pag. 670, no. 209, vol. 1, fol. 76r.
27. PC 2:509, no. 536, drafted by a committee chaired by Jacob Sturm.
28. Wehrmann, "Vom Vorabend des Schmalkaldischen Krieges," 191.
29. See this volume, chap. 9.
30. RTA, jR 8:259, 261. See Fabian, *Entstehung*, 194.
31. PC 2:22–23, no. 28, 42–43, no. 48; Fabian, *Entstehung*, 221–23; G. Schmidt, "Die Freien und Reichsstädte," 183–84.
32. PC 2:620, no. 628. In a letter to Elector John Frederick, Philip recommended that the Smalkaldic League imitate the Swabian League in its regulations for artillery. Fabian, *Entstehung*, 254. On the influence of the Swabian League on the Smalkaldic League, see ibid., 17, 133, 194, 215, 254, 293–94.
33. RTA, jR 8:56–57, no. 88, 58, no. 97.

22

The Smalkaldic League as Earthly Republic

191

34. E. Müller, "Die ernestinischen Landtage," 205.
35. Ibid., 209.
36. See this volume, chap. 7.
37. "Die Hulff, so dem Hertzogenn von Gulch, Cleff, Gerga vnnd Gellern beschehen solle, jst abgeredt, wie volget," Kassel, 15 February 1540, in StA Weimar, Reg. C, pagg. 493–95, no. 870, fol. 53r. The Saxon elector and his brother, Duke Henry of Saxony, Landgrave Philip of Hesse, Duke Ulrich of Württemberg, and Dukes Barnim and Philip of Pomerania were to supply 400 horse and 1,700 foot each; and the other princes and counts were to supply together 200 horse and 1,500 foot. If four cities—Strasbourg, Ulm, Bremen, and Hamburg—agreed to supply 1,000 foot each, the princes' contingents would be reduced correspondingly by 4,000 infantry.
38. Fabian, Entstehung, 296. See Brady, "Phases and Strategies," 164–65. An archive of the League had been founded in 1538.
39. Paetel, Organisation, 109–10.
40. Ibid., 107.
41. This point is made about the cities and the Swabian League by Naujoks, Obrigkeitsgedanke, 26–28.
42. See this volume, this chapter.
43. Brady, "Phases and Strategies," 174.
44. See this volume, this chapter.
45. Frey, "Das Gericht des Schwäbischen Bundes," 228. The following lines rest on this study.
46. Leonhard von Eck to Duke William of Bavaria, Ulm, 12 February 1519, quoted in Jörg, Deutschland in der Revolutions-Periode, 29 n. 2. Besides Reutlingen, Ulrich had designs on Esslingen already at this time, for which see Kittelberger, "Herzog Ulrichs Angriffspläne." For the background, see Brady, Turning Swiss, 92–100; Brady, "Princes' Reformation vs. Urban Liberty."
47. PC 2:217–18, no. 235.
48. Heyd, Ulrich, Herzog zu Württemberg 3:33. The following is based on G. Schmidt, Städtetag, 210–24; G. Schmidt, "Reichsstadt und Territorialstadt"; G. Schmidt, "Die Freien und Reichsstädte," 200–202; Naujoks, "Reichsfreiheit und Wirtschaftsrivalität."
49. Lenz, ed., Briefwechsel 3:136; and there (137), too, the following quote.
50. He was appointed, along with the Hessian Alexander von der Thann and Dr. Conrad Hel of Augsburg, by the Smalkaldic League's assembly at Regensburg in July 1541. There are many documents on this topic in StA Weimar, Reg. H, pagg. 383–84, fols. 126r–210r; and more in Reg. H, pagg. 394–400, no. 149, vol. 1, fols. 125r–194v.
51. PC 2:244–45, nos. 189–90; PC 3:596, no. 568.
52. G. Schmidt, "Die Freien und Reichsstädte," 201.
53. This difference of viewpoint is responsible for the criticism of G. Schmidt, "Die Freien und Reichsstädte," 179–81, of my position stated in "Phases and Strategies." My interpretation emphasizes the league's disruptive potential, based both on its weakened sense of legitimacy (a legacy of the early Reformation movement) and its potential for violent disruption, whereas Schmidt emphasizes—too much so, in my view—the continuity of legal forms and the league's lack of political achievement.
54. See Wiesflecker, Kaiser Maximilian I. 5:412, 418–22; and the overview of the French kingdom's economy by Knecht, Francis I, 305–25.
55. Poland and Hungary figured into the league's dreams from 1531, when Jerome Laski came to the Empire to make contact with the Smalkaldeners on their behalf. See Wolfram, "Gegenstände," 88–89.

56. It is worth noting that the league originally took the initiative with both France and England. See the exchange of letters in StA Weimar, Reg. H, no. 51, fols. 25r–68r, with drafts, some in Melanchthon's hand; no. 52, fols. 10r–36v.

57. Knecht, *Francis I*, 275–76. See Bourrilly, *Guillaume du Bellay*; Zeller, *La réunion de Metz* 1:75–107; Seidel, *Frankreich*, 137–65; Mariotte, "François Ier et la Ligue de Smalkalde"; Pariset, *Relations*, 8–82.

58. Knecht, *Francis I*, 248–52, whence the quoted phrases. On the implications of the affair for France, see Kelley, *Beginning of Ideology*, 13–19; and see Seidel, *Frankreich*, 71–76.

59. Elector John Frederick to Gregor Brück, Lochau, 19 August 1535, in StA Weimar, Reg. H, no. 104, fol. 9r–v.

60. Quoted by Tjernagel, *Henry VIII and the Lutherans*, 155.

61. Hasenclever, *Politik der Schmalkaldener*; Seidel, *Frankreich*, 177; Potter, "French Policy," 540–42.

62. A clear overview is given by Elton, *England under the Tudors*, 150–59; Elton, "England and the Continent." For details see Tjernagel, *Henry VIII and the Lutherans*, which is relatively full but uncritical, and Doernberg, *Henry VIII and Luther*, on the theological side; but Prüser, *England und die Schmalkaldener*, is the best study.

63. *Letters and Papers* 9:336, 344–45, nos. 994, 1014, from CR 2: nos. 1012, 1028. Langey's speech is also described by Jacob Sturm and Batt von Duntzenheim, in *PC* 2:319, no. 330. StA Weimar, Reg. H, no. 104, contains a very full documentation of this assembly.

64. Tjernagel, *Henry VIII and the Lutherans*, 155–62. The articles were so insignificant that they were utterly forgotten and were rediscovered only at the beginning of this century. See also Prüser, *England und die Schmalkaldener*, 85–92.

65. Prüser, *England und die Schmalkaldener*, 93–103. The members were to be Prince George of Anhalt, Jacob Sturm, Georg Drach of Hesse, and Bucer and Melanchthon.

66. Specklin, "Collectanées," no. 2346, which is the likely source of similar notices in Saladin, "Chronique," 343 (dated to 1535), and Hertzog, *Chronicon Alsatiae*, pt. 6:279.

67. The quoted phrase expresses the judgment of Elton, *England under the Tudors*, 153.

68. Ibid., 156; Scarisbrick, *Henry VIII*, 408–10; Tjernagel, *Henry VIII and the Lutherans*, 195. The Smalkaldic embassy to London in the summer of 1538 was headed by the Saxon chancellor, Franz Burckhardt.

69. Elton, *England under the Tudors*, 155; Prüser, *England und die Schmalkaldener*, 276–81.

70. *PC* 4:71–72, no. 53. See Petri, "Straßburgs Beziehungen, I," 161.

71. This can be followed in *Letters and Papers* 11:158, no. 388; vol. 12, pt. 1:262, no. 564; vol. 12, pt. 2:382, nos. 1088–89.

72. Prüser, *England und die Schmalkaldener*, 129, notes that the Smalkaldic chiefs in 1538 asked for as large a subsidy from England as they expected from France.

73. This point, emphasized by Elton, "England and the Continent," 11, is one on which the most detailed study, Tjernagel, *Henry VIII and the Lutherans*, 249–54, offers only confessional effusions.

74. *Letters and Papers*, vol. 12, pt. 2:130, no. 315; 156, no. 410; 338–39, no. 969. See Rott, *Correspondance de Martin Bucer*, 27, 32.

75. *PC* 2:371, no. 381, Mathis Pfarrer's instruction for the southern Smalkaldic cities' diet at Ulm, 1 June 1536.

76. Luther recalls this in his eloquent and moving preface to Barnes's "Articles

of Faith," quoted by Doernberg, *Henry VIII and Luther*, 125.

77. PC 2:627, no. 635 (1 August 1539).
78. Ibid., 630, 632, nos. 639, 642–43; Eells, *Martin Bucer*, 254, who points out the contrast between Bucer's enthusiasm and Luther's pessimism about England.
79. Baumgarten, *Jakob Sturm*, 4.
80. Mertens, "Maximilian I. und das Elsaß"; PC 1:55, 122, 153. Fundamental is Petri, "Straßburgs Beziehungen," though it is not free from the patriotic polemics that mar much of the literature on this subject. See also Hachtmann, *Straßburgs Beziehungen*.
81. PC 2:280, 295.
82. The first privilege, dated 14 March 1516, was confirmed in 1542, 1548, 1551, and 1559. Bresard, *Les foires de Lyon*, 121–22. See Pfeiffer, "Die Bemühungen der oberdeutschen Kaufleute," 408–16; and Vial, "Jean Cleberger," 277, who prints a list of German merchants living at Lyon in 1529—it contains no Strasbourg names. A list of German and Swiss creditors of the French king at Lyon in 1533 also contains no Strasbourg names. Ehrenberg, *Zeitalter der Fugger* 2:99 n. 46. Jacob Sturm was nonetheless well acquainted with the privileges, for he cited them correctly in a letter of 4 April 1541, in PC 3:176, no. 186.
83. See Fuchs, "Les foires," 304–5, 316.
84. PC 2:442, no. 464, in the hand of the city secretary, Johann Meyer, with additions by Jacob Sturm.
85. Ibid., 443, no. 464.
86. Ibid., 3:467–68, no. 443.
87. Ibid., 471–72, no. 445.
88. Ibid., 472–73, no. 446. See, for example, the petition of leading merchants with business in France on the occasion of King Francis's death in 1547, in AMS, XXI 1547, fols. 311v–313r; XXI 1548, fol. 37r. The men involved were Friedrich von Gottesheim, Hans Hammerer, Philips Ingold, Hans von Duntzenheim, Mathis Wecker, and Mattheus Geiger.
89. Trausch, "Straßburgische Chronik," no. 2682, which rests on tradition.
90. Hortleder, ed., *Ursachen* (ed. 1645) 1:1813 (= bk. 4, chap. 47): "Welcher Sturm sich auch vnlangst in des H. Reichs Versamblung mit trutzigen, pochenden, dräwlichen Worten gegen etlicher Ständ Gesandten, . . . offentlichen hören vnd vernehmen lassen hat: Daß ihme der Frantzoß ein guter Herr oder Haupt sey: Daß kan er nicht verneinen." This refers to a session of 23 April 1544 in the presence of Charles V and King Ferdinand. Gereon Sailer described it thus to Georg Herwart: "Den frommen her jacob Sturmen hat er [= Duke Henry] gar hitzig vnd scharpff angriffen, als ain furdrer des frantzhosen, vnd das her jm radt solt gesagt haben, der frantzhose sey jme ain guter herr." Roth, "Briefwechsel Gereon Sailers," 123 (25 April 1544). Sturm reported this incident to his masters (on 25 April 1544, in PC 3:488–89, no. 463), who insisted on the charges being answered, though they considered them absurd (ibid., 495, no. 468, 500–502, nos. 470–72). In a letter of 1 May 1544, Sailer identifies the object of the charge as "der Sturm, so ain leser zw Straspurg ist" (F. Roth, "Briefwechsel Gereon Sailers," 135), another case of confusion between the two Sturms.
91. PC 3:474, no. 448 (23 March 1544).
92. Landgrave Philip of Hesse to Elector John Frederick of Saxony, Spangenberg, 29 December 1545, in StA Weimar, Reg. H, pag. 670, no. 209, vol. 1, fol. 16r: "Was auch, freundlicher, lieber vetter unnd bruder, Johannes Sturm an seinen bruder, [H]er Jacob Sturm gein Franckfurt geschrieben, . . ." He refers to a letter of Jean Sturm to Jacob Sturm, 10 December 1545, of which a

copy is enclosed (ibid., fols. 17r–25r); it is printed (though without the ad-dendum on fol. 25r) in *PC* 3:679–89, no. 643. Others shared the confusion such as Cardinal Otto Truchsess von Waldburg, bishop of Augsburg, who identified one of the Smalkaldic envoys to England in 1545 (it was Jean Sturm) as "Jacomo Sturmio cittadino di Argentina." *NBD,* I 8:305, no. 62. The error was repeated by Girolamo Dandolo, bishop of Caserta, who wrote to Alessandro Farnese from Hertogenbosch, 18 December 1545, that "il Sturmio da Argentina, ch'è uno delli tre ambasciatori de Protestanti che sono ancora in Cales." Ibid., 500, no. 108.

93. Bourrilly, "Jean Sleidan et le Cardinal du Bellay," 241–42; Pariset, *Relations,* 40–44, 57–59, 64–68, 89–92, 103–5, 119–20.

94. Rott, "Le recteur strasbourgeois," 46. Another teacher in the Latin school, Michael Toxites, entered the chancellor's service in 1547. Van Durme, *Antoon Perrenot,* 346.

95. Wagner, *Graf Wilhelm von Fürstenberg,* 169–70. See Landgrave Philip to Elector John Frederick, Spangenberg, 26 January 1540, in StA Weimar, Reg. H, pagg. 348–52, no. 136, fols. 2r–3v, in which he recommends that the princes' letter to King Francis be sent to Strasbourg for translation, "dartzu si dan, wie vns ehr Jacob Sturm geschrieben, eyn geschickte person haben sollen."

96. Emperor Charles V to his ambassador in France, Brussels, 28 May 1549: "Et aussy qu'l'on entend que ledicts François publient qu'ils ont des principaux de ladicte ville [i.e., Strasbourg] à leur dévotion, et mesmes Jacques Sturmius, que l'on a tousjours trouvé obstiné lesdicts François." Weiss, ed., *Papiers d'état* 3:365.

97. See Pariset, "L'activité de Jacques Sturm," 261–63, who, though he recog-nizes (261) the purely instrumental character of Sturm's approaches to France ("pour Strasbourg, et pour Jacques Sturm surtout, une alliance avec la France ne peut être que temporaire"), later (263) spins out a mythic Sturm: "Jacques Sturm a, toute de sa vie, voulu conserver à Strasbourg son rôle de ville de passage, de ville frontière, à cheval sur deux civilisations, neutre dans les conflits et dans les disputes, mais gardant les privilèges et les libertés qui font sa richesse." This is a strange thing to write about a man who led his city into three wars (1534, 1542, 1546), of which one, the Brunswick cam-paign of 1542, hadn't the slightest connection with Strasbourg's trade or im-mediate security. But the same author also calls (257) Charles V an "espagnol."

98. Quoted by Bourrilly, "Jean Sleidan et le cardinal du Bellay," 227 n. 2, with-out source. On Guillaume du Bellay at Strasbourg and Smalkalden, see Bourrilly, *Guillaume du Bellay,* 205–13; Wagner, *Graf Wilhelm von Fürstenberg,* 80–81; Seidel, *Frankreich,* 172–77.

99. There is no literature on Jean Sturm's French background and his political activities. On Sleidan, see Bourrilly, "Jean Sleidan et le Cardinal du Bellay"; Hasenclever, "Johann Sleidan und Frankreich."

100. Ficker-Winckelmann 1:25–26. Geiger was already working for Guillaume du Bellay in the Empire in the summer of 1534. Seidel, *Frankreich,* 15–46, 77–87.

101. Petri, "Straßburgs Beziehungen, I," 140–41; Seidel, *Frankreich,* 176–77.

102. Pollet, *Correspondance* 2:488–527, is fundamental. See Petri, "Straßburgs Beziehungen, I," 143–45; Knecht, *Francis I,* 232–33.

103. For German reactions, see Seidel, *Frankreich,* 64–76.

104. Quoted by Knecht, *Francis I,* 249.

105. Analyzed by Seidel, *Frankreich,* 88–122.

106. Petri, "Straßburgs Beziehungen, I," 148–49.

107. *PC* 2:258, no. 280.

108. Ibid., 470, no. 493.

109. Franz Burckhardt to Elector John Frederick, Worms, 22 November 1540, in StA Weimar, Reg. H, pagg. 329–34, no. 133, vol. 1, fols. 191r–94r. See also Burckhardt's report of 29 November 1540 (ibid., fols. 235r–237r), which contains documents he got from Sturm on the factions at the French court. Ibid., pagg. 335–44, no. 134, vol. 3, fols. 138r–145v, contains further reports, which Jacob Sturm and Martin Bucer passed on to Gregor Brück at Naumburg in January 1541. Their information came from Guillaume Farel. There is another such document, which Sturm passed around at Worms in the autumn of 1540, in StA Weimar, Reg. H, pagg. 367–72, no. 141, fols. 182r–184v.

110. Knecht, *Francis I*, 194, and see 245–46, 299–300, 376; Bourrilly, "Jean Sleidan et le Cardinal du Bellay," 225–30; Seidel, *Frankreich*, 126–30.

111. PC 3:630, no. 639; Mentz, *Johann Friedrich* 2:250–51.

112. The best analysis from the league's point of view is by Mentz, *Johann Friedrich* 2:250–53, 268–73.

113. PC 3:14, no. 11, 17, no. 14; Lenz, ed., *Briefwechsel* 1:143, 146, 150; Mentz, *Johann Friedrich* 2:251; Petri, "Straßburgs Beziehungen, I," 150–54.

114. PC 3:67, no. 53.

115. Baumgarten, ed., *Sleidans Briefwechsel*, nos. 4–10. This edition must be used with the corrections and additions of Jean Rott, "Jean Sleidan." Rott's notices of lost letters (576) show that Sleidan's contacts to the Strasbourgeois date to 1539, that is, to just after Jean Sturm settled at Strasbourg. Sleidan's mission of 1540 is not mentioned in Batt von Duntzenheim's minutes of the colloquy, in PC 3:77–82, no. 77. That he was sending news to Strasbourg was noted by the Hessian envoys at Hagenau to Landgrave Philip, Hagenau, 23 July 1540, a copy of which is in StA Weimar, Reg. H, pagg. 359–64, no. 139, fols. 93r–94r.

116. They spread at Hagenau. See Batt von Duntzenheim to Daniel Mieg, Hagenau, 23 June 1540, in PC 3:68, no. 63.

117. Ibid., 125–28, nos. 134–35.

118. He proposed this to Franz Burckhardt in a letter written from Worms around Christmas Day 1540, in ibid., 151, 160. The documents on his involvement in the issue at this time are in StA Weimar, Reg. H, pagg. 329–34, no. 133, vol. 1, fols. 235r–237r; pagg. 335–44, no. 134, vol. 1, fols. 105r–18v; pagg. 367–72, no. 141, fols. 182r–85v. The final document cited is Sturm's draft of the memorial to be sent to King Francis on behalf of the Evangelicals. In addition, the Saxon agenda on the French matter for the league's diet at Naumburg is in ibid., Reg. H, pag. 335, no. 134, vol. 1, fols. 105r–18v.

119. Lenz, ed., *Briefwechsel* 1:254, no. 92.

120. PC, vol. 3:474–75, no. 448, from which the following quotes also come.

121. Petri, "Straßburgs Beziehungen, II," 139–57; Pariset, *Relations*, 44–72.

122. The document is printed in PC 4:553 n. 1.

123. I rely on Knecht, *Francis I*, 376.

124. Geiler, *Die Emeis*, 8v–9v. See Brady, "'You Hate us Priests,'" 182.

125. Schindling, "Die Reformation in den Reichsstädten," 83. See G. Schmidt, "Die Freien und Reichsstädte," 183.

126. I will focus on this court as the principal instance for such suits, though the Imperial High Court (*Hofgericht*) at Rottweil also accepted and heard suits for restitution. Fabian, *Entstehung*, 282.

127. Schlüter-Schindler, *Der Schmalkaldische Bund*, 26–30; and the following quote is at 30.

128. See, above all, the pioneering study by M. Schulze, *Fürsten und Reformation*, esp. 192–97, based on Saxony but attuned to the general state of the question; and for Württemberg, the suggestive study by Sieglerschmidt, *Territorialstaat*.

129. The following is based on Sieglerschmidt, *Territorialstaat*, 1–4.
130. As is admirably demonstrated by M. Schulze, *Fürsten und Reformation*.
131. Schlüter-Schindler, *Der Schmalkaldische Bund*, 31–36, which supersedes Körber, *Kirchengüterfrage*, 97–99.
132. Dolazalek, "Assessoren" and "Argumentation"; Sprenger, *Viglius van Aytta*, esp. 61–96. It is worth mentioning that the recent literature, based on a reconstruction of the Chamber Court's archives by legal historians headquartered at Frankfurt am Main, has made obsolete all the older evaluations of the court. See Diestelkamp, "Stand der Arbeiten"; Battenberg, "Reichskammergericht und Archivwesen."
133. Dolazalek, "Argumentation," 26–28, 57–58.
134. Sprenger, *Viglius van Aytta*, 63, identifies three main points of view among the judges.
135. Schelp, *Reformationsprozesse*, 79; Dolazalek, "Assessoren," 90–92.
136. PC 2:172–80, nos. 162, 166–67, 178. Strasbourg's Senate & XXI outlined the idea of recusing "partisan" judges in a letter to the landgrave, 12 November 1532, in ibid., 176–77, no. 169. See Schlüter-Schindler, *Der Schmalkaldische Bund*, 39–59; Schelp, *Reformationsprozesse*, 205–7. Already in 1533, the Saxon elector had ordered the judge, whom he had appointed to the Chamber Court, to have nothing to do with the suits of restitution. Elector John Frederick to Landgrave Philip, Weimar, 21 March 1533, in StA Weimar, Reg. H, no. 81, fols. 31r–32v.
137. Schlüter-Schindler, *Der Schmalkaldische Bund*, 41–45.
138. UARP, 211, no. 76 (28 December 1533), the landgrave's announcement of the meeting to discuss recusation of the court. An excerpt is in PC 2:202, no. 209.
139. UARP, 217–19, no. 81 (8 January 1534); PC 2:204–5, no. 212. On this important committee meeting at Speyer, see Schlüter-Schindler, *Der Schmalkaldische Bund*, 52–59. Daniel Mieg represented Strasbourg. His instruction is in UARP, 219–33, no. 82; PC 2:202–3, no. 210.
140. The act is printed in UARP, 262–74, no. 99 III. For interpretation, see Dommasch, ed., *Religionsprozesse*, 15–17; Schlüter-Schindler, *Der Schmalkaldische Bund*, 61–63. There is a large mass of documents on the southern cities' restitution suits in StA Weimar, Reg. H, nos. 86–87.
141. SBA 1:19, 25–26. A tax of 435 fl. was levied to pay the attorneys. Ibid., 17–28. Schlüter-Schindler, *Der Schmalkaldische Bund*, 65–73, with data on the lawyers at 68–69; Sprenger, *Viglius von Aytta*, 359–72.
142. PC 3:218, no. 214 (16 December 1541).
143. "Reformirung des Chamergerichts," in StA Weimar, Reg. E, pagg. 48–50, no. 99, vol. 1, fols. 52r–60v. I am grateful for the text to Katherine G. Brady, who transcribed this document. It is in the electoral Saxon acts about the Imperial Diet of Regensburg in 1541 and is signed (60v) "Theophilus subscripsit." Winckelmann (PC 3:218 n. 2) could not find in AMS the document Sturm describes as "ain bedenken, . . . so mir ain gut freund zugestellt" (ibid., 218), and its identity with the Weimar document is my hypothesis. A look at the court's personnel confirms the presence on the bench at this time of a disproportionately large number of Swabians. Another document, "Rathschlag sess Cambergerichts halben etc." from the same source and also from 1540, is in StA Weimar, Reg. H, pagg. 306–11, no. 126, vol. 4, fols. 17r–27v.
144. The acts of this case are in AMS, AA 1723, and the case is described by Winckelmann in PC 2:462 n. 2; Beinert, "Geschichte des Schloßes zu Willstätt," 36–37; Schelp, *Reformationsprozesse*, 223–27; Schlüter-Schindler, *Der Schmalkaldische Bund*, 138–41. Jörg Harder (or: Hörder) apparently moved to

Strasbourg because of his involvement in the Peasants' War in 1525.
145. PC 2:461–63, no. 485, 462 n. 2, 463 n. 1, 468, no. 490, 472, no. 494, 474, no. 495, 547, no. 570, 547 n. 2. Copies of the printed dossier are to be found in HStA Stuttgart, A 149/1, and StA Weimar, Reg. H, pagg. 265–67, no. 112, fols. 10r–27r. It contains many interesting depositions by eyewitnesses, including peasants.
146. "Von der Strasburgisken sake (1538)," in StA Weimar, Reg. H, pagg. 167–70, no. 79, fols. 83r, 84r (from which the quote): "De Straßburische sake is kein Religion sake belanget de weltlike jurisdiction . . . scholde de nu vor eine Religion sake anghenommen werden, . . . were mehre argerlich vnnd der conscientien entiegen alse forderlich. Vnnd hadde woll den schyn, alse wolde man de weltlikenn saken ock mit der Religion saken ghemenget hebbenn."
147. Württemberg councilors to Duke Ulrich, Stuttgart, 12 July 1538, in StA Weimar, Reg. H, pagg. 167–70, no. 79, fols. 54r–57v, against the Strasbourg memorial in ibid., fols. 58r–67v.
148. This point is made by Schelp, *Reformationsprozesse*, 243.
149. StA Weimar, Reg. H, pagg. 170–73, no. 80, vol. 2, fols. 3r–5v; and see PC 2:515, no. 537. The case involved the right of free movement (*freier Zug*), just as in the Hanau-Lichtenberg suit.
150. Schlüter-Schindler, *Der Schmalkaldische Bund*, 109–45, who describes suits against Strasbourg, Constance, Lindau, Augsburg, Frankfurt, Ulm, Memmingen, Isny, Bremen, Hesse, Saxony, and Brunswick-Lüneburg. The list of complaints against suits of this, or alleged to be of this, kind is much longer (ibid., 165–66).
151. Ibid., 155–75. She lists (165–66) the suits mentioned in the negotiations that led to the Truce of Frankfurt in 1539.
152. Ibid., 177–86. Strasbourg stood with Hesse, Saxony, Brunswick-Lüneburg, and Anhalt.
153. Schelp, *Reformationsprozesse*, 172–98, 235–39. The Carthusian monastery stood outside the walls but in the urban district. It lay on a rise on the left bank of the Breusch River on the road from Strasbourg toward Wasselonne and Saverne.
154. Ibid., 67–75.
155. AMS, II 28/17, undated but between 13 and 23 August 1540. See Schelp, *Reformationsprozesse*, 180.
156. Copies of the general complaint and the protest against the court's decision in the Hanau case are in StA Weimar, Reg. H, pagg. 265–67, no. 112, fols. 10r–27r, 28r–34v.
157. PC 3:174–76, nos. 185–86. In November 1540, Caspar Hedio had broached the case with Jean de Naves, who assured him that "es [i.e., the Chamber Court] seind buben; der kaiser waiss umb ihr handlung nichts, kan ihme auch nit gefallen." Ibid., 120, no. 128.
158. This point is cogently made by Schelp, *Reformationsprozesse*, 241–42.
159. Ibid., 243.
160. At Naumburg in early January 1541, for which see PC 3:156 n. 3; Schlüter-Schindler, *Der Schmalkaldische Bund*, 202 n. 186.
161. PC 3:164, no. 172. For the southern cities' reaction, see Schlüter-Schindler, *Der Schmalkaldische Bund*, 205–7.
162. The connection is clearly made by Schlüter-Schindler, *Der Schmalkaldische Bund*, 212–13.
163. On the league's diet and its decision, see ibid., 230–36, with the quote at 232. Strasbourg recommended total tax refusal until the courts were reformed. PC 3:330, no. 315 (17 October 1542), from Strasbourg's instruction for Ulman Böcklin and Michel Han (Jacob Sturm was attending the Upper Rhenish Circle's diet at Worms, for which see ibid., 334–35, no. 321); and see Michel

Han's oral report to the Senate & XXI at Strasbourg on 4 December 1542, in AMS, XXI 1542, fol. 485r, excerpted in PC 3:338, no. 326.

164. The protest, signed on 30 September 1543 at Frankfurt, and the envoys' instruction, dated 2 October 1543, are in StA Weimar, Reg. H, pagg. 490–97, no. 169, vol. 1, fols. 150r–153r, 138r–149v.

165. For details, see Rabe, Reichsbund und Interim, 303–21.

166. Körber, Kirchengüterfrage, 189.

167. Wiesflecker, Kaiser Maximilian I. 1:79. See Willoweit, "Das landesherrliche Kirchenregiment," 361–62; and the important study by Sieglerschmidt, Territorialstaat.

168. Winckelmann, Der Schmalkaldische Bund, 102–3, 125; Körber, Kirchengüterfrage, 93–94.

169. See Grimm, Lazarus Spengler, 114–18. The ordinance is printed by Sehling, ed., Kirchenordnungen, vol. 11, pt. 1:140–305.

170. I agree with Sieglerschmidt, Territorialstaat, 283–84, on the timing. The basic studies on this question are Körber, Kirchengüterfrage; and Köhler, Reformationspläne. There are very useful surveys by Schindling, "Reformation in den Reichsstädten"; Cohn, "Church Property." The work by Lehnert, Kirchengut und Reformation, is too doctrinal to give much idea of what happened, though it supplies some useful legal definitions.

171. Schindling, "Reformation in den Reichsstädten," 82–83; Körber, Kirchengüterfrage, 152–53 (there the example of Brunswick).

172. Brady, Ruling Class, 146, 226. Close investigation would turn up other examples at Strasbourg and elsewhere.

173. Cohn, "Church Property," 167–68, who surveys (168–72) Hesse, the two Saxonies, Württemberg, the Palatinate, the Welf (Brunswick) lands, and Brandenburg. For more details, see the older work by Körber, Kirchengüterfrage, 154–63. This paragraph rests on these two studies, plus, Deetjen, Studien, 106–256, for Württemberg; and the quotes are from Cohn's article.

174. There is a useful list of Imperial dioceses with dates of the foundation, secularization, or dissolution in Gebhardt, ed., Handbuch 2:621–23.

175. Quoted by Körber, Kirchengüterfrage, 182.

176. Quoted by ibid., 187–88.

177. PC 2:413. On Held's appearance and its effects, see ibid., 424 n. 1; Köhler, Reformationspläne, 63–70; Körber, Kirchengüterfrage, 150–51. The preachers' memorial of 24 February 1537 is in CR 3:288–90, no. 1532; MBW 2:297, no. 1852.

178. The chronology is laid out by F. Roth, ed., "Zur Kirchengüterfrage," 299–301. The diets were held at Smalkalden (February–March 1537), Brunswick (March–April 1538), Eisenach (July–August 1538), Arnstadt (November–December 1539), and Smalkalden (April 1540).

179. Their instruction, drafted by a committee of Sturm, Duntzenheim, and Pfarrer, is in PC 3:508–10, no. 536, here from 509. F. Roth, ed., "Zur Kirchengüterfrage," 299, believed that Jacob Sturm submitted Bucer's memorial on church property to the diet at Brunswick in March–April 1538, but Körber, Kirchengüterfrage, 167 n. 5, disagreed, and the Strasbourg documents support him. PC 2:471–80, nos. 494–96, 509 n. 3. The recess of Brunswick orders the allies to have opinions on the subject prepared for the next diet. F. Roth, ed., "Zur Kirchengüterfrage," 299 n. 3; PC 2:480.

180. I allude to the crisis provoked by the outlawry of Minden, which the Truce of Frankfurt ended in 1539. See Brady, "A Crisis Averted." The recess of Eisenach of 16 April 1538 (the relevant passage is printed by F. Roth, ed., "Zur Kirchengüterfrage," 299 n. 3) repeats the decision of 1537 to debate the matter at a future date. An attendance list for Eisenach is in StA Weimar,

Reg. H, pagg. 167–70, no. 80, fol. 35r–v; and Bucer's memorial on church property is in ibid., 201r–16r, which ends: "Martinus Bucer admonet ... presentatum Eissenach denn erstenn Augustj durch Er Jacob Storm. 1538."

181. The text is printed by Hortleder, ed., *Ursachen* (1617), book 5, chap. 8. Quotes and summaries are in Lenz, ed., *Briefwechsel* 1:48 n. 1; F. Roth, ed., "Zur Kirchengüterfrage," 304–19, and Körber, *Kirchengüterfrage*, 167–69.

182. F. Roth, ed., "Zur Kirchengüterfrage," 316–36; Körber, *Kirchengüterfrage*, 171.

183. Körber, *Kirchengüterfrage*, 174–75; Mentz, *Johann Friedrich* 3:436–37, no. 25.

184. PC 2:652, no. 653 (Duntzenheim's report on the Arnstadt diet). The account of the diet of Smalkalden is based on notes by Sturm and Duntzenheim in ibid., 3:27–43, no. 25, here at 35–38, from which come the quotes in this paragraph. See Körber, *Kirchengüterfrage*, 177–81; F. Roth, ed., "Zur Kirchengüterfrage," 301–2.

185. PC 3:40–41; Mentz, *Johann Friedrich*, 2:221. Melanchthon's opinion is printed in CR 4:1040–46, no. 1532. See Körber, *Kirchengüterfrage*, 177–78. The relevant passage of the diet's recess, based on this opinion, is printed by F. Roth, ed., "Zur Kirchengüterfrage," 301–2.

186. Perhaps because of Strasbourg's own hostage to fortune, the league's recognition of its suit concerning St. Stephan's, which it acquired on 6 April 1540. PC 3:26–27, 42; Schelp, *Reformationsprozesse*, 146–48.

187. The landgrave's view is in his instruction for the Diet of Speyer in 1544, in Lenz, ed., *Briefwechsel* 2:198 n. 1. For the princes' attitude and the Naumburg question, see Körber, *Kirchengüterfrage*, 182.

188. For accounts of Bucer's tract, "Von den kirchengütern," which he published under a pseudonym, see Körber, *Kirchengüterfrage*, 128–31; Lenz, ed., *Briefwechsel* 1:397–99. Max Lenz, who spotted the point about a Protestant emperor, called it (399) "die Errichtung *der* nationalen Monarchie" (emphasis added). On this whole topic, see Duchhardt, *Protestantisches Kaisertum*, 8–42.

189. Lenz, ed., *Briefwechsel* 2:168–93, 217–18; Körber, *Kirchengüterfrage*, 143–46.

190. Lenz, ed., *Briefwechsel* 2:242, no. 118.

191. PC 3:676, no. 642 (quote). See Hasenclever, *Politik der Schmalkaldener*, 143; Körber, *Kirchengüterfrage*, 181.

192. As Duke William of Bavaria pointed out in an especially keen way in 1547, for which see Druffel, ed., *Beiträge* 3:70–73, no. 159 VIII (autumn 1547).

193. There is no adequate history of Metz in this era. For an overview, see Zeller, *La réunion de Metz* 1:181–283. For the course of the struggle over religion at Metz in the early 1540s, see Kleinwächter, *Der Metzer Reformationsversuch*; Winckelmann, "Der Anteil der deutschen Protestanten"; Mazauric, "La Réforme au Pays Messin"; and Tribout de Morimbert, *La Réforme à Metz*, vol. 1, the most recent and, in some ways, the least satisfactory account.

194. Winckelmann, "Der Anteil der deutschen Protestanten," 208–9; Roussel, "Les premières dissidences religieuses," 38–39.

195. PC 1:296; Tribout de Morimbert, *La Réforme à Metz* 1:65–66.

196. On Niedbruck, see Ficker-Winkelmann 1:26; ADB 62:621–29.

197. PC 2:516, no. 540; 579, no. 590; 614, no. 620; 633, no. 644; 665, no. 662; Tribout de Morimbert, *La Réforme à Metz* 1:123.

198. Winckelmann, "Der Anteil der deutschen Protestanten," 211–12; Zeller, *La réunion de Metz* 1:229–30.

199. Winckelmann, "Der Anteil der deutschen Protestanten," 210–11; Mazauric, "Une famille réformée messine," 31–34, who believes that Gaspard was a very recent convert to Evangelical religion. His elder brother, Robert, had long possessed ties to the elector of Saxony.

200. The request is noted in *PC* 3:310 n. 1, and summarized by Kleinwächter, *Der Metzer Reformationsversuch*, 44–46.
201. The embassy is described by Tribout de Morimbert, *La Réforme à Metz* 1:142–43, based on documents in Archives Municipales de Metz, AA 13, which are often French translations, contemporary or modern, of documents printed in *PC*, vol. 3. The author favors French texts over original texts to a degree that sometimes undermines confidence in his interpretations. The first official action for the Evangelical Messins is the letter of the XIII to Elector John Frederick and Landgrave Philip, 31 August 1542, in ibid., 310–12, no. 298.
202. *PC* 3:317, no. 303. See Wagner, *Graf Wilhelm von Fürstenberg*, 208–24; and Winckelmann, "Der Anteil der deutschen Protestanten," 214–19, who believed that the rumor of a coup fit William's character and may well have been true.
203. *PC* 3:316–17, no. 302. Tribout de Morimbert, *La Réforme à Metz* 1:142–43, gives the contents of the Senate & XXI's letter to Metz's regime of 13 September 1542 (it could not be found for inclusion in *PC*, vol. 3–see 319 n. 1). The letter, which warns the Messins to allow free preaching and worship, was promptly turned over to Duke Antoine and his brother, who was cardinal and bishop of Metz.
204. *PC* 3:317 n. 3. The embassy was fully formed before 24 September, when it was announced by the XIII of Strasbourg to the Privy Council of Metz, in ibid., 319, no. 306. The instruction is also dated 24 September, for which see Tribout de Morimbert, *La Réforme à Metz* 1:145–46, who gives excerpts in French.
205. AMS, XXI 1542, fol. 380r (24 September 1542), cited in *PC* 3:319 n. 4.
206. I rely on the envoys' documents (*PC* 3:319–21, nos. 308–9), Sturm's oral report to the Senate & XXI of Strasbourg on 1 October (AMS, XXI 1542, at 9 October), and the account by some Catholic notables of Metz, which is quoted by Tribout de Morimbert, *La Réforme à Metz* 1:146–48. I agree with Winckelmann (*PC* 3:320 n. 2) that Bucer's report to Calvin (Herminjard, ed., *Correspondances* 8:150), is full of errors. It was written on the day (6 October 1542) of Sturm's return. See Kleinwächter, *Der Metzer Reformationsversuch*, 50–55; and Winckelmann, "Der Anteil der deutschen Protestanten," 220–21.
207. Tribout de Morimbert, *La Réforme à Metz* 1:147.
208. *PC* 3:320–21, no. 309.
209. I agree on this point with Winckelmann, "Der Anteil der deutschen Protestanten," 221–22.
210. Quoted in ibid., 222.
211. *PC* 3:323–24, no. 312; Tribout de Morimbert, *La Réforme à Metz* 1:152–53.
212. Elector John Frederick to his envoys at Schweinfurt, Lochau, 22 November 1542, in StA Weimar, Reg. H, pagg. 418–21, no. 153, fols. 97r–101v, here at 97v; and another copy is in ibid., Reg. H, pagg. 418–21, no. 154, vol. 1, fols. 155r–158v. On the very same day, the elector instructed his envoys at Schweinfurt, where the league was meeting, to adopt the same policy. Ibid., Reg. H, pagg. 421–24, no. 154, vol. 1, fols. 155r–158v.
213. Sturm reported to the Senate & XXI on 9 September 1542, so he probably arrived home on the seventh or eighth. *PC* 3:307 n. 1.
214. Dr. Niedbruck may have picked this argument up from Bucer. At any rate, he told the Saxon elector that the Evangelicals represented the "besseren und vermöglichen Teil" of the Messins, the meaning of which is unmistakable. Kleinwächter, *Der Metzer Reformationsversuch*, 43 n. 1.
215. The XIII of Strasbourg to Landgrave Philip, 24 October 1542, in *PC* 3:370, no. 349. Bucer wrote that Heu had said that in one year the whole city

would be "gar herbei gebracht." Lenz, ed., *Briefwechsel* 2:87.

216. PC 3:332, no. 317; and the following quote is at ibid., 311, no. 298.

217. Lenz, ed., *Briefwechsel* 2:84.

218. WA B 10:191. The Wittenbergers' responses are treated by Wolgast, *Wittenberger Theologie*, 271–72.

219. WA B 10:195.

220. Winckelmann, "Der Anteil der deutschen Protestanten," 225, says that the decision was mainly influenced by the elector of Saxony; but see Mentz, *Johann Friedrich*, 2:338–39, 371.

221. StA Weimar, Reg. H, pagg. 442–44, no. 158, fols. 63r–68v, and the league's reply on fols. 69r–74r. There is a list of Evangelical Messins in a letter of Caspar Gamank (?) and Jean Karchien to the Smalkaldic League, Strasbourg, 5 April 1543, in ibid., fols. 80r–90v.

222. Reply to "those of Metz," Nuremberg, 9 February 1543, a copy in StA Weimar, Reg. H, pagg. 421–34, no. 154, vol. 3, fols. 111r–12v. PC 3:352 n. 2; Winckelmann, "Der Anteil der deutschen Protestanten," 224–25; Tribout de Morimbert, *La Réforme à Metz* 1:173.

223. Reply to "those of Metz," in StA Weimar, Reg. H, pagg. 421–34, no. 154, vol. 3, fol. 111v; and there, too, the following quote at fol. 112r.

224. Ibid., fol. 112r.

225. See Jacob Sturm's diary and report from Nuremberg, January–April 1543, in which Metz is not mentioned, in PC 3:323–50, nos. 330–31.

226. The incident was widely reported, but see Peter Sturm's report of 26 March 1543, in PC 3:359–61, no. 342. On the negotiations and the raid, see also Tribout de Morimbert, *La Réforme à Metz* 1:173–78. An instruction for Count Dietrich von Manderscheid and Peter Sturm, envoys to Metz, Torgau, 8 March 1543, which Otto Winckelmann believed lost (PC 3:359 n. 1), is in StA Weimar, Reg. H, pagg. 458–63, no. 162.

227. Wagner, *Graf Wilhelm von Fürstenberg*, 221–23, 239–44. The landgrave promised his aid (PC 3:371, no. 352), but Strasbourg's Senate & XXI refused the count's request (ibid., 372–74, nos. 355, 357).

228. The minutes of the negotiations are printed in PC 3:380–83, no. 366. Twenty-eight persons, including two women, signed the exiles' petition to the delegated Smalkaldic powers at Strasbourg on 5 April 1543, in ibid., 367–68, no. 347.

229. Clemen, "Die Schmalkaldener und Frankreich," 224–27, printed their letter and the king's reply.

230. Wolgast, *Die Wittenberger Theologie*, 269. His treatment (269–76) is by far the best informed analysis of this case.

231. PC 2:257–58, no. 280. See ibid., 526–27, no. 551, and vol. 3:176–77, no. 187; Wagner, *Graf Wilhelm von Fürstenberg*, 79–80, 147. Sturm's relations with the count went back at least to 1538. Jacob Sturm to Landgrave Philip, Strasbourg, 31 October 1538, in StA Weimar, Reg. H, pagg. 214–18, no. 96, fols. 57r–58r.

232. Jacob Sturm's memorial on improvement of the league, September 1543, in StA Weimar, Reg. H, pagg. 490–97, no. 169, vol. 2, fols. 44r–46v; it was forwarded by Franz Burckhardt to Elector John Frederick, Frankfurt, 25 September 1543, in ibid., fols. 36r–45v.

233. The political setting for this program is discussed in this volume, chap. 7.

234. He supported this belief by gathering copies of the essential documents concerning the league's history, which he took along to Frankfurt. PC 3:675 n. 5.

235. The rest of this account rests on the instruction, which is printed in ibid., 675–78, no. 642.

236. PC 3:676; Hasenclever, *Politik der Schmalkaldener,* 141–44; Körber, *Kirchengüterfrage,* 181.

237. PC 2:655, no. 654 (28 November 1539).

238. Ibid., 3:677.

239. On the financial structure of the league, see in general, Heuschen, *Konstanz,* 124–28, which contains important corrections to the standard work by Schaffhausen, *Die Geldwirtschaft des Schmalkaldischen Bundes.* See also this volume, chap. 7.

240. PC 3:677.

241. Ibid.

242. This is clear from his diary, in ibid., 702–3. The beginning of this debate was reported by Thomas Blarer to Constance, Frankfurt am Main, 15 December 1545, in Fabian, ed., *Quellen zur Geschichte Reformationsbündnisse,* 192–93.

243. The following rests on the memorial that Sturm and Aitinger drafted on Christmas Day and submitted to the committee two days later, and that the allies approved "upon referral [*auf hindersichbringen*]" on 29 December. It is printed in PC 4:7–8, no. 9.

244. This memorial was drafted on 9 January 1546, read on 5 February, and tabled until the next diet at Worms. It is printed in ibid., 22–23, no. 23, and is the basis of the remainder of this paragraph.

245. Ibid., 2:586–88, nos. 597–99.

246. Ibid., 4:82, no. 62. This virtually repeats a statement at the head of his instruction for Frankfurt in December 1545: "So auf ainer statt Straßburg gelegenhait allain gesehen [wird], derselbigen ain solche weitleufig verstendnus beschwerlich." Ibid. 3:675–76, no. 642.

247. Ibid., 4:22–24, no. 23. He said this in the session (5 February 1545) in which surfaced the major opposition to the Common Penny. Hasenclever, *Politik der Schmalkaldener,* 138, says that Duke Ulrich of Württemberg's envoy supported the reform, but Sturm's diary says the opposite. PC 3:711, no. 651. Sturm reported from Frankfurt on 19 February 1546 that the Württembergers favored the Common Penny, though at Worms in April 1546 he noted that they had earlier argued against the idea that the league appropriate the Imperial Common Penny (Ibid. 4:31, no. 29; 82, no. 62).

248. PC 4:54, no. 49.

249. Ibid., 61, no. 49: "Derhalben besser, es wurd ein pen bestimpt, die ein yeden tribbe, sein gelt zu rechter zeyt zu erlegen." See Hasenclever, *Politik der Schmalkaldener,* 115–24, 139–41, 147–49.

250. Hasenclever, *Politik der Schmalkaldener,* 120–22, who believed that it would have been disastrous to the Protestant cause if the two commanders had yielded to Sturm's attempt to subordinate the War Council to the assembly rather than to the commanders.

251. See this volume, chap. 6.

252. See Sebastian Schertlin von Burtenbach to the Burgomaster of Augsburg, Rothenburg o.d.T., 21 December 1545: "Es were dann sach [i.e., to deal with the ecclesiastical territories] das der hauptkrieg (wie er [Landgrave Philip] selbs achtet) angeen solt." Herberger, ed., *Briefe,* 44.

253. Based on Rublack, "Political and Social Norms."

254. Dickens, "Johannes Sleidan," 41–42; Dickens and Tonkin, *Reformation,* 84–85, 99, 101–2, 142. The following is based on Friedensburg, *Johannes Sleidanus,* the most important study; Hasenclever, *Sleidan-Studien;* Dickens, "Johannes Sleidan and Reformation History."

255. Burke, *Renaissance Sense,* 124.

256. Sleidan's early contact at Strasbourg was Martin Bucer, who may well have

conceived the idea of an official history. See Rott, "Jean Sleidan," 576–81, whose reconstruction of Sleidan's correspondence shows him to have been in touch with Bucer since 1539 and with Jacob Sturm only since January 1545.

257. Sleidan, *Zwei Rede*; contents by Friedensburg, *Johannes Sleidanus*, 23–28.
258. Quoted by Prüser, *England und die Schmalkaldener*, 305. See Baumgarten, ed., *Sleidans Briefwechsel*, 143; Hasenclever, *Sleidan-Studien*, 34–35.
259. Lenz, ed., *Briefwechsel* 2:262, no. 174. See Friedensburg, *Johannes Sleidanus*, 84–88, the only reliable study of this question.
260. Baumgarten, ed., *Sleidans Briefwechsel*, 34, no. 18.
261. Ibid., 46–47, no. 23. His appointment was made by the two Smalkaldic commanders in the entire league's name. See Friedensburg, *Johannes Sleidanus*, 38 n. 2.
262. Baumgarten, ed., *Sleidans Briefwechsel*, 72, no. 38.
263. Hasenclever, *Sleidan-Studien*, 34 n. 3, quoting the elector's letter to his chancellor, Franz Burckhardt, Weida, 14 June 1545, from StA Weimar, Reg. H, pagg. 603–9, no. 194, fols. 146–47. He found the translation of the treaty, apparently in Sleidan's hand, in StA Weimar, Reg. C, no. 385.
264. Hasenclever, *Sleidan-Studien*, 35–36; Hasenclever, ed., "Neue Aktenstücke"; Friedensburg, *Johannes Sleidanus*, 41–43.
265. Friedensburg, *Johannes Sleidanus*, 49. Partly because of his brave words in the preface to the *Commentaries*, Sleidan's faithfulness to the sources has long been a matter of discussion. Mostly, however, the comments concern his truthfulness, though no one denies that he suppressed unpleasant truths. See Menke-Glückert, *Geschichtsschreibung*, 79. The issue raised here, however, of the sources he did use, has never been investigated in detail.
266. Heinrich Walther to Bernhard Meyer, Strasbourg, 29 November 1555, in Baumgarten, ed., *Sleidans Briefwechsel*, 309, no. 162. Sleidan confirms this in a letter to Elector John Frederick, Strasbourg, 24 June 1553 (ibid., 262, no. 127): "Denn die acten worden mir hie von meinen hern mitgetheilt."
267. Johannes Sleidan to the Senate of Augsburg, Strasbourg, 19 May 1555, in ibid., 276, no. 139.
268. Ibid., 309, no. 162.
269. Sleidan, *Commentarii*, bk. 4. See Baumgarten, ed., *Sleidans Briefwechsel*, 257, no. 124 (end of October 1552), where he sends Sturm his passage on the Peasants' War: "Quid regimentum tunc temporis egerit cum illis, audiam ex dignitate tua, quum vacuerit."
270. Rabe, *Reichsbund*, 182 n. 13.
271. Sleidan, *Commentarii*, bk. 19.
272. Ibid., bk. 20, 546.
273. Quoted by Dickens, "Johannes Sleidan," 21, from the preface to the Latin translation of Froissart.
274. This tone, once grounds for praising Sleidan's detached "modernity," has also created problems for some commentators. This is especially true of Sleidan's portrayal of Luther's thought, which grasps at the apparently superficial and often ignores what is now held to be the essence of the reformer's thought. An ingenious, though hardly convincing, solution to this puzzle has recently been offered by Vogelstein, *Johann Sleidan's Commentaries*, who argues that because Sleidan was what she calls "a second-generation Lutheran," he simply assumed that everyone knew these things and he thus didn't need to mention them.
275. This is such an axiom of modern interpretations of sixteenth-century Lutheran theology that it needs no documentation.
276. This is the chief point of Moeller, *Imperial Cities*; and see Brady, "In Search of the Godly City."

Part III

6

The Struggle for Peace, 1539–1545

Therefore, heed my warning
And keep your spirits high;
Rich or poor, you have the task
To protect our fatherland
From the Turkish dogs.
They come with great array,
Whose like I have not seen,
As I must tell you now,
They fear no mortal man.*

On 9 October 1538, Minden, a smallish city just north of where the Weser River debouches from the Central Highlands into the North German plain, became the first Protestant power to be outlawed by the Chamber Court for changes in religion.[1] When the news reached Strasbourg, six days later, the Smalkaldic chiefs were already preparing for war.[2] The Catholic party of action followed suit, and by early winter the Empire lay closer to civil war, perhaps, than at any time since the Bavarian War of 1504.[3] There were voices of prudence, however, and among them spoke Jacob Sturm, who told the landgrave that "we have seen all sorts of examples of how badly things went, when the sword was taken in hand," and though he admitted the danger of waiting for the other side to strike first, he thought the prospects for victory poorer than they earlier had been.[4] Sturm's view, which his regime supported, was that although the Minden affair was surely a "religious matter" in the league's understanding of that term, the Smalkaldeners must not strike first. The Empire did not go to war in 1539, and the Truce of Frankfurt and the ensuing religious colloquies confirmed Sturm's judgment that diplomacy was safer than war.

THE TRUCE OF FRANKFURT, 1539

General accounts of the German Reformation long served up a picture of the Holy Roman Empire between 1530 and 1546 as a land in which an alien emperor and his militant bishops pressed relentlessly for religious war. This picture is mostly legend.[5] The truth is that the wave of militancy, which the breakdown of confessional negotiations at Augsburg in 1530 provoked, soon cooled, and very quickly the Imperial political system began to adjust to the existence of confessionally based parties among the Imperial estates. The Truce of Nuremberg in July 1532, in which the emperor suspended judicial suits against the Protestant powers in return for their financial aid, began a process of reintegration that continued into the following decade. It was severely disrupted only once, during the winter of 1538–39, when the Minden affair nearly precipitated a confessional war.[6] Shortly thereafter, however, the reaffirmation of the confessional peace by the Truce of Frankfurt set in motion a quest for lasting peace by means of official negotiations, called "colloquies," about the religious schism and for resumed meetings of the Imperial Diet.

A close look at the crisis of 1538–39 reveals some powerful barriers to a German confessional war. The German question had to be seen, and was seen, within the larger frameworks of the international political situation. The two Habsburg brothers, Charles and Ferdinand, divided over the international situation and the German problem's place within it. Charles V gave highest priority to the Turkish threat to Aragonese interests in the central and western Mediterranean basins, which tended to marginalize the German problem in his policy between 1533 and 1542—a view that his Burgundian grand chancellor, Nicolas Perrenot de Granvelle, encouraged. The emperor's policy of promoting an end to the schism by means of relatively safe negotiations among theologians fitted very well the place of the nagging German schism—neither central nor peripheral—in his grand scheme.[7]

Meanwhile, King Ferdinand shared Charles's lack of enthusiasm for pressing the German question, only his view of things gave highest priority to the Turkish front in Hungary. From Charles he got soft words but little else.[8] This divergence broke into plain view in 1541, when Charles fled Regensburg for Italy just as Buda and Ofen were falling to the sultan's army.[9] By that time Ferdinand had begun to work on the German problem. More intelligent, politically more astute, and more tolerant than Charles, he began to rebuild his grandfather's system of South German clientele as a basis for reviving Catholic fortunes in the Empire.[10] The key was improved relations with the Bavarian dukes, which led to Ferdinand's sponsorship in January 1535 of the Nine Years' League, a successor to the defunct Swabian League.[11] The surge of free cities, including Protestant ones, toward this league illustrates the natural role of the monarchy as their protector. "Nuremberg is only Nuremberg," boasted Mayor Sebald Pfintzing, as he declared his city's entry into the league, "because it has always supported its lords, the Roman emperors and kings, as is right and just."[12] Based on this modest revival of Catholic and Habsburg fortunes in the mid-1530s, a new Catholic League of Nuremberg arose in 1537–38 under the command of Dukes Louis of Bavaria and Henry of Brunswick-Wolfenbüttel; it aimed to rally the prince-bishops in defense of Catholic territories, properties, and religion.[13]

The formation of a confessional alliance nevertheless did not lead to a religious war. The main reason it did not was because the vast majority of the Catholic estates, including most of the prince-bishops, did not want a war. They formed a standing Catholic "peace party," which could be relied on to support the leadership of the "neutrals." This group of electors, princes, and prelates had formed in 1531 after the Diet of Augsburg, and its leaders, the electors of Mainz and the Palatinate, had mediated the Truce of Nuremberg in 1532.[14] By the late 1530s, the party's leadership lay with electors Louis V of the Palatinate and Joachim II of Brandenburg, plus other "confessionally not unambiguously committed rulers," such as the duke of Cleves-Jülich and the margraves of Baden.[15] During the war fever of 1538–39, this party worked for peace, and its leaders mediated the Truce of Frankfurt between the emperor and the Smalkaldic League on 11 April 1539.[16]

On the Protestant side, too, prudent voices dampened the ardor for war during the crisis over Minden. It is easy to exaggerate the sense of threat the situation during the 1530s posed to rulers and magistrates who had altered their religious establishments, and some Evangelical powers never even joined the league. The cases of Nuremberg and Margrave George of Brandenburg-Ansbach are well known, but there was also Nördlingen, a middling southern free city, whose magistrates hoped that the issue might go away, if only they asserted often enough how unimportant it was.[17] The Smalkaldic League nonetheless attracted sooner or later most of the Evangelical powers, who were thus caught up in the drift toward war in the winter of 1538–39. The league's assembly met at Frankfurt on 14–18 February 1539 to debate the wisdom of making a preventive first strike. The two Smalkaldic chiefs were acting on the Wittenberg theologians' advice that "a preventive war is a defensive war."[18] "Saxony and Hesse are open, unfortified lands," Philip of Hesse explained, and "if the foe strikes first and invades them, he will take all the money, artillery, horses, etc., while if we strike first, we will occupy their lands." If the Smalkaldeners could not quickly get a tolerable peace, he thought, "then we should not await their first strike."[19]

At Frankfurt Jacob Sturm stood against the landgrave, perhaps for the first time in public, and argued for peace. He knew how grave the situation was, and that it was aggravated by the fact that, as he had reported to the Smalkaldeners at Eisenach in the summer of 1538, "there is currently no one among the emperor's German councillors or other people, who knows even a little about the Empire's affairs."[20] Sturm threw his weight on the side of peace during the Frankfurt debate, gambling that the mediators would offer terms acceptable enough to prolong the Truce of Nuremberg.[21] The news of war preparations was not conclusive, he said, "and in such doubtful situations, one should pursue the course that is in principle the best. Peace is better than war."[22] Next day (17 February) Sturm delivered the major address of the proceedings. "We should seek peace now," he urged, "for the [mediating] electors' attitude will tell us what the other side intends to do."[23] If a new truce can be reached, "then reunion might be achieved by a national assembly, though little is to be hoped from a general council, since foreign countries still regard the pope as the head of the church and accord him the authority to call such a council." Whoever strikes first, he warned, "the damage to the German nation will be so great that it will last for a hundred years." Sturm hoped that even if no national assembly met to heal the schism, the Smalkaldeners might participate in "a particular meeting with the princes and other rulers who are not entirely opposed to unity [*so der sachen nit gar ungewogen*]." Otherwise, "if a war breaks out in Germany, the pope will say to the Spaniards, the French, and the Italians, 'See, that's what comes from Luther's teachings; stick to my obedience, etc., for you don't need such trouble.'" If the Smalkaldeners could be certain that the Catholic princes were planning an attack, then it would only be a matter of forestalling it by attacking them, but if the emperor's mobilizations were aimed not at the Protestants but at the Turks, as all reports suggested, a first strike would rouse the foe into a catastrophic war. If the league struck first, Sturm believed, "then the emperor would exert all his might against us, also the pope, Portugal, and perhaps even France. The bishops in the Nuremberg League would also act, for they would fear attacks from us." In such matters, Sturm piously admonished his hearers, "one must not trust too much to human foresight but also trust God and look to him." Therefore, he concluded, "we should not start a war, but we should pursue every means, embassies and others, to see if these negotiations can't bring peace. In this cause we should deal with the emperor, the mediators, the other side, or anyone else."

Sturm, who carried the majority against the league's chiefs at Frankfurt, believed that if the Protestants began a German war, which they could win, it would widen into a European war, which they could not win. Conciliation, even if fruitless, would supply the Protestants with time for their cause to creep slowly over the entire Empire, an idea characteristic of Sturm. Among those who disagreed with it was Martin Bucer, who trumpeted that "we are in as much danger of attack from the king of Calicut as from the emperor, . . . We know from experience that if we strive to advance Christ's kingdom in the right way, it goes forward." "Just think," he chided Landgrave Philip, "of the aid you received from God and men in the Württemberg affair!"[24] In 1534, replied Philip, "we had our own money and troops and relied on no one else," but now the conflict would be general, and "many cooks seldom make a good soup."[25]

Like Sturm, most of the Smalkaldic powers wanted to pay the emperor's price for the Truce of Frankfurt: their consent to negotiations about the schism and to taxes against the Turks, in a word, a resumption of Imperial political life.[26] King Ferdinand wanted to convene a special assembly at Worms, but the clamor for tax revision made it clear that the Imperial Diet would have to meet if taxes were to flow again.[27] Supported by Imperial councilors, neutrals, and (more or less) the Catholic peace party, the Truce of Frankfurt opened a new path, the *via colloquii* or "way of discussion," to confessional peace and reunion.

COLLOQUIES: THE QUEST OF UNITY

During the war scare over Minden, Elector Joachim of Brandenburg and other neutrals recommended holding a colloquy, and shortly thereafter Charles V sent Johann von Weeze, the exiled archbishop of Lund, to the Empire to pursue a "lasting peace, an extended truce, or an agreement."[28] The surprising success of the first unofficial talks, held at Leipzig in January 1539, encouraged many, especially in the Catholic peace party, to anticipate the beginning of an end to the decade of hostility and menace.[29] The Truce of Frankfurt provided that the talks would continue under Imperial sponsorship at Nuremberg on 1 August 1539, though delays, partly because of opposition from the Catholic party of action and the Roman Curia, meant that another ten months passed before the participants assembled in June 1540 at Hagenau in Alsace under King Ferdinand's eye.[30] Disrupted by an epidemic, the Hagenau Colloquy nonetheless reached an agreement on procedure before it adjourned until 28 October 1540 at Worms. Here, unofficial talks sponsored by Chancellor Granvelle produced a provisional text on one disputed point, justification, before the colloquy was again translated, this time to Regensburg, where the Imperial Diet began to meet in January 1541.[31] The colloquy's concluding phase at Regensburg proved, despite the remarkably irenic "Regensburg Book," that no union was possible on essential points, such as the eucharist, although the colloquy yielded just enough progress to secure from Charles V what the Smalkaldeners really wanted, an extension and updating of the Truce of Nuremberg. Here the *via colloquii* ended, and although it brought an end to the German schism no nearer, it did slow the consolidation of Imperial politics along confessional lines and make possible a revitalization of Imperial political life.

As human drama, the colloquies of the early 1540s were impressive events. For the churchmen, more than for the hardened politicians, the ghost of Christian unity flitted hither and yon, taking on more substance as the two sides' theologians began to respect one another as persons and, occasionally, as Christians. This atmosphere helps to explain actions that went well beyond tactics. At Worms, for example, the tough Ingolstadt theologian Johann Eck suddenly shifted to the Protestants' view that religious truth, not disciplinary reforms, were the real matter at issue.[32] The most extraordinary scene, however, unfolded at Worms on 18 January 1541: after Melanchthon, Bucer, Eck, and Bishop Mensing of Halberstadt signed the formula on justification, they hugged and kissed one another like reunited brothers.[33] The intense, if fleeting, impact of such events helps to explain the colloquies' reputation for successes better than does a shared Erasmian culture, the practical importance of which is difficult to assess.[34] It is difficult to say, for example, whether Bucer, whose normal attitude toward Catholics was one of violent intolerance, momentarily believed in genuine reunion, or to what degree such experiences may have awakened a more-than-political attitude toward the colloquies.[35]

The colloquies were from first to last political events: the participants were rulers—princes, bishops, and urban regimes, assisted by theologians. The form established at Hagenau—four presidents named by the king, eleven voting rulers or regimes on each side—made it less a "national council" than a biconfessional commission of the Imperial Diet. Its major achievement was not toward reunion but toward the restoration of the Imperial Diet, which now resumed with impressive regularity for the next fifteen years.[36] It is hardly true, as has been alleged, that the colloquies arose from "the rulers' and theologians' common service to a divided Christendom," only to be later subverted by politics.[37] The colloquies *were* politics.

Their driving force came not from the Protestants, who felt confident about their cause's future, but from the neutrals and the Catholic peace party, who put their trust in Charles and his advisers on Imperial affairs, mostly Netherlanders and Burgundians.[38] The neutrals aimed to secure through mediation "the security of religious peace," as one Jülich opinion put it, though their momentum halted when the business came—as the Protestants insisted it must—to focus on Christian doctrine.[39]

Against this coalition for confessional peace stood powerful forces on either side. The Catholic party of action followed Henry of Brunswick-Wolfenbüttel and the Bavarian dukes, whose chancellor told Duke William that "the cause of religion rests chiefly on you, for the bishops are all asleep."[40] For this party spoke Johann Fabri, bishop of Vienna and grizzled veteran of the anti-Reformation struggle in southwestern Germany, who held that "there was nothing to be done, except to reveal and display to them their crimes, sins, and errors."[41] Such men feared that Charles V was risking the faith for purely dynastic advantage, and they viewed the entire enterprise with great skepticism.[42]

Although far more united than the Catholics, the Protestants displayed just enough cracks to encourage the conciliators. In principle, probably, most of the Smalkaldeners shared the views of the bluff Constancers, who said that "it is impossible to find any agreement or common ground with the pope and his followers, nor is any Christian power obliged to seek it."[43] Most, however, thought that the Protestants must make use of the opportunity to display their faith, and even if doctrinal compromise was unthinkable, discussion and disputation might hasten the day of total victory. Martin Luther spoke for them all: "The attempted agreement on religion is pure trickery by Mainz and the papists, for it is impossible to bring peace between

Christ and serpents. Nothing is sought [in these talks] but our discomfiture." Luther nevertheless wanted "to see our doctrine argued, explained, and recognized, as happened at Augsburg [in 1530]."[44] If the emperor or his agents seriously intended "to make a peace or agreement," Luther mused, "it would have to happen with God, or in His name, which, to speak plainly, means that they must hitherto reconcile themselves with God and publicly confess their errors and abuses." Their heinous crimes aside, the Catholics must surrender their errors and accept the Confession of Augsburg, just as the sacramentarians had done.[45]

Luther's attitude, coupled with his prince's readiness for action in 1538–39, reveals a shift in the center of Protestant militancy from the southwest to Saxony. In the league's early days, Landgrave Philip and Jacob Sturm had argued for the widest possible membership, looser doctrinal tests for admission, and a relatively aggressive policy, whereas the Saxon elector had striven for reconciliation with the Catholics and the emperor and opposed aggressive action, such as the Württemberg campaign of 1534. Now the roles had reversed, for Landgrave Philip, supported by Jacob Sturm and Martin Bucer, favored the *via colloquii* far more strongly than Elector John Frederick and his theologians did. This shift supplies important clues to the restoration of Imperial politics during the first half of the 1540s.

Jacob Sturm never expected a reformed, reunited Christian church to emerge from discussions among theologians. Between 1529 and 1536, from the Schwabach Articles to the Wittenberg Concord, Sturm had witnessed the consequences of relying on formulas rather than on what he had described to the Ulmers as "the proper sort of love for one another." Verbal agreement alone was useless, thought this old Scotist, for "it has often happened in discussions that people agreed in substance [*in der substanz*], but not in words."[46] When preparations were being made for talks at Leipzig in the autumn of 1538, Sturm had no very high hopes for them, even though Landgrave Philip of Hesse believed that "by means of such a gathering, the way may be found to draw Duke George [of Saxony] and his land over to our camp."[47] In January, when the landgrave urged him to go to Leipzig, because "this affair is more a political matter than a theological one," Sturm emptied his pockets of excuses: "The time is so short, the weather is so bad, the roads so poor, and the days so short. By the time I arrived at Leipzig, the talks would be over and the participants dispersed, and I will have traveled this long, tough, burdensome way for nothing."[48] Sturm did not attend the Leipzig meeting, which had as much to do with the future of the Saxon lands as with the situation in the Empire.

The emperor's official colloquy was another kettle of fish, and against his colleagues, who thought the enterprise hopeless and therefore worthless, Sturm supported the preachers' view that not only would Strasbourg's absence look bad, but "when we come together face-to-face, and if our princes are there, perhaps through God's grace the cause will be helped."[49] At first a committee of magistrates thought that "we should stand fast on doctrine and push for a proper reform of the church," but when a second committee met on 8 October 1540, it adopted Sturm's view that "the meeting must in any case be attended."[50]

Sturm's advocacy of the colloquy illustrates his consistent preference for diplomacy over other forms of strife and his hope that diminished strife over religion might lead to a more enduring, perhaps permanent, peace. Sturm stated his view of what was happening during a discussion at Smalkalden in March 1540, after Georg Nusspicker, a Hessian agent, reported on his mission to Chancellor Granvelle at Brussels.[51] Granvelle, Sturm responded,

> enjoys great prestige, is favorably disposed, and knows about the matter; if the emperor had displayed a tyrannical attitude toward us, Granvelle would hardly have acted in such a friendly manner. However, Granvelle has adopted this manner deliberately and given us fine words, so that we will think in the future that he is responsible for whatever [concessions] we receive. Even so, Sir Jacob [believes] . . . that Granvelle should be repaid in words just as fine, with elaborate thanks and other gestures.

If Granvelle really were good-hearted and well disposed, Sturm thought, "the attitudes of other Imperial councillors toward us would also have changed. We can therefore infer that Granvelle lacks a [true] knowledge of God."

With such men, Sturm believed, open rather than secret negotiations offered the only safe path. The Protestants should send Granvelle a confession of their common faith so as

> to display our belief that we are concerned for nothing but His honor. Further, how good and useful it would be for the German nation, if an agreement could be reached, but such agreement cannot be fruitfully attained, except in a general Imperial Diet or national council. This would bring His Majesty great prestige and produce, among other useful things, a strong will to resist the Turks—all of which would redound to the support, improvement, and welfare of the whole German nation.[52]

Because Granvelle was a Burgundian, Sturm added, "and by heritage a German who wishes the German nation well, he should be all the more active in this cause." Above all, Sturm warned, "this should not be allowed to become a matter for private negotiations [*particularsach*]."

Sturm saw that Granvelle, who presided over the colloquy at Worms in the winter of 1540–41, represented the emperor's peace policy, but he also felt that the chancellor's lack of sincerity made it dangerous for the Protestants to respond too eagerly to him. "If we fail to show him what we really want," Sturm warned the Hessians at Smalkalden in March 1540,

> and what it will require to satisfy our demands about religion, our willingness to negotiate and our appearance of softness will lead them to think us much more pacific than we are. We must be concerned that, if seems likely, they understand nothing of the true needs of the church,

purity of religion, duty, or the constraints of a believing conscience, but seek religious conciliation solely for worldly reasons, they will hope for concessions from us in matters, in which we can make none.[53]

The Protestants had nonetheless to disguise their true aims, for "if we tell this man [Granvelle] and others like him, what our cause is truly about, I worry that he will be too frightened to permit us to have this hearing and these negotiations."

Jacob Sturm thus entered the colloquy deeply skeptical about the motives of the emperor, Granvelle, and the Catholics and about the possibility of reunion on the basis of compromise with the Church of Rome, and with a correspondingly firm confidence in the ultimate triumph of the gospel in a Protestant sense. There is no evidence that he believed at all in the possibility of reunion through doctrinal concord. So long as time worked for the Protestants, negotiation—at any and every level and opportunity—was the correct policy. If it led to a restoration of Imperial politics, well and good, so long as the Smalkaldeners protected Protestant rights and interests. Sturm's was a policy of temporizing in the truest sense of the word.

Sturm's confidence rested, in the first place, on the Smalkaldic League's solid achievements since 1531. It also rested on favorable prospects for Protestantism in the Palatinate, which until 1504 had traditionally been Strasbourg's good neighbor. Elector Louis, one of the Catholic "neutrals" who labored to head off confessional strife, lacked a male heir, and next in line was Count Palatine Frederick, brother to Henry, Sturm's old employer.[54] On his way through Strasbourg in July 1539, Frederick revealed his Protestant leanings to Sturm in most expressive language. Back at Heidelberg, he invited Strasbourg's regime to send Sturm to him, and Michel Han, who went in Sturm's place, heard the frankest revelations about the emperor's intentions.[55] These gestures sparked hope for a future conversion of the Palatinate to the Protestant side and its admission to the Smalkaldic League, which would make the Smalkaldic League arbiter of the religious and political fate of South Germany. This would require time, which for the Smalkaldeners was the most attractive benefit to be expected from the colloquies.

When the colloquy opened at Hagenau in June 1540, the two parties stood in very different situations. The deeply divided Catholics voted to leave the procedural details to the king, and from the start, the two sides met separately, communicating only through the royally appointed presidents.[56] The Protestants, by contrast, found themselves in a very strong position because of their unity, because they had little at risk, and because they were fully informed about the Catholics' disunity.[57] They hence took a very strong stand, refusing negotiations on any basis except the Confession of Augsburg, though in return they had to agree to begin the colloquy's main phase on 28 October 1540 at Worms.[58] Jacob Sturm thought these talks at Hagenau had strengthened the Catholics and done little for conciliation, but probably he put too little weight on the neutrals' accomplishments.[59] Hagenau, after all, was merely the preparation for Worms, as the colloquy at Regensburg in 1541 was its aftermath. Sturm, however, put little hope in the coming colloquy, for he doubted that the papal legate, the emperor, and the Catholic princes would appoint theologians able or honest enough to conduct a true disputation with the Protestants, for "the antichristians will flee the light of truth, if they can."[60]

Despite Sturm's misgivings, he and his colleagues prepared for Worms with a new sense of seriousness. He presided over the committee that on 11 October selected an imposing battery of divines to accompany Sturm and Mathis Pfarrer to Worms: Bucer, Wolfgang Capito, John Calvin, "who is learned in the Church Fathers," and Jean Sturm, "because of his Greek." They would all go down together by boat to Worms.[61] The theologians could agree to changes in the wording of past doctrinal statements, Sturm and his colleagues decided, but only if concessions came on other fronts, such as ecclesiastical property, "since one Christian can give way to another, just as in a worldly matters; for if the other side is serious about the chief points, an agreement is well possible."[62] Sturm recommended a civic day of prayer, "because the matter is in itself so weighty and serious," a clear sign that he expected more of Worms than of Hagenau.[63]

So did Chancellor Granvelle, the colloquy's president, who headed the party of pacification around Charles V, and who now began to court the Strasbourgeois.[64] Imperial Vice-Chancellor Jean de Naves, a Luxembourgeois and Granvelle's agent, spoke with Dr. Caspar Hedio, an old acquaintance, on his way through Strasbourg in early November 1540.[65] Naves, as Hedio wrote Sturm and Pfarrer, said that Granvelle "seeks a true reformation of the church and peace among the Germans, and nothing else, for as head of the Imperial state council he is well aware what he may expect from this strife." Indeed, the chancellor told the emperor that if the Empire were not pacified, "he will lose the Imperial crown." Hedio opined that "as Granvelle is to the emperor, so this Naves is to Granvelle." When he asked Naves if the Catholics would begin the colloquy at Worms by insisting on the restitution of ecclesiastical property, the Luxembourgeois replied, "No, not at all. We proceed on the basis of the truth; then we determine good or bad usage and what is to be restored, and what not. Christian doctrine is far more important than the temporal affairs." The bishops, after all, "have nothing to fear from the colloquy or reform, for they will in any case remain lords, as before." Granvelle, Naves reported, had a high opinion of Jacob Sturm, whom he knew. Naves thought that Granvelle would not let three days pass at Worms before he invited Sturm to dinner, "and he [Naves] asked me to write to you, so that he can establish contact all the easier." Hedio was impressed. "I found this Naves a good man," he told Sturm and Pfarrer, "who sees the matter rightly, and who speaks best to the Protestant cause. He is a frank man and a good Strasbourgeois, and he thinks our theologians are by themselves a match for the Spanish theologians and sophists." Naves gave Hedio an introduction to Granvelle, who was soon to arrive with his son, the bishop of Arras, and the two men parted on most friendly terms.

A few days later, Granvelle himself arrived at Strasbourg. This Franche-Comtois had risen at court to become one of Europe's great figures. Suave, learned, extremely able in diplomacy, and ambitious in the extreme, Granvelle was coming to make peace, so as to fill the treasury and free his master's hands for greater tasks. He came to Strasbourg on 18 November—he had been due at Worms on 28 October—with his two sons, and they lodged in Conrad Joham's great mansion in Jews' Street. The Senate & XXI gave them handsome gifts, worthy of princes, though the greeting by Johann Meyer, the city secretary, probably did not meet Granvelle's standard of Latinity. The chancellor assured the magistrates of his good will and commanded them, in the emperor's name, to help him in securing the peace. Then he rode away toward Worms.[66]

The Strasbourgeois took a leading role in the Protestant delegation at Worms, in which the free cities secured a higher proportion of votes—originally five of eleven—than in any other mixed assembly of the era.[67] The theologians were parceled out: Johann Brenz of Schwäbisch Hall to Duke Henry of Saxony's delegation, Jean Sturm and John Calvin—the only Protestants present who were fluent in Granvelle's native tongue—to Brunswick-Lüneburg, and Martin Bucer to the landgrave.[68] The Hessian prince instructed his envoys that they should

> in all things act only after consultation with Sir Jacob Sturm and Dr. Martin Bucer, about how the colloquy should be begun. You should also hear what the other allies' envoys say, especially those of the Saxon elector, but you should always listen more to Sturm's and Bucer's opinions than to anyone else's.[69]

The Hessian prince's instruction elevated to a central role those in the Protestant delegation who were most avid for the colloquy's success. This was perhaps known to Granvelle, who, when negotiations at Worms reached an impasse, turned to the Strasbourgeois to help him break it. He probably had divined what the landgrave had learned, that "Bucer can steer Jacob Sturm and the magistrates of Strasbourg."[70]

The impasse arose in December from a demand by Catholic neutrals—Brandenburg, the Palatinate, and Cleves-Jülich—that the assembly vote as one body rather than as two.[71] If Granvelle agreed, he confessed to Chancellor Feige of Hesse, "he would take home less to the emperor than he had brought here, namely, that the German princes went over in numbers to our [the Protestant] side."[72] Sturm, who probably knew about the rift well before it became public knowledge around 19 December, reported that the Catholics "fear that a public colloquy will bring these three princes over to us," and Bucer, ever more extravagant than Sturm, held that a successful colloquy must bring them closer to total victory.[73] Such sanguine Protestant expectations hindered Granvelle's frantic attempt to flank the deadlock, caused by the split on the Catholic side. His Netherlandish secretary, Gerard Veltwyk, told Bucer on 14 December that "Granvelle wants to invite me and Capito to see him, but that's all hooey."[74] Veltwyk also suggested that Bucer and Capito should begin secret talks with Johann Gropper of Cologne, "who is not unfavorable to reform," about the disputed articles.[75] Bucer discussed the proposal with Jacob Sturm and Johann Feige, who pointed out "the danger in this matter, because these folk are against the colloquy and otherwise behave so oddly; and this proposition ought to be discussed with the allies." Bucer and Capito nevertheless decided to explore this overture, and on the next afternoon Bucer spoke for an hour with Granvelle, who revealed "how anxious he is for peace and reform," how highly he regarded the landgrave, and how impossibly the Catholic theologians were behaving. If, Granvelle warned him, the emperor lost hope of a peaceful compromise, there would be war. Bucer replied that though the Protestants could not yield on essential doctrines, on unessential matters of faith, and on ecclesiastical property, they wished nothing so much as "to preserve peace and quiet among Christians in Christ's name." Buoyed up by these comments, Bucer and Capito twice met secretly with Gropper and Veltwyk and nearly reached agreement on original sin and justification.

Jacob Sturm, who was party to this remarkable departure, didn't dare authorize Bucer to proceed, especially as the allies knew nothing of what they were doing. Even Sturm was not told the substance of the secret conversation with Granvelle and Veltwyk, which Bucer undertook not on Strasbourg's behalf but on behalf of Landgrave Philip, who sent him a backdated instruction "as his appointed theologian" and ordered him to meet with Capito, Gropper, and Veltwyk for secret talks.[76] "You have done the right thing," thought the landgrave, and "what harm can come from trying it?"[77]

Bucer, too, came gradually under Granvelle's spell, for on Christmas Day he reported that "it looks as if things are not so hopeless concerning the chief points of doctrine," and later that he had changed his mind about the chancellor: "I think that this man, though he does not follow our religion, is also no papist or defender of abuses, but that he truly wants to help bring a reformation, and that he sees how useful and honorable this would be for the emperor."[78] When, however, Granvelle asked Bucer to take to Landgrave Philip the formula, on which the theologians had secretly agreed, Bucer feared to tell Jacob Sturm the reason for this mission.[79] When he did, Sturm would not let him go, almost certainly because the secret talks had violated the Protestant party's policy. Sturm had already circumvented that policy, and he also favored accepting Granvelle's proposal that Bucer, Melanchthon, Capito, Chancellors Franz Burkhardt of Saxony and Johann Feige of Hesse, and Sturm should meet unofficially with six from the Catholic side. This time his colleagues at home ordered him "to stick to the recess of Hagenau and not to depart from the form it prescribes."[80] Sturm nonetheless continued to favor participation in Granvelle's informal talks, "so that the other side cannot say, as they are doing, that we fear the light."[81] Most of the other Protestant envoys disagreed, and they voted on 5 January to proceed with direct discussions through only one speaker on each side. It was too late for that, and soon the colloquy was adjourned to Regensburg, its sole positive accomplishment a formula on original sin, which subsequently became the basis of what was called the "Regensburg Book."[82]

Why did Sturm violate his instructions and flout the Protestant majority's will by permitting Bucer and Capito to participate in the unauthorized talks that salvaged at least a possibility from the colloquy of Worms? Possibly, like Bucer and Johann Feige, Sturm also came under the spell of the Burgundian's charm.[83] It was certainly not because he thought the confessional fronts were dissolving, for a sharply unpleasant encounter at Worms with Johann Eck, his old friend from Freiburg days, reminded him of how irrevocable the split was. One evening during the colloquy, Sturm met Eck in Worms's cathedral.[84] "Oh, Sir Jacob," Eck sighed, "we are no longer good comrades, as we used to be"—a point Sturm acknowledged. "Whose fault is that," Eck replied, "if not yours? You abandoned the church and left us, because you were not one of us, while I remained in the fold." "It is a damned sorry fold," responded Sturm, "and since you abandoned true doctrine and the apostolic church, the true departure was made by you, not by us, who desire only to hold to the apostolic church and evangelical truth." Eck charged that Sturm had been misled by wicked men, to which Sturm replied that "I read the writings of both sides and was persuaded by those of our side." "No," jibed Eck, recalling the young Sturm's fruitless pursuit of preferment, "in those days you expected preferment to a benefice," failing which, "you turned against the clergy."[85] Eck asked if Sturm hadn't read his writings and knew his reputation, to which Sturm responded with irony, "yes, I know you to be a man of great fame." The talk then moved on to the Protestant theologians, whom Eck called "apostates and whoremongers, not husbands," and he cursed Bucer in particular. Finally, Eck lapsed into Swabian, which Sturm, of course, well understood: "If you don't die in my faith, you can go to the Devil!"[86] Although others talked of reunion and reconciliation, this scene must have jolted Sturm back into the real world of the bitter acrimony between the confessions.

Always in the past, Martin Bucer had appeared outside Strasbourg as the stalwart supporter of Jacob Sturm, under whose orders he worked. The artisan's son from Sélestat had by the beginning of the 1530s surpassed Capito as Strasbourg's leading churchman, and by 1536 he was clearly the leading churchman of South German Protestantism.[87] At Worms he emerged for the first time from Sturm's shadow to appear as a theologian and churchman of Imperial standing, chief theologian of Hesse, chief spokesman—ahead of Melanchthon—for the Protestant side, and confidant of the Imperial chancellor. His connection to the landgrave, now no longer mediated by

Jacob Sturm, was opening Bucer's eyes to the Reformation's prospects on an Imperial scale at a time when his program had experience total blockage at Strasbourg. This change—recognition abroad, frustration at home—thrust Bucer both into the Protestant struggle to win northwestern Germany and into the conventicle movement inside the parishes of Strasbourg. If the beginnings of the North German reformation opened the Strasbourgeois' eyes to the wider church's needs, the need to come to grips with changes in the North also began to drive a wedge between Martin Bucer and Jacob Sturm.

It was not such considerations, but the Hessian problem, that lay behind the actions of Bucer and Sturm at Worms. The Hessian problem was very simple: in 1538 the landgrave had jeopardized his role as leader of the German Protestants by committing the crime of bigamy.

THE HESSIAN BIGAMY

No affair of this era caused more bad feeling among the leaders of the Smalkaldic League than did the Hessian bigamy.[88] The landgrave's marriage in 1523 to one of Duke George of Saxony's daughters had only briefly interrupted his long career of libertinage, one fruit of which was a severe case of syphilis. In the summer of 1539 he fell head over heels in love with a seventeen-year-old Saxon noblewoman, Margarethe von der Sale, who was to be had, her mother stipulated, as a wife but not as a mistress. The smitten landgrave soon decided to accept the terms and thought to seek support and protection from his Protestant allies; failing that, from the Catholics.[89] This determination made the planned bigamy a political act of gravest concern to the Protestant powers, and the landgrave's confession of bad conscience over his libertinage—he attended the Lord's Supper, he said, not more often than once a year—was bound to impress their theologians.[90] The theologians, in fact, formed in his view the key to gaining Protestant support, and thinking to approach Wittenberg via Strasbourg, he sent his physician, Dr. Gereon Sailer of Augsburg, to consult Martin Bucer. After several days of talks, Bucer, "who was terribly upset with the matter," agreed to go to Hesse and then on to Wittenberg, though he didn't dare tell Jacob Sturm or the Senate & XXI the real reason for the leave he requested.[91] Indeed, Bucer did not tell Sturm at all, for the stettmeister first learned of the planned bigamy—rumors had been flying for months—at Smalkalden in March or early April 1540, after the landgrave's betrothal had taken place (4 March). Chancellor Brück of Saxony took him for a walk in the churchyard and revealed the bigamy and his fear that if the elector and the allies did not support the landgrave, he "will leave the Christian alliance."[92] "If such a division, split, and bad will arise among us now," Brück said with some understatement, "this will truly be a bad time." True enough, for bigamy was a capital crime, as Jacob Sturm well knew, for in 1533 he had interrogated Claus Frey, the Swabian furrier who paid for his bigamy with his life.[93]

Sturm learned the terrible story, he later wrote to Brück, "with a heavy heart. The news itself did not please me; its consequences will please me even less. Every day I have thought about what great trouble and how many losses it will cause, even among those who are mostly closely attached to or are favorable to our religion."[94] Sturm thought the landgrave should not admit his bigamy openly or "tell of it and defend it before all the world. For while it has happened that some persons in some cases have been allowed dispensations out of need, few if any will be persuaded that His Princely Grace was *in casu necessitatis*." Therefore, "the longer it can be kept quiet, the better. If not, then it were better to void the contract, for all pious and good-hearted people will regard it with horror, while our foes will use it to divide us and to suppress the Word of God as best they can." The very knowledge of the bigamy terrified Sturm, as he confessed, for "I have no idea how to handle it with my own colleagues, and if it cannot be defended by the scholars, especially Dr. Martin Luther, from the Bible, I cannot imagine what the consequences might be. May God grant His grace and free the weak, feeble, reviving church from this terrible burden."

The bigamy could not be kept secret, of course, for already it was known at Rome, and gossip about it amused the Bavarian dukes and enraged important people in Saxony and Württemberg.[95] As Bucer and Sturm worked to soften the allies' attitudes, Landgrave Philip poured out his bitterness. "If they won't treat me as a comrade in the alliance for our religion," he wrote to Bucer on 15 July 1540, "and won't have me as its commander, they should say so openly. Then we will have to consider other ways to maintain ourselves and stick to the gospel."[96] One such way would be "for us to declare obedience to the emperor in all temporal matters, rather than to treat 'the person' [i.e., his second wife] and her friends so dishonorably." The landgrave made light of his difficulty to Sturm and Bucer and asked them "not to be so faint-hearted in this matter, which is not against God, but trust God and not fear the world so much. If someone wants to bag us, he will have to use both hands—and his thumbs, too." Good as his word, the landgrave was already deep in secret negotiations with the emperor, who restored him to favor six days after the colloquy adjourned at Worms.[97]

The knowledge of this secret affair formed a gigantic mortgage on Jacob Sturm's policy toward the colloquy, peace with the emperor, and the Catholics. Sturm never defended the bigamy publicly, as Bucer did, nor did he believe that support for Landgrave Philip's action could be justified except by the landgrave's vital role in the defense of German Protestantism. The Hessian prince knew this, and when he told Chancellor Feige at Worms to show Sturm and Bucer the proposed articles of his reconciliation with the emperor, he told Bucer, "Please give them to Sir Jacob Sturm that he may judge them himself, for I am confident that if he looks into his own conscience, he cannot turn his back on us."[98] Yet the landgrave needed Sturm and continued to court his confidence, as when he wrote Bucer that the emperor's declaration of favor must be kept "in deepest secrecy, though you may show it in confidence to Jacob Sturm."[99] In return, Sturm did advise the prince on how to defend the bigamy, though he did it through Bucer, who by this time was far deeper in Philip's counsels than Sturm was.[100] Much too deep, for Bucer's open defense of the bigamy, the most colossal act of bad judgment in his career, rested on the naïve expectation that Landgrave Philip would keep faith with the theologians and hold the bigamy a secret.

Bucer's poor judgment encouraged his numerous enemies at home—he blamed the Schwenckfelders—and abroad.[101] One of them was the Badener Michel Han, a city attorney, son-in-law of an ammeister, and one of Jacob Sturm's close collaborators. "A few Schwenckfelders have turned the entire magistracy and many pious, good-hearted burghers against me in the most terrible way," Bucer wrote in 1542. "I discovered today that Michel Han rails against me and has a great following here."[102] Among his followers, perhaps, was the anonymous author of a pamphlet in which Bucer was accused of authoring a notorious work defending the landgrave's bigamy. He accused Bucer of being

> A sort of Jew and false Christian,
> Full of verbal tricks, a true sophist ...
> A hypocrite and false exegete,
> Who perverts God's words and works.[103]

The landgrave, loyal to those who were loyal to him, thought to compensate Bucer for his damaged reputation with five hundred fl. per year to become "a superintendent over the clergy of our land," and a little later he suggested that Bucer come work for him and for Duke Moritz of Saxony "and help to establish good Christian discipline and ordinances in both of our lands."[104] Surely tempted by these offers to become head of the church in a major territory, Bucer nonetheless decided to remain at Strasbourg, even though his defeats there and the backlash about the bigamy were beginning to take their toll on his reputation and on his relations with Sturm. Indeed, the controversy over the bigamy began the deterioration in the relations between these two men, whose partnership had begun ten years earlier at the Marburg Colloquy.

Despite his horror, Sturm found that the bigamy had its welcome consequences as well, for while the landgrave sought reconciliation with the emperor, Elector John Frederick's ardor for combat began to cool. Like Landgrave Philip in his palmier days, the Saxon prince had been toying with plans to organize a great anti-Habsburg league among the kings of England, France, and Denmark, and German princes. "The great danger and threat," he instructed his envoys to England in 1538, "is that sometime in the future Austria might attempt to subject the neighboring kings and the Empire of the German Nation to a hereditary monarchy."[105] To yield at all to King Ferdinand's requests for taxes to fight the Turks, he wrote to the landgrave, would not only constitute tacit recognition of his illegal royal election but also put him in a position as victor to move against the Protestants. "Even if, God forbid," he wrote, "Austria and the king's dynastic lands fell to the Turks, the German nation would not be so badly damaged or threatened as it would through the establishment of such a hereditary servitude."[106] The partnership, thinking ran at the Saxon court, between the Protestant princes and the French king was especially apt, because the princes needed money and the wealthy king wanted German troops and influence in the diet.[107]

Even before alarm bells sounded over the Minden affair, therefore, John Frederick of Saxony had begun to embark on the activist path that so distinguished him from his stolid father. By early 1539 he was certain that war was not far off, and he meant to strike first.[108] Saxon envoys flattered the English king; Saxon councilors dreamed of a French alliance. Chancellor Brück told the elector that "it would be very useful to join hands with the French Crown, to speak in terms of worldly wisdom, in order to ward off such servitude and burdens. Just remember what help the Swiss got from this Crown for the preservation of their own freedom." This was a change, when the Saxons praised the Swiss as rebels! Gregor Brück, one of the most conservative men at court, even dreamed of the day when with French aid the Protestants could seize the Imperial crown and destroy Catholicism:

> In time our party could set up its own King of the Romans, to whom the whole Empire could be made subject and obedient, and other good laws could be made. And there should be no more priests, for otherwise the royal crown will remain in their hands, and we will have to endure their eternal oppression.[109]

At this time, therefore, the elector and his men foresaw a new struggle between princes and emperor, as in Emperor Maximilian's day, and they scented a chance of total victory. This mood shaped Saxon coolness toward Charles V's overtures to the Protestants in 1539–41 and toward the colloquies as a possible remedy for the schism. The Saxons saw in the schism not tragedy but opportunity for a final victory of the gospel over idolatry, of "German liberty" over "Latin tyranny," of Christ over Antichrist.

Most of the other Smalkaldeners had grave reservations about this aggressive Saxon policy, and even more about the hopes it placed on the king of France.[110] The persecution of French Evangelicals filled them with dismay, especially at Strasbourg, the nodal point of German Protestant communications with France.[111] Bucer, however, ever the man of action, sought to win Landgrave Philip away from the emperor and for a French alliance. To aid Charles V against France, he wrote, "is in my opinion no Christian path. For the emperor holds much that belongs to France, while France holds nothing that belongs to Austria."[112] "Whatever France may be," Bucer went on, "it has for a long time behaved well toward the entire Empire, which Austria has nearly destroyed and has driven into irreparable servitude and ruin." The emperor seeks taxes, he warned, "not to aid the Empire . . . but to swell the power which is already too great for the Empire to bear." This was a message from the old days, Zwingli's days, when the Reformation presented a golden opportunity to defeat the House of Austria. And though this dream contradicted the Smalkaldic League's professed religious basis and defensive purpose, it represented now as then a moderately realistic policy. Its high point, perhaps, coincided with the French envoys' arrival at Hagenau, come to fire John Frederick's commitment to a grand anti-Habsburg alliance.[113] The revelation of the landgrave's bigamy, of course, dealt this policy a mortal blow, though John Frederick continued his French negotiations, confident that he could later draw the Smalkaldeners into the scheme.[114] The elector even suggested that the reports of religious persecutions in France were Hessian fabrications, but the Strasbourgeois, who knew better, continued to plead for the league's intercession on the French Evangelicals' behalf.[115] At the beginning of the 1540s, therefore, the conjunction of forces scuttled the new Saxon dream of grand Franco-German war against the House of Austria, which might have put John Frederick on the throne for which his grandfather had longed. These forces—the landgrave's bigamy, the French persecutions, Granvelle's charm, and Jacob Sturm's influence—kept the Smalkaldeners on the path that led through the colloquies to Regensburg and the emperor they had not seen for nearly a decade.

CONCORD AT REGENSBURG, 1541

Charles V entered Regensburg on 23 February 1541, Granvelle at his side, in high expectation of ending the schism.[116] High time, too, for Charles had secret plans to strike at Algiers, and Ferdinand's Hungarian army was trying to take Ofen before Turkish forces arrived to relieve it. En route from the Netherlands, Charles advertised his attitude by suspending the decrees of outlawry against Minden and Goslar and all the suits of restitution against Protestant powers. When the diet opened on 5 April, Charles confirmed this impression by appointing to the Catholic team for the colloquy's last phase almost exclusively men who supported his reunion policy. On the Protestant side were appointed as theologians Melanchthon, Bucer, and Johann Pistoris, and as lay auditors the two commanders' chancellors, Burkhardt and Feige, plus Jacob Sturm.[117] To the partial agreements from Worms on free will and original sin, this group added statements on some relatively unproblematic topics—baptism, confirmation, and marriage—but no amount of good will could produce agreement on transsubstantiation, the authority of the hierarchy, the mass, penance, or the veneration of the saints, and the Protestants raised new objections to the formula on justification.[118] The results, collected in the Regensburg Book, pleased few but its authors.

Faced with his colloquy's failure, Charles V grasped at a declaration of toleration, the project for which had earlier been discussed with the Protestant leaders, including Jacob Sturm, though by this time—early July—the

Protestant peace party was clearly losing ground to Saxon intransigence. On the Catholic side, too, the opponents of conciliation were on the attack, and Charles, caught between two fires, decided to move against both of them. On the one hand, he issued on 29 July a secret declaration of toleration conceding to the Protestants the right of "Christian reformation" in return for their acceptance of the diet's recess; on the other, the recess confirmed both the Truce of Nuremberg and the recess of Augsburg of 1530. The two documents, which were perfectly incompatible with one another, also provided that if no general council met within eighteen months, the decision on the religious question should revert to the diet.[119] This incongruous medley of measures complete, Charles slipped southward toward Italy and his Mediterranean campaign, leaving Ferdinand and his army to face the oncoming Turks.

At Regensburg Jacob Sturm crowned the evolution of his role since early 1539 as leader of the Protestant peace party. When the emperor appointed him one of the three Protestant lay colloquents, Sturm was not especially hopeful, for "without God's special help, the prospect looks bleak. With Him, however, all things are possible."[120] With Sturm stood Dr. Conrad Hel of Augsburg and, of course, Johann Feige of Hesse, whose prince was formally restored to Imperial grace during the diet. This Protestant peace party was playing for time, for, as Dr. Hel admitted, through a mild policy "the opposition, or at least many of them, may through God's grace be won over, and the negotiations would thus not be fruitless."[121] Martin Bucer, on whom the Venetian cardinal Gasparo Contarini made a profound impression, saw the light of total victory and swung over again to this side.[122] "Germany is moving toward the gospel," Bucer declared at a critical point in the negotiations, "and for that reason I am driven by zeal to enlighten those in error."[123]

On the other side stood the elector of Saxony's men, headed by Franz Burkhardt and Prince Wolfgang of Anhalt.[124] Though they rode out on 27 March to greet Landgrave Philip and dined with him that evening, their instructions set them dead against the Hessian's policy. Melanchthon and Bucer were soon at loggerheads, separated by "fundamental" differences of policy and sympathy,[125] for although the Saxons regarded themselves as standing between God and the Devil, the Strasbourgeois and Hessians sensed the nearness of a reform-minded majority in the diet. As Sturm put it, the Protestants should hold to "the substance of the confession [of Augsburg]," because "in the colloquy it has happened, that often they are agreed in substance, but not in words."[126] John Frederick would have none of such talk, and he found the Protestants' formulations on episcopal power and the clergy "much too soft."[127]

In the end, it was Sturm and Feige who helped to make the settlement at Regensburg, secured by what the Hessian chancellor called "a good, suitable declaration [of toleration], which contains many good points never before conceded."[128] When the Protestants could not agree to accept or refuse, under Granvelle's pressure Sturm and Feige specified the Protestants' grievances and proposed the declaration of toleration, which unexpectedly gained support even from the recalcitrant Saxons and Württembergers. Sturm and Feige wanted the concessions included in the diet's recess, not in a separate declaration, but there was no other way. "So," Feige reported,

> Sir Jacob and I took on the task, and he took in hand the proposed recess and the draft of a declaration, and I took up my pen, and we drafted the declaration. . . . It was simply so that Sir Jacob and I would not budge: either the declaration or we would refer the recess to our masters [instead of signing it].[129]

"The declaration compensates for the recess," Feige asserted, for "had we not received the declaration, we would not have approved the recess. We did all we could under these conditions."[130]

If the Regensburg Book of 1541 represented, as has been said, "a new beginning" toward Christian unity in the Empire, it did so by fostering bad will and divisions in both confessional parties.[131] On the Protestant side, Jacob Sturm and Martin Bucer bore the brunt of criticism from those who thought the Protestants had conceded too much. Some feared that the partial rapprochement itself would cause new splits among the allies and among Protestant peoples. "Who will then explain it to the Common Man," asked Augsburg's leaders, "or convey it to the clergy who were not parties to it?" The compromises aroused dissension among Augsburg's clergy, "in all of which, to speak confidentially, Martin Bucer and Jacob Sturm are suspected of being the chief culprits."[132] Encouraged by Granvelle and the Imperial court, which they had once called "the greatest enemy of all liberty and justice in the German nation," Sturm and Bucer had become the spokesmen of conciliation, accommodation, and reunion. Sturm aimed to soften the consequences of the landgrave's bigamy and to put off a settlement into the indefinite future, and for the moment his temporizing policy coincided with Granvelle's. They held the day in 1541 because of the split between the Smalkaldic chiefs, which, in an ironic reversal of roles, found the Hessian landgrave for conciliation and the Saxon elector against it. No matter, for these shifted alignments opened the way for a resurgence of the preconfessional patterns of Imperial political life.

THE RECOVERY OF IMPERIAL POLITICS

When the estates came together under Charles's eye at Regensburg in 1541, no diet had sat since 1532.[133] The revitalization of Imperial governance during the first half of the 1540s, like the colloquies that preceded it, rested on a convergence of the Protestant peace party's policy with those of the emperor, the neutrals, and the Catholic peace party. For a time, until forces arising from the Reformation struggles in northern Germany broke through, the old political patterns recovered year by year. They engaged no one more completely than they did Jacob Sturm, who participated in every important political assembly of the era—Imperial Diet, circle assembly, urban diet, Smalkaldic League diet—and strove to restore the free cities' old solidarity from pre-Reformation days. Even when the league's problems again became paramount in 1545, a single issued united his efforts in the diet with those in the league: the free cities' struggle to be treated with fairness and respect by the princes.

Three closely related changes made the Imperial recovery possible. First, from 1542 onward the Habsburg brothers faced a two-front war against the Turks in Hungary and against France, and their need for taxes coincided with the neutrals' need for promotion of "moderation and order," as a Palatine instruction put it, and the Protestants' desire for security against legal suits.[134] Second, the menace posed by the French war to the Netherlands was so great—"since the days of our grandfather, Emperor Maximilian, the Netherlands never stood in such danger," Queen Mary wrote—that Charles could no longer neglect the German question.[135] The French war focused on Gelderland, that ancient thorn in the flesh of the Habsburg Netherlands, but Charles had to compete for German resources with King Ferdinand, whose forces were very hard pressed after the fall of Ofen and Pest in 1541.[136] Third, despite their differences, the Habsburg brothers collaborated to rebuild the Habsburg system of clientele, especially among the free cities and minor powers such as the free knights, into a new system of peace-keeping leagues.[137] This policy, aimed less to make the Empire a "monarchy" à la française than to establish Charles as, in Granvelle's words, "lord of Germany [padron di Germania]."[138]

These changes encouraged the shift away from the Reformation pattern of Imperial politics—direct bargaining with confessional blocs about concessions—to the main pre-Reformation pattern—bargaining with the Imperial Diet about taxes. If the free cities, long split by the schism, were to have any voice in this restored process, they had to resurrect their institutions, the Imperial Diet's Cities' House and the urban diet, both of which had been undermined by the formation of confessional parties at the end of the 1520s. The cities met together only once between 1529 and 1538, but thereafter they came together with something like the old frequency, and for much the same reasons.[139] The key, of course, to a new urban solidarity was avoidance of the confessional issue, and at the Diet of Regensburg in 1541, where the reconstitution of the cities' corporate policy really began, the separate meetings of the confessional parties made this difficult.[140] The restoration of urban unity vitally interested the Catholic free cities, who had no separate, confessionally organized association, and the crucial step came when the four major Catholic free cities of the Rhine Valley—Cologne, Worms, Speyer, and Metz—joined the Protestant towns to protest the diet's recess because it did not recognize the free cities' rights. The Catholic electors and princes rejected the claim that the cities "have such a separate house like our own, which may veto our proposals and decisions, for ancient custom dictates that they must not only agree with us, but that they must accept and obey whatever is decided by the majority among us, just as in our houses the weaker party must yield to the stronger."[141] This attitude brought the cities together behind a policy that linked the granting of taxes to recognition of their rights, and the leading urban politicians quickly saw what had happened and seized the opportunity. At the next urban diet at Speyer in November 1541, they urged the cities to search their archives for documentation of urban rights.[142] From this point on, regular sessions of the urban diet—eight between 1541 and 1545—reestablished a permanent network of communications among the free cities, especially the larger southern ones. Its effectiveness depended on the major communes' ability to prevent confessional loyalties from interfering with actions in the common urban interest, which they did with remarkable success. At the Diet of Speyer in 1542, for example, the Protestant cities chose corporate over confessional solidarity, when they rejected their co-religionists' demand for a separate Protestant sector of the Imperial army.[143]

Except for Cologne, the leaders of this new urban front, like those of the old one, came from the principal southern communes: Strasbourg, Augsburg, Nuremberg, Ulm, and Frankfurt.[144] Among them one voice carried weight in every Imperial assembly, that of Jacob Sturm, on whom, as Elector John Frederick remarked in 1541, "the southerners all depend."[145] Sturm moved into the forefront of the free cities' struggle for their rights during the Diet of Nuremberg in 1542, for which his (self-drafted) instruction recommended that the cities protest any recess framed without their participation.[146] Sturm was no legalist—he considered, for example, the distinction between "free" and "Imperial" cities to be "purely external" and therefore of no moment[147]— and his engagement for the cities' corporate constitutional rights had a very practical object: taxation. The issue of tax revision, on which all urban interests converged, made Jacob Sturm the free cities' undisputed spokesman in Imperial politics.[148]

Pecunia nervus belli ran a favorite saying of the sixteenth century, and taxation for war had dominated Imperial political life all through the Habsburg era.[149] In the Empire, taxation without consent was still tyranny, a point the Burgundian writer Philippe de Commynes had made long before:

> Is there any king or lord in this world who has the power, outside of his own domain, to levy a single penny [*denier*] on his subjects without the approval and consent of those who are to pay it, unless he does it by tyranny or violence?[150]

The Imperial estates had so successfully resisted taxation at western European levels that during Emperor Maximilian's long, war-torn reign they paid only a tenth to a fifteenth of his expenses, the remainder falling on Austria.[151]

In those days, about 70 percent of all tax revenues went for war, and it was no different in Charles's time. The wars of the 1540s produced so many diets—Regensburg in 1541, Speyer in 1542, Nuremberg in 1542 and again in 1543, Speyer in 1544, Worms in 1545—and such long parliaments that the Imperial Diet was sitting approximately half the time between April 1541 and August 1545.[152] What is more, this tempo continued at a reduced but nonetheless still rapid pace through the two wars of 1546–47 and 1552, right down to the Peace of Augsburg in 1555.[153] And whereas the diets held after 1547 necessarily focused on the religious schism, those of the early 1540s centered on war and taxes.

Behind the issue of urban rights, kept aboil by the diet's frequent and long sessions, stood the diabolically complex problems of Imperial taxation. The Holy Roman Empire since Maximilian's day had known two principal ways of assessing taxes.[154] The older and more usual one was the matricular levy, based on an army of standard size (twenty thousand foot and four thousand horse), granted in multiples called "Roman months," and assessed on the estates according to registers (Reichsmatrikeln), the currency and fairness of which were matters of endless debate. The second, newer method was the Common Penny, a direct property tax on all Imperial subjects, both immediate and mediate, granted as a rate on property and graduated by tax classes. Though the diet had experimented with this direct method in 1495, under Charles military taxes were granted (except for 1542 and 1544) according to the matricular system, based on the registers drawn up at Worms in 1521.[155] Between 1521 and 1550, this procedure yielded a total of about 2 million fl., whereas an average major campaign against the Turks devoured about 3 million fl. for one year.[156] The collection system was chaotic, for the taxes, when paid at all, were collected in the larger free cities or by the circles, there being no central oversight and no audits.[157] The granting of taxes, therefore, and even more the payment of taxes granted, formed a good if rough gauge of the temper of the estates and their enthusiasm for the king's and the emperor's military projects. This was especially true of the "long-term levy [beharrliche Hilfe]," the Empire's nearest thing to a permanent tax, as opposed to the cheaper, separately debated, and more readily granted "emergency levy [eilende Hilfe]." Both were assessed in "Roman months" and according to the Worms registers, the fairness and accuracy of which occasioned endless complaints and requests for exemptions and reductions, the net effect of which was to reduce the total yield by about a quarter during Charles's reign.[158]

Two issues dominated the tax debates of the first half of the 1540s: the choice between the matricular system and the Common Penny, and the fairness of the Worms registers. Commenting on the former issue in 1542, Jacob Sturm judged that the wealthier, more centralized powers preferred the indirect way of the matricular levy, whereas the mass of small estates, the weaker large ones, and the free cities favored the direct way of the

Common Penny.[159] Since its initial appearance in 1495, the Common Penny had always possessed a certain antiprincely flavor, because direct taxation established a direct connection between the Imperial government and the common people, whereas the alternative, matricular system confirmed the Empire's feudal character.[160] In the past, the major princes' opposition to the Common Penny had been decisive.

It would be so again in the mid-1540s.[161] The debates at the Diet of Speyer in 1544 found Bavaria, the two commanders of the Smalkaldic League, and Augsburg in favor of the matricular levy and the other Smalkaldic cities, including Strasbourg, aligned with most of the bishops, prelates, and counts for the Common Penny.[162] The electors and princes condemned the Common Penny as having a "curiously Swiss appearance" and alleged that the cities intended through it to "make all things in common."[163]

The second issue, unfair assessments under the matricular system, was a perennial source of grievance. Some years before, at Eisenach in 1538, Sturm had raised the issue of unfair assessment to the allies, arguing that "the electors and princes, who have wide lands and many subjects, should pay more than the cities."[164] So long as the old system was in force, the Strasbourgeois vied with other estates for reductions in their assessment, complaining of "how burdensome and unfair it is that Strasbourg's wealth is estimated much too high, yes, even as high as an elector's."[165] This was true, for the register of 1521 assessed Strasbourg 225 foot and 40 horse—which converted to cash at 1,380 fl.—whereas the electors were each assessed 277 foot and 60 horse.[166] The Worms register also contained remarkable discrepancies among the free cities—Metz, for example, was assessed much higher than Augsburg—and assessed cities that were no longer, or never had been, free.[167] The Worms register contained, in fact, fewer and less glaring discrepancies among urban assessments than had earlier registers, though this does not mean that it distributed taxes more fairly between the cites and the "higher" estates.

Both of these issues—the method of assessment and the discrepancies in the Worms register—grew more acute for the cities during the early 1540s, because the dampening of confessional tensions brought the princes more squarely behind the Imperial wars. At Regensburg the Catholic princes had declared their support for a long-term levy for three years, and the leading Protestant princes, assembled at Naumburg in October 1541, recommended that the long-term levy be doubled to forty thousand foot and eight thousand horse at the next diet at Speyer.[168] This biconfessional princely support for the war reflected both the alarm that the fall of Buda and Ofen evoked from the Germans and the movement of younger princes, even Protestant ones, toward Habsburg service. Something similar had happened in Maximilian's reign, when the emperor had striven to win over the younger princes to Imperial service, having alienated most of their seniors.[169] As Chancellor Granvelle courted the princes, Landgrave Philip responded, followed by younger men, such as the Hohenzollern prince Margrave Hans of Küstrin. The biggest catch, however, was Duke Moritz of Saxony, the strong, able, vibrant young Lutheran who had succeeded in 1541 to the rule of Albertine Saxony, which George the Bearded had so long guarded for the old faith.[170] After his accession at the age of twenty in August 1541, Moritz, who took part in the Hungarian campaign of 1542, sought the emperor's favor against his cousin and rival, Elector John Frederick, with an openness that worried his father-in-law, Landgrave Philip. "If you and I and Duke Moritz," the landgrave wrote Elector John Frederick,

> were as evangelical as we give ourselves out to be, we would not quarrel so much among ourselves but behave just as Christ and St. Paul teach us to do. We would also consider the dangers we see now all around us. For I truly fear that through this quarreling it will happen to us as it did in the war of the mice and the frogs, and the stork came and ate them all up.[171]

The landgrave's fears were fully justified, for their common religion did nothing to dampen the House of Wettin's division, now in its third generation, and the two cousins soon fell to quarreling over a prize piece of Reformation plunder, the bishopric of Meissen.[172]

The Protestant princes' support for war taxes angered Jacob Sturm, who declared in 1542 that Strasbourg simply could not pay at this level. The princes' proposal would require from Strasbourg alone the sum of 120,000 fl., more than from Duke Moritz with his vast lands and rich mines, and more than from the bishop of Würzburg, "who is just about the richest bishop in Germany."[173] He prudently did not mention the Hessian assessment, which was only slightly higher than Strasbourg's. Indeed, the landgrave was the only prince who displayed any sympathy for the free cities' bitter complaints against the scale and inequities of Imperial taxation.[174]

The existence of the confessional fronts made little difference to the free cities' political situation. Their treatment at Speyer in 1542 replicated their experiences in the Imperial Diets of the early 1520s. "After the electors' and princes' houses had conferred and agreed on the levy against the Turks," the Hessian envoys reported to their prince, "their unanimous decision was presented to the cities, who replied that the procedure followed by this Diet, and in particular the presentation of this decision, violates ancient custom; and they asked that their opinions be heard in open session, and then the matter could be decided."[175] For Sturm and the other Protestant politicians from the cities, the most grievous aspect of this entire procedure must have been the biconfessional consensus among the electors and princes. "The most important thing so far," Bucer wrote to the landgrave, "is how the cities are stripped not only of their right of consultation, but also of all their property and money . . . At this Diet the Protestant princes as well as the others have recommended and voted for the suppression of the cities; and many papists mock the cities for having put so much trust in the Protestant princes."[176] The villain behind it all, Bucer thought, was Chancellor Eck of Bavaria, who aimed "to tear the cities away from the Christian princes. For, if the Saxons, Duke Moritz's men, Lüneburgers, Württembergers, and Brandenburgers are all so set against the cities, what will happen then?" This time the shadow passed, for the Diet of Speyer levied the Common Penny, which most cities favored, for the first time in Charles's reign, and the urban delegates signed the recess.[177] The Common Penny, however, had to be collected through a laborious procedure of local assessment, the money came in slowly, and King Ferdinand, desperate for funds to support the army he was assembling to retake Buda, recalled the diet to Nuremberg for a month in midsummer.[178]

When Sturm reflected on the coming fight over taxation, he recommended that the urban envoys at Nuremberg protest any tax granted without their prior consent.[179] This was the tactic, of course, the Protestants had used so successfully at Speyer in 1529 and since, and which Sturm now offered to the revitalized urban front. He assumed, correctly, that the princes and electors would fall back on the matricular system, and his arguments against this system show that he understood why the tax burden was climbing so rapidly. The upper estates, he began, argue that the matricular system is traditional, and that the cities used to pay without protest. "Although the cities were always unfairly assessed," he responded,

> the unfairness was small then compared to what it now is. This can be easily proved from the old recesses. Now the levies are doubled, tripled, and quadrupled and have grown so burdensome to us that while a prince must send every hundredth man to the front, a city must send every fourth, third, or even every other man. Then, too, the old Imperial levies were employed only for emergency purposes, not for long campaigns. It was bearable then, but now the higher levies are being proposed for longer and even long-term aids, which the cities cannot endure. Many cities listed in the old registers are no longer even in the Empire, and their taxes are piled on the remaining ones. It was more bearable then, when there were many of us, to contribute to an army of thirty or forty thousand men, but now that we are fewer, it is to be feared that if the burdens are not reduced to fair levels, more cities will be forced to break away or to free themselves in other ways from this ruinous levy.[180]

A fair apportionment, it was thought, would assess Strasbourg at about a fourth the share of an elector.[181]

Sturm did not lack sympathy with those who fought the Turks in Hungary—he later advised his skeptical colleagues to pay two more "Roman months" for the army[182]—but he was frightened by the skyrocketing rise of military costs, propelled by the mercenary system, larger armies, and new weaponry.[183] The matricular system was figured on an army of twenty thousand foot and four thousand horse for one month, or around 125,000 fl. for wages and salaries alone. By 1542, however, it was reckoned that the cost of a long-term levy for the Turkish War would cost about 3 million fl. per year.[184] This from a diet that had granted about fifty thousand fl. per year in the previous generation. Where were such sums to be found? The Germans, understandably, scanned the vast Habsburg-Trastamara inheritance, saw realms fabled for their wealth or their military strength—Milan, Tuscany, Castile, Brabant, and Flanders—and expected rivers of cash to flow from them toward Christendom's common project in Hungary. Sturm shared this expectation, and he had once declared that the cities should balk at paying unless "such taxes are assessed on all the estates of Christendom, or at least on the whole German nation."[185] This expectation, however, contradicted both the place of the Empire in Charles's imperial vision—he did send two thousand Spanish foot to the Hungarian war in 1538, a mere gesture—and the deeper relationships between taxation and wealth in the Netherlands, Castile, and Italy.[186]

What could Sturm and the other urban representatives do in the face of this massive escalation of taxation through a system that weighed heavily on their burghers' wealth and trade? They could protest, of course, as Sturm did the recesses of Nuremberg in 1542 and 1543, only to find his name inserted among those of the signatories.[187] When he protested, Dr. Jacob Jonas, the chancellor of Mainz, sighed, "Who can tell me, when you are going to obey for a change?" Sturm retorted, "when you make fair recesses and enforce them, we will accept them. But you make unfair, incorrect recesses, which contradict earlier ones, and you don't enforce them. Therefore, we cannot accept them, though this is not disobedience on our part."[188]

Protests against the upper houses' obdurate rejection of their right to participation in the diet's decisions, protests against the decisions taken and fixed in the recesses—protests without teeth, protests based on tradition alone—could never succeed, but failure meant that taxation would grind the free cities down. What to do? As the Cities' House had admitted so long ago as 1524, it was impossible for them or anyone else to document "old, irrefutable tradition" by means of authenticated charters. At Nuremberg in the summer of 1542, the leading urban politicians nevertheless decided to comb their cities' chancelleries and archives for documentary evidence of urban rights, and to hand it over to the lawyers to draw up their case.[189] The Strasbourgeois, which meant Jacob Sturm, were asked to oversee this process.[190] Now began a new search for the practice of the past, for once before, in 1523, the free cities' politicians had ordered a search for evidence of what was essentially a legend, namely, that the practice of the past had been the free cities' full participation as a third house of the diet.[191] On the contrary, despite several lapses in practice, the upper estates had always defended the principle, which Elector Richard of Trier had thrown in Sturm's face at Speyer in 1526, that it was their place to command, the cities' to obey.[192]

Once the cities decided to make a historical and legal case, Jacob Sturm threw himself into the search for those "private or unofficial documents," that were "obviously old, being composed many years ago," and of which copies were now to be found in "the archives, chancelleries, or vaults of the cities."[193] He hunted through Strasbourg's chancellery, which his brother Peter had helped to put in order and inventory more than ten years before,[194] and he consulted—how is not known—the archives of at least seven other free cities.[195] He cast his net back to 1427 and documented as well as he could the free cities' decisions and actions at Imperial and urban diets concerning their parliamentary rights and taxation. He must have sighed as he read how Matern Drachenfels, Strasbourg's envoy to the Diet of Nuremberg in 1479, exclaimed in his report that "the cities are the sleepiest folk of all."[196] He must have marvelled, too, to read how Emperor Frederick III had come to an urban diet at Speyer in 1486 to beg the cities to pay their taxes. In Sturm's day the emperor as often as not failed to appear at Imperial Diets.[197] Year by year he followed the great assemblies of the 1490s, when so much of the diet's procedure had been formed, and when his own father and uncles had helped to rule Strasbourg.[198] Everywhere he looked for evidence that the free cities had taken part in the deliberations of Imperial Diets, sat in their committees, and signed their recesses.[199] He ended his notes in 1517, well within the memory of those living.

Jacob Sturm's investigations formed one step in the process that led to a 1544 decision to establish an archive of the free cities at Speyer.[200] They also served more immediate political purposes. At Nuremberg in early 1543, the materials were pulled together by a committee of lawyers from Nuremberg, Frankfurt, and Strasbourg into historical and legal brief on the cities' parliamentary claims. Sturm called Dr. Ludwig Gremp, a Swabian who was Strasbourg's city attorney, to Nuremberg, where he and a Frankfurt attorney, Hieronymus zum Lamm, compiled a "Summary and substance of all documents submitted, and the opinions based on them, concerning the honorable free cities' parliamentary rights."[201] Based on whatever turned up during unsystematic searches in the civic archives, and particularly on Sturm's own researches, the jurists sought to prove that the free cities' claims "are well grounded in all natural law, law of nations, civil and canon law, the Golden Bull, the emperor's reform decree of 1442, the Imperial ordinances, ancient custom and tradition, and also reasonable, reliable, and weighty reasons."[202] The lawyers' task became ever more urgent, as the upper houses excluded the cities from the Diet of Nuremberg's decision on taxes, which forced the urban delegates to draw another leaf from the Protestant book and to enter a protest against the recess.[203]

One sign of the recovery of traditional Imperial politics was that the free cities once more resorted to their old tactic of appeal from the diet to the emperor.[204] In May 1543 Charles had sailed from Spain—he would never see it again as emperor—for Genoa and Germany, bent on throwing his whole system's weight against France.[205] He came not as peacemaker, his role in 1530 and 1541, but as warlord, determined to dissuade his subjects from rebellion. A swift campaign in the Netherlands brought young William of Cleves to his camp seeking mercy, while the Smalkaldeners, led by William's own brother-in-law, Elector John Frederick, stood by and did nothing. Charles seized Gelderland, which had so long eluded his grandfather and so plagued the Habsburg Netherlands, and turned his eye westward toward France. Tortured by gout, he campaigned on into the winter, until in the new year's first days he moved back to the Rhine and southward toward Speyer, where he planned to marshal the German princes for the war against France.

Charles came to Speyer in 1544, therefore, much as his grandfather had come to Cologne in 1505, as a victorious warlord at the peak of his glory. There the parallel ended, for whereas Maximilian had faced a broken princely opposition, the Smalkaldic League was still very much intact. Heavy mortgages nonetheless burdened the Smalkaldic chiefs' power to resist—their illegal occupation of Brunswick-Wolfenbüttel, the submission of William of Cleves-Jülich, and Duke Moritz's good standing at court—and brought them to Speyer ready to compromise. Landgrave Philip set the tone with his anti-French outbursts, the leading Protestant theologians joined in to denounce the alliance of pope, French king, and sultan, and the diet quickly and with little rancor voted Charles twenty-four thousand foot and four thousand horse for six months.[206] The emperor then neatly finessed the religious question, issued the recess, and headed for Metz, where he assembled his troops for a lightning campaign on the Marne. On 19 September 1544, Charles concluded the Treaty of Crépy with France, having profited more from the Imperial Diet's generosity, perhaps, than he had ever done before or ever would again.

Jacob Sturm faced a terrible problem in January, when the Diet of Speyer voted taxes for the French war. "The Strasbourgeois are quite frightened," Gereon Sailer of Augsburg reported, at the prospect of an Imperial campaign over the Rhine.[207] It was true, for the panicked Strasbourg merchants knew that a campaign on their front "would be most burdensome and damaging to Strasbourg and to Alsace; for because they lie so close to France, on which they nearly border, they not only trade in France but gain a good part of their livelihood from Lorraine."[208] The princes' solid support for both wars, against the sultan and against France, made outright resistance impossible, for "if Strasbourg were to resist alone, or with a few allies," Sturm wrote home, "you can imagine how that would fuel the charges of those who are already crying that we are good Frenchmen."[209] Sturm thought Granvelle might allow the cities to pay their taxes in secret, "but without the damages to Strasbourg and the land of Alsace, which will surely follow from our consent [to the taxes]," or they might pay the entire sum against the Turks and remain neutral in the French war.[210] In any case, he advised, they should stick to the other free cities, for Strasbourg "cannot stand alone."[211]

The war fever at Speyer made the tax question all the more urgent, and the free cities turned to the only audience they possessed, the emperor himself.

When he arrived in the Empire in 1543, the leading southern cities—Augsburg, Ulm, Nuremberg, and Strasbourg—had sent an embassy, headed by Jacob Sturm, to warn him that they would not supply troops for the Hungarian war unless he would guarantee the cities and the Smalkaldeners a "solid peace."[212] On 6 March 1544, the urban envoys submitted a memorial in German and Latin, with a French summary for Charles, on their parliamentary rights, based on the brief prepared the year before by Gremp and the other lawyers, to the emperor as their sole lord and protector.[213] Charles responded with a confirmation, weaker than they wanted, of their right to participate in the diet, though this was not recognized by the diet until 1548, four years later.[214]

On the second issue, taxation, the Diet of Speyer tried to square the circle, voting to support the French war by the matricular system and the Turkish war by the Common Penny—a sure sign that confusion and disagreement had reached a level at which reform might be possible. The task of reform had been assigned at Nuremberg in 1543 to a relatively new form of assembly, a meeting of all the circles, whose delegates were to study the tax registers and propose a reform. Jacob Sturm represented Strasbourg and the Upper Rhenish Circle in this assembly, which opened at Worms on 28 October 1544 and sat until February 1545.[215] For nearly a third of a year, the delegates discussed and debated the countless proposals for reform and demands for lowering assessments.

Jacob Sturm played a central role in this assembly, which, despite its meager achievements, issued the most important tax reform under Charles V and fixed the pattern of Imperial tax assessment until 1803. At first Sturm thought the assembly would accomplish nothing, for even if the electors' envoys eventually appeared, "hardly anything can be done, for the delegates who have assembled have no instructions to make binding decisions."[216] Gradually, however, he began to change his mind. The Upper Rhenish Circle's delegation elected him their speaker, "and even though I would gladly lay this business aside, they won't let me do it, for we are all especially engaged in this business."[217] Unlike the diets of Empire, free cities, or league, and against all traditional practice, this Imperial assembly for tax reform (*Reichsmoderationstag*) tried to release the delegates from their instructions and bind them to the assembly through a special oath, a remarkable step toward the (never completed) transformation of the Imperial Diet into a true parliament. This commitment was reflected in a decision, which Sturm reported—and obeyed—to bind the delegates to secrecy, even toward their own governments and rulers, "on which account I cannot tell you any news."[218] Secrecy seems to have helped, for soon Sturm could report that "the work goes on strictly and seriously enough."[219]

Sturm could by no means achieve everything the free cities wanted. Their total assessment, he thought, was still too high, because the other powers tended to believe that all cities were as wealthy as Augsburg and Nuremberg.[220]

With Sturm as their voice, the Upper Rhenish Circle's delegates argued for an entirely new register, though they had to settle for a "quite positive" revision of the Worms register.[221] It lowered the cities' total assessment by about a quarter, raised (Augsburg, Lübeck) or lowered (Metz, Regensburg) relative ranks, and shifted the collective burden away from the middling and toward the larger cities.[222] This outcome was a modest reform of the matricular system—the Common Penny now disappeared forever—not the thoroughgoing tax reform favored by many urban politicians.

Tax reform and urban rights brought Jacob Sturm to the fore in the years 1542 to 1544 in a new role, as leader of something like a reconstituted urban front operating both in the Imperial Diet and through the circles. Sturm helped to shift Imperial politics back into constitutional channels and away from the pattern of direct negotiations between the emperor and the confessional parties. This movement diminished, for the moment, the confessional split's effects on the functioning of Imperial government, but it revived, too, the old strife between the free cities and the princes. Imperial political life was moving back into the channels marked out as goals by the reform era between 1495 and 1512: regular sessions of the Imperial Diet, the direct property tax, and functioning Imperial circles. It was a remarkable restoration, only twenty years after the Diet of Worms and ten after that of Augsburg, and it signaled a provisional closure of the Reformation—in its South German phase—as a transforming force in Imperial political life. Even the split over religion, the colloquies seemed to promise, would soon be composed, either within the Empire or on a grander scale.

There could be, however, no simple return to pre-Reformation patterns, for something else had changed: some of the Imperial circles had begun to function as more or less effective regional institutions. This development, long overlooked by the political historians, had its roots in the emergency mobilization of the western Imperial regions to put down the Anabaptist kingdom at Münster, but it began to take on regular shape during the early 1540s, taking over for the smaller powers of the Rhine Valley, Swabia, and Franconia the political role of the great regional leagues of the past—the Swabian League and the Lower Union.[223]

In this latter change, the development of an effective structure for *regional* political security and administration, Jacob Sturm played a central role during the 1540s. It meant the emergence of a political system of which, at least in theory, Strasbourg lay near the center, because the Upper Rhenish Circle stretched from Hesse and Baden in the east to Lorraine and Savoy in the west—an expanse very like the political world of Great-grandfather Peter Schott.[224] The religious schism aside, it was a world that suited Strasbourg's political traditions far better than did the stilted Smalkaldic League, with its conglomeration of powers who possessed no common interests except their religion. As the Reformation's strains on the Imperial system eased, therefore, politics began to run back into roughly traditional channels. In the Empire's southwest, the good old days seemed to have returned, and for his role in bringing them back, Jacob Sturm was honored by the free cities of the Upper Rhenish Circle. On 31 July 1545, they sent him a letter of thanks, and at year's end they presented him with an expensive (472 fl.) silver bowl and a contribution to his expenses while at Worms.[225] This greatest honor of Sturm's career came not from the Protestant powers but from the good old friends and neighbors, the free cities of Strasbourg's home region. In 1526 Strasbourg had marked Sturm's launching into the world of Imperial politics by striking a medal in his honor; in 1545 the region's free cities—Strasbourg, Metz, Frankfurt, Speyer, Worms, Hagenau, Colmar, and all the other little free cities of Alsace, neighbors all—honored Sturm's role in the protection of their interests through regional solidarity. It was a grand gesture, one Old Peter Schott would have understood and enjoyed.

It was also a gesture based on illusion, for, despite the restoration of familiar patterns in Imperial political life, the Reformation was not over. In South Germany, true, the movement had exhausted its power to disrupt and transform Imperial politics, but in the north, where the Reformation movement had begun later and developed more slowly, during the first half of the 1540s it was just getting up a fair head of steam. In 1542 Sturm and his southern allies had taken the fateful step of approving the Smalkaldic League's invasion of far-off Brunswick-Wolfenbüttel, a place about which the Strasbourgeois knew less than they did about Venice or Milan. It was a step they would live to regret.

Notes

* "Darumb so seit gewarnet/und seind eins guten muts;/er sei reich oder arme,/ daß er sein vaterland behut/vor den türkischen hunden,/sie fieren ein großen bracht,/desgleichen han ich nicht funden,/red ich zu disen stunden,/keiner ehr nemen sie nit acht." Liliencron, ed., *Historische Volkslieder* 4:156–57, no. 469, stanza 4, a song of unity composed at the time of the colloquy at Hagenau in 1540.
1. Hölscher, "Mindener Reichsacht"; Petri, "Karl V. und die Städte." Minden was not, as is commonly assumed (e.g., by Lauchs, *Bayern*, 134), a free city. See G. Schmidt, *Städtetag*, 38–42.
2. The news came to Strasbourg on 15 October. PC 2:523, no. 548. For the Protestant princes' reactions, see PC 2:525, no. 550; Mentz, *Johann Friedrich* 3:408–13, no. 19, and 417–27, no. 21; Duchhardt, *Kaisertum*, 29–30.
3. ARCEG 3:12–13, no. 8; 23, lines 29–34, no. 12; 28–29, no. 16; and 32, lines 20–27, no. 18.
4. PC 2:519–22, no. 545; 530, no. 554. John Frederick, to whom the landgrave passed the first letter, responded sourly about the southerners, "Das sie aber gleichwol und zuvorderst Jacob Sturm uf seinem angezeigten bedenken also beruhet hat, befrembdet uns etwas, nachdem er wol verstehet und hat erachten konnen, dieweil ain stant ader stadt unserer mitverwanten umb klare

religionsachen geechtiget, das wir uns des schutzes und rettung halben derselben acht im grunde auch mussen teilhaft machen und das unser schutz und rettung dafur angesehen wirdet werden, als wolten wir die execution kais. Mt acht und urteil verhindern." Mentz, *Johann Friedrich* 3:409, no. 19. An opinion by a Strasbourg jurist (probably Franz Frosch), who gives a negative response, is in AMS, AA 468. Ibid., 530 n. 4.

5. The most important studies in this revision are G. Schmidt, *Städtetag*; Kohler, *Politik*; Luttenberger, *Glaubenseinheit*; Lauchs, *Bayern*. For general orientation, see Lehmann, "Universales Kaisertum."

6. See Aulinger, "Verhandlungen," esp. 210–27.

7. The most important study of the colloquys from the Imperial point of view is still Cardauns, *Unions- und Reformbestrebungen*.

8. Kohler, *Politik*, 337–38; Fichtner, *Ferdinand*, 102–17, a chapter eloquently entitled "Waiting"; Csáky, "Karl V.," 233–35; Schweinzer, "Vorgeschichte," 246–48.

9. See Granvelle's memorial of November 1541 on the Habsburgs' situation, in Friedensburg, "Aktenstücke," 45–57, no. 5, discussed by Schweinzer, "Vorgeschichte," 236.

10. This picture of Ferdinand emerges from Fichtner, *Ferdinand*; Aulinger, "Verhandlungen"; and Schweinzer, "Vorgeschichte."

11. This chain of events began with the Treaty of Linz (11 September 1534) between Ferdinand and the Bavarian dukes, on which see Lauchs, *Bayern*, 34–48; Kohler, *Politik*, 370–73. What follows is based on Endres, "Der Kayserliche neunjährige Bund," 85–103; Salomies, *Pläne*, 74–83; Lauchs, *Bayern*, 48–63.

12. Quoted by Endres, "Der Kayserliche neunjährige Bund," 92. On Nuremberg's loyalism, see Brady, *Turning Swiss*, 217–20.

13. The history of this League of Nuremberg, which Held organized in June 1538, has not yet been written. See Press, "Bundespläne," 69–70. The degree of conformity between Held's actions and Charles's intentions is debated. See Petri, "Herzog Heinrich," 138–40.

14. Luttenberger, *Glaubenseinheit*, 152–61; Aulinger, "Verhandlungen," 198.

15. Luttenberger, *Glaubenseinheit*, 96–139; and on the composition of the large peace party, I follow ibid., 139–41.

16. Ibid., 185–99.

17. Rublack, *Nördlingen*, 237, who calls dissimulation the fundamental principle ("Grundsatz") of Nördlingen's policy.

18. Meinardus, "Verhandlungen," 646. What follows is based chiefly on the minutes taken by Balthasar Clammer, councillor (and later chancellor) of Duke Ernest of Brunswick-Lüneburg, published by Meinardus, "Verhandlungen," 636–54. A list of princes and envoys attending is in StA Basel, Kirchen-Akten A 6 ("Religions-Sachen 1532–1536"), which came from Strasbourg. For the Protestants' relations with the emperor in the preceding years, see Rosenberg, *Der Kaiser und die Protestanten*.

19. Meinardus, "Verhandlungen," 640–42. The landgrave's militancy is suspect, for he already lay deep in negotiations with the emperor. See Lanz, *Staatspapiere*, 255–63, no. 53; 269–77, nos. 55–57; Brandi, *Kaiser Karl V.* 1:366–68, 375–76.

20. Electoral Saxon envoys to Elector John Frederick, Eisenach, 1 August 1538, in StA Weimar, Reg. H, pagg. 170–73, no. 80, fol. 56r.

21. On 17 February, Duke Francis of Brunswick-Lüneburg quoted Sturm's first speech of the previous day, whereas Bremen's spokesman cited with approval Sturm's second speech (17 February). Meinardus, "Verhandlungen," 648–52. I do not mean to suggest that the two sides' estimation of the situation were

incompatible. Sturm seems, for example, to have regarded the threat of war to be serious enough that he supported the Saxon elector's decision to resume alliance negotiations with the king of England around this time. See "Bedenken Johann Friedrichs über die Gegenwehr, [ca. 12 January 1539]," in Mentz, *Johann Friedrich der Großmütige* 3:426.

22. Meinardus, "Verhandlungen," 642.

23. This speech is in ibid., 651–52. From it come the remaining quotes in this paragraph. Sturm's companions at Frankfurt were Ulman Böcklin and Batt von Duntzenheim.

24. Lenz, ed., *Briefwechsel* 1:75, no. 24.

25. Ibid., 85, no. 26.

26. ARCEG 3:53, lines 22–24, no. 34. The truce suspended the decree against Minden and other (named) actions and obliged the parties to participate, under exclusion of the pope, in a colloquy to be called to Nuremberg on 1 August 1539; and the Protestants agreed to attend the next assembly on the taxes for the Turkish War and to obey the majority's decisions. The treaty's text is summarized in *PC* 2:601–3; and by Fuchtel, "Anstand," 185–86. On the assembly on military taxes, which opened at Worms on 6 June 1539 and adjourned without reaching a decision, see Neuhaus, *Repräsentationsformen*, 169–85.

27. *PC* 2:610–12, no. 616. Sturm's list of participants at Worms is lost, but there survives a (probably similar) list in HStA Marburg, PA 517, fols. 41r–42v. See Neuhaus, *Repräsentationsformen*, 180–81; Ziehen, "'Frankfurter Anstand' und deutsch-evangelischer Reichsbund."

28. Neuser, *Vorbereitung*, 10–11, who identifies the first formulation of the plan in Joachim's letter of November 1538 to the commanders of the Smalkaldic League: "Noch solchen abgehandelten articeln wölten sein churf. gnaden hoffen, auch die wege finden zu sein, domit man durch bequeme wege einmall zu einem einmuthigem vorstand und vergleichung unsern christlichen religion und glaubens kommen möchten." Quoted from *NBD*, I 4:492.

29. On the policy and conduct of the colloquies as a whole, see Pastor, *Reunionsbestrebungen*, still the most detailed treatment; Luttenberger, *Glaubenseinheit*, 200–41; Augustijn, "Religionsgespräche." On their connections with the Diet of Augsburg, see Honée in *Libell des Hieronymus Vehus*, 25–48.

30. Fuchtel, "Anstand," 160–88; and the text of the truce is in Neuser, *Vorbereitung*, 75–85. Clemen, "Vergleichsartikel," 229–32, prints a document prepared for the colloquy scheduled for 1 August 1539 at Nuremberg.

31. On the shift to Regensburg, see Friedensburg, "Zur Geschichte des Wormser Konvents."

32. This act opened the way to the formula known as the "Regensburg Book." Fraenkel, *Einigungsbestrebungen*, 52–53; Ziegelbauer, *Johannes Eck*, 236–38.

33. The scene is described in the report of one of the nuncios, Bernardo Sanzio, bishop of Aquila, to Rome on 20 January 1541: "Et tutto ab omnibus non sine lachrimis fu acceptato et laudato et omnes recesserunt post longos amplexus, signum pacatae voluntatis." *NBD*, I 6:130. See also Laemmer, *Monumenta Vaticana*, 344; Fraenkel, *Einigungsbestrebungen*, 63–64.

34. The influence of Erasmus on the colloquys was accepted by Stupperich, *Humanismus*, and Lortz, *Reformation* 2:227–30, both of whom deplored it; it was generalized and put in a more positive light by Augustijn, *Godsdienstgesprekken*, though he is now more cautious ("Religionsgespräche," 49–51). See, however, Luttenberger, *Glaubenseinheit*, 96–116, 250–56; Schulze, "Concordia, Discordia, Tolerantia," 52–54.

35. Paulus, *Protestantismus und Toleranz*, 142–75, describes Bucer's normal attitude.

36. That this continuity reached all the way back to 1532 and the negotiations that led to the Truce of Nuremberg is the cogent thesis of Aulinger, "Verhandlungen," which provides the best overview. Fundamental, too, is Luttenberger, *Glaubenseinheit*, esp. 714–24.

37. Fraenkel, *Einigungsbestrebungen*, 38.

38. Including his sister, Mary, the widowed queen of Hungary and regent in the Netherlands, whose views resembled those of the neutrals. Luttenberger, *Glaubenseinheit*, 251–52; Schweinzer, "Vorgeschichte," 255–56.

39. An apologia for this position is contained in Elector Palatine Louis's negative reply to King Ferdinand, who at Hagenau in July 1540 asked him to join the League of Nuremberg. He mentions his age, his useful reputation as a "non-partisan," his hereditary alliances with Saxony, Hesse, and Württemberg, and the exposed position of the Palatine lands. ARCEG 3:162–64. See Luttenberger, *Glaubenseinheit*, 139–50, on the chief neutrals.

40. ARCEG 3:57, lines 18–19, no. 37; and a similar view is expressed by Johann Eck in ibid., 124 n. 168.

41. Quoted by Pfnür, "Einigung," 61. On Fabri and his views, see ibid., 56–57; on his work against Protestantism, see Oberman, *Masters*, 240–44, 254–60.

42. See ARCEG 3:53, lines 1–10, no. 33; 97, lines 6–33, no. 60B. For further Catholic criticisms of Habsburg policy, see ibid. 3:1; Duchhardt, *Kaisertum*, 27 n. 113. And for the contrast between the policy of Albert of Mainz and that of the Bavarian dukes, see ARCEG 3:38–40, no. 23; 112, lines 17–39, and 104–7.

43. BOSS 3:310.

44. WA, B 9:460, lines 3–7, and the following quote is from ibid., lines 15–25.

45. Augustijn, "Religionsgespräche," 45–46. Fraenkel, *Einigungsbestrebungen*, 39, describes the Saxon and Bavarian instructions for the Colloquy of Worms.

46. Lenz, ed., *Briefwechsel* 2:28. The passage is quoted by Augustijn, "Religionsgespräche," 47–48.

47. Landgrave Philip to Elector John Frederick, Kassel, 6 November 1538, in StA Weimar, Reg. H, pagg. 214–18, no. 96, fols. 98r–100v, here at 98v.

48. PC 2:532–33, no. 556; and Sturm's reply is in ibid., 534–35, no. 559. The landgrave wrote in the same sense to Elector John Frederick, Spangenberg, 8 December 1538, in StA Weimar, Reg. H, pagg. 211–14, no. 95, fols. 95r–96r. Two days later, he asked the XIII of Strasbourg to order Sturm to Leipzig; they merely forward the request to Sturm at Esslingen. PC 2:533 n. 3. On the Leipzig talks, see Fraenkel, *Einigungsbestrebungen*, esp. 7–26.

49. PC 3:48–49, no. 33. The committee consisted of three magistrates (Sturm, Claus Kniebis, and Batt von Duntzenheim), two preachers (Bucer and Capito), and a secretary (Michel Han).

50. AMS, R 26/8, fol. 27r–v. The committee was Hans Bock, Jacob Sturm, Daniel Mieg, and Mathis Pfarrer, "jn beÿ sein d. Wolffen Capitons vnd herrn martin Butzers."

51. Lenz, ed., *Briefwechsel* 1:156 n. 8; there, too, the remaining quotes in this paragraph. The remarks respond to a report drafted by the Hessian councillor Georg von Boyneburg, which is printed by Neudecker, *Aktenstücke*, 210. See PC 3:39.

52. Lenz, ed., *Briefwechsel* 1:156 n. 8; and there, too, the following quote. At the end Nusspicker notes that Jörg Besserer (typically) agreed with Sturm.

53. Ibid., 162–63, no. 61.

54. Press, *Calvinismus*, 179–83.

55. Lenz, ed., *Briefwechsel* 1:408–9.

56. See Batt von Duntzenheim's record of the colloquy, PC 3:77–82, no. 77, here at 78.
57. See the reports in ibid., nos. 59, 64, 68, 71. The king's negotiations with the Protestants began on 28 June (ibid., no. 77). The Protestants agreed not to budge from the "Wittenberg Memorial" of 18 January 1540. On the two sides' preparations, see Honée, Libell, 33–44; and for the events and recess of the meeting (28 July 1540), see Neuser, Vorbereitung, 16–18, 96–107.
58. Honée, Libell, 44–46. The talks on other subjects—restitution of church property, renewal of the truce, and a moratorium on expansion of the Smalkaldic League—foundered, "wie nicht anders zu erwarten, am unnachgiebigen Widerstand der protestantischen Seite." Luttenberger, Glaubenseinheit, 217.
59. PC 3:79 n. 1; Luttenberger, Glaubenseinheit, 218.
60. Lenz, ed., Briefwechsel, 188–9, no. 73, reporting Sturm's judgment about the procedural agreement reached at Hagenau.
61. PC 3:108–10, no. 111, from AMS, XXI 1540, fol. 378.
62. Elector John Frederick, by contrast, ordered his envoys to brush aside any proposal to discuss ecclesiastical property, though Landgrave Philip instructed his envoys to entertain general proposals for a settlement of the property question. Körber, Kirchengüterfrage, 135–36.
63. The Senate & XXI set this day of prayer for Sunday, 24 October, and declared that the taverns should be closed. PC 3:109 n. 4.
64. The favorable remarks on Granvelle, which Stupperich, Humanismus, 72–73, attributes to Jacob Sturm, are from letters written by Dr. Heinrich Kopp from Brussels to Strasbourg, in PC 3:103, 117, 118. Granvelle, of whom there is no adequate modern biography, has been variously judged. See, e.g., Friedensburg, "Zur Geschichte des Wormser Konvents," 113, who concedes that although he was hostile to Protestantism, Granvelle accurately estimated its political potential. On dating the change in Imperial policy toward the Protestants, I follow Luttenberger, Glaubenseinheit, 252–53.
65. PC 3:117–20, no. 127; and see BOL 4:xxv–xxvi. On Naves, see Hasenclever, "Johann Naves," his visit to Strasbourg at 297–98; and on his attitude, see the anonymous letter to Jacob Sturm and Mathis Pfarrer, undated but after 18 January 1540, in Neudecker, Urkunden, 601–5, no. 161.
66. PC 3:131, no. 140, which summarizes the entry in AMS, XXI 1540, at 9 November 1540. Sturm and Pfarrer also got reports from Joham and Caspar Hedio, who spoke with Granvelle, but these letters are lost. On Joham, a wealthy banker whom the emperor had knighted in 1536, see Brady, Ruling Class, 68, 102, 106–7, 109, 116–17, 155–56, 187–88, 281–89, 323–24.
67. On the atmosphere at Worms, see ARCEG 3:228–30. The Protestants' organizational sessions can be followed in Mathis Pfarrer's notes (4–26 November), which are printed by Neuser, Vorbereitung, 168–76; and see ibid., 19–24, 199–200. For Strasbourg's encouragement of other cities to send their theologians, see PC 3:110, no. 111; Lenz, ed., Briefwechsel 1:217, no. 85.
68. Jean Sturm and Simon Grynaeus were appointed among the Protestants' three recorders (notarien), mainly because of their command of languages. Neuser, Vorbereitung, 170. On the selection of the Strasbourg delegation for linguistic skills, see Lenz, ed., Briefwechsel 1:217, no. 85; Herminjard, ed., Correspondance 6:328 n. 14.
69. Franz, ed., Urkundliche Quellen 2:31–48, no. 420, here quoted from 341; and the delegation is listed at 341 n. 1. The landgrave flattered Bucer, who did not possess a doctorate. He sent Alexander von der Tann, his chief bailiff at Darmstadt, to Worms, though he shortly sent Chancellor Johann Feige to head the delegation. On Feige, see Müller, "Johann Feige."

70. Landgrave Philip to Elector John Frederick, Zapfenburg, 12 November 1538, in StA Weimar, Reg. H, pagg. 214–18, no. 96, fol. 117r: "Dan der Bucer ist Jacob Sturmen vnnd deren von Straspurk mechtig."

71. Luttenberg, *Glaubenseinheit,* 221–24.

72. ARCEG 3:274 n. 354: "Besorgend, er werd seinem hern dem keiser mynder heimbringen, dan er herbracht hat, das ist das die fursten von theutscher nation zu unserm theil so stattlich fallen." This would have meant, of course, the collapse of the emperor's policy of conciliation. See Friedensburg, "Zur Geschichte des Wormser Konvents," 114.

73. PC 3:147, no. 157. If Sturm did know, it was probably through the Palatine grand chamberlain (*Großhofmeister*), Ludwig von Fleckenstein, who was thought to have pro-Lutheran sympathies. Brady, *Ruling Class,* 302; Press, *Calvinismus,* 177; ARCEG 3:239, no. 99, 301, no. 101, and 336, no. 105a; Laemmer, ed., *Monumenta Vaticana,* 325, no. 198. For Bucer's view, see Lenz, ed., *Briefwechsel* 1:268–70, no. 98; and for the Protestants' expectation of victory, see Fraenkel, *Einigungsbestrebungen,* 64; Luttenberger, *Glaubenseinheit,* 219–20.

74. Lenz, ed., *Briefwechsel* 1:269, no. 98: "Der Granvel wollte D. Capiton und mich zu sich beruffen; es will aber wasser sein." On Bucer and Veltwyck, whom Bucer thought "ein feiner mensch," see Pollet, ed., *Relations* 1:35–49, quote at 38.

75. Lenz, ed., *Briefwechsel* 1:274–79, no. 101, on which the remainder of this paragraph is based. See also Müller, "Regensburger Buch," 101–2.

76. Much later, Sturm confessed that "Buceri halb, was er privatim mit ime [Granvelle] et Gerardo [Veltwyck] gehandelt, wuste ich nit." PC 3:605, quoted by Pollet, ed., *Relations* 1:39 n. 2. On Bucer's new Hessian instructions, see Lenz, ed., *Briefwechsel* 1:278–79, and 517: "Nun hett er [= Bucer] solichs mit hern Jacoben Sturmen geredt. Der wolte sich wol von wegen der von Strasburgk desselbigen nicht mechtigen, doch so wer es ime, hern Jacoben, nicht sonderlich zuwidder."

77. Lenz, ed., *Briefwechsel* 1:281–82, no. 103. The credential is in Varrentrapp, *Hermann von Wied* 2:42.

78. Lenz, ed., *Briefwechsel* 1:286, 287–91, nos. 104, 106.

79. Ibid., 289, no. 107 (1 January 1541): Although he is willing to undertake the mission, "Ich were aber nit mein selb, muste von h. Jacoben erlaubnuss haben, dem dorffte ich aber die ursachen nit anzeigen, wolte mit E. f. g. cantzler [Feige] reden, ob er auff sich nemen wolte, das er mich hinsante, alss ob E. f. g. mich berufen hette."

80. PC 3:154, no. 153, in response to Sturm's letter from Worms on 29 December 1540. The proposal is described by Johann Feige, Lenz, ed., *Briefwechsel* 1:520. The landgrave rejected both further private negotiations on the union formula and the proposal for a smaller meeting. Ibid., 309, no. 112.

81. PC 3:158, no. 166.

82. Neuser, *Vorbereitung,* 22.

83. The nuncio, Morone, wrote to Rome about "Martin Bucero, et un Giacomo Sturmio, non quel dotto, uno de quali è capo della città sua nel temporale, l'altro nelli dogma, sono di mala natura." Laemmer, ed., *Monumenta Vaticana,* 326. See also the harsh remarks attributed to Bucer and "Ioannes Sturmius Argentinae civitatis deputati consiliarii" by Robert Vanchop, the blind archbishop of Armagh, in ibid., 305, no. 188. The confusion of the two Sturms was very common.

84. This story is recounted by the Bremen theologian Johannes Timannus (d. 1557), called "Amsterodamus" from his birthplace, to his colleagues at Bremen, 18 November 1540; the extract was published by Spiegel, "Johannes Timannus

Amsterodamus," 42–44. The original was found by Ernst-Wilhelm Kohls in the Stadtbibliothek Bremen, a. 9, no. 13, and Jean Rott made a copy of his transcription available to me (for which my thanks to both scholars). The incident is not mentioned in the accounts of Eck at Worms in 1540. Iserloh, *Johannes Eck,* 77; Luttenberger, "Johannes Eck"; Ziegelbauer, *Johannes Eck,* 237–38.

85. See this volume, chap. 2. Neuser, *Vorbereitung,* 42, does not recognize the personal barb in this passage.

86. But which Tilmann, the reporter of this incident, tried to render into Low German.

87. See Greschat, *Martin Bucer;* Brady, "'The Earth is the Lord's.'"

88. *PC* 3:715–18; Rockwell, *Doppelehe,* 1–36; Eells, *Bigamy.* The best introduction to this affair is still Lenz, ed., *Briefwechsel* 1:327–91.

89. Lenz, ed., *Briefwechsel* 1:354, though he may have said this to put pressure on Bucer.

90. He revealed this in his instruction for Bucer to Luther and Melanchthon, Melsungen, 30 November 1539, the relevant passage from which is quoted by Rockwell, *Doppelehe,* 5–6. This key document is printed in CR 3:851–56, no. 1888; WA B 8:631–36, no. 3423.

91. Lenz, ed., *Briefwechsel* 1:345–46. Bucer did not disclose the secret to Sturm at Arnstadt, where the league was meeting in early December 1539, and he dissembled to Sturm his reason for going to the elector at Weimar. Ibid., 118–19, no. 39; 356–58, nos. 8–10. See Rockwell, *Doppelehe,* 23–24, 71–73.

92. *PC* 3:716.

93. See this volume, chap. 4.

94. *PC* 3:716–17; and there, too, the remaining quotes in this paragraph.

95. Laemmer, ed., *Monumenta Vaticana,* 277; ARCEG 3:178–79, no. 85; PC 3:717; Mentz, *Johann Friedrich* 2:253–64.

96. Lenz, ed., *Briefwechsel,* 1:186–87, no. 72. For the efforts of Sturm and Bucer, see ibid., 263, no. 95; 269, no. 98; 270–71, no. 99; 294, no. 106.

97. Ibid., 1:541–42, no. 17. See G. Müller, "Karl V. und Philipp der Großmütige."

98. Lenz, ed., *Briefwechsel* 1:266, no. 96.

99. Ibid., 2:9, no. 117. This refers to the declaration printed in ibid. 1:541–42, dated 24 January 1541.

100. Ibid., 2:20, no. 119 (10 March 1541). See Eells, *Bigamy,* 228–40, who, though he tries to put the best light on it, recognizes the error.

101. The center of the controversy was an anonymous pamphlet, the "Dialogus Neobuli," which defended polygamy. Eells, *Bigamy,* 164–70. On Michel Han, see Ficker-Winckelmann 1:19; Brady, *Ruling Class,* 190 n. 77, 255–56, 314.

102. Lenz, ed., *Briefwechsel* 2:65, no. 135, and 81, no. 140. Bucer suspected Sebastian Aitinger, a Hessian secretary, of being in cahoots with Han.

103. Quoted by Greschat, *Martin Bucer,* 212, from TAE 3:518, lines 4–5, 7–8.

104. Lenz, ed., *Briefwechsel* 2:68–69, no. 136, and 82, no. 141.

105. Elector John Frederick's supplementary instruction for Franz Burkhardt and Bernhard von Mila to the King of England, in Mentz, *Johann Friedrich* 3:376–83, no. 12, here at 379.

106. Ibid., 383–87, no. 13, here at 385.

107. Ibid., 387–94, no. 14.

108. Ibid., 417–27, no. 21.

109. Ibid., 464–68, no. 40, here at 467.

110. This is based on ibid. 2:249–85.

111. Ibid., 251; PC 2:630.

112. Lenz, ed., *Briefwechsel* 1:224, no. 86; and there, too, the following quotes.

113. Mentz, *Johann Friedrich* 2:253. One of the French agents at Hagenau was Johannes Sleidan. *PC* 3:62.
114. Mentz, *Johann Friedrich* 2:253–69. This calculation rested on the common interest of the German Protestants and France to support Duke William of Cleves-Jülich, John Frederick's brother-in-law.
115. Jacob Sturm to Franz Burkhardt, in StA Weimar, Reg. C, no. 870, fol. 59; *PC* 3:151; Mentz, *Johann Friedrich* 2:270.
116. Brandi, *Kaiser Karl V.* 1:370–77. On the negotiations on religion at Regensburg, see Vetter, *Religionsverhandlungen;* Luttenberger, *Glaubenseinheit,* 228–41.
117. Luttenberger, *Glaubenseinheit,* 229–30.
118. See *PC* 3:183, no. 192.
119. Schmauss, ed., *Reichs-Abschiede* 2:429–44.
120. *PC* 3:181, no. 190.
121. Roth, "Zur Geschichte des Reichstages," 62–63. Hel, city syndic of Augsburg, was a close associate of Wolfgang Rehlinger, Sturm's kinsman and a burgomaster of Augsburg. Sieh-Burens, *Oligarchie,* 146, 159.
122. See Augustijn, "Religionsgespräche," 47–48.
123. Neuser, *Vorbereitung,* 219.
124. The instruction for this delegation is in StA Weimar, Reg. E, 48r–50r, no. 99, vol. 1, fols. 2r–71v. Their greeting of the landgrave is described in their report to Elector John Frederick of 27 March 1541, in ibid., fol. 123r.
125. The quoted word is Augustijn's in "Religionsgespräche," 47.
126. Sebastian Aitinger's account of the Protestant deliberations on 11 July, in Lenz, ed., *Briefwechsel* 3:28–29. Sturm also said of the Protestants' comment on episcopal power, "Das solichs milter zu stellen sei, weil es nit vil bessert, sonder die leut schärpflich anreg."
127. Elector John Frederick to his councillors at Regensburg, Liebenwerda, 26 July 1541, in StA Weimar, Reg. E, 48r–50r, no. 99, vol. 3, fol. 236r.
128. Lenz, ed., *Briefwechsel* 3:130. The following paragraph is based on Feige's report.
129. Ibid., 134.
130. Ibid., 129. He mentions as the leaders in these negotiations himself, Sturm, and Burkhardt and Doltzig of Saxony.
131. Augustijn, "Religionsgespräche," 47.
132. Roth, ed., "Zur Geschichte des Reichstages," 276.
133. Though King Ferdinand had experimented in 1539 with another type of assembly. Neuhaus, *Repräsentationsformen,* 169–85.
134. I follow here Luttenberger, *Glaubenseinheit,* 250–61, with the quote at 258. The (unpublished) recess of the Smalkaldic League's diet at Frankfurt in April 1539 made security the absolute condition for voting taxes. G. Schmidt, *Städtetag,* 381.
135. Schweinzer, "Vorgeschichte," 269, writes that a survey of the Habsburg correspondence at the time of the Diet of Speyer in 1542 leads to the conclusion "daß Karl die Bedeutung der deutschen Probleme unterschätzte und ihnen nicht gebührend Raum in seinem Überlegungen hab." Queen Mary's comment is quoted by Brandi, *Kaiser Karl V.* 1:398, who also describes (393–401) the outbreak and course of this war.
136. Fichtner, *Ferdinand I of Austria,* 126–33.
137. On relations between Charles and Ferdinand, see the overview by Rodríguez-Salgado, *Changing Face,* 33–40. The Habsburgs' new mobilization policy in the 1540s may be followed in Press, "Bundespläne"; Press, *Reichsritterschaft;* and Roth, *Augsburgs Reformationsgeschichte* 3:17–18, 108–10, 319–24.
138. *NBD,* I 8:733.
139. Brady, *Turning Swiss,* 233; G. Schmidt, *Städtetag,* 96.

140. G. Schmidt, *Städtetag*, 276–78, 382–84.
141. Ibid., 278.
142. Ibid., 278.
143. Ibid., 519.
144. Brady, *Turning Swiss*, 134; G. Schmidt, *Städtetag*, 28–29, 38–39, 54, 124–25, according to whom these five cities, plus Speyer and Hagenau, attended nearly every urban diet of this era; they also furnished most of the important urban diplomats (125). The lawyers who prepared the cities' case for the Diet of Speyer in 1544, all came from these five cities. Isenmann, "Reichsstadt und Reich," 152–65; Isenmann, "Reichsstandschaft," 95; G. Schmidt, *Städtetag*, 251–52, 281–82.
145. Lenz, ed., *Briefwechsel* 2:43 n. 2: "Dweil an [h]er Jacob Sturmen, wie e. l. wissen, die oberlender gemeiniglich alle hangen." Compare the judgment of G. Schmidt, *Städtetag*, 375.
146. PC 3:no. 230.
147. Winckelmann, "Verfassung," 489, quoted by G. Schmidt, *Städtetag*, 86 n. 71.
148. G. Schmidt, *Städtetag*, 375: "Die Straßburger Gesandten, allen voran Jakob Sturm, waren die unbestrittenen Sprecher des Städtecorpus; sie saßen in den inneren Entscheidungszirkeln der Reichstage, sofern die Städte an Beratung und Beschlußfassung beteiligt waren."
149. Stolleis, *Pecunia nervus rerum*, 63–65.
150. Commynes, *Memoirs* 1:358 (bk. 5, chap. 19).
151. Wiesflecker, *Kaiser Maximilian I*. 5:563–75, is authoritative on Maximilian's finances.
152. Based on the table in Neuhaus, *Reichstag*, 318–19, and counting from the actual (not the announced) opening until the reading of the recess.
153. Ibid., based on the Diets of Regensburg in 1546 and Augsburg in 1547–48, 1550–51, and 1555.
154. Schmid, "Reichssteuern," is the best overview; see also Schulze, "Reichstage und Reichssteuern," and Isenmann, "Reichsfinanzen."
155. Schmid, "Reichssteuern," 163–73; Steglich, "Reichstürkenhilfe in der Zeit Karls V."
156. Over the same period the tax to support the Governing Council and Chamber Court yielded an additional 8–900,000 fl. Schmid, "Reichssteuern," 179.
157. Ibid., 176–78.
158. See the overview by Laufs, *Der Schwäbische Kreis*, 208 n. 196.
159. Jacob Sturm to the Senate of Strasbourg, 11 April 1542, in AMS, AA 513, fols. 84r–89v. See Eltz, "Zwei Gutachten," 277, 296, 298, 300. All the free cities except the two richest, Nuremberg and Augsburg, favored the Common Penny. Ibid., 275 n. 12. Eltz's analysis agrees in the main with the highly informed judgment of Isenmann, "Reichsfinanzen," 212.
160. Schulze, "Reichstage und Reichssteuern," 50; Blickle, "Gemeiner Pfennig und Obrigkeit (1495)," 181, and 193 for Blickle's generally negative appraisal of the tax's political effects.
161. For orientation, see Schulze, "Reichstage und Reichssteuern," 47–48, 50–51.
162. Eltz, "Zwei Gutachten," 275 n. 12, 277 n. 19, 277 n. 20, gives the divisions in the diet's three houses at Speyer in 1544.
163. Quoted by G. Schmidt, *Städtetag*, 401.
164. PC 2:508, no. 536, composed by Sturm, Duntzenheim, and Mathis Pfarrer.
165. In ibid., 3:611–12, no. 616, composed by Sturm, Duntzenheim, and Ulman Böcklin.
166. Ibid., 2:611 n. 1. The assessments were considerably higher for Cologne (322 and 30), slightly higher for Nuremberg and Metz (250 and 40), and lower for Augsburg (150 and 29) and Ulm (150 and 25). Schmauss, ed., *Reichs-Abschiede*

2:220-21. On the cities' assessments under the system of 1521, see Dollinger, "Charles Quint et les villes d'Empire," 184-87.

167. See G. Schmidt, *Städtetag*, 36-45.

168. Recess of Naumburg, 24 October 1541, in Lenz, ed., *Briefwechsel* 3:161-67. On this meeting, see Schweinzer, "Vorgeschichte," 238-40, 245-46. On the action of the Diet of Regensburg 1541, see Steglich, "Reichstürkenhilfe," 50.

169. Wiesflecker, *Kaiser Maximilian V.* 5:8-9. What follows is based on Brandi, *Kaiser Karl V.* 1:416-17.

170. Wartenberg, *Landesherrschaft*, 268-69. For Moritz's youth, accession, and relations with the emperor during the first half of the 1540s, see Blaschke, *Moritz von Sachsen*, 12-25, 43-46; and the older studies by Simon Ißleib listed in the Bibliography.

171. Quoted by Brandi, *Kaiser Karl V.* 1:417.

172. Wartenberg, *Landesherrschaft*, 94; Blaschke, *Moritz von Sachsen*, 40-42. I allude to the "Wurzen Feud" between the two princes.

173. PC 3:221-22, no. 216, Sturm's instruction for the Diet of Speyer of 1542, written in secretarial hands but corrected by Sturm. Landgrave Philip told the Strasbourgeois about the Protestant princes' decision, in ibid., 216-17, no. 211.

174. Lenz, ed., *Briefwechsel* 2:62 n. 5. When the landgrave heard this news, he sent Bucer an extract from this instruction, to prove his sympathy, which Bucer showed to Sturm. See ibid. 2:67, no. 136.

175. Lenz, ed., *Briefwechsel* 2:62 n. 5.

176. Ibid., 60-62, no. 134 (16 March 1542); and the remaining quotes in the paragraph are from this same letter.

177. G. Schmidt, *Städtetag*, 390. Only three times in this entire era was the Common Penny granted: 1495, 1542, and 1544. Schmid, "Reichssteuern," 168. The recess of Speyer 1542 contained very detailed stipulations for this tax, in Schmauss, ed., *Reichs-Abschiede* 2:453-60, para. 50-96.

178. Fichtner, *Ferdinand I of Austria*, 131.

179. PC 3:279-80, no. 269, from a draft by Jacob Sturm in AMS, AA 501, fols. 5-19.

180. PC 3:280-81, no. 269. Sturm may well have had Metz in mind, whose high assessment reflected its wealth in the distant past. See Dollinger, "Charles Quint et les villes d'Empire," 187-88.

181. The memorial to this effect, which is in Michel Han's hand with Sturm's corrections, was prepared for the diet but not submitted. It is in AMS, AA 501, fols. 75-92.

182. PC 3:334 n. 5; 335 n. 2. Later, stirred (but not too strongly) by news of the army's disintegration and suffering, they decided not to send another "month" but to give each of the city's soldiers a gulden, "not because it is owed, but as though for God's sake."

183. Wiesflecker, *Kaiser Maximilian I.* 5:563-75; Parker, *Military Revolution*, 9-24.

184. Schmid, "Reichssteuern," 155-56.

185. PC 2:611-12, no. 616. The instruction was composed by Sturm, Batt von Duntzenheim, and Ulman Böcklin. AMS, XXI 1539, fol. 137r. On this assembly, see Neuhaus, *Repräsentationsformen*, 169-85.

186. On German expectations and Charles's performance, see Fichtner, *Ferdinand I of Austria*, 127-33; and on finance and taxation in the Habsburg lands, see now Rodríguez-Salgado, *Changing Face*, 50-72, who sheds some light on this intractable subject.

187. His name appears in the list of those approving the recess of Nuremberg on 26 August 1542 (Schmauss, ed., *Reichs-Abschiede* 2:481), though no representatives sealed the recess in the name of the cities, but not in the recess of

Nuremberg of 23 April 1543 (ibid., 494). Indeed, Aulinger's lists, which are based chiefly on the recesses, has Strasbourg unrepresented at the Diet of Nuremberg in 1543, though Sturm certainly did attend it. Aulinger, *Bild*, 374.

188. *PC* 3:350, no. 331, from Sturm's report to the Senate & XXI on 14 May 1543.
189. Isenmann, "Reichsstadt und Reich," 152.
190. *PC* 3:339, no. 327. For what follows, I rely on Isenmann, "Reichsstadt und Reich," 152–62; G. Schmidt, *Städtetag*, 281–86.
191. G. Schmidt, *Städtetag*, 269–72.
192. See this volume, chap. 3. An intercurial committee, called a "Large Committee [*Großer Ausschuß*]," was formed at the diets of 1521, 1522, 1522/23, 1526, and 1529—in the latter two of which Jacob Sturm himself had sat. Neuhaus, *Reichstag*, 31–37; Neuhaus, "Wandlungen," 121–25, and the tables on 136–38.
193. Quoted by Isenmann, "Reichsstadt und Reich," 161 n. 481, from Gremp and zum Lamm, *Svmma vnnd innhalt*, 77–79.
194. Between 1528 and 1531, together with Caspar Rumler. *Ann. Brant*, nos. 4728, 4748, 4928, 3571. Jacob Sturm had also taken part in 1537 in the reform of civic chancellery. Eheberg, *Wirtschaftsgeschichte* 1:562, no. 302.
195. Jacob Sturm, "Außzug," edited by Wencker and printed (separately paginated) at the end of Knipschildt, *Tractatus de juribus*. It is described briefly by G. Schmidt, *Städtetag*, 251, who doubts that Sturm was the sole author. The answer to his question, why Sturm had it sent to Gremp, may be that it was sent to Gremp at Strasbourg before he was called to Nuremberg, though Schmidt's suggestion, that Sturm composed the first part and Gremp the second, is also possible. The work refers to acts preserved at Hagenau, Schwäbisch Hall, Speyer, Memmingen, Worms, Heilbronn, and Nuremberg. Sturm, "Außzug," 5–8, 10–12, 16, 27, 29, 32–35.
196. Sturm, "Außzug," 13: "Es seyen kein grössere Schläfer denn die Fryen Richs-Stette." Matern Drachenfels (d. 1491), elder son of Hans Drachenfels (d. 1469) and Katharina Hapmacher; ammeister (Salzmütter Guild) in 1483 and 1489; married Ottilia von Künheim (d. 1484). His younger brother Lienhart (d. 1501), called "Drach," commanded 600 Strasbourg foot in the relief of Neuss in 1475. Lienhart's son, Andreas (d. ca. 1535) married Irmelgard Schenckin of Obernai, by whom he had five daughters; ammeister (Salzmütter Guild) in 1500, 1506, 1512, and 1518, and resigned "because of old age" in January 1524. AST 1655, fols. 103v–104r; BMS, MS. 844, fol. 332v; Sturm, *Quarti Antipappi*, 40–41; Kindler, *Buch*, 373–74; Lehr, *L'Alsace noble* 3:467–68; Hatt, *Liste*, 556–57, 616.
197. Sturm, "Außzug," 18.
198. From 1492 onward the notices become very full and sometimes amount to day-by-day accounts of the proceedings. Ibid., 22–35.
199. Ibid., 37, on the Diet of Augsburg in 1510: "Nun kan ich in den Acten nit finden, wer in Vßschutz gewölt, finde woll die Bedencken ettlicher Verordneten uff Sontag Jubilate, vß welchem die Stend nachmaln Jr Antworten, so sie Kays[erlicher] Maj[estät] geben, gemacht haben, wer aber die Verordneten gewesen, find ich nit."
200. G. Schmidt, *Städtetag*, 102–4; Huber, "Städtearchiv."
201. Ludwig Gremp, born at Stuttgart in 1509 and died at Strasbourg in 1583; studied at Tübingen and Orleans; professor of law at Tübingen, 1537–41; called to Strasbourg as city attorney in 1541; ennobled as "Gremp von Freudenstein." See Ficker-Winckelmann 1:28; Feine, "Ludwig Gremp von Freudenstein," 199–219. Isenmann, "Reichsstadt und Reich," 152 n. 461, calls him the "chief author [*Hauptverfasser*]" of the brief. On its composition and contents, see ibid., 152–59; G. Schmidt, *Städtetag*, 251–52, 281–82.

202. Quoted by Isenmann, "Reichsstadt und Reich," 152–53, from Gremp and zum Lamm, *Svmma vnnd innhalt*, 19–20. Schubert, *Die deutschen Reichstage*, 145, makes the connection between this tract and Sturm's researches.
203. G. Schmidt, *Städtetag*, 282–83.
204. They took this decision at the urban diet of Frankfurt in July 1543, for which see ibid., 283–84. On the embassy's handling at court, see Sturm's report in *PC* 3:385, no. 401.
205. Brandi, *Kaiser Karl V.* 1:412–22; Wiesflecker, *Kaiser Maximilian I.* 3:198–220.
206. For details see de Boor, *Beiträge*; there is a very good, brief overview of this diet by Tyler, *Charles the Fifth*, 97–98. Eltz, "Gutachten," 275–76, attributes Charles's success to able diplomacy; Druffel, *Beiträge* 3:19 n. 2, to the princes' patriotism; but Sturm (in *PC* 3:467, no. 443) to the princes' concern for their "private affairs."
207. Roth, "Briefwechsel Gereon Sailers," 143.
208. *PC* 3:472–73, no. 446.
209. Ibid., 467–68, no. 443.
210. Ibid., 471–72, no. 445.
211. Ibid., 476, no. 451: "Es kond sich ein stadt Strasburg nit wol söndern." See ibid., 468, no. 443, with 493, no. 466.
212. Arbenz, ed., *Vadianische Briefsammlung*, no. 1300 (4 August 1543). Charles had stopped at Ulm in July on his way to the Netherlands. Pollet, ed., *Relations* 2:72 (2 August 1543).
213. Isenmann, "Reichsstadt und Reich," 159–61, who documents (160 n. 477) the dominance of Sturm.
214. See Gerber, "Augsburger Reichstag"; Isenmann, "Reichsstadt und Reich," 162–66; G. Schmidt, *Städtetag*, 287.
215. Neuhaus, *Repräsentationsformen*, 328–59, is definitive on this assembly, called a *Reichsmoderationstag*. For briefer views, see Laufs, *Der Schwäbische Kreis*, 207–9; G. Schmidt, *Städtetag*, 402–3. The revisions of the Worms register were completed by 12 February 1545. *PC* 3:563–64, no. 529.
216. *PC* 3:536, no. 506.
217. In ibid., 543, no. 515, quoted by Neuhaus, *Repräsentationsformen*, 354–55.
218. *PC* 3:545, no. 517. The Augsburg delegate, who reported this measure to his government, said he would violate it. Neuhaus, *Repräsentationsformen*, 342 n. 127.
219. *PC* 3:551, no. 522. One month earlier, he had complained that the work moved forward "vast langsam . . . von wegen der vile der personen und auch der stend, so ringerung begeren." Ibid., 545, no. 517.
220. *PC* 3:no. 529.
221. G. Schmidt, *Städtetag*, 402.
222. Ibid., 409–12.
223. See the lists of meetings assembled by Dotzauer, *Reichskreise*, 345–58.
224. For the membership, see Dotzauer, *Reichskreise*, 238–40.
225. *PC* 3:622–23, no. 590. The bowl was made by the Strasbourg goldsmith Martin Krossweiler, whom Winckelmann could not identify. Krossweiler married in 1530 Magdalena Murschel (b. 1511), daughter of the wealthy merchant Ulrich Murschel and Barbara von Weida, who bore eleven or more children; he was senator from the Guild Zur Steltz in 1547/48. BMS, MS. 1024, fol. 69; Hatt, *Liste*, 477.

7

The Road to War, 1541–1545

In fifteen hundred and forty-two
I tell now, and I tell true,
Of a lord of wealth and fame;
Duke of Wolfenbüttel is his name,
And he'll be taught the gospel's rule.

Duke Henry, are you a Christian man?
You've done much evil in your time,
For which you'll now get your reward.
The landgrave is coming into your land
And you'd best take to your heels.*

When the grateful free cities honored him in 1545, Jacob Sturm stood at the summit of his career. His fellow magistrate Hans Baldung Grien painted him full length just about this time, the lost original for all the many portraits by which the Strasbourgeois and others remembered Sturm in after years.[1] It reveals Sturm in his prime as short in stature and full of figure. He wears a squarish beard and is dressed in a beret, gentleman's mantle, hose, and sword; he holds a glove in one hand, while with the other he closes his cloak and prominently displays his seal ring.[2] He resembles, as one historian has charmingly written, "a middle-class Henry VIII."[3] His face, however, if we can trust the reproductions of Baldung's lost portrait, is grave and somewhat ascetic, as though his shoulders bear the republic's entire weight.

And so they nearly did, for twenty years of Senate and privy council sessions, committee work, long travels by boat and on horseback, and endless negotiations with theologians and magistrates, lawyers and princes, bishops and electors, and a king and an emperor had exacted their price. Rarely did he sleep more than a few months at a stretch in his own bed, and even more rarely could he relax at the family's chateau in Breuschwickersheim.[4] For the rest, the pace of business moved on with terrible relentlessness. As long ago as 1532, Sturm had "excused himself on account of ill health [leibsblödigkeit] and asked to be spared the ride" to Regensburg, though in the end he had vowed "to spare neither health nor wealth for the city's sake."[5] The following years brought no relief, for as older colleagues withdrew from diplomatic work, few younger ones came forward who possessed the requisite education, languages, speaking skills, and willingness to serve this commune in this way.[6] Despite frequent appeals by the senior magistrates to "do the best thing," the situation got no better. When Peter Sturm reported in February 1545 that Jacob, then at Worms, had fallen ill with a swelling of the ankles every evening, the alarmed magistrates dispatched a physician to treat him.[7] In June, still at Worms, Sturm wrote that "nothing would suit me better now than to get free of these difficult doings and rest up at home, so as to recover more peace and health in body and mind."[8] He yielded to compassion, however, and sent home Michael Schwencker, whose daughter had died and whose wife lay ill. Sturm stayed on to the end, a pillar of the free cities and of the Protestant cause. Yet time and care told on him, and rumors circulated to the effect that "Sir Jacob Sturm is said to be weakening mentally and not so sharp as he used to be."[9]

Now in his mid-fifties, Sturm was keenly aware of how completely Strasbourg's policy rested on his shoulders alone. When he agreed in 1545 to travel to the league's diet at Frankfurt, Sturm warned his colleagues of his own mortality.[10] "I have always placed, and will continue to prefer, the common good [gemein nutz] ahead of all my own affairs, and even of my health [ja eigne leibsgescheft]," but "gradually everything has come to rest on one man, which is not the case in other cities. You should reflect whether it is good to have everything in one man's head." The other magistrates, he complained, had come to leave business in the hands of a few, and "if the affair goes well, they say, 'How could it have gone otherwise?' If it goes badly, they say, 'It is not good that the whole city's welfare lies in the hands of one man.'" "More men are needed," he concluded, "for one day soon I will no longer be able to travel, or I may even be dead, and someone else must be acquainted with these matters." And yet he continued to travel, year in and year out, on horseback or by boat, until 1548, when he was fifty-nine years old. Sometimes a journey required several modes of transportation. On 22 February 1541, for example, Sturm left Strasbourg in the company of Martin Bucer and John Calvin, headed for Regensburg. They rode across the Rhine Bridge, up the Kinzig Valley, over the crest of the Black Forest, down across the Neckar basin, and crossed the Swabian Jura to Ulm—a five-day ride. There, after resting for a week, they boarded a boat and went downstream to Regensburg.[11]

How burdensome was Sturm's life as a diplomat can easily be grasped from the record of a single meeting, the Worms assembly on tax reform in 1544-45.[12] The Upper Rhenish Circle selected Sturm in August 1544 to be one of its four envoys to the meeting on tax reform. Sturm came to Worms, an easy trip by water from Strasbourg, to find no one there, and when the assembly opened on 28 October, nearly a month late, four circles were still unrepresented. The deliberations opened on 10 November and moved forward "very slowly," as Sturm reported, and completed its recommendations in about six months—longer than all but four of the Imperial Diets held in the sixteenth century.[13] Its proposals then came before the diet itself, at Worms in 1545, at Regensburg in 1546, and at Augsburg in 1547–48. Having spent six months on this project alone, Sturm did not live to see the reform, in which he had a major hand, pass into Imperial law.

It can hardly surprise, therefore, that most urban regimes, which were composed of honorary magistracies, found it impossible to recruit enough able diplomats from their own ranks. With few exceptions, they simply could not meet the new demands generated by the Reformation era and the confessional age. Nuremberg generally acquitted itself well, as Sturm confessed in 1526 with the remark that the Nurembergers "will perform in grand style, because they have the people for it."[14] Later in the century, most free cities turned over their diplomacy to paid civil servants, but during the Reformation era it was still in the hands of magistrates, most of whom turned in mediocre performances at best. Jacob Sturm was in no way typical of such men, and even the most prominent of the rest, such as Ulm's Bernhard Besserer and Constance's Thomas Blarer, were usually overshadowed by him.[15] Sturm's unique combination of qualities—personal integrity, dedication, education, eloquence, and patience—commanded respect from all sides, but especially from the great princes and their councilors.[16] His stature had increased since the 1530s, when the northward shift of political struggle quickened the tempo of the league's activities and strained the human resources of most southern members. The greater distances taxed the burghers' sense of dedication, and the cultural differences between South and North tested both their grasp of wider affairs and their linguistic abilities. In such company, Jacob Sturm had few peers and no superiors, and his reputation for easy discourse with the great and the powerful long clung to his memory. It is illustrated by a story that can no longer be substantiated.[17] At the Diet of Augsburg in 1530, the story goes, during an audience at which Sturm submitted the Tetrapolitan Confession to the emperor, Charles chided him about Strasbourg's eviction of the local Carmelites, who were colloquially called "Our Dear Lady's Brothers." "Stürmel, Stürmel," the emperor cried in French, "why have you evicted Our Lady's Brothers?" "Most Gracious Majesty," Sturm replied, "so long as they remained Our Dear Lady's Brothers, we loved and treasured them; but when they wanted to become our ladies' men as well, we could tolerate them no longer." This made Charles and his courtiers laugh, the story goes, as well it might have. It is nonetheless difficult to imagine such banter to an emperor coming from any of the mill-run urban politicians of the era.

The Reformation era burdened the southern urban magistrates in at least two new respects. For one thing, divided religious loyalties within the urban regimes weakened their credibility as political allies. The princes preferred to deal with individuals, not with councils. When he was preparing in November 1538 for the Leipzig colloquy, for example, Landgrave Philip of Hesse expressed his wishes to deal only with trusted leaders of Strasbourg, Ulm, and Augsburg:

> At Strasbourg it [the negotiations] should be conducted with Jacob Sturm and Mathis Pfarrer; at Ulm with Bernhard and Jörg Besserer, father and son; and at Augsburg with Wolfgang Rehlinger, for he knows who can be trusted with such matters, and we believe him to be the most knowledgeable about it.[18]

He was especially worried about Ulm, where in the privy council of the V sat "a man named [Ulrich] Neithart, who enjoys great prestige, even though he is a papist, and he is said to be reliable in all of Ulm's affairs, even those concerned with the gospel."[19] At Augsburg the situation was more complicated, for although the last prominent Catholic in the regime, Anton Fugger, withdrew in 1539, the magistrates were split into factions. Wolfgang Rehlinger, the leading figure until his fall in 1543, pursued a moderate foreign policy, whereas Jakob Herbrot, whose faction subsequently came to power, conducted a more militant Evangelical policy. This change, which occurred out of phase with the landgrave's policies, nonetheless did not disrupt his relations with the city, which were managed by able civic servants, such as the city attorney Dr. Conrad Hel, under Rehlinger until his fall in 1543, and the city secretary Georg Fröhlich and city physician Gereon Sailer, under Herbrot.[20] Dealing with urban regimes, however, remained a time-consuming, relatively insecure business for the princes.

The Reformation also increased the southern urban politicians' burdens by throwing their leading diplomats frequently into the company of distant princes and, what was more burdensome yet, of politicians from the far reaches of the North. An Alemannic speaker from, say, Strasbourg, probably had no spoken tongue in common with a Lübecker, except perhaps for Latin. Somehow, they managed to communicate. Sturm, for example, whose knowledge of North Germany came entirely from books, nonetheless knew enough to astonish the Stralsunders at Augsburg in 1548 with his grasp of Pomeranian history.[21] Most southern politicians, however, knew less of the far North than they did of Italy, and the eruption of northern affairs into their political world during the later 1530s strained their abilities. The North was different in every way, from the densely urbanized landscapes of the Northwest to the vast, gloomy plains of the Northeast, where self-governing towns were few, the states were huge and poor, communal institutions were weak, rural insurrections were rare, and regular Imperial governance was practically unknown. Different, too, was the Reformation in North Germany, for as the southern reformation began to stabilize in the mid-1530s, its northern counterpart was just getting underway.

Yet the Reformation did not come peacefully to the North, no more than it had to the South, and the great revolution of 1525 found its northern counterpart in the upheavals that from 1533 set all of northern Europe in motion and exerted a catalytic effect on the northern reformation quite comparable to 1525's effects in the South. At Münster in Westphalia arose a millenarian commune called "the Anabaptist kingdom," the crushing of which involved the whole apparatus of Imperial governance and sent shock waves as far south as Strasbourg.[22] In March 1533 another revolutionary leader, the Hamburg-born merchant Jürgen Wullenwever, came to power at Lübeck, and over the next two years he made seaborne war on the Hollanders and the English, gained control of the regime through a revolutionary coup (January 1534), and led Lübeck into a disastrous intervention in the war for the Danish succession.[23] Seen on a large scale, these events were merely adjustments in the northern balance of power, mainly in response to the decline of the Hanseatic system and the rise of the Dutch. The local effects could be extreme, however, as when a beaten, sobered Lübeck left the Smalkaldic League in 1536, never to return.[24] And on a middling scale, the events of 1533–35 resonated through the northern world, shaking loyalties and creating a general atmosphere of uncertainty and opportunity.

In this atmosphere the northern reformation made its first great spurt, comparable to the southern reformation's growth between 1521 and 1525. Three conditions of the movement merit attention here. First, the arm of Imperial government, hesitant enough in the South, barely reached the North, where Charles V's power rested more on his dynastic resources as ruler of the Netherlands than on his Imperial office. Second, across the northwest an arc of great prince-bishoprics formed an impressive but temptingly vulnerable shield between the Habsburg Netherlands and the Protestant heartlands. Third, the Smalkaldic chiefs held a strategically interior position between the two Habsburg centers in Austria and the Netherlands. Their eastern flank gradually became apparently more secure through the excruciatingly deliberate passage of Elector Joachim II's Brandenburg, and, since 1539, the more rapid movement of Albertine Saxony, toward Lutheranism.[25] In the west, on the other hand, the richest opportunities presented themselves during the first half of the 1540s: Duke William of Cleves-Jülich's determination to claim the duchy of Gelderland, Elector Herman's desire to introduce Lutheran reforms into the state of Cologne, and Bishop Franz von Waldeck's very similar intentions for his states of Münster and Osnabrück.[26] Unsettled by the tremendous mobilization against the Anabaptists at Münster, by the spectacular career of Wullenwever at Lübeck, and by unmistakable signs of Habsburg expansion, most of the northern Imperial princes either adopted Lutheranism or joined the party of Catholic "neutrals," which cooperated with the Protestants in temporal matters.[27] By the early 1540s, the opposing Catholic party of action had but one champion among the lay princes of the North, Duke Henry II of Brunswick-Wolfenbüttel. The Smalkaldic chiefs, who held back from war over Gelderland and Cologne, struck twice at Henry in 1542 and 1545. This "Brunswick affair," a direct prelude to the decisive war of 1546–47 between the emperor and the German Protestants, drew fuel from Protestant disappointments in the contests for Gelderland, Cologne, and Münster-Osnabrück.

THE STRUGGLE FOR THE NORTHWEST: CLEVES-JÜLICH

Cleves-Jülich, a conglomerate creation of the later Middle Ages, formed by the sixteenth century a potential major power in the Empire's northwestern sector.[28] The state's position—its core lands lay along both banks of the Lower Rhine, and its other holdings reached far into neighboring Westphalia—made it a natural rival to the Habsburg Netherlands and a natural target of Protestant attentions. A Protestant Cleves-Jülich would become a fox in the Lower Rhenish–Westphalian henhouse, whose plump laying hens included the sees of Cologne, Trier, Münster, and Osnabrück. Although Dukes John III (r. 1521–39) and William V (r. 1539–92) flirted with Protestantism, in their own lands they sponsored a reformist, Erasmian Catholicism and tried to maintain good relations with both the Habsburgs and the Smalkaldeners.[29] The dukes' beacon on this middle way was their expectancy on the duchy of Gelderland. When the duchy's estates elected Duke William in 1538 to succeed the last Egmont duke, no one expected that Charles V, whose dynasty had claimed the duchy since 1473, would allow him to keep it.[30]

Whereas the old dukes of Gelderland had maintained their independence with French aid, the new one found a natural ally in the Smalkaldic League. The league easily slipped once more, as in Württemberg in 1534, into the historic role of a German princely opposition, because Duke William was thought to favor Lutheranism, and because his sister, Sybil, was married to John Frederick of Saxony. Already at William's accession in 1539, John Frederick had proposed that the league either admit him, if he would allow the true religion to be freely preached in his lands, or make a separate alliance with him.

Jacob Sturm, who spotted the opportunity from the first, favored the more aggressive course of admitting William, for "we should not oppose rendering him adequate aid [gebuerende hilf], because we would thereby bring these powerful lands all over to our side."[31] In exchange for Duke William's pledge of freedom for preaching the gospel, Sturm's colleagues at Strasbourg agreed that "according to conscience and the terms of our alliance, we could not exclude him but must, on grounds of fairness, take him in, ... for even we, the [current] members, have no bond among ourselves except for the defense of religion." Then, too, "we won't soon find another Imperial prince who has such power and such good cavalry, with which he could support and aid us when we need him," whereas to reject him might drive him into the other camp. The issue of Gelderland thus laid bare the dilemma at the heart of Jacob Sturm's grand policy: the structure and goals of the Smalkaldic

League encouraged an identification of the gospel with its chiefs' interests and power, and the stabilization of the Reformation in South Germany tended to blind the southern Smalkaldic politicians to the dangers of aggressive action in far North Germany. It began to seem reasonable, even to these perennial advocates of peace and diplomacy, to risk strife in remote regions for the sake of the gospel. Then, too, the Strasbourgeois were old hands at blurring the boundaries between religious and secular causes, and they recognized that if the emperor moved against William of Cleves-Jülich, "Saxony and Hesse as his dear kinsmen cannot easily abandon him. And if it goes badly for him and the emperor wins, these two could be drawn into the conflict and suffer losses in it, which would weaken us through damage to our two mightiest princes and leave us open to future attacks."[32] Just as he had in Württemberg in 1534, in Gelderland Sturm favored an aggressive policy of cooperation between the gospel and dynastic interests. Just as typically, however, when war seemed imminent, Sturm backed away.

In 1540, as the struggle over Gelderland mounted toward its first crisis, Duke William and the Smalkaldic chiefs coordinated a plan for war: twelve thousand foot and a large cavalry force would seek out Charles's army, crush it, and raise the Netherlandish towns and provincial estates against the Habsburg regime.[33] They had grand hopes. "Once we have the Netherlands in hand," the speculation ran, "England and Denmark will join us, and with their aid we can stand off the French king" and win "prestige and benefit for the cause of the gospel and preserve the freedom of the German nation." This grand scheme, the destruction of Habsburg power "for the cause of the gospel and . . . the freedom of the German nation," resembled nothing so much as a northern reprise of the southern drama plotted years ago by Landgrave Philip and Huldrych Zwingli.

Would the southern Smalkaldeners back the play on the Lower Rhine? The landgrave sounded out Sturm in early January 1540 about a war for the gospel, German liberty, domination of northern Germany, and the friendship of all northwestern Europe. If the emperor seized Gelderland and Cleves-Jülich, Philip predicted,

> the consequence would be his control of Münster, Osnabrück, and the lands all the way to Paderborn, also the neighboring territories of Cologne and Trier. Then, when bishops are elected, the chapters will have to accept and elect bishops approved by the emperor and the House of Burgundy.[34]

This, in turn, would give Charles control of all the best sources of good cavalry. Would Sturm and his government support the landgrave, the Saxon elector, Württemberg, and, perhaps, the king of Denmark to aid Duke William against the emperor? The landgrave's proposal would have the league remain formally neutral, while its chiefs made war on the Habsburgs on behalf of Duke William, whose admission would strengthen the league. In effect, a Württemberg campaign in northern dress. If it worked in the North, subsequent gains might easily transform the Empire into the aristocratic republic that was the stuff of princely dreams. As earlier in Württemberg, as later in Brunswick-Wolfenbüttel, the Cleves affair called on the Smalkaldeners to accept and support the linkage of their alliance's purpose, the defense of religion, to their chiefs' ambitions and to the greater cause of aristocratic power in the Empire.

In the meantime, second thoughts cooled Sturm's ardor for the north-western enterprise. He told the landgrave that the XIII were "not disin-clined [nit ongewegen]" to back a war to prevent even greater harm, but they didn't dare bring the proposal before the Senate & XXI or the Schöffen. As for himself, Sturm thought that

> Your Princely Grace ought to proceed cautiously and with careful plan-ning [vorbetrachtlich und gewarsamlich] in this affair, so that Your Grace, out of loyalty and a desire to preserve the German liberty, does not get himself, alone or with a few allies, into a position from which he cannot easily get out.[35]

No talk of "we" and "the gospel" in Sturm's dovish words, and the other southern Smalkaldeners, the landgrave thought, were "even more off the mark." "Therefore," he complained, "Jülich won't join the Protestant league, he won't come over to our religion or faith, . . . and everything is so con-fused, that we don't know what to do."[36] Yet the Strasbourgeois would stand by the chiefs, the landgrave had from Martin Bucer in March 1540, even though Jacob Sturm "is a reasonable man, who cannot decide so quickly about such important affairs. He looks at the situation just like a man who sees many paths open and can't decide, which to take."[37] The rest of the XIIIers, Bucer told the landgrave, did not all share Sturm's caution and would back the war to support Duke William. Indeed, Sturm's own fears were calmed by his brother, Peter, who wrote home from Ghent that "I hope from all signs here, that we need have little fear of the emperor tak-ing military action against us this summer."[38]

As storm clouds gathered, the normally pliant and indecisive Duke William, perceiving his peril, drew closer to the French king—historically the main backer of Gelderland against Brussels—whose niece, Jean d'Albret, he mar-ried.[39] These steps drew him inevitably into the Imperial war against France in 1542, without, however, supplying the French succor he needed. William and his territorial levies had to face alone an international force of nearly forty thousand, which invaded his left-bank lands in August 1543 and brought him, after two weeks of hopeless resistance, from Düsseldorf to the emperor's camp at Venlo, where he made his submission on 7 September.

The Smalkaldeners, once so hot to aid the young duke, left him to his fate. Landgrave Philip, for the moment a loyal Habsburg client, remarked laconically that though the duke might deserve his reputation as "a good, pious lord," he had intrigued with France and "has now got his reward," a shame, but hardly God's punishment for Protestant sins. Martin Bucer replied in the same smug tone that God had punished William "for not doing more to advance His kingdom" and for helping to bring on "this devilish French war."[40] When matters became desperate in the following spring, and Duke William took communion under both kinds, the landgrave blocked his entreaty for admission to the Smalkaldic League. The Smalkaldeners' inaction had the gravest consequences, for the Treaty of Venlo eclipsed their greatest hopes in the whole arc of Lower Rhenish and Westphalian bishoprics from Liège to Münster and Paderborn and robbed them of a potential base from which to threaten the Netherlands.[41]

Sometime during the Cleves-Jülich affair, Jacob Sturm began to revise his views about the advisability of backing in North Germany the combination—the gospel and German liberty—that had proven so successful in the South. He was beginning to unlearn the lesson of Habsburg weakness, which Austrian inaction had taught him in 1525 and 1534, as Charles V in the early 1540s had come to resemble his grandfather, Maximilian, at his peak in the 1500s. Sturm noted this change as he reflected on the Cleves affair: "The black eagle is a powerful bird, and he does not tolerate contempt—as the Palatine elector discovered years ago [in 1504]."[42]

THE STRUGGLE FOR THE NORTHWEST: COLOGNE

In contrast to Cleves-Jülich, where the Protestants could gain influence only by dealing with the ruling duke, in the neighboring prince-archbishopric of Cologne they hoped to gain commanding influence in the elector's lands through their own theologians' preaching, pamphleteering, and ecclesiastical reorganization. Cologne was a very good example of what Jacob Sturm had had in mind in 1526, when he had chided Capito and others for "relying more on worldly power than on Christ alone."

Herman, count of Wied and since 1515 prince-archbishop and elector of Cologne, was one of those pre-Reformation prelates who tried to move with the times.[43] At the end of the 1530s, from motives that are not entirely clear, he joined Elector Joachim of Brandenburg as a zealous mediator between the confessional fronts and an enthusiastic promoter of the colloquys.[44] Johann Gropper, the Catholic theologian whose cooperation with Bucer saved the colloquy of Worms, was his chief advisor on reform and theology. After the end of the colloquy at Regensburg, which in vague terms loaded the task of reform on the Catholic bishops, Herman turned to the Smalkaldeners for aid in reforming the church in his lands.[45]

The situation at Cologne was confusing. The lay estates of Elector Herman's territorial diet supported his program of reform, whereas against it stood the cathedral chapter, the magistrates, and most of the burghers of the city of Cologne. The city's magistrates, a Hessian councillor groused in 1543, "are an ignorant folk, who understand plenty about business, pleasure, and prosperity, but little about God," though they might be converted with the

help of God, "who makes the children of Abraham out of stones and clods."[46]
A Protestant reformation in the territory of Cologne—the archdiocese, much
of it ruled by other princes, was a different story—could therefore be introduced only from above, and the involvement of the Protestants, including
the Strasbourgeois, rested entirely on their influence with the elector.

Though no warrior, Herman was in one respect a greater catch for the
Smalkaldeners than Duke William of Cleves-Jülich, for all of his cavalry,
or even Ulrich of Württemberg. For Herman was an elector, one of the
great lords who elected the Empire's monarchs, and his reforms and flirta-
tions with the league during the first half of the 1540s quickened in the
hearts of Protestant princes, politicians, and churchmen that most gripping
of their secret hopes, a Protestant on the Imperial throne.[47] The Ernestine
Saxon chancellor, Gregor Brück, for example, saw in it the key to wiping
out Catholicism in the Empire, for

> in time our party could set up its own King of the Romans, to whom the
> whole Empire could be made subject and obedient, and other good laws
> could be made. And there should be no more priests, for otherwise the
> royal crown will remain in their hands, and we will have to endure their
> eternal oppression.[48]

Two of the lay electors, Joachim of Brandenburg and Louis of the Palatinate, were among the neutrals, and Herman's conversion might give the
Protestants a majority in the electoral college, providing always that they
could help him retain his offices as a Protestant prince.[49] When Herman of
Cologne and Bishop Franz von Waldeck of Münster and Osnabrück, who
made signs of imitating Herman's course, entered the Protestant fold, the
old church would be doomed in the whole arc of prince-bishoprics across
northwestern Germany.[50]

Strasbourg's Martin Bucer became the Protestants' chief agent for Cologne.[51] Some years before, Bucer had developed a program for the ecclesiastical principalities: they should be reformed rather than secularized, and
their bishops should become elective, that is, nonhereditary, lay rulers.[52]
When Elector Herman's call to Bonn came in early 1542, Bucer's enthusiasm for the project was doubtless heightened by the prospect of serving, for
a change, a lord who was as much churchman as prince. A first glance
confirmed, as he triumphantly declared, that the elector "is entirely ours."[53]
He returned with Hedio in December 1542 for an eight-month stay, for a
few months of which Philip Melanchthon came over from Saxony to lend
a hand in reforming Cologne.[54] Bucer drafted the main plan of reform, called
the "Simple Opinion [*Einfaltigs Bedencken*]," which Elector Herman might
have introduced into his state, as the territorial diet empowered him to do
in July 1543. The fall of Cleves-Jülich, however, visibly cooled Herman's
ardor for reform, and Bucer's work remained an impressive but lifeless monument to the failed reformation of the prince-archbishopric of Cologne.

Jacob Sturm took no direct part in the efforts to bring Cologne over to the Protestant side, though the spread of the Protestant cause through loans of clergymen was a policy he had often supported in the past.[55] When Elector Herman's call came, therefore, Sturm requested that Bucer be relieved of his local duties, though it is worth noting that during his long stay at Bonn, Bucer kept Landgrave Philip of Hesse better informed than he did Sturm.[56] Sturm's view of the reform at Cologne is unknown, though likely he favored spreading the gospel by all means short of war.

The Cologne affair, like the Cleves business, taught the Smalkaldeners to temper enthusiasm with prudence. Even as the league's assembly voted in the winter of 1545–46 to aid Herman if he were attacked, the Smalkaldic chiefs drew back. John Frederick of Saxony wrote to the landgrave in February 1546 that "it would in our view have been better, had the estates [of the league] not promised to help him [Herman], for you know how these things go," alluding to their experiences in the two Brunswick campaigns of 1542 and 1545. Philip agreed and thought "it would have been wiser to investigate the matter more thoroughly or to have been more prudent in assuring the [arch]bishop of our support."[57] The landgrave had told Sturm and Bucer that if the league could raise thirty thousand foot and six thousand horse, "in a few weeks the entire principality [of Cologne], or the largest and best parts of it, could be brought over to our religion."[58] But could it then be held and governed? The weakness of Herman's regime, typical of the Empire's ecclesiastical states, made success doubtful, and the potential for resistance was far greater than in Brunswick-Wolfenbüttel. As Landgrave Philip pointed out to Sturm and Bucer in September 1545, "The land is divided against itself, for the majority of the cathedral chapter stands against the bishop, and many nobles, also the coadjutor and the city of Cologne, hold to the old religion." The Catholics knew that Elector Herman "is not very powerful, but just a good, pious, simple man, that few of his councillors are truly loyal to him, and that he has few fortresses and little artillery or cash."

It was all speculation, for although the Smalkaldeners did commit the league's aid to Herman in the winter of 1545–46, they did so too late to do more than help Charles V decide to go to war. When they lost the war, Herman lost the see and electorate he had held for more than thirty years. What was true of Cologne held mutatis mutandis for the Westphalian prince-bishoprics of Münster and Osnabrück, whose incumbent, like Herman of Cologne, feared that the emperor would incorporate Münster, Osnabrück, and Cologne into the Netherlands, as he had done to Utrecht.[59]

Although Strasbourg's merchants traded with Cologne and Antwerp, these events in the far northwest evoked no great enthusiasm from the city's magistrates, who still preferred, as they said in 1545, the old sort of alliance "when neighbor allies with neighbor."[60] Two decades of Sturm's far-flung diplomacy had nonetheless developed at Strasbourg a broader political horizon, and the perception of a common religion lent energy to policy. The magistrates *did* support action in far Westhphalia, a land they knew less well than they did northern Italy or France, and they did it so decisively that in 1545 Bucer could report to Philip of Hesse that the Senate & XXI "are unanimous, that [the bishop of] Münster should not be abandoned."[61] Under Sturm's direction, the regime had come to believe that "the estates [of the league] should act together wholeheartedly, so we can see clearly, who opposes us and how long, so long as the German nation does not turn entirely to God's Word." Had the entire Smalkaldic League agreed, its forces might have cracked the Netherlandish shield in Cleves-Jülich, Cologne, or Münster and Osnabrück, or all along the line. Instead, the Smalkaldic chiefs shied from war in the northwest and turned their eyes toward an easier prey of much lesser strategic value, the duchy of Brunswick-Wolfenbüttel.

THE BRUNSWICK WAR

The death of Duke Eric of Brunswick-Calenberg in 1540 left his cousin, Duke Henry of Brunswick-Wolfenbüttel, as the last firmly Catholic lay prince on the North German plain.[62] Vigorous, able, ambitious, and vain, loyal but not more pious than need be, Henry, who was just Jacob Sturm's age, proved a capable ruler and became the founder of the modern Guelph state.[63] Henry was also a stalwart in the Catholic party of action and a commander of the League of Nuremberg, though his staunch loyalty to the House of Austria had been badly strained by the emperor's policy of conciliating the Smalkaldeners. By the early 1540s, Henry was both Catholicism's last, best hope in the North and Lutheranism's last, toughest barrier to victory there.[64]

The Brunswick affair's roots lay, on the one hand, in Duke Henry's feuds with the cities of Goslar and Brunswick and, on the other, in his personal quarrels with the Smalkaldic chiefs. His conflicts with the two cities, which had nothing to do with religion, encouraged them to introduce Lutheranism in 1528 and to become very early recruits to the Smalkaldic League.[65] Henry pursued his cases at law, supplemented by occasional acts of violence, and when the Smalkaldeners first reviewed the cases during their diet at Brunswick in April 1538, they recommended mediation rather than action.[66] Even when Henry disrupted Goslar's mining operations in the Harz Mountains, the Smalkaldeners could not act, for the southern cities insisted that the issues at stake were mundane and not religious ones.[67] At Regensburg in July 1541, however, the league yielded to Saxon-Hessian pressure and recognized Goslar's case as a "religious matter" and therefore eligible for military support under the compact of the league.[68] When the Chamber Court handed down decrees of outlawry against Duke Henry's foes, therefore, the obligation to defend the threatened cities led to the Brunswick affair.

It was not the league, however, that decided to make war on Duke Henry, but the trio of Elector John Frederick, Landgrave Philip of Hesse, and Duke

Moritz of Saxony, who conferred on the matter at Naumburg on 26 October 1541.[69] Although the league decided to back the princes' play, the Brunswick affair was essentially an interdynastic war fueled by the wildly personal feud between Duke Henry and his old comrade, Philip of Hesse.[70] Religious differences fanned, but did not cause, the princes' blind hatred, and so did the roles of Henry and Philip as commanders of their respective confessional alliances. The bad blood between them went back to 1538, when the landgrave, then en route to the league's diet, which had provocatively been called to Brunswick, rode right under the walls of Castle Wolfenbüttel and was fired upon from its battlements. Elector John Frederick returned the compliment next year by attacking Henry and his escort, who were crossing Wettin lands without permission. Meanwhile, while he was hunting wolves near Kassel at the end of 1538, the landgrave's men caught a Brunswick courier, in whose pouch they found papers that retailed ducal charges against the Hessian prince.[71]

These acts set off a fierce war of words between Duke Henry and the Smalkaldic chiefs and their respective partisans, the chief effect of which was to inflame passions on both sides. In this scurrilous symphony of hatefulness—more than sixty titles appeared in 1542 alone, and nearly a hundred by 1546—the writers and ghostwriters pulled out all stops, dwelling with particular glee on real and alleged sexual delicts.[72] Much was heard, from the one side, about Duke Henry's mistress, Eva von Trott, who after a sham funeral was said to have borne him seven children; also much, from the other side, about Margarethe von der Sale and the Hessian bigamy.[73] The battle in print was entertaining because of the wildness of the charges, the coarseness of the language, and the satisfying sight of great princes, lords of human kind, railing at one another like fishwives in the marketplace. The theologians often behaved as badly as their lords, and sometimes worse. "You should not write a book," Luther mocked Duke Henry in his infamous *Wider Hanswurst*, the most ribald of his pamphlets, "until you have heard an old sow fart. Then you should gape in wonder and say, 'Thank you, beautiful nightingale, there I hear a text for me!'"[74] However entertaining, the feud was dangerous as well, because the stream of charges and countercharges, slanders, rumors, gossip, and lies soaked up and focused all the resentments, hatreds, and griefs—but also the senses of righteousness and triumph—of the confessional parties against the Habsburg policy of conciliation, which was now approaching its zenith.

The role of the printing press in ripening the Brunswick affair illustrates an important feature of Reformation politics in Germany: the tremendous explosion of pamphleteering during the 1520s had swelled German printing capacity, readership, hunger for news, and means of distribution to new and irreversible levels. The Brunswick affair sparked a second flood of pamphleteering on this new, massive scale, and helped to turn a princely feud toward the long-expected confessional Armageddon. Some of the polemics were simply amusing, as when Elector John Frederick unleashed a blast "against the Calpurnian scandal and book of lies by the blockheaded, godless, perjured, damned scoundrel, wicked Barrabas, and Holfernes of Brunswick, who calls himself 'Henry the Younger.'"[75] From such language it was no great step to talk of Christ and Antichrist, especially after the princes moved from words to actions. Witness Luther's reaction to the initial conquest of Brunswick-Wolfenbüttel in 1542: "This is a truly divine victory, for God has done it all. He is the *fac totum*, and we may now hope that the last days are at hand!"[76] The general view was nonetheless more sober, especially on the Catholic side, for neither the Habsburgs nor the Catholic League of Nuremberg stirred a hand to save Duke Henry from the Smalkaldeners.[77]

On 13 July 1542 the Smalkaldic chiefs declared war on Duke Henry and began to invade his lands, and by mid-August they had conquered the duchy as easily as the landgrave had taken Württemberg eight years before.[78] Supported by their Smalkaldic allies, they installed a governor, who under their instructions organized a Lutheran transformation of the duchy's church, much as Duke Ulrich had done in Württemberg, except that in Brunswick-Wolfenbüttel there could be no legitimate right to reform (*jus reformandi*). Once in control, the Smalkaldic chiefs could not let go, partly because they could not decide whether to partition the lands or to hold them for the legitimate heirs, Henry's sons, much as the Bavarians had once planned in Württemberg. They feared, too, a widely supported proposal to place the duchy in receivership ("sequestration") with its feudal lord, the emperor.[79] Most of all, the Smalkaldic chiefs held on to the duchy so as to press their allies to cover their war debts.

The invasion of Brunswick, more than any other event, made the North German reformation impossible to contain, as its South German counterpart had been contained since 1534, even though the restoration of Imperial politics around 1540 made the times more propitious. This is not to say that without Brunswick there would have been no German civil war in 1546–47, much less in 1552. But the invasion of Brunswick, a pure act of aggression, belied the Smalkaldeners' avowed purpose and standard defense, that they were loyal to both the Empire and emperor and to the true religion. Brunswick also weakened the Smalkaldic League, for it evoked dissension and strengthened suspicions between South and North and between cities and princes, which poisoned the negotiations in 1545–46 for the league's renewal and intensified Charles V's temptation to settle the German question through force.

The debilitating effects of the victory in Brunswick-Wolfenbüttel can be traced in the attitudes of Jacob Sturm and his Strasbourg colleagues. Since about 1539, Sturm and his government had supported the league's engagement in North Germany more strongly than did any other southern Protestants. In April 1539, for example, Sturm asked his government for a voluntary contribution of several thousand florins to soften by example the other southerners' opposition to a militant policy in North Germany.[80] In 1540–41, when the southern Smalkaldic cities balked at aid for Goslar against Duke Henry, the Strasbourgeois undertook to change their minds. Led by Sturm, they recommended in December 1540 both financial and diplomatic support for the city of Brunswick and argued that Duke Henry's religious hatred for Goslar made the city's cause a "religious matter."[81]

Though strong for aid to the league's northern members, the Strasbourgeois also insisted that the league honor its own constitutional procedures, which the three princes' plan to invade Brunswick-Wolfenbüttel surely violated. For this reason, probably, the landgrave wanted to initiate Jacob Sturm into the secret even before the princes signed the highly confidential agreement at Naumburg to attack Duke Henry. The landgrave now sat at the center of a highly complicated web of double games, reconciled to the emperor, deceiving his southern allies, and preparing to strike at his most bitter foe. This duplicity was vital to the adventure into which he wanted to drag Sturm. "It would not be a bad thing," he wrote Elector John Frederick toward the end of 1541,

> that at the coming diet [Speyer 1542] we secure the suppression of the Edict of Worms and the recess of Augsburg [1530] and allow the other side to accept the religious articles agreed upon at Regensburg. It would also be all right to allow the other side to accept, concerning the articles not agreed upon, the emperor's book [Regensburg Book]—though our side musn't approve it—in order to move them over closer to our religion.[82]

The whole business was a cover for the plan against Brunswick, so far as the landgrave was concerned. He was worried that Jacob Sturm's opinions concerning the decrees against Minden and Goslar "may be detrimental to what we intend," and he recommended that Sturm be let in on the secret, "because, as is well known, the southerners all follow Jacob Sturm." And so, when Sturm came on 1 February 1542 to Speyer for the Imperial Diet, a Hessian agent came to him and, "on special orders and under his sworn oath of loyalty" to the landgrave, revealed the three princes' plan of campaign. Sturm, the agent reported, "judged the matter very positively and answered in the enclosed [lost] document, which is composed in hidden words [in cipher?] by [Rudolf] Schenck."[83] The landgrave proposed to tell other southern politicians of the plan—"though not Augsburg"—on Jacob Sturm's advice, "so that they will be mobilized ahead of time to support the aid of 7,000 foot and 3,000 horse for Goslar." Jacob Sturm, therefore, had known since early February 1542 that the three princes would invade Brunswick very soon and only thereafter assemble the league's war council. Bucer, who may have learned of the plan even earlier than Sturm did, confirmed in mid-March that "Sir Jacob recognizes Your Grace's proposal as the best and swiftest, . . . and he doesn't doubt that the estates will be glad to take part in it."[84] What is more, at the same time that he was giving the Hessians this impression, Sturm was recommending to his colleagues at home a peaceful solution to the entire quarrel.[85] Sturm also played his double games.

Sturm had decided to support the invasion of Brunswick-Wolfenbüttel, which was illegal according to the laws of both the Empire and the league. On 3 July 1542 he and Mathis Pfarrer told their colleagues that if Strasbourg supported the war and paid its share, a victory would relieve the city from the threat of attack, though a defeat would bring blame on "us as a cause of this evil."[86] Following Sturm's recommendation, the Senate & XXI decided that "we should not abandon the princes" and instructed their war councillor, Ulman Böcklin, that "he should voice our complaint [against the unconstitutionality], but even if this or that ally withdraws, the aid must be given to the commanders. And although the princes ignored the majority and exceeded the terms of the alliance, the aid should be paid according to the league's rules."

Once decided, the Strasbourgeois followed words with deeds, and in July 1542, when the invasion was underway, they threw their whole weight against the southern allies—Duke Ulrich and the Swabian cities—who voted only half the aid Landgrave Philip requested.[87] Soon the landgrave complained that the southerners owed him 130,000 fl. and asked Bucer to remind his masters "that we borrowed money for this campaign, which must be repaid."[88] Indeed, by this time the Strasbourgeois were having second thoughts about the war, for in August they proposed that the second doubled "month" be retained at Ulm, in case it were needed in the South.[89] According to Hessian accounts, the southerners owed for two double-months—the first levied by the commanders, the second by the war council—a total of 207,600 fl., of which by autumn they had paid less than half.[90] By October, when Strasbourg's regime approved its share of the second double-month, the commanders were asking for a third double-month, and Duke Ulrich of Württemberg, who had refused to pay anything, was voicing doubts that the Brunswick affair was either defensive or constitutional.[91] Landgrave Philip felt insulted and injured by the southerners. "If this is the way we are to operate," he wrote to Bucer, "that the money doesn't come in until after the war, and then only begrudgingly, we'll soon tire of this alliance."[92]

Jacob Sturm had entered the Brunswick affair with his eyes open, his normal prudence tempered by the magnitude of the opportunity. The more volatile Bucer greeted the invasion of Brunswick with the same joy he had voiced over Württemberg in 1534, though triumphant elation soon gave way to anxiety and misgivings. In early fall, when the duchy was won, he rejoiced and gave "eternal praise and thanks to God, our Father Almighty, who through His Son, Jesus Christ, has granted this gracious victory to His people. He will also assure that this victory will serve to greatly expand His kingdom."[93] A month later, Bucer had caught the southern mood, and he lectured Landgrave Philip about equity. "Our alliance is a Protestant alliance," he wrote, in which no one should make money or seek to become richer than he is, but in which everyone should maintain the highest standards of loyalty and equality [*gleichmessigkeit*]. Equality is the basis of all communities, inequality is like the very quicksilver, which destroys everything, especially religious community.[94]

Six weeks later, Bucer warned the prince against those who "wanted to slip quicksilver among our princes and estates, just as Your Grace was able to do in the Swabian League."[95] That the language of "equality" and "community" had much effect on the landgrave, may well be doubted.

The whole thing happened so quickly, as the brief moment of exaltation gave way to an eternity of wrangling about money. The occupation of Brunswick-Wolfenbüttel sucked up enormous sums, nurtured the southern allies' sullen resentment, and prevented the issue of unconstitutionality from being laid to rest. Reports of Hessian and Saxon plundering of the duchy's churches intensified the allies' fears of being branded "church robbers" and enemies of the public peace.[96] By year's end, even the loyal Strasbourgeois began to grumble against the landgrave's financial irresponsibility, how he had pocketed Duke Moritz's gift of fifty thousand thalers, how the booty had not been assigned to the war's expenses, and how the princes "remain in the field with large forces and at great expense."[97]

For their part, once they had properly plundered the conquered duchy, the Smalkaldic chiefs found themselves in the position of the dog who chases cars and finally catches one. What to do with it? By March 1543, when he began to face this issue, Jacob Sturm thought that "it would be much better, and do more for our reputation, to sign a treaty with Duke Henry's children, to restore the land to them, and with the duke himself. That is our first choice, and so we have advised."[98] Failing this, the Smalkaldeners should grit their teeth and deal with Duke Henry himself, "so that the affair may be put to rest." If the allies could raze Henry's fortresses, require his estates to go surety for his conduct, and bind him through a treaty confirmed by the emperor, "we can trim his claws, so that he cannot start anything, or, if he does, he must lose." The religious argument, Sturm confessed, was phony, for though Henry would probably restore Catholicism, "this is not sufficient reason to deprive him of his lands. This is not the reason they were taken." Once Goslar and Brunswick were secure and the Smalkaldeners recovered their costs, "we will have no claims on the land or his subjects, which are his hereditary fief and property of His Majesty and the Empire. It is none of our affair, what religion is established in such a land." So much for the Brunswick war as a "religious matter," so much for confessional Armageddon. Jacob Sturm was at heart a conservative legalist, and he recognized that Henry must be restored, whatever the religious consequences, "for otherwise we could take other papist princes' lands from them, bring the people over to our religion, and then refuse to restore the lands."[99] As for Henry's undoubted crimes, "we are not his lord or judge, but only His Imperial Majesty has such jurisdiction. If he will not punish the duke, we may not."

Some months later, Sturm returned to his ruminations in a secret opinion written for Landgrave Philip of Hesse. "I wish to God I could give abundant and useful advice in this matter, which I would dearly love to do," he began,

> but how should I advise in the face of so many different opinions that the proposal seems best and most rational, which is most eloquently stated? Your Princely Grace knows that I never wanted this affair begun without a prior decision by the league's assembly or at least its war council. I was worried about just the kind of split which the affair has subsequently caused. And we must be concerned that more and worse divisions will occur, if the matter is not pursued and laid to rest.[100]

After stating his opinions on a possible solution, Sturm urged that settling the quarrel would not only bring the Smalkaldeners back together but "law may be reestablished in the Empire, if the matter can be settled, and an equitably assessed aid against the Turks can then be voted." If not, then, because of the struggles amongst the Germans, "the Turk will become our master."

The irony of the Brunswick affair as the northern counterpart of the Württemberg affair of 1534, cannot have been lost on Sturm. In 1534 he and his government had backed restoration in Württemberg on the legal grounds that Duke Ulrich had been unjustly dispossessed;[101] nine years later, Sturm advanced a similar argument in favor of Duke Henry against the Smalkaldic chiefs. That Ulrich had turned a Catholic land to Lutheranism and Henry would restore a Lutheranized land to Catholicism, if he could, did not change the legality of the case in Sturm's eyes. The gospel, after all, was purely spiritual, not a godly law that superseded and broke the law of this world. Sturm had learned this lesson in 1525, and though he could sometimes be tempted to join in an aggression that promised rich rewards, he always fell back on conservative legalism.

When the allies met at Smalkalden in July 1543 to decide the fate of Brunswick-Wolfenbüttel, they agreed to let the duchy's ecclesiastical lands be sold off to cover the war costs. Bitter words nonetheless flew about the Saxon-Hessian domination of the occupation government, which the princes refused to allow to be sworn to the league rather than themselves, and about the princes' objection to razing the duchy's fortifications—a clear indication that they intended to retain the conquered lands. Sturm confessed that although the fortifications' fate was "not very important, because the land is far away, . . . the costs of the occupation are unbearable."[102] During the league's next diet at Frankfurt in the autumn, the conflict became a quarrel, for after the southern envoys departed, the others excised from the league's letter to Charles V a passage suggesting that, under certain conditions, Duke Henry might be restored. Though the Strasbourgeois sighed that "since it has happened, we must put up with it," the argument raged on into winter.[103]

The quarrel over Brunswick revealed to Landgrave Philip, as he wrote to Bucer, "how ramshackle [*baufellig*] our alliance's affairs have become."[104] For this outcome he chiefly blamed Jacob Sturm, whose "timid [*cleinmutig*]" view of the matter was that the Brunswick invasion had violated the public peace.[105] Bucer, who agreed with Philip, nonetheless defended Sturm and blamed the lawyers,[106]

> who have become truly mighty tyrants over the laws of the German nation. They regard only their written, Roman, tyrannical law, which they employ to inflate their reputation among all estates. They can do this, because such law is so complicated and is so buried in enormous tomes, that they alone can use it.

By means of this jurisprudence, Bucer complained, the Chamber Court's judges gathered all matters into the emperor's hands, and "while these doctors sit on the highest court, all princes and estates must beg them for justice." He condemned those who, like Sturm, "don't just look at the matters as they are, but listen to the lawyers about what will and won't be approved by the Chamber Court, which makes them either happy or timid." Roman law, he thought, contradicted the right of free Germans to depose tyrants:

> Sir Jacob [Sturm] knows as well as anyone does, that by means of the Franks, God broke the Roman law of tyranny in the German lands, and He gave us the free, Frankish law, which should now be the German law, according to which the free princes and estates may drive out such an unbearable tyrant [i.e., Duke Henry], even without the sovereign's permission.

It was the learned lawyers who, since the founding of the Chamber Court,

> reined in and suppressed the free, Frankish law and brought in and replaced it with the tyrannical Roman law. And now that this powerful emperor grows ever stronger, and this learned court remains so obdurate, well, now Sir Jacob will see what coin has value, and what sort of law will be enforced. There is a proverb: A willing audience is more important than a good singer. The point is: what counts is not how many rights you have, but how much you give the judge.

Bucer here voiced one of the most common public sentiments of the day, the fear of Roman law and the hatred of learned lawyers.[107] The sentiment had its conservative side—protection of traditional rights and privileges under the "old law"—but it could also fuel a radical advocacy of the gospel as a "godly law" over all other kinds of law. Sturm took one side, Bucer the other, and the split between them widened.

In February 1544 at Speyer, Sturm and Landgrave Philip finally stood face to face on the Brunswick affair.[108] Sturm led the opposition to the princes' demand that the league throw its whole weight behind their campaign to have Duke Henry condemned for his crimes. Three times the landgrave sent for Sturm and lectured him about Brunswick. The first time, he berated Sturm for worrying about the local merchants' money and sneered that he would rather the business were in the hands of the XIII or the Senate than in Sturm's.[109] Sturm gravely took the diplomat's defense: he followed his instructions; if he received different ones, he would follow those. In a subsequent interview the landgrave poured out his resentment on Sturm.[110] "We are truly astonished," he hectored Sturm, that

> Henry's violent acts against Goslar and his intentions against Saxony and us don't persuade you, but that you recommend that we make a treaty with him and let him come back into his lands. We know, however, that you were ever of such a mind, since the day when Rudolf Schenck told you in confidence what the elector, Duke Moritz, and we were planning to do. Even then you concluded that we wanted to make war and were using defense merely as an excuse. If you now search your own conscience, you will surely see that we had this revealed to you because we trusted you; for you know that we have never kept anything from you, about war or anything else. We expect, therefore, since we have so trusted you, that you should not criticize but praise us.

Then, at great length, the landgrave recounted his own motives in this affair, the decision to support the cities of Brunswick and Goslar, the princes' rejection of offensive war, and the league's authorization of action by its commanders. "These were the origins of the entire affair," he said, "and this is its true history." The prince pointed out that Sturm had told Schenck, the Hessian agent, that he would prefer that the princes attack Duke Henry alone, "without expense to the other estates, and that it not be done for the sake of religion or for reasons connected with religion," so that the Catholics would not be moved to help Henry. The landgrave had concurred, but "God did not want that to happen" but brought it about in quite a different way, so that "Sir Jacob must reasonably conclude that this affair is an act of God. And he must then not regard the affair with the eyes of this world alone."

The Hessian prince's "vehement [*heftig*]" words revealed, Sturm thought, "that the two, elector and landgrave, have decided to retain the duchy and thus want to prevent a peaceful settlement of this affair, no matter what we think of it."[111] His view, by contrast, was that if the Brunswick affair came before the emperor, "there are many reasons why Duke Henry would find in this matter a more favorable judge than we would. If the judgment goes against us, we will have pay all the costs and restore the lands."[112] The league's majority, however, backed the princes' stand against arbitration, though over Sturm's protest. "The princes," he wrote home, "lead us ever deeper into this game. . . . It would be grievous to handle the affair in such a way that no treaty is possible; it would also be grievous to part company over this affair."[113] Sturm pleaded that to defer a settlement would only favor Duke Henry and endanger the league, because the emperor was more likely to have a free hand later than he did at the moment, "but this argument has no effect on our princes, because they are too hot and emotional against Duke Henry."[114]

By 1544 at the latest, therefore, Jacob Sturm came to realize how deeply irrational the Smalkaldic chiefs' engagement against Duke Henry had become, how recklessly they were dragging the league into conflict with the emperor, and how feeble were the league's defenses against exploitation by its own chiefs. Their aggression threatened to strip the Smalkaldic League of the respect of those who, whatever their motives—reformism, neutralism or anti-Habsburg policy—opposed the use of force against the Protestants. The league posed, as Sturm believed, a military match for the staunch Catholics alone, but it could not fight the emperor except in the broader fellowship of the German opposition, the friends of aristocratic liberty. If Charles and Ferdinand could catch the Smalkaldic League isolated from the rest of this German opposition, they would settle the German schism once and for all in their own sense. The situation of 1544, therefore, curiously replicated that of 1525—the Reformation stood or fell with German liberty—though "liberty" in an aristocratic, not a popular, sense.

The Brunswick affair also drove a permanent wedge between Sturm, on the one hand, and Bucer and Philip of Hesse, on the other. For although Sturm consistently favored the sequestration of Brunswick-Wolfenbüttel in the emperor's hands, the Smalkaldic chiefs wanted to allow Henry's sons some lands and, it was widely believed, retain "the choicest parts" for themselves.[115] Bucer, who favored this path, once more reported on Sturm's legalism. "He is hindered by the public peace's provision," Bucer wrote to the landgrave,

> that the lands taken from a violator of the peace must revert to the feudal lord, and that the protectors of the peace may recover only their costs. From this he concludes that according to the law, we may not retain possession of the land except by force.[116]

As for the Christian duty of reformation, Sturm held that

> if we have no right to retain possession, then we are obliged to keep hands off the religion of the land as we found it, as we have done in other regions in which we've had considerable claims and connections, such as the prince-bishoprics, which according to all the laws of their church belong not to their possessors but to the people of God. That was the case in Metz and with others, whom we turned away, as you well know.

Indeed, Sturm saw very clearly where breaking human laws for the gospel's sake would lead. He did not need to be reminded of Metz.

Sturm's agony over Brunswick reached its climax during the Diet of Speyer in 1544. Not only did the Smalkaldic chiefs rush to support the French war—so dreaded at Strasbourg—hoping thereby to soften the emperor on the Brunswick question, but Duke Henry, who prowled about demanding his rights, singled out Sturm and accused him, both orally and in print, of having said publicly at Nuremberg in 1543 that "the French king is a good lord and chief to me."[117]

The Smalkaldic chiefs' rush to back the emperor's war against France further deepened the breach between Sturm and the landgrave. Bucer pleaded with the prince,

> Please don't be angry with Sir Jacob's timidity. He is loyal, and he is more afraid of illegality than of violence.... He looks deeply into the matters and fears God's wrath, if things are not kept properly and in correct order. Then, too, he always goes further than he can promise to go, and our masters will truly stand by Your Princely Grace to the last.[118]

Yet the quarrels plunged Sturm into a state of deepest depression, so deep, Bucer wrote in February 1545, that he considered renouncing his citizenship and leaving Strasbourg.[119] From Worms, where the Imperial Diet was sitting, Sturm wrote home in an uncharacteristically sarcastic tone that the war was "an enterprise from which the cities certainly will not become rich."[120]

The tension was also splitting Sturm from his colleagues at home, who tended to support the Hessian-Saxon policy of holding the duchy if the path of sequestration failed.[121] The landgrave, hearing of this disagreement, exploited it to undermine Sturm's role as leader of the league's opposition party, a tactic that led Sturm to write home in April from Worms in a spirit of deep resignation: "I can only commend the matter to God. I could well tolerate that someone else were sent here, who could do better than I can." If they yielded to the princes, he insisted, "we would have ... given out fifty or sixty thousand florins more, all in vain."[122] Bucer, as usual, sided with the landgrave against him.[123]

And yet the southerners prevailed, and the league decided to deliver Brunswick-Wolfenbüttel into the emperor's hands within one month, providing that Duke Henry were not allowed into the land, and that for the time being no changes were made in the regime of occupation.[124] Henry, however, would not wait, and in mid-September he invaded his lands with eight thousand foot and fifteen hundred horse.[125] His lack of heavy guns proved his undoing, for he had to break off unsuccessful sieges of the city of Brunswick and Castle Wolfenbüttel to prevent the Smalkaldic chiefs from uniting with Duke Moritz. Near Kalefeld on 14 October 1545, Landgrave Philip used his superior artillery to blast the Brunswick troops. "If I fell into your power, as you have into mine," he told the captured duke, "you would not let me live. I, however, will treat you better than you deserve from me. You have been very foolish to disobey His Imperial Majesty by rejecting the sequestration, for otherwise you would not have come to this bad end."[126]

While Henry was coming to his bad end, Jacob Sturm sat down at home, weary from spending eleven of the last thirteen months at Worms, to draft an apology of his views for the landgrave's eyes.[127] "Your councillors and envoys have often heard my reasons," he began, "for I believed ... it would be best to negotiate even if both sides were already mobilized, in order to prevent terrible damage to the German nation." If the Smalkaldeners win and keep the land,

> we must either place it in His Majesty's receivership or hold it, which will involve such expense and trouble that our allies cannot bear it in the long run; then, I fear, the allies will be further divided. Therefore, even if we win, we will gain greater expenses and nothing more, which we cannot recover from Duke Henry or from his land or officials.

Henry had been ruined, Sturm thought, and he would never be dangerous again, whereas the occupation of Brunswick was a continuing burden to the league, not only because of the land's debts, but even more because its occupation would dissuade other Protestant powers from joining the league. In sum, "the burden and expense rests on a few of us alone, and day-by-day we become fewer."

Next Sturm turned to the landgrave's charges against him. He denied that

> I look only to the advantage of my masters or of other cities, rather than to the common cause. As far as I can judge, if this affair continues, my masters here will perform whatever burdens the alliance places on them, if they are able—just as they have always done. It is hard, however, and in the long run will be impossible, for those of good will to bear the load alone, while others slip the harness. I am afraid it will ruin them all. May it please Your Grace to accept these words of mine and consider them. May God Almighty give Your Grace and us all grace and understanding, so that we may find the right path through this burdensome and difficult affair and the way that will praise His holy name, expand His kingdom, and advance His honor and His holy Word. May He also give Your Grace a long, happy reign.

Sturm's uncharacteristic effusion in the letter's closing betrays how low relations had sunk between the Smalkaldic League's two architects. They would never recover.

In for a penny, in for a pound, and the costs of the second Brunswick campaign had to be piled on earlier debts and, one hoped, spread as widely as possible. On the day of the Battle of Kalefeld, when Sturm, Martin Herlin, and Conrad Joham met to draft a recommendation to their colleagues, they allowed the emergency to override their scruples. Because this action

> is too expensive for those powers who are engaged in the defense of Brunswick, the landgrave should circularize the other allies and tell them that the affair concerns not only those now involved but all the allies and the whole cause of true religion. They should, therefore, give aid and support and are obliged to do it. We should also send to all Protestant powers and others of the Augsburg Confession, just as to the allies, and draw them into deliberations about this common religious matter, so that the affair does not end in trouble and damages for us, and thus for our religion as a whole.[128]

This had been Landgrave Philip's view from the start—whether sincere or hypocritical, is beside the point—that the welfare of the Protestant powers was itself a "religious matter," and the distinction between "religious" and "worldly" therefore merely a tactical matter. Sturm and his colleagues had essentially accepted the same principle, when they insisted that the suits against Strasbourg, whatever their objects, were "religious matters." A committee of Strasbourg's regime said as much in 1546, when it recommended that envoys from the northern Smalkaldic cities be reminded "how loyally we helped them against Brunswick, which was basically [im grund] not a religious matter."[129]

UNRAVELING: REFORM OF THE LEAGUE

While the Brunswick affair crackled and boiled, the Smalkaldic League neared the point at which the issues of its own renewal and reform would have to be faced. So bad had relations become, wrote Augsburg's envoys from the Imperial Diet of Worms in early 1545, that no one any longer knew who belonged to the league or who wished to remain in it.[130] Some smaller members were drifting toward the Protestant neutrals, such as Nördlingen, whose regime eschewed all alliances and prayed for peace and toleration.[131] By this time, the splits—South vs. North, cities vs. princes—were beginning to unhinge the league. Elector John Frederick, whom some southerners thought "lazy," contemplated giving up his command and even leaving the league, and the landgrave complained repeatedly about having to neglect his own lands for the league's sake.[132] The Strasbourgeois, on the other side, reminded themselves that except for the common religion, they had no reason to continue membership in "so widely scattered an alliance [eines so weitläufigen verständnisses]."[133] At Augsburg in July 1545, the regime even predicted that the Brunswick affair might even destroy the league. "Because the [quarrels about] the audit and the [cities'] ingratitude have made princes, especially Saxony and Hesse, who risked life, land, and people [in Brunswick], just as diffident as the cities," they wrote in alarm, "it could easily happen that if the cities simply wait for the princes to open the question, the [league's] treaty will elapse and the two groups will become estranged from one another."[134]

   This plunge into apathy and pessimism, plus the impending expiration of the league's treaty in September 1546, prompted the Smalkaldic chiefs to act. On 20 October 1545, the day before they captured Duke Henry at Kalefeld, they called the Smalkaldeners and other Protestant powers to assemble on 6 December at Frankfurt, where they would deliberate on renewal and reform of the league.[135]

   The problem of reform, and Jacob Sturm's role in it, has to be seen in a larger context.[136] The tensions over the Brunswick affair illuminate the Smalkaldic League's three major weaknesses. First, the league suffered from the social division between the cities, whose trade-oriented regimes naturally favored peace over war, and the princes, who regarded war as a natural, if risky, path of expansion. Second, the league suffered from its immense extent and inadequate density, for it literally marched with the Empire itself, from Strasbourg to Pomerania and from Constance to Hamburg. Third, the league suffered from an ideological confusion, which the Reformation had intensified but not created, about acceptable boundaries between "religion" and "temporal affairs." Underlying all of these weaknesses, the league rested on a common religion alone, unsupported by common economic interests, common political traditions, or common problems of regional security. It had no palpable interests to foster what Jacob Sturm had called "the proper sort of love for one another."

All these weaknesses came to the fore when the urban politicians began to think about renewal, about reform, and about alternatives to the present order of security. Sturm thought about such things in March 1544, when King Ferdinand's men talked up a new league of southern powers under royal leadership. Such a revival of the old Swabian League, he thought, would be good for such rulers and cities as "lie near one another," but otherwise

> such a league would be of little use [*wenig erschiessen*], for the federation and system of legal arbitration, which the allies establish together, covers only the members. If such a league should include Strasbourg but not its neighbors, with whom the city might any day come into conflict, membership would have little purpose—as we saw some years ago, when Strasbourg for a while joined the Swabian League [in 1512].[137]

His colleagues added that the new league would involve Strasbourg in Austrian affairs and would, in any case, contain a Catholic majority. Their basic objection, however, applied to all such federations, "unless neighbor should ally with neighbor."[138] Strasbourg needed this kind of protection less than others, for

> we don't have so much civic and private wealth, manufactures, and trade as exist in Nuremberg, Augsburg, Ulm, and other cities, so that we also don't have, thank God, so many factions, feuds, and enmity as others. Most of our enemies and conflicts, so far as we know, arise because of the Christian religion and God's holy Word, and for this purpose we already have a league.

Besides, "if we should join alliances for secular reasons, they would profit us little, since the public peace forbids the use of force, even if violence is used against us."[139] Here they echoed Strasbourg's ancient tradition of political self-sufficiency, based on its role as the metropolis of a region that lacked powerful princes.

Elsewhere, the matter looked very different. At Ulm, for example, where mounting Smalkaldic dissent over Brunswick prompted Bernhard Besserer and others to advocate an entirely different alliance, two federated leagues of Protestant and Catholic powers, one northern and one southern.[140] This total repudiation of the Smalkaldic ideal frightened the Augsburgers and made them work harder for the league's renewal and reform. The crisis of 1545–46 transformed the question of renewal into an issue of reform, for many members advocated, and some demanded, changes in the Smalkaldic League's way of doing business and even its structure. The leadership in this campaign to save the league through reform fell to Jacob Sturm.

The principal negotiations for renewal and reform of the Smalkaldic League took place at Frankfurt between 7 December 1545 and 7 February 1546, which Sturm attended in the company of Heinrich von Mülnheim, his kinsman, and the guildsman Michael Schwencker.[141] The league took no decision, either at this long meeting or at Worms in April 1546.[142]

Well aware that his grand policy lay at risk, Jacob Sturm wearily agreed to go to Frankfurt, for "on the issues which will be treated now depend our city's prosperity or ruin."[143] The Strasbourg plan for reform, almost certainly his work, has already been presented.[144] It aimed to promote the league's statelike qualities, to strengthen its administrative and judicial apparatus, to redistribute its votes, and to cultivate fairness in taxation through adoption of the Common Penny.[145]

At Frankfurt in December 1545 a surprising consensus emerged for reform, and the two commanders declared that although "the multiplication of business and affairs causes them to neglect their own lands and people," and they "have become targets of great displeasure and resentment [grossen ungunst und unwillen]," nevertheless "the League must not be allowed to die."[146] Sturm, supported by the Saxons, asked for a point-by-point review of the constitution; the Augsburgers declared themselves "ready for anything"; and all of the cities' and most of the princes' envoys complained about taxes. The committee quickly deadlocked on the constitutional issues, especially Sturm's proposals that cities and princes have parity in votes and that members of the league's assembly be sworn on the constitution and be relieved of their oaths to their principals.[147] It was the issue of taxation, however, that brought a storm of complaints, especially from the league's senior members, so that the Saxons, fearing that tax reform would leave the elector to swallow the costs of the Brunswick campaign, allowed that "the situation was never so desperate as now."[148] Sturm hauled out all of his arguments for the Common Penny, many of which he had used in the Imperial Diet, and repeated them at the diet of Worms in April 1546. Again and again, he hammered away at what, in his eyes, had been and remained the only important reason for the league's formation and survival: the community of religion. "If his masters look only to themselves," he wrote, "they could well dispense with this league. But when they regard the common cause [den gemainen handel] and the dangerous state of current affairs, they believe that this league can best be preserved through loyal cooperation."[149] "On this account," he told the allies, "rather than indulging so much mistrust in the league and its business, it should be enough that we are dealing with honorable and Christian persons, who rest the matter on trust and faith, . . . for then God will make the cause flourish."[150] It was all in vain, for the league would not accept direct taxation, and Sturm returned to the revision of the matricular lists, according to which the league voted a new levy at Worms in April 1546.[151] The size of this levy, 900,000 fl., symbolizes the depth of the league's financial plight and the solidity of its political deadlock. But, then, no one regarded this sum as anything more than a fantasy.[152] It was a bitter defeat for Sturm, who came to the diet of Worms with powers "to make an agreement here [*dann sie haben bevelh hie ze schliessen*]."[153] The issue of the league's reform was dead, and it died over centralization and especially taxation, for some of the allies held the Common Penny to be "the path to a despotism of the cities . . . and to ruin."[154]

Despite the reformers' sense of urgency, the league rejected reform and approved a slightly revised version of the constitution of 1536.[155] To make matters worse, at Frankfurt the allies refused to accept more than a third of the huge war debt—seventy-five thousand fl.—claimed by Philip of Hesse.[156] In the spring of 1546, therefore, the Smalkaldic League lay near shipwreck, how near is revealed by the fact that its two architects, Jacob Sturm and Landgrave Philip, considered scrapping this league for some new alliance arrangements. They agreed, however, only on the league's plight, not on the reasons for it. The landgrave opposed Sturm's centralizing reforms and declared if delegates were sworn on the constitution, as Sturm proposed, he "would rather form a different league with some of the powers."[157] The old league, he said, "was well ordered, and it should be left alone; but if that cannot be, he would consider himself well out of the whole mess." Jacob Sturm, on the other hand, so disheartened by the failure of reform and the northern cities' selfishness, thought that "the honorable southern cities alone might ally with His Princely Grace [the landgrave]."[158] On the eve of the league's last peacetime diet, he analyzed the failed cooperation between Protestant North and Protestant South. "They have been so slow and dilatory with their payments," he thought,

> though the Brunswick affair concerned them more than it did the southerners and was undertaken for their benefit. Possibly, since they behave so slowly and improperly in their own cause, they would act even more slowly and improperly if the action took place in the South.[159]

Perhaps, he concluded, the Protestant cause might better be served by two separate, federated leagues, a southern one under the landgrave of Hesse and a northern one under the elector of Saxony.

On the eve of the Smalkaldic War, therefore, the Protestant alliance was succumbing to the same forces that kept the Empire from evolving into a centralized monarchy of the western European type. The regional differences and the heritage of successful particularism were simply too powerful to enable rulers and magistrates from different corners of the Empire to maintain a politically effective body, even when a common faith encouraged them to develop, in Sturm's phrase, a "proper sort of love for one another."[160] Like the Empire, the league was too large and too lacking in centralism to act like an effective state in the sixteenth-century manner.

Such was the unraveling condition of the alliance, when the allies met at Worms in the spring of 1546 for the last and largest of the Smalkaldic League's regular assemblies: fifty-six chancellors, councillors, mayors, and attorneys represented thirty of the league's thirty-six members and eleven other Protestant or sympathetic nonmembers.[161] But no princes, for the princes stayed home to sharpen their swords, and within a matter of weeks after Jacob Sturm came home from Worms, the league and the emperor were at war.

UNRAVELING: DISSENT AT STRASBOURG

The unraveling of the league's fabric in the mid-1540s corresponded to analogous disruptions on all other levels—city, region, and Empire. At Strasbourg, the unraveling hung on the growing fissure between Sturm and Martin Bucer. The Sélestat saddler's son now stood at the pinnacle of his career. Bucer, who had for years played second fiddle to Wolfgang Capito, rose between the Marburg Colloguy in 1529 and the Wittenberg Concord in 1536 to the chieftainship of Strasbourg's reformed church. Capito himself announced in 1534 that "Bucer is our bishop."[162] By the early 1540s, Bucer was also one of the two or three most influential Evangelical clergymen in the Holy Roman Empire, as his hand reached out from Strasbourg to touch reformations all across South Germany in both cities—Bern, Basel, Nuremberg, Ulm, Frankfurt, and Augsburg—and leading territories, Württemberg and Hesse, where he had a freer hand than he ever got at Strasbourg.[163] Like Sturm, and in partnership with Sturm, Bucer thus served as a regional leader of great stature, but he also broke out of the South to play parts in the reformations of other places, such as Cleves-Jülich, Hamburg, and, above all, Cologne.[164]

Bucer's expanded horizons, his sanguine, often aggressive, temperament, and his haste of judgment sometimes led him to advocate political solutions more radical, because more heedless of existing laws and rights, than Sturm could swallow.[165] In the Smalkaldic League, for example, Sturm characteristically tried to strengthen conciliar government, whereas Bucer just as characteristically called for a dictatorship. If the league should move to aid Elector Herman, he wrote to the landgrave in September 1545,

> then it would be better to have only one head with full authority [vollen gewalt], and to give him some councilors. The Romans did this, and so did everyone who ever accomplished great deeds. They established a dictator [einen dictatorem] without charge or limits but to assure that the city came to no harm. He had power over all money, people, and everything. May God grant Your Princely Grace what is needed to help this cause.[166]

Bucer and Sturm also differed about the enemy within. The preacher held that godly discipline formed a precondition to the Protestants' hope of defeating the pope and his minions. Christian religious discipline thus preceded and nourished political and military discipline. "We must revive and most zealously uphold moral discipline [*zuchtordnung*] and conduct our common prayers most faithfully," Bucer wrote, "for otherwise the Lord will not be with us. Our contributions of money, men, and whatever else is needed must have no other purpose or goal than to secure a proper peace and general, true reformation for the whole German nation."[167] Bucer's crusading vision of a godly nation marshaled behind an armed and godly ruler, pointed toward a world, the Puritan world, that the conservative Jacob Sturm could never enter.[168]

The expansion of his horizons beyond Strasbourg, the Upper Rhine, and South Germany liberated religious energies and ecclesiological dreams that Bucer turned back in a critical spirit on Strasbourg's own truncated and compromised reformation.[169] Sometime in the later 1530s, Bucer had begun to advocate a "second reformation" to revitalize the stalled reformation of doctrine and abuses in the church.[170] The clash with the dissenters during the first half of the 1530s had unleashed in Bucer's thoughts a new confidence in the church as an instrument of the Holy Spirit, which took shape in his great treatise on pastoral theology, "On the True Cure of Souls and Correct Pastoral Service" (1538), in which he searched for a theological principle to overcome the magistrates' rule of the church through their churchwardens.[171] Wolfgang Capito's death in 1541 may have encouraged Bucer in his search, for Capito had remained to the end a staunch defender of the Marsiglian ideal of magisterial authority over the church.[172] During the first half of the 1540s, though he possessed all the marks of success—the deanship of St. Thomas, a big house, a handsome salary, and a new wife—Bucer's yearning for a purer, more disciplined church gnawed away at him. As it left him no peace, so he left the magistrates none, for,

> truly, if we do not acknowledge, accept, hold to, and enforce God's holy covenant better than we do now, God will break it and will no longer be our God and Savior. He will deliver us most terribly into the hands of our enemies, to our ruin, both temporal and eternal, just as He did His people of old.[173]

Sometime before 1545, Bucer and some colleagues began to develop a new approach to the godly discipline they had been denied in 1534 and again in 1539. They formed conventicles of devout laymen—later called "Christian communities"—not outside the parishes, as their Anabaptist foes had done, but within them.[174] About the same time, the preachers formed a new type of purely clerical commission (*Konvent*) to deliberate on church business under Bucer's presidency.[175]

The issue of a continuing reformation at Strasbourg came to the surface toward the end of 1545, while the general council was convening at Trent and the league's diet sat at Frankfurt.[176] As the first conventicles appeared in two of the city's parishes, Bucer labored away on the second reformation's manifesto, "On the Church's Defects and Failings," which the preachers submitted to the Senate & XXI on Epiphany (6 January) 1546.[177] Its tone is set by the first sentence:

> One of the leading causes of the current ignorance of the difference between ecclesiastical and civil government is the people's feelings of great disdain and outrage, whenever the church's power of the keys is mentioned. They have insufficient knowledge of how the two governments differ from one another and the limits of each, imagining that they are subject to the authority of the temporal ruler alone.[178]

The church as a distinct kind of government! A very different song from what Bucer and his colleagues had sung against the Catholics in the 1520s and against the sects in the 1530s, for Bucer and his colleagues now demanded the power to excommunicate, stricter religious discipline, and the right of the parishioners to manage their parishes without magisterial interference.[179] They wanted permission to "visit" their parishioners in order "to examine their faith," which the Senate & XXI predictably refused to allow. From this confrontation a straight line led to the growth of active conventicles in at least four parishes during the years of the Smalkaldic War (1546–47) and to a decisive confrontation between regime and clergy at war's end.[180]

Because Jacob Sturm was away at Frankfurt and Worms that winter and spring, he took no part in the beginnings of this struggle—the third of the Reformation era—for the church's future at Strasbourg.[181] Indirect evidence nonetheless suggests that he supported his colleagues against Bucer and the younger clergy.[182]

Just as Bucer was attacking Sturm's ecclesiastical settlement, one of his oldest colleagues, Claus Kniebis, was working against Sturm's alliance policy. Once the political chief of Strasbourg's reformation, Kniebis had come to feel that Sturm had sold the cities, their liberty, and their devotion to the gospel into the clutches of the selfish, heedless, violent princes. Kniebis began to work against Sturm's policy in 1542, the year in which the league invaded Brunswick-Wolfenbüttel and the free cities began the new struggle for their rights in the Imperial Diet. Everything—except his failing health—suited Kniebis for the role of Sturm's opponent, for though Kniebis had ample wealth and a university education, he was a "new man" who had few ties to Strasbourg's past and none at all to the aristocratic world in which Sturm so easily moved. He nonetheless stood for the old way, the tradition of regional security through urban solidarity, and he turned his mind back to the dream of "turning Swiss."[183] His confidant was Basel's mayor, Bernhard Meyer, whom Kniebis asked to warn the Swiss that "we must not wait until we have been stripped clear of our wealth . . . or until some of us have been mediatized," but they must "care for one another with true brotherly love . . .

[and] take the trouble of one as the concern of all and support one another's just and equal rights." Kniebis proposed to revive "the good, old neighborliness, which Strasbourg many years ago had with your friends, the confederates, and especially with your city of Basel" to protect it from the princes, who "want the lion's share and treat us without fairness or justice. May Almighty God help us to free ourselves from these raging wolves!" For Kniebis, Duke Ulrich's oppression of Esslingen, the electors' and princes' behavior toward the free cities in the diet, and the Smalkaldic chiefs' expensive adventurism in the North, all converged toward the same end, the plundering and eventual subjugation of the free cities. Burghers, Protestants and Catholics alike, ought to stand together against this menace. Claus Kniebis thus proposed to fold Strasbourg's reformation into its political traditions, to wed, that is, the gospel to the burghers' politics of communal liberty, just as the landgrave and other princes tried to unite it with the aristocratic politics of "German liberty." He differed with Sturm chiefly in that his conception of liberty was genuinely communal in the traditional sense, whereas Sturm's was not. This distinction explains why Kniebis wanted to revitalize the Reformation version of "turning Swiss" against Sturm and his advocacy of the Smalkaldic League.

By the mid-1540s, therefore, domestic opponents were hammering away at Sturm's ecclesiastical and foreign policies. What might have helped to stabilize both fronts was a neighborly Protestant prince, whose strengths and needs might complement those of Strasbourg. This had once been the Palatine elector's role, then, briefly, that of the Austrian regime at Ensisheim. Next, the Reformation had brought the role to the Hessian landgrave, though on economic and geographical grounds—but on no others—Duke Ulrich would have been more suitable. The southern Protestant cities needed an active, friendly, and powerful Protestant prince, who might lead and speak for the southern Protestants and give them a sense of worth in the league's affairs. As if roused by this need, such a figure appeared on the stage in the mid-1540s. After nearly forty years of policy so cautious that it was hard to distinguish from somnolence, the Elector Palatine began to stir again, as the German Reformation began to knock at Heidelberg's gates.

UNRAVELING: THE PALATINE PROJECT

Long the most powerful dynasty in the southwest, the Rhenish branch of the House of Wittelsbach had stuck its long arm into Lower Alsace and Middle Baden during the fifteenth century. Long after Emperor Maximilian crushed the Palatine power in 1504, Strasbourg's elites kept close ties to Heidelberg.[184] Policies, however, diverged, for with the coming of the Reformation, Elector Louis V (r. 1508–44) followed a policy of "laisser faire, laisser allez" in religion at home and confessional neutrality abroad.[185] Now, however, changes could be expected from his brother and successor, Count Palatine Frederick.

Frederick, called by some "Frederick the Wise" and by others "Freddy the Penniless," has been called an "elderly playboy and incorrigible spendthrift."[186] Long in Habsburg service, in 1519 he had carried the news of his election to Charles V in Spain, and he later wooed several Habsburg princesses and married one, Dorothy, whose dowry contained a hopeless claim on the Danish throne. Frederick had headed the Imperial Governing Council in the early 1520s and commanded the relief of Vienna in 1529, and for twenty-six years he had held court at the provincial town of Neumarkt in the Upper Palatinate.[187] In accordance with Palatine custom, he made few changes in Heidelberg upon his succession in 1544, and his Danish claims also dictated a prudently pro-Habsburg policy and confessional neutrality.[188] By the end of 1545, however, he seemed to be drifting toward Evangelical religion and the Smalkaldic League.

Or so it seemed to Jacob Sturm, who had discussed religion with Frederick at Strasbourg in October 1538.[189] Sturm had studied at Heidelberg, he and his brothers were Palatine vassals, and through his dead wife's family, the Bocks, he had ties to several of the most powerful figures in the late elector's regime.[190] Familiar connections may, indeed, have prompted a small group of Frederick's officials to approach Sturm, behind their prince's back, during the Imperial Diet at Worms in 1545.[191] One of them, Philipp von Helmstett, later arranged for a secret meeting with Sturm at Neckarhausen, where they talked in the mayor's house on 4 or 5 December.[192] Their plan, kept secret from all but two or three others at Heidelberg, was that Elector Frederick should be invited to the league's diet at Frankfurt, where the landgrave would persuade him to initiate religious reforms in his lands and to join the league.[193] Sturm would broach this plan in the diet's committee, as though it were merely his own idea, and recruit the landgrave and others for the scheme.[194]

For a time it looked as if they would succeed. "We must strike," Helmstett pressed and Sturm echoed, "while the iron is hot."[195] Sturm pressed the Hessian landgrave to lay aside his differences with the elector and his friendship with the Bavarian duke.[196] "I have no doubt," Sturm told him, "that it would be more useful to the league and the Protestants to bring the Palatinate in than to refuse to do so on account of Bavaria." Sturm planted the idea of inviting Frederick to Frankfurt and volunteered to head the embassy the league sent to Heidelberg on 11 January.[197] In response, the elector did send envoys to Frankfurt, and though no agreement was reached, the whole matter looked very promisng when the league's diet rose in February.

When the allies reassembled at Worms in April, the situation had changed. Sturm believed that the Elector Palatine's admission to the league would draw others after him; if he refused, they would refuse.[198] By 22 April Sturm thought that "with the elector Palatine the matter is doubtful," and he was right, for the emperor's June agreement with Duke William of Bavaria drove Frederick back toward the Imperial camp.[199] In truth, Frederick proved as lukewarm a Protestant as he had been a Catholic.[200]

By late April, therefore, Jacob Sturm saw slip from his grasp the Palatine possibility, for the sake of which he had dissembled to his colleagues in the league and at Strasbourg. The project lay close to his heart on both religious and political grounds, as he told Helmstett in a characteristically Sturmian way:

> Personally, I view [the project] as both good and useful, and I will gladly and faithfully do whatever I can to help it forward. For if it comes to be, I can well imagine what it will mean to have the Palatinate firm for the gospel, and I hope that others will feel the same. For whatever furthers God's Word and serves to preserve the peace of the German nation, I will ever support with my poor ability. I firmly believe that if everyone wholeheartedly seeks and clamors [for it], we will do it. If, however, some one looks for this advantage and the other for another, it will go on such as we now see. May the Lord change it all for the better.[201]

This was not all, of course, for in the long run another great prince in the league's Southern District would have balanced Landgrave Philip's ambitions and Duke Ulrich's intransigence.[202] In the shorter run, the Palatine admission would have greatly strengthened the Smalkaldic League against the coming storm.

As spring turned to summer 1546, the storm lay on the horizon, and in mid-May Landgrave Philip wrote gloomily to his Strasbourg friends:

> It seems to me that we no longer possess the spirit and the feeling that we all used to have. In those days we were far fewer in number, but we formed the League, assumed large tax burdens, and with God's help we accomplished many things, both great and small. But now, when fortune smiles on us and our cause's need is greatest and comes to its critical point, we are so small-minded and so stingy with our money, our possession of which is not secure for an hour's time. If we are stingy in this crisis, we will save it only for our enemies' use, when we and our lands come under their yoke.[203]

Now, a quarter-century since Luther had journeyed to the Diet of Worms, it was time to determine who was going to live under whose yoke.

Notes

* "Als man zalt zwei und virzig jar,/was ich euch sing wan das ist war/von einem großen herren,/herzog von Braunschweig ist er gnant,/die schrift wird man in leren!/Herzog, bistu ein christen mann?/du hast vil böser stück gethan,/darumb wird man dich strafen;/der landgraf leit dir in deim land,/darauß mustu entlaufen." Liliencron, ed., *Historische Volkslieder* 4:192, no. 481, stanzas 1, 3.
1. We know that Strasbourgeois kept portraits of Mathis Pfarrer, Sturm's colleague, and presumably they did of Sturm as well. Ungerer, *Hausaltertümer* 2:140, 156.
2. C. Koch, "Über ein verschollenes Gemälde," 107–13; Ficker, *Bildnisse*, 9; Haug,

"Notes et documents," 92–111, here at 102 n. 1; Brady, "Social Place," 314. The painting is now in the Chapître de St-Thomas in Strasbourg, an oil measuring 1.95m x 0.94m, which was executed posthumously, based on Baldung's lost original; it was the model for all subsequent portraits of Jacob Sturm.

3. Chrisman, *Strasbourg and the Reform*, 94.
4. I have found but one letter dated from Breuschwickersheim, a letter from Sturm to Chancellor Johann Feige of Hesse, "Wickersheim," 12 October 1541, of which a copy is in StA Weimar, Reg. H, pagg. 501–6, no. 171, vol. 1, fols. 101r–104r.
5. *Ann. Brant*, no. 4963.
6. The story is assembled in Brady, *Ruling Class*, 250–57.
7. *PC* 3:566 n. 1, from AMS, XXI 1545, fols. 70, 72. Sturm reported some improvement and declined to come home.
8. *PC* 3:601, no. 572.
9. Lenz, ed., *Briefwechsel* 3:318.
10. *PC* 3:675 n. 5, from AMS, XXI 1545, fol. 453r. The remaining quotes in this paragraph come from Brady, *Ruling Class*, 254.
11. Lenz, ed., *Briefwechsel* 2:21 n. 4, based on letters in CR 39:nos. 281, 284–85, 288.
12. This paragraph is based on Neuhaus, *Reichsständische Repräsentationsformen*, 330–47.
13. Neuhaus, *Reichstag*, 318–19. The recommendations are in HStA Marburg, PA 725, fols. 88r–132r.
14. Friedensburg, *Reichstag*, 371–74; and see *PC* 1:267, no. 470.
15. On Besserer, see Walther, "Bernhard Besserer"; M. Ernst, "Bernhard Besserer." On Thomas Blarer, see Rublack, *Konstanz*, 167, 333 n. 100.
16. See Sebastian Schertlin von Burtenbach to the Burgomaster of Augsburg, 12 December 1545: "Her landgraf offtermals geclagt, das die von Augspurg jre gesante offter verenderen, vnnd nit solche leut die er gern hette schicken, vnnd so es zu ernstlichem thun kumm, so müessen die stett ander leut senden." Herberger, ed., *Briefe*, 40.
17. The story comes from Johannes Friese, *Neue Vaterländische Geschichte der Stadt Straßburg* 2:224, from which it is quoted by Hermann, *Notices historiques* 1:176–77; Stein, *Jacob Sturm*, 24 n. 1.
18. Landgrave Philip to Elector John Frederick, Zapfenburg, 12 November 1538, in StA Weimar, Reg. H, pagg. 214–18, no. 96, fol. 117r.
19. Ibid. He had this information from the two Besserers' letter of 30 May 1548, in StA Weimar, Reg. H, pagg. 218–20, no. 97, fol. 43.
20. Sieh-Burens, *Oligarchie*, 156–64.
21. This volume, chap. 9.
22. Vogler, "The Anabaptist Kingdom of Münster."
23. On Lübeck and the northern wars of the first half of the 1530s, see Hauschild, "Früheneuzeit und Reformation," 391–411; Häpke, *Die Regierung Karls V. und der europäische Norden*, 96–230; Korell, *Jürgen Wullenwever*.
24. Virck, "Lübeck und der Schmalkaldische Bund."
25. On Joachim's policies, see C. Meyer, "Kurfürst Joachim II. von Brandenburg im Schmalkaldischen Kriege"; Luttenberger, *Glaubenseinheit*, 129–39, 398–418.
26. For this situation, see Petri, "Karl V. und die Städte," 9–17; and on the prince-bishoprics and the Reformation movement, see the very good survey by Schindling, "Reichskirche," esp. 83–86.
27. Petri, "Norwestdeutschland," 10–11, takes seriously the threat of Habsburg expansion in northwestern Germany; he also follows (9–10) Hubert Jedin, "Fragen um Hermann von Wied," in ascribing purely religious motives to Elector Herman of Cologne.

28. Petri, "Landschaftliche und überlandschaftliche Kräfte," 91.
29. Dolan, The Influence of Erasmus; Luttenberger, Glaubenseinheit, 116–24.
30. Struick, Gelre en Habsburg; Wiesflecker, Kaiser Maximilian I. 1:158, 378–80, 2:140–6, 3:280–88; Tracy, Politics of Erasmus, 71–88.
31. PC 2:549, no. 571.
32. Ibid., 554–56, no. 573.
33. Lenz, ed., Briefwechsel 1:411–12, from which come the following quotes. A fairly detailed plan for aid from the Protestants was drawn up at Kassel on 15 February 1540. It provided for 1,700 foot and 400 horse from each Saxon ruler, the landgrave, Württemberg, and Pomerania; 1,500 foot and 200 horse from the lesser princes and counts together; and 1,000 foot each from Strasbourg, Ulm, Bremen, and Hamburg. The cities' contributions, which are speculative, would reduce the princes' total by 4,000. If the cities think the force too large, "we should negotiate with them for half this number." StA Weimar, Reg. C, 493–495, no. 870, fol. 53r.
34. PC 3:4, no. 4.
35. Ibid., 13–14, no. 11; an excerpt by Lenz, ed., Briefwechsel 1:412 n. 2.
36. Lenz, ed., Briefwechsel 1:150, no. 56.
37. Landgrave Philip to Elector John Frederick, Rottenberg, 4 March 1540, in StA Weimar, Reg. H, pagg. 348–52, no. 136, 93r–94v, here at 93r, reporting Bucer's remarks: "Er Jacob Sturm sei ein vernunfftiger man, wilcher jn so wichtigenn hendelen nicht palt sich entlichen erclere. Er sehe dj leuffte ahn, vnnd thue gleich wie einer, der vff vielen wegenn siehe vnnd nit wisse, wilchen weg er gehen wolt."
38. PC 3:24, no. 21.
39. For these ties and the coming of the war, see Petri, "Landschaftliche und überlandschaftliche Kräfte," 107–9.
40. Lenz, ed., Briefwechsel 2:103–4, no. 148 and 106–7, no. 149.
41. Brandi, Emperor Charles V, 503; and see Petri, "Karl V. und die Städte," 15, on the importance of this Imperial victory for the revival of Catholicism in the region. The Treaty of Venlo, 7 September 1543, is printed in Papiers d'état 2:669–77.
42. Mentz, Johann Friedrich 3:492, no. 43 (February 1543).
43. On Herman von Wied, see Franzen, Bischof und Reformversuch.
44. Ibid., 57–69, the quoted phrase at 62.
45. Ibid., 70.
46. Quoted by Varrentrapp, Hermann von Wied 1:208 (29 July 1543). See Scribner, "Cologne"; and on the general failure of Protestantism in the cathedral towns with resident bishops, see Rublack, Gescheiterte Reformation.
47. For what follows, see Duchhardt, Kaisertum, 30–33.
48. Mentz, Johann Friedrich 3:464–68, no. 40, here at 467.
49. See Duchhardt, Kaisertum, 33–35, for Catholic fears of the subversion of Mainz and Trier as well.
50. Varrentrapp, Hermann von Wied 2:60 n. 1: "Das aber die Trierschen wider christum von tagen zu tagen frecher werden, das horen wir ungern, hoffen aber, wann Coln und Münster zu den Evangelischen dreten, es werde Trier mit der zeit sich auch schemen."
51. On Bucer's role in Hermann von Wied's reform, see the account by Köhn, Entwurf. Pollet greatly expands the known sources, in Relations 1:83–243; 2:34–164.
52. Körber, Kirchengüterfrage, 128–31, 167–72; Lenz, ed., Briefwechsel 1:397–99. The opinions for Eisenach (not for the earlier diet at Brunswick, as Roth thought) are printed by Roth, "Zur Kirchengüterfrage," 304–19.

53. Martin Bucer to Nikolaus Pruckner, 24 January 1542, in BNUS, Thes. Baum., vol. 13:151; Varrentrapp, *Hermann von Wied* 1:118; Köhn, *Entwurf,* 41. There is no doubt, however, that Pruckner was acting for the elector, for Jean Sturm wrote to the Cardinal du Bellay from Cologne, 8 February 1543: "Haec ego Coloniae scripsi. Venit mecum Bucerus, qui ab episcopo Coloniensi religionis ergo vocatus est." *PC* 3:223, no. 218. On Bucer at Bonn in 1542–43, see Köhn, *Entwurf,* 44–60; Pollet, ed., *Relations* 1:134–38.

54. Köhn, *Entwurf,* 41–44, 49–66.

55. Much of this work is documented by Pollet's volumes, *Correspondance* and *Relations.*

56. AMS, XXI 1542, fol. 17r; Pollet, ed., *Relations* 1:140–48; 2:42–43. In Pollet's lists, I count three letters to Sturm, fifteen to the landgrave, and twenty-one to Conrad Hubert and the other clergymen at Strasbourg. Elector Herman's only known letter to Sturm is lost. Pollet, ed., *Relations* 1:139.

57. Varrentrapp, *Hermann von Wied* 2:109–11, and the landgrave's reply quoted in 111 n. 1.

58. Ibid., 103–9; and there, too, the remaining quotes in this paragraph.

59. See Stratenwerth, *Osnabrück,* 99 n. 4. On other aspects of the struggle in this region, see F. Fischer, *Reformationsversuche;* Petri, "Nordwestdeutschland."

60. *PC* 3:568, no. 540. On Strasbourg's northwestern trade, see Fuchs, "Les foires," 275–90.

61. Lenz, ed., *Briefwechsel* 2:332–33, no. 209; and there, too, the following quote.

62. Petri, "Herzog Heinrich."

63. Scheel, "Kurbraunschweig," 746, 752, 755–56, 760. There is a good overview of the Guelph states in this generation in Mörke, *Rat und Bürger,* 52–59.

64. Reller, *Kirchenverfassung,* 94. Henry's deep skepticism about Charles V's conciliation policy is expressed in a memorial he submitted to Charles V at Ghent, in *ARCEG* 3:89–90, no. 55, here at 89, lines 20–30: "In bedenckung das die Schmalcaldischen, wann sie gesehen, das der vorteil nit auf ir seiten gewesen, yeder zeit demutiglich zu gebarn und sich viel zu erpieten wol gwent seindt, haben aber daneben das widderwertig gesucht, auch fur und fur mehrern abfal gemacht."

65. Blume, *Goslar,* 19–33; Gebauer, "Die Stadt Hildesheim," 208–10; Mörke, *Rat und Bürger,* 55. Their entries, and that of Einbeck, swelled the number of northern Smalkaldic cities to seven. The others were Magdeburg, Bremen, Lübeck, and Göttingen. Blume, *Goslar,* 35.

66. Blume, *Goslar,* 51–52.

67. Ibid., 81–82. This occurred at the league's diet at Naumburg (19 December 1540–16 January 1541).

68. Ibid., 91–92.

69. Lenz, ed., *Briefwechsel* 1:155–60, discusses the secret plan of campaign at great length, but the text of the agreement, dated 26 October 1541, was first printed by *PKM* 1:225–31, no. 228. There is a good, brief discussion in Blume, *Goslar,* 96.

70. The secret plan provides "dass beide kur- und fursten als hauptleut die krigsreth [i.e., of the Smalkaldic League] nicht anderst oder nicht ehr fordern sollen oder werden, dann so sie schon das volk im werk versammlet haben, oder im werk sein, dasselb zu versammlen; alsdann sollen sie solche krigsrethe auch erfordern." *PKM* 1:227, lines 1–5.

71. Brady, "A Crisis Averted," 51.

72. Edwards, *Battles,* 143–62, offers by far the best account of this pamphlet war. I can only reinforce his warning (236 n. 5) that the texts printed by Hortleder, *Ursachen,* useful as they are—most of the pamphlets are now accessible in no other form—contain many bowdlerized passages.

73. Rockwell, *Doppelehe*, 101–12.
74. "Wider Hans Worst," in *WA* 51:561, lines 9–12, here in English from Edwards, *Battles*, 154. On the context, see Brecht, *Martin Luther* 3:219–22.
75. Printed at Wittenberg by Georg Rau in 1541. I use a copy in StA Weimar, Reg. H, pagg. 207–17, no. 102ab. It is bound with several other blasts into a stout volume of 906 pages.
76. For references, see Edwards, *Battles*, 158; Wolgast, *Wittenberger Theologie*, 277–78. H. A. Oberman, *Luther*, has taught us to take seriously Luther's apocalypticism, and Luther's "interpretation of the victory in terms of his theology of history" (Wolgast, *Wittenberger Theologie*, 277) was not rhetorical excess; as Edwards argues (*Battles*, 162), Luther's verbal excesses were quite deliberate.
77. Petri, "Herzog Heinrich"; Lauchs, *Bayern*, 217–38.
78. Bruns, *Die Vertreibung Herzog Heinrichs*.
79. This legal term meant "to deposit a controversial thing with a third person as *sequester*." Berger, *Dictionary*, 701.
80. *PC* 2:586–87, no. 597.
81. Ibid. 3:135–38, no. 148; 156, no. 165. Jacob Sturm was then at Worms. When the other southern cities demurred, the Strasbourgeois pressed the same policy on them at Esslingen in February 1541. Ibid., 164–65, no. 172.
82. Lenz, ed., *Briefwechsel* 2:43 n. 2; and there, too, the following quote. Lenz reports that he did not find in the StA Marburg the three opinions by Jacob Sturm, which were sent to Saxony via Hesse. I did not find copies of them in StA Weimar.
83. Ibid., 56 n. 2; and there, too, the following quote. The Hessian agent was Rudolf Schenck zu Schweinsberg, known to Sturm from the days of the Württemberg campaign of 1534. See Brady, "Princes' Reformation," 274 n. 43.
84. Lenz, ed., *Briefwechsel* 2:64, no. 134. The subject is a bit obscure, but the following passage is about Duke Henry.
85. This fact was noticed by ibid., 64 n. 7, who refers to the exchange between Sturm and Meyer at Speyer and the XIII on 5 and 7 April, AMS, AA 498, now in *PC* 3:261–63, nos. 247–49.
86. *PC* 3:275, no. 265, from AMS, XXI 1542, fol. 245v; and there, too, the remaining quotes in this paragraph. Unfortunately, the opinion by Sturm and Pfarrer is lost.
87. Michel Han's report on the southern allies' meeting at Ulm to the Senate and XXI of Strasbourg is printed in ibid., 277–78, no. 267. The growth of the southern reaction can be followed in the exchange between Strasbourg and Ulm in July and August 1542, in ibid., 278, 283–84, no. 271, 287, no. 277, 289–90, no. 281, 291. By mid-August the resentment had grown so strong that southern allies demanded that southern league funds remain in the South. Ibid., 296–97, no. 288.
88. Lenz, ed., *Briefwechsel* 2:97, no. 146.
89. Ibid., 97 n. 2. This was but a minor lapse. For the main line of Strasbourg's policy, see *PC* 3:329–30, no. 315, where the regime approves paying both the second and the third doubled "months," the razing of Castle Wolfenbüttel, a southern representative in the occupation council, and allowing Saxon-Hessian occupation to continue for at least one year before facing the question of how to dispose of the duchy.
90. Lenz, ed., *Briefwechsel* 2:97 n. 2.
91. Ibid. The landgrave's receipt for Strasbourg's share of the second doubled "month" is dated 12 November 1542, and he also bought 1,500 pikes at Strasbourg.
92. Lenz, ed., *Briefwechsel* 2:101–3, no. 148.

93. Ibid., 83, no. 142, 90–91, no. 143, with the quote from the former letter.
94. Ibid., 96, no. 145.
95. Ibid., 106, no. 149.
96. For which there was good enough ground in the Hessian-Saxon plundering the duchy's church. See Körber, *Kirchengüterfrage*, 183–87.
97. PC 3:340, no. 327, drafted by Jacob Sturm.
98. Ibid., 346–47, no. 330, sent on 10 March and read to the Senate & XXI on 17 March 1543; the remaining quotes in this paragraph are also from this document. With it Sturm sent a Saxon-Hessian opinion that opposed restoration under any circumstances.
99. When the landgrave, some months later, used this as an argument for keeping the lands, Sturm agreed that this would be the certain consequence of restoration. PC 3:439, no. 415 (18 October 1543), and Sturm's marginal comment at 439 n. 3.
100. Jacob Sturm to Landgrave Philip, Strasbourg, 3 September 1543, here from the copy in StA Weimar, Reg. H, pagg. 555–63, no. 182, fols. 99r–101r, here at fol. 99r; and the remaining quotes in the paragraph are from ibid., fol. 100r.
101. Brady, "Princes' Reformation," 282–83.
102. Sturm's notes on the league's diet at Smalkalden, July 1543, in PC 3:418–21, no. 394, the quote at 420.
103. Ibid., 445, no. 420, and 452 n. 2; Lenz, ed., *Briefwechsel* 2:191–97, no. 178.
104. Lenz, ed., *Briefwechsel* 2:195.
105. See his letters to Bucer, in ibid., 200, no. 179; and to Sturm, in PC 3:445, no. 420. Sturm expressed his view in a (lost) letter to the landgrave of 28 October 1543.
106. Lenz, ed., *Briefwechsel* 2:208, no. 181, and 213–15, no. 183, from which the quotes in the paragraph come.
107. Strauss, *Law*, 3–30. It appears in a radicalized form in Hans Hergot's 1527 pamphlet, "Von der neuen Wandlung eines christlichen Lebens." See Laube and Seiffert, eds., *Flugschriften der Bauernkriegszeit*, 547–57, here at 553, line 5–554, line 32.
108. Schlüter-Schindler, *Der Schmalkaldische Bund*, 250–52. Landgrave Philip's rejection of sequestration was shared by Elector John Frederick, for whom see Mentz, *Johann Friedrich* 2:388–90. For the landgrave's instruction for the diet of 1544, see de Boor, *Beiträge*, 31–32.
109. PC 3:460–61, no. 437, in Sturm's hand.
110. I rely on the account taken down by Simon Bing, the Hessian secretary, which is in Lenz, ed., *Briefwechsel* 2:252 n. 4, and on Sturm's account to the XIII of Strasbourg, in PC 3:454–55, no. 432.
111. PC 3:455, no. 432.
112. Ibid., 462, no. 437.
113. Ibid., 463–64, no. 439.
114. Ibid., 468–69, no. 443: "Aber dise argument gelten alle bei unsern fursten nichts, als die zu gar gegen h. Heinrichs person erhitzigt und affect sind. vermeinen, wir wollen alle obenteur mit inen beston, es gang recht under oder uber sich, wir gewinnen oder verlieren es im recht."
115. F. Roth, "Briefwechsel Gereon Sailers," 144.
116. Lenz, ed., *Briefwechsel* 2:259–60, no. 194, with the quotes at 258–59. This letter is central to understanding the breach between Sturm and the landgrave.
117. Hortleder, ed., *Ursachen* (1645) 1:1813 (= bk. 4, chap. 47): "Welcher Sturm sich auch vnlangst in des H. Reichs Versamblung mit trutzigen, pochenden, dräwlichen Worten gegen etlicher Ständ Gesandten, ... offentlichen hören

vnd vernehmen lassen hat: Daß ihme der Frantzoß ein guter Herr oder Haupt sey: Daß kan er nicht verneinen." This refers to a session of 23 April 1544 in the presence of Charles V and King Ferdinand. Gereon Sailer described it thus to Georg Herwart: "Den frommen her jacob Sturmen hat er [= Duke Henry] gar hitzig vnd scharpff angriffen, als ain furdrer des frantzhosen, vnd das er jm radt solt gesagt haben, der frantzhose sey jme ain guter herr." F. Roth, "Briefwechsel Gereon Sailers," 123 (25 April 1544). Sturm reported this incident to his masters (on 25 April 1544, in PC 3:488–89, no. 463), who insisted on the charges being answered, though they considered them absurd (ibid., 495, no. 468, 500–502, nos. 470–72). In a letter of 1 May 1544, Sailer identifies the object of the charge as "der Sturm, so ain leser zw Straspurg ist" (F. Roth, "Briefwechsel Gereon Sailers," 135), which suggests that this was another case of confusion between the two Sturms.

118. Lenz, ed., *Briefwechsel* 2:263, no. 194.
119. Ibid., 307, no. 204: "Er ist so betriebt in der sachen, das er etwan gedencket, darvon zu fliehen und sein burgerrecht uffzusagen. Darumb ich E. f. g. umb Gottes willen bette, wie wolle uff diesen frommen, getrauen man kein ongnad werffen, nach uff unser stadt."
120. PC 3:559–60, no. 526.
121. Ibid., 576–77, no. 546. It is worth noting that during the allies' deliberations on 10 April, Sturm recommended his own position ahead of his government's. See his record of the session, in ibid., 580, no. 550; and see the exchange in ibid., 590–91, no. 563, 593–95, no. 566, and 596, no. 568.
122. PC 3:588, no. 560. The landgrave knew of the differences by 24 April. See Lenz, ed., *Briefwechsel* 2:340 n. 1 (24 April 1545; the date is corrected in PC 3:588 n. 2). That the landgrave's informant was Bucer can hardly be doubted, especially in the light of Lenz, ed., *Briefwechsel* 2:307, no. 204.
123. Lenz, ed., *Briefwechsel* 2:346–47, no. 213, 350–51, no. 214, 352–53, no. 215; PC 3:598–99, no. 570; Lenz, ed., *Briefwechsel* 2:352–53, no. 215. All doubt that Bucer stood with the landgrave on Brunswick in the summer of 1545 is dispelled in PC 3:598–99, no. 570, where he writes: "Horrendum quidem est cogitatu, tradere religione fratres talis tyranno. Et quia societas germanici imperii est christiani imperii, equidem non dubito, victoria contra tyrannum eius culpa a nostris extorta hoc officii nostris esse impositum, ut, si valere eos id [?] dominus fert, in religione Christi hanc provinciam conservent."
124. Blume, *Goslar*, 128. The text of the Capitulation of Worms, dated 10 July 1545, is printed by Hortleder, *Ursachen* (1645), bk. 4, chap. 49.
125. Blume, *Goslar*, 129–34, gives a good overview of this campaign; and see Brandenburg, *Die Gefangennahme Herzog Heinrichs*; Ißleib, *Der Braunschweigische Krieg*.
126. Quoted by Blume, *Goslar*, 133.
127. PC 3:644–45, no. 606, from which the quotes in this and the following paragraph come.
128. Ibid., 658–59, no. 620.
129. Ibid., 4:446, no. 422.
130. L. Müller, *Die Reichsstadt Nördlingen*, 162, app. 6.
131. Rublack, *Nördlingen*, 245.
132. See Lenz, ed., *Briefwechsel* 2:166, no. 173. In the same year, John Frederick had proposed to the landgrave that they replace the Smalkaldic League with a new Saxon-Hessian alliance; Philip, however, had defended the league as God's instrument and a surer defense against aggression, despite the southern cities' recalcitrance. PKM 1:622 n. 4.
133. PC 3:676, no. 642.

134. Quoted by F. Roth, *Augsburgs Reformationsgeschichte* 3:325–26.
135. Summarized in PC 3:661, no. 623, printed by Neudecker, *Aktenstücke*, 488. See F. Roth, *Augsburgs Reformationsgeschichte* 3:326. The treaty was to expire on 29 September 1546, because although the original constitution is dated 24 December 1535 (SBA 2:74), it was not fully ratified until the following September.
136. See this volume, chap. 5.
137. PC 3:479–80, no. 454, and the Senate's reply in 482–83, no. 456.
138. Ibid., 568, no. 540, and 572, no. 543.
139. Ibid., 572.
140. See Hasenclever, *Politik Karls V.*, 136–38; F. Roth, *Augsburgs Reformationsgeschichte* 3:327.
141. PC 4:30, no. 29; the Strasbourgeois left home on 1 December, arrived in Frankfurt on 7 December, and remained until 9 February 1546 (the recess was signed on 7 February). The principal Strasbourg documents are the instruction (ibid. 3:675–78, no. 642), Sturm's diary (ibid., 697–712, no. 651), and his report of 19 February (ibid. 4:30–37, no. 29). The best account of the reform efforts at Frankfurt is by Hasenclever, *Politik der Schmalkaldener*, 115–39. The very large attendance, including many Protestant powers who were not members, is documented in StA Weimar, Reg. H, pagg. 612–30, no. 196, vol. 1b, fols. 105r–106r; vol. 2, fols. 1r–4v.
142. PC 4:83–92, no. 63; the Strasbourgeois (including a secretary, Barthel Meyer) left home on 31 March, attended the diet from 3 to 23 April, and came home on 25 April.
143. He supported this belief by gathering copies of the essential documents concerning the league's history, which he took along to Frankfurt. Ibid., 3:675 n. 5.
144. See this volume, chap. 5.
145. The remainder of this account rests on the instruction for the Frankfurt diet, in PC 3:675–78, no. 642.
146. Ibid., 698, from Sturm's diary. The reference here is to a theologians' opinion printed in CR 5:720–22.
147. PC 3:700. See Hasenclever, *Politik der Schmalkaldener*, 117, 120–22, who thought it salutary for the league that its commanders did not accept Sturm's proposal to subordinate the war council to the diet.
148. PC 3:700. The Saxon envoys wrote to Elector John Frederick from Frankfurt on 18 January 1546, "Dieweil shier ydermann durchauss ringerung suchet." StA Weimar, Reg H, no. 196, vol. 1, quoted by Hasenclever, *Politik der Schmalkaldener*, 125. The Constance instruction begins, "Erstlich belangende erstreckung der verainigung soll unser gsanter in die erstreckung bewilligen ouch der zu raten. Er soll sich aber zuvor unser halb der größe unserer anlag beclagen und unser armuet und klains vermegen anzaigen in maßen vorher ettwan vor der kay. und ko. Mten und sunst ouch beschehen ist." Fabian, ed., *Quellen zur Geschichte Reformationsbündnisse*, 180–81. See Sturm's diary, in PC 3:699, which reveals that he also made this point.
149. PC 4:82, no. 62. This virtually repeats a statement at the head of his instruction for Frankfurt in December 1545: "So auf ainer statt Straßburg gelegenhait allain gesehen [wird], derselbigen ain solche weitleufig verstendnus beschwerlich." Ibid., 3:675–76, no. 642.
150. PC 4:24, no. 23. He said this in the session (5 February 1545) in which surfaced the major opposition to the Common Penny. Hasenclever, *Politik der Schmalkaldener*, 138, says that Duke Ulrich of Württemberg's envoy supported the reform, but Sturm's diary says the opposite. Ibid., 3:711, no. 651. Sturm reported from Frankfurt on 19 February 1546 that the Württembergers

favored the Common Penny, though at Worms in April 1546 he noted that they had earlier argued against the idea that the league appropriate the Imperial Common Penny (ibid., 4:31, no. 29; 82, no. 62).

151. PC 4:52–54, no. 49, documents Sturm prepared for the league's diet at Worms in April 1546. The second document, clearly a draft for his own instruction, allows the envoys to Worms to accept Strasbourg's old levy (5,000 fl.), if the total for a "month" were at least 100,000 fl. The absolute sum was less important than Strasbourg's relative share, which under the old matricular list was 5,000 fl. of 105,000 fl., or about 5 percent of the total. The highest new proposal laid on Strasbourg 4,000 fl. of 139,000 fl., or less than 3 percent of the total, but its probable yield was only about 100,000 fl., which would have Strasbourg paying a "tolerable" 4 percent. For Sturm's and Schwencker's instruction for Worms, which the Senate & XXI approved on 22 March 1546, see ibid., 52, no. 49. Sturm's own account of this diet is in ibid., 83–92, no. 63.

152. The sum actually proposed at Frankfurt would yield 896,000 fl., which was apportioned nearly evenly to the northern (51.1 percent) and southern (48.9 percent) districts. At Worms the total yield of one "month" was first raised from 105,020 fl. to 127,300 fl. and then lowered to 84,720 fl. PC 4:91, no. 63 n. 51. The matricular list approved at this time had another fantastic side, for, as Sturm pointed out, it included assessments on many powers (such as the Elector Palatine) who were at best possible members; their inclusion prompted estimates of a "month" to climb as high as 139,000 fl. in ibid., 53, no. 49.

153. Ibid., 4:81, no. 62, from Aitinger's protocol of the league's diet at Worms. He nonetheless continued to insist that the Common Penny was "the fairest" method of taxation, though he also saw that given the uncertainty about the emperor's intentions, it would be better not to conclude a reform by vote of so few members of the league. Ibid., 82, no. 62.

154. Quoted by Rommel, *Philipp der Großmütige* 2:475.

155. The new constitution is compared with that of 29 September 1536 in PC 4:31, no. 29 n. 12; the old one largely follows the original version of 23 December 1535, which is printed by Fabian, *Entstehung*, 357–76. The strength of reform sentiment is reported by Sebastian Schertlin von Burtenbach, in Herberger, ed., *Briefe*, 41. Sturm lists those who came to Worms with full powers, in PC 4:85, no. 63. See the Hessian envoy's comments about the outcome at Worms, in Lenz, ed., *Briefwechsel* 2:439 n. 4.

156. On the landgrave's claim, see StA Weimar, Reg. H, 670, no. 209, vol. 1, fols. 41r–45v, dated Kassel, 7 January 1546. The first audit of accounts occurred at Frankfurt from 2 to 8 February 1546. The two princes were voted the remainder of the third doubled "month" plus 10,000 fl. See Jacob Sturm's diary and report in PC 4:32, no. 29.

157. PC 4:30, no. 29, from the discussion in AMS, XXI 1546, fols. 53r–59r; and the following comment is quoted by Schertlin, in Herberger, ed., *Briefe*, 52–53.

158. PC 4:30, no. 29 n. 5.

159. Ibid., 58, no. 49.

160. See Martin Bucer to Landgrave Philip, [Strasbourg], 29 May 1546: "Dise onrightikeit der sechsischen stenden macht die oberlendischen seer irenthalben kleinmietig, das sie sich irer nit fil wissen zu getrösten, weil sie in diesem handel, er doch inen zum besten komet vor anderen, so onrichtig sind." Lenz, ed., *Briefwechsel* 2:454, no. 238. On the Empire in this respect, see Brady, *Turning Swiss*, 218–19; Rabe, *Reichsbund*, 136–42, 152–54; Endres, "Der Kayserliche neunjährige Bund," 100.

161. See the list in G. Schmidt, "Zur Geschichte des Schmalkalder Bundes," 72–73.
162. Wolfgang Capito to Simon Grynaeus, Strasbourg, 13 September 1534, in BNUS, Thes. Baum. 8:219. For Bucer's earlier acknowledgement of Capito's primacy, see BCorr 1:16, 251–52, no. 66.
163. See Pollet, ed., Correspondance 2:53–438; Guggisberg, "Strasbourg et Bâle"; Weyrauch, "Strasbourg et la Réforme en Allemagne du Sud"; Bornkamm, Martin Bucers Bedeutung, 15–16; Greschat, Martin Bucer, 161–71; and BDS 7:249–57, 321–38, for references on Bucer and the Hessian reformation.
164. Pollet, ed., Relations 1:83–233; Stupperich, "L'influence de Bucer en Europe du Nord"; Hall, "Bucer et l'Angleterre."
165. Fundamental on Bucer's view of politics and government is de Kroon, Studien; and Schultz, Martin Butzer's Anschauung, is still of some value.
166. Lenz, ed., Briefwechsel 2:373, no. 220. It is worth noting that Bucer wrote this in the midst of the second Brunswick campaign.
167. Ibid., 373, no. 220.
168. This point was long ago recognized by August Lang, Puritanismus und Pietismus, esp. 13–38.
169. On the patristic, Thomistic, and Erasmian elements in Bucer's theology, see Hammann, Entre la secte et la cité, 388–94, who quite independently confirms the connection Heiko Oberman has drawn between the urban reformation and the scholastic via antiqua. Oberman, Masters, 276–95.
170. The quote is from Bellardi, in BDS 17:156. Bucer's universalism has often been celebrated (e.g., by Bornkamm, Martin Bucers Bedeutung, 25–31), and the theological basis of his sectarianism has been uncovered (by Hammann, Entre la secte et la cité, esp. 103–74), but few have marked the connection between them. See also Stephens, Holy Spirit, 165, who recognizes the dualism in Bucer's ecclesiology.
171. BDS 7:67–245, edited by Robert Stupperich, who connects (84) the work directly to Bucer's dissatisfaction with the settlement of 1534. The theological development is treated by Stephens, Holy Spirit, 156–66.
172. Paulus, Protestantismus und Toleranz, 125–41, based on a work published in 1537 and reprinted in 1540.
173. Quoted from Bucer's catechism of 1543 by Greschat, Martin Bucer, 211, who links Bucer's mood at this time with "the decline of his physical powers."
174. See this volume, 9.
175. Bellardi, Geschichte, 22; Lienhard, "La Réforme à Strasbourg, I," 412. Perhaps they were spurred on by their failure to win the new bishop, Erasmus of Limburg, for a program of reform. See Chrisman, Strasbourg and the Reform, 256–59; Lienhard, "La Réforme à Strasbourg, I," 404.
176. Bellardi, in BDS 17:157, though his monograph (Geschichte, 39) puts the beginnings during the Smalkaldic War.
177. BDS 17:151–95.
178. Ibid., 159, line 3–160, line 3.
179. See the analysis by Bellardi, Geschichte, 24–25.
180. This history is recounted in ibid., 38–107. See Lienhard, "La Réforme à Strasbourg, I," 412.
181. Bellardi, in BDS 17:157, suggests that a loosening of the bonds between church and regime at Strasbourg might have given Sturm a freer hand in negotiations with the emperor. Perhaps, but everything speaks against Sturm's complicity with this movement.
182. The younger clergy mostly backed Bucer, whereas the older ones, including Mathis Zell, supported the magistrates against them. Bellardi, Geschichte, 48.
183. What follows is taken from Brady, Turning Swiss, 207–9, with references.

184. See Brady, *Ruling Class*, 83, 89–90, 134, 137, 153–54, 156.

185. Luttenberger, *Glaubenseinheit*, 129–39; Press, *Calvinismus*, 170–80.

186. Tyler, *Emperor Charles the Fifth*, 100 n.

187. Press, *Calvinismus*, 181–84.

188. On Frederick's policy toward the Reformation, see H. Rott, *Friedrich II. von der Pfalz.*

189. PC 2:519–20, no. 545 (11 October 1538, incorrectly dated to July 1539 by Lenz, ed., *Briefwechsel* 1:408). A chronicle notes that Frederick was accompanied by his wife, Dorothy, "so ein königin uss Denmarckt war." Mone, ed., *Quellensammlung* 2:143. The hope for a restoration in Denmark, of course, kept Frederick tied to Palatine neutralism, the grounds of which are laid out in a memorial in ARCEG 3:162–64, no. 77, Beilage 2.

190. Brady, *Ruling Class*, 350–53; Brady, "La famille Sturm," 35. For the connections, see Hans Bock von Gerstheim's testament in ADBR, G 841 (9 October 1542); Irschlinger, "Landschaden von Steinach," tables 2–3.

191. H. Rott, *Friedrich II. von der Pfalz*, 27–28; Hasenclever, "Kurfürst Friedrich," 59; Press, *Calvinismus*, 187, 187 n. 27, 188. The incident is not mentioned in Sturm's correspondence during the diet, which portrays the elector entirely in the traditional role of a neutral and mediator between the parties. See PC 3:nos. 569, 579, 583. There is also no mention of the Palatinate in the memorial that Sturm, Martin Herlin, and Conrad Joham drew up for their colleagues on 17 October 1545, in ibid., 658–59, no. 620. On the course of Palatine policy at this time, the best study is by Hasenclever, *Die kurpfälzische Politik.*

192. The documents are printed by Hasenclever, "Kurfürst Friedrich," 73–76. Winckelmann, who edited PC, vol. 3 (see 707 n. 4), found nothing at Strasbourg about the whole business; nor did I.

193. Hasenclever, "Kurfürst Friedrich," 75 (7 December 1545).

194. Sturm wrote to Helmstett: "So hab ich dise sach also gehandelt, als ob es allein vor mir on einich vorwissen, was der pfaltz gelegenheit were, sachen zu gut geschehe." Hasenclever, "Kurfürst Friedrich," 80.

195. Helmstett wrote to Sturm that "unser gutbedoncken were, wyll das eyssen warm, man forderlich geschmit hette." Sturm replied from Frankfurt: "Weil das eysen warm ist, man furderlich geschmidt hette." Hasenclever, "Kurfürst Friedrich," 76, 80.

196. PC 3:692–94, no. 647, from which the following quote is taken. The situation and changes in religious practice are detailed by Hasenclever, "Kurfürst Friedrich," 59–62. For the landgrave's position, see F. Roth, *Augsburgs Reformationsgeschichte* 3:328.

197. Sturm's diary, in PC 3:707, no. 651; Voigt, *Briefwechsel*, 332. Sebastian Schertlin von Burtenbach came to Heidelberg and went on to Hesse; working in Augsburg's service, he urged the two princes to settle their differences and work together, though the Augsburgers, apparently, did not want Frederick to join the league. Hasenclever, "Kurfürst Friedrich," 67–68.

198. PC 4:83, no. 62: "Dann so Pfalz heraus beleiben, so werden vil stend heraus beleiben."

199. Duchhardt, *Kaisertum*, 36.

200. Hasenclever, "Kurfürst Friedrich," 70–71.

201. Ibid., 80–81.

202. Ibid., 64, suggests this motive.

203. Lenz, ed., *Briefwechsel* 2:441, no. 235.

8

The Smalkaldic War, 1546–1547

Woe to you, you poor free cities,
What arrogance from you
That without cause you raise your banner
Against our pious monarch,
The highest in the land.
Truly, you should have considered
How better to behave.
Lord have mercy! The Spaniards are in our land.*

Charles, tell us truly,
What you want with our poor land.
You want to bring poor Germany
Into the House of Austria's hand
And make of it a "monarchy,"
So that "Plus ultra" will ever stand.
There's where the dog is buried.**

Shortly after Easter (25 April) 1546, the story went around that at the end of March the Emperor Charles V had stopped at Speyer on his way to the Imperial Diet at Regensburg. Among the many who sought him out there came Landgrave Philip of Hesse, hawk on arm, with two hundred men. At dinner after a hunt, Charles asked the Hessian how things stood with the Smalkaldic League. "My Gracious Lord Emperor," he replied, "I am missing only one man." When the sovereign inquired whom he meant, Philip responded, "Why, I mean to have Your Imperial Majesty among the pious folk." The two men chuckled, and Charles retorted, "No, no, I will not join the party of error."[1]

His bold words aside, by this time Landgrave Philip and his allies found themselves in a very tight corner, for in sad disarray they faced an impending trial by combat. The league's diet at Worms in April had tabled all outstanding issues until the Imperial Diet of Regensburg had met.[2] Rumors circulated that the southern cities, as Augsburg's city secretary told the landgrave in

March, "are in a state of great mistrust and misunderstanding, and especially Sir Jacob Sturm is said to have become mistrusted [*in ain unglauben gezogen werden*], which greatly threatens the whole common enterprise and especially the southern cities." The Strasbourgeois were reported to be negotiating "a privilege from the king of France, which will favor their affairs to the disadvantage of the other cities."[3] The rumors were wrong, for the cities, unlike princes, had no freedom to shift their loyalties as they would.[4]

The coming contest appeared so unequal. On the one side, the Catholics: with the French and Turkish fronts now at peace, pope, emperor, and Bavarian duke were creating the financial and strategic basis of a successful German campaign.[5] On the other side, the Protestants: the Smalkaldic League seemed to have deteriorated into a state of *sauve qui peut*.[6] And so, by Eastertide 1546 conditions seemed very favorable to a solution by force to the German schism in a Catholic sense. Martin Luther had foretold a great war between the princes and the emperor, to which the Peasants' War of 1525 would seem in retrospect but a prelude, and his death on 18 February 1546 now seemed a portent of this coming cataclysm.

Active participation in a war meant great risk and little prospect for gain for sixteenth-century urban regimes.[7] On the one hand, cities were strong in defense, because, although the superior and frightfully expensive new fortifying system, called the *trace italienne*, had hardly established itself yet in the Empire, no German prince, not even the emperor, possessed the guns to break the walls of the great South German cities. On the other hand, cities were weak in offense, because, although they possessed the financial skills and credit on which the new mercenary system depended, sixteenth-century command systems had outgrown the ability of urban regimes or urban leagues to control them, and when cities allied with princes, the latter, naturally, assumed all the command functions. To engage in war, however, posed great dangers for cities, because armies plundered the countryside and disrupted production and trade, the cities' two sources of wealth. To these sources of ruin, a war against the emperor added another, for outlawry, the usual treatment for rebels, removed all protections of the law from the citizens' goods, lands, and lives. War could be extremely profitable to cities, but only if they supplied money, men, munitions, and foodstuffs to the belligerents without becoming one. For a hundred years, except for 1499, 1504, and 1525, the large South German cities had flourished in a zone of peace that supplied the wars that raged on three sides—Italy, Hungary, Burgundy, Lorraine, and the Netherlands, and the German North. These wars, capped by the Habsburgs brothers' titanic struggle with the Ottoman sultan and their four wars against France, fueled Augsburg's great wealth and fattened the other cities' traffic in money, arms, and foodstuffs as well.[8] With the single, if spectacular, exception of Bern, however, where since 1536 a city of five thousand inhabitants ruled over a quarter of a million subjects, no German-speaking city-state could aggrandize itself from war in

the way that the princes did.[9] This was the paradox of city-state development in the Empire, that the burghers could grow rich from war, but only
if they did not fight. For this reason, at Strasbourg, as at Augsburg, Ulm,
and Frankfurt, the deterioration of the Imperial political order and the coming
of war, win or lose, spelled defeat.

THE DANUBE CAMPAIGN, 1546

Regensburg, where Charles V arrived on 10 April, hummed with the fre-
netic heedlessness that often signals a belief that catastrophe is imminent.[10]
The theologians' colloquy had resumed on 27 January 1546 and dragged on
for six weeks in a spirit of meanness, acrimony, and intransigence on both
sides, and when the emperor arrived to open the diet, the poisoned atmosphere and sparse attendance quashed all his remaining doubts about using
force against the Protestants.[11] The recent behavior of the Smalkaldic chiefs
encouraged his resolve, for they had supported the French war in 1544, and
their provocative talk about Cologne would likely prove—as it had about
Cleves-Jülich in 1543—more words without deeds.[12] Even so, their (reluctant) decision to back Elector Herman may have tipped the balance toward
war. "This war chiefly began over the reformation in Cologne," the landgrave
thought, "when the allies supported the bishop's appeal so bravely to the
emperor." Concerned to protect the Netherlands from Protestantism, "he
also feared that the other bishops would imitate the bishop of Cologne,
and all the electors would belong to our religion, which might lead to his
deposition and the election of another."[13] Although Charles V insisted from
the first that he aimed only to punish rebels, the Smalkaldeners never doubted
that this was a war "on account of religion" in the league's meaning of the
term.[14] When the Strasbourgeois, for example, responded in Sturm's words
to Charles's declaration against the Smalkaldic chiefs, they blamed the failure of the negotiations since 1541 on "the opposition" alone and portrayed
the coming conflict as the inevitable outcome of Catholic resistance to
reform.[15] By May it was clear to Jacob Sturm, as he wrote the landgrave,
"that by means of these colloquys, national assemblies, diets, or other institutional paths, no truly Christian concord can be hoped for at this time."
"Just as religion in the time of Jesus, the apostles, and the martyrs spread
against the will and consent of the Jewish and pagan authorities," he mused,
"so today a household, tomorrow another, then a village, and finally a whole
land receives the faith, which gradually comes to prevail despite all persecution."[16] Strong stuff, this talk of martyrdom and ultimate victory.

The emperor, too, concluded that the German schism would yield neither to colloquys, to the diet, nor to the Council of Trent, which had
convened with sparse attendance on 13 December 1545.[17] When he left
the Netherlands for Regensburg the following March, Queen Mary warned
him about what had happened to Emperor Sigismund in the Hussite Wars,
and Charles promised her that he would do his utmost to avoid a war. At

Regensburg the situation looked much clearer, and by Eastertide the Empire was abuzz with news of mobilizations on all sides; by mid-June Charles was asking Queen Mary and the bishops to prepare for war; and on 3 July he published the sentence of deposition (dated 16 April) against Elector Herman.[18] Meanwhile, the pieces of his plan fell into place. The marriages of two of Charles's nieces, to the Bavarian heir, Albert, and Duke William of Cleves-Jülich respectively, sealed the agreements securing the southeastern and northwestern flanks of his strategic plan.[19] Meanwhile, treaties with the pope and with Duke Moritz of Saxony supplied money and troops to support his own forces in the coming campaign.

The emperor sent out his mobilization orders on 10 June 1546, by which time his well-informed military specialists were drafting plans of campaign.[20] By the beginning of July, while the diet droned on at Regensburg and the papal troops started for Germany, the Smalkaldic chiefs were meeting at Ichtershausen near Erfurt, where they issued orders for the league's mobilization and began to send embassies abroad for aid.[21] The league's southern cities responded to the chiefs' call with great enthusiasm, offering to pay even more than the three double-months that constituted the league's initial levy for the war.[22] Schertlin marched eleven thousand foot and twenty-six guns from the southern cities to the Upper Lech, where he hoped to disrupt the emperor's musters and prevent the papal troops from joining the emperor.[23]

Schertlin's deft but indecisive raid aside, the Danube campaign began much as envisaged by Charles and his advisers.[24] His Germans and Spaniards and the pope's Italians—about thirty-six thousand foot, six thousand horse, and seventy guns—united at Landshut in Bavaria on 13 August, only three weeks after the diet had risen on 24 July. They faced the league's somewhat stronger army with more than one hundred guns, which had united near Ingolstadt at the beginning of August. At the leaguers' backs, however, came another force. Twelve thousand foot and eight thousand horse under Maximilian Egmont, count of Buren, slipped by Oldenburg's shadowing forces, crossed the Rhine unhindered at Bingen, and marched southeastward to form the anvil against which Charles would hammer the leaguers. Rarely in sixteenth-century warfare did a strategic plan so nearly succeed as this one did, as the two reinforced armies came to face each other for a battle of decision on the Danube near Ingolstadt.[25] After testing Charles's forces with a two-day preparatory bombardment on 31 August–1 September, the leaguers should have attacked, but at Buren's approach they decided to move off upstream and try to keep him from linking up with Charles. They failed, and there ensued a running play of feint-and-duck, the leaguers afraid to stop and give battle, Charles afraid to risk his entire force against them.[26] Eventually, the Smalkaldic chiefs pitched camp outside of Giengen, while Charles moved off toward Ulm and also pitched camp. To the astonishment of all observers, there was no more combat, and the two encamped armies were gradually eaten to bits by bad weather, poor rations, lack of pay, and disease. The Danube campaign was a superb example of the sixteenth-century art of war, except that the battle of decision never took place.

Strasbourg played three roles in the Danube campaign. First, it supplied three men for the administrative conduct of the war: Ulman Böcklin von Böcklinsau, who accompanied the army as war councillor; his brother, Wolff, who served as delegate to the league's Southern District at Ulm; and the secretary Michel Han, who served in both the Southern District's diet and the treasury (*Kammerrat*), which was created at Ulm to manage the army's finances.[27] Second, Strasbourg's regime played a major role in the financing of the campaign. It paid more than 210,000 fl. in direct levies (*Anlagen*) to the treasury, plus the loans it took up at home and in Switzerland, and it co-signed, along with Ulm and Augsburg, for the league's enormous loans raised at Lyon. Third, Strasbourg served as the point of departure and arrival for all of the league's quests for allies and loans abroad, including Jean Sturm's three missions to France and Johann von Niedbruck's mission to England. In addition to these main roles, Strasbourg also served as a supply point for mercenary infantry, a center for the gathering and transmission of news to the front and the allies, and a source of advice and loans to the smaller free cities.[28]

For most of the Danube campaign, Jacob Sturm stayed home. He did not leave Strasbourg between Easter Sunday (25 April), when he returned from the league's diet at Worms, and the beginning of November, when he visited Ulm and the army's camp near Giengen, and in the meantime he resisted all calls and pleas to ride in the league's service.[29] Finally, on 3 November, as the Smalkaldic chiefs were preparing to decamp for their own lands, Sturm came to Ulm, where the league's diet had been sitting continuously since late September.[30] By then conditions in camp were so bad that the mutinous Hessian troops would no longer even stand sentry duty.[31]

Why did Jacob Sturm not take a more prominent role in the Danube campaign, for example, as member of the league's and the Southern District's diets at Ulm? On 4 July the XIII replied to a request that Sturm go to Switzerland with the remark that "for special reasons he cannot be available at this time."[32] This excuse may signify illness or poor health, and it is true that the previous March his health had been poor.[33] Sturm nonetheless played a very active role at Strasbourg all through the Danube campaign. He framed Strasbourg's public apologies for the war, first to the emperor himself and later to the Swiss assembly, and through his hands ran the entire correspondence with the league's agents in France and England.[34] Sturm nonetheless took a less prominent role in the Danube campaign than in any other major operation of the league, and he did not go to the front— despite repeated entreaties that he come—until the war was nearly lost. Even the sending of envoys to France and England was inaugurated directly by the Smalkaldic chiefs during their meeting at Ichtershausen in early July without consulting Jacob Sturm.[35] These actions bore fruit too little and too late to influence the course of the war.[36] Four times Jean Sturm journeyed to France to offer alliance and beg royal permission to borrow money from the bankers at Lyon, and Niedbruck went three times to England, the last time accompanied by Franz Burkhardt of Saxony. The French connection, on which the Protestants set such great hopes—and the management of which lay naturally in the province of the Strasbourgeois—proved a terrible disappointment, as French royal diffidence and the bankers' tight-fistedness drove the allies into a dubious relationship with Piero Strozzi, an exiled Florentine at Lyon. When the merchants of Augsburg, Ulm, and Strasbourg flatly refused to guarantee the loans Strozzi offered, the regimes of those cities had to step in, albeit reluctantly, and give guarantees.[37] All in vain, for the French alliance collapsed, and French money failed to arrive in time.[38]

One piece of evidence sheds light, if indirectly, on Jacob Sturm's absence from the leadership of the league until the Danube campaign was lost. In the first part of November, the league's delegates came to the army's camp near Giengen, where they and the commanders debated three courses of action: give battle, go into winter camp, or sue for peace. Sturm offered his opinion on the third path, suing for peace. "Since this war began last summer between the emperor and the Christian allies," he told the league's combined political and military leadership,

> a great deal of damage has been done to both sides and to the German nation. I have observed this with deep sadness, and I would much rather, had it been God's will, that this terrible war had never been begun. In that case, I would have stayed at Strasbourg. Now, however, I see that the war has become a long one, and may become longer, on which account I decided to leave Strasbourg on behalf of the peace, order, and unity of the German nation, and place myself at the service of the elector of Saxony, the landgrave of Hesse, and the war council and to demonstrate to them how the continuation of the war will ruin and destroy all law and order, nobility, property, and morals in the German nation.[39]

Sturm's statement breathes a spirit of dejection, weariness, and defeat, laden with the bitterness of past quarrels and missed opportunities.[40] It also echoes his foreboding of disaster at the war's beginning. In July, even as the preparations for war were underway, Sturm had written to Count Palatine Otto Henry of his apprehension:

> Otherwise the mobilization is in full swing. And if it must come, we on our side are determined to stick to God and His Word, and to risk all that we have for their sake. May the Lord grant us His grace, and that, if we must suffer, we bear it with Christian forbearance, so that we do not betray Our Lord Jesus Christ for the sake of worldly advantage.[41]

Sturm's statement at Giengen on 10 November 1546 helps to explain why Strasbourg sent to the front men who were at best middling figures, at worst political nonentities. The ablest was Michel Han, a secretary rather than a magistrate, who had always served Sturm well. He made a good impression on the other councillors at Ulm, who asked Strasbourg to let them keep Han, "whom we regard as truly competent."[42] The same, alas, could not be said of Sturm's kinsmen, the Böcklin brothers, who represented the city at the front and at Ulm. Ulman Böcklin did send fairly regular reports home from the front, but both he and his brother complained frequently about their pay, and Ulman's behavior during the two days' cannonade before Ingolstadt gave rise to ugly stories at Strasbourg. Elector John Frederick was said to have complained that "the Strasbourgeois ought to have sent someone else as war councillor."[43] Strasbourg's regime, ever a pillar of the Smalkaldic League, served it rather poorly in its hour of greatest need.

Sturm knew perfectly well, when he came to Ulm at the beginning of November, how poorly things stood. Only two months earlier, when the two armies had faced each other near Ingolstadt, Cousin Ulman had written in high spirits that "by God's grace we have many good troops, and everyone is ready to attack."[44] The battle did not come then, nor did it come later, though the stream of pleas for money never stopped. On 16 September the Smalkaldic chiefs and their war council announced a third levy of six double-months, making eighteen in all, and proposed a proclamation of general confiscation of ecclesiastical properties.[45] Sturm and his colleagues favored paying the new levy, but only if the other allies would pay their shares, for it was becoming ever more apparent that a few, mainly southern, allies were paying the lion's share of the costs.[46] Table 8.1 shows that this appearance was correct.

Disregarding the two commanders' outlays, the primary financial burden of the Danube campaign fell on the duchy of Württemberg and the three leading southern cities, Strasbourg, Augsburg, and Ulm, who together paid 72.4 percent of all funds collected for this operation. They alone, plus Heilbronn and little Ravensburg, the league's newest member, paid the full eighteen double-months, and the Southern District's overall performance— 83.1 percent of its assessments—contrasts very favorably with the Northern District's 26.7 percent. As the southerners had always said, the North complained and the South paid. No wonder the XIII of Strasbourg complained so bitterly that "if all members of the league paid their eighteen double-months, we reckon, it would yield more than 3,000,000 fl., with which the army could be maintained for some time [ain gute zeit]."[47] The large southern cities also raised most of the supplementary sums through loans from their own citizens and subjects and from foreign powers. The total sums were very large. Strasbourg's levies alone—180,000 fl.—were more than double the city's total Imperial assessments for the Turkish wars during the entire reign of Charles V.[48]

More money, indeed, and not more troops formed the key to the Danube campaign. As Claus Kniebis wrote, "If we cannot raise large sums for our

TABLE 8.1

Payments (in fl.) of Smalkaldic League Levies
for the Danube Campaign, 1546

SOUTHERN DISTRICT: 3 × 6 DOUBLE-MONTHS

Member	Levied	Paid (%)
Hesse	504,000	
Württemberg	327,240	357,336 (109.8)
Tecklenburg	14,400	?
Strasbourg	180,000	180,000 (100)
Augsburg	180,000	180,000 (100)
Ulm	180,000	180,000 (100)
Frankfurt	108,000	?
Memmingen	52,200	24,123 (46.2)
Constance	46,800	21,900 (46.8)
Esslingen	45,000	30,220 (67.2)
Schwäbisch Hall	43,200	28,860 (66.8)
Biberach	39,600	27,883 (70.4)
Heilbronn	36,000	36,000 (100)
Lindau	32,400	18,780 (57.9)
Reutlingen	32,400	17,221 (53.2)
Kempten	25,200	16,800 (66.7)
Isny	21,600	11,900 (55.6)
Ravensburg	14,400	14,400 (100)
Total	1,882,440	1,145,423

NORTHERN DISTRICT: 1 × 6 DOUBLE-MONTHS

Member	Levied	Paid (%)
Elector of Saxony	168,000	
Other princes	114,000	
Hamburg	43,560	13,878 (33.1)
Brunswick	42,720	37,794 (88.5)
Magdeburg	42,720	18,976 (44.4)
Bremen	38,400	5,309 (13.8)
Goslar	22,560	7,984 (35.4)
Göttingen	11,640	0 (00.0)
Einbeck	8,400	0 (00.0)
Hanover	7,680	3,186 (41.5)
Hildesheim	6,000	3,314 (55.2)
Minden	4,800	808 (16.8)
Total	510,480	91,249

Source: Gerber, "Die Kriegsrechnungen."[49]

side, it will go badly for us."[50] Not only did the league's assembly at Ulm
send incessant pleas for funds, Strasbourg's treasury had also to pay out
retainers and traveling money (*Laufgeld*) for many bands of mercenaries headed
for the front, expenses for envoys abroad on the league's business, and fees
for couriers and diplomats.[51] These smaller sums, to be sure, which came to
approximately 8,000 fl., were deducted from the city's payments of levies to
the league, but at the campaign's end the Strasbourgeois estimated that the war
had cost their city about 210,000 fl.[52] Their commitment to the war is further
illustrated by their offer on 14 August to co-sign notes for 800,000 fl. to be
borrowed at Lyon.[53] The league's need, however, knew no measure, and so
desperate was the shortage of money among the southern allies, that in
August, just as the Strasbourgeois were seeking a loan at Basel, envoys came
from Frankfurt and Constance to ask for loans from Strasbourg.[54]

Financial desperation, therefore, was one reason Jacob Sturm came to
Ulm at the beginning of November; the other was the military situation.
Once the campaign was over, there were excuses and recriminations aplenty,
but they all pointed to one fact: the Smalkaldeners ought to have struck
the Imperial forces early and hard, and they had failed to do so. This was
clear to all experienced observers from the beginning, to the Saxon "old
warrior," for example, who had counseled the allies to strike into Bavaria
and make Charles defend it.[55] It was no less clear to the war councillors of
the Southern District, who at the end of July had recommended crossing
the Danube to the south bank and moving on Regensburg.[56] Indeed, the
allies had been well warned by an experienced fighter, Count William of
Fürstenberg, who after an inspection of the allied troops and guns told the
allies what to expect. "Dear lords and friends," Count William said,

> you have laid your preparations very well. But Emperor Charles is a warrior
> not for a summer but for several years, if he must. You are lost, for Charles
> is a fighter and can stand a long war, which you cannot. In the end,
> though you don't see it now, you will not prevail against him.[57]

Not only did the league fail to strike either Charles's army or Bavaria, their
blocking force also failed to hold Buren's army on the Rhine's west bank or
to intercept him on the way to Charles. "If these [Buren's Netherlandish]
cavalry had been beaten," a Prussian nobleman judged, "this war would
have been over, for the emperor could not have replaced them."[58] Even so,
though the Smalkaldic chiefs had missed their main chances to strike either Charles or Buren before they united, the campaign was not yet lost.

JACOB STURM AT THE FRONT

Sturm came to the front in November to press two causes: to raise sufficient
funds to continue the war through a general direct tax, the Common Penny,
for which he had earlier fought so hard, and to urge a decisive battle before
breaking up the league's army. Whereas Strasbourg's regime had proposed

"a general tax on the subjects of all the league's members, rich and poor," their envoys at Ulm had joined others to urge a kind of *lévée en masse* in Swabia: every eighth burgher and every fourth peasant from allies' lands.[59] When Sturm arrived, he told the diet that his lords were willing to levy a direct tax of 1 percent on their subjects, though "it would not be enough," and said that "if, at the beginning of the war, the southern allies had sat quietly at home, which they could have done, the war would have taken place in Saxony and Hesse."[60] "In these most important negotiations," Württemberg's war councillor wrote to Stuttgart,

> I was glad to have had Sir Jacob Sturm, a partisan of the gospel and a talented and experienced man, come here and speak devoutly, ably, moderately, and impartially. His words, however, were disheartening and without consolation, and neither I nor the other allies got counsel from him how this whole situation is to be dealt with.[61]

The diet wrote the Common Penny into its recess on 16 November, but Sturm's victory was meaningless, for the Danube campaign was over.[62]

On 10 November Sturm and the other members of the diet's committee visited the army and met with its commanders, the Smalkaldic chiefs.[63] At Giengen they found no psalm-singing host of fighters for the Lord but a tough, hard-drinking army of typical sixteenth-century mercenaries. "We live such a life," the Prussian envoy wrote,

> full of eating, drinking, blaspheming, and bad conduct, that it would be no wonder if God, instead of sparing his elect, would punish us. The clergy preach fiercely and admonish us to penance, but to little effect. . . . I hope that, like David, we will be punished by God and not by the enemy.[64]

Sturm told the league's commanders that his government wanted to continue the war and would approve no "dishonorable settlement."[65] As things stood, he admitted, "perhaps they will have to alter their policy." Sturm nonetheless pressed for an attack, for the emperor

> has an agreement with the pope not to negotiate a treaty. His inquisitions and edicts show that he wants to uproot the whole religion. Besides, to sue for peace would diminish our stature and drive away potential allies. Therefore, the best policy is to give battle, though I cannot tell whether it is feasible. I have hope, however, that if we attempt it, God will grant us good fortune.

If this were impossible, then they must sue for peace, though Sturm refused a request that he ride in this cause to Chancellor Granvelle.[66] Sturm and the other southerners pleaded with the princes not to leave the South without giving battle, "for the enemy will thereby gain courage to recoup his strength."[67] Their idea, rather, was that the league must first attack the emperor, "who is tired and weak, and drive him from the field, and then what the elector of Saxony has lost can easily be recouped." They pointed out that "we can do far more against the enemy with a united army than can be done once it is divided and dispersed to several places." If the princes retreated from the South, the Strasbourgeois warned, the emperor would force all the Rhenish neutrals into his camp, and "the Common Man would probably refuse to pay the Common Penny." To attack now "would be better than to let the army sit in camp and be ruined and die from the cold and wet and other causes." They thought it useless to winter over the southern troops alone, "for the enemy will easily gain new strength from the bishops and others, who until now have been dissuaded by fear, and will attack Württemberg and the southern cities with forces greater than they can withstand." The meeting at Giengen was supposed to formulate recommendations for action by the full diet at Ulm, but the delegates could not agree, and no one even bothered to make a proper recess out of Sturm's draft.[68]

Returning to Ulm, Sturm addressed the league's diet on 19 November. "What my lords and others have done here in the South," he told the envoys,

> concerns both temporal and eternal life, and the matter now stands so, that we must either lay down our tools or see how we can rescue it. . . . Each of us must now regard not his own interest but the common enterprise. My own lords have approved the Common Penny. If that will help the situation, well and good; if not, then I know no other way.[69]

Neither did the others, and Sturm, now at the end of his tether, declared, "Here is how it stands. The cities cannot pay another assessment, and there is no other solution. Either we pay the Common Penny or nothing!"[70] But the southerners were deadlocked, and the diet dispersed without agreement about how to encamp their troops for the winter or how to pay them. One more time, Sturm pleaded with Landgrave Philip to stay long enough to attack Charles's army:

> For otherwise, if you retreat and leave the enemy the field and the freedom to crush us one after another, and if God shows us no way to help His people and His churches, we Germans will lose our reputation among all other nations, and the just cause of the Holy Gospel will be besmirched, as though we deserved this punishment from God through our unbelief.[71]

Sturm even resorted on this occasion, his last chance, to highly uncharacteristic language to dissuade the landgrave from treating for peace, "for you will deal not alone with His Imperial Majesty, but also with the Antichrist at Rome, who instigated and organized this business against all of us." Landgrave Philip did not heed Sturm's pleas. He had a belly full of this kind of war, he said, in which "the doctors and secretaries want to be soldiers, and the soldiers want to be doctors."[72] Bitterly unfair words, of course, for the southern cities had paid, and some smaller ones bled themselves white, for the common cause. At Constance, the only city whose financial outlays for the league and the war have been studied, the Danube campaign came as a disaster, plunging the city into one of the deepest financial crises of its entire history.[73] These sacrifices were of no moment to the landgrave, who on 22 November wrote that Sturm simply didn't understand the military situation and that "whoever told you the emperor was weak, he surely was wrong, for we know from some of our nobles, whom the emperor had captured, and from our spies that he is very strong." On that same day, the two Smalkaldic chiefs broke camp for home.[74]

In November's waning days, Jacob Sturm and Wolff Böcklin rode westward over the Swabian Jura and across Württemberg toward home. Stopping at Stuttgart on 27 November, they found Landgrave Philip, who had come on a last, desperate mission to beg more money from Duke Ulrich, for whom he risked so much in 1534. After Duke Ulrich had refused to lend him fifty thousand fl., Jacob Sturm came to see the Hessian prince,

> and we asked him if such a sum couldn't be raised at Strasbourg. He replied, this is surely impossible, and even if the regime were willing, they could not raise such a sum in the city; the sums they have spent on this war were raised from their own citizens.[75]

Then the landgrave pleaded with the duke once more, reminding him of his own promise, that if the three cities—Augsburg, Ulm, and Strasbourg—and the two Smalkaldic chiefs would raise a further 100,000 fl. each for the cause, he would do the same. Ulrich replied that he remembered the letter, but it hadn't been done, "and if he now advanced the 50,000 fl. asked for, he would lose his money, but the cause would not be helped." There the matter stood—no more money for a lost cause. The landgrave rode away to rejoin his army, Sturm headed for home, and the two men never met again.

Homeward bound, Sturm retraced the path over the Black Forest and down the Kinzig Valley to the Rhine, which he had traveled in the year of the great rebellion, 1525. His mood was desperate, almost apocalyptic, and oppressed by a sense of martyrdom and doom. He had tried to communicate this sense to the landgrave in a letter he wrote from Ulm after their last meeting at Giengen. "Your Princely Grace should reflect on the matter," Sturm wrote,

> and not allow yourself to be persuaded that we can secure, now or ever, any acceptable peace from the enemy, unless we surrender God and His word. You are dealing not only with the emperor but with the Antichrist at Rome, who instigated and organized this whole thing against us.[76]

Meanwhile, at home the XIII deliberated the possibility of continuing the war by means of French gold,

> for it can be argued that it would be good for the common cause of religion and the German nation, if we could conclude such an alliance with France and other powers, so that we could block the emperor's project for a monarchy [*des keisers furnemen der monarchi*].[77]

There were still stout hearts among the southern Smalkaldeners, men such as Mattheus Molkenbur of Constance, who at Giengen had shouted against suing the emperor for peace, "I'd rather be struck by lightning!"[78] At that time, Sturm, who felt the same, had hammered the allies with angry words. "My dear sirs," he said,

> if you are so little committed that, for the sake of money alone, you are willing to sacrifice your people instead of accepting minor damages [ein kleinen schaden], then, truly, I don't know what to say. I do believe, however, it is a great foolishness to let this army withdraw from the South.[79]

The "great foolishness" prevailed nonetheless, and the southern Smalkaldeners had now to face its consequences.

SURRENDER OR RESISTANCE?

It was the morning of 8 December 1546, and in the council chamber of Strasbourg's city hall, all eyes glued on Jacob Sturm, as the aging statesman reported on his mission to the Danube front.[80] It was bitter to report how meanly the northern allies had repaid the southerners' generous support of the Brunswick campaigns of 1542 and 1545. Sturm recounted the meeting near Giengen and the debates about attack, negotiation, or wintering over the troops. At the end, the magistrates appointed Sturm and three other veteran magistrates to consider what to do: "Whether the war should be continued, or we should seek peace, and whether and how the Common Penny should be collected."[81] To some envoys from Speyer, who arrived three days later with an offer to mediate, Sturm admitted that "it is clear that negotiations might be a good thing," but he asked that it be done "so that none will know that we want to treat."[82] Meanwhile, the XIII pointed out to the Smalkaldic chiefs that the league's diet could hardly meet, as scheduled, at Frankfurt on 12 January 1547, as that city had already fallen to the enemy. In fact, the Smalkaldic League was shattered, and the 300,000 fl., which belatedly arrived from France, served only to help tidy up the situation.[83] After Christmas Sturm received a long, self-serving letter, in which Landgrave Philip suggested that if he made peace with Charles, he could intercede for the others.[84] Ulm had surrendered, and Duke Ulrich and other southern allies lay deep in peace negotiations.[85]

On the fourth day of the new year, Sturm and his three colleagues laid out the arguments for and against the two possible courses of action, surrender or resistance.[86] If the Strasbourgeois made peace with the emperor, they would betray their allies and, "according to the custom of the Latin nation, little or none of his terms would be honored." Eventually, the emperor would require attendance at the papal council, and "we would then have to reestablish the mass and all papal ordinances and to restore the ecclesiastical properties." The city would also lose its ancient immunity from paying homage to the emperor, it would have to submit to the Imperial Chamber Court and its Catholic judges, and it would be taxed "according to the emperor's pleasure, just as in his hereditary lands." Further, the Imperial troops quartered in Strasbourg would "harm women and children, levy contributions, and do as they please, to which we are quite unaccustomed," and the bishop would recover his "old rights."

The alternative course, resistance, would lead to ruin.[87] A siege would bring threats from the city's own mercenaries, shortage of money and provisions, and devastation of the countryside, "on which the city mostly depends for its rents and dues." Even without a siege, Imperial cavalry would still harry the countryside, "so that the rich burghers, merchants, and also the common burghers and artisans could not do their business." If the emperor outlawed the city, which was likely, no one would pay his debts to the city or its citizens, and all payment of interest by foreigners would cease. Further, "if the nobles and rich burghers received no interest, rents, or other dues, they would hardly be able to maintain their standing, nor would the common artisan, who depends on the nobles and the rich and lives from them." Finally, there was "the unreliability of the Common Man, who perhaps at first favored the cause, but, now that things have gone badly, might suddenly turn about and favor a treaty, since he has little to lose—unlike the rich." Finally, if Strasbourg resisted, it would resist alone, "for it is not to be expected that our allies will be able to raise another army."[88]

At the end of both paths, surrender and resistance, lay possible ruin. The Senate & XXI had nonetheless to recommend a policy to the three hundred Schöffen of the guilds, "though it is to be feared that among them are some who would tolerate making the emperor lord here, no matter what the consequences for the whole city's religion and liberty." If the Schöffen advised the regime to negotiate, or if they were badly divided, the emperor might hear of it "through opponents" and decide to besiege the city or take other actions against it. The committee's opinion was read to the patricians and to the Schöffen on 13 January 1547, and on the nineteenth five squads of senators made the rounds to poll the Schöffen, three-fifths of whom (188 of 300), opposed any dealings with the emperor, because, they said, whatever he promised, he would not keep his word.[89] Who could trust those slippery Latins?

Sturm and some other leading senators already realized that Strasbourg would have to treat, but why did so many of the city's notables favor resistance? Initially, the Smalkaldic War had not evoked strong enthusiasm, for although the preachers had ordered the bells to be rung each morning at 9 o'clock, when everyone, "whoever he may be, in the streets or at home, should fall on his knees and ask God to grant His grace that we may beat the emperor," the painter Sebald Büheler reports that "I never saw anyone, in the streets or elsewhere, fall on his knees."[90] Martin Bucer admitted to the landgrave that "alas, we convince few people that something great is happening; they grumble about the costs, ... If everyone had to bear the burdens every day, and eat and drink less, they would pray better and learn better. ... We have, alas, too long and too much presumed on the immeasurable grace of Christ."[91] One citizen called Bucer a "thief" and refused to sell to him, and another, Gilg Sollern from Solothurn, said "the landgrave is a thief and a rascal, who stole 100,000 fl. from the allies, and in two weeks we'll have a new lord here."[92] Others were simply confused or worried that "my lords are doing nothing about the situation."[93] Still others whispered that "my lords are divided, and that Sir Mathis Pfarrer two or three times tried to run out of the chamber, saying that he had to tell this to the commune, but he was pulled back by his coattails."[94]

Gradually, however, opinion was being mobilized for resistance through preaching and pamphleteering, the unsettling play of rumor and report, native bigotry against Charles's "Latin" troops, lurid antipapalism and acerbic anticlericalism, disappointing reports about the army's inaction, and sincere concern for the future of Evangelical religion. Early on, when the war went well, it was preached as a crusade. "Our war is God's war," Bucer wrote the landgrave, "a war for heaven and eternal life, not alone for its undeniably worldly aims. For no Christian wishes to live under the antichristian tyranny of these people. . . . If the rulers would take the lead, I believe that wonderful things would happen, for the affair is truly God's affair."[95] The crusading spirit encouraged the formation about this time of the first conventicles—"Christian communities," they would be called—circles of disciplined Christians under clerical leadership.[96] Meanwhile, Bucer and some of his colleagues labored from their pulpits to weld together the two motives, anti-Imperialism and Christian militancy. They warned that the recent defeat and impending peace would initiate a religious persecution, by means of which God would punish the lack of discipline among the Protestants. Instead of making peace, therefore, a godly discipline must arise at Strasbourg, not through the government solely, or even principally, but through the committed Christians who composed the heart of the church. The lost war thus supplied an opportunity for an assault on Sturm's Marsiglian church settlement of 1534.

The preachers' cause was aided by the warming effects of a massive outpouring of the printed word, which in 1546–47 achieved a verbal violence and a volume unknown in Germany since the great pamphleteering of the mid-1520s. The printing press, by now a normal tool of political struggle in the Empire, had gone to war on both sides. The emperor's declaration of outlawry against the Smalkaldic chiefs had also proclaimed his case against them as open rebels and church robbers, and the princes' propagandists replied in kind.[97] While the leaguers appealed to "the Germans" to rise up against the alien "Latin" hegemony, the Imperialists warned them that the league represented the same forces—Luther and the princes—who had slaughtered the common people in 1525. At Strasbourg, naturally, mostly Protestant propaganda was heard, and it was filled with hatred for the faithless emperor, behind whom stood the pope, the bishops, and the whole Catholic clergy, whose sole aim was to slaughter the Protestants and restore Germany to clerical tyranny.[98] The authors called the pope, bishops, and priests "shameless whoremongers and adulterers, drunkards and gamblers, who are vicious, jealous, quarrelsome, and greedy."[99] Whereas the pamphleteers of 1525 had spared the emperor and his office, the more apocalyptic Protestant mood of 1546–47 judged the emperor and all other temporal rulers according to their militancy for God and the true gospel and against Satan and his minions, the pope and the emperor. It was easy to argue, by late winter 1547, that the gospel had gone down not because the forces of Satan were invincible, but because the Christians were weak and half-hearted in their militance and zeal.[100]

This verbal ferocity distinguished the Smalkaldic War, which in a military sense was far less destructive and bloody than, say, the Bavarian War of 1504. This is not to say that the league's propagandists aimed to instigate a general insurrection, nor that their words were not judged critically. The Smalkaldic War was a struggle for the liberties of princes and free cities, not for any general kind of freedom, and the peasants sometimes deliberately defended the emperor and Catholicism against Lutheran burghers. Around Hildesheim during the Smalkaldic War, for example, the peasants rejoiced that the victorious emperor would punish the arrogant burghers and bring them so low that a harrow could be run over them.[101] During the Smalkaldic War much depended, as it had during the 1520s, on traditional social and political animosities and solidarities. Where the Reformation had arisen as a popular cause, the defense of the gospel against the papal Antichrist and the bishops possessed quite specific political implications, which could be mobilized in favor of resistance and a more godly regime. This was true at Strasbourg, the Anabaptists' New Jerusalem, where during the first weeks of 1547 anti-Imperial militance, a vocal clerical leadership, and popular sentiments for a purer church began to flow together and to disrupt civic life as the revolution of 1525 never had done. It surfaced when the Danube campaign was lost and the southern allies were surrendering, while far to the northeast, Elector John Frederick, the Smalkaldic chief, braced himself against his oncoming foes—Charles, Ferdinand, and Duke Moritz.[102] The Smalkaldic chiefs would now stand alone, cut off from the sources of hard money and good infantry in the South.[103]

Meanwhile, behind closed doors at Strasbourg, Sturm and his colleagues were at this moment planning Strasbourg's surrender. The first peace feelers came at the end of January via Sturm's kinsman, Wolfgang Rehlinger, the immigrant ex-burgomaster from Augsburg. Rehlinger had played a key role in Augsburg's decision for the Reformation, led his city into the Smalkaldic League in 1535, and dominated the city's politics from 1539 until 1543, when the rise of a more militant party under Jakob Herbrot drove him from the regime and from the city.[104] He settled in his mother's home, Strasbourg, where his kinsman, Jacob Sturm, had played a similar political role with more lasting success. Now, as the wealthy immigrant tried to mediate between his adopted city and the emperor, militant Evangelicals began to call him "a traitor to this city."[105] The terms he forwarded from Chancellor Granvelle required Strasbourg to "make formal submission [*ein zimblichen fusfall thon*]," abandon the league and agree not to enter another, support and obey the Chamber Court, and pay "a tolerable fine [*ein leidliche geltstraff*]." In return, Charles would restore the city and citizens to grace, forgive them their actions as belligerents, confirm their privileges, and promise not to suppress their religion by force.[106] These very generous terms reflected Granvelle's recognition of Strasbourg's strength and proximity to France. They had to be handled in strictest secrecy until the Schöffen could be brought around.[107]

The decision for peace fell on 31 January, when Sturm and his committee of three—all staunch Evangelicals since the mid-1520s—recommended, after much hemming and hawing, that Granvelle should be told "that we will enter negotiations."[108] For this step they needed the Schöffen's consent, and when they presented Granvelle's terms on 3 February, the magistrates referred to the vote of 19 January, in which, they declared—with some bending of the truth—"many of you . . ., nearly a majority," advised negotiation. This time they got their way, though the majority was slim— 162 of 300 votes—and they were forbidden to make peace without consulting the Schöffen again.[109] Several of the Schöffen nevertheless had the courage to point out the duplicity of the regime in general and Jacob Sturm in particular, whom Hans Mennlich of the Tailors accused of having said last summer that "the emperor has never kept faith." When Mennlich continued to heckle Sturm during the peace negotiations, he was ordered "to shut his mouth."[110]

SURRENDER

The negotiation of the surrender to the Emperor Charles V in February 1547 was one of Jacob Sturm's greatest political triumphs, for by its terms Strasbourg, a principal belligerent, escaped from the Smalkaldic War with its liberties and its Evangelical religion intact. In return, Strasbourg's leaders transformed it by 1549 from a citadel of militant Protestant resistance into a loyal Protestant free city with an unwanted but tolerated Catholic minority and a church once more firmly in governmental hands. Sturm defeated the party of resistance by rallying the guilds' notables to a policy of peace. The initial poll of 19 January 1547 reveals that the hard division for peace or resistance ran roughly along class lines: the patricians, the merchants, and the rich generally favored peace, whereas the militant resisters mostly came from poor trades and poor guilds.[111] One bastion of resistance was the Masons' Guild, whose Georg Büheler demanded that "the whoredom so prevalent among the rich and poor must be punished, and it would not hurt to purge the regime of evil-doers, both nobles and commoners."[112] In the middle, however, was a considerable group that wanted peace, if it could be had "with honor," that is, without compromising the city's liberties and religion. Sturm and the others won their cause by rallying this middle to their side and pushing the party of resistance into isolation.

The vote on 3 February did not settle the issue, for it was followed by agitation from the city's pulpits, by Mathis Zell at the cathedral, by Bucer at St. Thomas, and especially by young Paul Fagius at New St. Peter's. They prompted, a report ran, "the burghers to say subversive things [*unnutz reden treiben*]" and "try to establish the right of excommunication in their own hands [*und understanden den bann fur sich selbs ufzurichten*]."[113] It was understood, clearly, that the clergy were using this occasion to revise the Marsiglian settlement of 1534 in a clerical and communitarian sense. Abroad, it was reported that Strasbourg, along with Augsburg, Constance, and Duke Ulrich, would "turn Swiss" and join the confederacy rather than submit to the emperor.[114] This was false, for the leaders of Strasbourg's resisters offered no alternative policy, neither to "turn Swiss" nor—the natural resort of every form of German opposition—to "turn French," despite feverish efforts by Strasbourg's Francophile agents, Jean Sturm and Dr. Ulrich Geiger, to tie the city to France's dying king.[115] There simply was no pro-French party at Strasbourg, and those who might have played the French card in late winter 1547, Bucer and his friends, despised King Francis as a bloody persecutor of their French religious brethren.[116] Far from being a popular cause, the French alliance was merely a fall-back position kept open by Jacob Sturm, who in early February, when the first feelers came from the Imperial court at Ulm, drafted and had sent to Paris a plan, "how the king of France might be approached about an alliance, if the emperor advances on and besieges the city."[117] Something might have come of this option, except that at the critical moment King Francis lay ill at Castle Rambouillet, where he died on the last day of March 1547.[118] France influenced Strasbourg's surrender only in a negative sense, for the remarkable mildness of the terms reflected, as Antoine Perrenot remarked, the fact that "the Strasbourgeois have French envoys in their city."[119] The French king's persecutions of French Protestants, which had never disqualified him as an ally in the eyes of the Smalkaldic chiefs, did so in those of the Strasbourgeois.

The peace negotiations crept on in deepest secrecy, while letter after letter arrived from the Smalkaldic chiefs, full of reproach for Duke Ulrich and the southern allies who had surrendered, full of praise for Strasbourg's staunch resistance. No one in the South believed now in John Frederick's promised victory over Ferdinand, Charles, and Duke Moritz.[120] After dark on 10 February, a forester named Veltin slipped into Strasbourg to give Sturm and Conrad Joham the emperor's safe-conduct and letters from Jean de Naves and Wolfgang Rehlinger, which Sturm read next day to the Senate & XXI.[121] The instruction prepared for Sturm, Mathis Pfarrer, and a young patrician named Marx Hag, told them to reject the renunciation of the league, as the league would expire in two weeks' time (on 27 February

1547), but to concede the prohibition against new alliances and the pledge to support the Chamber Court.[122] The oath of allegiance posed a difficult problem, for

> Emperor Frederick [III] and Emperor Maximilian came often in person to Strasbourg, and when they were informed that it was the custom of Strasbourg, as a free city of the Empire, to swear no oath to a [Holy] Roman emperor, the city was relieved of this obligation and left to enjoy its freedom and custom.[123]

If the oath must be taken, it should be taken by the ammeister and XXI alone "in the name of the whole city." The other symbolic act, the submission (*Fußfall*), should be conceded, though if possible with a confession of having acted against the emperor but not criminally. In return, the regime hoped that Charles would promise to station no troops in Alsace and to restore all the burghers to grace and confirm them and the city in their traditional liberties. As for religion, he should be asked to pursue a settlement not through force but "through a regular, Christian, amicable way in an Imperial Diet."[124] The Senate & XXI accepted, therefore, most of the terms Rehlinger had relayed from Granvelle, because, as they wrote Landgrave Philip, "now all princes and cities in the South have surrendered, except for us and Constance, which has no hope of saving itself through the Swiss or any other way and will not be able to hold out."[125]

As Sturm and his companions rode eastward toward Ulm and the emperor, they left a city poised between the hammer of the victorious emperor's will and the anvil of popular opposition to a negotiated peace.[126] They crossed the Rhine bridge and rode via Pforzheim across Württemberg and over the Swabian Jura to the Danube at Ulm, where they found the emperor in the company of his court and twenty-four thousand veteran troops.[127] The lord of all South Germany was a man in a hurry, for Ferdinand and Moritz awaited his approach to strike John Frederick's army and lands, and Charles needed a swift victory over the Protestant chiefs in order to stave off decisions by the Council of Trent (now meeting at Bologna) that might trump his plan for a German settlement. When they came to occupied Ulm on 19 February, the Strasbourgeois saw and heard much about the handiwork of Charles's troops in Swabia and about his plans for a speedy departure for Saxony.[128] Granvelle was away, and Jean de Naves died on the eve of their arrival, "so that the emperor has no eminent German councillors now," but Rehlinger put them in touch with Granvelle's son, Bishop Antoine Perrenot of Arras, who promised to forward their instruction to Charles and discussed the terms informally with them.[129] The terms, the bishop said, came not from Charles but "from his father and himself, who hadn't favored this war and had counselled against it, and who were especially friendly toward Strasbourg."[130] The talks revealed two major points of dispute, the oath and religion, though the thirty thousand fl. in fine offered by Strasbourg was found to be puny.[131] Charles's reply—"the emperor's final word," the bishop warned—came to Sturm and the others on 23 February; it compromised on several points but demanded artillery—seven to nine large guns— renunciation of the league and all other alliances, and the oath of loyalty. When Sturm and the bishop had agreed on the details, Perrenot warned him to fetch his regime's assent as soon as possible, "for if you delay one day more than absolutely necessary, some will get angry and suspect that you are intriguing with the French."

After the Senate & XXI heard these terms on 2 March, they instructed the envoys, plus Conrad Joham and Hans Lindenfels, to prepare the case for the Schöffen.[132] Three days later, the regime convened the Schöffen for the third time on the issue of peace or resistance. The long address is a masterpiece of Sturmian rhetoric.[133] The Schöffen were told of the negotiations at Ulm and the terms "on which the whole city of Strasbourg and its people might be reconciled with the emperor." The immediate price would be thirty thousand fl., much less than the other former allies had to pay, plus six siege guns and six field pieces. To refuse these terms, the regime warned in Sturm's words, would be to condemn the city and its burghers "plus the whole neighboring countryside to war and total ruin and to the humiliation and crimes to women and children, which war brings with it." The main points—submission, renunciation of alliances, Chamber Court, oath of loyalty, garrison, fine in cash and guns—were then described in the best light. When he came to the oath, Sturm wrote into the speech the story of how his great-grandfather, Old Peter Schott, and Philips von Mülnheim, his father's kinsman, had journeyed in 1473 to Metz to see Emperor Frederick III, after the monarch had demanded that Strasbourg swear an oath to him as other "free and Imperial cities" did. They told Frederick that he might have his oath from them or, if this did not suffice, the entire Senate & XXI, as was customary in other cities. That would have occurred, Sturm wrote, except for the intervention of the Burgundian Wars. The point of this little lesson in civic history was that if their ancestors had been willing to surrender this liberty then, "when the emperor was not so powerful," how much more was this course advisable "now, with this very powerful emperor and in these circumstances." Sturm used this little story, which he had from his family's traditions or from his researches in the civic archives, to argue that an oath of homage, even if uncustomary and humiliating, was preferable to resistance, for "when we are destitute and ruined, to whatever onerous conditions the enemy desires and, as they say, we will have to surrender unconditionally [*auf gnad und ungnad ergeben*]." "Dear friends," the speech concluded, "you can easily understand why we are inclined more to peace than to war." Stripped of human powers to resist, the city could not expect aid from above, for "because we see . . . how little preaching of the Gospel has changed our lives, we cannot presume that the Almighty will uphold His honor and name in other ways and, because of our devotion, perform a special miracle." The emperor's terms "will be better and less costly for the city of Strasbourg and its citizens than war against such a popular emperor, who now has almost half the German nation in his grip."

Moved by Sturm's words and other motives, 243 Schöffen voted to empower the Senate & XXI to conclude peace on the stipulated terms.[134] In the six weeks since 19 January, support for the regime's peace policy had increased from one-third (32.9 percent) to more than four-fifths (81 percent) of the merchants, shopkeepers, artisans, and officials who made up the notables of the guilds. The third vote shows that Sturm and his colleagues had brought together the peace party and the middling party of "peace with honor" to form the majority their peace policy required. They now plunged ahead toward the most grievous political humiliation any of them had ever witnessed.

The magistrates still hoped they might avoid the worst by finessing the oath of homage in return for money, "because the Rhenish cities are free [france und libere], and they have never performed an oath, such as the Swabian and Franconian cities swear," so perhaps "His Majesty will dispense Strasbourg from such an oath, for such free Rhenish cities as Cologne, Worms, and Speyer have never sworn one."[135] They also hoped to save some of the artillery, "because Strasbourg lies on the frontier, as His Majesty knows, the envoys should ask him graciously to leave them their guns" or at least let them ransom the guns from him.[136] On the most sensitive point, the intergrity of Strasbourg's religious establishment, Jacob Sturm candidly told the Senate & XXI that "the bishop of Arras said that the emperor would give no assurance concerning religion other than he gave to . . . others, namely, that the debate would continue as before."[137] In order to speed the negotiations, Sturm was authorized to present Antoine Perrenot with a gift of up to two thousand fl.

Jacob Sturm rode out again on 9 March, this time accompanied by young Marx Hag and a wealthy merchant named Friedrich von Gottesheim.[138] All three of the envoys were noblemen; two of them, Hag and Gottesheim, spoke fluent French; but only Jacob Sturm possessed any real diplomatic experience. At Pforzheim, where they stopped on their way to intersect the emperor's journey northward, Sturm heard the hair-raising story of Duke Ulrich's submission.[139] When Ulrich came before Charles on 4 March at Ulm, before the army broke camp, the gouty old sinner had to be carried in a chair into the emperor's presence and "to beg forgiveness for his inability to make his submission on his knees [also sitzen sich entschuldigt, das er den fussfal libs halb nit thon möge]." Sturm and his companions found the emperor at Nördlingen on 13 March, and though he and the bishop of Arras quickly agreed on the terms, an attack of Imperial gout delayed the ceremony of submission.[140] Early in the afternoon on 21 March, Sturm and the others knelt and made their city's submission in the presence of only thirty persons. Then Charles got back in his litter to begin the painful passage of Franconia toward Nuremberg and on to Saxony.[141]

The treaty of 21 March 1547 "composed [*verglichen*]," as Sturm put it, the breach between emperor and free city in terms that closely followed those Granvelle had proposed in February.[142] Though they also approximated what had been told the Schöffen on 5 March, the question remained whether they could now be sold to a broader public at Strasbourg. Many believed not, including some who claimed to have heard it from Johann Meyer, Strasbourg's city secretary.[143] Rumors flew: Bucer had hailed the young king of England as a champion of the gospel, the Swiss were ready to move, France was on the move, the emperor was gravely ill. Bucer did see the treaty as a portent of doom, though he looked for inspiration not to England but to the Swiss. "Look how God made and kept the Swiss free!" he wrote to the landgrave on 29 March, the day after Sturm and his companions reported to the Senate & XXI.[144] "One needs only Biblical courage and willingness to fight, for all else—money, food, supplies—God will provide!" Why had Strasbourg not learned this lesson? Because, Bucer thought, "the fear of God has for some time been neglected here, which compelled me to urge in various ways and to various audiences, that religion ought to be properly ordered and maintained. But not much was said or done." All those who shared the blame, he said with some satisfaction, "must share in the punishment, which will truly be severe." Though many boast of the city's wondrous reconciliation with the emperor,

> those who really understand are in great fear of God and the Common Man. Everyone, even our enemies, so the envoys who went to the emperor report, praises the elector's courage. That is the right way, even if it leads to death, for [such a] death will place him high in esteem before God and men—which, surely, is the highest thing a pious and godfearing man can desire. . . . The landgrave, however, is cursed at Strasbourg, as the elector is praised.

After his review of the treaty's terms, Bucer closed with a terrible cry,

> But, dear God, where is the proper and free confession of God's Son and the true duty [of the ruler] to the subjects? God's punishment must come. Blessed is he who now finds death through his trust in God! God's Son will now surely show Himself and proclaim and enforce *His* treaty, which says that all lordship is His alone.

The landgrave replied with characteristic sarcasm that "I marvel at how the wise, godfearing folk at Strasbourg could do no better, for they have never seen a foe or suffered a siege, and they have such a strong, well provisioned and populated city, with the Swiss and French at their backs."[145] The senior Smalkaldic chief did not believe, no more than Sturm did, that a pious death was better than an ignominious peace.

Sturm, to whom fell the task of convincing the Senate & XXI, warned them of Antoine Perrenot's remark, "I would not bet 100,000 crowns that the emperor will moderate any of the terms for money, nor will he remit the oath or the artillery."[146] There were small concessions, for example, about the guns, some of which they might have cast at Augsburg, "where it is done cheaper and better than here." On the two most threatening points, however, the emperor's freedom to enter the city with as large a force as he chose and the guarantee of established religion, no concessions could be had. After his report Sturm convened his committee to frame recommendations on a wide variety of outstanding points, such as public security, for the storm of criticism that greeted his return led to measures to control the preachers and their followers' "meetings [convocationen]."[147] Bucer, Zell, Fagius, and Marbach clearly intended to exploit the uproar over the treaty to force a revision of the church ordinance and the institution of excommunication, that is, to secure the governance of the church for its "better part" and to push through their plan for a compulsory regime of religious discipline at Strasbourg.[148] Bucer still believed that with popular support the preachers could defeat the treaty, as he wrote to the landgrave about this time:

> Strasbourg's subjects [underthanen] are much put out with their envoys, who went to the emperor. The treaty has not yet been made public, perhaps out of fear, and the envoys are trying to portray it as less significant than it truly is. . . . The Common Man here at Strasbourg wants to resist [ist unwillig]; he demands to be consulted both individually and as a whole and not just through the guilds. For it was the Common Man who was the cause of [the restoration of] religion.[149]

It was indeed. Desperate to defend this restoration against, as he saw, defeatists and temporizers, Bucer flung this uncomfortable truth at Jacob Sturm and the other magistrates, most of whom well remembered the 1520s and did not want them repeated.

As the agitation began to put the treaty before the whole commune, not just the Schöffen, rumors arose about an impending upheaval at Strasbourg. Jean Sturm admitted to the French ambassador that he feared an insurrection,[150] while Jakob Lersner, a Hessian official, spread a story about the revolutionary mood at Strasbourg. "At Strasbourg there are many good-hearted folk," he reported to the landgrave, "who don't want this treaty. . . . We may expect that all sorts of disturbances and rebellion might occur against those who promoted this treaty for their own purposes [umb aignes nutzes]."[151] The fact that one of the negotiators, Friedrich von Gottsheim, was trying to secure his confiscated goods, now that "we are reconciled with the emperor," lent credence to Lersner's charge.[152]

The civic crisis over the treaty came to a head in mid-April, just as Dr. Gremp was negotiating final details with Antoine Perrenot.[153] On 18 April Jakob Lersner wrote to the Saxon elector that

> in Strasbourg, gracious Lord, there is great hostility [vnwill] between the common citizens and those who have produced [verursachet] and accepted the treaty. It must soon come, I think, to a revolt or uprising, for the common citizens and many honorable folk are criticizing them [the magistrates].[154]

The latter, though tempted to yield the point and consult the entire commune, decided to address the Schöffen alone for the fifth time on 20 April. This time the case was prepared by a committee composed of magistrates who had originally favored resistance, untainted by Sturm's peace policy. Headed by the aging Claus Kniebis, they recommended consultation not of the commune as a whole, but only of the Schöffen guild by guild, in order to explain the situation and prevent further agitation.[155] The address they drafted concentrated on the chief reason for anxiety, the future of religion, and explained that because the emperor had not conducted his war on account of religion, he had dismissed the subject from the treaty. His Majesty had nevertheless assured the envoys "that concerning religion" everything would remain as it was until the whole matter was decided "by a general council or through other, proper ways and means." The committee also denied the danger of an Imperial garrison and reminded the Schöffen that on each Schwörtag they promised to obey the regime and uphold the city's welfare.

With the situation now in hand, the regime made ready to receive the Imperial commissioner, Christoph von Schauenburg, who arrived to receive as proxy Strasbourg's oath of homage to the emperor.[156] Once lodged in the city, he sent for Jacob Sturm to display his credentials and ask how to proceed. When he also offered to depart and return when the burghers had calmed down, Sturm replied that "my lords are agreed about this [*mein hern heten sein kein irrung*]."[157] Sturm and Mathis Pfarrer then escorted Schauenburg to the town hall, where he announced his instructions "that my lords shall swear and do homage to His Majesty." Then, reserving the city's traditional liberties, the Senate & XXI swore the oath to Schauenburg as the emperor's proxy.[158] The date was 25 April 1547, and no one at Strasbourg knew that on the previous day, the emperor and his allies had crushed Elector John Frederick's army at Mühlberg on the River Elbe.[159]

Sturm and his colleagues soon heard from the victorious emperor, who commanded that "you proceed with all speed and dispatch against the conspiracies, rebellions, and disturbances which have broken out there, and you are to prosecute, try, and punish severely the leaders and instigators, . . . and maintain your citizenry and commune in peace, quiet, and due obedience."[160] This is what happened. The senators sought out and warned those cited for "harmful talk [*unnutze reden*]," admonished spreaders of rumors and grumblers against the preachers, investigated dereliction among guards at the city gates, arrested and jailed obdurate agitators, and forbade public gatherings, such as the annual parade of the bakers' apprentices on Ascension Day.[161] Odd things were happening in the churches, such as outbursts by a country woman called "Longnails," who during the service cried out that "the emperor is coming, the altars and the mass will be restored." She was taken and ejected from the city.[162] The atmosphere was further troubled by prejudice against the "Latins," an old problem at Strasbourg, with its many French-speaking residents. The natives tended to "make no distinctions among Spaniards, Italians, and Frenchmen," even "though some have been driven from their own lands because of their faith."[163] Such feelings colored the agitation against the emperor and the treaty, for the resistance party tended to emphasize the Latin foreignness of the emperor and his troops. The cooper Arbogast Keller, for example, "who is a very old fellow," was punished for saying that "a foreign army is coming here, and my lords have letters from the emperor, which they will post on their houses, so they won't be harmed; and when that happens, he will put some timbers under the town hall and set them afire, so the building will be destroyed."[164] Most difficult to discipline, of course, were those preachers who involved themselves in agitation against the treaty. For one thing, they held the upper hand through their campaign for moral reform, which Jacob Sturm admitted was necessary, and for stricter religious discipline.[165] One could not jail a Mathis Zell or Bucer without trial, as one did lesser folk, but when Zell during the annual fair in late June 1547 preached "an improper sermon . . ., which might stir up the common folk and especially the foreigners, who come here at this time," the senators warned him and other preachers "to preach the Word of God . . . and say nothing about the news that runs about."[166]

By the end of May 1547, informants, denunciations, investigations, warnings, arrests, jailings, and threats had brought the situation well enough in hand that Sturm and his colleagues felt they could turn urgently needed attention to public finance. On the last day of May, a commission of six privy councillors under Sturm's chairmanship reported that the financial crisis could be helped in three ways: reduction or elimination of debt service, increase of revenues, and reduction of expenditures.[167] The central problem concerned the war debt, for the city had borrowed at 5 instead of the customary 4 percent, and 99 percent of the redeemable current debt of 174,099 fl. was being paid at the higher rate. The committee recommended that before the next due date (25 July), creditors must either accept conversion to 4 percent, which would reduce annual debt service by nearly eight thousand fl., or repayment of the principle. The magistrates decided to bully the town's creditors as they bullied its preachers, but it did not work, and by autumn they fell back on the tried-and-true expedient of raising indirect taxes, chiefly the Umgelt levied on wine.[168]

It is difficult to overestimate the explosive potential in post-war Strasbourg of the linkage between the clerical campaign for stricter moral discipline, the burghers' sense of humiliation over the lost war, and the Evangelical sense that to submit to an emperor who served the papal Antichrist would violate the commune's duty to uphold God's honor and the gospel. The social source of this danger lay in the world of the artisans, their guilds and their shops, where the Reformation movement had given voice to a deep longing for what has been called "Evangelical moralism," a burghers' ethic based on the suppression of immorality, especially sexual immorality, and the ideal of the pious, patriarchal household.[169] The early and relatively easy victory of the Reformation movement at Strasbourg had meant that, in contrast to Augsburg, the Evangelical reconstruction of the church had occurred through the struggle with the sects. Unity, therefore, was achieved through the formal proclamation of doctrinal orthodoxy, which was desultorily enforced, and the sterner Evangelical moralism did not emerge, as it did at Augsburg, to be the hallmark of allegiance to Protestantism. Although the magistrates at Strasbourg, like the Augsburgers, issued new laws against immorality, the stern ethos of moral conformity gained less of a hold on them than it did on the magistrates of embattled Augsburg, which meant that, in a sense, when the tests of war and defeat came, the magistrates had still to prove the strength of their Evangelical commitment through a strict suppression of immorality and promotion of civic godliness. This is what Bucer's campaign for stricter discipline was all about, and it lent his oppositional stance in 1547, and again over the interim in 1548, great political potential because of its broad religious appeal to those burghers on whose loyalty the regime most depended.

By high summer 1547, Sturm and his fellow magistrates had this first phase of the postwar struggle well in hand. They had a grip on the financial crisis the campaign of 1546 had created, and it seemed time to close the books on the war—providing the triumphant emperor also wanted to close them. At Wittenberg on 19 May, John Frederick of Saxony signed away his electorate and parts of his lands in order to save his sons' succession and his own head, and the booty was made over to his cousin, Duke Moritz, known now to German Protestants as "the German Judas" or "the Judas of Meissen."[170] Then, the Hessian landgrave knelt before his enthroned emperor while his chancellor read his plea for mercy. The Holy Roman Empire was no England, Charles V was no Henry VIII, and the Smalkaldic chiefs kept their heads—but, for the moment, little else. By early July, the two captive princes in tow, Charles was moving southward through eastern Franconia toward the Danube and Augsburg. Now at the summit of his career, just as Titian painted him—though in fact confined by his gout to a litter—the forty-seven-year-old monarch was coming back to the Imperial heartlands of the South, where he meant to settle the German schism.

Notes

* "Weh euch, ir armen reichstet,/wie groß vermeßenhait,/daß ir euch widern frommen kaiser,/die höchste oberkait,/on ursach dorften setzen/auß besonderm neid und haß!/furwar, ir solten wöllen,/ir hettens betrachtet baß./Kyrie, die Spanier seind im land!" Liliencron, ed., *Historische Volkslieder* 4:369, no. 539, stanza 1.

** "Karle, sag an die sachen,/die heimlich treiben dich!/Deutschland wilt eigen
machen/dem haus zu Ostereich,/ein monarchie wilt richten an,/Plus ultra soll
noch weiter gan,/do ligt der hund begraben." Ibid., 333, no. 527, stanza 5.

1. So Sebastian Erb told the story: "[Philip] respondit facetia: gn. her kaiser, es
   manglet mir nit mer dann noch ein man. caesare percunctante, qui esset,
   respondit: e. K. Mt. hätte ich auch gern under the die frommen leute.
   subridentem ferunt caesarem dixisse: nein, nein, ich kum nit under die verwürten
   leute. at Cattus in pace dimussus ad suos rediit." PC 4:93, no. 65 n. 1; and
   see ibid. 4:93, no. 65. Charles stopped at Speyer on 24 March, which was
   Holy Saturday, and remained until the twenty-ninth. Brandi, Kaiser Karl V.
   1:452; 2:366–67. Philip wanted Jacob Sturm to take part in this interview,
   but the latter pleaded poor health and too short notice. PC 4:51, no. 48, and
   69, no. 50; Druffel, ed., Beiträge 3:4, no. 6.

2. See Sturm's diary of this meeting, PC 4:83–92, no. 63, covering 31 March–25
   April 1546.

3. Lenz, ed., Briefwechsel 3:400, 404.

4. G. Schmidt, "Die Freien und Reichsstädte," 205–6, emphasizes this difference.

5. See Brandi, Kaiser Karl V. 1:453–55, 2:368–69.

6. In his portrayal of the landgrave's meeting with Charles V at Speyer,
   Hasenclever, Die Politik Karls V., 18–32, emphasizes Philip's bravado.

7. This paragraph is based on Parker, Military Revolution; Hale, War and Society.

8. Wiesflecker, Kaiser Maximilian I. 5:62–63, 583–92; and Körner, Solidarités,
   studies the rise of Basel in a similar context.

9. The calculations for Bern are based on Mattmüller, Bevölkerungsgeschichte der
   Schweiz, pt. 1, vol. 1:121–24, 199. The Bernese state thus contained about as
   many persons as the Florentine state at the time of the great cadaster of
   1427.

10. Brandi, Kaiser Karl V. 1:453–54, describes the atmosphere.

11. Hasenclever, Politik der Schmalkaldener, 217–28; F. Roth, "Der offizielle Bericht,"
    1–30, 374–97; Brandi, Kaiser Karl V. 1:453, 2:267–68. On the emperor's
    mentality, see his letter to Prince Philip in Maurenbrecher, Karl V. und die
    deutschen Protestanten, app. 4, 37–39, no. 2. Kannengiesser, Karl V. und
    Maximilian Egmont, 11–12, believed that Charles had decided by August 1545
    to make war, but others, including Tyler, Emperor Charles the Fifth, 99–100,
    emphasize the difficulty with which Charles made up his mind.

12. On the decisive effect of their inaction in 1543, see Hartung, Karl V. und die
    deutsche Reichsstände, 18, who also offers (14–25) a very fine analysis of the
    origins of the Smalkaldic War; and see Heidrich, Karl V. und die deutschen
    Protestanten.

13. Lenz, ed., Briefwechsel 2:475, no. 244.

14. See Charles V to the Senate of Strasbourg, in Lanz, ed., Correspondenz 2:496–
    500, summarized in PC 4:132, no. 98, in which he justifies his mobilization
    as an action to punish disrupters of the public peace.

15. PC 4:205–10, no. 181, which compares Sturm's draft with the version sent
    to Charles.

16. Quoted by Baumgarten, Jacob Sturm, 32 n. 23, and extracted by Lenz, ed.,
    Briefwechsel 2:450 n. 2. The passage is omitted from PC 4:103, no. 76.

17. Brandi, Kaiser Karl V. 1:437–47, on background and opening of the council;
    and, on a grander scale, Jedin, Council of Trent 1:545–81.

18. Lanz, Correspondenz 2:486, quoted by Brandi, Kaiser Karl V. 2:369–70. See
    ibid. 1:455–56.

19. The reconciliation of Wittelsbach and Habsburg, the keystone of the war
    against the Protestants, is made clearer by Metzger, Leonhard von Eck, 287–98.

20. See, for example, the plan by Giangiacomo de' Medici (?), Marchese di Marignano, in Friedensburg, "Am Vorabend des Smalkaldischen Krieges." On the first phase of the war, see Baumgarten, "Zur Geschichte des Schmalkaldischen Krieges"; Schüz, *Donaufeldzug*.

21. See Mentz, *Johann Friedrich* 3:9–12 on mobilization; and Queen Mary's description of the forces, in *Papiers d'état* 3:238–39.

22. Or so was reported by Chancellor Burkhardt of Saxony. See Moritz von Damwitz to Duke Philip I of Pomerania-Wolgast, Arnstadt, 18 July 1546, in Wehrmann, "Vom Vorabend," 195–200. Damwitz came as Pomeranian war councillor to Arnstadt in Thuringia, where the war council of the league's Northern District was meeting.

23. Schüz, *Donaufeldzug*, 11. There is a good, brief account of the Danube campaign and its consequences in Brecht and Ehmer, *Südwestdeutsche Reformationsgeschichte*, 285–90.

24. See Friedensburg, "Am Vorabend des Schmalkaldischen Krieges." The sources and modern literature on the Danube campaign are given by Brandi, *Kaiser Karl V.* 2:371–72. The best studies of the campaign are by Mentz, *Johann Friedrich* 3:1–52; and Schüz, *Donaufeldzug*. On the vital role of Buren, see the very helpful study by Kannengiesser, *Karl V. und Maximilian Egmont Graf von Büren*, esp. his estimate on 194 n. 477 of the size of Buren's forces. The southern forces and their initial campaign are described by Brecht and Ehmer, *Südwestdeutsche Reformationsgeschichte*, 285–86, who also give (285–90) a good overview of the war and its effects on southwestern Germany.

25. The various estimates of the forces are collated by Schüz, *Donaufeldzug*, 89–94.

26. See ibid., 46–77, who gives a clear account of this movement and dispels many myths about it.

27. See *PC* 4: nos. 183, 251, 257. On these men, see Brady, *Ruling Class*, 255–56, 304–5, 336. Some possible confusion arises from the fact that there existed two war councils, one with the army and one of the Southern District at Ulm, and two assemblies, one of the Southern District which met continuously at Ulm, and the diet of the entire league, which was called to Ulm on 20 September (*PC* 4:nos. 433, 437, 440; Möllenberg, "Verhandlungen," 32). In addition, Heinrich von Mülnheim undertook missions to raise funds and troops in Switzerland.

28. Based on *PC* 4:132–549, nos. 98–508.

29. Ibid., 114, no. 82, 128, no. 95, 148, no. 118, 198, no. 175, 214, no. 184, 249, no. 226, and 417, no. 392 n. 2, document such requests.

30. Ibid., 475, no. 449 n. 2.

31. Paetel, *Organisation*, 113–14.

32. *PC* 4:214, no. 184: "Us sondern ursachen diser zeit nit abkommen kan."

33. When the landgrave asked that Sturm take part in a Smalkaldic embassy to the emperor at Speyer, the XIII reported that Sturm declined "because of his health [leibs halben]." Ibid., 51, no. 48; 69, no. 50; Druffel, *Beiträge* 3:4, no. 6.

34. The statement to the emperor is in *PC* 4:205–21, no. 181 (3 July 1546). On the approach to the Swiss, see ibid., 299–303, no. 280; *EA* vol. 4, pt. 1d: 668–69; Geiser, "Haltung der Schweiz," 169–89; Brady, *Turning Swiss*, 210–11. For the missions abroad, see *PC* 4:nos. 187, 251, 263, 270, 283, 290, 297, 303, 323, 344, 350, 360, 369, 376, 391, 428, 436, 442, 444, 457.

35. *PC* 4:215–16, no. 186, and the instructions, in the princes' names alone, in 216–18, no. 187. The prince had renewed contacts with France and England in late winter 1545.

36. On French policy, see Pariset, *Relations*, 44–82; Knecht, *Francis I*, 374–76; Mariotte, "François Ier et la Ligue de Smalkalde," 206–42. On English policy,

see Scarisbrick, *Henry VIII*, 466–70. Niedbruck, a Messin, is the man whom the English called "Dr. Hans Bruno."
37. Pariset, *Relations*, 63–64.
38. See Potter, "Foreign Policy," 540–42, for the best analysis of why these efforts failed.
39. PC 4:479–80, no. 451, noticed by Gerber, "Jakob Sturms Anteil," 166 n. 2. My translation transposes the text into the first person.
40. In fact, Sturm had come to the front to press for a battle of decision.
41. PC 4:235, no. 208.
42. Ibid., 243, no. 219.
43. Ibid., 367, no. 345 n. 3. Böcklin's reports are in ibid., nos. 142–43, 150, 177, 296, 309, 330, 345, 354, 362, 372, 380, 391, 393, 396, 417, 432.
44. PC 4:348, no. 330 and his more subdued report after Buren's army arrived, in ibid., 375, no. 354.
45. PC 4:386–88, no. 363. The Strasbourgeois replied that in their view the proclamation would do more harm than good. Ibid., 392–93, no. 369. Ulman Böcklin and the Ulm envoy took the same position, when the subject was debated on 19 August in the princes' war council. See Sebastian Schertlin von Burtenbach and Matthaeus Langenmantel to the Burgomaster of Augsburg, Camp near Ingolstadt, 19 August 1546, in Herberger, ed., *Briefe*, 142. Landgrave Philip wrote bitterly to Bucer about this decision, in Lenz, ed., *Briefwechsel* 2:469, no. 242: "Uns verwundert nit wenig, das ewere hern und ezliche mer der meinung sein, auch uns, disen stenden schreiben, das man die bischove und andere, wilch disen krieg verursacht, nit angreifen soll, bei denen wol vil gelts zu machen were zu erhaltung dises vereines, das wir sonstet itzo uns selbst [mit] kriegen ausmergeln und erschepfen."
46. PC 4:389, no. 365 n. 2. See Heuschen, *Konstanz*, 134–47, the only detailed study of the war's impact on a city's finances.
47. PC 4:398–99, no. 375, based on a calculation by Jacob Sturm (ibid., 398, no. 375 n. 3).
48. Strasbourg paid at least 53,848 fl. and perhaps as much as 88,788 fl. in taxes for the Turkish wars. Hunyadi, "Participation de Strasbourg," 237.
49. The league's commanders did not remit their assessed shares of the levies, which together came to about 1 million fl., and the northern allies sent at best the first six double-months. On 31 January 1547, Landgrave Philip estimated that he had laid out "funfmal hundert thausend gulden" for the war, which had cost the league as a whole "mehr den in die zwantzig hundert thausend gulden." Rommel, *Philipp der Großmütige* 3:197, no. 45. Hessian accounts indicate that the campaign of 1546–47 cost the landgrave and his lands 622,650 fl., so the figure for the Danube campaign alone may be too high. Paetel, *Organisation*, 157. According to the league's accounts, the army cost about 400,000 fl. per month, but Gerber thinks this is a bit too high. Gerber, "Kriegsrechnungen, I," 45–47. The landgrave's estimate suggests that Gerber is right.
50. PC 4:260, no. 239.
51. See ibid., 265–66, no. 245; and the final accounts in Gerber, "Kriegsrechnungen, I," 49–55.
52. This sum includes a loan to the league of 30,000 fl. Gerber, "Kriegsrechnungen, I," 49. The XIII recounted Strasbourg's contributions in a letter to Elector John Frederick, Landgrave Philip, and the Smalkaldic war councillors, Strasbourg, 23 September 1546, in StA Weimar, Reg. I, pagg. 214–16, K, no. 3, fols. 13r–15r.
53. PC 4:311, no. 290.

54. The proposal to borrow money from other Protestant powers originated with the Southern District's council at Ulm, for whom Michael Han and others drafted a recommendation, in ibid., 274–75, no. 257. For Strasbourg's efforts to raise money and troops at Basel, see ibid., nos. 317, 323, 326–27, 333, 335, 347. For Frankfurt's plight, see ibid., nos. 313, 329; and see the report of Mattheus Molkenbur to Constance, in ibid., 356–58, no. 339. Strasbourg borrowed at Basel a total of 12,000 fl. at 5 percent, of which 4,000 fl. went to Constance. Körner, *Solidarités*, 388–89.

55. "Eines Kriegserfahrnen Bedencken, warumb man den Krieg aus dem Land zu beyern nicht versetzen lassen, vnnd wie man verhüten solle, daß durch die ergangene Keyserliche Acht der Leute Gemüther nicht abwendig gemacht werden mögen," Weimar, 23 August 1546, in Hortleder, ed., *Ursachen* (1645) 2:bk. 3, chap. 26.

56. Hortleder, ed., *Ursachen* (1645), 2:bk. 3, chap. 18. The desire to link up with the southern allies at Donauwörth, however, was responsible for the fact that the Saxon-Hessian forces did not march on the direct line via Nuremberg to Regensburg, which Charles's councillors had expected them to do. For an excellent overview, see Kannengiesser, *Karl V. und Maximilian Egmont*, 43–50.

57. I conflate two versions of this story from Barack, ed., *Zimmerische Chronik* 3:19, line 28–20, line 4, and 425, lines 14–23.

58. Asverus von Brandt to Duke Albert of Prussia, Camp near Donauwörth, 18 October 1546, in Brandt, ed., *Berichte und Briefe* 2:210, no. 72.

59. PC 4:399, no. 375, 413, no. 388, 426–27, no. 400. Strasbourg's envoys reported that "almost all the allies here favor the Common Penny in the form recommended by Jacob Sturm's memorial," though "Saxony, Hesse, and Augsburg are against it." Ibid., 448–49, no. 425 (27 October 1546).

60. PC 4:475, no. 449 n. 2.

61. Ibid., 476, no. 449 n. 5.

62. Ibid., 477, no. 449 n. 10.

63. On what follows, see Möllenberg, "Verhandlungen."

64. Asverus von Brandt to Duke Albert of Prussia, camp near Giengen, 20 October 1546, in Brandt, *Berichte und Briefe* 2:212, no. 73. See Landgrave Philip in Lenz, ed., *Briefwechsel* 2:475, no. 244: "Das in diesem glaubenskrieg kein glaubenszucht gehalten, solchs ist ubel gnug gethan, aber das kriegsvolk ist wie es ist."

65. PC 4:478, no. 450.

66. The instruction drafted for Sturm around 10 November in the camp near Giengen is in ibid., 479–81, no. 451. The notes to this and the preceding document adequately relate the context and subsequent history of this affair. Adam Trott seems to have been the choice of Landgrave Philip, though at first the allies spoke with near unanimity for Sturm.

67. Ibid., 488–90, no. 458, from which come the remaining quotes in this paragraph.

68. Ibid., 488, no. 458, in which Strasbourg's XIII refers to the recess of the meeting in camp near Giengen, which Sturm drafted on 14 November, though the version printed by Hortleder, ed., *Ursachen* (1645) 2:374–76, bk. 3, chap. 49, is dated 16 November 1546. Already on 16 November the envoys of Strasbourg, Ulm, and Augsburg wrote to Duke Ulrich to announce the decision to split the army and ask that he join their regimes in supplying funds for wintering over their troops. PC 4:485–86, no. 456. See Möllenberg, "Verhandlungen," 56.

69. PC 4:491–92, no. 460, from Sebastian Aitinger's minutes.

70. Ibid., 492, no. 460 n. 2.

71. Ibid., 494–95, no. 462; and there, too, the following quote.
72. In a letter to his chancellor, Dr. Günterode, and Sebastian Aitinger, 3 November 1546, quoted by Möllenberg, "Verhandlungen," 34.
73. Heuschen, *Konstanz*, 147–48.
74. PC 4:495–97, no. 463, from which the following quote comes. See Mentz, *Johann Friedrich* 3:46–49; Schüz, *Donaufeldzug*, 85–88; Brandi, *Kaiser Karl V.* 1:463–64.
75. Landgrave Philip to Elector John Frederick, Stuttgart, 27 November 1547, in StA Weimar, Reg. I, pagg. 190–93, J, no. 1, fols. 57r–60r, here at 58r; and the following quote is at 58v.
76. PC 4:495, no. 462.
77. Ibid., 501, no. 468. Sturm and Böcklin were at Plochingen on 25 November and at Stuttgart on the twenty-eighth. PC 4:497–98, no. 464, 499, no. 465 n. 2. For Ulrich's refusal to take part in the French project, see PC 4:505–6, no. 472.
78. He actually said "thunder [*dunner*]," but his meaning is clear. Möllenberg, "Verhandlungen," 54.
79. Lenz, ed., *Briefwechsel* 2:494–95, no. 252, quoting Sturm's words from memory.
80. The minutes of Sturm's report are in PC 4:507–8, no. 474, from AMS, XXI 1546, fols. 598–99.
81. PC 4:508, no. 474. The committee consisted of Jacob Sturm, Mathis Pfarrer, Hans von Lindenfels, and Conrad Joham.
82. Ibid., 513–14, no. 482.
83. Gerber, "Kriegsrechnungen, I," 47. See PC 4:516–17, no. 484, about the progress of the loan.
84. PC 4:536–40, no. 500. Möllenberg, "Verhandlungen," contains important corrections to Max Lenz's scathing indictment of the landgrave's apology, in Lenz, *Rechenschaftsbericht*.
85. PC 4:559, no. 516. Augsburg, unbeknownst to its allies, had made peace feelers while the league's diet was still meeting at Ulm. See Giovanni Verallo to Guidascanio Sforza, Dillingen, 19 November 1546, in NBD, pt. 1, vol. 9:357, no. 108: "La città d'Augusta fa negociare con Sua Maestà di ritornare in gratia, et questo con il mezzo d'uno qui, che stà nel campo nostro, nel quale confidiamo."
86. The document, which is in Conrad Joham's hand, is printed in PC 4:556, no. 514.
87. Ibid., 556–57, no. 514, from which come the quotes in this paragraph.
88. Ibid., 558, no. 515, from AMS, XXI 1546, fols. 649–50, from which come the quotes in this paragraph.
89. PC 4:558, no. 515 n. 3. See Holländer, *Straßburg im Schmalkaldischen Krieg*, 48–53.
90. Büheler, *Chronique* nos. 302–3. Büheler, a Catholic, was no friend of the preachers.
91. Lenz, ed., *Briefwechsel* 2:460, no. 240.
92. AMS, XXI 1546, fols. 545v, 547v (8 November 1546), 610r (15 December 1546).
93. Ibid., fols. 644r (4 January 1547), 648v–49r (5 January 1547), 653r (8 January 1547).
94. AMS, XXI 1547, fol. 22r (24 January 1547).
95. Lenz, ed., *Briefwechsel* 2:460, no. 240: "Es ist ja unser krieg ein krieg Gottes ... Und warlich, fiengen die oberen das an, ... es solte wunderbarlich von statten gohn, dann der handel ja Gottes ist." The presence of a crusading spirit during the early stages of the war is confirmed by Waldeck, "Publizistik, II," 70.
96. In his tract, "Von der kirchen mengel und fahl," of 1546. See Bellardi, *Geschichte*,

38–39. The principal Bucerian texts of this time are now superbly edited by Bellardi in *BDS* 17:153–345; to which should be added Hedio's piece in Bellardi, "Ein Bedacht Hedios."

97. The standard study, Waldeck, "Publizistik, I–II," is extremely one-sided. Hühns, "'Nationale' Propaganda," shows that the Imperial propagandists were just as active and effective as those of the league.

98. See Waldeck, "Publizistik, I," 9–36, and "Publizistik, II," 46–59.

99. Quoted by Waldeck, "Publizistik, II," 71. The most radical attack on the emperor's legitimacy came in the Smalkaldic commanders' second apology, or "Verwahrungsschrift," of 11 August 1546, which is printed by Hortleder, ed., *Ursachen* (1645), bk. 3, chap. 24, and described by Waldeck, "Publizistik, I," 25–26.

100. See Barnes, *Prophecy and Gnosis*, chap. 1, who suggests the role of the lost war in the growth of Lutheran apocalypticism.

101. Gebauer, "Die Stimmung katholischer Bauern," 437.

102. The best detailed account of the peace process is by Holländer, *Straßburg im Schmalkaldischen Krieg*, 56–94, which is now supported by the documents in *PC* 4. The most stalwart opponent of peace was, as usual, Constance. Its regime wrote angrily of the Swabian Smalkaldic cities' deliberations on the issue in a letter to Strasbourg, Constance, 11 January 1547, of which a copy is in StA Weimar, Reg. I, pagg. 710–20, AA, no. 7, fols. 26r–29r.

103. As Landgrave Philip noted to Elector John Frederick, Kassel, 4 February 1547, in StA Weimar, Reg. I, pagg. 710–20, AA, no. 7, fols. 18r–20r, here at 18r.

104. Sieh-Burens, *Oligarchie*, 157.

105. Brady, *Ruling Class*, 85 n. 111, 273, 273 n. 52.

106. *PC* 4:585–86, no. 542. See Holländer, *Straßburg im Schmalkaldischen Krieg*, 59–61. Some hints as to how important Charles's councillors thought Strasbourg to the pacification of South Germany are contained in the Italian reports, in *NBD*, pt. 1, vol. 9:427, no. 128, 427 n. 1, and 440, no. 130. Peace overtures also came from Jean de Naves, who sent an Imperial paymaster, Wolfgang Haller von Hallerstein, to speak with Sturm and Conrad Joham. Jakob Sturm to Wolfgang Rehlinger, Strasbourg, 4 February 1547, in *PC* 4:593, no. 547.

107. *PC* 4:585, no. 542 n. 2.

108. Ibid., 588–91, no. 545, from AMS, XXI 1547, fols. 77r–83r.

109. Holländer, *Straßburg im Schmalkaldischen Krieg*, 62–63; *PC* 4:591, no. 545 n. 9. The incriminating passage is quoted by Holländer (53) and in *PC* 4:559, no. 515 n. 3.

110. *PC* 4:656, no. 586 n. 8. Another opponent, the mason Conrad Kruss, was thrown in jail for two months and then banished for five years (though he was let back in after one year's exile).

111. The following is based on Brady, *Ruling Class*, 259–75, which analyzes this document and places the replies in their social context.

112. Quoted in ibid., 271.

113. AMS, XXI 1547, fols. 41r, 63v, 64r, 65r; *PC* 4:656, no. 586 n. 7.

114. Philip Melanchthon to King Christian of Denmark, [Wittenberg], 3 February 1547, in *MBW* 6:37, no. 4576, though in the accompanying report (ibid., 38, no. 4577), Melanchthon noted that Duke Ulrich had, in fact, already submitted.

115. See Jean Sturm and Ulrich Geiger to King Francis I, Strasbourg, 19 February 1547, in *PC* 4:608–9, no. 559, in which they try to put the best face on the city's negotiations for peace and ask for another French envoy to Strasbourg. They also explain to the king how the negotiations began through a mediator, "qui ad biennium in hac civitate habitavit, vir copiosus et locuples, unus

ex sociis Fuggerianis et caesaris creditoribus, caesaris etiam consiliarius; Rellingerus ei cognomen est." What they were telling the French agents is revealed in a letter of Sébastian de l'Aubespine, abbot of Bassefontaine, to King Francis I, Ligny, 26 March 1547: "J'ay laissé Mr. Celius [= Ulrich Geiger] là, & depuis renuoyé [Johannes] Sturmius, afin d'y faire la plus grande poursuite qui'il sera possible: bien entendant que ce coup rompu, jamais la Ville n'entrera en negotiation auec l'Empereur." Ribier, ed., *Lettres et Mémoires* 1:634, quoted in *PC* 4:671–72, no. 597 n. 2.

116. Lenz, ed., *Briefwechsel* 2:460–61, no. 240. There was no popular pro-French sentiment among the native Strasbourgeois. In the poll of 19 January 1547 only one patrician, Bernhard Wurmser, suggested that Strasbourg might seek French protection. Holländer, *Straßburg im Schmalkaldischen Krieg*, 54. This Bernhard Wurmser was not the member of the XIII of this name, who had died in 1540. Brady, *Ruling Class*, 356–57. Pariset, "L'activité de Jacques Sturm," 261, is simply wrong to write that in January and February 1547, "Strasbourg est partagée entre deux partis: l'un favorable à la France."

117. *PC* 4:599, no. 553 n. 1, where the German text of Sturm's document is printed for the first time. The king sent an agent, who arrived too late to accomplish anything. Ibid., 599–600, no. 553, and n. 3 on 601.

118. Knecht, *Francis I*, 416–18.

119. Druffel, ed., *Beiträge* 1:57, no. 96, quoted in *PC* 4:655, no. 586 n. 4.

120. *PC* 4:605–6, no. 556, 615–16, no. 563. Landgrave Philip had written to Jacob Sturm from Spangenberg, 23 January 1547, about how poor the elector's prospects really were. Ibid., 578–79, no. 533. John Frederick had invaded Moritz's lands on 24 December and attempted a badly prepared and fruitless siege of Leipzig. See Mentz, *Johann Friedrich* 3:62–69. On Duke Ulrich's surrender, see ARCEG 5:6 lines 5–7, no. 5, and 10, no. 7; Lanz, ed., *Correspondenz* 2:524–28; Stälin, *Wirtembergische Geschichte* 4:456–58; Press, "Herzog Ulrich," 132–33.

121. *PC* 4:593, no. 547 n. 4.

122. The instruction of 12 February 1547 is in ibid., 603–5, no. 555. See Holländer, *Straßburg im Schmalkaldischen Krieg*, 63–64, on the envoys' selection. Marx Hag(en) was the son of Philips Hag(en), a merchant who had tried to force his way into the Constofel zum Hohensteg in 1514–23. The young man had studied law in France and in Italy and had entered the Senate in 1546; this mission opened his way into the XXI in May 1547. His knowledge of Latin, Italian, and French was admired, and his death in 1551, three years after his mental health had begun to fail, was much mourned. See *PC* 3:521, no. 486; ibid., 4:612, no. 561; Ridderikhoff, et al., eds., *Les livres des procurateurs . . . d'Orléans*, 1, pt. 2, sect. 2:198–99, no. 864; Hatt, *Liste*, 446; AMS, XXI 1547, fol. 256v; AMS, XXI 1548, fols. 307v, 48r; Ficker-Winckelman 1:12; Brady, *Ruling Class*, 64–66.

123. *PC* 4:604, no. 555.

124. Ibid., 604–5.

125. Ibid., 600, no. 554. The landgrave's reply from Kassel on 19 February expressed concern for his son, whom he had sent for safety to Strasbourg, and for the shipments of French money that were expected to pass via Strasbourg to him. Ibid., 610–12, no. 560.

126. See ibid., 612, no. 561. The writer, Heinrich Walther, was secretary to the Small Senate, that is, the Senate minus the XXI, which sat as the city's Chamber Court.

127. For Charles's situation at this time, see Brandi, *Kaiser Karl V.* 1:464–66, from whom I take the phrase, "lord of South Germany." On the situation of Charles

and the Council of Trent, see Jedin, *Council of Trent* 2:396–443.

128. PC 4:623–24, no. 562.
129. Antoine Perrenot de Granvelle (1517–86), bishop of Arras, later bishop of Utrecht, cardinal, and grand chancellor. See the biography by Van Durme, *Antoon Perrenot*. The Perrenots and Naves counted as "Germans," because their places of origin lay in the Empire.
130. PC 4:620–24, no. 566, here at 620.
131. See Antoine Perrenot de Granvelle's report to his father, in *Papiers d'état* 3:251–52, quoted in *PC* 4:621, no. 566 n. 2. The fine offered by Strasbourg was indeed puny, for very small Swabian towns, such as Ravensburg, Dinkelsbühl, and Biberach, paid this amount. Brecht and Ehmer, *Südwestdeutsche Reformationsgeschichte*, 288–89.
132. PC 4:624, no. 566 n. 9.
133. Ibid., 625–33, no. 569, draft by Johann Meyer with corrections by Jacob Sturm. From it come the quotes in this paragraph.
134. PC 4:633, no. 569 n. 33.
135. This and the remaining quotes in this paragraph come from the envoys' instruction, ibid., 635–40, no. 572.
136. The Strasbourgeois clearly appreciated the fact that the city's frontier position was responsible for the relatively mild terms they were offered. An anonymous letter to Hesse, probably from Bucer's circle, noted on 9 March that "den Straspurgern geht keiser so gutig entgegen in bedenken der gelegenheit mit Frankrich." Ibid., 644, no. 576.
137. Ibid., 639, no. 572 n. 14.
138. Ibid., 654, no. 577 n. 1. Friedrich von Gottesheim, member of a wealthy family of ennobled (in 1513) Hagenau merchants, purchased citizenship at Strasbourg in 1528 and married Agnes von Duntzenheim, Conrad's daughter and sister to Batt and Jacob. He had extensive properties and ties to mercantile and noble families, and he succeeded Jacob Sturm as scholarch in 1553. Brady, *Ruling Class*, 315–16. This embassy provides an interesting check on local tradition. Writing a generation later, Bernhard Hertzog substitutes Mathis Pfarrer for Gottesheim and says that Jacob Sturm was sent, "dieweil er dem Kayeser bekant, vnnd vmb seiner Tugendt willen angenem war." Hertzog, *Chronicon Alsatiae*, pt. 6, 279.
139. PC 4:649, no. 580. Charles V's Treaty of Heilbronn with Ulrich had been signed on 3 January 1547. See ARCEG 5:6, lines 5–7, no. 5, and 10, lines 9–11, no. 7; Press, "Herzog Ulrich," 132–33; Brecht and Ehmer, *Südwestdeutsche Reformationsgeschichte*, 287.
140. PC 4:654–57, no. 586. Charles was to rejoin his army at Nuremberg, which he left on 28 March to join King Ferdinand and Duke Moritz a few days later at Tirschenreuth on the edge of the Bohemian Forest. From there they moved via Plaun and down the Mulde River toward the decisive battle with John Frederick's forces at Mühlberg on 27 April 1547. Brandi, *Kaiser Karl V.* 1:471–73.
141. PC 4:658, no. 587. Among those present was Prince Maximilian, King Ferdinand's heir.
142. The terms are printed in ibid., 658–60, no. 588, a text that bears Sturm's own corrections. There is no evidence that either Hag or Gottesheim had any part in this event, though Gremp was sent on to Nuremberg to secure from the Imperial chancellery the documents of "absolution." Ibid., 658, no. 587.
143. See Heinrich Schetzel's report to Landgrave Philip, in PC 4:661, no. 590: "Item der stadtschreiber solt gesagt haben, die von Strasb[urg] werden den vortrag nicht annemen." He also collects most of the other stories.
144. Lenz, ed., *Briefwechsel* 2:490–92, no. 250. The letter is dated "Basel" and

signed "Alban Kreutzach." From it come the three following quotes.
145. Ibid., 498, no. 253. On the landgrave's own betrayal of John Frederick, see Brandi, *Kaiser Karl V.* 1:476–77.
146. PC 4:662–65, no. 592.
147. The notices about the preachers are collected in ibid., 668–69, no. 593 n. 10. See Bellardi, *Geschichte*, 30–31.
148. See the long interview of the Senate & XXI with them on 11 April 1547, in AMS, XXI 1547, fols. 178v–183r. Their memorial is edited in *BDS* 17:207–44; and see the analysis by Strauss, *Luther's House of Learning*, 44–45. On 23 May 1547 the Senate & XXI appointed Peter Sturm, Claus Kniebis, Bastian Erb, and Jacob Meyer to deliberate on the memorial, which they did for several months. AMS, XXI 1547, fols. 265v, 267v, 275r, 326r–v, 348v, 403v–404r, 414r. See also Bucer's "Ein Summarischer vergriff," in *BDS* 17:132 line 23–133, line 2, plus Bellardi's introduction at 207.
149. Lenz, ed., *Briefwechsel* 2:493, no. 251.
150. Jean Sturm to Sébastian de l'Aubespine, abbot of Bassefontaine, Strasbourg, 4 April 1547, in PC 4:672, no. 597: "Nos hic motum plebis et seditionem metuimus; causam coniicis." Bishop Erasmus conveyed the same fears to the Imperial commissioner, Christoph von Schauenburg, who stopped at Saverne on 22 April. Ibid., 694, no. 615.
151. PC 4:683, no. 608 n. 1. Lersner wrote much the same thing to Elector John Frederick, Kassel, 18 April 1547, in ibid., 680, no. 604 n. 1. Already from Nördlingen on 19 March, Sturm had written his colleagues about the rumors circulating at court about Strasbourg and asked them to curb the preachers. Ibid., 655–56, no. 586. The Bernese regime wrote on 6 April that they had heard "landmärs wis . . ., (wiewoll wir dem keinen glouben geben), das ir mit kei. Mt. vertragen und den füssvall gethan söllend haben." Ibid., 674, no. 600. See also the news from Nuremberg, that most of the pro-Imperial party had left the city. Ibid., 692, no. 614 n. 2.
152. PC 4:669, no. 593 n. 11.
153. His report of 9 April 1547 is in ibid., 676–77, no. 602, and his instruction for the next round of talks is in ibid., 677–79, no. 603. There was also a mandate announcing to the Empire and the hereditary lands that Strasbourg was reconciled and that its burghers were to be allowed to trade and enjoy their property as usual. Ibid., 677, no. 602 n. 8.
154. Jacob Lersner to Elector John Frederick, Kassel, 18 April 1547, in StA Weimar, pagg. 177–182, H, no. 6, fols. 124r–125r.
155. Kniebis's opposition to Sturm's grand policy is described in this volume, chap. 7. The other three members, Jakob Meyer (XIIIer), Bastian Erb (XVer), and Gregorius Pfitzer (XXIer), all counseled resistance in the survey of 19 January 1547. See Brady, *Ruling Class*, 261–62 for Meyer and Erb. Their recommendation is in PC 4:679–80, no. 604, and the address they drafted is in ibid., 685–88, no. 610.
156. Based on the minutes of the Senate & XXI, in PC 4:691–93, no. 614, and on Schauenburg's report to the Emperor Charles V, Geissbach bei Schauenburg, 26 April 1547, in ibid., 694–95, no. 615.
157. PC 4:692, no. 614; and Sturm and Pfarrer repeated this assurance a little later (693). In his report to the emperor, Schauenburg remarked on "die varlichkeit, das die herren noch in stond, . . . und damit die vorgemelten hern mitler zeit das böss kraut ausreiten mögen und die widerwilligen, wie si schon angefangen zu thon, straffen, die den hetten mögen gleich uf einmal ufrurisch sein, so hett ich mit dem eid lenger still gestanden." Ibid., 694, no. 615.
158. The oath is quoted by Holländer, "Straßburgs Politik im Jahre 1552," 6 n. 3.

Its constitutional significance is discussed by Winckelmann, "Straßburgs Verfassung," 499–50.

159. This news seems to have arrived at Strasbourg on 2 May, according to Ulrich Geiger, in PC 4:698, no. 620.

160. Emperor Charles V to the Senate & XXI of Strasbourg, Camp near Wittenberg, 12 May 1547, in ibid., 700–701, no. 623.

161. AMS, R 29/110; AMS, XXI 1547, fols. 221r–22v, 231r–v, 232r–v, 233r, 240r, 242v–43r, 248r, 250r–v, 253v, 255r, 261v, 265v, 271r–v, 274v, 292r–v, 301r, 345v, 362r; PC 4:688, no. 610 n. 17, all from late April through July 1547.

162. AMS, XXI 1547, fols. 363v–64r (13 July 1547).

163. Ibid., fol. 4v.

164. Ibid., fol. 419r–v.

165. Ibid., fols. 274r–75r (30 May 1547), where Sturm admits that he has done nothing for the committee to advise about "vicious living and the destruction of sound doctrine."

166. Ibid., fol. 345r–v (27 June 1547), and see fols. 347v–48v (28 June 1547).

167. Their report of 31 May 1547 is in PC 4:702–3, no. 626. The origins of this commission lie in a report from the treasury board (*Drei auf dem Pfennigthurm*) of 2 April 1547, in AMS, XXI 1547, fols. 156r–57r.

168. PC 4:765, no. 668. They also suggested debasement of the treasury's store of "old, good coins" and plundering the ecclesiastical corporations, convents, and welfare and school funds.

169. The following is based on Roper, *Holy Household*, esp. 56–82. Her judgment on the urban reformation (3) is this: "Heir to the master craftsmen's own politics, articulated by their guilds, the politics of the Reformation gave voice to the interests and perceptions of the married craftsmen who ruled over their wives and organized the household's subordinate labour force of men and women."

170. Brandi, *Kaiser Karl V.* 1:475–78. The phrase comes from one of the many reformation parodies of the late medieval German hymn, "O du armer Judas, was hast du getan." Examples in Liliencron, *Historische Volkslieder* 4:175, no. 476; 464–67, no. 572; 575–76, no. 609; and the melody in 5:25–26. Luther parodied it twice at the end of "Wider Hans Worst," in WA 51:570, line 28, 571, line 17. On the history of this song, see the references in ibid., 570 n. 2. On the landgrave's submission, see Preuschen, ed., "Bericht."

9

The Reformation Crisis, 1547–1549

Interim, we will hear
Of terrible deeds of war;
Interim, the Common Man
Will suffer all through the land;
Interim, Christianity will groan;
Interim, Christ will come,
To save us from all ills.*

The pall of defeat over Charles V's last years as emperor—the princes' revolt of 1552, Charles's abdication, the Peace of Augsburg in 1555—makes it difficult to imagine how invincible he appeared in mid-1547. His victory over the Protestants left three questions open. Would Charles retain military control of Augsburg, Ulm, and Württemberg's castles, add Strasbourg and Constance, and thereby dominate South Germany? Would he reconstruct Imperial authority in a centralized, "Latin" manner or secure his victory in a traditional German manner through federations? Would he settle the German schism via negotiations in the Empire or by forcing the Protestants to attend and obey the Council of Trent?

THE "ARMORED DIET" AT AUGSBURG

As the emperor traveled southward in the summer of 1547, Jacob Sturm reflected on the strategic situation.[1] If the emperor came as near as Ulm or Speyer, Sturm thought, "he will not neglect to visit this city, too, for he some time ago expressed the wish to see it. His desire, too, to enhance his reputation abroad, especially in France, will bring him hither to display his power over this city, which has abroad a greater reputation for strength than it deserves."[2] In all of southwestern Germany, "there is hardly a fortified place not in his hands, except for Strasbourg, and it is to be feared that he will want to have this one as well." Charles had many reasons for revenging himself on Strasbourg, which "was the principal city in the league and was more disobedient than any other."[3] What, then, to do? In the event of a siege, "in the end, as one says, the city must 'come to the stake' [*zur stangen kommen*] and surrender." Sturm, a man of words rather than weapons, thought of approaching the emperor through the Granvelles, father and son, but he needn't have bothered. Charles V did not come to Strasbourg, for he had something much grander in mind: an Imperial political settlement as an opening, he hoped, to a religious one.

The beaten Protestants misjudged the emperor's intentions, perhaps because the Latin character of his court played to their deep prejudices against Latin ways, which they identified with "monarchy," that is, centralized, military absolutism. This, however, was not Charles's way. After discussions with King Ferdinand, he decided to negotiate both a general political settlement along federal lines, the traditional way in the Empire, and an interim agreement on religion.[4] This meant an Imperial Diet, which he called to Augsburg in late summer. It was called "the armored diet," since, as Jacob Sturm noted, "because of the many soldiers present, this Diet is not like others."[5] This longest diet of the sixteenth century sat at Augsburg from 1 September 1547 until 30 June 1548—ten full months, Sturm's longest Imperial Diet and his last.[6] The diet's agenda was very long, but for Sturm and Strasbourg the central item was the future of religion, the one subject not covered by their recent treaty with the emperor.[7]

Before the diet sat, the emperor proposed to establish a vast Imperial league (*Reichsbund*).[8] Although many southern powers favored something like a reconstituted Swabian League, Sturm pointed out that Strasbourg had "experienced more harm and disadvantages from the most recent [i.e., Smalkaldic] league and from the Swabian League and other past alliances," and he advised against bringing the emperor's scheme before the Schöffen, "who just now have no more desire for alliances, and since the terms of the league are unknown, it could not be brought before the Large Senate."[9] Strasbourg was moving back toward the old policy of nonalignment, a fact suggested, too, by the city's failure to send Sturm to the assembly on the Imperial league, which the emperor called to Ulm before the diet.[10] His absence made no difference, for the emperor's scheme, which he revealed on 28 July 1547, offered not a reconstituted Swabian League based on the South but a grand union of the Empire with the hereditary lands, Austria, Burgundy, and the Netherlands.[11] He embodied this idea in his "Burgundian Treaty," which he announced to the diet on 27 March 1548, proposing Imperial protection for the Netherlands (against France) in return for (unspecified) Netherlandish contributions to the Empire's expenses.[12] In this intelligent plan, Charles of Ghent proposed to rule the Empire from its richest part, the Netherlands, rather than from one of its poorest, Austria.[13]

Not Charles's plan but the fate of religion was on Jacob Sturm's mind as he hurried off to Augsburg, where he arrived on 6 September 1547 in the company of Hans von Odratzheim, a rich young member of the XXI of no special experience.[14] The war had cost the fifty-nine-year-old Strasbourgeois none of his old prestige among the urban politicians. Stralsund's mayor, Bartholomäus Sastrow, captured in his memoirs Sturm's image and mood at this time. One day during the diet, he relates, the Stralsunders entertained Sturm, who astounded them with his knowledge of the histories of Pomerania and the bishopric of Cammin—a region about as remote from Strasbourg as one could get and still be in the Empire:

> In short, it was as lucid, complete and accurate a summary of the subject as if he had just finished studying it. Our counsellors greatly admired his wonderful memory. Verily, he was a superior, experienced, eloquent, and prudent man, who had had his share in many memorable days from an Imperial as well as from a provincial view. . . . Without him, Sleidan could never have written his *History*. . . . Nobody throughout the empire realized to the same degree as he did the motto, "*Usus me genuit, mater me peperit memoria.*"[15]

Sastrow continued with a story that characterizes Sturm's attitude and temperament perfectly: "When a person of note asked him if the towns of the League of Smalkalden were all at peace with the emperor, he answered: "*Constantia tantum desideratur.*" "Constance alone holds out." This critical but sympathetic comment perfectly sums up both Sturm's mistrust of radical aims and his preference for discussion, argument, negotiation, delay, compromise, and political tactic.

The diet's ten-month session tested to an extraordinary degree Sturm's faith in such means. For nine months, against pressure from the Imperial court, rebuffs by the electors and princes, and bullying by everyone, Sturm held the urban envoys together behind his triple policy of refusing to recognize the Council of Trent as a "free Christian council," requesting that the schism be settled by a truly free council, and opposing the diet's direct consideration of religion. Sturm aimed to separate the schism and its settlement from the business of political reconstruction by the diet, which, in his view, concerned "how peace and quiet can meanwhile be maintained among the rulers."[16] He managed to maintain urban solidarity behind his policy until mid-January 1548, when Cristoforo Cardinal Madruzzo of Trent reported that Pope Paul would neither return the council to Trent nor allow the emperor to settle the German question in Germany. This news turned Charles's policy from the Council of Trent to the solution Sturm most feared—an interim religious settlement.[17] Sturm, sensing that Charles would announce resumption of the colloquies, wrote home on 15 January that "it would not be unhelpful, my lords, if you would send Martin Bucer as soon as possible to Ulm, . . . where he could wait to see if we need him here."[18] He guessed wrong, for the emperor announced not a colloquy of theologians but a sixteen-member committee of the diet to frame a recommendation on the regulation of religion.[19]

Although the committee, in which Sturm and Jörg Besserer sat for the cities, met only three times in February, its minutes throw important light on Jacob Sturm's view of the causes of the German Reformation. In the first session he tried to establish his main point, the distinction between the political competence of the diet and the religious competence of a council, colloquy, or other assembly containing clerical experts. "I am not equal to this task," he began,

> but for obedience's sake I will try to do it. Since the matter has been referred to a general council and our task is to deal with an interim arrangement alone, I will serve and am content to let others propose ways and means. If religion is to be dealt with, however, it is necessary to include others and in proper form.[20]

In the committee's second session on 11 February, Sturm responded to provoking comments by the Carmelite Eberhard Billick of Cologne and Chancellor Eck of Bavaria, stating more strongly the need for a German national council to heal the schism in the Empire.[21] "There can be no lasting peace without composition of the religious schism," he warned, but because the pope has blocked the general council, "the German nation must make a beginning and not wait for other peoples to act." "The German nation is sick," Sturm said, "and I cannot imagine why it should not heal itself through a national council."

Now the committee's deliberations turned to the cause of the schism, which, Sturm asserted in reply to Chancellor Eck of Bavaria, was not the alleged "robbery of the church [*spolium*]" the many, grievous, and irreformable abuses. "For many centuries," he said,

> all pious churchmen have described and complained of the church's fall and its need for reformation. But nothing happened, and the worse the abuses became, the worse conditions were, and the abuses have now thoroughly penetrated doctrine and Christian life, as everyone knows, and the failure to improve them, despite the writings and preaching, has caused this schism.

Since the bishops would not act, Sturm continued, the temporal rulers had done so, and justly, for the Bible and the canons taught how the church's properties should be employed to support the churches, the schools, and the poor. If the Empire were to have peace, "improvement of the abuses in teaching and way of life" had to come before restoration of properties. But, "first we must find a way to live together"—a political settlement—before the religious settlement could be taken in hand. Sturm had in mind a reinstatement of the old truce and then a resumption of the old colloquys, for before there could be a restoration of properties, "first we must agree about religion and what constitutes an abuse of it, for no restitution can precede an agreement on religion." Otherwise, he warned, there might be another rebellion, though "I don't want to speak of rebellion, for I know my duty to obey the emperor, but freely, and on that I will stake my life. Whether it [rebellion] can be justified before God, I don't care to say, but I believe that we must speak again about reaching agreement on religion and about what is and is not an abuse." His own Strasbourg had nothing to fear from this procedure, he said, for "I have never taken anyone's property; the city of Strasbourg has never driven anyone out; and the goods have been employed there, where they belong. For 400 years there has been no serious effort at reform."[22] In these remarks Sturm framed his triple policy: peace, reform, and reunion—in that order.

Sturm realized that his strategy rested on the central issue of the Reformation's legitimacy, and he turned to this point during the committee's final session on 20 February. "If it were true that we have abandoned the 1,500-year-old Apostolic religion," he began, "and the other side has maintained it, not only would restitution . . . be just, but His Majesty ought to force us to recant and accept again the same old Catholic faith." The Protestants naturally deny that "and hope that we have the true, old, Apostolic faith. Our theologians offer to explain how this can be so." This "chief dispute about religion . . . has been referred to a free, Christian council to be decided according to God's Word and the writings of holy teachers." Premature restitution—property, churches, episcopal jurisdictions—before reform would leave the Protestants without pastors or churches. That is no peaceful interim arrangement."

Sturm now turned from defense to attack. Although the plaintiffs claim to have been expropriated, he argued, it is well known that the properties belong not to them

> but to the church, which is why they are variously called *bona ecclesiae, pauperum, patrimonium Christi oder crucifixi*—those are the true owners. A "church," however, is the community of believers in one place, so that a principality has many churches, and each city and village has one. The clergy are the administrators [*dispensatores*] of these common properties as public properties [*bona publica*], not their lords; and many laws, rules, and written confessions specify how they may use the properties. . . . All other uses are sacrilegious.

If restitution should precede a doctrinal concord and reform, he noted, "we at Strasbourg must imitate St. Ambrose, who said to the emperor: 'If you take the church's goods, we will take up collections and see how to support our poor.'"

In his closing remarks to the committee, Sturm unsheathed the sharpest weapon in his armory, the memory of 1525. "If the common people, who want the true Christian religion, would see it suppressed, they would suffer and even die to prevent it [*darumb werden sie leiden und sterben*], which would lead to insurrection [*uffruhr*] and much suffering by innocent people." He contrasted this popular zeal with his own broad-mindedness.

> I am not impassioned about what is done in public [*was publicum betrifft*]. I would like to see worship follow the teachings of the old Fathers, and I

would not resist, except in spirit [*dan mit dem gemütt*]. If I cannot say "yes," I will obey and suffer whatever the emperor commands. But the common people will not do that. To live a Christian and godfearing way of life requires unity in religion, which is why it was decided to hold a general council, or, lacking that, a national one or a diet. . . . And even if there is no council, why should we not help to suppress the abuses and thereby quiet the common people?[23]

No matter how the theologians disputed doctrine, no matter how the clergy lived, Sturm warned the committee, the only guarantee of religious peace was popular consent. It was an argument calculated to impress, above all, Chancellor Eck, whom Sturm had first met at Ulm during the terrible spring of 1525. In playing "the card of 1525," Sturm tried to revitalize the emotions of those days and to manipulate them through the artful contrast between common people's fanaticism for the gospel and his own aristocratic tolerance. One of his best performances, this masterpiece of Sturmian oratory.

All to no avail, for when the reform commission stalled, Charles V turned to direct measures and issued a mandate regulating ritual, property, and doctrine, which was to be enforced until a general council should end the schism. Hence the name *interim*.[24] His councillors, as they rallied support for it through negotiations with the estates *ad partem*, lobbied the free cities in three groups: the Catholic cities, the Protestant cities, and Strasbourg.[25] Sturm, of course, resisted from the first, and at the end of an audience on 23 March, Chancellor Granvelle took him by the arm to ask, "But how can such matters be resolved?" Sturm's characteristic reply, that "it might be helped if learned men came together and discussed it without quarreling [*gezenk*]," caused a rare crack in the chancellor's charm, and he poured out his anger at the Protestants for having brought on this terrible schism. "Think," he shot at Sturm,

> how this split had damaged our religion. For the German nation was esteemed before all others for its virtue, which has all run into the sand. The princes have neither faith nor honor, the nobles are mere bandits, and the cities contain only usurers. Thus the Germans have lost the virtues for which their ancestors were famed.[26]

If Jacob Sturm really wanted to know his own reputation, Granvelle offered, "it is said that you are one of the chief causes of this thing." Realizing he must not rise to this provocation, Sturm replied, "I must bear whatever is said of me. It is said unjustly, however, because those who know my deeds and thoughts, would speak differently of me." Now Granvelle's voice grew darker, and he warned Sturm that "you must see how the thing can be mended, for if you do not, it will redound to great personal disadvantage for you." Once more Sturm refused the provocation and said, "A Christian may suffer what he cannot accept." Martin Luther, now more than a year in his grave, could not have said it better.

This exchange between men who had once, in the palmier days of the colloquies, collaborated in a spirit of mutual admiration, seemed to portend menace for resisters to the interim. Sturm probably wanted to sign the interim, for he got the emperor's permission for Bucer to come over from Ulm—Charles said he would tolerate no Wittenbergers in these discussions— to confer with the Brandenburg and Palatine electors about the document.[27] At first glance Bucer admired the text. This is hardly surprising, for, contrary to legend, the Interim of Augsburg embodied the views not of the Catholic militants but of the Catholic "mediating theology," whose spokesmen still believed reunion was possible.[28] Gradually, however Bucer's attitude hardened, and on 13 April he wrote to Bishop Julius Pflug of Naumburg his reasons why the formula could not be accepted. This led on the same day to his arrest, from which he was released on the twentieth after signing the formula—"under duress," he later wrote. He started immediately for home.[29] This incident began a backfire to Sturm's strategy, for whatever propaganda value Bucer's signature—however obtained—had to the interim's proponents, the bitter memory of his humiliation at Augsburg launched Bucer into a campaign against the interim that brought Strasbourg to the brink of revolution.

For the moment Sturm had heavy sledding at Augsburg, for the two upper houses' favorable responses to the interim put tremendous pressure on the cities, whose solidarity was weakened, in any case, by other issues.[30] The most damaging defection came from Nuremberg, whose envoys refused, Sturm wrote home, "to give us at least a summary of their instructions, saying only that the instructions were appropriate and that their lords took the matter as seriously as others did. We have heard, however, that they will neither accept nor refuse the interim."[31] The other cities fell away one by one, until only Strasbourg, Frankfurt, Constance, and Lindau held out against the interim.[32]

Sturm was the obvious key to the situation, and on 28 June 1548, Granvelle tried to break his resistance. Eschewing the familiarity of their previous encounters, the Burgundian addressed Sturm through Heinrich Hass, an Imperial councillor formerly in Palatine service.[33] To Hass's opening remark, that the emperor "is not a little displeased" at Strasbourg's resistance, Sturm replied with a petition—he handed over a copy—which asked the emperor not to force the interim on Strasbourg.[34] Granvelle, a French speaker, asked Hass to interpret the petition for him, and after a brief interruption Hass pointed out that the majority of the diet had placed this decision in the emperor's hands, and that the chancellor could not forward to him Strasbourg's request for an exception. Sturm replied—in Latin for Granvelle's benefit—that the referral to the emperor had been intended to cover "only external matters, which concern peace and justice, and not the disputed articles on religion, which have been referred to a free, Christian council to judge after hearing both sides." These words repeated Sturm's basic line: temporal affairs belonged before the diet, spiritual ones before a council, though not the papal one. This defense of two jurisdictions sounded odd from one whose government wielded both swords, temporal and spiritual, but Sturm nonetheless stuck to it. He told Granvelle,

My government asks this only because they are convinced in their consciences, that if they accept all provisions of the Interim, they will act against God and their souls' salvation, so that His Majesty should tolerate the other side until a settlement by a free, Christian council. For it is a grievous thing for a Christian to act against his conscience. And even if one errs, still he wants to be heard and instructed by a free council, for St. Paul says, *"wer wider sin gewissen handelt, bauet zu der hollen."*[35]

To this he added the aristocratic tolerance, nearly a Sturmian trademark, first expressed in his 1525 memorial on public worship in the exclamation, "Both sides are Christians, may God have mercy!"[36] "We believe," he said, "that there are godfearing people on both sides, whose consciences are entirely opposed to each other. From this sprang the religious schism, and it is difficult for any pious Christian to confess or act other than as he holds for right and Christian in his conscience." As his government was prepared to obey the emperor "in all other matters, which concern life and property," Sturm asked Granvelle to lay Strasbourg's petition before the monarch.

In response the chancellor offered his view—as radical in its own way as Sturm's—that Strasbourg promised to accept whatever contributed to peace and justice in the Empire, and because this interim conformed to Catholic doctrine and could not, therefore, be opposed on grounds of conscience, it must be accepted as a decision of the Imperial Diet. He mockingly asked Sturm and Odratzheim, "Are you so clever that you wanted to believe and stand alone against all Christendom and thereby separate yourselves from it? You had no right to make such changes without the permission of Christendom and its heads." Sturm countered this argument—precisely Charles V's riposte to Luther at Worms in 1521—with his well-thumbed "card of 1525." Because the matters at issue "concern the soul's salvation and eternal life," he said, "it would be a terrible thing to force people against their consciences, especially as it would burden only the pious, who fear to displease God. For the others, who care nothing about religion [*die nichts nach der religion fragen*], it's all the same." To force the believers, however, "would not only not contribute to peace and harmony, it would create a great movement."

Granvelle had had enough of this sparring with Sturm. Now visibly upset ["*etwas bewegt*"], he warned the Strasbourgeois that more was at stake here than getting the diet's unanimous acceptance of the interim, namely, their own city's future relations with the emperor, and he repeated the old charges of Francophilia. "Let the French say what they will," Sturm responded, "we have no bond [*gemeinschaft*] with the French"—to which the chancellor replied, "He who knows the French, will not much rely on them."

At this point the interview ended, but as Sturm and Odratzheim were leaving the building, a servant called them back for one last exchange.

"When we said that faith cannot be forced," Sturm reported, "Granvelle replied, 'yes, one cannot force a non-Christian, but an apostate may be forced with fire.' We responded that while one might kill such a person with fire, he couldn't be made thereby to change his beliefs." Here the interview ended, and it ended with a significant victory for Sturm, for the chancellor did not set a date by which Strasbourg must conform to the interim.

Sturm's interview with Granvelle at Augsburg on 28 June throws a revealing light on the emerging language of confessional discourse. Sturm employed two highly characteristic two-edged weapons. One was the slippery appeal to conscience, which appeared now as an individual, now as a magisterial, attribute. Sturm's usage of "conscience" was vulnerable, as he well knew, to the Anabaptists' retort that if the magistrates wouldn't obey the emperor in religion, why should the burghers obey them?[37] Sturm's second two-edged weapon was the "card of 1525," the argument that reform was the only sure preventative of revolution. A further point confirmed by this interview is that Sturm, a consistent ecclesiological particularist, was content with the promise that a nebulous "free, Christian council" would meet "sometime in the distant future," when, presumably, the gospel's progress would have made it possible for Christians to unite once more. The unifying experience behind all three principles—conscience, revolution, particularism—was the Peasants' War, which had demonstrated the importance of local control of religion. The difference between Granvelle and Sturm on the persecution of heresy confirms this point. When Granvelle mentioned fire, he meant not that the threat of death would make all heretics recant, but that persecution would free Christendom of pernicious and recalcitrant error—a view typical of an age that had not yet discovered spiritual regeneration through incarceration and punishment. Sturm, too, believed in suppressing heresy, as the Anabaptists could testify, but his particularist perspective was satisfied if heretics were banished into someone else's lands or, in extreme cases, jailed for life, as Melchior Hoffman was at Strasbourg. Whether his view is called magisterial, Marsiglian, or Erastian, Jacob Sturm believed in the enforcement of religious uniformity and the close control of the church by the state, and most of the deep differences between his policy and Granvelle's, which the Augsburg interview reveals, arose from the incompatibility of his civic-particularist view of the church with the imperial-universalist—or "neo-Ghibelline"—one advanced by the Catholic Imperial chancellor.[38] The two men agreed that the church, whether conceived as the devout commune or as Christendom, had no independent authority, but they disagreed about whether primary authority over the church lodged with the magistrates or with the emperor. Only once did Jacob Sturm compromise his Marsiglian ecclesiology, when he advocated a positive religious policy for the Smalkaldic League, but with the alliance's demise, he reverted to the uncompromising particularism he represented in 1548. This position fitted not only his city's postwar situation but also its political tradition.[39]

And it was not shared by everyone at Strasbourg, especially not by Martin Bucer, whose humiliation at Augsburg had fixed his conviction that the time had come to rescue Strasbourg's church from Strasbourg's reformation.

THE INTERIM, SUMMER 1548

The diet rose on 30 June 1548, two days after Sturm's interview with Granvelle.[40] Sturm and Odratzheim arrived home on 4 July, just ten months after their departure, and on the ninth Sturm reported to the Senate & XXI.[41] He tried to recreate for his colleagues the atmosphere that had dictated his failure.

> In sum, the emperor was so well supplied with German and Latin troops that the electors and princes dared not resist. We burghers, however, stood fast and protested our grievances, but to no effect, for the threats assured that we could accomplish nothing.[42]

In fact, the outcome was more menacing than Sturm said, or perhaps at this point knew, for the regime faced the emperor's demand for conformity to the interim while at their backs Martin Bucer was kindling the flames against it.[43] "See, dear Christians," Bucer sneered, "what the pope and his gang have done this time with their interim."[44] Although he knew better, Bucer portrayed the interim as a diabolical thrust from Rome rather than what it was, a failed effort of the pro-Imperial Catholic theologians, and he closed with words that set the tone for his whole crusade against the interim: "[God] does not know or accept those who cry, 'Lord, Lord,' and reject the pope's yoke, but who won't obey the will of our only, eternal Saviour and His Father, and won't submit to His yoke. May He give us grace and help and remain with us, for evening is nigh. Amen."[45]

When Sturm and his companion arrived at Strasbourg on 4 July, therefore, the battles lines over the interim were already forming. When an anonymous pamphlet, printed at the Catholic town of Molsheim, accused Bucer and his colleagues of spreading "the spirit of Münster," the magistrates noted laconically that "most think that it is not so far off the mark [*nit so weitleuffig vsgestrichen ist*]."[46] Recognizing his peril, Bucer drafted his greatest oppositional tract, the "Attempt at Summary of the Christian Doctrine and Religion, which has been taught at Strasbourg for 28 Years," to demonstrate "that we have nothing to do with the spirit and teaching of Münster."[47] Perhaps not, but Bucer expounded an ecclesiology based on the divine authority of the devout, for

> these true servants of Christ, whatever may be their rank in the churches, high or low, great or small, have received from the Lord the same spiritual authority and charge [*geistlichen gewalt und befelch entpfangen*] to establish the whole of the church's life, including doctrine, the sacraments, discipline, poor relief, and they, therefore, must feed Christ's flock in every needful way, for the sake of eternal life.[48]

Autonomous, divine authority for Christians "to establish the whole of the church's life," and in the name "of the whole community, to which Our Lord Christ gave the keys to heaven and the power to forgive sins"— this was either "a new papacy" or Müntzerite revolution.[49] And Bucer, who preached in the light of what he called "the evening," had fellows, for old Claus Kniebis wrote on 16 July 1548, "I believe that in the past hundred years things were never so dangerous as they are right now."[50] The magistrates were caught between two fires, which Kniebis well recognized, because he remembered the very similar situation in 1524–25:

> If we refuse the emperor's demand and reject the interim, we will fall into disgrace with him and into the greatest danger. For there are many papists here, but few who are determined to do God's will for the sake of religion. If, therefore, we obey the emperor, we will do so believing that the papacy is against God and the Bible, and knowing that we must love God above all creatures and with our whole soul and goods, and that we must fear God more than men and sooner lose all—father, mother, house and lands, everything—than disobey Him. And if we nevertheless submit, the Lord will say that we are unworthy of Him. The emperor demands an answer, yes or no, and we have not yet consulted our Schöffen. Oh, if only the Almighty, for the sake of His honor, would relieve us from this trial, so that we could remain in His divine grace and not provoke the emperor's wrath.[51]

The division ran through the commune, through the parishes, and even through Kniebis's own breast on 23 July, as he and his colleagues brought the matter of the interim to the Schöffen for the first time.[52] The ammeister informed the Schöffen of the Interim of Augsburg and of the regime's efforts to have it mitigated or vacated, and he asked their approval for a new embassy to the emperor for this purpose.[53] The Schöffen unanimously approved, though this vote was no proper test of support, because at this time few expected the interim to be forced upon Strasbourg. On 9 August, however, on the heels of reports about the submissions of former allies, the news arrived that Charles would neither make new concessions to Strasbourg nor grant a hearing to its theologians.[54] The interim must be accepted.

This news sparked a new stage of resistance and risked insurrection, because, said Paul Fagius, Capito's successor as pastor at New St. Peter's, the Senate & XXI refused to make a decision and left the people in the dark.[55] Fagius and other younger clergy, such as Ludwig Rabus, Zell's successor in the. cathedral parish, supported Bucer's fight from their pulpits and in the conventicles, despite all official attempts to stop their mouths.[56] Bucer captured the mood of these days in a letter to John Calvin: "There is no choice; either we must accept the Antichrist completely and give him back everything and pay him homage, or we must place everything in gravest jeopardy. . . . My fellow clergymen stand bravely, and with them many from all classes."[57] So did a hymn sung in several parishes, which began, "Keep us,

O Lord, by your Word / And kill the pope and the Turks." This was too much, and Jacob Sturm was sent to warn the preachers that

> if you don't practice more moderation, the emperor will force our regime to send you all away. This has happened at Augsburg, Memmingen, and Ulm and in Württemberg, where all preachers but two have been dismissed. If the gospel is removed entirely from our city, after the regime has worked so hard to sustain it, that will be entirely on your consciences. Your office is to preach the gospel with love and gentleness, not to cause conflict and to insult others.[58]

It was Sturm's old lesson from the mid-1520s: the clergy should preach the gospel and leave politics to the magistrates. The trouble was, some of his own colleagues agreed with the preachers' assessment of the situation as presenting a choice between Christ and Antichrist. The veteran stettmeister and member of the XIII, Egenolf Röder von Dierspurg, for example, sighed that "there's nothing to be done, . . . though it is grievous to good men to have to abandon the truth and return to idolatry."[59] As feelings mounted, a report came that "many odd women go in and out of the city."[60]

By 29 August matters were clearly getting out of hand. As the magistrates settled on their benches at city hall that morning, all minds were fixed by the news of a daring attempt by fifteen hundred Spanish troops on the city of Constance in the night of 6 August and of the city's outlawry by the emperor on the same day.[61] On the ninth came another ominous sign, the first resignation by a magistrate, Sebastian Münch, member of the XV from the Tanners' Guild, while elsewhere in the city nearly two hundred citizens gathered that morning without permission.[62] Rumors about the emperor's Neapolitan cavalry on the Rhine's right bank inflamed local bigotry against the Latins, and in many places artisans—for all the men informed on were artisans—engaged in "harmful talk [*unnutze reden*]."[63] On the seventeenth Paul Fagius and a teacher named Michael Toxites met with an innkeeper and two others in Fagius's house, where they planned a direct action in the style of the mid-1520s: forty men, two from each guild, would appear before the Senate & XXI and "warn them not to be so dilatory [*schlefferisch*]."[64] Meanwhile, at New St. Peter's, Fagius's parish, some gardeners plotted to hold an illegal assembly of members of all the guilds. The magistrates knew what was up, and time and again they warned Fagius and other preachers "to stop stirring up the common people."[65] By now agitation against the interim had begun to merge with resentment of the upper classes, for, as the Walloon nobleman Valérand Poullain (d. 1558) told King Henry II of France, "the nobles, who are the minority, mostly accept the interim and the city's subjection to the emperor, . . . while the majority of the said Schöffen are wholly opposed to the interim."[66] This was true, for during the second half of August the movement against the interim turned against the rich nobles and merchants.

In the mansions of Strasbourg's elite, these signs were noted and decisions were made, and on 15 August the exodus began. The émigré Augsburger Wolfgang Rehlinger declared on that day that he must leave Strasbourg, where he no longer felt safe; on the eighteenth Philips Ingold, head of a great banking firm, did the same for his clan; and by the twenty-second Caspar Hedio reported that "the rich, the nobles, and the merchants are leaving the city in great numbers."[67] Not only had the local mood turned against them, they had so much to lose—trade goods, loans, fiefs, estates, and rents—were Strasbourg and its burghers outlawed. And so they departed, the cream of Strasbourg's financial and mercantile community— Ingolds and Ebels, Prechters and Miegs—and most of the nobles. Among them were many of Jacob Sturm's kinsmen and -women. Cousin Stephan Sturm went, and so did the Böcklin boys, the Wurmser men and women, the Bocks, the Mülnheims, and the Mieg cousins. Family after family, wagon after wagon, rumbled through the city's streets, trailed by the ordinary burghers' curses and threats. A precious eyewitness fixed this scene of a great commune in dissolution:

> Each day the Senate was deep in deliberation about the interim, while two or three thousand citizens were gathered constantly before the town hall, and nobody knew what to do. Again and again, the regime asked the people to trust them and to go their homes. . . . When the Senate & XXI met, many of them, fearing for their own skins and afraid of the emperor, wanted to flee; but Sir Jacob Sturm stood at the door and wouldn't let anyone out until a decision had been reached. Since some of them had Imperial sympathies and held Imperial fiefs, they were afraid of the people, realizing that they would be the targets of a possible rebellion. They decided to accept the book or interim, for the rumor was true that the emperor intended to come, just as he said. For the sake of civic peace, these men renounced their citizenship and went abroad until the crisis was over. The people cursed them and charged them with cowardice, following them through the streets with insults.[68]

The whole event is captured in one small scene, as the fifty-nine-year-old Sturm stands at the Senate chamber's door, barring the way out to younger men, whose nerve had broken. Yet nearly two-thirds of the Senate & XXI did leave, including two members of the XIII, eight of the XV, one of the XXI, two stettmeisters, and five patrician and three guild senators.[69] As one of them, old Conrad Joham, the only veteran of the 1520s who emigrated, left the chamber, Ammeister Jacob von Duntzenheim, Batt's brother, flung terrible words after him: "I would love to stick a knife through your heart!" Joham retired to his country seat at Mundolsheim, and he never came back.

As his beleaguered, crippled regime sagged around him, Jacob Sturm rose to the zenith of his career. He drafted the great address for the Schöffen on 27 August, when the tide began to turn in the regime's favor. Throwing secrecy to the winds—"among the Schöffen there are men of papal or episcopal sympathies, who will not keep it quiet"—Sturm's text began with a notice that the emperor had given Strasbourg a month to decide.[70] Although the interim contained much that was good, the errors and the restoration of episcopal jurisdiction made it unacceptable.[71] Resistance was nonetheless impossible, for a siege would ruin the burghers. Thus, "so long as the emperor commands obedience in the Empire of the German Nation, as he now does, it is unthinkable that the city can hold out against him, for at last we must surrender and obey him, as others have done, or seek a lord outside the Empire." Although no one spoke the word "France," Sturm cautioned that no foreign lord possessed both the power and the will to protect Strasbourg, and if Strasbourg embraced the French king, a persecutor of true religion, Alsace would become a theater of chronic war, just like Lombardy, Piedmont, and Hungary. "You know well," the Schöffen were told, "what sort of religion and fear of God would be maintained and practiced in such a state of war."

Sturm's text then examined the arguments for and against resistance. It is not certain, he noted, that resistance is allowed "without an explicit command [from God] and biblical authority,

> for in the past, when He has wished to save His people, God has always shown them the way and means in terms that human reason can comprehend. There is no such path now, and our whole experience teaches us that almost certainly we are not such as God will save through a miracle. And since He intends to save and preserve His own honor in some other way, we should meanwhile tolerate and endure arbitrary power and injustice and in suffering and patience to await deliverance by His hand, rather than resist them without God's command and biblical warrant. For on the latter course we ourselves, our wives and our children, plus those out on the land, will fall into misery, degradation, and total ruin.

Therefore, just as in Roman times "some good, stalwart Christians had to suffer for their faith with troubled consciences and perhaps even with their blood," so "we may hope that since the Christian faith came into the world through such staunch witness and confession, not through power and resistance," today "it will also be preserved and restored in the same way." Resistance or nonresistance, he thought, "on both paths lie danger and oppression." What, then, to do? Sturm's text now proposed to send an embassy to the emperor to tell him "why the introduction of the interim will burden our consciences" and to ask him to order "the bishop of Strasbourg, whom the emperor holds to be our ordinary and spiritual superior," and the canons and officials of the cathedral and some other collegial churches, "whose canons and officers mostly live here in the city," to install the interim "in some churches, about which we are willing to negotiate in a friendly manner with His Grace and the others." The Senate & XXI would promise that in the other churches, the preachers would be bridled, the sacrament administered in both kinds "in an intelligible language," the fasting holy days observed, and "external discipline and propriety" maintained, so that the emperor might observe "that we seek nothing else than what may promote God's honor and obedience to His Majesty." If this offer were accepted, the city would retain its reformed doctrine, sacraments, and liberty, all of which would be lost through resistance. Negotiation, on the contrary, would hold the future open, to be shaped by the burghers' devotion or, as in the past, by their sins.

The brilliance of this speech evokes wonder, for Sturm presented the proposed course of action—resistance means the certain loss of liberty and religion, negotiation means the possible salvation of both—in terms that linked God's providence to the individual burgher's responsibility for the situation. The civic common good was threatened not by alleged pollution through restored Catholic ceremonies but by the Evangelical burghers' lack of devotion. A powerful argument, this coupling of good conscience and the common good, but not powerful enough: 132 Schöffen voted with the regime, but 134 voted "to bring the matter before the commune, because it concerns the faith and the soul." The magistrates promised to consider this demand, though "it is not the custom or tradition here to refer anything from the Schöffen to the commune." The moment of truth had come. While the ammeister addressed the Schöffen in Jacob Sturm's words, Paul Fagius and others were meeting at New St. Peter's, and the rumor flew about "that before noon a stout body of folk will be together."[72]

Sturm did not record his feelings at this moment, the peak of the Reformation's worst crisis, when his world tottered around him: empty spaces on the magistrates' benches; friendships, born of a hundred committee meetings and a dozen diplomatic missions, broken; and most of Sturm's own class, including many of his kinsmen and -women, gone into exile, perhaps forever. Nothing like this had happened at Strasbourg since 1419, when most of the urban nobility had left the city forever.

In August's last days, Sturm needed a miracle, for everything stood against him: the government lay in shambles; the streets seethed with scenes reminiscent of the mid-1520s; the clergy led an opposition headed for insurrection; and except for Strasbourg and Constance, all South Germany lay in the emperor's hands. One thing, however, weighed in Sturm's favor: the opposition found no leader. Gone from city hall were the party divisions of the 1520s, for the regime's militants of those days were either too old and too sick, as Kniebis was, or they lacked stomach for sedition, as Mathis Pfarrer did, and the younger generation had produced no candidate for the tribune's role. Instead, the rump Senate & XXI decided to try again, after members were sent—for the how-manyeth time?—to warn the preachers not "to stir up the people against the pope, the king, and the emperor, for the honorable Senate will no longer tolerate that."[73]

On 30 August, when the Schöffen were summoned again, they were told that "it would be an unheard-of innovation for the Schöffen to bring something before the commune, for important matters have always been decided by the Schöffen and the ammeister."[74] Clearly, the speech went on, "you misunderstood our intention [on 27 August] and thought that we want to accept and tolerate the interim and allow our lord, the bishop of Strasbourg, to establish it in the whole city, so that the Word of God would be entirely suppressed." Having turned the supposition of misunderstanding into a fact, the ammeister—almost certainly again in Jacob Sturm's words—used it to disarm the Schöffen. "If you, the Schöffen, who are the principal persons of the guilds and of the commune," he said, "misunderstood our intention and proposal, how much less correctly would it be understood by the whole commune?" Not only would they have more difficulty to grasp it, "but the crush of persons in the guildhalls would be very great. Those of them who can understand it, will in those conditions have difficulty to hear, much less to understand, it." It would be even worse to call them all together in one place, instead of reading the proposal to them in the guildhalls, for everyone would want to speak, and each would have his supporters, "and each would say that his opinion was best." From such a procedure would arise "inequality and conflict, and perhaps something worse." If the vote were taken guild by guild, the large guilds would unjustly dominate the small ones. "This is why it has been justly arranged that the smallest guild has a senator and fifteen Schöffen, just like the greatest guild, so that equity shall be maintained among guilds in all things." Another reason against consultation was the need for secrecy, for

> it is dangerous to reveal the city's secrets to the whole commune, in which there are all sorts of people from all sorts of places and of all sorts of opinions. One fellow just came, the other will leave tomorrow, and no one knows what sort of loyalties such outsiders have and whether they can be trusted. . . . Therefore, our ancestors wisely established that no one can become a Schöffe unless he has been a citizen for ten years. . . . Who would want to put his and his friends' welfare, much less that of the whole city, into the hands of such inexperienced men in the commune? For you see that many good burghers, who provide much work [*narhafter*], have renounced their citizenship, just because you voted to refer the matter to the commune against all tradition and custom. Many others will doubtless leave, if things stay as they are.

Besides, as the vote on the twenty-seventh produced "only a two-vote majority," the magistrates were asking once more for permission to continue negotiations.

This superb speech, almost certainly written by Jacob Sturm,[75] forms a stunning complement to his speech for the assembly on 27 August. Then he had appealed to their faith, their trust in God, and their willingness to sacrifice for the common good; now he appealed to their dislike of foreigners and new settlers, their concern for their livelihoods, feelings of rivalry among trades and guilds, and respectable burghers' sense of superiority to the common herd. It was a moral Cannae, a double envelopment that did not fail of its purpose with the Schöffen, who this time voted 206 to 4 to give the regime permission to continue negotiations within the stated terms.[76] As if to seal the victory, that afternoon a clothworker named Rudolph Probst came up to Fagius in the cathedral square and said, "You rascally priest, haven't you preached enough subversive nonsense?" A bit later, when he saw the preacher again in the Franciscans' Square, he "struck Fagius to the ground."[77]

With the horse now standing at the gate, Sturm had to lead it in. No sooner had the Schöffen been dismissed than the Senate & XXI filed into their chamber and appointed Sturm, Mattheus Geiger, and Dr. Gremp to ride to Granvelle or his son for more time or for permission to negotiate the interim's terms with the bishop.[78] The envoys, who left the city on 2 September, missed Charles at Speyer and followed him downstream to Cologne, where on 10 September Granvelle conducted Sturm and Gremp to the emperor.[79] Sturm opened the interview with a long speech, presumably in Latin, about how the cities, though they had taken up arms to defend their liberties and their religion, had never abandoned their traditional obedience to the emperors or Imperial law. He also reminded the emperor of his claim to have made war not to change anyone's religion but merely to punish rebel princes and of his promise to respect Strasbourg's liberties and religion until a general council should heal the schism.[80] The emperor's ambiguous reply rejected, on the one hand, the proposal to preserve the present (i.e., Evangelical) order of worship in some of Strasbourg's churches and approved, on the other, that the interim's terms at Strasbourg should be negotiated between the city and the bishop and his clergy. Sturm, to whom Charles was unusually gracious on this occasion, could not withdraw without a parting shot, and he reminded the emperor that the free cities had never approved placing this decision in Charles's hands.[81]

Back at home, Sturm's committee held it fruitless to send another embassy, especially as "the emperor accepted far enough [genugens] the Senate's proposal that the bishop should be allowed to do it."[82] This was the main point, and the preachers must tolerate Catholic ceremonies in some of the churches and refrain from attacking the interim, so that true doctrine might be preserved until better times. Sturm's entire policy of negotiation rested on his expectation of getting easier terms from the bishop than from the emperor, and he doubtless remembered how, when he was a boy, his father's colleagues had handled Bishop William, the present bishop's predecessor. The chance to take advantage of the bishop's vulnerability, however, depended on the magistrates' ability to stop the turmoil in the city, and even as they took up contacts with Bishop Erasmus—on 3 November 1548 they asked him to set the date for the talks—they investigated the network of conventicles in the local parishes.[83] Rather than suppressing the groups, the magistrates took the wind from the movement's sails by forbidding them to keep rolls or to maintain a citywide network.

This two-pronged policy yielded its predictable fruit in the following year, though not without cost to its architect. Around Schwörtag (8 January 1549), wrote the indomitable Katharine Schütz, Mathis Zell's widow, Jacob Sturm visited her, and "when he tried to speak to me, he wept so that he could hardly speak. So he knows how things stand."[84] He surely did, for the city's side of the bilateral negotiations lay in Sturm's hand from start to finish.[85] Not until 23 January were the Schöffen officially informed of the negotiations with Bishop Erasmus and asked to accept what could "with good conscience" be accepted and to allow the bishop to deal with the rest. When the Schöffen voted 262 to 30 for the magistrates' proposal, the struggle against the interim at Strasbourg was finished. The negotiations continued until 23 November 1549, when the negotiators agreed on the terms under which Catholic worship would be restored on the first day of the year 1550.[86] Though mandated by Imperial authority, the interim was introduced at Strasbourg based on a treaty between equals, bishop and city, and on terms more favorable to the city's Evangelical majority than in any other former Smalkaldic power. This outcome was Jacob Sturm's greatest political triumph.[87]

Sturm's victory, which overcame the crisis his own policy had brought upon Strasbourg, cost him dearly. The social strife envigorated by the attack on the interim threatened to undermine the civic peace by fracturing the solidarity between the rich and the middling guildsmen, which Greatgrandfather Peter Schott had done so much to cement. The struggle severed Sturm's ties to some old comrades, such as Conrad Joham, soured relations with others, such as Claus Kniebis and Mathis Pfarrer, and destroyed the most important personal monument to Strasbourg's successful reformation, the partnership between Jacob Sturm and Martin Bucer. Bucer was dean of St. Thomas, and when he opposed the installation of the interim in that church, Bishop Erasmus demanded his deposition. On 1 March the Senate & XXI decided that Bucer and Fagius "shall be suspended for a while." Not "for a while," as it turned out, but forever. Bucer had come to Strasbourg in 1522 as a nobody, a homeless former friar hot for the gospel; he had risen under Capito's tutelage to become the leading figure in Strasbourg's church; and he had held back nothing in his loyal, unflagging support of Sturm's policy of union with the Lutheran princes, traveling up and down the land as advisor, theologian, and ecclesiastical politician, conscientiously performing his offices as pastor, dean, and teacher. All that counted for little now, as he lingered as a guest in Katharine Schütz's house, and on 6 April 1549 he and Fagius slipped out of the city they would never see again. Bucer would die amidst England's eternal fogs, and Sturm in his own bed in Fire Street.[88]

Brooding in English exile, Bucer reflected on the half-finished state in which he had left the German Reformation, a condition for which he mostly blamed the Protestant princes and magistrates. He passed bitter judgment on them in his *De regno Christi*, his last major work. After thirty years of the revived gospel in Germany, he thought, there still can be found only a few who have become entirely subject to Christ's gospel and Kingdom, indeed who have allowed the Christian religion and the discipline of the churches to be restored throughout according to the laws of our King.[89]

In particular, he complained, the princes and magistrates have denied to the ministers of the gospel the power to bind the people "through penance, and with the consent of the Church, pronounce those who refuse this remedy of salvation to be regarded as heathens and publicans." Furthermore, besides refusing the "discipline of penance," the rulers "have demanded that the ministers of the churches give the most holy sacrament of communion of Christ to anyone who asks, without probing into his faith and life." Penance and excommunication, the two tools of sound religious discipline for which Bucer had struggled since 1538, who can doubt that, as he puzzled over "how varied the ways are by which the Lord treats his churches in this world," his thoughts came again and again to rest on Strasbourg and Jacob Sturm?

"Oh, cursed Mammon," Bucer cried in a letter he wrote to friends at home on a day in mid-May 1549, seizing on that excessive respect for the world to which, he believed, Sturm had fallen prey.[90] The painful memory prompted him to pen on that very day a letter to Sturm, the last ever, to which no reply would come. He began with a gloomy meditation on the broken state of Christ's church at Strasbourg, "and I think of you, both because of that which was introduced [i.e., the interim], because of you personally, and mostly because of what I heard you say."[91] Reviewing the roots of their quarrel, Bucer lectured Sturm that "the earth is the Lord's [Ps. 24:1] and our homeland as well," and He is the source of all law and liberty. Rulers and leaders, he wrote, must observe and maintain the kingdom of Christ despite the people's weaknesses and the interests of "the rich [accumulandi mammonae]." The whole world must become a single godly order, in which Christ builds His kingdom, a regnum Christi founded on those "in whom Christ is most alive." Here was the theme, the world as the Kingdom of Christ, for which the experiences of opposition and exile had whetted Bucer's hunger. In this mood, he had every reason to judge and condemn Sturm as a slave to the interests of this world. At this point, however, the clergyman made a remarkable turn from censorious complaint to gentle affection, as the memory of better days crept over him, days when he and Jacob Sturm had formed a team beyond compare in the service of the German Reformation. "I beg you to accept my admonition as I intend it," Bucer wrote, "for I truly love you, . . . and I am terribly concerned for your welfare [pro tua salute]." He commended Strasbourg's church and school to Sturm's hands, added some news of his and Fagius's lives in exile, and, with a dramatically Bucerian touch, signed with a pseudonym. On his side, at least, something of the old partnership from the great days survived the pain of estrangement. But estranged they remained, for the interim, to Bucer the work of the Antichrist, was to Sturm a fruit of defeat to which the Protestants must regrettably but necessarily submit. The restoration of the Catholic mass might be divisive, but hardly idolatrous, for in Sturm's view, after all, "both sides are Christians. May God have mercy!" Politician and preacher, these two men who had labored for the same cause for twenty years, often together in the same harness of policy, saw the world with different eyes. Their long partnership concealed two, equally Evangelical, views of religion and the world, seen respectively from the pulpit and from city hall. For Bucer, as he wrote in his last letter to Sturm, "the earth is the Lord's, and our homeland as well"; for Sturm, as he had written in an address to the Schöffen, "our whole experience teaches us that we are not such as God will save through a miracle." Whereas his devotion to the church had taught the former friar that the world is destined to become "the Kingdom of Christ," a lifetime in politics had taught Jacob Sturm, who was not much younger than Niccolò Machiavelli, that the earth is not the Lord's, but the lords'.

Notes

* "Interim wirt man hören/von kriegen große streich,/interim wirt sich erbören/ der gemeine mann im reich,/interim leidet die christenheit,/interim wirt Christus kommen,/zu lösen von allem leid." Liliencron, ed., *Historische Volkslieder* 4:460, no. 570, stanza 18.

1. For the context, see PC 4:731, no. 650 n. 1.
2. Sturm's undated memorial, "which I wrote when the emperor was coming from Saxony to Swabia, after the elector's capture," is in PC 4:731–36, no. 650, here at 731; and there, too, the following quote.
3. PC 4:732; and there, too, the remaining quotes in this paragraph.
4. See Rabe, *Reichsbund*, 121–33; Press, "Bundespläne"; and Luttenberger, *Glaubenseinheit*, 425–33, who shows the continuity of the neutral princes' mediation (see 375–424). King Ferdinand's influence may well have been crucial in persuading Charles to call an Imperial Diet. See ARCEG 5:16–17, no. 9.
5. Quoted by Gerber, "Jakob Sturms Anteil," 169 n. 4, and paraphrased by him in PC 4:777, no. 680.
6. Because Harry Gerber, the editor of PC, vol. 4, gives a running account of Sturm's work in the diet, the following account can be abbreviated and quotes from the rich documentation accordingly reduced. See also Gerber, "Jakob Sturms Anteil," and "Die Bedeutung des Augsburger Reichstags," and more generally the studies by Rabe and Luttenberger.
7. Gerber, "Jakob Sturms Anteil," 168–69; Rabe, *Reichsbund*, 197–204. King Ferdinand and other leading Catholics also thought the religious question the central one. See ARCEG 5:29, lines 11–24, no. 12, 36–40, nos. 18–19.
8. Rabe, *Reichsbund*, 134–76, 199–200, 273–94, 361–98, on the entire course of negotiations, and 149–71, on the summer assembly at Ulm.
9. PC 4:704, no. 628; and there, too, the quotes in the following sentence. This document was edited by Sturm. See Rabe, *Reichsbund*, 154–55, for the southern cities' reactions.
10. PC 4:716, no. 635 and n. 1. Strasbourg sent Dr. Gremp and Marx Hag, an inexperienced patrician of uncertain mental health.
11. Rabe, *Reichsbund*, 168–69. See PC 4:753–54, no. 661, 754–56, no. 662.

12. Rabe, *Reichsbund*, 375–98. The "Burgundian Treaty" is printed in *Papiers d'état* 3:319–22.

13. Rabe, *Reichsbund*, 274–75; Petri, "Karl V. und die Städte," 18–20, for the centrality of northwestern Germany and the Netherlands to Charles's plan. For the Strasbourgeois' negative reaction to it, see PC 4:899–900, no. 744.

14. PC 4:762, no. 666. On Odratzheim, see Brady, *Ruling Class*, 338–39. The story of Sturm and the diet is related by Gerber, "Jakob Sturms Anteil." The two chief issues, the league and religion, dominated the preparations for the diet by Sturm, Pfarrer, and Andreas Mieg, in PC 4:744–51, no. 657.

15. This quote and the following one are from the translation in Sastrow, *Memoirs*, 233–35. So taken was Sastrow with Sturm that he inserted the latter's portrait into his memoirs, "should my children have a desire to know what Sturm was like facially."

16. Quoted by Gerber, "Jakob Sturms Anteil," 175. On the origins of this policy, see PC 4:750, no. 659.

17. Rabe, *Reichsbund*, 248–61; Luttenberger, *Glaubenseinheit*, 442–44.

18. PC 4:832, no. 716, written the day after Madruzzo's report was announced to the diet. The Senate on 21 January ordered Bucer to ride to Ulm. Ibid., 835–36, no. 719. Two weeks later, on 1 February, Sturm also sent for Dr. Ludwig Gremp to help him with the negotiations with the former Smalkaldic League's other members about the Brunswick affair. Ibid., 851, no. 726.

19. The very full sources are in PC 4:855–68, no. 729 (Sturm; Mainz); Druffel, ed., *Beiträge* 3:83–84, no. 159 (Saxon elector); ARCEG 5:208–22, no. 64 (Mainz); and the best accounts are by Rabe, *Reichsbund*, 407–24; Luttenberger, *Glaubenseinheit*, 451–65. For the following quotes, I have freely drawn from Sturm's own notes and from the fuller ones by Dr. Konrad Fisch of Mainz.

20. PC 4:857, no. 729; ARCEG 5:210 lines 34–42. Besserer, who spoke after Sturm, complained he was "a laymen and uneducated, and if theology and the disputed points are to be dealt with, he asks to be released in favor of others."

21. The hard Catholic line on restitution was taken by the Carmelite provincial Eberhard Billick, who sat for the (new) elector of Cologne, and Chancellor Eck of Bavaria, though the latter agreed with Sturm that the doctrinal schism was "das principal." Rabe, *Reichsbund*, 421; Metzger, *Leonhard von Eck*, 308.

22. PC 4:862–63; ARCEG 5:220, lines 19–39, but reading with Gerber, "besorg[en] mer dan er. will wol nit von rebellion reden."

23. PC 4:865–68; ARCEG 5:226–27. It is worth noting that this entire final passage is lacking in Sturm's own account of his speech.

24. On the origins of the Interim of Augsburg, see above all Rabe, *Reichsbund*, 425–26; Luttenberger, *Glaubenseinheit*, 463–66, with references to important documents in ARCEG, vol. 5. The text is presented in a bilingual edition by Mehlhausen, ed., *Das Augsburg Interim*, 28–160. To the other literature on the Catholic party of mediation should be added Decot, *Religionsfrieden und Kirchenreform*.

25. PC 4:920, no. 752: "Nun handlet kei. Mt. noch ad partem mit den stenden, ob er sie dahin bewegen möcht, irer Mt. fürschlag gutwillig anzunemmen." The lobbying of the estates is reconstructed by Rabe, *Reichsbund*, 427–49; Luttenberger, *Glaubenseinheit*, 442–76; and there is more detail about the free cities in Gerber, "Jakob Sturms Anteil," 182–89.

26. This exchange is known from the Nurembergers' report, cited by Gerber, "Jakob Sturms Anteil," 182–83, and published in PC 4:897, no. 743; Pflug, *Correspondance* 3:629 n. 4. Sturm's report of 26 March ignores the incident. Ibid., 898–900, no. 744.

27. The calling of Bucer and the development of his views on the interim can be

followed in PC 4:903–20, nos. 747–52, with the especially valuable reports by Nuremberg's envoys, who learned much through their close ties to Elector Joachim of Brandenburg's entourage. See also the reports of the papal legate, Francesco Sfondrato, to Alessandro Farnese, Augsburg, 29 March, 5 April, and 10 April, in *NBD*, pt. 1, vol. 10:288, no. 100; 295, no. 102; 302, no. 104. In the latter, Sfondrato reports that "Il Buccero debbe esser partito secretamente nè ho possuto intendere con qual risolutione o disegno." The very important documents from Bucer's pen are all edited in *BDS* 17:346–438, with Bellardi's helpful commentary.

28. This is one of the most important conclusions of Rabe and Luttenberger, who have taken advantage of the dense documentation in *ARCEG*, vol. 5. See also Metzger, *Leonhard von Eck*, 308–13, who shows what the Catholic party of resistance thought about the interim.

29. PC 4:918–19, no. 751 n. 7; *BDS* 17:347, with the letter to Pflug printed on 422–38. Pflug, a member of the committee that drafted the formula, was thought to be its author.

30. On issue of urban rights, see Gerber, "Die Bedeutung des Augsburger Reichstags," although Georg Schmidt's very detailed investigation of the issue (*Städtetag*, 247–319) passes over this diet in silence.

31. PC 4:996, no. 788; Gerber, "Jakob Sturms Anteil," 177, 187–88.

32. PC 4:997–98, no. 788, where Sturm describes this process. For Sturm's perspective on the disintegration of a Protestant-neutralist front in the Cities' House and in the diet as a whole, see his reports to Strasbourg from the month of June, in PC 4:967–70, 981–83, 986–90, 992–93, 996–1002, 1008–12, nos. 776–77, 780, 784, 786, 788, 790. The Nurembergers reported, perhaps not without malice, "und ischt ime gleich, als ob die kei. Mt. geen Strasburgh verrücken und die sachen daselbst handel wolte." PC 4:967, no. 776 n. 1.

33. Heinrich Hass (d. 1562) from Lauffen, served the Count Palatine of Zweibrücken, then became chancellor of the Palatinate before entering Imperial service. Sleidan calls him "rerum Germaniae valde peritus." Sleidan, *Commentarii* (ed. Frankfurt 1785) 2:580. On Hass, see Naujoks, *Zunftverfassung*, 169–70. Sturm's account (PC 4:1012–17, no. 791) speaks of "we," and Odratzheim certainly accompanied him but said nothing. Marx Hag had come back to Strasbourg on 28 April, after Sturm had reported on 26 March that he had been ill for three weeks and asked for a relative to be sent to fetch him home, for otherwise he would not go. By October the Senate ordered Hag to be bound with a chain, lest he injure (kill?) himself. PC 4:902, no. 745 n. 4.

34. In PC 4:1013, no. 791 n. 4, which asks the emperor to allow Strasbourg to retain "irer religion und der augspurischen confession bis zu erörterung eines allgemeine freien christlichen concilii." From the document come the quotes in this and the next three paragraphs.

35. Ibid., 1014, no. 791: "nun stund eins rats bitt allein doruf, dweyl sy in iren gewissen uberzeugt, das, so sy das interim in allen puncten annemen, das sy wider gott und ir selen heyl handelten, das dan kay. Mt. sy so woll als das ander teyl tulden wolt bis zu erorterung eins freien christlichen concilii; dan es wer ye ein schwer ding, das ein christ solt wider sein gewissen handeln. und ob schon einer ein irrig gewissen hett, begert er doch in eynem freyen concilio gehort und underricht zu werden, dan Paulus spricht: wer wider sin gewissen handelt, bauet zu der hollen." I cannot identify this citation.

36. See this volume, chap. 4.

37. See this volume, chap. 4.

38. Brady, "In Search of the Godly City," 15–16; Headley, "The Habsburg World Empire."

39. A point made long ago by Hans Baron, "Religion and Politics."
40. Schmauss, ed., *Reichs-Abschiede* 2:527–50.
41. *PC* 4:1023, no. 795 n. 1.
42. Ibid., 1025, no. 795. He said that at the end the emperor stationed a company of troops around the townhall, where the diet was meeting.
43. What follows is based on Bellardi, "Bucer und das Interim," and Bellardi, "Bucers 'Summarischer Vergriff.'" For the whole topic of the struggle against the interim at Strasbourg, see Weyrauch, *Krise*, esp. 133–62, on the events of 1548–49. The first blow in this campaign was the preachers' memorial of 3 June 1548, "Welcher Massen das Interim den Christlichen Stenden Augspurgischer Confession ist vorgegeben vnd vfferlegt," in *BDS* 17:439–67.
44. *BDS* 17:443, lines 13–14.
45. Ibid., 467, lines 24–28. The views of the other Catholic party, the militants, were voiced by the Bavarian chancellor, who thought that the enforcement of the interim in Bavaria and other Catholic territories would lead to mass defections from Catholicism. Metzger, *Leonhard von Eck*, 313.
46. *TAE* 4:253, lines 1–2, no. 1608; and see 250, 254–55, nos. 1603–5, 1610. The "H. Sturm" mentioned in the cited text cannot be Jacob Sturm, who was still at Augsburg, but is probably his brother, Peter, who was a member of the XV.
47. "Ein Summarischer vergriff der Christlichen lehr und Religion die man zu Strasburg hat nun in die xxviij. jar gelehret," in *BDS* 17:111–50, here at 122, lines 9–10. This tract is speckled with references to "Münster," "der Münsterischer geist" (122, lines 5–6), "Münsterisch lehren" (122, line 12), "wie die zu Münster" (125, line 12), "wie die falschen Propheten zu Münster gethon" (145, line 17), and "wie das die zu Münster gelehrt und gethon haben mit auffrur und enderung der ordenlichen Oberkeiten" (145, lines 7–8). Not only does this tract directly respond to and attack the (lost) Molsheim pamphlet, but Bucer also organized the pastors to preach against the pamphlet and its charge, "quia dogma es Epicuri." Almost certainly, therefore, the anonymous author came from the ranks of Bucer's Epicurean opponents, and was not a Catholic, though the distinction cannot be made with perfect sharpness. Bellardi, in *BDS* 17:114; *TAE* 4:250, no. 1604 n. 4.
48. *BDS* 17:132, lines 23–133, line 2.
49. Ibid., 133, lines 3–6.
50. *PC* 4:1034, no. 799. See Weyrauch, *Krise*, 134–37, on the apocalyptic mood.
51. In *PC* 4:1034–35, no. 799.
52. Joseph Münch von Rosenberg to Duke Ulrich of Württemberg, 6 July 1548, in *PC* 4:1022, no. 794; Justus Velsius to Don Cesar de Silva, Strasbourg, 14 July 1548, in ibid., 1033, no. 798: "Dum indies magis magisque per se alioqui satis concitati populares cum ardentibus nonnullorum concionibus inflammentur, quibis id studio esse videtur, ut secum multos, immo universam rempublicam in ruinam trahant." In the same vein, see also Trajanus Marii to Cardinal Cristoforo Madruzzo, Augsburg, 26 July 1548, in *NBD*, pt. 1, vol. 11:47 n. 1; Pietro Bertano to Alessandro Farnese, Augsburg, 29 July 1548, in ibid., 53, no. 15.
53. *PC* 4:1035–37, no. 800; the vote is given in 1037 n. 3, from the interesting letter of Paul Fagius to Johannes Ulstetter (his son-in-law), BNUS, Thes. Baum., 19:89 (30 July 1548). For Sturm's membership in the drafting committee, see *PC* 4:1025.
54. *PC*, vol. 4:1050–52, no. 810.
55. BNUS, Thes. Baum., vol. 10:93; *PC* 4:1053, no. 811 n. 2. Weyrauch, *Krise*, 137–39, gives an overview of this agitation. On Fagius, a native of Bergzabern in the Palatinate, see Ficker-Winckelmann 2:65; Raubenheimer, *Paul Fagius*.

56. Bellardi, *Geschichte*, 63. Fagius had been warned already in early May, after Assmus Böcklin reported that "Vagius hab nechsten ein so scharpffe predig gethon, das es jn hoch beschwerdt." Fagius preached against "alle die so jm vergangenen zug gewessenn," which included several of Böcklin's kinsmen. AMS, XXI 1548, fol. 236r–v. See other reports in ibid., fols. 364r, 374v–75v. Zell died on 9 January 1548 (*PC* 4:837, no. 720; Ficker-Winckelmann 2:55), and he was replaced by Ludwig Rabus (1524–92), a Memminger "welcher wieder das *Interim*, als eine Papistische Lehre hefftig geeyffert." Crusius, *Schwäbische Chronik* 2:269. See Ficker-Winckelmann 2:90.

57. Martin Bucer to John Calvin, Strasbourg, 10 July 1548, in *CR* 41:5. This was not simply hyperbole, for Claus Kniebis also understood the situation in these terms. He hoped "dass wir nit uns mussen in des entchrists gehorsam begeben wider die lehr, die wir us gottes wort entpfangen haben." Claus Kniebis to Bernhard Meyer, Strasbourg, 5 July 1548, in *PC* 4:1022, no. 793 n. 5. On the growth of apocalyptic attitudes among Lutherans after the war, see Barnes, *Prophecy and Gnosis*, 63–66.

58. This story is told by Friese, *Neue Vaterländische Geschichte* 2:275–76. He dates it to May 1548, which is impossible, because Sturm was not at Strasbourg in that month, and because the changes referred to had not yet taken place at that time. As Friese says that the preachers' reply "ist bey den Akten nicht befindlich," presumably Sturm's admonition was.

59. *PC* 4:1022, no. 794 n. 4.

60. AMS, XXI 1548, fols. 374v, 375v; and see the report of 18 July about the cooper Jacob Bötzell and "seiner unnutzen reden . . ., die er der religion und meiner herrn halben getriben," in ibid., fol. 368r–v.

61. The news came from Johann von Heideck to the Senate of Strasbourg, Basel, 8 August 1548, in *PC* 4:1048, no. 808, which arrived on the morning of 9 August and was read to the XIII on the same day. The decree of outlawry is printed by Fabian, ed., *Quellen zur Geschichte der Reformationsbündnisse*, 232–35 (6 August 1548).

62. AMS, XXI 1548, fols. 394v–98r. On Sebastian Münch (d. 10 November 1578), whose father, Claus (d. 1522), had sat in the XV and then in the XIII, see Brady, *Ruling Class*, 337–38.

63. I rely here on my analysis in *Ruling Class*, 271–75, 277–78.

64. AMS, XXI 1548, fols. 411v–12r (18 August 1548); and the following report is from the same source.

65. AMS, XXI 1548, fol. 429r (25 August 1548).

66. *PC* 4:1042–44, no. 804. On Poullain, see Ficker-Winckelmann 2:72; Zeller, "Valerand Poullain," esp. 344. He had briefly been pastor of the French parish.

67. Quoted from Brady, *Ruling Class*, 280. This account rests on *Ruling Class*, 280–86, and 377–80, where the émigrés are listed.

68. Specklin, *Collectanées*, no. 2387, slightly revised from my translation in *Ruling Class*, 284.

69. AMS, XXI 1548, fol. 440r–v.

70. The preparations took twelve days, and the drafts of the address are all by Sturm; Ammeister Jacob von Duntzenheim delivered it. The quotes are all from *PC* 4:1059–63, no. 816.

71. The following is all based on the text in ibid., from which the quotes come.

72. AMS, XXI 1548, fols. 413v–32r (27 August 1548).

73. *PC* 4:1065, no. 818 n. 1.

74. Ibid., 1065–68, no. 818. As the address exists only in a fair copy in the hand of the city secretary, its authorship is uncertain, though it is most probably the work of Jacob Sturm.

75. In reporting this vote to Philip Melanchthon on 7 September 1548, Bucer emphasized that the initiative in this whole process lay with Jacob Sturm. *MBW* 6:349, no. 5284.

76. The regime secured just under half (49.2 percent) the votes cast on 27 August and nearly all (98 percent) of those cast on the thirtieth. The undervote, however, climbed from 11.3 percent to a highly abnormal 30 percent. In the third vote on the interim, the undervote dropped to 2.7 percent.

77. AMS, XXI 1548, fols. 440v, 441v–42r. Fagius was reported to have said to a tinsmith, "Es were jme nyme anderst zethun, dann das man disen Rhat abthett unnd ein annderen Christlichen Rhat setzte." Bucer complained to Melanchthon on 7 September 1548 of the weak popular support the opposition enjoyed, and Melanchthon suggested that the theologians' quarrels had weakened the people's resolve. *MBW* 6:349, no. 5284; 361–62, no. 5310.

78. PC 4:1071–73, no. 820; the envoys were appointed on 30 August. The Senate & XXI sent after the envoys a letter to the emperor, in which the proposal is spelled out in detail. Ibid., 1077–78, no. 825.

79. PC 4:1076, no. 824; 1079, no. 826 n. 1. Present at this audience were the two Granvelles, father and son, and two German-speaking councillors, Heinrich Hass and Georg Seld.

80. We have Sturm's speech only from a letter of the French ambassador, Charles de Marillac, to King Henry II, in Druffel, ed., *Beiträge* 2:158–59, no. 214. The rest of the audience is recounted in PC 4:1079–81, no. 826.

81. PC 4:1081–82, no. 827, referring to the urban delegates' memorial to the emperor at Augsburg on 30 January 1548.

82. Ibid., 1085–86, no. 829. The other members were Claus Kniebis, Dr. Ludwig Gremp, Mattheus Geiger, and Caspar Rumler.

83. Ibid., 1086–88, nos. 830, 832–33; Bellardi, *Geschichte*, 63–67.

84. Katharine Schütz (Zell) to Conrad Pellikan, Strasbourg, 4 January 1549, in BNUS, Thes. Baum., vol. 20:4–5, printed by Bainton, "Katherine Zell," 25–26 n. 40.

85. For Sturm's central role from the beginning through the signing of the treaty on 23 November 1549, see PC 4:1094–95, no. 836; 1114–18, no. 851 and n. 14; 1265–66, no. 933; 1269–70, no. 937.

86. The text is printed in PC 4:1259–64, no. 931. For commentary, see Weyrauch, *Krise*, 150–55.

87. I judge the potentially disruptive power of this crisis to have been much greater than does Erdmann Weyrauch, *Krise*, 147.

88. Martin Greschat looks at this relationship realistically, a rare thing in the historiography of Reformation Strasbourg. Greschat, *Martin Bucer*, 103: "Wollte Sturm also vor allem Straßburgs Stellung und Einfluß bewahren und sichern, … konnte [Bucer] Straßburg nur als einen Brückenkopf für die Ausbreitung des Evangeliums und die Durchsetzung des Reiches Gottes betrachten."

89. Bucer, "De regno Christi," 211; and there, too, at 212–13, the following quotes in this paragraph (original: *BOL* 15a:40–42).

90. Martin Bucer to Katherine Schütz (Zell) and Lux Hackfurt, Croydon, 13 May 1549, in Pollet, ed., *Correspondance* 1:254–56, no. 38, here at 256, line 1.

91. Martin Bucer to Jacob Sturm, Croydon, 13 May 1549, in Rott, "Un receuil," 809–18, no. 10, here at 809; also in Rott, *IH* 1:303. See Oberman, *Masters*, 238 n. 137, who quotes and comments on this letter.

10

The Last Years, 1549–1553

Awake, noble emperor grand
And take the matter in your hand
Down here, on this earth;
The margrave wants your title and land,
Along with your life,
And your throne as well.

He has hatched some evil plans
And brought Frenchmen into German lands
So as to frighten all good men.
God will help the emperor well
And give that chap his just deserts.*

For two decades the Reformation had thrust Jacob Sturm, Strasbourg, and the southern free cities into the whirlpool of Imperial and European politics, and the experience had brought them all to defeat, humiliation, and the brink of revolution. Little wonder, then, that Sturm's final years witnessed a return to the old policy of magisterial control, armed particularism, and provincial security.

STURM'S LESSON

One sign of his postwar retrenchment was Sturm's desire to lessen the subjection of the magistrates to fickle popular opinion. Sturm had always mistrusted the political sense of the common people, who, he believed, even when devout and good hearted, were too volatile and too ignorant to be politically responsible. They were easily confused by contradictory preaching, he often said, but when once gripped by an idea, as he warned Chancellor Granvelle at Augsburg in 1548, forcing a contrary rule, such as the interim, on them "would create a great movement" à la 1525.[1] This was the "card of 1525," but also his lifelong conviction. Sometime, probably before Schwörtag 1549, when city hall's empty benches were filled by new magistrates, Sturm drafted a plan for altering Strasbourg's constitution in favor of the upper classes.[2] He would create a new (but not unprecedented) constitutional category of "citizens" or "notables [cives, optimates, Bürger]," which,

TABLE 10.1

Jacob Sturm's Proposal for a Constitutional
Reform at Strasbourg, 1548 (?)

Category	Existing	Sturm's Proposal
Patricians (*nobiles/Adel*)		
Stettmeisters	4	4
Senators	6	6
Subtotal	10	10
Notables (*optimates/Bürger*)		
Senators		10
Subtotal		10
Guildsmen (*tribus/Handwerker*)		
Senators	20	10
Subtotal	20	10
Total	30	30

Source: AMS, VI 491/3; Brady, *Ruling Class*, 108–9.

as his lists of families show, would comprise the rich merchants and rentiers of the guilds, and he would redistribute the magisterial offices as shown in table 10.1.

Sturm's reform would give two-thirds of the magistracies to mercantile, noble, and other rentier families, who together counted, perhaps, fifty to seventy adult males eligible for office, and the remaining third to the some thirty-seven hundred members of the guilds.[3] Such a regime would provide security to those who, in Sturm's view, alone possessed the experience, education, and wisdom to protect the social order and maintain a stable policy abroad. As such, the plan (which remained on paper) was both the logical capstone on the growth of oligarchy in late medieval Strasbourg and Sturm's critique of the domestic political consequences of his own reformation policy.

The most striking thing about Sturm's constitutional revision is that it coincides almost exactly with the new constitutions, which Charles V's councilors installed at Augsburg and Ulm in August 1548 and in twenty-five other southern free cities during the following years. On the surface, this coincidence seems bizarre, for Charles V had become notorious in his treatment of urban liberties in consequence of his pacification of Ghent in 1540, at which time Strasbourg's Senate & XXI had noted: "Reflect on the example of Ghent. In every way we should be more careful."[4] The emperor, to be sure, revised the South German urban constitutions to protect the Catholic minorities, but he also aimed to reform the southern cities according to the model of loyal, Lutheran Nuremberg.[5] His policy arose chiefly from his mistrust of the common people and their influence on government, which is why his agents forced the revisions on Catholic and Evangelical free cities alike, not just on the former Smalkaldic powers. This motive, mistrust of the commons, Sturm shared with his monarch, which is why their constitutional revisions look like peas in a pod. Building up oligarchy, after all, was a logical response to Sturm's self-fulfilling prophecy to Granvelle at Augsburg in 1548 that forcing the interim on the towns "would create a great movement."[6] And he had the advantage that he understood, as Charles did not, the political importance of religious matters in the cities.[7] They nonetheless shared the belief that the urban regimes needed to be better insulated from the ordinary citizens. The proof for Sturm, of course, lay in the breakdown in relations between the magistrates and the Schöffen during August 1548.[8] From this experience he drew this lesson, though he got no opportunity to put it into practice. In the event, Strasbourg escaped a dictated constitutional revision and came away from the postwar era far more intact than, say, loyal Catholic towns, such as Leutkirch, Wangen, and Überlingen.

The postwar retrenchment, returning Strasbourg's policy to simpler, more restricted contexts, is visible in many aspects of Sturm's last years. His own journey to Cologne in the autumn of 1548 marked his final appearance on the stage of Imperial politics, and thereafter he traveled infrequently, and then very briefly, beyond his native city's environs.[9] Although his age—he was fifty-nine in 1548—and health partly account for this change, the patterns of civic diplomacy were also changing. For one thing, the subjects changed, for with few exceptions the city's missions of the half-decade between 1547 and 1552 dealt with leftover subjects from the Smalkaldic League. Meeting after meeting was held among the dead league's southern members, or among the free cities alone, to deliberate on debts from the Brunswick campaigns, peace with Duke Henry of Brunswick, the costs of the Danube campaign of 1546, and claims for damages from the war.[10]

The agents of civic diplomacy also changed, as with Sturm's withdrawal from active service the conduct of affairs passed swiftly and permanently from the magistrates to the lawyers. After the Smalkaldic War, the Senate & XXI placed most of its diplomatic affairs in the hands of its lawyers, a process illustrated by table 10.2.

In these years only one magistrate, Gottesheim, moved from the privy council's benches into the diplomatic harness in the old way. Even Jacob Sturm's rank in this table is deceptive, for two-thirds of his diplomatic tasks did not require him to leave Strasbourg.[11] In the main, the salaried civil servants took over the city's diplomatic operations, and in 1550, for the first time, Strasbourg sent only such men and no magistrates to an Imperial Diet.[12] The central figures in this change were two lawyers, the Alsatian Bernhard Botzheim and the Swabian Ludwig Gremp, who for decades after Jacob Sturm's death acted as Strasbourg's chief agents in Imperial politics. Negotiations with the Imperial court during Sturm's last years rested in the

TABLE 10.2

Strasbourg's Diplomatic Missions,
October 1548–November 1553

Name	Status	Missions
Dr. Ludwig Gremp	advocate	14
Dr. Bernhard von Botzheim	advocate	12
Friedrich von Gottesheim	XVer	12
Jacob Sturm	XIIIer	6
Dr. Heinrich Kopp	advocate	5
Johannes Sleidan	historian	3

Source: PC, vols. 4–5.

hands of another lawyer, Dr. Heinrich Kopp, a local boy whom the magistrates had sent to Bourges to learn French and the law.[13] It was Kopp who
handled the very delicate negotiations on the interim with Granvelle during
1549–50 and who came to the emperor's camp before Metz in November
1552.[14] The rise of these men completed a dramatic professionalization of
diplomacy during Jacob Sturm's last years.[15]

THE COUNCIL OF TRENT

Strasbourg could not simply sink back into its provincial nest, of course,
because at least one major issue, the schism, remained on the emperor's
agenda. Charles V's great postwar plan for the Empire and Christendom
required that the general council should complete the settlement the
Smalkaldic League's defeat had begun, and it sustained a grievous setback
on 11 March 1547, when Pope Paul translated the council from Trent to
Bologna. The Protestant electors and the free cities had set two conditions
on their agreement to attend the council: it must not meet under papal
leadership, and they should not be obliged to accept its earlier decisions.[16]
Charles seized on their "yes," ignored their "but," and told the new pope,
Julius III, that he had achieved the sine qua non of the council's return to
Trent. Julius, though he probably suspected the truth, nonetheless called
the council to reconvene at Trent on 14 November 1550. When, in the
following March, the diet drew to its close at Augsburg, it was time for the
Protestants to act out their part in the conciliar charade.[17]

Strasbourg's regime had from the first dismissed the papal council as neither
general, free, nor Christian, and Jacob Sturm agreed. When the council did
open at Trent in 1545, and Charles V pressed the German Protestants to
attend, Sturm declared that "the allies cannot entrust their cause to this
council," from which he expected only that "our teachings will surely be
condemned."[18] The contradiction, he told Chancellor Granvelle during the
Diet of Worms in 1545, was fundamental:[19]

Other nations and rulers consider the pope to be head of the church and vicar of Christ, from whom they expect decisions in controversies about the faith, so that this is a true and legitimate council. Our side, however, considers the pope and his adherents to be enemies of Christ, who, contrary to His teaching, introduced the abuses, so that we cannot refer our case to this council, which is neither free nor Christian.

Who, he asked, "can find a middle way which is acceptable to both sides?" Much reflection had suggested

only one way. There should be held such a council or assembly, in which pious, godfearing, learned men from both sides come together and organize themselves, free of all oaths and other loyalties; and that they should be sworn and obliged that, apart from all human passion and without fear or favor, they should consider what would conform to the Bible and usages of the early, still pure churches [*ersten reinen kirchen*]; they should then bring their views before the assembly.

Granvelle responded, naturally enough, that such a body—a grand version of the colloquies held in the early 1540s—had no authority of its own, and that a binding decision could be reached only "through the authority of a general council." Sturm retorted that the pope had shown through his actions that his council was illegitimate, especially in how "he has persecuted our people through the Spanish Inquisition in France, Italy, and the Netherlands." Sturm's view, that a council under papal presidency or leadership could not be "proper, free, and Christian," conforms to the general view of the matter among German Protestants, though he did not share the belief, which Martin Luther's last writing keynoted, "that the papal abomination did not come from God nor did it begin in God's name, but rather through God's wrath as punishment for sins [it was] founded by the devil and came into the church in his name."[20] Such absolute thinking was foreign to Sturm, who in 1546 thought that the Council of Trent might be tolerable, if the emperor would transform it from a papal into an Imperial assembly.[21] This was not to be, for Charles V held to his chosen line, and by 1551 it had become clear that the Protestant powers would have to send envoys to the current council, which had resumed sessions at Trent.[22]

A fortuitous event made this distasteful course safer and more palatable to Sturm and other politicians of the southern Protestant free cities. With Duke Ulrich's death at Tübingen on 6 November 1550, Württemberg came under the rule of his only son, Duke Christoph.[23] Now thirty-five years old, Christoph had been reared and educated at the Imperial, Bavarian, and French courts, and though reconciled to his difficult father in 1542, the young duke remained a stranger in his native land. He nonetheless moved easily into the niche of Strasbourg's friendly neighboring prince, which in the deeper past had belonged to the Elector Palatine and more recently to Landgrave Philip of Hesse. The long association between Lutheran Strasbourg and Lutheran Württemberg began with joint preparations for attendance at Trent, for, though reared at three Catholic courts, Christoph in his years at Montbéliard had become a zealous Lutheran.

Jacob Sturm knew by late January 1551 that the Protestants would have to attend the Council of Trent, and he began casting his net to mobilize the leading Protestant cities of the South, Elector Moritz, Duke Christoph, and other princes "of our religion."[24] Sturm wanted a broad coalition, but Duke Christoph, who feared "raising suspicions and mistrust," thought it would be good "if the theologians met beforehand."[25] On 4 May 1551 theologians from Strasbourg met their Württemberg counterparts at Dornstetten, a little town on the duchy's western border, and accepted their confessional statement (the "Confessio Virtembergica") as the beginning of the Strasbourg-Württemberg cooperation on religion.[26] At Strasbourg, Sturm hoped this agreement could be expanded until all the southern Protestants would come "to stand as one person with others of this religion."[27] It was not to be. "There is so much fear in Germany," wrote the English agent Christopher Mount, "that people dare not confer together lest they be suspected of renewing conspiracies."[28] Separate embassies, therefore, were sent to Trent by Strasbourg, Duke Christoph, and Elector Moritz of Saxony.

At Strasbourg the selection of envoys proved perplexing, for only Caspar Hedio remained of the older clergymen, and the younger ones were entirely untried. As Jacob Sturm observed in January 1551, "The lack of persons qualified for this task is such that we have no one to send. If Martin Bucer, Dr. Peter Martyr, or Calvin were still here, we would not consider them unqualified to be sent with the other theologians."[29] The most likely choice was Johann Marbach, the young Lindauer and graduate of Wittenberg, who since Bucer's departure was emerging as the coming man among the local clergy.[30] Sturm, however, hit on another idea, as the XIII told Frankfurt's regime:

> we think that at first one or two persons, not theologians, should go in the names and at the common expense of the cities who agree with us in this matter; they should have instructions to follow the lead of [sich . . . anhengich zu machen] the Saxons and Württembergers and take counsel and make common cause with them. And if it should later become necessary to send learned men, we'll send someone from among the theologians.[31]

But whom to send? The unexpected choice fell on Johannes Sleidan, the Paris-educated historian of the Smalkaldic League. Though relatively inexperienced in diplomacy, the trilingual Sleidan had for some years served as secretary to Cardinal Jean du Bellay, and his father-in-law was Johann von Niedpruck of Metz, a very experienced diplomat.[32] That Jacob Sturm made the choice is clear from the fact that Sleidan reported from Trent separately to the XIII and to Sturm.[33] He set off on 3 November 1551, made a late autumn passage of the Brenner down to Trent on the twenty-ninth, where he lodged in a German inn called "The Red Rose."[34]

Jacob Sturm and the preachers in the meantime prepared a document that sheds much light on their view of the Council of Trent.[35] Strasbourg should be represented at Trent, they declared "not because we hoped to pluck grapes from among the thorns at Trent, or figs from among the thistles [Mt. 7:16, Lk 6:44], but to proclaim, both orally and in writing, the Confession of Augsburg . . ., which is the true doctrine of Our Lord Jesus Christ, before the Council of Trent, that piece of whoremongery, and to do so stalwartly but with proper Christian modesty."[36] They could think nonetheless of no Strasbourgeois whom they wished to recommend for this mission, and it was not until February 1552 that the Senate & XXI decided to send two of its clergymen, Johann Marbach and Christoph Söll, to Trent.[37] They arrived on 8 April and stayed just under three weeks. Marbach put the best light on their mission:

> Although no negotiations were conducted, yet we accomplished what was originally conceived, namely, to show that we don't avoid the light, and we maintain the doctrine we have held until now and have given a good account of it.[38]

Sleidan and the preachers returned to a city seething with preparations for war: King Henry of France was coming to the Rhine at the head of an enormous army; German princes, having raised the standard of revolt, were marching to meet him near the Rhine bridge at Strasbourg.[39] The last major event of Jacob Sturm's career was about to take place, right on his doorstep.

THE YEAR OF THE FRENCH, 1552

The French War of 1552 played out a classic scenario: German princes in league with France revolted against the emperor. King Henry II did not merely send money this time, as his father had done in 1534, he came at the head of his army across Lorraine and toward the Rhine. At the head of his German allies stood Elector Moritz of Saxony, the tall, lean, sybaritic prince who had benefitted so hugely from the Smalkaldic War.[40] Since the summer of 1550, Moritz lay in touch with Henry II, the young king of France, to whom he proposed offensive action against the emperor; a little later he made contact with a princes' conspiracy that was forming under the leadership of Margrave Hans of Brandenburg; and in the autumn of 1551 they formed an alliance to make war on the emperor.[41] Their strategic plan called for the king to bring his army to the Rhine, while Moritz and his allies cut their way across Franconia to meet him near Frankfurt. They made war in the names of "German liberty" and of the Empire, of which they pledged to make King Henry the emperor. Henry, the new Arminius, his propaganda proclaimed, was coming to defend the Germans against the Habsburg Varus's legions. By mid-March 1552, when the princes proclaimed their war against Charles V, the French royal army already lay in camp at Joinville. Then, with about forty thousand foot and ten thousand horse— not eighty thousand foot and twelve thousand horse, as one nobleman reported at Strasbourg—the king crossed into the Empire and traversed Lorraine toward Metz, which his generals entered on Palm Sunday (10 April) 1552.[42] On 21 April, Metz's magistrates appeared before him to swear their recognition of the royal mission "for the good of the Holy Empire and the restoration and preservation of its liberty."[43]

At Strasbourg the preparations began well before Metz fell. Apparently, it never crossed Jacob Sturm's mind to regard King Henry as a liberator, for Sturm was no Francophile, and he once remarked that the Smalkaldic League's experience had shown that "the French are fickle."[44] He and his colleagues decided early to defend "fortress Strasbourg," for as "the land cannot resist a large force, we must consider how we can hold this place . . . for the protection of everyone, both laymen and clergy."[45] If the French king took the city, "he will strengthen, provision, and garrison it and use it to hold the entire land," and the emperor's attempts to retake it would turn the entire province into a battleground. The Strasbourgeois could not bear the expense of this policy alone, however, so the regime decided to consult the other Alsatian powers about "how the place may be held at common expense and protected from force. If the city alone must bear the costs, that will mean a levy [schatzung], which the burghers will oppose because the clergy are exempt from it."[46] Sturm's committee recommended immediate talks with the region's other powers, such as the city of Basel, the bishop and cathedral chapter of Strasbourg, the counts of Hanau-Lichtenberg and Bitsch, the other free cities, and the free knights, with the aim of organizing a collective provincial defense centered on Strasbourg.[47] When Sturm talked with envoys of the bishop and the free knights at the end of March and beginning of April, he tried to rally them for his policy of "fortress Strasbourg."[48] Though they listened, the other Alsatian powers promised nothing and gave nothing.

The French invasion of 1552 thus thrust Strasbourg back into its old role of regional metropolis, and Sturm slipped into the role of provincial leader as easily as his great-grandfather had done eighty years ago. At the end of his long career at the highest levels of Imperial politics, during which time he had dealt with princes on an intimate basis, spoke for an entire house of the Imperial Diet, traded jokes and barbs with the Imperial grand chancellor, and received honors and praise from the Empire's free cities, Jacob Sturm sat down with countrified squires and politicians from petty towns to talk of purely provincial interests. That it came to this was a sign of how completely the Protestant cause had been defeated; that he should undertake such work no less willingly than he had earlier dealt with great lords is a measure of Sturm as a man of the city. He brought to this task the same calm sense that he had spread among the allies and among the free cities: "We should try to compose the quarrels among us and dispel all ill will, for otherwise . . . there will come not good will but much misfortune."[49] As he had told the Ulmers so many years before, political solidarity depended on "the proper sort of love for one another."

At the beginning of April, as Sturm tried to scrabble together a provincial defense organization, Strasbourg already lay isolated between two theaters of war. Eastward, Elector Moritz and his allied princes were marching southward from Franconia to try to snare the fleeing emperor at Augsburg; westward, the French army entered Metz—the news came to Strasbourg on 13 April—and prepared to invade Alsace via Saarbrücken with thirty thousand men.[50] "We are caught between two armies," Sleidan wrote on 16 April, "the princes threaten us from Swabia, the Frenchman from Metz, where today, it is said, he will enter the city.... We have only 2,000 troops. Oh, poor Germany!"[51] Two days later, a French herald came to announce the king's imminent arrival and his desire for provisions, and next day the magistrates consulted the Schöffen, who "unanimously gave my lords, the senators, powers and said they would stick by them through thick and thin."[52]

Peter Sturm, Jacob's brother, headed the embassy that left Strasbourg for the French camp on 18 April. It brought back mixed news. Although, as Dr. Kopp reported, the city could well withstand a siege at the hands of this army, there was great danger from agents and sympathizers among the resident French at Strasbourg.[53] "Rascals," Jacob Sturm had once called such men, "who act against God and their country for the sake of money."[54] And yet, the French speakers had their uses, as a second embassy discovered, when it found Anne de Montmorency, constable of France, on 2 May at Saverne, where the king was about to descend the Vosges Mountains' east face. Peter Sturm, Gottesheim, and Sleidan found a Catholic merchant from Saint-Nicolas-de-Port in Lorraine, Michel Berman, who could identify them to the French as "men from the regime at Strasbourg."[55] The approach of the French army nevertheless inflamed anti-Latin feelings among the native Strasbourgeois, so much so that when the Schöffen were called on 2 May, it was decided "to gather all the Latins in the inn, eat with them, and ask them to stay, because the people are somewhat upset."[56]

When the envoys returned from Saverne with the king's terms—200,000 loaves of bread, 100 casks of wine, and other provisions—the regime decided for negotiation, reported to the Schöffen, and sent the envoys back.[57] This time Peter Sturm and the others entered camp under protection of Basel's envoys and were brought to see Montmorency in the bishop's garden.[58] They gave him the disagreeable message that the city could neither supply much food nor allow French troops to enter, whereupon the constable, unaware, perhaps, that "German liberty" was a purely princely ideal, lectured the Strasbourgeois about how much his king had done for them. Next they were called before the king in the presence of the cardinal of Lorraine and the Duc de Vendôme, and when Sleidan said that Strasbourg would supply fruit, oats, and wine (double yesterday's offer), Montmorency cried, "We are no cows who can live on fruit! We need bread!"[59] The envoys returned to Strasbourg on the same day, 5 May, and on the sixth the French broke camp for the Rhine.[60] Next day the king camped at Brumath, from which he could see the spires of Strasbourg, though the well-known story of a French patrol fired on by cannon from the walls of Strasbourg is probably a legend.[61] One week later, when king and army moved off northward, the storm was past. When King Henry wrote to Strasbourg in November 1552, he had recovered his lofty tone, speaking no more of bread and wine but only of old friendship and the cause of "German liberty."[62]

Meanwhile, Moritz and his allies, too, had struck blows for "German liberty." They aimed to secure lasting security for the German Protestants, but also to oppose the "Spanish succession," Charles's plan to leave all his lands and titles to his son, Prince Philip.[63] "You princes ought to watch out," Moritz warned, "for someone with catch you by a rope around the horns and then lead you where he will."[64] This was a language all princes could understand, so when Moritz plunged southward in the spring of 1552, few hands lifted to help the emperor, who, "paralysed by a mixture of fear and pride" and at odds with his brother, sat motionless at Innsbruck until the rebel army was literally at the city's gates.[65] In May, finally, King Ferdinand and the neutral electors brought together peace proposals that, though with very bad grace, Charles had to accept. The Treaty of Passau (15 August 1552) ended the main German phase of the war and shaped relations between emperor and princes until the settlement of 1555.

The Strasbourgeois followed these events with great interest, once the French army left the city and its province in relative peace. The rebellion and war made their security once again a problem of regional scope, and in June the Senate & XXI sent an envoy down to the regional center to which their ties had once been firmest, Heidelberg. Someone else could have done it, or the message could easily have gone by post, but they sent Jacob Sturm to visit once more the university town he had first seen in 1504.[66] His mission was merely to tell the elector, who would pass it to the other princes, of the city's determination to remain loyal and have nothing to do with the rebel princes.

1552, the year of the French, a year of surprises, had one more surprise in store for Jacob Sturm and Strasbourg. On 7 September an Imperial official named Haug Engele von Engelsee appeared at Strasbourg to ask for provisions for the Imperial army, which then lay near Bretten.[67] Two days later, an Imperial quartermaster wrote that Charles himself would arrive with his army on the fifteenth.[68] Goaded by his wounded honor, a thirst for revenge, and his hatred of France, the failing monarch aimed to cross the Rhine with seventy thousand men and retake Metz.[69] At Strasbourg, the Schöffen were informed, and on 13 September an embassy went out to meet and greet the emperor before he reached the city.[70] It was Sturm's last journey. Finding Charles V near Rastatt, he delivered his masters' plea that the emperor spare the city and region and send at least some of his troops by other routes. They would receive him in person in a fitting manner, though they begged him to bring only a small bodyguard and to respect their liberties.[71] Charles praised the city for its stand against the French, excused his quick passage by the lateness of the season, promised to lead his army around the city, and dismissed the envoys.

The embassy's return touched off a frenzy of preparations: burghers in armor and weapons, gunners on the walls, towers, and bastions, strengthened guards at the gates, and three hundred extra guards at night in the suburbs. Next day, Imperial troops appeared on the Rhine bridge, mounted Spaniards and Italians in the van, followed by German foot and artillery. They camped in the nearby villages, with the usual consequences for the peasants' life, limb, and property. The Schöffen and the guilds had been warned to keep peace, doubly necessary with so many "Latin" troops about, and many hundreds of men, women, and children climbed the city's walls to view this wildly colorful array of warriors. For nearly four days the army camped, as their emperor rested in headquarters near Auenheim, and on the nineteenth they began to march off. Just at midday, the emperor appeared at Butchers' Gate, entered the city, and was received by the magistrates "in a most affectionate and respectful manner," as Sleidan put it.[72] With Charles came great lords, among them the Duke of Alba, Margrave Hans of Brandenburg-Küstrin, Duke Emmanuel Philibert of Savoy, and Granvelle, plus Bishop Erasmus of Strasbourg and eight hundred troopers. They moved between lines of armed burghers, stiffened with mercenaries, until they came to the cathedral, where Charles met the city's clergy before lunching in the mansion of Conrad Meyer, the rich member of the XV.[73] About five o'clock Charles mounted his "little brown" and rode away through the rain, the magistrates accompanying him as far as the Good Folk's House, where the lepers lived. He bedded down that night in the mayor's house at Bischheim, which belonged to the Böcklins, and next day he was gone. "I departed Strasbourg," he later wrote Prince Philip, "where I received the very finest demonstrations of love and good will."[74] He was leaving the German-speaking lands forever—Strasbourg was the last large German-speaking city he ever saw—headed for the ruin of his army and the rest of his reputation before the walls of Metz.

Thus, forty-eight years after King Maximilian had come overnight to Strasbourg to get aid for the Bavarian War, the Strasbourgeois greeted his grandson and sent him gratefully on his way. His treatment symbolizes Strasbourg's return to the good, old, safe policy: respectful loyalty to the emperor; strong regional ties symbolized by Bishop Erasmus's presence; and sturdy self-reliance, embodied in the long ranks of armed burghers. The policy suited the city, and if the magistrates needed this fact confirmed, they could recall that during the entire afternoon of that September day in 1552, Charles V never once mentioned religion.

STURM'S END

When Charles V left Strasbourg, Jacob Sturm had just over one year to live. His only missions in this last year were three meetings of the Lower

Alsatian association for regional defense (*Landesrettung*), all held at Strasbourg.[75] Their discussions of a regional defense system frame Sturm's end, as the far-flung Smalkaldic League had his prime. Such meetings reassembled the world in which his father, his uncles, and his great-grandfather Schott had grown old, the small world of Imperial councilors from the Austrian regime at Ensisheim, episcopal vassals (like himself), cathedral canons (as he might have been), city secretaries, and free knights (again, like himself). Indeed, some others who took part were his own kinsmen, Wolff Zorn von Plobsheim and Ludwig Bock von Gerstheim, Hans's son.[76] It was a familiar, comfortably provincial world, where everyone came from nearby places and spoke in familiar accents, a great and welcome relief from the long journeys on horseback, the weeks of waiting for something to happen, and the months of lodging in inns and eating overpriced, hastily prepared food and drinking sour wine. In this familiar Upper Rhenish world, by contrast, Jacob Sturm was thoroughly at home.

And there he died. Pastor Johann Marbach, who stood at Sturm's deathbed, as Sturm had stood at Geiler's in 1510, left us a picture of the stettmeister's end. "On 30 October at four o'clock in the morning," he tells,

> I was summoned to Sir Jacob Sturm, who had been ill with a quartain fever for about ten days. As I came into the room, he lay already in his death agony, and though his tongue was so dry that he could no longer speak, his mind was clear. To every passage I read from the Bible, he answered, "yes," and he prayed with us with folded hands and at end said audibly, "Amen." It was now six o'clock, and after a quarter of an hour I said to him, "Sir, will you hear some more from God's Word?" He turned his open eyes to me and looked, as I now said these words from John [3:17]: "For God did not send his Son to judge the world but to save it; and whoever believes in Him will not be judged but given eternal life." Then he closed his eyes again, opened his mouth, and with two breaths he was gone and moved no more.[77]

Marbach, Bucer's heir as chief of Strasbourg's church, mourned this greatest member of what they would all come to think of as the Reformation's heroic generation. "For myself," the pastor from Lindau wrote, "in him I lost my best friend, yes, my father in this city."

That afternoon Ammeister Hans Hammerer of the Cobblers' Guild spoke the terrible news at city hall, "that Sir Jacob Sturm, father of his country and an ornament of this republic [*pater patriae et ornamentum huius Reipublicae*], has fallen asleep in the Lord (may He grant him a happy resurrection), and that we will bury him tomorrow at two o'clock. Sir Mathis Pfarrer says that it is customary for all magistrates to attend."[78] Next day they all gathered at the Dominicans' and walked over to the Sturms' mansion in Fire Street. Then they set out—magistrates, civil servants, clergymen, schoolmasters, and pupils—to guide the dead stettmeister and scholarch to rest, his coffin carried by teachers and civic employees. Through the city's gates they walked and past the Good Folk's House, where the lepers lived, for as the Reformation had banished Strasbourg's dead from its churches, Sturm had to be buried outside the walls. After Marbach preached in German on the text "For to me to live is Christ, and to die is gain" (Phil. 1:21), in early afternoon on the last day of October 1553, Jacob Sturm was laid to rest. The magistrates and teachers filed by the open grave and cast clods of earth on him.[79]

Very soon after Jacob Sturm's burial—he lay alone, for his wife was nearly twenty-five years dead, so long that many Strasbourgeois believed that, like his brothers, he had never married[80]—the rector of the Latin school, Jean Sturm, declaimed before the Senate & XXI a eulogy for his namesake.[81] His speech was an epitaph for the generation that had established the Reformation at Strasbourg. The rector tolled the names of those who had preceded the great stettmeister in death: the ammeisters Daniel Mieg, Batt von Duntzenheim, Martin Herlin, Hans Lindenfels, Mattheus Geiger, and Claus Kniebis, plus the stettmeisters Hans Bock and Egenolf Röder von Diersburg. The age belonged, however, to Jacob Sturm. "I have in mind," the rector said, "what service he performed after the Peasants' War, namely, in changing the religion and suppressing useless rituals and false worship." Perhaps the rector overemphasized the importance of individuals in the regime, as he described how the torch of leadership had passed from old Ludwig Böcklin, Jacob Sturm's uncle, the eminent stettmeister who had died in 1529, but his description emphasized the dominance of Jacob Sturm through most of the Reformation era. With grand words and in the fashion of the day, he compared the dead statesman to the Greek and Roman statesmen of old— straining the historical knowledge, no doubt, of some of his hearers—and praised the deceased's faultless private life, his gentle decency, "his eloquence, his learning, his wisdom [*oratio, doctrina, sapientia*]," his combination of "sweetness and gravity [*in suavitate grauitas*]," and his fine appearance. Above all, the rector associated the dead stettmeister's reputation with the founding and growth of the Latin school, far more than with the reconstruction of the church and the defense of the faith. He recounted Jacob Sturm's steadfast behavior after the Smalkaldic War and in the crisis of the Interim of Augsburg, proclaiming that he was responsible for the fact that "you have your republic; you have your religion; you have your liberty; you have your citizens safe and sound."

Nothing characterizes Jacob Sturm's legacy more than his passing, blessed by the words of Johann Marbach, future leader of Strasbourg's church, and lauded by the eloquence of Jean Sturm, rector of its Latin school. For these two men would one day, not long in the future, become bitter enemies in the struggle for possession of the reputation and the future of Strasbourg's reformation. Marbach represented the ties to Luther and Wittenberg, the development of which into Lutheran orthodoxy grew from roots fostered by Jacob Sturm's alliance policy; Jean Sturm represented the ties to the world of humanism and the Gallicized culture of Calvinism, which was nurtured

by Jacob Sturm's policies as scholarch. When Strasbourg's reformation heritage became an object of struggle between these two forces, both sides
could claim with justice to be guardians of the great stettmeister's legacy.
Jacob Sturm had been a man of late medieval politics, Reformation piety,
and Renaissance culture.

Notes

* "Wach auf, du edler keiser gut/und halt dein sach in vester hut/iezunder auf
diser erden;/der marggraf stelt dir nach ehr und gut,/sein beger stet im nach
deinem blut,/vermaint, er wöll keiser werden.//Etlich practik hat er geschwind
erdacht,/hat den Franzosen in das Deutschland gebracht,/die leut darmit zu
erschrecken;/got weißt dem keiser sein hilf zu thon,/daß er im geb den rechten
lon." Liliencron, ed., *Historische Volkslieder* 4:538, no. 596, stanzas 1–2.

1. PC 4:1016, no. 791.
2. This paragraph rests on Brady, *Ruling Class*, 108–9, though I failed there to
recognize the similarity of Sturm's plan to the Caroline revision of free cities'
constitutions in 1548–56.
3. Based on figures in Brady, *Ruling Class*, 73, 109; Rott, "Artisanat," 159 (also
in Rott, *IH* 1:154).
4. AMS, XXI 1540, fol. 188r. See Brandi, *Kaiser Karl V.* 1:322–59; Pirenne, *Histoire
de Belgique* 3:117–28.
5. Naujoks, *Zunftverfassung*, 18, 37–45; Brady, *Turning Swiss*, 211–21.
6. PC 4:1016, no. 791.
7. Petri, "Karl V. und die Städte," 21–25; Naujoks, *Zunftverfassung*.
8. See Brady, *Ruling Class*, 162, 195–96.
9. Sturm went to Speyer in February 1549 and to Heidelberg during the French
invasion of Alsace in June 1552. PC 4:1138–40, 114–43, nos. 861, 863; ibid.
5:337–38, no. 251.
10. PC 4:nos. 860, 874, 890, 895, 915, 928, 938; ibid. 5:nos. 10, 78, 84, 115–16,
121–22, 135, 139–40, 145, 159, 161, 175, 183, 370, 390. This carries the
story beyond Sturm's death. The chief exceptions were embassies to the Imperial Diet of Augsburg in 1550–51 and to the Council of Trent's second session.
11. PC 5:nos. 295, 327, 333, 337.
12. Ibid., 117–18, no. 76; Ficker-Winckelmann 1:28, 33.
13. Ficker-Winckelmann 1:27.
14. PC 4:1222–23, no. 911; ibid. 5:45–46, no. 30, 306, no. 222, 314, no. 228,
413–14, no. 311.
15. For prewar tendencies, see Brady, *Ruling Class*, 255–57.
16. Jedin, "Die Deutschen," 143–48. Fundamental on German Protestant participation in the Council of Trent are Jedin, *Geschichte*, 3; Bizer, *Confessio
Virtembergica*, 10–62; H. Meyer, "Die deutschen Protestanten"; Brecht,
"Abgrenzung."
17. Luttenberger, *Glaubenseinheit*, 553–65, and the Recess of Augsburg 1551, in
Schmauss, *Reichs-Abschiede* 2:611–14, and CT 3,3:21–22. Though Brecht,
"Abgrenzung," questions this view, the documents bear out Jedin's conclusion
("Die Deutschen," 145) about "die—in Wirklichkeit nur scheinbare—Anerkennung des Trienter Konzils durch die deutschen Protestanten."
18. Lenz, ed., *Briefwechsel* 2:342 n. 2; PC 3:570. On the regime's attitude, see ibid
2:191, no. 194.

19. The following is taken from Sturm's account of the interview, in PC 3:604–6, no. 574.

20. Quoted by Edwards, Last Battles, 186. Bucer's view, which was similar, is in Lenz, ed., Briefwechsel 2:385, no. 223. See, in general, Edwards, Last Battles, 182–200; Oberman, Luther, 246–71; Kirchner, "Luther und das Papsttum," 444–55.

21. PC 4:94–95, no. 67. Note that Sturm could not recommend the proposal in the document he enclosed, which had been written by Conrad Hubert and Johann Lenglin of Strasbourg, and which suggested a new colloquy under elaborate safeguards. Ibid., 95, no. 67 n. 2.

22. The best account of preparations among the Protestant powers of southwestern Germany is by Bizer, Confessio Virtembergica, 10–31. For Strasbourg's role, see Friedensburg, "Zur Konzilspolitik," which rests on his editorship of PC, vol. 5.

23. Maurer, "Herzog Christoph."

24. PC 5:111, no. 72. See Friedensburg, "Zur Konzilspolitik," 194–98.

25. PC 5:115–16, no. 75; Ernst, ed., Briefwechsel 1:156–65, no. 165; CT, vol. 7, pt. 3: 49–59, no. 20, 75–76, no. 36. See Bizer, Confessio Virtembergica, 14–15.

26. PC 5:156–58, no. 104; Ernst, ed., Briefwechsel 1:82–84, no. 179; and the best account is by Bizer, Confessio Virtembergica, 18–20. Strasbourg's regime wanted a wider collaboration, including Duke Moritz, the free cities, and the Protestant free nobles, whereas Duke Christoph favored a much narrower operation.

27. PC 5:169, no. 114, and 176–77, no. 117. The story is well told by Bizer, Confessio Virtembergica, 21–27.

28. Quoted by Bizer, Confessio Virtembergica, 31 n. 105.

29. PC 5:111, no. 72. See Friedensbrug, "Zur Konzilspolitik," 195, 199.

30. Friedensburg, "Zur Konzilspolitik," 199–200, 208–9. Marbach had been tainted by the episode of the conventicles, but he possessed good connections to the Saxons. Ficker-Winckelmann 2:89, Bellardi, Geschichte, 96, 106.

31. PC 5:219, no. 153. This passage contains an ominous reference to the safe-conduct for the Saxon envoys being in the form, "Wie daz concili zu Basel die Behem vergleitet hat."

32. Sleidan remained in French service after coming to Strasbourg. See Cardinal du Bellay to King Henry II, Rome, 13 August 1547, who recommended that the king retain Sleidan in royal service. Sleidan, Briefwechsel, 143–44, no. 80. Sleidan had gone to England on the league's behalf in 1545. Sleidan, Briefwechsel, 81–89. It is sometimes said that he taught history in the Latin school at Strasbourg, but this is false. Schindling, Gymnasium, 271 n. 2. Sleidan's reputation at Strasbourg may be gathered from a comment of Heinrich Walther, a secretary, who called him a "fürtrefflich gelehrten mann bei uns." PC 5:240 n. 5.

33. For example, on 29 November 1551, the days of his first official report from Trent. Sleidan, Briefwechsel, 173–80, nos. 94–95. See the note in Rott, "Jean Sleidan," 632 (also in Rott, IH 2:444).

34. Based on his reports, in Sleidan, Briefwechsel, 167–69, 171–78, nos. 91, 93–94. His original instruction is lost, though the XIII sent him a supplementary instruction after his report on the interview with Duke Christoph. Ibid., 169–70, no. 92. For the efforts to gather powers from other towns, see PC 5:nos. 153–54, 159, 163; CT, vol. 7, pt. 3:352, no. 247. Sturm used personal ties to promote this effort, for an example of which, see CT, vol. 7, pt. 3:368, no. 260.

35. PC 5:252–55, no. 173, Hedio's draft with Sturm's corrections. From the time of their arrival, the Protestants were pressed about why their masters had sent no theologians. Sleidan, Briefwechsel, 176, no. 94.

36. Grapes, of course, do not have thorns, and in Swabian-Alemannic "träuble" are currants, which do.

37. *PC* 5:282, 284, nos. 200, 202. On 15 January 1552, the XIII wrote to Sleidan that they still hadn't decided whether to send theologians. Sleidan, *Briefwechsel*, 194, no. 99. On Söll (d. 1552), a Tyrolean who married one of Bucer's step-daughters, see Ficker-Winckelmann 2:68.
38. *PC* 5:308, no. 223, from their report. They returned on 22 April 1552. Crusius, *Schwäbische Chronik* 2:282.
39. See *PC* 5:nos. 203, 209–15.
40. For what follows, the fundamental study for the Imperial side of the story is Lutz, *Christianitas afflicta*; for the French side, see Zeller, *Réunion*, vol. 1, and Pariset, *Relations*; and for Strasbourg's involvement, see Holländer, *Straßburg im Französischen Krieg*, and Petri, "Straßburgs Beziehungen." The war figures importantly in the long debate about the origins of French expansionism to-ward the Rhine, on which see the overview by Hübinger, "Die Anfänge der französischen Rheinpolitik."
41. Born, "Moritz von Sachsen"; Schlomka, *Kurfürst Moritz*, 5–10; Pariset, *Relations*, 107–15; H. Weber, "Le traité de Chambord."
42. *PC* 5:300–301, no. 219; Zeller, *Réunion* 1:345–66; Pariset, *Relations*, 129–31. The larger figure came to the XIII from Count Philip of Nassau-Saarbrücken, who wrote on 20 March, and who, given the location of his little territory in Henry's path, may be forgiven his exaggeration. *PC* 5:294 n. 3. On Stras-bourg's relations with France after the Smalkaldic War, see Petri, "Beziehungen," 164–81; on the situation in Alsace before the campaign, see Holländer, *Straßburg im Französischen Krieg*, 7–9; and on the situation in the Empire, see Lutz, *Christianitas afflicta*, 64–81.
43. The text of the oath is printed by Zeller, *Réunion* 1:466.
44. *PC* 4:76, no. 56.
45. *PC* 5:295–97, no. 214; there, too, the remaining quotes in this paragraph. The idea of "fortress Strasbourg" was formulated already in January 1552 in the first consultation on defense. Ibid., 276–77, no. 194. See Holländer, *Straßburg im Französischen Krieg*, 9.
46. See Craemer, "Wehrmacht Straßburgs," 56–57. The regime later claimed to have spent "mehr als 100,000 gulden" to keep Alsace out of French hands. Holländer, *Straßburg im Französischen Krieg*, 58 n. 3.
47. The free cities Sélestat and Hagenau are not mentioned in this document but in the following one, which was read in council on 26 March 1552. *PC* 5:298, no. 215. In the talks on regional defense at the end of March, Sturm empha-sized the need to hold these three strong places—Strasbourg, Sélestat, and Hagenau. Holländer, *Straßburg im Französischen Krieg*, 17–18.
48. These negotiations are described by Holländer, *Straßburg im Französischen Krieg*, 16–22. Strasbourg's envoys were instructed approximately as Sturm had rec-ommended in his memorial of March 1552.
49. *PC* 5:296, no. 214.
50. Ibid., 300–301, no. 219.
51. Sleidan, *Briefwechsel*, 242, no. 116.
52. *PC* 5:306, no. 222, and the quote is from note 1. See Pariset, *Relations*, 138–39, who dates the appointment of the embassy to 20 April. Just at this time Marbach and Söll returned from Trent, made their report, and presented their bills. Ibid., 307–10, nos. 223–24.
53. *PC* 5:314, no. 228.
54. Ibid. 3:511 n. 3, quoted by Wagner, *Wilhelm von Fürstenberg*, 22. In a letter to King Henry II, Charles de Marillac speaks of operations "comme aussy à Stras-bourg par voz serviteurs secretz." Druffel, ed., *Beiträge* 1:42, no. 458 (29 July 1550). Charles V had earlier complained of French "pensionnaires, mesmes

ceulx qui se trouvent à Strasbourg ayan adhéré zu rebelles." Ibid., 41, no. 81.
55. PC 5:320, no. 234. See Holländer, *Straßburg im Französischen Krieg*, 42; Kammerer, "Réforme et grand commerce," 54. His brother, Jehan, was at Strasbourg, whence he reported to the Duc de Guise, French governor at Metz, on movements in the Imperial army. Zeller, "Marchands-capitalistes," 275. See also Holländer, "Straßburgs Politik," 23 n. 1, on French spies. Sleidan accompanied these embassies of 2 and 5 May as interpreter, though Gottesheim could also understand French. Brady, *Ruling Class*, 316. Peter Sturm, of course, knew Latin.
56. PC 5:321. The "inn [*herberg*]" was probably the tavern in the guildhall Zur Möhrin, where the ammeister dined.
57. Ibid., Holländer, 321; *Straßburg im Französischen Krieg*, 45, who notes that 162 voted to support the regime, and 84 wanted to give the king nothing.
58. This is based on their report in PC 5:325–26, no. 236.
59. Ibid., 326; Holländer, *Straßburg im Französischen Krieg*, 46–48.
60. Holländer, *Straßburg im Französischen Krieg*, 51–52.
61. Ibid., 52–54; Holländer, *Eine Straßburger Legende*.
62. Kentzinger, ed., *Documents historiques* 1:36–37, noticed in PC 5:410, no. 306. Pariset, "L'activité des Jacques Sturm," 262–63, holds that Strasbourg's policy toward France at this time was determined by the desire of the city's merchants for good relations with France in case of French control of the Rhine Valley, and he concludes: (263) "Mais au XVIe siècle il est encore trop tôt pour changer de zone économique." While not wrong, his comment breathes a national point of view.
63. Lutz, *Christianitas afflicta*, 80–81; Duchhardt, *Protestantisches Kaisertum*, 39–43.
64. Brandenburg, *Politisches Korrespondenz* 1:no. 373, art. 2. Moritz's words had their effect on, for example, Duke Christoph of Württemberg, though he shared Sturm's view of the French, whom he knew very well. See Ernst, ed., *Briefwechsel* 1:511–12. For Charles's project, which revived the failed scheme of 1547–48, see Lutz, *Christianitas afflicta*, 114–20, 190–99.
65. Rodríguez-Salgado, *Changing Face*, 45–47, gives an especially dramatic picture of these events. The fundamental account is Lutz, *Christianitas afflicta*, 81–105. For Ferdinand's side of the estrangement, see Fichtner, *Ferdinand I*, 192–99; and for Charles's side, see Brandi, *Kaiser Karl V.* 1:505–12.
66. His instruction is in PC 5:337–38, no. 251; simultaneously Botzheim was sent to Stuttgart with the same instruction. Elector Frederick informed Duke Christoph of Sturm's visit, in Druffel, ed., *Beiträge* 2:601. See Holländer, "Straßburgs Politik," 5–8.
67. For what follows, see Holländer, "Straßburgs Politik," 20–37.
68. PC 5:389–90, no. 292.
69. The campaign to Lorraine is marked by Rodríguez-Salgado, *Changing Face*, 47–48, as the turning point toward Charles's enfeeblement and abdication. She essentially restates the position of Brandi, "Karl V. vor Metz." For the campaign itself, see Finot, "Le siège de Metz," 260–70.
70. Holländer, "Straßburgs Politik," 23–29, on this mission.
71. The instruction is in PC 5:392–93, no. 295.
72. Quoted by Holländer, "Straßburgs Politik," 32 n. 3. There, too, is quoted Charles's comment.
73. On Conrad Meyer (d. 6 March 1556), see Brady, *Ruling Class*, 330–31.
74. Quoted by Holländer, "Straßburgs Politik," 32 n. 3.
75. They met on 8 February, 22 March, and 12 April. PC 5:426–27, no. 327, 432, no. 333, 434–36, no. 337.
76. Brady, *Ruling Class*, 302, 352, 372. See the lists in PC 5:432, 435–36.
77. AST 198, fols. 99v–100r; and there, too, the following quote. My thanks to

James M. Kittelson for this text. It is now printed in Lebeau and Valentin, eds., *L'Alsace au siècle de la Réforme*, 147–48.

78. AMS, XXI 1553, at 30 October 1553, printed in Fournier and Engel, eds., *Statuts et privilèges*, pt. 2, vol. 4, fasc. 1:64 n. 2; PC 5:481, no. 386.

79. AST 198, fols. 100v–101r. Marbach says that he preached at one o'clock, but the Senate & XXI were to gather at two. The detail about the clods of earth is from Crusius, *Schwäbische Chronik* 2:287, who was a student at Strasbourg.

80. Büheler, *Chronique*, no. 347: "Und er . . . hat auch sein leben lang, wie wol er uff die 63 jar oder mehr worden, nie kein eheweib gehabt."

81. *Ioannis Sturmii Consolatio ad senatum Argentinensem. De morte clarissimi et nobilissimi viri D. Iacobi Sturmij, odae etiam aliquae et epitaphia de eodem* (Strasbourg: Wendelin Rihel, 1553), from which come the following quotes. On the German version, which appeared from the same publisher in 1554, see Brady, "Contemporary German Version."

11

Jacob Sturm and the Fate of German Protestantism

News of Jacob Sturm's death moved swiftly through Evangelical networks across the Empire. First to the southerners, of course, and Ambrosius Blarer, the exiled reformer of Constance, passed the sad news to Heinrich Bullinger, Zwingli's successor at Zurich.[1] The news spread eastward, too, and at Weimar one preacher responded, "what you wrote me about Jacob Sturm's death shocked and deeply disturbed not only me but also many other honorable people at [Duke John Frederick's] court."[2] This was the general reaction in Evangelical circles to the news. The historian Johannes Sleidan spoke his grief more simply, "You know how much we lose in him." And Ulrich Geiger, a long-time Strasbourg agent with whom Sturm had worked closely, put it most simply of all: "He was the pilot and the driver [register und wagenman]."[3] Many years later, Thomas Blarer, Ambrosius's brother, reminisced about those days and said that if he could, he would conjure Jacob Sturm back from the past.[4]

The news of Sturm's death evoked less happy memories of the stettmeister for Landgrave Philip of Hesse. The landgrave, ever one to blame others for his troubles, never forgave Sturm and the other burghers for his own defeat in 1547. On 20 January 1554, the lawyer Jacob Hermann of Strasbourg was in Kassel on government business. When he was called in to see Landgrave Philip, Hermann reported,

> the prince drew me away from the statthalter and chancellor, who were also present, into a little turret [erker] and asked me all sorts of things about the late Sir Jacob Sturm, Sir Mathis Pfarrer, and the preachers, how they were living, and especially whether Sir Jacob Sturm had re-mained steadfast in our religion to the end.[5]

This scene, in which one architect of the Smalkaldic League expressed his doubts about the other's steadfastness in the Evangelical faith, evokes the atmosphere of uncertainty that clouded the prospects of Protestant politics during the years between its defeat in the Empire and its rise in France and the Netherlands. The landgrave's question also suggests how utterly, in his last years, Sturm's persona had withdrawn from the Imperial stage back into the local milieu from which he had come.

Seen as distinct but coupled stories, the braided patterns of Sturm's career and the fate of German Protestantism display similar patterns of great early effects followed by war, defeat, and retreat. Sturm arose on the tide of the Evangelical movement from provincial obscurity to Imperial prominence, only to sink after the war back into the local history of Strasbourg. And German Protestantism, despite its spectacular early history, found no form adequate to its dream—an Empire reformed in an Evangelical Christian sense—and it therefore missed the moment that, in Goethe's phrase, once past, history would never give back. The Holy Roman Empire would never recapitulate, as Sturm imagined, the Roman Empire's experience of slow but irresistible Christianization through the Spirit's hidden workings; nor would it ever experience, as Martin Bucer imagined, a revolutionary transformation into the "Kingdom of Christ."

It is easy to see these "defeats" as the outcomes of a profound ambiguity at the core of the German Reformation, which sought both to enhance the importance of religion in everyday life and to resolve the structural tension between spiritual and temporal authority in the laity's sense. This is why the Evangelical sense of being a community under the Cross came to clash with the Protestant leaders' respect for historic structures of authority and right; why the Evangelical burghers' conflation of the gospel with the idea of a Christian common good contradicted the princes' conflation of it with their aristocratic idea of "German liberty"; and why the Evangelicals' sense of universal mission crumbled before the disparities between the densely structured lands of the Reformation's southern infancy and the vast, loosely structured regions of its northern maturity. Each of these tensions worked at critical moments to enhance the Protestant leaders' indecision about how much of the present to risk for the future's sake.

Yet movements to change the world do change it, if not always to the degrees or in the ways their actors imagine, and outcomes can only be appreciated in terms of a dialectic of human agency and enduring structures, which will yield different outcomes from the interplay of similar programs with different structures. The German Reformation unfolded on a stage of many levels and compartments, the relationships among which it altered, sometimes permanently, sometimes temporarily or not at all. The movement both fostered and exploited a new kind of public consciousness in the Empire, and it created entirely unprecedented bonds of engagement and cooperation between previously unrelated entities, such as Strasbourg and Hesse, not to speak of Strasbourg and Saxony. Loyalty to a common faith alone prompted the hard-eyed merchants of Strasbourg, Ulm, and Augsburg to finance the invasion of Brunswick-Wolfenbüttel in 1542, though it did not kindle a zeal hot enough to make them throw law and order to the winds for the sake of the Evangelicals of Metz. It was powerful, this Reformation movement, even though it lacked stamina. It made obscure clergymen, such as Martin Luther and Martin Bucer, into churchmen of Imperial influence, and local magistrates, such as Jacob Sturm, into leading Imperial politicians. It then cast them down again, and Sturm and Bucer lived to experience the defeat and humiliation that Luther, by his death, escaped. Worse, the aftermath of defeat threatened in the summer of 1548 to destroy everything Sturm's ancestors, especially Old Peter Schott, had achieved in the way of stable oligarchical rule and law and order. It was here, on this local stage in 1547–48, and not on the great stage of Imperial politics, that Sturm faced his greatest test—as a local magistrate, not as an Imperial politician. Sturm's greatest achievement was not the ephemeral Schmalkaldic League but Strasbourg's post-war settlement of surrender, submission, and interim in the face of revolution-minded opposition.

Viewed on this broad Imperial canvas, Protestant politics looms as a failure.[6] On the local canvas, however, a very different story, a success story, unfolds. On this scale we see how the Reformation movement took early and deep root in a soil prepared by the profound geographical and social devolution of governance during the later Middle Ages. Had the Reformation not gripped people who were accustomed to demanding a say in their own fates, Evangelical religion could never have taken political shape as German Protestantism. The connection between particularism and the local success of Evangelical religion helps to explain why the nursery of German Protestantism was not its birthplace, Saxony, but the deeply fragmented German Southwest. The Reformation truly changed the world in these parts, but it did not change the whole world, nor did its power to change things radically endure for very long.

This pattern of Protestant politics, Imperial failure and local success, frames perfectly the career of Jacob Sturm. The Reformation transformed Jacob Sturm from an insignificant gentleman-clergyman, a simulacrum of the great-uncle he was encouraged from boyhood to imitate, into a politician of Imperial stature. This change did not arise simply out of his personal evolution from Wimpheling's "mediocre program" through Erasmianism to Evangelical religion, a passage which did not distinguish him from dozens of other young clergymen of his generation. From Strasbourg's city hall, Sturm moved upward into the forums of Imperial political life. What made Sturm a politician of Imperial rank, however, was not primarily his personal abilities but the direct consequence of the Reformation's impact on Imperial political life, namely, the formation of confessional parties. Sturm moved through the formative experiences of Protestant politics—the Peasants' War of 1525, the diets of Speyer in 1526 and 1529 and Augsburg in 1530, and the founding of the Smalkaldic League—into a new set of solidarities—the Swabian cities, Hesse, and Saxony—and a new circuit of venues—Franconia, Hesse, Thuringia, and Saxony. This entire development crashed down after the failure of the

Danube campaign in November 1546 and the "armored" Diet of Augsburg in 1547–48, and the backwash of defeat carried Sturm back into his native city's deepest crisis of the age, the struggle over the interim. Thereafter, Sturm spent his last years hobnobbing with small-town lawyers and countrified knights—much the sort of provincial notables with whom Old Peter Schott had been at home.

The expansive phase of this odyssey exploded Jacob Sturm's political horizons with breathtaking speed. From his great–grandfather's cozy Alemannic–speaking world, Sturm's gaze vaulted eastward across Swabia into Franconia, Thuringia, and Saxony; northward through Hesse to Cleves-Jülich, Cologne, and Brunswick-Wolfenbüttel, and beyond to Hamburg and Denmark; and westward to France and England. Sturm's grasp of this broad world astounded his contemporaries, such as the mayor of Stralsund, who marveled at his knowledge of a region that was nearer to Warsaw than it was to Strasbourg. And when the experience of defeat and the threat of insurrection drew him back into his local world, this greater world followed, for the secure, bounded world of his great-grandfather no longer existed. From a regional metropolis, Sturm's city had become a frontier fortress, as any Strasbourgeois could plainly see from the city's walls over the course of a few months in 1552: first, came the French king and his army, headed eastward toward the Rhine; then, came Emperor Charles V and the Imperial army, headed westward toward Metz. Two monarchs, two directions, but a single new European order of dynastic rivalry and struggle, and a single new system of international warfare and finance. The change is mirrored by the contrast between Charles's reception at Strasbourg in 1552 and that of his grandfather in 1504. Maximilian entered the city as armed sovereign, surrounded by his commanders and councilors and prepared to see and be seen; Charles, who was also on campaign, rode in as a tourist, looked around, took a bit of lunch and rode away.

Imperial Protestant politics and local Evangelical reformation, two moments united in the career of one man. In Sturm's person, too, flowed together two powerful experiences of crisis and disorder. The Peasants' War of 1525, which he witnessed more intimately than did any other politician of his age, taught Sturm to fear the volatile cacophony of the popular will to justice and liberty, an experience Sturm carried as a political mortgage for the rest of his life. The interim crisis of 1548, which arose largely from the defeat of Sturm's own alliance policy, was a purely local event, yet it brought Strasbourg nearer to revolution than the Peasants' War had. Jacob Sturm single-handedly extricated Strasbourg from this dangerous situation, saving its regime and its elite—many of whom deserted him—from revolution and its reformation from a thoroughgoing Catholic restoration. At this moment and in this small forum, his full capabilities as a politician unfolded. Only the fruits of political devolution—particularism—made this triumph possible, but it was a very near thing. How near may be gauged by comparing the situations of 1525 and 1548. During the Peasants' War, Strasbourg towered like a great rock over a plain swept by the storms of insurrection, because the social bedrock of its regime, the trust and alliance between the rich and the middling guildsmen, held firm. In 1548, by contrast, this trust and alliance, the fruit of a local political evolution over the last stage of which Old Peter Schott had presided, fractured in such a way as to allow the clerically led opposition to grasp for the custody of the commune's two great legitimating principles, religion and the common good. All the opposition lacked in early August 1548 was able, determined leadership.

The struggle, therefore, over the nature of the Reformation occurred not on the Imperial level but on the local one, not between the Smalkaldic League and Charles V but between Jacob Sturm and Martin Bucer. The struggle itself supplies a precious clue to the affinity of the Erasmian Sturm to the Lutheran reformation. For Bucer in 1548 was making his bid for a second reformation, an attempt to transform this city of mixed religion—as Claus Kniebis admitted in 1543, "there are many papists here"—into a "Kingdom of Christ" on earth. Whether, had he succeeded, the result would have looked more like Anabaptist Münster or more like Calvin's Geneva, is beside the point, for his essential goal was to restore the religious supremacy of a clergy, now reformed and disciplined to Evangelical standards, over a largely unreformed laity. Jacob Sturm, who believed that compulsion produced order but not devotion—"laws make hypocrites"—was not about to permit these "new popes" to rule Strasbourg's church. On this fundamentally Marsiglian principle, that laymen should rule the church, Sturm, whatever his theology, was at one with the Lutheran reformation. And, despite the defeat of Protestant politics on the Imperial level, on this local level Sturm successfully defended Protestant politics against this second reformation.

If Sturm's victory over Bucer seems inevitable in retrospect, the victory of Calvin—inspired by Bucer's failures—at Geneva prompts caution on this score. It cannot have seemed inevitable to Jacob Sturm in August 1548, as he watched his kinsmen and -women, his friends, and many long-time colleagues stream out of the city, while his regime, discredited by defeat and the evident loss of God's favor, faced the tide of Evangelical militancy and social rage. Here, not on the Danube in November 1546, Protestant politics stood its test and carried the day, as Sturm defended the urban reformation's legacy against the Evangelical movement's radical agenda. He did so drawing on the political heritage of his family and his class, the legacy of Strasbourg's successful particularism, as he worked to restore trust between magistrates and leading guildsmen, the merchants, shopkeepers, and artisans who made up both the most natural partisans of Evangelical religion and the vital basis of oligarchical rule. The magistracy's triple address to the Schöffen was almost entirely Sturm's work, the restoration of confidence in the regime almost entirely his doing. It was his finest hour as a magistrate, a man of the city.

Jacob Sturm's experience shows how the urban reformation, in which late medieval political particularism sheltered, nurtured, and shaped the Evangelical movement, also became the movement's captor, defining the permissible limits and the instruments of its mandate to reshape social religion. The outcome of this convergence of movement and structure was a religious settlement in a magisterial sense, which was itself a type of local Protestant politics that did not depend on the success of Protestant politics on an Imperial scale. The proof of this assertion of local success despite Imperial failure is the case of Nuremberg, originally a bulwark of Evangelical militancy, but since 1529 a citadel of Evangelical loyalism. The shift had been sealed by the formulation of the doctrine of non-resistance. Not only did loyal, Lutheran Nuremberg come away entirely unscathed from German-speaking Protestantism's political downfall in 1546–47, but the emperor adopted its oligarchy as his model for reforming the other southern urban regimes. Would Nuremberg's policy have succeeded, had there been no Smalkaldic League and no truces in 1532 and 1539? Difficult to say, although it is worth noting that Evangelical Nuremberg stuck to its pre-Reformation policy of loyalism, whereas Evangelical Strasbourg abandoned both loyalism and its historic pro-Swiss policy for Protestant politics. Nuremberg's fate demonstrates that it was this step, Jacob Sturm's step, which thrust Strasbourg between two fires—on the one side, the emperor's wrath and the courts; on the other, exploitation of the burghers by the princes in the service of aristocratic liberty flying the banner of the gospel.

From Sturm's point of view, Protestant politics succeeded not as a preparation for war but as a way of avoiding war. Jacob Sturm's personal preference for diplomacy over war is expressed in the motto on the medal struck to honor him in 1526: Patience Conquers Fortune. His preference corresponded to the position of the burghers, whose strengths lay in finance and in their walls, and who were therefore peculiarly unsuited to making offensive war. Jacob Sturm violated this principle on several occasions—for Württemberg in 1534, in principle for Cleves–Jülich in 1540, and for Brunswick–Wolfenbüttel in 1542—when the prospect of quick, cheap gains overcame his burgher's scruples and caution. Otherwise, as in the crisis over Minden in 1538–39, Sturm's version of Protestant politics always favored diplomacy over military action.

Sturm's attitude helps to explain why he normally regarded the Smalkaldic League less as a military alliance than as a political body in the burghers' sense, possessing a common good and requiring equity in its internal dealings and fairness and honesty in its finance. Sturm also recognized the vital need for a moral basis, what he called "the proper sort of love for one another," if the Smalkaldeners were to grow together. This, too, was typical of the corporate thinking of the burghers' political discourse. When the Smalkaldic League came into being in 1531, however, it remained to be seen if this moral basis could be sufficiently supplied by an unprecedented factor of association in the Empire, a confession of Christian doctrine, to overcome the social differences between burghers and nobles and the geographical differences between South and North. The Reformation's chance to transform the Empire arose from a revolutionary quickening of the widespread desire for something which late medieval particularism could not supply, namely, a program of religious and secular reform on the Imperial level. Protestant politics failed to realize this potential, because the burghers balked at the illegality and risk required by a transformative politics, while the princes turned Protestantism's power to the only politics they knew, dynastic advantage under the name of "German liberty." It is easy to see that the shock of the Peasants' War of 1525 had a great deal to do with this fixing of these traditional burghers' and princes' politics, from which the ideal of Evangelical community could not break free.

This is not to deny the innovative political aspects of Protestant politics as embodied in the Smalkaldic League, which broke new ground in four respects. First, its basis, a reformed religion, transcended in a new way differences of economic and legal interest. Second, the league ignored old boundaries between regions and brought together, to an unprecedented degree, powers from the far corners of the Empire. Third, the league assumed a definite, if vague, responsibility for the defense of all Evangelicals in the Empire and even, though more vaguely yet, sought solidarity with Evangelicals in other European countries. Fourth, the Smalkaldic League crippled an entire branch of Imperial government, the judicial branch, and long provided adequate protection against the most widespread threat to Evangelical religion, the suits for the restitution of ecclesiastical properties. These four achievements demonstrate the German Reformation's political creativity, but they also reveal its political limitations and the episodic nature of its power for political transformation.

The root of this episodic nature of Protestant politics lay in the Evangelical movement's inability to nurture a powerful enough sense of community outside of the cities and villages it affected. The Smalkaldic League proved ever so much more fragile than the tough solidarities, which the Reformation movement was to inspire in France and the Netherlands. In the Empire it created no broad fellowship of religious practice to complement its community of faith, for the league was unable to create norms of worship, ecclesiastical governance, and the deployment of the church's properties. One might argue, of course, that it had never been the movement's goal to create such common elements, but the experience of Protestants elsewhere in Europe suggests that this argument is a post facto rationalization. Indeed, the peculiarity of German Protestantism seems to have been that political particularism, which allowed it to become established permanently in the Empire, became the prison that prevented it from developing into a united, powerful force on an Imperial scale. Later on, of course, the Calvinist challenge would encourage German Lutheranism to consolidate itself, but only into a confession, never a church. Neither in the first nor in subsequent generations did it create an institutional infrastructure for its common faith, an outcome which, one may argue, owes much less to Luther's alleged separation of religion from politics than to the political culture and structures that made Protestant politics possible. That culture and those structures determined that the Smalkaldic League would be led by princes and financed by burghers, and that it would be drawn into the historic role of the aristocratic opposition to the Imperial monarchy. The league's major actions—the campaign against Ferdinand's royal election, the restoration of Duke Ulrich in Württemberg, and the vengeance taken on Duke Henry of Brunswick–Wolfenbüttel—all fit this role. Protestant politics thus succumbed to a political order it could exploit but not transform. The bitterly ironical embodiment of this situation was the Lutheran "Judas of Meissen," Duke Moritz of Saxony.

The fate of Protestant politics in the German Reformation, therefore, was an outcome of the intersection of a social and religious movement, the Reformation, with a structure, the Holy Roman Empire. Unlike Ranke's narrative, this one does not depend on invoking the mysterious spoiling power of "Rome" to thwart the destiny of the German nation. Then, too, because it is attentive to the society and governance of that age, this new story does not depend on the common but dubious argument that German Protestantism was by nature authoritarian and conservative, which, like most idealist explanations in history, carries more verbal than explanatory weight. There is no reason to single out the Evangelical religion of Luther, Bucer, and Zwingli as inherently different from that of Calvin, who considered himself their brother in the service of the Word. Whatever its later development, German-speaking Lutheranism was the child of Protestantism, not its parent, and it differed from the Protestant religions of other peoples not so much in its beliefs as in its political experience.[7] That experience contained, in European terms, two great peculiarities: the structural peculiarity of political particularism, and the dynamic peculiarity of the Peasants' War of 1525. The entire subsequent history of the German-speaking reformation unfolded in the shadow of 1525, which defined the limits of religion's right to call upon the law of God against the laws of this world. The experience of these peculiarities is what shaped the "timidity" of Jacob Sturm, who experienced 1525 with a chilling and unique intimacy. Reinforced by the Anabaptist enterprise of 1534, the memories of Müntzer and Münster bound the hands of Protestant politicians against revolutionary action. Each of the Smalkaldic League's critical decisions, therefore, whether about the definition of doctrine, the disposal of ecclesiastical property, or the succoring of fellow Evangelicals oppressed by Catholic rulers, was settled according to particularist principles in favor of the individual princes and the urban regimes. These decisions simply reminted the Imperial Diet's hapless decision in 1526 that each ruler should be responsible for religion in his own lands. They frustrated and blocked every subsequent attempt, including Jacob Sturm's, to supply the Protestants' hard-won religious unity with an adequate material basis and an appropriate political form, to unite, in a phrase, Protestant power with Evangelical imagination.

There is no reason to measure this outcome against Ranke's dream of a lost chance for a German Christian national state. Nations are created by states through the mobilizing agency of nationalism, and in the absence of a centralized state, there could be no German nation in the modern sense. Despite its title, the Holy Roman Empire had no center, neither a capital nor an effective monarchical government, and Sturm's idea of its reform through the Holy Spirit's percolation of the gospel into individual hearts was also an impossible dream. No sixteenth-century movement could have revolutionized such a vast, complicated, and flexible system, certainly not in one generation, but the same characteristic that precluded a Protestant victory via a grasp for the center—which succeeded in England, Denmark, and Sweden but failed in France—also guaranteed that a defeated Protestantism could survive to play a central role in German life during later centuries. Protestant politics failed as an Imperial force, because it succeeded as a local one and by that success helped to conserve the Empire for another 250 years, until it was revolutionized, finally, by Napoleon Bonaparte.

The interplay of structure, movement, motive, and outcome brings us back to the thread of this narrative, the career of Jacob Sturm. The great aim of his career was to unite sound religion with the civic common good, and his greatest fear arose from his belief that "in our times scarcely anything else so unites people's minds or drives them apart as unity or disunity in religion does."[8] It was a lesson he learned again and again in the storms of the Peasants' War, in the tumults of Strasbourg's own reformation, in the struggle against the sects, in the quarrels between Zwinglians and Lutherans, and in the fight over the interim. This sense of threat he shared with the ruling classes of his day.

Sturm's metier was politics, the formulation and execution of policy, and he understood the difference between policy and desires. Despite his Evangelical views, he opposed suppression of the mass in the late 1520s; despite the Swiss alliance, he tricked Zwingli during the Diet of Augsburg in 1530; despite his sacramentarian theology, he accepted the Confession of Augsburg in 1532; and despite his belief that "laws make hypocrites," he persecuted the sects during the early 1530s. When required, he was a master manipulator of others, a quality displayed nowhere more magnificently than in the speeches he drafted for the ammeister during the crisis over the interim in 1548. And he could be devious, as when he told Chancellor Granvelle in 1548 that he, for his own person, might tolerate a restoration of Catholicism, but that the common people would not hear of it. His own world view seems to have drunk far more deeply from the humanists' neo-Stoic vision of a world centered on the engagement of morality with fortune—Patience Conquers Fortune—than from the reformers' starkly neo-Augustinian vision of a world thirsting for grace. He was comfortable, therefore, as Martin Bucer was not, with the apparent distance between politics and true religion, which, as the Spirit's prompting of the individual heart, bore only an indirect connection to public doctrine, discipline, and worship. The meeting place between God and man is the hidden heart, not the world, which God mostly leaves to fortune's whim. To conquer fortune is the task of policy, the instrument of which is patience, as the motto of 1526 proclaimed, and not zeal for the truth or divine intervention.

The deep and abiding influence of the humanism of Wimpheling—"If I am a heretic, you made me one!"—and Erasmus on his view of the world does not mean that Sturm was anything less than a devoted Evangelical and a whole-hearted Protestant. His whole career as a Protestant politician testifies to his fidelity to these causes. To begin with, it was Sturm who pushed, against his city's traditions and his colleagues' inclinations, for an alliance based on religion. Further, he devoted much of his adult life to this policy, as more than ninety missions forced him to spend his days on horseback and his nights sleeping in strange beds. He rode for days, sometimes for weeks, to reach distant sites of meetings, living for months in rented quarters, surrounded mostly by people with whom he could converse only with difficulty. The worst was Thuringia, with its mean inns and sour wine, but many other provincial nests were not much better. And though he might well have begged off by pleading ill health, as most of his colleagues did, his unvarying answer to the call was, "he will ride, if he must."

At home, when he lived at home, Sturm resumed all of his normal duties in the XIII, in the Senate & XXI, and in his commissions and ad hoc committees. A tone of deep asceticism hangs over Sturm's adult life, a tone sounded by his life in the mansion in Fire Street. Here, in a mood of semi-monastic restraint and sobriety, he lived for a quarter of a century in the company of his sister, Veronica, and his two surviving brothers, Friedrich and Peter, and the rhythms of this childless household served not the Sturm lineage or the reformed church, but the commune. As his colleagues declared at his death, Jacob Sturm was "the father of his country," and he had no other children. Except for the schoolchildren, on whose welfare Sturm lavished his most precious asset, his spare time.

The interplay of religion and politics in Sturm's career helps to explain the interplay of liberty and repression in his policy. On the one hand, the deep attachment to received values of law and order, which colored Sturm's entire public face, fitted closely his status as a seignior, a feudal vassal, and a magistrate. About moral freedom and liberty of choice, on the other hand, he had learned from Wimpheling and Erasmus, but his reaction to the Peasants' War permitted them no place in his policy alongside order, obedience, and conformity. He was capable of appealing for fraternal spirit and liberty of conscience for the sacramentarians in the Smalkaldic League, and for the Protestant powers in the Empire, but not for the Anabaptists at Strasbourg. Indeed, Sturm did not believe that liberty for the common people was compatible with the demands of public order, an attitude confirmed both by his own statements and by his antipopular proposal of 1548 to revise Strasbourg's constitution. Only in the schools, at a safe social and linguistic distance from the common people, did Sturm cultivate liberty in the sense not of local independence but of individual moral development. Sturm lavished his love for moral freedom on an institution, the Latin school, which gave him a kind of pleasure the church did not. He made daring recruitments of scholars whose learning brought fame to the city, just as their heterodoxy made trouble with the preachers; he bought books for the library and bequeathed his entire collection of books; and he kept the School Board's records with care and attention to detail. Most importantly, by hiring Jean Sturm and supporting his Strasbourg pedagogy of "eloquent piety," Jacob Sturm made Strasbourg into a nexus of the international republic of letters. In this environment, Jacob Sturm cultivated the spiritual liberty he could not tolerate in the closely corporate environment of Strasbourg's communal life, though he thereby sowed the seeds of all the later controversies between school and church. Strasbourg's Latin school, the one great innovation of Sturm's career, supplied the bachelor's need to spend his love on the future. Not only did the fugitive moments, which he dedicated to the school's affairs, provide his sole relief from the crushing burdens of diplomacy and the atmosphere of well-worn benches and broad Alemannic vowels at city hall, they also brought him back to the world in which Wimpheling had nurtured him so long ago. That world had changed very little. How little is symbolized by the only book that remains from the large library with which he endowed the civic schools. It contains the writings of Clement of Alexandria, a late second-century convert to Christianity, whose ideas are characterized by serenity and hopefulness. The Greek text was printed in 1550 at Florence, a Catholic city the Reformation movement had hardly touched.

It is idle, of course, to analyze a human life into "ages," as though it were a reducible chemical compound, and as though the "ages" were something more substantial than codified arguments about the past. Yet, for the sake of our perceptions it is helpful to see Jacob Sturm as a person in whose life the late Middle Ages, the Renaissance, and the Reformation flowed together. The grandson of Old Peter Schott, he served a free city, one of late medieval particularism's most successful political forms. The pupil of Jacob Wimpheling, he made Strasbourg a center of the republic of Renaissance letters. The political partner of Landgrave Philip of Hesse, he raised the Reformation's local achievements by means of the Smalkaldic League to an Imperial level of significance.

In 1866, the year after Appomattox, James Bryce confessed that his age, standing too close to the Middle Ages ever to do justice to that era, had to leave this task to a later generation.[9] The same was true, even truer, of Ranke and the German Reformation. The world has changed profoundly since Bryce wrote, and in some ways we can come closer to the women and men of the sixteenth century than Ranke could, seeing the uncertainty of fortune, which only patience may overcome, where Ranke saw the mighty hand of God in history. We can recognize the sigh of Jacob Sturm, who was a younger contemporary of Niccolò Machiavelli, that "our whole experience teaches us that we are not such as God will save through a miracle."

Notes

1. Schiess, ed., *Briefwechsel* 3:217, no. 1897: "Iacobum Sturmium illum, incomparabilis prudentiae virum, Argentoratensis reipublicae decus et ornamentum, vita excessisse non ignoras."
2. Cornelius Friedsleben to Dr. C. F. Curio, Weimar, 21 November 1553, in AMS, AA 601, fol. 94r–v. The news of Sturm's death was passed by Ambrosius Blarer to Heinrich Bullinger in Zurich on 22 November. Schiess, ed., *Briefwechsel* 3:215–16, no. 1879. His brother, Thomas Blarer, also wrote a eulogy of Jacob Sturm. Ibid. 3:361, no. 2054.
3. Johannes Sleidan to John Calvin, Strasbourg, 28 December 1553, in CR 42:719, no. 1881.
4. Thomas Blarer to Conrad Hubert, Gyrsberg, 25 February 1564, in Schiess, ed., *Briefwechsel* 3:799, no. 2589: "Tu Bucerum revocas, ego N. Kniebissum et consimiles, ipsum etiam Sturmium, qui in meticulosis est habitus nec sine causa; sed floruit eo vivente tamen civitas christiana adhuc, quae nunc, nisi respirarit fortassis dante deo, videtur magis quam antea labascere explusis nuper viris tam doctis quam piis ob non meritam invidiam."
5. PC 5:504, no. 404.
6. I mean "failure" as measured against the concrete opportunities, which seem to me to have lain open to the political leaders of German-speaking Protestantism in its first generation. This issue is quite distinct from that of judging the German Protestants' achievements against the reformers' programs, which is the subject of the controversy provoked by Gerald Strauss' *Luther's House of Learning*. See Strauss, "Success and Failure in the German Reformation." The current state of this debate is presented soberly by M. Schulz, *Fürsten und Reformation*, 3–6; and broadly and even-handedly by Parker, "Success and Failure."
7. See the pithy remarks of Schilling, *Civic Calvinism*, 1–10, 98–104.
8. PC 2:237, no. 259.
9. Brady, "'Special Path,'" 198.

Bibliography

ABBREVIATIONS

ADB   *Allgemeine Deutsche Biographie*.
ADBR   Archives Départementales du Bas-Rhin
AEKG   *Archiv für elsässische Kirchengeschichte/Archives de l'Église d'Alsace*, n.s.
AGBR   Emil Dürr and Paul Roth, eds, *Aktensammlung zur Geschichte der Basler Reformation*
AKG   *Archiv für Kulturgeschichte*
AMC   Archives Municipales de Colmar
AMS   Archives Municipales de Strasbourg
Ann. Brant   Léon Dacheux, ed., *Annales de Sébastien Brant*
ARCEG Georg Pfeilschifter, ed., *Acta reformationis catholicae ecclesiae Germaniae concernantia saeculi XVI. Die Reformverhandlungen des deutschen Episkopats von 1520 bis 1570*
ARG   *Archiv für Reformationgeschichte*
ASAVS *Annuaire de la Société des Amis de Vieux-Strasbourg*
AST   Archives du Chapître de St.-Thomas de Strasbourg
BCorr Martin Bucer, *Correspondance*
BDLG   *Blätter für deutsche Landesgeschichte*
BDS   *Martin Bucer's Deutsche Schriften*
BHR   *Bibliothèque d'Humanisme et Renaissance*
BIHR   *Bulletin of the Institute of Historical Research*
BLVEL *Beiträge zur Landes- und Volkeskunde von Elsaß-Lothringen und den angrenzenden Gebieten*
BLVS   Bibliothek des Litterarischen Vereins in Stuttgart
BNUS   Bibliothèque Nationale et Universitaire de Strasbourg
BMS   Bibliothèque Municipale de Strasbourg
BOL   *Martini Buceri Opera Latina*
BOSS   Ekkehart Fabian, ed., *Die Beschlüße der oberdeutschen schmalkaldischen Städtetage*
BPH   *Bulletin philologique et historique (jusqu'en 1610) du Comité des travaux historiques et scientifiques*
BSCMHA *Bulletin de la Société pour la Conservation des Monuments Historiques de l'Alsace*
BSHPF *Bulletin de la Société pour l'Histoire du Protestantisme Français*
BWKG   *Blätter für württembergische Kirchengeschichte*
CEH   *Central European History*
CH   *Church History*
CR   *Corpus reformatorum*
       —Philip Melanchthon, *Opera quae supersunt omnia*
       —Jean [John] Calvin, *Ioannis Calvini opera quae supersunt omnia*
CS   Chester David Hartranf and Elmer Ellsworth Schulz Johnson, eds, *Corpus Schwenckfeldianorum*
CT   *Concilium Tridentinum. Diarorum, actorum, epistolarum, tractatum nova collectio*
CWE   Desiderius Erasmus, *Collected Works of Erasmus*
EA   *Amtliche Sammlung der älteren eidgenössischen Abschiede*
EHR   *The English Historical Review*

ELJb   *Elsaß-Lothringisches Jahrbuch*
FDG   *Forschungen zur deutschen Geschichte*
Ficker-Winckelmann   Johannes Ficker and Otto Winckelmann, eds., *Handschriften-
proben des sechszehnten Jahrhunderts nach Strassburger Originalen*
GLAK   Generallandesarchiv Karlsruhe
HAMNG   Heidelberger Abhandlungen zur mittleren und neueren Geschichte
HJ   *Historisches Jahrbuch der Görres-Gesellschaft*
HJLG   *Hessisches Jahrbuch für Landesgeschichte*
HStAD   Hessisches Staatsarchiv Darmstadt
HStAM   Hessisches Staatsarchiv Marburg
HZ   *Historische Zeitschrift*
JGF   *Jahrbuch für Geschichte des Feudalismus*
JGOR   *Jahrbuch für Geschichte der Oberdeutschen Reichsstädte*
JHKGV   *Jahrbuch der hessischen kirchengeschichtlichen Vereinigung*
JWOS   Jacob Wimpheling, *Opera Selecta*
Letters and Papers   Great Britain, Public Record Office, *Letters and Papers, Foreign
and Domestic, of the Reign of Henry VIII, 1509–1547*
MBW   *Philipp Melanchthon, Briefwechsel. Kritische und kommentierte Gesamtausgabe*
MIÖG   *Mitteilungen des Instituts für Österreichische Geschichtsforschung*
MKH   Mitteilungen der Kommission für Humanismusforschung
MVGN   *Mitteilungen des Vereins für Geschichte der Stadt Nürnberg*
NBD, I   *Nuntiaturberichte aus Deutschland nebst ergänzenden Aktenstücke*, part 1,
1533–1559
NBD, I, suppl. 1   *Nuntiaturberichte aus Deutschland nebst ergänzenden Aktenstücke*,
supplementary vol. 1, *Legation Campeggios 1530–1532 und Nuntiatur Girolamo
Aleandros 1531*
NBD, I, suppl. 2   *Nuntiaturberichte aus Deutschland nebst ergänzenden Aktenstücke*,
supplementary vol. 2, *Legation Lorenzo Campeggios 1532 und Nuntiatur Girolamo
Aleandros 1532*
Papiers d'état   Charles Weiss, ed., *Papiers d'état du Cardinal de Granvelle*
PC   *Politische Correspondenz der Stadt Straßburg im Zeitalter der Reformation.*
PKM   Erich Brandenburg, et. al., eds., *Politisches Korrespondenz des Herzogs und
Kurfürsten Moritz von Sachsen*
Pollet, *Correspondance*   J. V. Pollet, ed., *Martin Bucer. Études sur la correspondance
avec de nombreux textes inédits*
Pollet, *Relations*   J. V. Pollet, ed., *Martin Bucer. Études sur les relations de Bucer
avec les Pays-Bas, l'électorat de Cologne et l'Allemagne du Nord*
PP   *Past and Present*
PSSARE   Publications de la Société Savante d'Alsace et des Régions de l'Est
QFIAB   Quellen und Forschungen aus italienischen Archiven und Bibliotheken
QFKKEL   Quellen und Forschungen zur Kirchen- und Kulturgeschichte Elsaß-
Lothringens
QFRG   Quellen und Forschungen zur Reformationsgeschichte
RA   *Revue d'Alsace*
Reichs-Abschiede   Johann Jakob Schmauss, ed., *Neue und vollständigere Sammlung
der Reichs-Abschiede*
Rott, *IH*   Jean Rott, *Investigationes historicae. Eglises et société au XVIe siècle.
Gesammelte Aufsätze*
RPHR   *Revue de philosophie et d'histoire religieuses*
RST   Reformationsgeschichtliche Studien und Texte
RTA, jR   *Deutsche Reichstagsakten, jüngere Reihe*
SBA   Ekkehart Fabian, ed., *Die Schmalkaldische Bundesabschiede 1530–1536*
SCJ   *Sixteenth Century Journal*

SCSE   Sixteenth Century Studies & Essays
SFN   Spätmittelalter und Frühe Neuzeit. Tübinger Beiträge zur Geschichtswissenschaft
SHCT   Studies in the History of Christian Thought
SHKBA   Schriftenreihe der Historischen Kommission bei der Bayerischen Akademie der Wissenschaften
SHKK   Schriften des Historischen Kollegs, Kolloquien
SKRG   Schriften zur Kirchen- und Rechtsgeschichte
SMRT   Studies in Medieval and Reformation Thought
StA   Stadt(Staats)archiv
SVRG   Schriften des Vereins für Reformationsgeschichte
SWIEL   Schriften des Wissenschaftlichen Instituts der Elsaß-Lothringer im Reich (an der Universität Frankfurt)
TAE   Manfred Krebs, et al., *Elsaß*
· TKT   Texte zur Kirchen- und Theologiegeschichte
UARP   Ekkehart Fabian, ed., *Urkunden und Akten der Reformationsprozesse am Reichskammergericht, am kaiserlichen Hofgericht zu Rottweil und an anderen Gerichten*
VIEG   Veröffentlichungen des Instituts für Europäische Geschichte Mainz
VKLBW   Veröffentlichungen der Kommission für geschichtliche Landeskunde in Baden-Württemberg
VSWG   *Vierteljahrschrift für Sozial- und Wirtschaftsgeschichte*
WA   *Luthers Werke. Kritische Gesamtausgabe*
WA B   *Luthers Werke. Kritische Gesamtausgabe. Briefe*
WA TR   *Luthers Werke. Kritische Gesamtausgabe. Tischreden*
WF   Wege der Forschung
Wittmer-Meyer   Charles Wittmer and J. Charles Meyer, eds., *Le Livre de Bourgeoisie de la Ville de Strasbourg 1440–1530*
ZfG   *Zeitschrift für Geschichtswissenschaft*
ZGO   *Zeitschrift für die Geschichte des Oberrheins*
ZHF   *Zeitschrift für historische Forschung*
ZKiG   *Zeitschrift für Kirchengeschichte*
ZVHG   *Zeitschrift des Vereins für Hessische Geschichte und Landeskunde*
ZW   Emil Egli, et al., eds., *Huldrych Zwinglis sämtliche Werke*
ZWLG   *Zeitschrift für württembergische Landesgeschichte*
ZRG, GA   *Zeitschrift der Savigny–Stiftung für Rechtsgeschichte, Germanistische Abteilung*
ZRG, KA   *Zeitschrift der Savigny–Stiftung für Rechtsgeschichte, Kanonistische Abteilung*

UNPUBLISHED SOURCES

Augsburg. Stadtarchiv
   Literaliensammlung, "1528 Dezember und Nachtrag": "Correspondenz des Dr. Gereon Sailer, 1528–1544"
Basel. Staatsarchiv
   Kirchen-Akten A 6: "Religions-Sachen 1532–1536"
Bremen. Stadtbibliothek
   MS. A 9, no. 13: "Johannes Timannus Amsterodamus to the Preachers of Bremen, Worms, 18 November 1540"
Chicago. The Newberry Library
   MS. 63: "Oraciones varies"
Constance. Stadtarchiv
   Reformations-Akten 4
Copenhagen. Danish Royal Library
   MS. Thott 497,2°
Darmstadt. Hessisches Staatsarchiv

F 26, nos. 18, 19, 49, 133
Göttingen. Niedersächsische Staats- und Universitätsbibliothek
    MS. Theol. 184
Karlsruhe. Generallandesarchiv
    44, no. 818
    67/1007, 1010, 1013, 1016, 1023, 1057–58
Lindau. Stadtarchiv
    6, 17
Ludwigsburg. Staatsarchiv
    Bestand 387 aus Band 14, nos. 194, 216–17
    Bestand 396 aus Büschel 171; Büschel 172, no. 2
Marburg. Hessisches Staatsarchiv
    Series K: 29
    Politisches Archiv des Landgrafen Philipp: PA 269, 389, 517, 725, 1793, 2915
Paris. Bibliothèque de la Société de l'Histoire du Protestantisme Français. Collection Labouchère
Strasbourg. Archives Départementales du Bas-Rhin
    Series E: 578; 2764(1)
    Series G: 653c; 675; 802–4
    Series 3B: 1484
    Series J: 12 J 2006; 12 J 2022; 16 J 154
Strasbourg. Archives du Chapître de St.-Thomas
    19/37; 38; 47/I, no. 18; 70/1; 75; 157; 176; 198; 319/42; 324/7; 372/VI; 1351; 1352; 1655; Supplement 35; Supplement 41/I–II, IV, VI; Supplement 42, XV, XXIV, XXV
Strasbourg. Archives Municipales de Strasbourg
    Series II: 28/17
    Series IV: 86/17; 1053
    Series AA: 155; 319; 374a; 393a; 396; 407a; 409; 409a; 425; 425a; 427; 462; 468; 498; 501; 513; 530; 601; 1552; 1723; 1808
    Series H: 590
    Series KS: 11; 14; 20; 23/I; 27/I
    Series R: 26/8
    Series XXI (= Procès-verbaux du sénat et des XXI): 1539–53, 1559
    MS. 85
Strasbourg. Bibliothèque Municipale
    MSS. 435; 844; 1024; 1223
Strasbourg. Bibliothèque Nationale et Universitaire
    MS. 1058; "Thesarus Baumianus sive epistolae reformatorum Alsaticorum"
Stuttgart. Hauptstaatsarchiv
    A 149/1
Uppsala. University Library
    Cod. C 687
Weimar. Staatsarchiv, Ernestinisches Gesamtarchiv
    Reg. C: nos. 385; 870; 1069
    Reg. E: pagg. 48–50, no. 99
    Reg. H: nos. 12, 35, 42, 47, 51–52, 59, 80, 89, 104; pagg. 167–70, no. 79; pagg. 170–73, no. 80; pagg. 211–14, no. 95; pagg. 214–18, no. 96; pagg. 218–20, no. 97; pagg. 265–67, no. 112; pagg. 306–11, no. 126; pagg. 329–34, no. 133; pagg. 335–44, no. 134; pagg. 348–52, no. 136; pagg. 359–64, no. 139; pagg. 367–72, no. 141; pagg. 383–84, no. 145; pagg. 394–400, no. 149; pagg. 418–521, no. 153; pagg. 421–34, no. 154; pagg. 442–44, no. 158; pagg. 442–44, no. 158; pagg. 458–63, no. 162; pagg. 490–97, no. 169; pagg. 501–6, no. 171; pagg.

555–63, no. 182; pagg. 603–9, no. 194; pagg. 612–30, no. 196; pag. 670, no. 209; Reg. I: pagg. 177–82, H, no. 6; pagg. 190–93, J, no. 1; pagg. 214–16, K, no. 3; pagg. 710–20, AA, no. 7
Wolfenbüttel. Herzog August Bibliothek
MS. 181.16 Theol. 4to

PRINTED SOURCES AND LITERATURE

Abray, Lorna Jane. *The People's Reformation: Magistrates, Clergy, and Commons in Strasbourg, 1520–1599.* New Haven: Yale Univ. Press, 1985.

Adam, Johann. *Evangelische Kirchengeschichte der Stadt Straßburg bis zur französischen Revolution.* Strasbourg: J. H. Ed. Heitz (Heitz & Mündel), 1922.

Adam, Paul. *L'humanisme à Sélestat: l'école, les humanistes, la bibliothèque.* Sélestat: Imprimerie Alsatia, 1962.

Alioth, Martin. *Gruppen an der Macht: Zünfte und Patriziat in Straßburg im 14. und 15. Jahrhundert. Untersuchungen zu Verfassung, Wirtschaftsgefüge und Sozialstruktur.* 2 vols. BBG, 156. Basel: Helbing & Lichtenhahn, 1988.

Allen, P. S., and H. S. Allen, eds. *Opus epistolarum Des. Erasmi Roterodami denuo recognitum et auctum.* 12 vols. Oxford: Oxford Univ. Press, 1906–46.

Allgemeine Deutsche Biographie. Edited by the Historische Kommission der Bayerischen Akademie der Wissenschaften. 56 vols. Leipzig: Duncker & Humblot, 1875–1912. Reprint. Berlin: Duncker & Humblot, 1967–71.

Amtliche Sammlung der älteren eidgenössischen Abschiede.
Vol. 3, pts. 1–2, *1478–1520.* Edited by A. Philipp Segesser. Zurich, 1858. Reprint. Lucerne: Meyer'sche Buchdruckerei, 1869.
Vol. 4, pts. 1a–1b, *1521–1532.* Edited by Johannes Strickler. Brugg: Fisch, Wild und Comp., 1873–76.
Vol. 4, pts. 1c–1e, *1533–1555.* Edited by Karl Deschwanden. Lucerne: Meyer'sche Buchdruckerei, 1878–86.

Angermeier, Heinz. *Die Reichsreform 1410–1555. Die Staatsproblematik in Deutschland zwischen Mittelalter und Gegenwart.* Munich: C. H. Beck, 1984.

―――. "Das Reichsregiment in der deutschen Geschichte." In *Das Wappenbuch des Reichsherolds Caspar Sturm,* edited by Jürgen Arndt, 43–49. Wappenbücher des Mittelalters, 1. Neustadt an der Aisch: Bauer & Raspe, 1984.

Annales de Sébastien Brant. Edited by Léon Dacheux. In BSCMHA, 2d ser. 15 (1892): 211–79, nos. 3238–3645bis; 19 (1899): 33–260, nos. 4391–5132.

Arbenz, Emil, ed. *Vadianische Briefsammlung.* Pt. 4, *1526–30.* In *Mitteilungen zur vaterländischen Geschichte* [St. Gallen] 28 (1902).

Arndt, Jürgen. "Organisation und Besetzung des Reichsregiments unter Kaiser Karl V. (1521–1531)." In *Das Wappenbuch des Reichsherolds Caspar Sturm,* edited by Jürgen Arndt, 51–61. Wappenbücher des Mittelalters, 1. Neustadt an der Aisch: Bauer & Raspe, 1984.

Augustijn, Cornelis. *De godsdienstgesprekken tussen rooms-katholieken en protestanten van 1538 tot 1541.* Haarlem: De Erven F. Bohn N.V., 1967.

―――. "Die Religionsgespräche der vierziger Jahre." In *Die Religionsgespräche der Reformationszeit,* edited by Gerhard Müller, 43–53. SVRG, 191. Gütersloh: Gerd Mohn, 1980.

Aulinger, Rosemarie. *Das Bild des Reichstages im 16. Jahrhundert: Beiträge zu einer typologischen Analyse schriftlicher und bildlicher Quellen.* SHKBA, 18. Göttingen: Vandenhoeck & Ruprecht, 1980.

―――. "Die Verhandlungen zum Nürnberger Anstand 1531/32 in der Vorgeschichte des Augsburger Religionsfriedens." In *Aus der Arbeit an den Reichstagen unter Kaiser Karl V.: Sieben Beiträge zu Fragen der Forschung und Edition,* edited by

Heinrich Lutz and Alfred Kohler, 194–227. SHKBA, 26. Göttingen: Vandenhoeck & Ruprecht, 1986.

Avila y Zuniga, Luis de. *Geschichte des Schmalkaldischen Krieges.* Berlin: E. S. Mittler, 1853.

Bainton, Roland H. "Katherine Zell." *Medievalia et Humanistica,* n.s. 1 (1970): 3–28.

Barack, Karl August von, ed. *Zimmerische Chronik.* 4 vols. BLVS, 91–94. Tübingen: Litterarischer Verein, 1869.

Barnes, Robin Bruce. *Prophecy and Gnosis: Apocalypticism in the Wake of the Lutheran Reformation.* Stanford: Stanford Univ. Press, 1988.

Baron, Hans. "Religion and Politics in the German Imperial Cities during the Reformation." *The English Historical Review* 52 (1937): 405–27, 614–33.

Barraclough, Geoffrey. *The Origins of Modern Germany.* 2d ed. rev. Oxford: Basil Blackwell, 1947.

Battenberg, Friedrich. "Reichskammergericht und Archivwesen. Zum Stand der Erschließung des Reichskammergerichtsakten." In *Das Reichskammergericht in der deutschen Geschichte: Stand der Forschung, Forschungsperspektiven,* ed. Bernhard Diestelkamp, 173–94. Quellen und Forschungen zur höchsten Gerichtsbarkeit im alten Reich, 21. Vienna: Böhlau, 1990.

Bauer, Johannes Joseph. *Zur Frühgeschichte der Theologischen Fakultät der Universität Freiburg i. Br. (1460–1620).* Beiträge zur Freiburg Wissenschafts- und Universitätsgeschichte, 15, Freiburg im Breisgau: Albert, 1957.

Baum, Adolf. *Magistrat und Reformation in Straßburg bis 1529.* Strasbourg: J. H. Ed. Heitz, 1887.

Baum, Johann Wilhelm. *Jacob Sturm, Straßburgs großer Stettmeister und Scholarch.* Strasbourg: J. H. Ed. Heitz, 1870.

Baumann, Franz Ludwig, ed. *Akten zur Geschichte des Bauernkrieges aus Oberschwaben.* Freiburg im Breisgau: Herder, 1877.

Baumgarten, Hermann. *Geschichte Karls V.* 3 vols. Stuttgart: J. G. Cotta, 1885–92.

———. *Jacob Sturm. Rede gehalten bei Übernahme des Rektorats der Universität Straßburg am 1. Mai 1876.* Strasbourg: Karl J. Trübner, 1876.

———. "Karl V. und der katholische Bund vom Jahre 1538." *Deutsche Zeitschrift für Geschichtswissenschaft* 6 (1891): 273–300.

———, Hermann, ed. *Sleidans Briefwechsel.* Strasbourg: Trübner, 1881.

———. "Zur Geschichte des Schmalkaldischen Krieges." HZ 36 (1876): 26–82.

Beinert, Johann. "Geschichte des ehemaligen hanau-lichtenbergischen Schloßes zu Willstätt." *Die Ortenau. Mitteilungen des historischen Vereins für Mittelbaden* 1/2 (1910/1911): 29–47.

Bellardi, Werner. "Anton Engelbrecht (1485–1558), Helfer, Mitarbeiter und Gegner Bucers." ARG 64 (1973): 183–206.

———. "Ein Bedacht Hedios zur Kirchenzucht in Straßburg aus dem Jahre 1547." In *Bucer und seine Zeit. Forschungsbeiträge und Bibliographie,* edited by Marijn de Kroon and Friedhelm Krüger, 117–32. VIEG, 80. Wiesbaden: Steiner, 1976.

———. *Die Geschichte der "christlichen Gemeinschaften" in Straßburg (1546/1550): Der Versuch einer "zweiten Reformation."* Quellen und Forschungen zur Reformationsgeschichte, 18. Leipzig: M. Heinsius Nachfolger, 1934. Reprint. New York: Johnson Reprint Corp., 1971.

———. "'Summarischer Vergriff' und das Interim in Straßburg. Die Bedeutung der letzten deutschen Schrift Martin Bucers im Kampf um die Einführung des Interims in Straßburg 1548." ZKiG 85 (1974): 64–76.

———. *Wolfgang Schultheiss: Wege und Wandlungen eines Straßburger Spiritualisten und Zeitgenossen Martin Bucers.* Schriften der Erwin-von-Steinbach-Stiftung, 3. Frankfurt am Main: Erwin-von-Steinbach-Stiftung, 1976.

Bender, Wilhelm. *Zwinglis Reformationsbündnisse: Untersuchungen zur Rechts- und*

Sozialgeschichte der Burgrechtsverträge eidgenössischer und oberdeutscher Städte zur Ausbreitung und Sicherung der Reformation Huldrych Zwinglis. Zurich and Stuttgart: Zwingli Verlag, 1970.

Berger, Adolf. *Encyclopedic Dictionary of Roman Law.* Transactions of the American Philosophical Society, 43, pt. 2. Philadelphia: American Philosophical Society, 1953.

Berler, Matern. "Chronik." In *Code historique et diplomatique de la Ville de Strasbourg,* edited by Louis Schnéegans, vol. 2, 71–130. Strasbourg: Silbermann, 1845–47.

Berman, Harold J. *Law and Revolution: The Formation of the Western Legal Tradition.* Cambridge, Mass.: Harvard Univ. Press, 1983.

Bernays, Jacob. "Jakob Sturm als Geistlicher." ZGO 59 (1905): 350–57.

Bernhardt, Walter. *Die Zentralbehörden des Herzogtums Württemberg und ihre Beamten 1520–1629.* 2 vols. VKLBW, ser. B, 70–71. Stuttgart: W. Kohlhammer, 1973.

Birnbaum, Marianna D. "Humanism in Hungary." In *Renaissance Humanism: Foundations, Forms, and Legacy,* edited by Albert Rabil, Jr. Vol. 2: *Humanism beyond Italy,* 293–334. Philadelphia: Univ. of Pennsylvania Press, 1988.

Bischoff, Georges. "La Haute-Alsace et la Guerre des Paysans." In *La Guerre des Paysans 1525,* edited by Alphonse Wollbrett, 111–20. Saverne: Société d'Histoire et d'Archéologie de Saverne et Environs, 1975.

Bizer, Ernst. *Confessio Virtembergica: Das württembergische Bekenntnis von 1551.* BWKG, Sonderheft 7. Stuttgart: Quell-Verlag, 1952.

———, ed. "Die Wittenberger Konkordie in Oberdeutschland und der Schweiz. Unbekannte Aktenstücke aus der Vermittlertätigkeit Martin Butzers." ARG 36 (1939): 214–52.

Blaich, Fritz. *Die Wirtschaftspolitik des Reichstags im Heiligen Römischen Reich: Ein Beitrag zur Problemgeschichte wirtschaftlichen Gestaltens.* Stuttgart: Gustav Fischer, 1970.

Blanke, Fritz. "Zwinglis 'Fidei ratio' (1530). Entstehung und Bedeutung." ARG 57 (1966): 96–101.

Blarer, Gerwig. *Briefe und Akten.* Edited by Heinrich Günter. 2 vols. Württembergische Geschichtsquellen, 16–17. Stuttgart: W. Kohlhammer, 1914–21.

Blaschke, Karlheinz. *Moritz von Sachsen: Ein Reformationsfürst der zweiten Generation.* Persönlichkeit und Geschichte, 113. Göttingen and Zurich: Muster-Schmidt Verlag, 1983.

———. "The Reformation and the Rise of the Territorial State." Translated by Thomas A. Brady, Jr. In *Luther and the Modern State in Germany,* edited by James D. Tracy, 61–76. SCES, 7. Kirksville, Mo.: Sixteenth Century Journal Publishers, 1986.

———. *Sachsen im Zeitalter der Reformation.* SVRG, 185. Gütersloh: Gerd Mohn, 1970.

Blickle, Peter. "Alternativen des Feudalismus 1525. Die Bedeutung des Elsass für die Konzeption einer korporativ-bündischen Verfassung im 'Bauernkrieg.'" In *La Guerre des Paysans 1525,* edited by Alphonse Wollbrett, 9–12. Saverne: Société d'Histoire et d'Archéologie de Saverne et Environs, 1975.

———. *Communal Reformation: The Quest for Salvation in Sixteenth-Century Germany.* Translated by Thomas Dunlap. Studies in German Histories. Atlantic Highlands, N.J.: Humanities Press, 1992.

———. *Deutsche Untertanen: Ein Widerspruch.* Munich: C. H. Beck, 1981.

———. *Gemeindereformation: Die Menschen des 16. Jahrhunderts auf dem Weg zum Heil.* Munich: R. Oldenbourg, 1985.

———. "Gemeiner Pfennig und Obrigkeit (1495)." VSWG 63 (1976): 180–93.

———. *Landschaften im Alten Reich: Die staatliche Funktion des gemeinen Mannes in Oberdeutschland.* Munich: C. H. Beck, 1973.

————. *Die Reformation im Reich*. Uni-Taschenbücher, no. 1181. Stuttgart: Eugen Ulmer, 1982.

————. *The Revolution of 1525: The German Peasants' War from a New Perspective*. Translated by Thomas A. Brady, Jr., and H. C. Erik Midelfort. Baltimore: Johns Hopkins Univ. Press, 1981.

————. *Unruhen in der ständischen Gesellschaft 1300–1800*. Enzyklopädie deutscher Geschichte, 1. Munich: R. Oldenbourg, 1988.

————, ed. *Zugänge zur bäuerlichen Reformation*. Bauer und Reformation, 1. Zurich: Chronos, 1987.

Blume, Gundomar. *Goslar und der Schmalkaldische Bund 1527/31–1547*. Beiträge zur Geschichte der Stadt Goslar, 26. Goslar: Selbstverlag des Geschichts- und Heimatschutzvereins, 1969.

Bock, Ernst. *Der Schwäbische Bund und seine Verfassung 1488–1534. Ein Beitrag zur Geschichte der Zeit der Reichsreform*. Aalen: Scientia Verlag, 1968.

Bofinger, Wilhelm. "Kirche und werdender Territorialstaat. Eine Untersuchung zur Kirchenreform Herzog Ulrichs von Württemberg." *BWKG* 65 (1965): 75–149.

Bog, Ingomar. "Betrachtungen zur korporativen Politik der Reichsstädte." *Ulm und Oberschwaben* 34 (1955): 87–101.

Boor, Albert de. *Beiträge zur Geschichte des Speirer Reichstages vom Jahre 1544*. Strasbourg: J. Schneider, 1878.

Bopp, Marie-Joseph. *Die evangelischen Geistlichen und Theologen in Elsaß und Lothringen von der Reformation bis zur Gegenwart*. Bibliothek familiengeschichtlicher Quellen, 14. Neustadt an der Aisch: Degener, 1959.

————. *Die evangelischen Gemeinden und Hohen Schulen in Elsaß und Lothringen von der Reformation bis zur Gegenwart*. Bibliothek familiengeschichtlicher Quellen, 16. Neustadt an der Aisch: Degener, 1963.

Borchardt, Frank L. *German Antiquity in Renaissance Myth*. Baltimore: Johns Hopkins Univ. Press, 1971.

Born, Karl Erich. "Moritz von Sachsen und die Fürstenverschwörung gegen Karl V." *HZ* 191 (1960): 18–66. Reprint. Darmstadt: Wissenschaftliche Buchgesellschaft, 1972.

Bornert, René. *La réforme protestante du culte à Strasbourg au XVIe siècle (1523–1598): Approche sociologique et interprétation théologique*. SMRT, 28. Leiden: E. J. Brill, 1981.

Bornkamm, Heinrich, ed. *Luther im Spiegel der deutschen Geistesgeschichte*. 2d ed. Göttingen: Vandenhoeck & Ruprecht, 1970.

————. *Luther und der deutsche Geist*. Sammlung gemeinverständlicher Vorträge und Schriften aus dem Gebiet der Theologie und Religionsgeschichte, 170. Tübingen: J. C. B. Mohr (Paul Siebeck), 1934.

————. *Martin Bucers Bedeutung für die europäische Reformationsgeschichte*. SVRG, 169. Gütersloh: Gerd Mohn, 1952.

Bourrilly, Victor-Louis. *Guillaume du Bellay, seigneur de Langey, 1491–1543*. Paris: Société nouvelle de librairie et d'édition, 1905.

————. "Jean Sleidan et le Cardinal du Bellay. Premier séjour de Jean Sleidan en France (1533–1540)." *BSHPF* 50 (1901): 225–42.

Brady, Thomas A., Jr. "Architect of Persecution: Jacob Sturm and the Fall of the Sects at Strasbourg." *ARG* 79 (1988): 262–81.

————. "The Common Man and the Lost Austria in the West: A Contribution to the German Problem." In *Politics and Society in Reformation Europe: Essays for Sir Geoffrey Elton on his Sixty-Fifth Birthday*, edited by E. I. Kouri and Tom Scott, 142–57. London: Macmillan, 1987.

————. "A Contemporary German Version of Johann Sturm's Funeral Eulogy of Jacob Sturm." *BHR* 28 (1965): 680–81.

————. "Continuity in Gerhard Ritter." In *Continuity and Change in German Historiography, 1933–1950s*, edited by James Van Horn Melton and Hartmut Lehmann, 109–17. Cambridge: Cambridge Univ. Press, 1994.

————. "A Crisis Averted: Jacob Sturm and the Truce of Frankfurt, 1539." In *Krisenbewußtsein und Krisenbewältigung in der Frühen Neuzeit: Festschrift für Hans-Christoph Rublack*, edited by Monika Hagenmaier and Sabine Holtz, 47–60. Frankfurt am Main: Peter Lang, 1992.

————. "'The Earth is the Lord's, and Our Homeland as Well': Martin Bucer and the Politics of Strasbourg." In *Martin Bucer et l'Europe du XVIe siècle. Colloque International, Strasbourg, 28–31 août 1991* ed. 129–43. Leiden: Marc Lienhard, Christian Krieger and E. J. Brill, 1993.

————. "La famille Sturm aux XVe et XVIe siècles." *RA* 108 (1982): 29–44.

————. "From the Sacral Community to the Common Man: Reflections on German Reformation Studies." *CEH* 21 (1988): 229–45.

————. "In Search of the Godly City: The Domestication of Religion in the German Urban Reformation." In *The German People and the Reformation*, edited by R. Po-chia Hsia, 14–31. Ithaca: Cornell Univ. Press, 1988.

————. "Jacob Sturm and the Lutherans at the Diet of Augsburg, 1530." *CH* 42 (1973): 183–202.

————. "Jacob Sturm and the Seizure of Brunswick-Wolfenbüttel by the Schmalkaldic League, 1542–1545." In *Festschrift for DeLamar Jensen*, ed. Paul B. Pixton and Malcolm R. Thorp. Sixteenth Century Studies & Essays, Kirksville: Sixteenth Century Journal Publishers, 1994.

————. "Phases and Strategies of the Schmalkaldic League: A Perspective after 450 Years." *ARG* 74 (1983): 162–81.

————. "Princes' Reformation vs. Urban Liberty. Strasbourg and the Restoration of Duke Ulrich in Württemberg, 1534." In *Städtische Gesellschaft und Reformation*, edited by Ingrid Bátori, 265–91. SFN, 12. Stuttgart: Klett-Cotta, 1980.

————. "The Rise of Merchant Empires, 1400–1700: A European Counterpoint." In *The Political Economy of Merchant Empires*, edited by James D. Tracy, 117–60. Cambridge: Cambridge Univ. Press, 1991.

————. "Rites of Autonomy, Rites of Dependence: South German Civic Culture in the Age of Renaissance and Reformation." In *Urban Culture in the Renaissance and Reformation*, edited by Steven Ozment, 9–24. SCSE, 11. Kirksville, Mo.: Sixteenth Century Journal Publishers, 1989.

————. *Ruling Class, Regime and Reformation at Strasbourg, 1520–1550.* SMRT, 22. Leiden: E. J. Brill, 1978.

————. "'Sind also zu beiden theilen Christen, des Gott erbarm.' Le mémoire de Jacques Sturm sur le culte publique à Strasbourg (août 1525)." In *Horizons européens de la Réforme en Alsace: Mélanges offerts à Jean Rott pour son 65e anniversaire*, edited by Marijn de Kroon and Marc Lienhard, 69–79. PSSARE, 17. Strasbourg: Librairie Istra, 1980.

————. "Social History." In *Reformation Europe: A Guide to Research*, edited by Steven Ozment, 161–81. St. Louis: Center for Reformation Research, 1982.

————. "The Social Place of a German Renaissance Artist: Hans Baldung Grien (1484/5–1545) at Strasbourg." *CEH* 8 (1975): 295–315.

————. "'Special Path'? Peculiarities of German Histories in the Early Modern Era." In *Germania Illustrata: Essays on Early Modern Germany Presented to Gerald Strauss*, edited by Susan Karant-Nunn and Andrew Fix, 197–216. SCSE, 18. Kirksville, Mo.: Sixteenth Century Journal Publishers, 1991.

————. "The Themes of Social Structure, Social Conflict, and Civic Harmony in Jakob Wimphelings *Germania*." *SCJ* 3 (1972): 65–76.

————. *Turning Swiss: Cities and Empire, 1450–1550.* Cambridge Studies in Early

Modern History. Cambridge and New York: Cambridge Univ. Press, 1985.

———. "'You Hate Us Priests': Anticlericalism, Communalism, and the Control of Women at Strasbourg in the Age of the Reformation." In *Anticlericalism in the Late Middle Ages and Reformation*, edited by Peter Dykema and Heiko A. Oberman, 167–207. Leiden: E. J. Brill, 1993.

Brandenburg, Erich. *Die Gefangennahme Herzog Heinrichs von Braunschweig durch den Schmalkaldischen Bund (1545)*. Leipzig: Gustav Fock, 1894.

———. *Moritz von Sachsen*. Vol. 1, *Bis zur Wittenberger Kapitulation (1547)*. Leipzig: B. G. Teubner, 1898.

———, ed. *Politisches Korrespondenz des Herzogs Moritz von Sachsen*. Vols. 1–2. Leipzig: Teubner, 1900–1904. Reprint. Berlin: Akademie-Verlag, 1982.

Brandi, Karl. *Kaiser Karl V.: Werden und Schicksal einer Persönlichkeit und eines Weltreiches*. Vol. 1, *Darstellung*. 6th ed. Munich: F. Bruckmann, 1959.

———. *Kaiser Karl V.: Werden und Schicksal einer Persönlichkeit und eines Weltreiches*. Vol. 2, *Quellen und Erörterungen*. 2d ed. Munich: F. Bruckmann, 1967.

———. "Karl V. vor Metz." *ELJb* 16 (1937): 1–30.

Brandt, Asverus von. *Berichte und Briefe des Rats und Gesandten Herzog Albrechts von Preußen*. Edited by Adalbert Bezzenberger. 2 vols. Königsberg in Preussen: Gräfe und Unzer, 1904.

Brann, Noel L. "Humanism in Germany." In *Renaissance Humanism: Foundations, Forms, and Legacy*, edited by Albert Rabil, Jr. Vol. 2: *Humanism beyond Italy*, 123–55. Philadelphia: Univ. of Pennsylvania Press, 1988.

Brant, Sebastian. "Bischoff Wilhelm von Hoensteins waal und einritt. Anno 1506 et 1507." In *Code historique et diplomatique de la Ville de Strasbourg*, edited by Louis Schnéegans, vol. 2, 239–99. Strasbourg: Silbermann, 1845–47.

Brecht, Martin. "Abgrenzung oder Verständigung. Was wollten die Protestanten in Trient?" *BWKG* 70 (1970): 148–75. Also in *Concilium Tridentinum*, edited by Remigius Bäumer, 161–95. WF, 313. Darmstadt: Wissenschaftliche Buchgesellschaft, 1979.

———. "Ambrosius Blarer's Wirksamkeit in Schwaben." In *Der Konstanzer Reformator Ambrosius Blarer 1492–1564: Gedenkschrift zu seinem 400. Todestag*, edited by Bernd Moeller, 140–71. Constance and Sigmaringen: Jan Thorbecke, 1964.

———. "Die gemeinsame Politik der Reichsstädte und die Reformation." *ZRG*, KA 94 (1977): 181–263.

———. *Martin Luther*. 3 vols. Stuttgart: Calwer Verlag, 1981–87.

———. "Luthers Beziehungen zu den Oberdeutschen und Schweizern von 1530/ 1531 bis 1546." In *Leben und Werk Martin Luthers von 1526 bis 1546: Festgabe zu seinem 500. Geburtstag*. 2 vols. Vol. 1, edited by Helmar Junghans, 497–518. Berlin: Evangelische Verlagsanstalt, 1983.

———. "Ulm und die deutsche Reformation." *Ulm und Oberschwaben* 42/43 (1978): 96–116.

Brecht, Martin, and Hermann Ehmer. *Südwestdeutsche Reformationsgeschichte. Zur Einführhung der Reformation im Herzogtum Württemberg 1534*. Stuttgart: Calwer Verlag, 1984.

Brem- und Verdische Bibliothek, worin zur Aufnahme der Wissenschaft insonderheit der theologischen, philologischen und historischen, allerley brauchbare Abhandlungen und Anmerkungen mitgetheilt werden. 4 vols. Hamburg: Christian Wilhelm Brandt, 1758.

Brendler, Gerhard. *Das Täuferreich zu Münster 1534–35*. Leipziger Uebersetzungen und Abhandlungen zum Mittelalter, ser. B, 2. Berlin: VEB Deutscher Verlag der Wissenschaften, 1966.

Bresard, Marc. *Les foires de Lyon aux XVe et XVIe siècles*. Paris: A. Picard, 1914.

Brunner, Otto. *Land and Lordship. Structures of Governance in Medieval Austria*. Translated by Howard Kaminsky and James Van Horn Melton. Philadelphia: Univ. of Pennsylvania Press, 1992.

Bruns, Friedrich. *Die Vertreibung Herzog Heinrichs von Braunschweig durch den Schmalkaldischen Bund.* Pt. 1, *Vorgeschichte.* Dissertation, Marburg. Marburg: Georg Schirling, 1889.

Bucer, Martin. *Correspondance.* Edited by Jean Rott. Martini Buceri Opera Omnia, ser. 3. Leiden: E. J. Brill, 1979–.

———. "De regno Christi." In *Melanchthon and Bucer*, edited by Wilhelm Pauck, 155–394. The Library of Christian Classics, 19. Philadelphia: Westminster Press, 1969.

———. *Martin Bucers Deutsche Schriften.* Edited by Robert Stupperich. Martini Buceri Opera Omnia, ser. 1. Gütersloh: Gerd Mohn, 1960–.

———. *Martini Buceri Opera Latina.* Edited by Robert Stupperich. Martini Buceri Opera Omnia, ser. 2. Paris: Presses Universitaires de France; Leiden: E. J. Brill, 1955–.

Bucholtz, Franz Bernhard von. *Geschichte der Regierung Ferdinands des Ersten.* 9 vols. Vienna: Schaumburg, 1831–38. Reprint. Graz: Akademische Druck- und Verlagsanstalt, 1971.

Buck, Hermann. *Die Anfänge der Konstanzer Reformationsprozesse: Österreich, Eidgenossenschaft und Schmalkaldischer Bund 1510/22–1531.* SKRG, 29–31. Tübingen: Osiandersche Buchhandlung, 1964.

Büheler, Sebald. *La chronique strasbourgeoise*, edited by Léon Dacheux. BSCMHA, 2d ser. 13 (1888): 23–149, nos. 85–599.

Bullinger, Heinrich. *Werke.* Edited by the Zwingli-Verein in Zurich. Pt. 2, *Briefwechsel.* Edited by Ulrich Gäbler for the Zwingli-Verein. Zurich: Theologischer Verlag, 1972–.

———. *Reformationsgeschichte nach dem Autographon herausgegeben.* Edited by Johann Jakob Hottinger and H. H. Vögeli. 3 vols. Frauenfeld: Christoph Beyerl, 1838–40. Reprint. Zurich: Theologische Buchhandlung, 1985.

Burg, André-Marcel. "La Guerre des Paysans dans la région de Hagenau." In *La Guerre des Paysans 1525*, edited by Alphonse Wollbrett, 49–54. Saverne: Société d'Histoire et d'Archéologie de Saverne et Environs, 1975.

Burger, Heinz-Otto. *Renaissance, Humanismus, Reformation: Deutsche Literatur im europäischen Kontext.* Bad Homburg v. d. H., Berlin, and Zurich: Gehlen, 1969.

Burke, Peter. *The Renaissance Sense of the Past.* London: Edward Arnold, 1969.

Calvin, John. *Ioannis Calvini opera quae supersunt omnia.* Edited by Johann Wilhelm Baum, Eduard Cunitz, and Eduard Reuss. 59 vols. *Corpus Reformatorum*, 29–87. Brunswick: C. Schwetzschke, 1863–1900.

Capito, Wolfgang. *In Habakuk prophetam V. Capitonis enarrationes.* Strasbourg: Wolf Köpfel, 1526.

Cardauns, Ludwig. *Zur Geschichte der kirchlichen Unions- und Reformbestrebungen von 1538–1542.* Bibliothek des Königlich Preußischen Historischen Instituts, 5. Rome: Loescher & Co. (W. Regenberg), 1910.

Cargill Thompson, W. D. J. *The Political Thought of Martin Luther.* Hassocks: Harvester Press, 1984.

Chickering, Roger. *Karl Lamprecht.* Studies in German Histories. Atlantic Highlands, N.J.: Humanities Press, 1993.

Chrisman, Miriam Usher. *Bibliography of Strasbourg Imprints, 1480–1599.* New Haven: Yale Univ. Press, 1982.

———. "James Sturm of Strasbourg." In *Contemporaries of Erasmus: A Biographical Register of the Renaissance and Reformation*, edited by Peter G. Bietenholz, vol. 3:293–94. Toronto: Univ. of Toronto Press, 1987.

———. *Lay Culture, Learned Culture: Books and Social Change in Strasbourg, 1480–1599.* New Haven: Yale University Press, 1982.

———. "La pensée et la main: Mathias Schürer, humaniste-imprimeur." In *Grandes figures de l'humanisme Alsacien: Courants, milieux, destins,* edited by Francis Rapp and Georges Livet, 159–72. PSSARE, Collection "Grandes Publications," 14. Strasbourg: Librarie Istra, 1978.

―――. *Strasbourg and the Reform: A Study in the Process of Change.* New Haven: Yale University Press, 1967.

―――. "Women and the Reformation in Strasbourg, 1490–1530." *ARG* 63 (1972): 143–67.

Clasen, Claus Peter. *Anabaptism: A Social History, 1525–1618. Switzerland, Austria, Moravia, South and Central Germany.* Ithaca: Cornell Univ. Press, 1972.

Clemen, Otto. "Die Schmalkaldener und Frankreich im Mai 1543." *ARG* 37 (1940): 222–27.

―――. "Vergleichsartikel für das Religionsgespräch, das am 1. Aug. 1539 in Nürnberg beginnen sollte." *Zeitschrift für bayerische Kirchengeschichte* 15 (1940): 229–32.

Cohn, Henry J. "Church Property in the German Protestant Principalities." In *Politics and Society in Reformation Europe: Essays for Sir Geoffrey Elton on his Sixty-Fifth Birthday,* edited by E. I. Kouri and Tom Scott, 158–87. London: Macmillan, 1987.

Commynes, Philippe de. *The Memoires of Philippe de Commynes.* Edited by Samuel Kinser and translated by Isabelle Cazeaux. 2 vols. Columbia: Univ. of South Carolina Press, 1969–73.

Concilium Tridentinum. Diarorum, actorum, epistolarum, tractatum nova collectio. Edited by the Görres-Gesellschaft. 14 vols. Freiburg i. Br.: Herder, 1904–85.

Conrad, Franziska. *Reformation in der bäuerlichen Gesellschaft: Zur Rezeption reformatorischer Theologie im Elsass.* VIEG, 116. Wiesbaden: Franz Steiner, 1984.

Crämer, Ulrich. *Die Verfassung und Verwaltung Straßburgs von der Reformationszeit bis zum Fall der Reichsstadt 1521–1681.* SWIEL, n.s., 3. Frankfurt am Main: Selbstverlag des Elsaß-Lothringen Instituts, 1931.

―――. "Die Wehrmacht Straßburgs von der Reformationszeit bis zum Fall der Reichsstadt." *ZGO* 84 (1932): 45–95.

Crusius, Martin. *Schwäbische Chronik . . . aus dem Lateinischen erstmals übersetzt und mit einer Continuation vom Jahr 1596 bis 1733 . . . versehen.* Translated by Johann Jakob Moser. 2 vols. Frankfurt: Metzler und Erhard, 1733.

Csáky, Moritz. "Karl V., Ungarn, die Türkenfrage und das Reich." In *Das römisch-deutsche Reich im politischen System Karls V.,* edited by Heinrich Lutz, 223–37. SHKK, 1. Munich and Vienna: R. Oldenbourg, 1982.

Csezmiczei, János ("Janus Pannonius"). *Jani Pannonii Quinquecclesiensis Episcopi Sylua Panegyrica ad Guarinum Veronensem, praeceptorum suum.* Basel: Johannes Froben, 1518.

Dacheux, Léon, ed. *Fragments de diverses vieilles chroniques.* BSCMHA, 2d ser. 18 (1890): 1–181.

―――. *Un réformateur catholique à la fin du XVe siècle: Jean Geiler de Kaysersberg, étude sur sa vie et son temps.* Paris and Strasbourg: E. Delegrave, 1876.

Decker-Hauff, Hansmartin, and Rudolf Seigel, eds. *Die Chronik der Grafen von Zimmern.* 3 vols. Constance and Sigmaringen: Jan Thorbecke, 1964–72.

Decot, Rolf. *Religionsfrieden und Kirchenreform: Der Mainzer Kurfürst und Erzbischof Sebastian von Heusenstamm 1545–1555.* VIEG, 100. Wiesbaden: Franz Steiner, 1980.

Deetjen, Werner-Ulrich. "Licentiat Martin Frecht, Professor und Prädikant (1494–1556)." In *Die Einführung der Reformation in Ulm. Geschichte eines Bürgerentscheids,* edited by Hans Eugen Specker and Gebhard Weig, 269–321. Forschungen zur Geschichte der Stadt Ulm, Reihe Dokumentation, 2. Ulm: Stadtarchiv, 1981.

―――. *Studien zur württembergischen Kirchenordnung Herzog Ulrichs 1534–1550: Das Herzogtum Württemberg im Zeitalter Herzog Ulrichs (1498–1550): Die Neuordnung des Kirchengutes und der Klöster (1534–1547)*. Quellen und Forschungen zur württembergischen Kirchengeschichte, 7. Stuttgart: Calwer Verlag, 1981.

de Kroon, Marijn. "Die Augsburger Reformation in der Korrespondenz de Straßburger Reformators Martin Bucer unter besonderer Berücksichtigung des Briefwechsels Gereon Sailers." In *Die Augsburger Kirchenordnung von 1537 und ihr Umfeld: Wissenschaftliches Kolloquium*, edited by Reinhard Schwarz, 59–90. SVRG, 196. Gütersloh: Gerd Mohn, 1988.

———. *Studien zu Martin Bucers Obrigkeitsverständnis: Evangelisches Ethos und politisches Engagement*. Gütersloh: Gerd Mohn, 1984.

Dellsperger, Rudolf. "Zehn Jahre bernischer Reformationsgeschichte (1522–1532). Eine Einführung." In *450 Jahre Berner Reformation: Beiträge zur Geschichte der Berner Reformation und zu Niklaus Manuel*, edited by Historischer Verein des Kantons Bern, 25–59. Bern: Historischer Verein des Kantons Bern, 1980.

Demandt, Karl E. *Geschichte des Landes Hessen*. 2d ed. Kassel: Bärenreiter Verlag, 1959.

Denis, Philippe. *Les églises d'étrangers en pays rhénans (1538–1564)*. Bibliothèque de la Faculté de Philosophie et Lettres de l'Université de Liège, fascicle 243. Paris: Société d'Édition "Les Belles Lettres," 1984.

Deppermann, Klaus. *Melchior Hoffman: Soziale Unruhen und apokalyptische Visionen im Zeitalter der Reformation*. Göttingen: Vandenhoeck & Ruprecht, 1979.

———. "Melchior Hoffman à Strasbourg." In *Strasbourg au coeur religieux du XVIe siècle*, edited by Georges Livet, Marc Lienhard, and Jean Rott, 501–10. PSSARE, 12. Strasbourg: Librairie Istra, 1978.

Deutsche Reichstagsakten, jüngere Reihe. Deutsche Reichstagsakten unter Kaiser Karl V. Edited for the Historische Kommission bei der Bayerischen Akademie der Wissenschaften.

Vol. 1, edited by August Kluckhohn. Gotha: F. A. Perthes, 1893. Reprint. Göttingen: Vandenhoeck & Ruprecht, 1962.

Vol. 2, edited by Adolf Wrede. Gotha: F. A. Perthes, 1896. Reprint. Göttingen: Vandenhoeck & Ruprecht, 1962.

Vol. 3, edited by Adolf Wrede. Gotha: F. A. Perthes, 1901. Reprint. Göttingen: Vandenhoeck & Ruprecht, 1963.

Vol. 4, edited by Adolf Wrede. Gotha: F. A. Perthes, 1905. Reprint. Göttingen: Vandenhoeck & Ruprecht, 1963.

Vol. 7, edited by Johannes Kühn. Gotha: F. A. Perthes, 1935. Reprint. Göttingen: Vandenhoeck & Ruprecht, 1963.

Vol. 8, edited by Wolfgang Steglich. Göttingen: Vandenhoeck & Ruprecht, 1970–71.

Dickens, A. G. *Contemporary Historians of the German Reformation*. London: Univ. of London, Institute for Germanic Studies, 1978.

———. *The German Nation and Martin Luther*. New York: Harper & Row, 1974.

———. "Johannes Sleidan and Reformation History." In *Reformation Conformity and Dissent. Essays in Honour of Geoffrey Nuttall*, edited by R. Buick Knox, 17–43. London: Epworth Press, 1977.

Dickens, A. G., and John Tonkin. *The Reformation in Historical Thought*. Cambridge, Mass.: Harvard Univ. Press, 1985.

Diestelkamp, Bernhard, ed. *Forschungen aus Akten des Reichskammergerichts*. Vienna: Böhlau, 1984.

———. "Der Stand der Arbeiten zur Erschliessung der Quellen des Reichskammergerichts." In *Consilium Magnum 1473–1973. Herdenking van de 500e verjaardag van de oprichting van het Parlement en Grote Raad van Mechelen*, 199–213. Brussels: Algemeen Rijksarchief, 1977.

Dobel, Friedrich. *Memmingen im Reformationszeitalter*. 5 vols. Augsburg: Lamparter, 1877–78.

Doernberg, Erwin. *Henry VIII and Luther: An Account of their Personal Relations.* Stanford: Stanford Univ. Press, 1961.

Dolan, John Patrick. *The Influence of Erasmus, Witzel and Cassander in the Church Ordinances and Reform Proposals of the United Duchies of Cleve during the Middle Decades of the Sixteenth Century.* RST, 83. Münster: Aschendorff, 1957.

Dolazalek, Gero. "Die Assessoren des Reichakmmergerichts und der Nürnberger Religionsfriede vom 23. Juli 1532." In *Recht, Gericht, Genossenschaft und Policey: Studien zu Grundbegriffen der germanistischen Rechtshistorie. Symphosion für Adalbert Erler,* ed. Gerhard Dilcher and Bernhard Diestelkamp, 84–96. Berlin: Erich Schmidt, 1986.

———. "Die juristische Argumentation der Assessoren am Reichskammergericht zu den Reformationsprozessen 1532–1538." In *Das Reichskammergericht in der deutschen Geschichte. Stand der Forschung, Forschungsperspektiven,* ed. Bernhard Diestelkamp, 25–58. Quellen und Forschungen zur höchsten Gerichtsbarkeit im alten Reich, 21. Vienna: Böhlau, 1990.

Dollinger, Philipp. "Charles-Quint et les villes d'Empire." In *Charles-Quint, le Rhin et la France: Droit savant et droit pénal à l'époque de Charles-Quint,* 183–94. PSSARE, collection "Recherches et Documents," 17. Strasbourg: Librairie Istra, 1973.

———. *The German Hansa.* Translated by D. S. Ault and S. H. Steinberg. Stanford: Stanford Univ. Press, 1970.

———. "La tolérance à Strasbourg au XVIe siècle." In *Hommage à Lucien Febvre,* vol. 2, 241–49. Paris: Armand Colin, 1953.

———. "La ville libre à la fin du Moyen Age (1350–1482)." In *Histoire de Strasbourg,* edited by Georges Livet and Francis Rapp, vol. 2, 99–175. Strasbourg: Éditions Les Dernières Nouvelles, 1981.

Dommasch, Gerd. *Die Religionsprozesse der rekusierenden Fürsten und Städte und die Erneuerung des Schmalkaldischen Bundes 1534–1536.* SKRG, 28. Tübingen: Osiandersche Buchhandlung, 1961.

Dotzauer, Winfried. *Die deutschen Reichskreise in der Verfassung des alten Reiches und ihr Eigenleben (1500–1806).* Darmstadt: Wissenschaftliche Buchgesellschaft, 1989.

Douglass, E. Jane Dempsey. *Justification in Late Medieval Preaching: A Study of John Geiler of Keisersberg.* SMRT, 1. Leiden: E. J. Brill, 1966.

Druffel, August von, ed. *Beiträge zur Reichsgeschichte.* 4 vols. *Briefe und Akten zur Geschichte des 16. Jahrhunderts mit besonderer Rücksicht auf Bayerns Fürstenhaus.* Vols. 1–4, 1546–1553. Munich: M. Rieger, 1873–96.

Du Bellay, Martin, and Guillaume du Bellay. *Mémoires de Martin et Guillaume Du Bellay.* Edited by Victor-Louis Bourrilly and Fleury Vindry. 4 vols. Société de l'histoire de France (Série anterieure à 1789), 338, 350, 356, 387. Paris, Renouard, 1908–19.

Du Boulay, F. R. H. *Germany in the later Middle Ages.* New York: St. Martin's Press, 1983.

Duby, Georges. *The Three Orders: Feudal Society Imagined.* Translated by Arthur Goldhammer. Chicago: Univ. of Chicago Press, 1980.

Duchhardt, Heinz. *Deutsche Verfassungsgeschichte 1495–1806.* Stuttgart: W. Kohlhammer, 1991.

———. *Protestantisches Kaisertum und Altes Reich: Die Diskussion über die Konfession des Kaisers in Politik, Publizistik und Staatsrecht.* VIEG, 87. Wiesbaden: Franz Steiner, 1977.

Dueck, Abraham. "Religion and Politics in the Reformation. Philipp of Hesse and the Consolidation and Expansion of German Protestantism, 1531–1536." Ph.D. diss., Duke Univ., 1971.

———. "Religion and Temporal Authority in the Reformation. The Controversy Among the Protestants Prior to the Peace of Nuremberg, 1532." SCJ 13 (1982): 55–74.

Duggan, Lawrence G. "The Church as an Institution of the Old Reich." In *The Old Reich: Essay in German Political Institutions, 1495–1806*, edited by James A. Vann and Steven Rowan, 149–64. Studies Presented to the International Commission for the History of Representative and Parliamentary Institutions, vol. 48. Brussels: Éditions de la librairie encyclopédique, 1974.

Dülfer, Kurt. *Die Packschen Handel*. Pt. 1, *Darstellung*. Veröffentlichungen der Historischen Kommission für Hessen und Waldeck, 24, 3. Marburg: N. G. Elwert, 1958.

Dürr, Emil, and Paul Roth, eds. *Aktensammlung zur Geschichte der Basler Reformation in den Jahren 1519 bis Anfang 1534*. 6 vols. Basel: Verlag der Historischen und Antiquarischen Gesellschaft, 1921–50.

Edwards, Mark U., Jr. *Luther's Last Battles: Politics and Polemics, 1531–46*. Ithaca: Cornell Univ. Press, 1983.

Eells, Hastings. *The Attitude of Martin Bucer toward the Bigamy of Philip of Hesse*. Yale Historical Publications, Miscellany, 12. New Haven: Yale Univ. Press, 1924.

———. *Martin Bucer*. New Haven: Yale Univ. Press, 1931.

Eheberg, Karl Theodor, ed. *Verfassungs-, Verwaltungs- und Wirtschaftsgeschichte der Stadt Straßburg bis 1681*. Vol. 1, *Urkunden und Akten*. Strasbourg: J. H. Ed. Heitz, 1899.

Ehrenberg, Richard. *Das Zeitalter der Fugger: Geldkapital und Creditverkehr im 16. Jahrhundert*. 2 vols. Jena, 1896. Reprint. Hildesheim: Georg Olms, 1963.

Elton, Geoffrey R. "England and the Continent in the Sixteenth Century." In *Reform and Reformation: England and the Continent, c. 1500–c. 1750*, edited by Derek Baker. Church History: Subsidia, vol. 2:1–16. Oxford: Basil Blackwell, 1979.

———. *England under the Tudors*. History of England, 4. London: Methuen, 1956.

Eltz, Erwein. "Zwei Gutachten des Kurfürstenrates über die Wormser Matrikel und den Gemeinen Pfennig. Ein Beitrag zur Reichssteuerproblematik vom Reichstag in Speyer 1544." In *Aus der Arbeit an den Reichstagen unter Kaiser Karl V: Sieben Beiträge zu Fragen der Forschung und Edition*, edited by Heinrich Lutz and Alfred Kohler, 273–301. SHKBA, 26. Göttingen: Vandenhoeck & Ruprecht, 1986.

Endres, Rudolf. "Der Kayserliche neunjährige Bund vom Jahr 1535–1544." In *Bauer, Reich und Reformation: Festschrift für Günter Franz zum 80. Geburtstag am 23. Mai 1982*, edited by Peter Blickle, 84–103. Stuttgart: Eugen Ulmer, 1982.

Engel, Carl. *Das Schulwesen in Straßburg vor der Gründung des Protestantischen Gymnasiums, 1538*. Programm des Protestantischen Gymnasiums zu Straßburg für das Schuljahr 1886–1887. Strasbourg: J. H. Ed. Heitz (Heitz & Mündel), 1886.

Engel, Evamaria, and Bernhard Töpfer, eds. *Deutsche Geschichte*. Vol. 2, *Die entfaltete Feudalgesellschaft von der Mitte des 11. bis zu den siebziger Jahren des 15. Jahrhunderts*. 2d ed. Berlin: VEB Deutscher Verlag der Wissenschaften, 1986.

Engelhardt, Adolf. "Der Nürnberger Religionsfriede von 1532." MVGN 31 (1933): 17–123.

Erasmus, Desiderius. *Collected Works of Erasmus*. Toronto: Univ. of Toronto Press, 1974–.

Erasmus. *See* Allen, *Opus epistolarum Des. Erasmi*.

Ernst, Fritz. "Über Gesandtschaftswesen und Diplomatie an der Wende vom Mittelalter zur Neuzeit." AKG 33 (1951): 64–95.

Ernst, Max. "Bernhard Besserer, Bürgermeister in Ulm (1471–1542)." ZWLG 5 (1941): 88–133.

Ernst, Viktor, ed. *Briefwechsel des Herzogs Christoph von Wirtemberg*. 4 vols. Stuttgart: W. Kohlhammer, 1899–1907.

Eubel, Conrad, ed. *Hierarchia catholica medii aevi, sive, summorum pontificum, S. R.*

E. cardinalium, ecclesiarum antistitum series ab anno 1198 usque ad annum [1667] perducta et documentis tabularii praesertim Vaticani. 4 vols. Padua: Il Messaggero di S. Antonio, 1960.

Fabian, Ekkehart, ed. *Abschiede der Bündnis- und Bekenntnistage protestierender Fürsten und Städte zwischen den Reichstagen zu Speyer und zu Augsburg 1529–1530.* SKRG, 6. Tübingen: Osiander, 1960.

——, ed. *Die Beschlüße der oberdeutschen schmalkaldischen Städtetage.* Pts. 1–3, *1530–1536.* SKRG, 9/10, 14/15, 21/24. Tübingen: Osiander, 1959–60.

——. *Dr. Gregor Brück 1557–1957: Lebensbild und Schriftenverzeichnis des Reformationskanzlers.* SKRG, 2. Tübingen: Osiandersche Buchhandlung, 1962.

——. *Die Entstehung des Schmalkaldischen Bundes und seiner Verfassung 1524/29–1531/35: Brück, Philipp von Hessen und Jakob Sturm.* 2d ed. SKRG, 1. Tübingen: Osiandersche Buchhandlung, 1962.

——, ed. *Quellen zur Geschichte der Reformationsbündnisse und der Konstanzer Reformationsprozesse 1529–1548.* SKRG, 34. Tübingen: Osiandersche Buchhandlung, 1967.

——, ed. *Die Schmalkaldischen Bundesabschieden 1530–1536.* 2 vols. SKRG, 7–8. Tübingen: Osiander, 1958.

——, ed. *Urkunden und Akten der Reformationsprozesse am Reichskammergericht, am kaiserlichen Hofgericht zu Rottweil und an anderen Gerichten.* Pt. 1. SKRG, 16/17. Tübingen: Osiander, 1961.

Faulenbach, Bernd. *Ideologie des deutschen Weges. Die deutsche Geschichte in der Historiographie zwischen Kaiserreich und Nationalsozialismus.* Munich: C. H. Beck, 1980.

Feine, Hans-Erich. "Ludwig Gremp von Freudenstein." In *Schwäbische Lebensbilder,* vol. 3: 199–218. Stuttgart: W. Kohlhammer, 1942.

——. "Die Territorialbildung der Habsburger im deutschen Südwesten, vornehmlich im Mittelalter." ZSRG, GA 67 (1950): 176–308.

Fichtner, Paula Sutter. *Ferdinand I of Austria: The Politics of Dynasticism in the Age of the Reformation.* East European Monographs, 100. Boulder, Colo: East European Monographs, 1982.

Ficker, Johannes, ed. *Bildnisse der Straßburger Reformation.* Quellen und Forschungen zur Kirchen- und Kulturgeschichte von Elsaß-Lothringen, 4. Strasbourg: Trübner, 1914.

——. "Das größte Prachtwerk des Straßburger Buchdruckes. Zur Geschichte und Gestaltung des großen Straßburger Gesangbuchs 1541." ARG 38 (1941): 198–230.

——, ed. "Jakob Sturms Entwurf zur Straßburger reformatorischer Verantwortung." ELJb 19 (1941): 149–58.

Ficker, Johannes, and Otto Winckelmann. *Handschriftenproben des sechszehnten Jahrhunderts nach Straßburger Originalen.* 2 vols. Strasbourg: Karl J. Trübner, 1902–5.

Finot, J. "Le siège de Metz en 1552 et les finances de Charles Quint." BPH (1897): 260–70.

Fischer, Franz. *Die Reformationsversuche des Bischofs Franz von Waldeck im Fürstbistum Münster.* Beiträge für die Geschichte Niedersachsens und Westfalens, 6. Hildesheim: August Lax, 1906.

Fischer-Galati, Stephen A. *Ottoman Imperialism and German Protestantism, 1521–1555.* Harvard Historical Monographs, 43. Cambridge, Mass.: Harvard Univ. Press, 1959.

——. "Ottoman Imperialism and the Religious Peace of Nürnberg." ARG 47 (1956): 160–80.

Förstemann, Carl Eduard, ed. *Neues Urkundenbuch zur Geschichte der evangelischen Kirchen-Reformation.* Vol. 1. Hamburg: Perthes, 1842. Reprint. Hildesheim: Georg Olms, 1976.

———, ed. *Urkundenbuch zu der Geschichte des Reichstages zu Augsburg im Jahre 1530*. 2 vols. Halle: Verlag der Buchhandlung des Waisenhauses, 1833–35. Reprint. Osnabrück: Biblio-Verlag, 1966.

Fournier, Marcel, and Charles Engel, eds. *Les Statuts et privilèges des Universités françaises*. Pt. 2, vol. 4, fasc. 1, *Gymnase, Académie, Université de Strasbourg*. Paris: L. Larose et Forcel, 1894. Reprint. Aalen: Scientia, 1970.

Fraenkel, Pierre. *Einigungsbestrebungen in der Reformationszeit*. Vorträge des Instituts für europäische Geschichte Mainz, no. 41. Wiesbaden: Franz Steiner, 1965.

———. "Utraquism or Co-Existence: Some Notes on the Earliest Negotiations before the Pacification of Nurenberg, 1531–32." *Studia theologica* 18 (1964): 119–158.

Franz, Eugen. *Nürnberg, Kaiser und Reich: Studien zur reichsstädtischen Außenpolitik*. Munich: C. H. Beck, 1930.

Franz, Günther. *Der deutsche Bauernkrieg*. 12th ed. Darmstadt: Wissenschaftliche Buchgesellschaft, 1984.

———, ed. *Quellen zur Geschichte des Bauernkrieges*. Darmstadt: Wissenschaftliche Buchgesellschaft, 1963.

———, ed. *Urkundliche Quellen zur hessischen Reformationsgeschichte*. Vol. 2. Veröffentlichungen der Historischen Kommission für Hessen und Waldeck, 11, pt. 2. Marburg: N. G. Elwert, 1952.

Franzen, August. *Bischof und Reformation: Erzbischof Hermann von Wied in Köln vor der Entscheidung zwischen Reform und Reformation*. Katholisches Leben und Kirchenreform im Zeitalter der Glaubensspaltung, 31. Münster im Westfalen: Aschendorff, 1972.

Frey, Siegfried. "Das Gericht des Schwäbischen Bundes und seine Richter 1488–1534. Ein Beitrag zur Geschichte der Rechtsinsitutionen des Einungswesens und ihrer Entscheidungsträger." In *Mittel und Wege früher Verfassungspolitik*, edited by Josef Engel, 224–81. SFN, 9. Sttutgart: Klett-Cotta, 1979.

Friedensburg, Walter, ed. "Aktenstücke zur Politik Karls V. im Herbst 1541." *ARG* 29 (1932): 35–66.

———, ed. "Am Vorabend des Schmalkaldischen Krieges. Denkschrift aus der Umgebung Karls V." *QFIAB* 2 (1899): 140–51.

———. *Johannes Sleidanus. Der Geschichtsschreiber und die Schicksalsmächte der Reformationszeit*. SVRG, 157. Leipzig: M. Heinsius Nachfolger, 1935.

———. *Der Reichstag zu Speier 1526 im Zusammenhang der politischen und kirchlichen Entwicklung Deutschlands im Reformationszeitalter*. Historische Untersuchungen, 5. Berlin: Engelmann, 1887. Reprint. Nieuwkoop: B. de Graaf, 1970.

———. "Zur Geschichte des Wormser Konvents 1541." *ZKiG* 21 (1901): 112–27.

———. "Zur Konzilspolitik der Stadt Straßburg 1551." *ELJb* 8 (1929): 192–210.

Friese, Johann. *Neue vaterländische Geschichte der Stadt Straßburg bis 1791*. 2d ed. 6 vols. Strasbourg, 1792–1801.

Fuchs, François-Joseph. "Les catholiques strasbourgeois de 1529 à 1681." *AEKG*, n.s. 22 (1975): 142–69.

———. "Les foires et le rayonnement économique de la ville en Europe (XVIe siècle)." In *Histoire de Strasbourg des origines à nos jours*, edited by Georges Livet and Francis Rapp, 2, 259–361. Strasbourg: Librairie Istra, 1981.

———. "Les marchands strasbourgeois etaient-ils des épicuriens?" In *Croyants et sceptiques au XVIe siècle*, edited by Marc Lienhard, 93–100. PSSARE, collection "Recherches et documents," 30. Strasbourg: Librairie Istra, 1981.

———. "Noblesse et grand commerce à Strasbourg en 1490." In *Landesgeschichte und Geistesgeschichte: Festschrift für Otto Herding zum 65. Geburtstag*, edited by Kaspar Elm, Eberhard Gönner, and Eugen Hildenbrand, 257–64. VKLBW, ser. B, 92. Stuttgart: W. Kohlhammer, 1977.

Fuchs, Konrad. "Zur Politik der protestantischen Reichsstände vor der Eröffnung des Augsburger Reichstages von 1530." ZGO 118 (1970): 157–74.

Fuchtel, Paul. "Der Frankfurter Anstand vom Jahre 1539." ARG 28 (1931): 145–206.

Füglister, Hans. Handwerksregiment: Untersuchungen und Materialien zur sozialen und politischen Struktur der Stadt Basel in der ersten Hälfte des 16. Jahrhunderts. BBG, 143. Basel: Helbing & Lichtenhahn, 1981.

Fuhrmann, Rosi. "Die Kirche im Dorf: Kommunale Initiativen zur Organisation von Seelsorge vor der Reformation." In Zugänge zur bäuerlichen Reformation, edited by Peter Blickle, 147–86. Bauern und Reformation, 1. Zurich: Chronos Verlag, 1987.

Fürstenwerth, Ludwig. Die Verfassungsänderungen in den oberdeutschen Städten zur Zeit Karls V. Dissertation, Göttingen, 1893.

Garzoni, Giovanni. De miseria humana. Strasbourg: Johann Grüninger, 1505.

Gebauer, Johannes Heinrich. "Die Stimmung katholischer Bauern im Stift Hildesheim zur Zeit des Schmalkaldischen Krieges." ZKiG 37 (1918): 432–38.

Gebhardt, Bruno. Handbuch der deutschen Geschichte. 8th ed. by Herbert Grundmann. 4 vols. Stuttgart: Union Deutsche Verlagsgesellschaft, 1955.

Geiler von Kaysersberg, Johann. Die Emeis: Dis ist das buch von der Omeissen, und auch Herr der können ich diente gern. Strasbourg: Johann Grüninger, 1516.

———. Evangelia mit Ussleg. Strasbourg: Johann Grüninger, 1517.

———. Pater noster. Strasbourg: Matthias Hupfuff, 1515.

Gerber, Harry. "Die Bedeutung des Augsburger Reichstags von 1547/48 für das Ringen der Städte um Stimme, Stand und Session." ELJb 9 (1930): 168–208.

———. "Jakob Sturms Anteil an den Religionsverhandlungen des Augsburger 'geharnischten' Reichstags von 1547/48." ELJb 8 (1929): 166–91.

———. "Die Kriegsrechnungen des Schmalkaldischen Bundes über den Krieg im Oberland des Jahres 1546." ARG 32 (1935): 41–93, 218–47; 33 (1936): 226–55; 34 (1937): 87–122, 272–88.

Gerlich, Alois. Geschichtliche Landeskunde des Mittelalters: Genese und Probleme. Darmstadt: Wissenschaftliche Buchgesellschaft, 1986.

Giefel, Joseph A. "Streit um die gefürstete Propstei Ellwangen im Zeitalter der Reformation." Württembergische Vierteljahrshefte für Landesgeschichte 7 (1884): 170–81, 241–53.

Glitsch, Christoph. Die Bündnispolitik der oberdeutschen Städte des Schmalkaldischen Bundes vom Speyrer Protestationsreichstage bis zum sog. Nürnberger Religionsfrieden 1529/31 bis 1532. Dissertation, Tübingen, 1960.

Gottesheim, Jacob von. "Les éphemerides de Jacques de Gottesheim, docteur en droit, prébendier du Grand-Choeur de la Cathédrale (1524–1543)," edited by Rodolphe Reuss. BSCMHA, 2d ser. 19 (1898): 267–81.

Grandidier, Philippe A. Nouvelles oeuvres inédites. Edited by A. M. P. Ingold. 5 vols. Colmar: H. Hüffel, 1897–1900.

Graus, František. Pest—Geissler—Judenmorde: Das 14. Jahrhundert als Krisenzeit. Veröffentlichungen der Max-Planck-Gesellschaft für Geschichte, 86. Göttingen: Vandenhoeck & Ruprecht, 1987.

Great Britain, Public Record Office. Letters and papers, foreign and domestic, of the reign of Henry VIII, 1509–47, preserved in the Public Record Office, the British Museum. Edited by J. S. Brewer, James Gairdener, and R. H. Brodie. 21 vols. London: Longmans, 1862–1910. Reprint. Vaduz: Kraus, 1965.

Greiner, Christoph. "Die Politik des Schwäbischen Bundes während des Bauernkrieges 1524/25 bis zum Vertrag von Weingarten." Zeitschrift des Historischen Vereins für Schwaben 68 (1974): 7–94.

Gremp von Freudenstein, Ludwig, and Hieronymus zum Lamm. Svmma vnnd innhalt aller vndergebner Acten vnd darauff gestellter Radtschläg der Erbaren Frey vnd Reichstett Session Stand vnnd Stimm belangende. [Strasbourg, 1543].

Gresbeck, Heinrich. "Bericht von der Wiedertaufe in Münster." In *Berichte der Augenzeugen über das münsterische Wiedertäuferreich*, edited by C. A. Cornelius, 1–214. Die Geschichtsquellen des Bisthums Münster, 2. Münster: Theissing, 1853. Reprint. Münster: Aschendorff, 1965.

Greschat, Martin. *Martin Bucer: Ein Reformator und seine Zeit 1491–1551*. Munich: C. H. Beck, 1990.

Greyerz, Kaspar von. "Stadt und Reformation. Stand und Aufgaben der Forschung." ARG 76 (1985): 6–63.

Grimm, Harold J. *Lazarus Spengler: A Lay Leader of the Reformation*. Columbus: Ohio State Univ. Press, 1978.

Grube, Walter. *Der Stuttgarter Landtag 1457–1957: Von den Landständen zum demokratischen Parlament*. Stuttgart: Ernst Klett, 1957.

Grundmann, Annelies. "Die Beschwerden der Deutschen Nation auf den Reichstagen der Reformation: Erläuterung und Begründung der Sonder-Edition." In *Aus der Arbeit an den Reichstagen unter Kaiser Karl V.: Sieben Beiträge zu Fragen der Forschung und Edition*, edited by Heinrich Lutz and Alfred Kohler, 69–129. SHKBA, 26. Göttingen: Vandenhoeck & Ruprecht, 1986.

Grundmann, Herbert. "Deutsche Reichstagsakten, Jüngere Reihe." In *Aus Reichstagen des 15. und 16. Jahrhunderts. Festgabe dargebracht der Historischen Kommission bei der Bayerischen Akademie der Wissenschaften zur Feier ihres hundertjährigen Bestehens*, 132–57. SHKBA, 5. Göttingen: Vandenhoeck & Ruprecht, 1958.

———. *Landgraf Philipp von Hessen auf dem Augsburger Reichstag 1530*. SVRG, 176. Gütersloh: Gerd Mohn, 1959.

Guénée, Bernard. *States and Rulers in Later Medieval Europe*. Translated by Juliet Vale. Oxford: Basil Blackwell, 1985.

Guggisberg, Hans R. *Basel in the Sixteenth Century: Aspects of the City Republic before, during, and after the Reformation*. St. Louis: Center for Reformation Research, 1982.

———. "Strasbourg et Bâle dans la Réforme." In *Strasbourg au coeur religieux du XVIe siècle*, edited by Georges Livet, Marc Lienhard, and Jean Rott, 333–40. PSSARE, 12. Strasbourg: Librairie Istra, 1978.

Gumbel, Hermann. "Humanitas Alsatica: Straßburger Humanismus von Jakob Wimpfeling zu Johann und Jakob Sturm." ELJb 17 (1938): 1–36.

Haas, Martin. *Zwingli und der erste Kappelerkrieg*. Zurich: Verlag Berichthaus, 1965.

Hachtmann, Rüdiger. *Straßburgs Beziehungen zu Frankreich im 16. Jahrhundert*. Ph.D. diss., Munich. Göttingen: Göttinger Tageblatt, 1931.

Hall, Basil. "Bucer et l'Angleterre." In *Strasbourg au coeur religieux du XVIe siècle*, edited by Georges Livet, Marc Lienhard, and Jean Rott, 401–30. PSSARE, 12. Strasbourg: Librairie Istra, 1978.

Hamm, Bernd. "Stadt und Kirche unter dem Wort Gottes. Das reformatorische Einheitsmodell des Nürnberger Ratsschreibers Lazarus Spengler (1479–1534)." In *Literatur und Laienbildung im Spätmittelalter und in der Reformationszeit*, edited by Karl Stackmann and Bernd Moeller, 710–29. Germanistische Symposien—Berichtsbände, 5. Stuttgart: Metzler, 1982.

———. *Zwinglis Reformation der Freiheit*. Neukirchen-Vluyn: Neukirchener Verlag, 1988.

Hammann, Gottfried. *Entre la secte et la cité. Le projet d'église du réformateur Martin Bucer*. Histoire et société, 3. Geneva: Labor et Fides, 1984.

Häpke, Rudolf. *Die Regierung Karl V. und der europäische Norden*. Veröffentlichungen zur Geschichte der Freien und Hansestadt Lübeck, 3. Hildesheim: G. Olms, 1976.

Hartfelder, Karl. *Zur Geschichte des Bauernkrieges in Südwestdeutschland*. Stuttgart: J. G. Cotta, 1884.

Hartmann, Alfred, ed. *Die Amerbachkorrespondenz*. 6 vols. Basel: Verlag der Universitätsbibliothek, 1942–83.

Hartranf, Chester David, and Elmer Ellsworth Schulz Johnson, eds. *Corpus Schwenckfeldianorum.* 19 vols. Leipzig: Breitkopf & Härtel, 1907–61.

Hartung, Fritz. *Karl V. und die deutschen Reichsstände von 1546–1555.* Historische Studien, 1. Halle an der Saale: Max Niemeyer Verlag, 1910. Reprint. Darmstadt: Wissenschaftliche Buchgesellschaft, 1971.

Hasenclever, Adolf. "Balthasar Merklin, Propst von Waldkirch, Reichsvizekanzler unter Kaiser Karl V." *ZGO* 73 (1919): 485–502; 74 (1920): 36–80.

———. "Johann Sleidan und Frankreich." *ELJb* 10 (1931): 101–22.

———. "Johann von Naves aus Luxemburg, Reichsvizekanzler unter Kaiser Karl V." *MIÖG* 26 (1905): 280–328.

———. "Kurfürst Friedrich II. von der Pfalz und der schmalkaldische Bundestag zu Frankfurt vom Dezember 1545. Ein Beitrag zur pfälzischen Reformationsgeschichte." *ZGO* 57 (1903): 58–85.

———. *Die kurpfälzische Politik in den Zeiten des Schmalkaldischen Krieges (Januar 1546 bis Januar 1547).* HAMNG, 10. Heidelberg: Carl Winter, 1905.

———, ed. "Neue Aktenstücke zur Friedensvermittlung der Schmalkaldener zwischen Frankreich und England im Jahre 1545." *ZGO* 57 (1905): 224–51.

———. *Die Politik Karls V. und Landgraf Philipps von Hessen vor Ausbruch des Schmalkaldischen Krieges (Januar bis Juli 1546).* Marburg: Elwert, 1903.

———. *Die Politik der Schmalkaldener vor Ausbruch des Schmalkaldischen Krieges.* Historische Studien, 23. Berlin: Emil Ebering, 1901. Reprint. Vaduz: Kraus, 1965.

———. *Sleidan-Studien. Die Entwicklung der politischen Ideen Johann Sleidans bis zum Jahre 1545.* Bonn: Röhrscheid & Ebbecke, 1905.

Hatt, Jacques. *Liste des membres du grand sénat de Strasbourg, des stettmeistres, des ammeistres, des conseils des XXI, XIII, et des XV du XIIIe siècle à 1789.* Strasbourg: Mairie de la Ville, 1963.

———. *Une ville du XVe siècle. Strasbourg.* Strasbourg: Collection Historique de la vie en Alsace, 1929.

Haug, Hans. "Notes et documents sur Hans Baldung Grien et son entourage." *RA* 91 (1952): 92–111.

Hauschild, Wolf-Dieter. "Frühe Neuzeit und Reformation. Das Ende der Großmachtstellung und die Neuorientierung der Stadtgemeinschaft." In *Lübeckische Geschichte,* edited by Antjekathrin Graßmann, 341–432. Lübeck: Schmidt Römhild, 1988.

Hauswirth, René. *Landgraf Philipp von Hessen und Zwingli: Voraussetzungen und Geschichte der politischen Beziehungen zwischen Hessen, Straßburg, Konstanz, Ulrich von Württemberg und den reformierten Eidgenossen 1526–1531.* SKRG, 35. Tübingen: Osiandersche Buchhandlung, 1968.

———, ed. *Quellen zur Geschichte der Reformationsbündnisse und der Konstanzer Reformationsprozesse 1529–1548. Erstausgabe von ausgewählten Texten zur Bündnis- und Bekenntnispolitik reformierter Orte der Eidgenossenschaft mit den schmalkaldischen Bundesständen Konstanz, Straßburg und Hessen (sowie Ulrich von Württemberg) und zur kirchlichen Rechtsgeschichte der reformierten Reichsstadt Konstanz.* SKRG, 34. Tübingen: Osiander, 1967.

Headley, John M. "The Habsburg World Empire and the Revival of Ghibellinism." *Medieval and Renaissance Studies* 7 (1978): 93–127.

Hedio, Caspar. *Ein ausserleszne Chronick von angang der Welt bis auff das jar nach Christi unsers eynigen Heylands geburt MDXXXIX.* Strasbourg: Crato Mylius, 1539.

———. *Radts Predig. Wie die oberkeit für sich selbs die vnderthonen für jre oberkeiten in disser geuerlichen sorglichen zeit zu bitten haben.* Strasbourg: Johann Albrecht, 1534.

Heidrich, Paul. *Karl V. und die deutschen Protestanten am Vorabend des schmalkaldischen Krieges.* 2 pts. Frankfurter Historische Forschungen, 5–6. Frankfurt am Main: Joseph Baer & Co., 1911–12.

Heinemeyer, Walter. "Landgraf Philipps des Großmütigen Weg in die Politik." *HJLG* 5 (1955): 176–92.

Herberger, Theodor, ed. *Sebastian Schertlin von Burtenbach und seine an die Stadt Augsburg geschriebenen Briefe.* Augsburg: Verlag der von Jenisch und Stage'schen Buchhandlung, 1852.

Herminjard, Aimé-Louis, ed. *Correspondances des réformateurs dans les pays de langue française.* 9 vols. Geneva: H. Georg, 1866–97. Reprint. Nieuwkoop: B. de Graaf, 1965.

Herrmann, Johannes, and Günther Wartenberg, eds. *Politische Korrespondenz des Herzogs und Kurfürsten Moritz von Sachsen. Vol. 3, 1. Januar 1547–25. Mai 1548.* Abhandlungen der Sächsischen Akademie der Wissenschaft, Philologisch-historische Klasse, 68, pt. 3. Berlin: Akademie-Verlag, 1978.

Hertzog, Bernhard. *Chronicon Alsatiae. Edelsässer Chronik vnnd aussfürliche Beschreibung des untern Elsasses am Rheinstrom.* Strasbourg: Bernhard Jobin, 1592.

Hesslinger, Helmo. *Die Anfänge des Schwäbischen Bundes: Ein Beitrag zur Geschichte des Einungswesens und der Reichsreform unter Kaiser Friedrich III.* Forschungen zur Geschichte der Stadt Ulm, 9. Stuttgart: W. Kohlhammer, 1970.

Heuschen, Diethelm. *Reformation, Schmalkaldischer Bund und Österreich in ihrer Bedeutung für die Finanzen der Stadt Konstanz 1499–1648.* SKRG, 36. Tübingen: Osiandersche Buchhandlung; Basel: Basileia-Verlag, 1969.

Heyd, Ludwig Friedrich. *Ulrich, Herzog zu Württemberg: Ein Beitrag zur Geschichte Württembergs und des deutschen Reiches im Zeitalter der Reformation.* 3 vols. Tübingen: Laupp, 1841–44.

Hillerbrand, Hans, ed. *Radical Tendencies in the Reformation: Divergent Tendencies.* SCES, 9. Kirksville, Mo.: Sixteenth Century Journal Publishers, 1988.

Hoffmann, Konrad. "Konrad Sam (1483–1555), der Prediger des Rats zu Ulm." In *Die Einführung der Reformation in Ulm: Geschichte eines Bürgerentscheids,* edited by Hans Eugen Specker and Gebhard Weig, 233–68. Forschungen zur Geschichte der Stadt Ulm, Reihe Dokumentation, 2. Stuttgart: Kohlhammer, 1981.

Holländer, Alkuin. *Straßburg im französischen Krieg.* BLVEL, 6. Strasbourg: Karl J. Trübner, 1888.

———. *Straßburg im Schmalkaldischen Krieg.* Strasbourg: Karl J. Trübner, 1881.

———. *Eine Straßburger Legende: Ein Beitrag zu den Beziehungen Straßburgs zu Frankreich im 16. Jahrhundert.* BLVEL, 17. Strasbourg: Karl J. Trübner, 1914.

———. "Straßburgs Politik im Jahre 1552." *ZGO,* n.s. 9 (1894): 1–48.

Hölscher, Uvo. "Die Geschichte der Mindener Reichsacht 1541." *Zeitschrift der Gesellschaft für niedersächsische Kirchengeschichte* 9 (1904): 192–202.

Honée, Eugène, ed. *Der Libell des Hieronymus Vehus zum Augsburger Reichstag 1530. Untersuchungen und Texte zur katholischen Concordia-Politik.* RST, 125. Münster im Westfalen: Aschendorff, 1988.

Horawitz, Adalbert. *Michael Hummelberger.* Berlin: Calvary & Comp., 1875.

Hortleder, Friedrich, ed. *Der Röm. key.- u. königlichen Maiesteten, auch des Heil. Röm. Reichs geistl. und weltl. Stände, Churfürsten, Fürsten Handlungen und Ausschreiben, Sendbrieff, Klag und Supplikationsschriften von den Ursachen des Teutschen Krieges keyser Carls des Fünften wider den Schmalkaldischen Bundesoberste Chur- und Fürsten, Sachsen und Hessen und Mitverwandte anno 1546 u. 47.* 2 vols. Frankfurt am Main: Hartmann Palthenius, 1617.

———, ed. *Der Röm. key.- u. königlichen Maiesteten . . . Handlungen und Ausschreiben, Ratschlag, Bedenken . . . von Rechtmäßigkeit, Anfang, Forgang und endl. Ausgang des Teutschen Krieges keyser Carls d. Fünften wider die Schmalkaldischen Bundesoberste . . . vom Jahre 1526 bis auf das Jahr 1558.* Frankfurt am Main: Hartmann Palthenius, 1618.

———, ed. *Der Röm. key.- u. königlichen Maiesteten . . . Handlungen und Ausschreiben,*

Ratschlag, Bedenken . . . von den Ursachen deß Teutschen Kriegs Kaiser Carls des Fünfften wider die Schmalkaldischen Bundes-Oberste, Chur- vnd Fürsten, Sachsen vnd Hessen vnd Ihrer Chur- vnd F. G. g. Mitverwandte. Anno 1545 vnd 47. Gotha, 1645.

Huber, Max. "Städtearchiv und Reichsstandschaft der Städte im 16. Jahrhundert." *Ulm und Oberschwaben* 35 (1958): 94–112.

Hübinger, Paul Egon. "Die Anfänge der französischen Rheinpolitik als historisches Problem." *HZ* 171 (1951): 21–45.

Hühns, Erik. "Nationale Propaganda im Schmalkaldischen Krieg." *ZfG* 6 (1958): 1027–48.

Hunyadi, István. "Participation de Strasbourg à la défense de la Hongrie pendant les guerres turques (1521–1555)." *Études finno-ougriennes* 6/7 (1969/70): 171–237.

Ibn Kahldûn. *The Muqaddimah: An Introduction to History.* Translated by Franz Rosenthal. Abridged ed. by N. J. Dawood. Princeton: Princeton Univ. Press, 1967.

Iggers, George G. *The German Conception of History: The National Tradition of Historical Thought from Herder to the Present.* Rev. ed. Middletown, Conn.: Wesleyan Univ. Press, 1983.

Immenkötter, Herbert, ed. *Die Confutatio der Confessio Augustana vom 3. August 1530.* Corpus Catholicorum, 33. 2d ed. Münster im Westfalen: Aschendorff, 1981.

———. "Die katholische Kirche in Augsburg in der ersten Hälfte des 16. Jahrhunderts." In *Die Augsburger Kirchenordnung von 1537 und ihr Umfeld*, edited by Reinhard Schwarz, 9–32. SVRG, 196. Gütersloh: Gerd Mohn, 1988.

———. "Reichstag und Konzil. Zur Deutung der Religionsgespräche des Augsburger Reichstags 1530." In *Die Religionsgespräche der Reformationszeit*, edited by Gerhard Müller, 7–20. SVRG, 191. Gütersloh: Gerd Mohn, 1980.

Irschlinger, Robert. "Zur Geschichte der Herren von Steinach und der Landschaden von Steinach." *ZGO* 86 (1934), 421–508.

Isenburg, Wilhelm Karl, Prinz von. *Stammtafeln zur europäischen Staatengeschichte.* 2 vols. 2d ed. Marburg: J. A. Stargardt, 1953.

Isenmann, Eberhard. *Die deutsche Stadt im Spätmittelalter 1250–1500: Stadtgestalt, Recht, Stadtregiment, Kirche, Gesellschaft, Wirtschaft.* Stuttgart: Eugen Ulmer, 1988.

———. "Reichsstadt und Reich an der Wende vom späten Mittelalter zur frühen Neuzeit." In *Mittel und Wege früher Verfassungspolitik*, edited by Josef Engel, 9–223. SFN, 9. Stuttgart: Klett-Cotta, 1979.

———. "Reichsfinanzen und Reichssteuern im 15. Jahrhundert." *ZHF* 7 (1980): 1–76, 129–218.

———. "Die städtische Gemeinde im oberdeutsch-schweizerischen Raum (1300–1800)." In *Landgemeinde und Stadtgemeinde in Mitteleuropa*, edited by Peter Blickle, 191–261. Beihefte der Historischen Zeitschrift, 13. Munich: R. Oldenbourg, 1991.

———. "Zur Frage der Reichsstandschaft der Frei- und Reichsstädte." In *Stadtverfassung, Verfassungsstaat, Pressepolitik: Festschrift für Eberhard Naujoks*, edited by Franz Quarthal and Wilfried Setzler, 91–110. Sigmaringen: Jan Thorbecke, 1980.

Iserloh, Erwin, ed. *Confessio Augustana und Confutatio: Der Augsburger Reichstag 1530 und die Einheit der Kirche. Internationales Symposion der Gesellschaft zur Herausgabe des Corpus Catholicorum in Augsburg vom 3.–7. September 1979.* RST, 118. Münster im Westfalen: Aschendorff, 1980.

———. *Johannes Eck (1486–1543). Scholastiker, Humanist, Kontroverstheologe.* Katholisches Leben und Kirchenreform im Zeitalter der Glaubensspaltung, 41. Münster im Westfalen: Aschendorff, 1981.

Ißleib, Simon. *Der Braunschweigische Krieg im Jahre 1545.* Dissertation, Leipzig. Dresden: C. Heinrich, 1876.

———. "Moritz von Sachsen als evangelischer Fürst 1541–1553." *Beiträge zur sächsischen Kirchengeschichte* 20 (1906): 1–21.

————. "Moritz von Sachsen gegen Karl V. bis zum Kriegszuge 1552." *Neues Archiv für sächsische Geschichte* 6 (1885): 210–50.

————. "Moritz von Sachsen gegen Karl V. 1552." *Neues Archiv für sächsische Geschichte* 7 (1886): 1–59.

————. "Moritz von Sachsen und die Ernestiner 1547–1553." *Neues Archiv für sächsische Geschichte* 24 (1903): 248–306.

Jahns, Sigrid. *Frankfurt, Reformation und Schmalkaldischer Bund: Die Reformations-, Reichs- und Bündnispolitik der Reichsstadt Frankfurt am Main 1525–1536.* Studien zur Frankfurter Geschichte, 9. Frankfurt am Main: Kramer, 1976.

Janssen, Johannes, ed. *Frankfurts Reichscorrespondenz nebst andern verwandten Aktenstücken von 1376–1519.* Vol. 2. Freiburg im Breisgau: Herder, 1872.

Jedin, Hubert. "Die Deutschen Protestanten am Trienter Konzil 1551/52." *HZ* 188 (1959): 1–16. Also in *Concilium Tridentinum,* edited by Remigius Bäumer, 141–60. WF, 313. Darmstadt: Wissenschaftliche Buchgesellschaft, 1979.

————. "Fragen um Hermann von Wied." *HJ* 74 (1955): 687–99. Reprinted in Hubert Jedin, *Kirche des Glaubens—Kirche der Geschichte,* Vol. 1, 347–60. Freiburg im Breisgau: Herder, 1966.

————. *Geschichte des Konzils von Trient.* 4 vols. Freiburg im Breisgau: Herder, 1949–75.

————. *A History of the Council of Trent.* Translated by Ernest Graf, O.S.B. Vol. 1. Edinburgh: Thomas Nelson and Sons, 1957.

Jegel, August, ed. "Ein ungedrucktes Gutachten Andreas Osianders von der rechten Gestalt des weltlichen Regiments." *ARG* 40 (1943): 62–72.

Jeserich, Kurt G. A., Hans Pohl, and Georg-Christoph von Unruh, eds. *Deutsche Verwaltungsgeschichte.* Vol. 1, *Vom Spätmittelalter bis zum Ende des Reiches.* Stuttgart: Deutsche Verlagsanstalt, 1983.

Jung, Andreas. *Geschichte der Reformation in Straßburg und der Ausbreitung derselben in den Gemeinden des Elsasses.* Beiträge zu der Geschichte der Reformation, vol. 2. Leipzig: F. G. Levrault, 1830.

Kammerer, Odile. "Réforme et grand commerce à Saint-Nicolas-de-Port au XVIe siècle." In *Les Réformes en Lorraine 1520–1620,* edited by Louis Châtellier, 47–56. Centre des recherches en histoire sociale et religieuse, 2. Nancy: Presses Universitaires de Nancy, 1986.

Kannengiesser, Paul. *Karl V. und Maximilian Egmont, Graf von Büren. Ein Beitrag zur Geschichte des schmalkaldischen Krieges.* Freiburg im Breisgau and Tübingen: J. C. B. Mohr, 1895.

Kaufmann, Thomas. *Die Abendmahlstheologie der Straßburger Reformatoren bis 1528.* Beiträge zur historischen Theologie, 81. Tübingen: J. C. B. Mohr (Paul Siebeck), 1992.

Kawerau, Gustav. *Johann Agricola von Eisleben. Ein Beitrag zur Reformationsgeschichte.* Berlin: W. Hertz, 1881.

Kelley, Donald R. *The Beginning of Ideology: Consciousness and Society in the French Reformation.* Cambridge: Cambridge Univ. Press, 1981.

Kentzinger, Antoine de, ed. *Documents historiques relatifs à l'histoire de France, tirés des Archives de la Ville de Strasbourg.* 2 vols. Strasbourg: F. G. Levrault, 1818–19.

Kindler von Knobloch, Julius. *Das goldene Buch von Straßburg.* Vienna and Karlsruhe: Selbstverlag des Verfassers, 1885–86.

Kintz, Jean-Pierre. *La société strasbourgeoise du milieu du XVIe siècle à la fin de la Guerre de Trente Ans 1560–1650: Essai d'histoire démographique, économique et sociale.* Paris: Éditions Ophrys, 1984.

Kirchner, Hubert. "Luther und das Papsttum." In *Leben und Werk Martin Luthers von 1526 bis 1546. Festgabe zu seinem 500. Geburtstag,* edited by Helmar Junghans, vol. 1, 441–56. Berlin: Evangelische Verlagsanstalt, 1983.

Kittelberger, Gerhard. "Herzog Ulrichs Angriffspläne auf die Reichsstadt Eßlingen." *JGOR* 17 (1971): 116–19.

Kittelson, James M. "Strasbourg, the Landesherrlichekirchenregiment, and the Relative Autonomy of Lutheran Churches in Sixteenth-Century Germany." *Locus* 2 (1990): 131–43.

———. *Wolfgang Capito from Humanist to Reformer*. SMRT, 17. Leiden: E. J. Brill, 1975.

Klein, Kurt. "Der Bauernkrieg in der Ortenau und das Elsass." In *La Guerre des Paysans 1525*, edited by Alphonse Wollbrett, 129–32. Saverne: Société d'Histoire et d'Archéologie de Saverne et Environs, 1975.

Kleinwaechter, Emil. *Der Metzer Reformationsversuch 1542–43*. Pt. 1. Dissertation, Marburg, 1894.

Knecht, R. J. *Francis I*. Cambridge: Cambridge Univ. Press, 1982.

Knepper, Joseph. *Jakob Wimpfeling (1450–1528): Sein Leben und seine Werke*. Freiburg im Breisgau: Herder, 1902. Reprint. Nieuwkoop: B. De Graaf, 1965.

———. *Das Schul- und Unterrichtswesen im Elsaß von den Anfängen bis gegen das Jahr 1530*. Strasbourg: J. H. Ed. Heitz (Heitz & Mündel), 1905.

Knod, Gustav, ed. "Neun Briefe von und an Jakob Wimpfeling." *Vierteljahrsschrift für Kultur und Litteratur der Renaissance* 1 (1886): 229–43.

———. "Wimpheling und die Universität Heidelberg." *ZGO*, n.s. 1 (1886): 317–35.

Koch, Carl. "Über ein verschollenes Gemälde Hans Baldungs: Bildnis des Jacob Sturm." *Münchner Jahrbuch der bildenden Kunst*, n.s. 13 (1938/39): 107–13.

Kohl, Benjamin G., and Ronald G. Witt. "General Introduction." In *The Earthly Republic: Italian Humanists on Government and Society*, edited by Benjamin G. Kohl and Ronald G. Witt, 3–22. Philadelphia: Univ. of Pennsylvania Press, 1978.

Kohler, Alfred. *Antihabsburgische Politik in der Epoche Karls V.: Die Reichsständische Opposition gegen die Wahl Ferdinands I. zum römischen König und gegen die Anerkennung seines Königtums (1524–1534)*. SHKBA, 19. Göttingen: Vandenhoeck & Ruprecht, 1982.

———. "Der Augsburg Reichstag 1530. Von der Bilanz des Jubiläumsjahres 1980 zum Programm einer Edition der Reichstagsakten." In *Aus der Arbeit an den Reichstagen unter Kaiser Karl V.: Sieben Beiträge zu Fragen der Forschung und Edition*, edited by Heinrich Lutz and Alfred Kohler, 158–93. SHKBA, 26. Göttingen: Vandenhoeck & Ruprecht, 1986.

Köhler, Dietrich. *Reformationspläne für die geistlichen Fürstentümer bei den Schmalkaldenern: Ein Beitrag zur Ideengeschichte der Reformation*. Dissertation, Greifswald. Berlin: Emil Ebering, 1912.

Köhler, Walter, ed. *Das Marburger Religionsgespräch. Versuch einer Rekonstruction*. SVRG, 148. Leipzig: Heinsius, 1929.

———. *Zwingli und Luther: Ihr Streit um das Abendmahl nach seinen politischen und religiösen Beziehungen*. 2 vols. QFRG, 6–7. Leipzig: M. Heinsius Nachfolger, 1924. Gütersloh: Gerd Mohn, 1953.

Kohls, Ernst-Wilhelm. *Die Schule bei Martin Bucer in ihrem Verhältnis zu Kirche und Obrigkeit*. Heidelberg: Quelle & Meyer, 1963.

Köhn, Mechtild. *Martin Bucers Entwurf einer Reformation des Erzstiftes Köln*. Untersuchungen zur Kirchengeschichte, 2. Witten: Luther-Verlag, 1976.

Kolde, Theodor, ed. *Analecta Lutherana. Briefe und Aktenstücke zur Geschichte Luthers*. Gotha: Perthes, 1883.

Körber, Kurt. *Kirchengüterfrage und schmalkaldischer Bund*. SVRG, 111–112. Leipzig: Rudolf Haupt, 1913.

Korell, Günter. *Jürgen Wullenwever: Sein sozial-politisches Wirken in Lübeck und der Kampf mit den erstärkenden Mächten Nordeuropas*. Abhandlungen zur Handels- und Sozialgeschichte, 19. Weimar: Böhlau, 1980.

Körner, Martin H. *Solidarités financières suisses au XVIe siècle: Contribution à l'histoire monétaire, bancaire et financière des cantons suisses et des États voisins.* Bibliothèque historique vaudoise. Lausanne: Éditions Payot, 1980.

Krebs, Manfred, and Hans-Georg Rott, eds. *Elsaß.* Pt. 1, *Stadt Straßburg 1522–1532.* Quellen zur Geschichte der Täufer, 7. Gütersloh: Gerd Mohn, 1959.

——, eds. *Elsaß.* Pt. 2, *Stadt Straßburg 1533–1535.* Quellen zur Geschichte der Täufer, 8. Gütersloh: Gerd Mohn, 1960.

Krieger, Leonard. *Ranke: The Meaning of History.* Chicago: Univ. of Chicago Press, 1977.

Kühn, Johannes. *Die Geschichte des Speyrer Reichstags 1529.* SVRG, 146. Leipzig: M. Heinsius, 1929.

Laemmer, Hugo, ed. *Monumenta Vaticana historiam ecclesiasticam saec. XVI illustrantia, ex tabulariis Sanctae Sedis Apostolicae secretis.* Freiburg im Breisgau: Herder, 1861.

Lang, August. *Puritanismus und Pietismus: Studien zu ihrer Entwicklung von M. Butzer bis zum Methodismus.* Beiträge zur Geschichte und Lehre der Reformierten Kirche, 6. Neukirchen-Vluyn: Buchhandlung des Erziehungsvereins, 1941. Reprint. Darmstadt: Wissenschaftliche Buchgesellschaft, 1972.

Lanz, Karl, ed. *Correspondenz Kaiser Karls V. Aus dem königlichen Archiv und der Bibliothèque zu Brüssel.* 3 vols. Leipzig: Brockhaus, 1844–46. Reprint. Frankfurt am Main: Minerva, 1966.

——, ed. *Staatspapiere zur Geschichte Kaiser Karls V. aus dem königlichen Archiv und der Bibliothèque de Bourgogne zu Brüssel.* BLVS, 11. Stuttgart: Litterarischer Verein, 1845.

Laube, Adolf. "Radicalism as a Research Problem in the History of Early Reformation." In *Radical Tendencies in the Reformation: Divergent Perspectives,* edited by Hans J. Hillerbrand, 9–24. SCES, 9. Kirksville, Mo.: Sixteenth Century Journal Publishers, 1988.

——. *Studien über den erzgebirgischen Silberbergbau von 1470 bis 1546.* 2d ed. Forschungen zur mittelalterlichen Geschichte, 22. Berlin: Akademie-Verlag, 1976.

Laube, Adolph, and Hans Werner Seiffert, eds. *Flugschriften der Bauernkriegszeit.* Berlin: Akademie-Verlag, 1975.

Lauchs, Joachim. *Bayern und die deutschen Protestanten. Deutsche Fürstenpolitik zwischen Konfession und Libertät.* Einzelarbeiten aus der Kirchengeschichte Bayerns, 56. Neustadt an der Aisch: Degener & Co., 1978.

Laufs, Adolf. *Der Schwäbische Kreis: Studien über Einungswesen und Reichsverfassung im deutschen Südwesten zu Beginn der Neuzeit.* Untersuchungen zur deutschen Staats- und Rechtsgeschichte, n.s., 16. Aalen: Scientia, 1971.

Lebeau, Jean, and Jean-Marie Valentin, eds. *L'Alsace au siècle de la Réforme, 1482–1621.* Nancy: Presses Universitaires de Nancy, 1985.

Lehmann, Hartmut. "Universales Kaisertum, dynamische Weltmacht oder Imperialismus. Zur Beurteilung der Politik Karls V." In *Beiträge zur neueren Geschichte Österreichs,* edited by Heinrich Fichtenau and Erich Zöller, 71–83. Veröffentlichungen des Instituts für Österreichische Geschichtsforschung, 20. Vienna, Graz, and Cologne: Böhlau, 1974.

Lehmann, Hartmut, and James Van Horn Melton, eds. *Paths of Continuity: Central European Historiography, 1933–1950s.* Cambridge: Cambridge Univ. Press, 1994.

Lehnert, Hans. *Kirchengut und Reformation. Eine kirchenrechtsgeschichtliche Studie.* Erlangen: Palm und Enke, 1935.

Lehr, Paul-Ernest. *L'Alsace noble, suivie de la livre d'or du patriciat de Strasbourg.* 3 vols. Paris and Strasbourg: Berger-Levrault, 1870.

——. "Jacques Sturm de Sturmeck, stettmeistre, ambassadeur et scolarque de la ville libre de Strasbourg." In Paul-Ernest Lehr, *Mélanges de littérature et d'histoire alsatiques,* 147–228. Strasbourg: J. Noiriel, 1870.

Lenz, Max, ed. *Briefwechsel Landgraf Philipps des Großmüthigen von Hessen mit Bucer.* 3 vols. Publicationen aus den K. Preussischen Staatsarchiven, 5, 28, 47. Stuttgart: S. Hirzel, 1880–91. Reprint. Osnabrück: Zeller, 1965.

———, ed. *Der Rechenschaftsbericht Philipps des Großmütigen über den Donaufeldzug 1546 und seine Quellen.* Marburg: N. G. Elwert, 1885.

Levresse, René-Pierre. "Prosopographie du chapître de l'église cathédrale de Strasbourg de 1092 à 1593." *AEKG,* n.s. 18 (1970): 1–39.

———. "La survie du catholicisme à Strasbourg." In *Strasbourg au coeur religieux du XVIe siècle,* edited by Georges Livet, Marc Lienhard, and Jean Rott, 457–69. PSSARE, 12. Strasbourg: Librairie Istra, 1978.

Lienhard, Marc. "Les autorités civiles et les anabaptistes: Attitudes du Magistrat de Strasbourg." In *The Origins and Characteristics of Anabaptism,* edited by Marc Lienhard, 196–215. The Hague: Mouton, 1977. Reprinted in Lienhard, *Un temps,* no. 15.

———. "Les épicuriens à Strasbourg entre 1530 et 1550 et le problème de l'incroyance au XVIe siècle." In *Croyants et sceptiques au XVIe siècle,* edited by Marc Lienhard, 17–45. PSSARE, collection "Recherches et documents," 30. Strasbourg: Librairie Istra, 1981.

———. "Evangelische Alternativen zur Augustana? Tetrapolitana und Fidei Ratio." In *Bekenntnis und Geschichte,* edited by Wolfgang Reinhard, 81–100. Schriften der Philosophischen Fakultät der Universität Augsburg, 20. Munich: Ernst Vögel, 1981. Reprinted in Lienhard, *Un temps,* no. 11.

———. "Jakob Sturm." In *Gestalten der Kirchengeschichte.* Vol. 5, *Reformationszeit I,* edited by Martin Greschat, 289–306. Stuttgart: W. Kohlhammer Verlag, 1981. Reprinted in Lienhard, *Un temps,* no. 4.

———. "La Réforme à Strasbourg, I: les événements et les hommes." In *Histoire de Strasbourg,* edited by Georges Livet and Francis Rapp, vol. 2, 365–432. Strasbourg: Éditions Les Dernières Nouvelles, 1981.

———. "La Réforme à Strasbourg, II: Église, culture et société." In *Histoire de Strasbourg,* edited by Georges Livet and Francis Rapp, vol. 2, 437–540. Strasbourg: Éditions Les Dernières Nouvelles, 1981.

———. *Religiöse Toleranz in Straßburg im 16. Jahrhundert.* Abhandlungen der Akademie der Wissenschaften und der Literatur Mainz, geistes- und sozialwissenschaftliche Klasse, 1991, no. 1. Stuttgart: Franz Steiner Verlag, 1991.

———. "Strasbourg et la Guerre des Pamphlets." In *Grandes figures de l'humanisme alsacien. Courants, milieux, destins,* edited by Francis Rapp and Georges Livet, 127–34. PSSARE, Collection "Grandes Publications," 14. Strasbourg: Librarie Istra, 1978. Reprinted in Lienhard, *Un temps,* no. 7.

———. *Un temps, une ville, une Réforme. La Reformation à Strasbourg / Studien zur Reformation in Straßburg.* Aldershot: Variorum, 1990.

Lienhard, Marc, and Jean Rott. "Die Anfänge der evangelischen Predigt in Straßburg und ihr erstes Manifest: Der Aufruf des Karmeliterlesemeisters Tylman von Lyn (Anfang 1522)." In *Bucer und seine Zeit: Forschungsbeiträge und Bibliographie,* edited by Marijn de Kroon and Friedhelm Krüger, 54–73. VIEG, 80. Wiesbaden: Franz Steiner, 1976. Reprinted in Lienhard, *Un temps,* no. 1.

Liliencron, Rochus Freiherr von, ed. *Die historischen Volkslieder der Deutschen.* 5 vols. Leipzig: Vogel, 1865–96.

Livet, Georges. "Géographes et cartographes en Alsace à l'époque de la Renaissance." In *Grandes figures de l'humanisme alsacien: Courants, milieux, destins,* edited by Francis Rapp and Georges Livet, 183–201. PSSARE, Collection "Grandes Publications," 14. Strasbourg: Librarie Istra, 1978.

———. "Jacques Sturm, stettmeister de Strasbourg: formation et idées politiques (1489–1532)." In *Strasbourg au coeur religieux du XVIe siècle,* edited by Georges

Livet, Marc Lienhard, and Jean Rott, 207–41. PSSARE, 12. Strasbourg: Librairie Istra, 1978.

Locher, Gottfried W. *Die Zwinglische Reformation im Rahmen der europäischen Kirchengeschichte.* Göttingen: Vandenhoeck & Ruprecht, 1979.

Lucke, Helmut. *Bremen im Schmalkaldischen Bund 1540–1547.* Schriften der Wittheit zu Bremen, series F, 23. Bremen: Carl Schünemann, 1955.

Ludewig, Georg. *Die Politik Nürnbergs im Zeitalter der Reformation (von 1520–1534).* Göttingen: Vandenhoeck & Ruprecht, 1893.

Ludolphy, Ingetraut. *Friedrich der Weise, Kurfürst von Sachsen 1463–1525.* Göttingen: Vandenhoeck & Ruprecht, 1984.

Luther, Martin. *Luthers Werke. Kritische Gesamtausgabe.* 87 vols. Weimar: Böhlau, 1883–90.

 Pt. 1, *Werke.* 60 vols.

 Pt. 3, *Tischreden.* 4 vols.

 Pt. 4, *Briefe.* 17 vols.

Luttenberger, Albrecht Pius. *Glaubenseinheit und Reichsfriede: Konzeptionen und Wege konfessionsneutraler Reichspolitik (1530–1552) (Kurpfalz, Jülich, Kurbrandenburg).* SHKBA, 20. Göttingen: Vandenhoeck & Ruprecht, 1982.

———. "Johann Eck und die Religionsgespräche." In *Johannes Eck (1486–1543) im Streit der Jahrhunderte. Internationales Symposion der Gesellschaft zur Herausgabe des Corpus Catholicorum aus Anlaß des 500. Geburtstages des Johannes Eck vom 13. bis 16. November 1986 in Ingolstadt und Eichstätt,* ed. Erwin Iserloh, 192–222. Münster im Westfalen: Aschendorff, 1988.

———. "Karl V., Frankreich und der deutsche Reichstag." In *Das römisch-deutsche Reich im politischen System Karls V.,* edited by Heinrich Lutz, 189–221. SHKK, 1. Munich and Vienna: R. Oldenbourg, 1982.

———. "Reichspolitik und Reichstag unter Karl V.: Formen zentralen politischen Handelns." In *Aus der Arbeit an den Reichstagen unter Kaiser Karl V.: Sieben Beiträge zu Fragen der Forschung und Edition,* edited by Heinrich Lutz and Alfred Kohler, 18–68. SHKBA, 26. Göttingen: Vandenhoeck & Ruprecht, 1986.

Lutz, Heinrich. *Christianitas afflicta: Europa, das Reich und die päpstliche Politik im Niedergang der Hegemonie Kaiser Karls V. (1552–1556).* Göttingen: Vandenhoeck und Ruprecht, 1964.

———. *Conrad Peutinger. Beiträge zu einer politischen Biographie.* Abhandlungen zur Geschichte der Stadt Augsburg, 9. Augsburg: Verlag Die Brigg, 1958.

———. "Zur Einführung." In *Aus der Arbeit an den Reichstagen unter Kaiser Karl V.: Sieben Beiträge zu Fragen der Forschung und Edition,* edited by Heinrich Lutz and Alfred Kohler, 7–17. SHKBA, 26. Göttingen: Vandenhoeck & Ruprecht, 1986.

———, ed. *Das römisch-deutsche Reich im politischen System Karls V.* SHKK, 1. Munich and Vienna: R. Oldenbourg, 1982.

Lutz, Heinrich, and Alfred Kohler, eds. *Aus der Arbeit an den Reichstagen unter Kaiser Karl V.: Sieben Beiträge zu Fragen der Forschung und Edition.* SHKBA, 26. Göttingen: Vandenhoeck & Ruprecht, 1986.

Machiavelli, Niccolo. "Rittrato della cose della Magna." In *Arte della guerra et scritti politici minori,* edited by Sergio Bertelli, 209–15. Milan: Feltrinelli, 1961.

Marchal, Guy P. "Bellum justum contra judicium belli. Zur Interpretation von Jakob Wimpfelings antieidgenössischer Streitschrift 'Soliloquium pro Pace Christianorum et pro Helvetiis ut respiscant . . . ,' (1505)." In *Gesellschaft und Gesellschaften: Festschrift zum 65. Geburtstag von Professor Dr. Ulrich Im Hof,* edited by Nicolai Bernard and Quirinus Reichen, 114–37. Bern: Wyss, 1982.

Mariotte, Jean-Yves. "François Ier et la Ligue de Smalkalde de la trêve de Nice à la paix de Crespy 1538–1544." *Revue suisse de l'histoire/Schweizer Zeitschrift für Geschichte* 16 (1966): 206–42.

Mathis, Marcel. "Les origins de Jacques Sturm (1489–1553)." In Marcel Mathis, *Livre d'or de Strasbourg: Trois grandes familles strasbourgeoises, XIIIème siècle au XIXème siècle. Wetzel de Marsilien, Sturm, Oesinger*, 78–99. Strasbourg: Éditions Christian, 1991.

Matzinger, Albert. *Zur Geschichte der niederen Vereinigung.* Zurich-Selnau: Gebr. Leemann, 1910.

Maurenbrecher, Wilhelm. *Karl V. und die deutschen Protestanten 1545–1555.* Düsseldorf: Julius Buddeus, 1865.

Maurer, Hans-Martin. "Herzog Christoph (1550–1568)." In *900 Jahre Haus Württemberg. Leben und Leistung für Land und Volk*, edited by Robert Uhland, 136–62. Stuttgart: W. Kohlhammer, 1984.

Maurer, Justus. *Prediger im Bauernkrieg.* Calwer Theologische Monographien, 5. Stuttgart: Calwer Verlag, 1979.

Mayer, Hermann, ed. *Die Matrikel der Universität Freiburg im Breisgau von 1460– 1656.* 2 vols. Freiburg im Breisgau: Herder, 1907–10.

Mazauric, Robert. "La Réforme au Pays Messin." *BSHPF* 95/96 (1948): 157–83.

———. "Une famille réformée messine aux XVIe et XVIIe siècles: La famille de Heu." *BSHPF* 87 (1938) 27–40, 210–12.

McLaughlin, R. Emmet. *Caspar Schwenckfeld, Reluctant Radical: His Life to 1546.* New Haven: Yale Univ. Press, 1986.

Mehlhausen, Joachim, ed. *Das Augsburger Interim von 1548.* Neukirchen-Vluyn: Neukirchener Verlag, 1970.

Meinardus, Otto, ed. "Die Verhandlungen des Schmalkaldischen Bundes vom 14.–18. Febr. 1539 in Frankfurt a. M." *FDG* 22 (1882): 605–54.

Meinecke, Friedrich. *Cosmopolitanism and the National State.* Translated by Robert B. Kimber. Princeton: Princeton University Press, 1970.

Melanchthon, Philipp. *Melanchthons Briefwechsel. Kritische und kommentierte Gesamtausgabe.* Edited by Heinz Scheible. Vols. 1–6, *Regesten*, nos. 1–6690 (1514– 1552). Stuttgart-Bad Canstatt: fromann-holzboog, 1977–88.

———. *Opera quae supersunt omnia.* Edited by Carl Gottlieb Bretschneider and Heinrich Bindseil. 29 vols. *Corpus Reformatorum*, 1–29. Halle an der Saale: Schwetschke, 1834–60. Reprint. New York: Johnson, 1963.

Melton, James Van Horn. "Otto Brunner." In *Paths of Continuity: Central European Historiography, 1933–1950s*, edited by Hartmut Lehmann and James Van Horn Melton. Cambridge: Cambridge Univ. Press, 1994.

Menke-Gluckert, Emil. *Die Geschichtschreibung der Reformation und Gegenreformation: Bodin und die Begründung der Geschichtsmethodologie.* Leipzig: J. C. Hinrich, 1912.

Mentz, Georg. *Johann Friedrich der Großmütige 1503–1554.* 3 vols. Beiträge zur neueren Geschichte Thüringens, 1. Jena: Gustav Fischer, 1903–8.

Mertens, Dieter. "Maximilian I. und das Elsaß." In *Die Humanisten in ihrer politischen und sozialen Umwelt*, edited by Otto Herding and Robert Stupperich, 177–200. MKH, 3. Boppard: Harald Boldt, 1976.

———. "Reich und Elsass zur Zeit Maximilians I. Untersuchungen zur Ideen- und Landesgeschichte im Südwesten des Reiches am Ausgang des Mittelalters." Habilitationsschrift, University of Freiburg im Breisgau, 1981.

Mesnard, Pierre. "La 'pietas litterara' de Jean Sturm et le développement à Strasbourg d'une pédagogie oecumenique 1538–81." *BSHPF* 111 (1965): 281–302.

Metzger, Edelgard. *Leonhard von Eck (1480–1550): Wegbereiter und Begründer des frühabsolutistischen Bayern.* Munich: R. Oldenbourg, 1980.

Meyer, Christian. "Kurfürst Joachim II. von Brandenburg im Schmalkaldischen Kriege." *Forschungen zur deutschen Geschichte* 18 (1878) 1–17.

Meyer, Friedrich. *Die Beziehungen zwischen Basel und den Eidgenossen in der Darstellung der Historiographie des 15. und 16. Jahrhunderts.* Basler Beiträge zur Geschichtswissenschaft, 39. Basel: Helbing & Lichtenhahn, 1951.

Meyer, Gerhard. *Zu den Anfängen der Straßburger Universität. Neue Forschungsergebnisse zur Herkunft der Studentenschaft und zur verlorenen Matrikel.* Edited by Hans-Georg Rott and Matthias Meyer. Historische Text und Studien, 2. Hildesheim: Georg Olms, 1989.

Meyer, Helmut. "Die deutschen Protestanten an der zweiten Tagungsperiode des Konzils von Trient 1551/52." *ARG* 56 (1965): 166–209.

———. *Der Zweite Kappeler Krieg: Die Krise der Schweizerischen Reformation.* Zurich: Hans Rohr, 1976.

Meyer, Manfred. "Die Haltung der Freien und Reichsstädte auf den Reichstagen 1521 bis 1526." *JGF* 5 (1981): 181–236.

Minutoli, Julius von, ed. *Das kaiserliche Buch des Markgrafen Albrecht Achilles. Kurfürstliche Periode 1470–1486.* 2 vols. Bayreuth: Buchner, 1850–81. Reprint. Osnabrück: Otto Zeller Verlag, 1984.

Moeller, Bernd. "The German Humanists and the Beginnings of the Reformation." In *Imperial Cities and the Reformation: Three Essays,* translated by H. C. Erik Midelfort and Mark U. Edwards, Jr., 19–38. Philadelphia: Fortress Press, 1975.

———. *Imperial Cities and the Reformation: Three Essays.* Translated by H. C. Erik Midelfort and Mark U. Edwards, Jr. Philadelphia: Fortress Press, 1975.

———. "Problems of Reformation Research." In *Imperial Cities and the Reformation: Three Essays,* edited by H. C. Erik Midelfort and Mark U. Edwards, Jr., 3–16. Philadelphia: Fortress Press, 1975.

———. *Reichsstadt und Reformation.* SVRG, 180. Gütersloh: Gerd Mohn, 1962. New ed. Berlin: Evangelische Verlagsanstalt, 1987.

Möllenberg, Walter, ed. "Die Verhandlungen im Schmalkaldischen Lager vor Giengen und Landgraf Philipps Rechenschaftsbericht." *ZVHG* 38 (1904): 31–62.

Mommsen, Wolfgang J. "Ranke and the neo-Rankean School." In *Leopold von Ranke and the Shaping of the Historical Discipline,* edited by Georg G. Iggers and James M. Powell, 124–40. Syracuse: Syracuse Univ. Press, 1990.

Mone, Franz Joseph, ed. *Quellensammlung der badischen Landesgeschichte.* 4 vols. Karlsruhe: Macklot'sche Verlagshandlung, 1848–67.

Moraw, Peter. "Fragen der deutschen Verfassungsgeschichte im späten Mittelalter." *ZHF* 4 (1977): 59–101.

———. *Von offener Verfassung zu gestalteter Verdichtung: Das Reich im späten Mittelalter 1250 bis 1490.* Propyläen Geschichte Deutschlands, 3. Berlin: Propyläen Verlag, 1985.

Moraw, Peter, and Volker Press. "Probleme der Sozial- und Verfassungsgeschichte des Heiligen Römischen Reiches im späten Mittelalter und in der frühen Neuzeit (13.–18. Jahrhundert)." *ZHF* 2 (1975): 95–108.

Mörke, Olaf. *Rat und Bürger in der Reformation. Soziale Gruppen und kirchlicher Wandel in den welfischen Hansestädten Lüneburg, Braunschweig und Göttingen.* Veröffentlichungen des Instituts für historische Landesforschung der Universität Göttingen, 19. Hildesheim: August Lax, 1983.

Müller, Ernst. "Die ernestinischen Landtage in der Zeit von 1485 bis 1572 unter besonderer Berücksichtigung des Steuerwesens." *Forschungen zur Thüringischen Landesgeschichte,* 188–228. Weimar: Böhlau, 1958.

Müller, Gerhard. "Johann Feige, der Kanzler Philipps des Großmütigen." *JHKGV* 12 (1961): 175–82.

———. "Karl V. und Philipp der Großmütige." *JHKGV* 12 (1961): 12–19.

———. *Die römische Kurie und die Reformation 1523–1534: Kirchen und Politik während des Pontifikats Clemens VII.* QFRG, 38. Gütersloh: Gerd Mohn, 1969.

Müller, Gregor. *Bildung und Erziehung im Humanismus der italienischen Renaissance: Grundlagen—Motive—Quellen.* Wiesbaden: Franz Steiner, 1969.

Müller, Ludwig. *Die Reichsstadt Nördlingen im schmalkaldischen Kriege.* Nördlingen: C. H. Beck, 1877.

Nachtigall (Luscinius), Othmar. *Progymnasmata Grecae literaturae, . . . Epistola de utilitate graecarum literarum.* Strasbourg: Johann Knobloch, 1521.

Nauert, Charles G. "The Clash of Humanists and Scholastics: An Approach to Pre-Reformation Contoversies." *SCJ* 4 (1973): 1–18.

Naujoks, Eberhard. *Obrigkeitsgedanke, Zunftverfassung und Reformation: Studien zur Verfassungsgeschichte von Ulm, Eßlingen und Schwäbisch-Gmünd.* VKLBW, ser. B, 3. Stuttgart: W. Kohlhammer, 1958.

———. "Reichsfreiheit und Wirtschaftsrivalität. Eine Studie zur Auseinandersetzung Eßlingens mit Württemberg im 16. Jahrhundert." *ZWLG* 16 (1957): 279–302.

Neudecker, Christian Gotthold, ed. *Merkwürdige Aktenstücke aus dem Zeitalter der Reformation (1522–1548).* Nuremberg: F. N. Campe, 1838.

———, ed. *Urkunden aus der Reformationszeit.* Kassel: J. C. Krieger, 1836.

Neuhaus, Helmut. *Reichstag und Supplikationsausschuß: Ein Beitrag zur Reichsverfassungsgeschichte der ersten Hälfte des 16. Jahrhunderts.* SVG, 24. Berlin: Duncker & Humblot, 1977.

———. *Reichsständische Repräsentationsformen im 16. Jahrhundert: Reichstag—Reichskreistag—Reichsdeputationstag.* SVG, 33. Berlin: Duncker & Humblot, 1982.

———. "Wandlungen der Reichstagsorganisation in der ersten Hälfte des 16. Jahrhunderts." In *Neue Studien zur frühneuzeitlichen Reichsgeschichte,* edited by Johannes Kunisch, 113–40. Beihefte der Zeitschrift für Historische Forschung, 3. Berlin: Duncker & Humblot, 1987.

Neuser, Wilhelm H., ed. *Die Vorbereitung der Religionsgespräche von Worms und Regensburg 1540/41.* Texte zur Geschichte der evangelischen Theologie, no. 4. Neukirchen-Vluyn: Neukirchener Verlag, 1974.

Newald, Richard. "Elsässische Charakterköpfe aus dem Zeitalter des Humanismus: Johann Geiler von Kaisersberg, Jakob Wimpfeling, Sebastian Brant, Thomas Murner, Matthias Ringman." In *Probleme und Gestalten des deutschen Humanismus,* 326–457. Berlin: De Gruyter, 1963.

Nirrnheim, Hans, ed., "Aktenstücke, betreffend die Aufnahme Hamburgs in den schmalkaldischen Bund." *Mitteilungen des Vereins für Hamburgische Geschichte* 25 (1905/06): 27–42.

Nuntiaturberichte aus Deutschland nebst ergänzenden Aktenstücke. Pt. 1, *1533–59.* Edited by the Deutsches Historisches Institut in Rom. 12 vols. Gotha: F. A. Perthes, 1892–1910. Reprint. Frankfurt am Main: Minerva, 1968.

Nuntiaturberichte aus Deutschland nebst ergänzenden Aktenstücke. Supplementary vols. 1–2. Edited by Gerhard Müller. Tübingen: Max Niemeyer, 1963–69.

Oberman, Heiko A. *Luther: Man between God and the Devil.* Translated by Eileen Walliser-Schwarzbart. New Haven: Yale Univ. Press, 1989.

———. *Masters of the Reformation: The Emergence of a New Intellectual Climate in Europe.* Translated by Dennis Martin. Cambridge: Cambridge Univ. Press, 1981.

———. *The Roots of Antisemitism in the Age of Renaissance and Reformation.* Translated by James I. Porter. Philadelphia: Fortress Press, 1984.

———. *Werden und Wertung der Reformation: Vom Wegestreit zum Glaubenskampf.* 2d ed. Spätscholastik und Reformation, 2. Tübingen: J. C. B. Mohr (Paul Siebeck), 1979.

———. *Wurzeln des Antisemitismus: Christenangst und Judenplage im Zeitalter von Humanismus und Reformation.* Berlin: Severin & Siedler, 1981.

———. "University and Society on the Threshold of Modern Times: The German Connection." In *Rebirth, Reform and Resilience: Universities in Transition, 1300–1700,* edited by James M. Kittelson and Pamela J. Transue, 19–41. Columbus: Ohio State Univ. Press, 1984.

Oestreich, Gerhard. "Zur parlamentarischen Arbeitsweise der deutschen Reichstage unter Karl V. (1519–1556)." *Mitteilungen des österreichischen Staatsarchivs* 25 (1972): 217–243.

Oliger, Livarius. "Der päpstliche Zeremonienmeister J. Buckard von Straßburg, 1450–1506." *AEKG* 9 (1934): 199–232.

Overfield, James H. *Humanism and Scholasticism in Germany, 1450–1520.* Princeton: Princeton Univ. Press, 1984.

Ozment, Steven. "Humanism, Scholasticism, and the Intellectual Origins of the Reformation." In *Continuity and Discontinuity in Church History: Essays Presented to G. H. Williams,* edited by F. Forrester Church and Timothy George, 133–49. SHCT, 19. Leiden: E. J. Brill, 1979.

———. *The Reformation in the Cities: The Appeal of the Reformation to Sixteenth-Century Germany and Switzerland.* New Haven: Yale Univ. Press, 1975.

———, ed. *Reformation Europe: A Guide to Research.* St. Louis: Center for Reformation Research, 1982.

Pappus, Johann. *Christliche Leichpredig auss den Neundten Capitel der Apostel Geschichte, bey den Begrebniss der Edlen und Tugentreichen Frawen, Veronica Stürmin, welche den 9. Decembris, Anno. 1581, in Christo sälig entschlaffen. Gehalten den 12. Decembris . . . durch Johannem Pappus.* Strasbourg: Niclauss Wyriott, 1582.

Pariset, Jean-Daniel. "L'activité de Jacques Sturm, stettmeister de Strasbourg de 1532 à 1553." In *Strasbourg au coeur religieux du XVIe siècle,* edited by Georges Livet, Marc Lienhard, and Jean Rott, 253–66. PSSARE, 12. Strasbourg: Librairie Istra, 1978.

———. *Les rélations entre la France et l'Allemagne au milieu du XVIe siècle.* PSSARE, Série "Grandes Publications," 19. Strasbourg: Librairie Istra, 1981.

Parker, N. Geoffrey. *The Military Revolution. Military Innovation and the Rise of the West, 1500–1800.* Cambridge: Cambridge Univ. Press, 1987.

———. "Success and Failure during the First Century of the Reformation." *PP,* no. 136 (August 1992): 43–82.

Pastor, Ludwig. *Die kirchlichen Reunionsbestrebungen während der Regierung Karls V. aus den Quellen dargestellt.* Freiburg im Breisgau: Herder, 1879.

Pater, Calvin Augustine. *Karlstadt as the Father of the Baptist Movements: The Emergence of Lay Protestantism.* Toronto: Univ. of Toronto Press, 1984.

Paulus, Nikolaus. *Protestantismus und Toleranz im 16. Jahrhundert.* Freiburg im Breisgau: Herder, 1911.

———. "Religionsfreiheit und Augsburger Religionsfriede." In *Zur Geschichte der Toleranz und Religionsfreiheit,* edited by Heinrich Lutz, 17–41. WF, 246. Darmstadt: Wissenschaftliche Buchgesellschaft, 1977.

Pelikan, Jaroslav. "Leopold von Ranke as Historian of the Reformation: What Ranke Did for the Reformation—What the Reformation Did for Ranke." In *Leopold von Ranke and the Shaping of the Historical Discipline,* edited by Georg G. Iggers and James Powell, 89–98. Syracuse: Syracuse University Press, 1990.

Petri, Franz. "Herzog Heinrich der Jüngere von Braunschweig-Wolfenbüttel. Ein niederdeutscher Territorialfürst im Zeitalter Luthers und Karls V." *ARG* 72 (1981): 122–58.

———. "Karl V. und die Städte im Nordwestraum während des Ringens um die politisch-kirchliche Ordnung in Deutschland." *Jahrbuch für westfälische Kirchenge-schichte* 71 (1978): 7–31.

———. "Landschaftliche und überlandschaftliche Kräfte im habsburgisch-klevischen Ringen und im Frieden von Venlo (1537–1543)." In *Aus Geschichte und Landeskunde: Forschungen und Darstellungen, Franz Steinbach zum 65. Geburtstag gewidmet von seinen Freunden und Schülern,* 92–113. Bonn: L. Röhrscheid, 1960.

———. "Nordwestdeutschland im Wechselspiel der Politik Karls V. und Philipps des Großmütigen von Hessen." *ZVHG* 71 (1960): 37–60.

Petri, Franziskus. "Straßburgs Beziehungen zu Frankreich während der Reformationszeit." *ELJb* 8 (1929): 134–65; 10 (1931): 123–92.

Pfeiffer, Gerhard. "Die Bemühungen der oberdeutschen Kaufleute um die Privilegierung ihres Handels in Lyon." *Beiträge zur Wirtschaftsgeschichte Nürnbergs,* edited by the Stadtarchiv Nürnberg, Beiträge zur Wirtschaftsgeschichte Nürnbergs, 11, vol. 1:408–23. Nürnberg: Stadtarchiv Nürnberg, 1967.

———. "Albrecht Dürer und Lazarus Spengler." In *Festschrift für Max Spindler zum 75. Geburtstag,* edited by Dieter Albrecht, Andreas Kraus, and Kurt Reindel, 379–400. Munich: C. H. Beck, 1969.

Pfeiffer, Hans. *Verfassungs- und Verwaltungesgeschichte der Fürstpropstei Ellwangen.* VKLBW, ser. B, 7. Stuttgart: W. Kohlhammer, 1959.

Pfeilschifter, Georg, ed. *Acta reformationis catholicae ecclesiae Germaniae concernantia saeculi XVI. Die Reformverhandlungen des deutschen Episkopats von 1520 bis 1570.* 6 vols. Regensburg: F. Pustet, 1959–74.

Pflug, Julius. *Correspondance.* Edited by J.-V. Pollet. 5 vols. Leiden: E. J. Brill, 1969–82.

Pfnür, Vinzenz. "Die Einigung bei den Religionsgesprächen von Worms und Regensburg 1540/41 eine Täuschung?" In *Die Religionsgespräche der Reformationszeit,* edited by Gerhard Müller, 55–88. SVRG, 191. Gütersloh: Gerd Mohn, 1980.

Pirenne, Henri. *Histoire de Belgique.* 7 vols. Brussels: M. Lamertin, 1922–32.

Planitz, Hans von der. *Des kursächsischen Rates Hans von der Planitz Berichte aus dem Reichsregiment 1521–1523.* Edited by Hans Virck. Schriften der Königlich Sächsischen Kommission für Geschichte, 3. Leipzig: Teubner, 1899. Reprint. Hildesheim: Georg Olms, 1979.

Pollet, J. V., ed. *Martin Bucer. Études sur la correspondance avec de nombreux textes inédits.* 2 vols. Paris: Presses Universitaires de France, 1958–62.

———, ed. *Martin Bucer. Études sur les relations de Bucer avec les Pays-Bas, l'électorat de Cologne et l'Allemagne du Nord.* 2 vols. SMRT, 33. Leiden: Brill, 1985.

Post, R. R. *The Modern Devotion: Confrontation with Reformation and Humanism.* SMRT, 3. Leiden: E. J. Brill, 1968.

Potter, D. L. "Foreign Policy in the Age of the Reformation: French Involvement in the Schmalkaldic War, 1544–1547." *Historical Journal* 20 (1977): 525–44.

Press, Volker. "Die Bundespläne Kaiser Karls V. und die Reichsverfassung." In *Das römisch-deutsche Reich im politischen System Karls V.,* edited by Heinrich Lutz, 55–106. SHKK, 1. Munich and Vienna: R. Oldenbourg, 1982.

———. *Calvinismus und Territorialstaat: Regierung und Zentralbehörden der Kurpfalz 1559–1619.* Kieler Historische Studien, 7. Stuttgart: Ernst Klett, 1970.

———. "Herzog Ulrich (1498–1550)." In *900 Jahre Haus Württemberg. Leben und Leistung für Land und Volk,* edited by Robert Uhland (Stuttgart: W. Kohlhammer, 1984), 110–35.

———. "The Holy Roman Empire in German History." In *Politics and Society in Reformation Europe: Essays for Sir Geoffrey Elton on his Sixty-Fifth Birthday,* edited by E. I. Kouri and Tom Scott, 51–77. London: Macmillan, 1987.

———. *Kaiser Karl V., König Ferdinand und die Entstehung der Reichsritterschaft.* 2d ed. Institut für Europäische Geschichte Mainz, Vorträge, no. 60. Wiesbaden: Franz Steiner, 1980.

Preuschen, Erwin, ed. "Ein gleichzeitiger Bericht über Landgraf Philipps Fußfall und Verhaftung." In *Philipp der Großmütige. Beiträge zur Geschichte seines Lebens und seiner Zeit,* 144–54. Edited by the Historischer Verein für das Großherzogtum Hessen. Marburg: N. G. Elwert, 1904.

Prodi, Paolo. *The Papal Prince—One Body and Two Souls: The Papal Monarchy in Early Modern Europe.* Translated by Susan Haskins. Cambridge: Cambridge Univ. Press, 1987.

Prüser, Friedrich. *England und die Schmalkaldener 1535–1540*. Marburg: Elwert, 1928.

Puchta, Hans. *Die habsburgische Herrschaft in Württemberg 1520–1534*. Munich: UNI-Druck, 1967.

Raab, Heribert. "Die oberdeutschen Hochstifter zwischen Habsburg und Wittelsbach in der frühen Neuzeit." *BDLG* 109 (1973): 69–101.

Rabe, Horst. "Befunde und Ueberlegungen zur Religionspolitik Karls V. am Vorabend des Augsburger Reichstags 1530." In *Confessio Augustana und Confutatio: Der Augsburger Reichstag 1530 und die Einheit der Kirche. Internationales Symposion der Gesellschaft zur Herausgabe des Corpus Catholicorum in Augsburg vom 3.–7. September 1979*, edited by Erwin Iserloh, 101–12. RST, 118. Münster im Westfalen: Aschendorff, 1980.

————. *Reichsbund und Interim: Die Verfassungs- und Religionspolitik Karls V. und der Reichstag von Augsburg 1547/48*. Cologne and Vienna: Böhlau, 1971.

Rabil, Albert, Jr. "Preface." In *Renaissance Humanism: Foundations, Forms, and Legacy*, edited by Albert Rabil, Jr. Vol. 1, *Humanism in Italy*, xi–xv. Philadelphia: Univ. of Pennsylvania Press, 1988.

Ranke, Leopold von. *Deutsche Geschichte im Zeitalter der Reformation*. Edited by Willy Andreas. 2 vols. Wiesbaden: Emil Vollmer, 1957.

————. *History of the Popes in the Last Four Centuries*. 3 vols. Translated by E. Fowler. London: G. Bell and Sons, 1912.

————. *History of the Reformation in Germany*. Translated by Sarah Austin. London: George Routledge and Sons, 1905.

Rapp, Francis. *Le diocèse de Strasbourg*. Histoire des diocèses de France, 14. Paris: Beauchesne, 1982.

————. "Die elsässischen Humanisten und die geistliche Gesellschaft." In *Die Humanisten in ihrer politischen und sozialen Umwelt*, edited by Otto Herding and Robert Stupperich, 87–108. MKH, 3. Boppard: Harald Boldt, 1976.

————. "La guerre des paysans à Dorlisheim." *Annuaire de la Société d'histoire et d'archéologie de Molsheim et environs*, 1974: 51–60.

————. "Jean Geiler de Kaysersberg (1445–1510), le prédicateur de la cathédrale de Strasbourg." In *Grandes figures de l'humanisme alsacien. Courants, milieux, destins*, edited by Francis Rapp and Georges Livet, 25–32. PSSARE, Collection "Grandes Publications," 14. Strasbourg: Librarie Istra, 1978.

————. "Préréformes et humanisme. Strasbourg et l'Empire (1482–1520)." In *Histoire de Strasbourg des origines à nos jours*, edited by Georges Livet and Francis Rapp, vol. 2:177–254. Strasbourg: Éditions Les Dernières Nouvelles, 1981.

————. *Réformes et reformation à Strasbourg: Église et société dans le diocèse de Strasbourg (1450–1525)*. Collection de l'Institut des Hautes Études Alsaciennes, 23. Paris. Éditions Ophrys, 1974.

————. "Die soziale und wirtschaftliche Vorgeschichte des Bauernkriegs im Unterelsaß." In *Bauernkriegs-Studien*, edited by Bernd Moeller, 29–46. SVRG, 189. Gütersloh: Gerd Mohn, 1975.

————. "Les strasbourgeois et les universités rhénanes à la fin du Moyen Age et jusqu'à la Réforme." *ASAVS* 4 (1974): 11–22.

Rathgeber, Julius Friedrich Emil. *Die handschriftlichen Schätze der früheren Straßburger Stadbibliothek*. Gütersloh: Bertelsmann, 1876.

Raubenheimer, Richard. *Paul Fagius aus Rheinzabern. Sein Leben und Wirken als Reformator und Gelehrter*. Veröffentlichungen des Vereins für pfälzische Kirchengeschichte, 6. Zweibrücken: Verein für pfälzische Kirchengeschichte, 1957.

Rauch, Moriz von, ed. *Urkundenbuch der Stadt Heilbronn*. Vols. 2–4. Württembergische Geschichtsquellen, 15, 19, 20. Stuttgart: W. Kohlhammer Verlag, 1913–22.

Reeves, Marjorie. "Marsiglio of Padua and Dante Alighieri." In *Trends in Medieval Political Thought*, edited by Beryl Smalley, 86–104. Oxford: Basil Blackwell, 1965.

Reinhard, Wolfgang. "Die kirchenpolitischen Vorstellungen Kaiser Karls V., ihre Grundlagen und ihr Wandel." In *Confessio Augustana und Confutatio: Der Augsburger Reichstag 1530 und die Einheit der Kirche. Internationales Symposion der Gesellschaft zur Herausgabe des Corpus Catholicorum in Augsburg vom 3.–7. September 1979*, edited by Erwin Iserloh, 62–100. RST, 118. Münster im Westfalen: Aschendorff, 1980.

Reinhart, Rudolf. "Untersuchungen zur Besetzung der Propstei Ellwangen seit dem 16. Jahrhundert." In *Ellwangen 764–1964: Beiträge und Untersuchungen zur Zwölfhundertjahrfeier*, edited by Viktor Burr, vol. 1:316–78. Ellwangen: Schwabenverlag, 1964.

Reuchlin, Johannes. *Reuchlins Briefwechsel*. Edited by Ludwig Geiger. BLVS, 126. Stuttgart: Litterarischer Verein, 1875. Reprint. Hildesheim: Olms, 1962.

Rhenanus, Beatus. *Briefwechsel des Beatus Rhenanus*. Edited by Adalbert Horawitz. Leipzig: Teubner, 1900. Reprint. Nieuwkoop: B. de Graaf, 1966.

———, ed. *Jani Pannonii Quinquecclesiensis Episcopi Sylua Panegyrica ad Guarinum Veronensem, praeceptorem suum*. Basel: J. Froben, 1518.

Richter, Max. *Bremen im Schmalkaldischen Bund 1537–1540: Ein Beitrag zur Geschichte des Schmalkaldischen Bundes*. Dissertation Marburg. Marburg/Lahn: Buchdruckerei Robert Nostke (Borna-Leipzig), 1914.

Ridderikhoff, C. M., H. de Ridder-Symoens, and Chris. L. Heesakers, eds. *Les livres des procurateurs de la nation germanique de l'ancienne Université d'Orléans, 1444–1602*. 2 vols. Leiden: Brill, 1971–88.

Riederer, Johann Baptist. *Nachrichten zur Kirchen-, Gelehrten- und Bücher-Geschichte*. 4 vols. Altdorf: Lorenz Schüpfel, 1764–68.

Riegger, Joseph Anton. *Amoenitates literariae friburgenses*. 3 pts. Ulm: Stettin, 1775–76.

Ritter, Gerhard. *Die Heidelberger Universität. Ein Stück deutscher Geschichte*. Heidelberg: Carl Winter, 1936.

Robinson, Hastings, ed. *Original Letters Relating to the English Reformation*. 2 vols. Parker Society Publications, 38–39. Cambridge: Cambridge Univ. Press, 1846–47. Reprint. New York: Johnson Reprint Corp., 1968.

———, ed. *Zurich Letters*. 2d ser. Parker Society Publications, 52. Cambridge: Cambridge Univ. Press, 1845. Reprint. New York: Johnson Reprint, 1968.

Rockwell, William Walker. *Die Doppelehe des Landgrafen Philipp von Hessen*. Marburg: N. G. Elwert, 1904.

Rodríguez-Salgado, M. J. *The Changing Face of Empire: Charles V, Philip II and Habsburg Authority, 1551–1559*. Cambridge: Cambridge Univ. Press, 1988.

Roeck, Bernd. *Lebenswelt und Kultur des Bürgertums in der frühen Neuzeit*. Enzyklopädie deutscher Geschichte, 9. Munich: R. Oldenbourg, 1991.

Röhrich, Timotheus Wilhelm. *Geschichte der Reformation im Elsass und besonders in Strassburg*. 3 vols. Strasbourg: Friedrich Carl Heitz, 1830–32.

———, ed. *Mittheilungen aus der Geschichte der evangelischen Kirche des Elsasses*. 3 vols. Paris: Treuttel & Würtz, 1855.

Rommel, Christoph von. *Philipp der Großmütige, Landgraf von Hessen*. 3 vols. Giessen: Georg Friedrich Heyer, 1830.

Rommel, Franz. *Die Reichsstadt Ulm in der Katastrophe des Schmalkaldischen Krieges*. Stuttgart: W. Kohlhammer, 1922.

Roper, Lyndal. "'The common man,' 'the common good,' 'common women': Gender and Meaning in the German Reformation Commune." *Social History* 12 (1987): 1–21.

———. *The Holy Household: Women and Morals in Reformation Augsburg*. Oxford: Clarendon Press, 1989.

Rosenberg, Walter. *Der Kaiser und die Protestanten in den Jahren 1537–1539*. SVRG, 77. Halle: Max Niemeyer, 1903.

Rosenkranz, Albert. *Der Bundschuh: Die Erhebungen des südwestdeutschen Bauernstandes in den Jahren 1493–1517.* 2 vols. SWIEL. Heidelberg: Wissenschaftliches Institut der Elsaß-Lothringer im Reich, 1927.

Roth, Friedrich. *Augsburgs Reformationsgeschichte.* 4 vols. Munich: Theodor Ackermann, 1901–11.

———, ed. "Aus dem Briefwechsel Gereon Sailers mit den Augsburger Bürgermeistern Georg Herwart und Simprecht Hoser (April–Juni 1544)." *ARG* 1 (1903/04): 84–97.

———, ed. "Der offizielle Bericht der von den Evangelischen zum Regensburger Gespräch Verordneten an ihre Fürsten und Obern." *ARG* 5 (1907/08): 1–30, 375–97.

———, ed. "Zur Geschichte des Reichstages in Regensburg im Jahr 1541. Die Korrespondenz der Augsburger Gesandten Wolfgang Rehlinger, Simprich Hoser und Dr. Konrad Hel mit dem Rathe, den Geheimen und dem Bürgermeister Herwart nebst Briefen von Dr. Gereon Sailer und Wolfgang Musculus an den letzteren." *ARG* 2 (1904/05): 250–307; 3 (1905/06): 18–64; 4 (1906/07): 65–98, 221–304.

———, ed. "Zur Kirchengüterfrage in der Zeit von 1538 bis 1540. Die Gutachten Martin Bucers und der Augsburger Prädikanten Wolfgang Musculus und Bonifacius Wolfart über die Verwendung der Kirchengüter." *ARG* 1 (1903/04): 299–336.

Roth, Paul. *Die Reformation in Basel.* 2 vols. Basler Neujahrsblatt, nos. 114, 121. Basel: Helbing & Lichtenhahn, 1936–43.

Rott, Hans. *Friedrich II. von der Pfalz und die Reformation.* HAMNG, 4. Heidelberg: Carl Winter, 1904. Reprint. Nendeln/Liechtenstein: Kraus Reprint, 1976.

Rott, Jean. "L'ancienne Bibliothèque de Strasbourg, détruite en 1870: les catalogues qui en subsistent." In *Refugium animae bibliotheca: Mélanges offerts à Albert Kolb,* 426–42. Wiesbaden: Guido Pressler, 1969. Reprinted in Rott, *IH* 2:615–32.

———. "Artisanat et mouvements sociaux à Strasbourg autour de 1525." In *Artisans et ouvriers d'Alsace,* 137–70. PSSARE, 9. Strasbourg: Librairie Istra, 1965. Reprinted in Rott, *IH* 1:133–66.

———. "Bucer et les débuts de la querelle sacramentaire: l'instruction donnée à Grégoire Caselius pour sa mission auprès de Luther (octobre 1525)." *RPHR* 34 (1954): 234–54. Reprinted in Rott, *IH* 2:182–202.

———. "Clercs et laiques à Strasbourg à la veille de la Réformation: Les tragiques amours du Chanoine Jean Hepp et ses procès (1512–1521)." *ASAVS* 9 (1979): 15–52. Reprinted in Rott, *IH* 1:313–50.

———, ed. *Correspondance de Martin Bucer: Liste alphabétique des correspondants.* Strasbourg: Association des Publications de la Faculté de Théologie Protestant de l'Université des Sciences Humaines de Strasbourg, 1977.

———. "L'église des réfugiés de langue française à Strasbourg au XVIe siècle: aperçu de son histoire, en particulier de ses crises à partir de 1541." *BSHPF* 122 (1976), 525–50. Reprinted in Rott, *IH* 2:17–42.

———. "Erasme et les réformateurs de Strasbourg." In *Erasme, l'Alsace, et son temps: Catalogue de l'exposition réalisée à la Bibliothéque nationale et universitaire de Strasbourg,* 49–56. PSSARE, collections "Recherches et Documents," 8. Strasbourg: Palais de l'Université, 1971.

———. "Exposition de documents originaux concernant les anabaptistes à Strasbourg au XVIe siècle." In *Origins and Characteristics of Anabaptism,* edited by Marc Lienhard, 222–28. The Hague: Mouton, 1977.

———. "La guerre des paysans et la Ville de Strasbourg." In *La Guerre des Paysans 1525,* edited by Alphonse Wollbrett, 23–32. Saverne: Société d'Histoire et d'Archéologie de Saverne et Environs, 1975. Reprinted in Rott, *IH* 1:199–209.

———. *Investigationes historicae: Églises et société au XVIe siècle. Gesammelte Aufsätze.* Edited by Marijn de Kroon and Marc Lienhard. 2 vols. Strasbourg: Librarie Oberlin, 1986.

———. "Jacques Sturm, scolarque de la Haute-Ecole (Gymnase) de la ville de Strasbourg 1526–1553." In *Strasbourg au coeur religieux du XVIe siècle*, edited by Georges Livet, Marc Lienhard, and Francis Rapp, 243–51. PSSARE, Collection "Grandes Publications," 12. Strasbourg: Librairie Istra, 1977. Reprinted in Jean Rott, *IH* 2:461–69.

———. "The Library of the Strasbourg Humanist Thomas Wolf, Senior (+1511)." In *The Process of Change in Early Modern Europe: Essays in Honor of Miriam Usher Chrisman*, edited by Phillip N. Bebb and Sherrin Marshall, 33–58. Athens: Ohio University Press, 1988.

———. "Jacques Sturm, scolarque de la Haute-Ecole (Gymnase) de la ville de Strasbourg 1526–1553." In *Strasbourg au coeur religieux du XVIe siècle*, edited by Georges Livet, Marc Lienhard, and Jean Rott, 243–51. PSSARE, 12. Strasbourg: Librairie Istra, 1978.

———. "Nouveaux documents sur Jean Sleidan, historien de la Réforme (1506–1556)." In *BPH* 1967 (1970): 551–648. Reprinted in Rott, *IH* 2:363–460.

———. "Pfaffenfehden und Anfänge der Reformation in Straßburg. Die Streitigkeiten des Johannes Murner mit den Brüdern Wolff und dem Jung Sankt Peter-Stift daselbst (1519–1522)." In *Landesgeschichte und Geistesgeschichte: Festschrift für Otto Herding zum 65. Geburtstag*, edited by Kaspar Elm, Eberhard Gönner, and Eugen Hildenbrand, 279–94. VKLBW, ser. B, 92. Stuttgart: W. Kohlhammer, 1977. Reprinted in Rott, *IH* 1:351–67.

———. "Le recteur strasbourgeois Jean Sturm et les Protesants français." In *Actes du Colloque L'Amiral Coligny et son temps (Paris, 24–28 octobre 1972)*, 407–25. Paris: Société de l'histoire du protestantisme français, 1974. Reprinted in Rott, *IH* 2:43–62.

———. "La Réforme à Nuremberg et à Strasbourg. Contactes et contrastes (avec des correspondances inédites)." In *Homage à Dürer: Strasbourg et Nuremberg dans la première moitié du XVIe siècle*, 91–142. PSSARE, series "Recherches et Documents," 12. Strasbourg: Librairie Istra, 1972. Reprinted in Rott, *IH* 1:391–443.

———. "Sources et grandes lignes de l'histoire des Bibliothèques publiques de Strasbourg détruites en 1870." *Cahiers alsaciens d'archéologie, d'art et d'histoire* 15 (1971): 145–80. Reprinted in Rott, *IH* 2:633–68.

———. "Un recueil de correspondances strasbourgeoises du XVIe siècle à la Bibliothèque de Copenhague (MS. Thott 497,2°)." In *BPH* 1968 (1971), 2:749–818. Reprinted in Rott, *IH* 1:243–312.

Roussel, Bernard. "Les premières dissidences religieuses du XVIe siècle à Metz (Hiver 1523–Été 1525)." In *Les Réformes en Lorraine 1520–1620*, edited by Louis Châtellier, 11–45. Centre des recherches en histoire sociale et religieuse, 2. Nancy: Presses Universitaires de Nancy, 1986.

Rublack, Hans-Christoph. "Die Aussenpolitik der Reichsstadt Konstanz während der Reformationszeit." In *Der Konstanzer Reformator Ambrosius Blarer 1492–1564: Gedenkschrift zu seinem 400. Todestag*, edited by Bernd Moeller, 56–80. Constance and Stuttgart: Jan Thorbecke, 1964.

———. "Forschungsbericht Stadt und Reformation." *Stadt und Kirche im 16. Jahrhundert*, edited by Bernd Moeller, 9–26. SVRG, 190. Gütersloh: Gerd Mohn, 1978.

———. *Gescheiterte Reformation. Frühreformatorische und protestantische Bewegungen in süd- und westdeutschen geistlichen Residenzen.* SFN, 4. Stuttgart: Klett-Cotta, 1978.

———. "Is There a 'New History' of the Urban Reformation?" In *Politics and Society in Reformation Europe: Essays for Sir Geoffrey Elton on his Sixty-Fifth Birthday,*

edited by E. I. Kouri and Tom Scott, 121–41. London: Macmillan, 1987.
———. *Nördlingen. Eine bürgerliche Reformation*. QFRG, 51. Gütersloh: Gerd Mohn, 1982.
———. "Nördlingen zwischen Kaiser und Reformation." *ARG* 71 (1980): 113–33.
———. "Political and Social Norms in Urban Communities in the Holy Roman Empire." In Peter Blickle, Hans-Christoph Rublack, and Winfried Schulze, *Religion, Politics and Social Protest: Three Studies on Early Modern Germany*, edited by Kaspar von Greyerz, 24–60. London: George Allen & Unwin, 1984.
Rückert, Hanns. "Die Bedeutung der württembergischen Reformation für den Gang der deutschen Reformationsgeschichte." *BWKG* 38 (1934): 267–80.
Ryff, Fridolin. *Die Chronik des Fridolin Ryff 1514–1541 mit der Fortsetzung des Peter Ryff 1543–85*. Edited by Wilhelm Vischer and Alfred Stern. Basler Chroniken, 1. Leipzig: Teubner, 1872.
Saladin, Johann Georg. *Straßburg Chronik*. Edited by Aloys Meister and Aloys Ruppel. BSCMHA, 2d ser. 22 (1908): 137–206; 23 (1911): 182–281, 283–435.
Salomies, Martti. *Die Pläne Kaiser Karls V. für eine Reichsreform mit Hilfe eines allgemeinen Bundes*. Helsinki: Suomalainen Tiedeakatemia, 1953.
Santifaller, Leo. "Die preces primariae Maximilians I." In *Festschrift zur Feier des 200-jährigen Bestandes des Haus-, Hof- und Staatsarchivs*, edited by Leo Santifaller, vol. 1, 578–661. Vienna: Druck und Kommissionsverlag der Österreichischen Staatsdruckerei, 1949.
Sastrow, Bartholomäus. *Bartholomew Sastrow, being the Memoirs of a German Burgomaster*. Translated by Albert D. Vandam. London: Archibald Constable & Co., 1905.
Scarisbrick, Joseph J. *Henry VIII*. Berkeley and Los Angeles: Univ. of California Press, 1968.
Schaafhausen, Friedrich Wilhelm. *Die Geldwirtschaft des Smalkaldischen Bundes*. Ph.D. diss., Göttingen, 1921.
Schaub, Friedrich. "Elsässische Studenten an der Universität Freiburg im Zeitalter der Reformation und Gegenreformation." *ARG* 38 (1941): 279–82.
Scheel, Günter. "Kurbraunschweig und die übrigen welfischen Lande." In *Deutsche Verwaltungsgeschichte*, edited by Kurt G. A. Jeserich, Hans Pohl, and Georg-Christoph von Unruh. Vol. 1, *Vom Spätmittelalter bis zum Ende des Reiches*, 741–63. Stuttgart: Deutsche Verlags-Anstalt, 1983.
Scheible, Heinz, ed. *Das Widerstandsrecht als Problem der deutschen Protestanten 1523–1546*. TKT, 10. Gütersloh: Gerd Mohn, 1969.
Schelp, Robert. *Die Reformationsprozesse der Stadt Straßburg am Reichskammergericht zur Zeit des Smalkaldischen Bundes (1524)/1531–1541/(1555)*. 2d ed. Kaiserslautern: Buchhandlung Geschwister Schmidt (im Kommission), 1965.
Schiess, Traugott, ed. *Briefwechsel der Brüder Ambrosius und Thomas Blarer 1509–1548*. 3 vols. Freiburg im Breisgau: Friedrich Ernst Fehsenfeld, 1908–12.
Schilling, Diebold. *Berner Chronik*. Edited by Hans Bloesch and Paul Hilber. Bern: Aare Verlag, 1943–45.
Schilling, Heinz. *Aufbruch und Krise: Deutschland 1517–1648*. Berlin: Siedler, 1988.
———. *Civic Calvinism in Northwestern Germany and the Netherlands, Sixteenth to Nineteenth Centuries*. SCES, 17. Kirksville, Mo.: Sixteenth Century Journal Publishers, 1991.
———. "Die deutsche Gemeindereformation. Ein oberdeutsch-zwinglianisches Ereignis vor der 'reformatorischen Wende' des Jahres 1525?" *ZHF* 14 (1987): 325–32.
Schindling, Anton. *Humanistische Hochschule und freie Reichsstadt: Gymnasium und Akademie in Straßburg 1538–1621*. VIEG, 77. Wiesbaden: Franz Steiner, 1977.
———. "Die Reformation in den Reichsstädten und die Kirchengüter. Straßburg, Nürnberg und Frankfurt im Vergleich." In *Bürgerschaft und Kirche*, edited by Jürgen Sydow, 67–88. Stadt in der Geschichte. Veröffentlichungen des Südwestdeutschen

Arbeitskreises für Stadtgeschichte, 7. Sigmaringen: Jan Thorbecke, 1980.

————. "Reichskirche und Reformation. Zu Glaubensspaltung und Konfessionalisierung in den geistlichen Fürstentümern des Reiches." In *Neue Studien zur frühneuzeitlichen Reichsgeschichte*, edited by Johannes Kunisch, 81–112. Beihefte der Zeitschrift für Historische Forschung, 3. Berlin: Duncker & Humblot, 1987.

Schirrmacher, Friedrich Wilhelm, ed. *Briefe und Acten zu der Geschichte des Religionsgespräches zu Marburg 1529 und des Reichstages zu Augsburg 1530*. Gotha: Perthes, 1876. Reprint. Amsterdam: Rodopi, 1976.

Schlaich, Klaus. "Die Mehrheitsabstimmung im Reichstag zwischen 1495 und 1613." *ZHF* 10 (1983): 300–340.

Schlomka, Ernst. *Kurfürst Moritz und Heinrich II. von Frankreich von 1550–1552*. Halle: Max Niemeyer, 1884.

Schlütter-Schindler, Gabriele. *Der Smalkaldische Bund und das Problem der causa religionis*. Europäische Hochschulschriften, ser. 3, 283. Frankfurt am Main, Bern, and New York: Peter Lang, 1986.

Schmauss, Johann Jakob, ed. *Neue und vollständigere Sammlung der Reichs-Abschiede, Welche von den Zeiten Kayser Konrads des II. bis jetzo auf den Teutschen Reichs-Tagen abgefasst worden*. 2 vols. Frankfurt am Main: E. A. Koch, 1747. Reprint. Osnabrück: Otto Zeller, 1967.

Schmid, Peter. "Reichssteuern, Reichsfinanzen und Reichsgewalt in der ersten Hälfte des 16. Jahrhunderts." In *Säkulare Aspekte der Reformationszeit*, edited by Heinz Angermeier, 153–98. SHKK, 5. Munich and Vienna: R. Oldenbourg, 1983.

Schmidt, Charles Guillaume Adolphe. *Répertoire bibliographique strasbourgeois jusque vers 1530*. 9 vols. Strasbourg: J. H. Ed. Heitz, 1893–96.

————. *Histoire littéraire de l'Alsace à la fin du XVe et au commencement du XVIe siècle*. 2 vols. Paris, 1879. Reprint. Nieuwkoop: B. De Graaf, 1966.

Schmidt, Georg. "Die Freien und Reichsstädte im Smalkaldischen Bund." In *Martin Luther: Probleme seiner Zeit*, edited by Volker Press and Dieter Stievermann, 177–218. SFN, 16. Stuttgart: Klett-Cotta, 1986.

————. "Die Haltung des Städtecorpus zur Reformation und die Nürnberger Bündnispolitik." *ARG* 75 (1984): 194–233.

————. "Reichsstadt und Territorialstadt. Eßlingen, Württemberg und das Städtecorpus um die Mitte des 16. Jahrhunderts." *Esslinger Studien* 21 (1982): 71–104.

————. *Der Städtetag in der Reichsverfassung: Eine Untersuchung zur korporativen Politik der Freien und Reichsstädte in der ersten Hälfte des 16. Jahrhunderts*. VIEG, 113. Wiesbaden: Franz Steiner, 1984.

Schmidt, Gustav. "Zur Geschichte des Smalkaldischen Bundes (Der Tag zu Frankfurt Dezember 1545 bis Februar 1546)." *FDG* 25 (1885): 69–98.

Schmidt, Heinrich Richard. "Die Häretisierung des Zwinglianismus im Reich seit 1525." In *Zugänge zur bäuerlichen Reformation*, edited by Peter Blickle, 219–36. Bauer und Reformation, 1. Zurich: Chronos Verlag, 1987.

————. *Reichsstädte, Reich und Reformation: Korporative Religionspolitik 1521–1529/30*. VIEG, 122. Wiesbaden: Franz Steiner, 1986.

Schneider, Eugen, ed. *Ausgewählte Urkunden zur württembergischen Geschichte*. Württembergische Geschichtsquellen, 11. Stuttgart: W. Kohlhammer, 1911.

Schnelbögl, Fritz. "Ein Ratsmahl mit Dürer." *MVGN* 47 (1958): 446–51.

Schoenberger, Cynthia Grant. "The Development of the Lutheran Theory of Resistance, 1523–1530." *SCJ* 8 (1977): 61–76.

————. "Luther and the Justifiability of Resistance to Legitimate Authority." *Journal of the History of Ideas* 40 (1979): 3–20.

Schornbaum, Karl. *Zur Politik des Markgrafen Georg von Brandenburg vom Beginne seiner selbständigen Regierung bis zum Nürnberger Anstand 1528–1532.* Munich: T. Ackermann, 1906.

―――. "Zur Politik der Reichsstadt Nürnberg vom Ende des Reichstages zu Speier 1529 bis zur Übergabe der Augsburgischen Konfession 1530." *MVGN* 17 (1906): 178–245.

Schott, Peter. *Works of Peter Schott (1460–1490).* Edited by Murray A. Cowie and Marian L. Cowie. 2 vols. Univ. of North Carolina Studies in the Germanic Languages and Literatures, 41, 71. Chapel Hill: Univ. of North Carolina Press, 1963–71.

Schreiber, Heinrich, ed. *Der deutsche Bauernkrieg. Gleichzeitige Urkunden.* Urkundenbuch der Stadt Freiburg im Breisgau, n.s. 3 vols. Freiburg im Breisgau: Herder, 1863–66.

Schubert, Friedrich Hermann. *Die deutschen Reichstage in der Staatslehre der frühen Neuzeit.* Schriftenreihe der Historischen Kommission bei der Bayerischen Akademie der Wissenschaften, 7. Göttingen: Vandenhoeck & Ruprecht, 1966.

Schubert, Hans von, ed. *Bekenntnisbildung und Religionspolitik 1529/30 (1524 bis 1534). Untersuchungen und Texte.* Gotha: Perthes, 1910.

―――, ed. "Bucers Gegenbekenntnis zu den Schwabacher Artikeln vertreten durch Jakob Sturm, und Konrad Sams Glossen." *ZKiG* 30 (1911): 229–57.

―――. *Bündnis und Bekenntnis 1529/1530.* SVRG, 98. Leipzig: M. Heinsius, 1908.

Schuffenhauer, Werner, and Klaus Steiner, eds. *Martin Luther in der deutschen bürgerlichen Philosophie 1517–1945.* Berlin: Akademie-Verlag, 1983.

Schultz, Rudolf. *Martin Butzer's Anschauung von der christlichen Oberkeit, dargestellt im Rahmen der reformatorischen Staats- und Kirchentheorien.* Ph.D. diss., Freiburg im Breisgau. Zella-Mehlis: M. von Nordheim'sche Buchdruckerei, 1932.

Schulze, Manfred. *Fürsten und Reformation. Geistliche Reformpolitik weltlicher Fürsten vor der Reformation.* Spätmittelalter und Reformation, n.s., 2. Tübingen: J. C. B. Mohr (Paul Siebeck), 1991.

Schulze, Winfried. "Concordia, Discordia, Tolerantia. Deutsche Politik im konfessionellen Zeitalter." In *Neue Studien zur frühneuzeitlichen Reichsgeschichte,* edited by Johannes Kunisch, 43–80. Beihefte der Zeitschrift für Historische Forschung, 3. Berlin: Duncker & Humblot, 1987.

―――. "Reichstage und Reichssteuern im späten 16. Jahrhundert." *ZHF* 2 (1975): 43–58.

―――. "Soziale Bewegungen als Phänomen des 16. Jahrhunderts." In *Säkulare Aspekte der Reformationszeit,* edited by Heinz Angermeier, 113–52. SHKK, 5. Munich and Vienna: R. Oldenbourg, 1983.

―――, ed. *Ständische Gesellschaft und soziale Mobilität.* SHKK, 12. Munich: R. Oldenbourg, 1988.

Schüz, Alfred. *Der Donaufeldzug Karls V. im Jahre 1546.* Tübingen: Osiandersche Buchhandlung, 1930.

Schwarz, N. N., ed. "Johann Friedrich's des Großmüthingen Correspondenz mit Brück und Amsdorf vor dem Augsburger Reichstag 1547." *Zeitschrift des Vereins für thüringische Geschichte* 1 (1854): 395–414.

Schweinzer, Silvia. "Die Vorgeschichte des Reichstags von Speyer 1542 im Spiegel der politischen Korrespondenz Kaiser Karls V." In *Aus der Arbeit an den Reichstagen unter Kaiser Karl V.: Sieben Beiträge zu Fragen der Forschung und Edition,* edited by Heinrich Lutz and Alfred Kohler, 228–72. SHKBA, 26. Göttingen: Vandenhoeck & Ruprecht, 1986.

Scott, Tom. *Freiburg and the Breisgau: Town-Country Relations in the Age of Reformation and Peasants' War.* Oxford: Clarendon Press, 1986.

Scribner, Robert W. "The Reformation as a Social Movement." In *The Urban Classes, the Nobility and the Reformation: Studies on the Social History of the Reformation in England and Germany*, edited by Wolfgang J. Mommsen, Peter Alter, and Robert W. Scribner, 49–79. Publications of the German Historical Institute London, 5. Stuttgart: Klett-Cotta, 1979. Also in Robert W. Scribner, *Popular Culture and Popular Movements in Reformation Germany*, 145–74. London and Ronceverte: Hambledon Press, 1987.

———. "Ritual and Reformation." In *The German People and the Reformation*, edited by R. Po-chia Hsia, 122–44. Ithaca: Cornell Univ. Press, 1988.

———. "Why was there no Reformation in Cologne?" *BIHR* 48 (1975): 217–41. Also in Robert W. Scribner, *Popular Culture and Popular Movements in Reformation Germany*, 217–41. London and Ronceverte: Hambledon Press, 1987.

Sea, Thomas F. "Imperial Cities and the Peasants' War in Germany." *CEH* 12 (1979): 3–37.

———. "The Swabian League and Government in the Holy Roman Empire of the Early Sixteenth Century." In *Aspects of Late Medieval Government and Society: Essays Presented to J. R. Lander*, edited by J. G. Rowe, 249–76. Toronto: Univ. of Toronto Press, 1986.

Sebiz, Melchior, Jr. "Appendix Chronologica." In *Straßburgischen Gymnasii christliches Jubelfest 1638 celebrirt und begangen*, 210–20. Strasbourg, 1641.

Seebaß, Gottfried. "Die Augsburger Kirchenordnungen von 1537 in ihrem historischen und theologischen Zusammenhang." In *Die Augsburger Kirchenordnung von 1537 und ihr Umfeld*, edited by Reinhard Schwarz, 33–58. SVRG, 196. Gütersloh: Gerd Mohn, 1988.

Sehling, Emil, ed. *Die evangelischen Kirchenordnungen des XVI. Jahrhunderts*. Vol. 11, pt. 1, *Franken*. Tübingen: J. C. B. Mohr (Paul Siebeck), 1961.

Seibt, Ferdinand. *Karl V.: Der Kaiser und die Reformation*. Berlin: Siedler, 1990.

Seidel, Karl Josef. *Frankreich und die deutschen Protestanten. Die Bemühungen um eine religiöse Konkordie und die französische Bündnispolitik in den Jahren 1534/35*. RST, 102. Münster in Westfalen: Aschendorff, 1970.

Sender, Clemens. "Die Chronik von Clemens Sender von den ältesten Zeiten der Stadt bis zum Jahre 1536." In *Augsburg*, vol. 4, 1–404. *Chroniken der deutschen Städte*, 23. Leipzig: S. Hirzel, 1894. Reprint. Göttingen: Vandehoeck & Ruprecht, 1966.

Seyboth, Adolph. *Das alte Straßburg vom 13. Jahrhundert bis zum Jahre 1870*. Strasbourg: J. H. Ed. Heitz, 1890.

Sieglerschmidt, Jörn. *Territorialstaat und Kirchenregiment: Studien zur Rechtsdogmatik des Kirchenpatronatsrechts im 15. und 16. Jahrhundert*. Forschungen zur kirchlichen Rechtsgeschichte und zum Kirchenrecht, 15. Cologne and Vienna: Böhlau, 1987.

Sieh-Burens, Katarina. *Oligarchie, Konfession und Politik im 16. Jahrhundert: Zur sozialen Verflechtung der Augsburger Bürgermeister und Stadtpfleger 1518–1618*. Schriften der Philosophischen Fakultät der Universität Augsburg, 29. Munich: Ernst Vögel, 1986.

Singer, Bruno. *Die Fürstenspiegel in Deutschland im Zeitalter des Humanismus und der Reformation*. Humanistische Bibliothek, ser. 1, vol. 34. Munich: W. Fink, 1981.

Skinner, Quentin. *The Foundations of Modern Political Thought*. 2 vols. Cambridge: Cambridge Univ. Press, 1978.

Sleidan, Johannes. *Sleidans Briefwechsel*. Edited by Hermann Baumgarten. Strasbourg: Karl J. Trübner, 1881.

———. *De Statu religionis et reipublicae Carolo V Caesare commentarii*. Strasbourg: Wendelin Rihel, 1555.

———. *The General History of the Reformation of the Church*. Translated by Edmund Bohun. London: Edward Jones, 1689.

———. *Joanni Sleidani de Statu religionis et reipublicae Carolo V Caesare Commentarii*.

Edited by Christian Carl Am Ende. Frankfurt am Main: Johann Gottlieb Boehme, 1785.

———. *Zwei Reden an Kaiser und Reich.* Edited by Eduard Böhmer. Bibliothek des Litterarischen Vereins in Stuttgart, 145. Tübingen: Litterarischer Verein in Stuttgart, 1879.

Smend, Rudolf. *Das Reichskammergericht: Geschichte und Verfassung.* Quellen und Studien zur Verfassungsgeschichte des Deutschen Reiches in Mittelalter und Neuzeit, 4, pt. 3. Weimar: Böhlau, 1911. Reprint. Aalen: Scientia Verlang, 1965.

Smirin, Moisej Mendelevich. *Die Volksreformation Thomas Müntzers und der große Bauernkrieg.* Translated by Hans Nichtweiss. 2d ed. Berlin: Dietz, 1956.

Sohm, Walther. *Die Schule Johann Sturms und die Kirche Straßburgs in ihrem gegenseitigen Verhältnis 1530–1581: Ein Beitrag zur Geschichte deutscher Reniassance.* Historische Bibliothek, 27. Munich and Berlin: R. Oldenbourg, 1912.

Specklin, Daniel. *Les collectanées.* Edited by Rodolphe Reuss. BSCMHA, 2d ser. 13 (1888): 157–360, nos. 600–1299; 14 (1889): 1–178, 201–404, nos. 1300–2561.

Spiegel, N. N., ed. "Johannes Timannus Amsterodamus und die Colloquien zu Worms und Regensburg 1540, 1541." *Zeitschrift für historische Theologie* 42 (1872): 36–49.

Spitz, Lewis W. *The Religious Renaissance of the German Humanists.* Cambridge, Mass.: Harvard Univ. Press, 1963.

Sprenger, Regina Maria. *Viglius van Aytta und seine Notizen über Beratungen am Reichskammergericht (1535–1537).* Gerard Noodt Instituut, Rechtshistorische reeks, 13. Nijmegen: Gerard Noodt Instituut, 1988.

Stafford, William S. *Domesticating the Clergy: the Inception of the Reformation in Strasbourg, 1522–1524.* American Academy of Religion Dissertation Series, 17. Missoula, Mont.: Scholars Press, 1976.

Stähelin, Ernst, ed. *Briefe und Akten zum Leben Oekolampads.* 2 vols. QFRG, 10, 19. Leipzig: M. Heinsius, 1927–34. Reprint. New York: Johnson, 1971.

———. "Le édition de 1522 du Defensor Pacis." *RPHR* 34 (1954): 209–22.

Stälin, Christoph Friedrich. *Wirtembergische Geschichte.* Pt. 4. Stuttgart: Cotta, 1870–73.

Stayer, James M. *Anabaptists and the Sword.* Rev. ed. Lawrence, Kans.: Coronado Press, 1976.

———. *The German Peasants' War and Anabaptist Community of Goods.* Montreal: McGill-Queen's Univ. Press, 1991.

Steglich, Wolfgang. "Die Reichstürkenhilfe in der Zeit Karls V." *Militärgeschichtliche Mitteilungen,* no. 1 (1972): 7–55.

———. "Die Stellung der evangelischen Reichsstände und Reichsstädte zu Karl V. zwischen Protestation und Konfession 1529/30. Ein Beitrag zur Vorgeschichte des Augsburgischen Glaubensbekenntnisses." *ARG* 62 (1971): 161–91.

Steiff, Karl, and Gebhard Mehring, eds. *Geschichtliche Lieder und Sprüche Württembergs.* Stuttgart: W. Kohlhammer, 1912.

Stein, Friedrich Alexander. *Jakob Sturm, Stettmeister von Straßburg: Ein Lebensbild aus der Zeit der Kirchenverbesserung in Deutschland.* Leipzig: F. A. Brockhaus, 1878.

Steinmetz, Max. "Die dritte Etappe der frühbürgerlichen Revolution. Der deutsche Bauernkrieg 1524 bis 1526." In *Der Bauernkrieg 1524–1526: Bauernkrieg und Reformation,* edited by Rainer Wohlfeil, 655–89. Munich: Nymphenburger Verlagshandlung, 1975.

———. "Reformation und Bauernkrieg—die deutsche frühbürgerliche Revolution." In *Die frühbürgerliche Revolution in Deutschland,* edited by Max Steinmetz, 9–30. Studienbibliothek DDR-Geschichtswissenschaft, 5. Berlin: Akademie Verlag, 1985.

Stephens, W. P. *The Holy Spirit in the Theology of Martin Bucer.* Cambridge: Cambridge Univ. Press, 1979.

Stokes, Francis G., ed. *The Letters of Obscure Men.* London: Chatto & Windus, 1909. Reprint. Philadelphia: Univ. of Pennsylvania Press, 1972.

Stolleis, Michael. *Pecunia nervus rerum: Zur Staatsfinanzierung der frühen Neuzeit.* Frankfurt am Main: Vittorio Klostermann, 1983.

Stoy, Stephan. *Erste Bündnisbestrebungen evangelischer Stände.* Jena: Gustav Fischer, 1888.

"Strassb[urgische]. Archiv-Chronik." In *Code historique et diplomatique de la Ville de Strasbourg,* edited by Louis Schnéegans, vol. 2, 131–220. Strasbourg: Silbermann, 1845–47.

Stratenwerth, Heide. *Die Reformation in der Stadt Osnabrück.* VIEG, 61. Wiesbaden: Franz Steiner, 1971.

Straub, Alexandre. "Notes généalogiques sur une ancien famille patricienne de Strasbourg [Schott]." *BSCMHA,* ser. 2, 9 (1872): 80–88.

Strauss, Gerald. "The Holy Roman Empire Revisited." *CEH* 11 (1978): 290–301.

———. *Law, Resistance, and the State: Opposition to Roman Law in Reformation Germany.* Princeton: Princeton Univ. Press, 1986.

———. *Luther's House of Learning: Indoctrination of the Young in the German Reformation.* Baltimore: Johns Hopkins Univ. Press, 1978.

———, ed. and trans. *Manifestations of Discontent in Germany on the Eve of the Reformation.* Bloomington: Indiana Univ. Press, 1971.

———. "Protestant Dogma and City Government: The Case of Nuremberg." *PP,* no. 36 (April 1967): 38–58.

———. *Sixteenth-Century Germany: Its Topography and Topographers.* Madison: Univ. of Wisconsin Press, 1959.

———. "Success and Failure in the German Reformation." *PP,* no. 67 (May 1975): 30–63.

Strickler, Johannes, ed. *Actensammlung zur Geschichte der schweizerischen Reformation im Anschluß an die gleichzeitigen eidgenössischen Abschiede.* 5 vols. Zurich: Meyer & Zeller, 1878–84. Reprint. Zurich: Theologischer Verlag, 1989.

Struick, J. E. A. L. *Gelre en Habsburg, 1492–1528.* Arnhem: Brouwer en Zoon, 1960.

Stupperich, Robert. *Der Humanismus und die Wiedervereinigung der Konfessionen.* SVRG, 160. Leipzig: Duncker & Humblot, 1936.

———. "L'influence de Bucer en Europe du Nord, de l'Est et en Europe centrale." In *Strasbourg au coeur religieux du XVIe siècle,* edited by Georges Livet, Marc Lienhard, and Jean Rott, 379–90. PSSARE, 12. Strasbourg: Librairie Istra, 1978.

———. "Die Reformatoren und das Tridentinum." *ARG* 47 (1956): 20–63.

Sturm, Caspar. *Das Wappenbuch des Reichsherolds Caspar Sturm.* Edited by Jürgen Arndt. Wappenbücher des Mittelalters, 1. Neustadt an der Aisch: Bauer & Raspe, 1984.

Sturm, Jacob. "Außzug aller gehaltener Reichs–Tage und Summarie, dabey beschrieben wie und waß uff einem jeden gehandelt worden vom Jahre 1427. biß ad annum 1517. inclusive." Edited by Jakob Wencker. In Philipp Knipschildt, *Tractatus politico-juridicus de juribus et privilegiis civitatum imperialium.* 3d ed. Strasbourg: Johann Beck, 1740.

Sturm, Jean. *Classicae epistolae sive scholae Argentinenses restitutae.* Edited by Jean Rott. Paris: Librairie E. Droz; Strasbourg: Éditions Fides, 1938.

———. *Ioannis Sturmii Consolatio ad senatum Argentinensem. De morte clarissimi et nobilissimi viri D. Iacobi Sturmij, odae etiam aliquae et epitaphia de eodem.* Strasbourg: Wendelin Rihel, 1553.

———. *Quarti Antipappi tres partes priores.* Neustadt an der Hardt: Matthias Hupfuff, 1580.

———. *Trostschrifft Joannis Sturmij an einen Ersamen Rhat der Statt Straßburg belangendt das leyd vnd tödtlichen abgang des Edlen vnd Ehrenvesten Herren, Herr Jacob Sturmen, newlich auß dem Latein verteutscht.* Strasbourg: Wendelin Rihel, 1554.

Tjernagel, Neelak Serawlook. *Henry VIII and the Lutherans: A Study in Anglo-Lutheran Relations from 1521 to 1547.* St. Louis: Concordia Publishing House, 1965.

Toepke, Gustav, ed. *Die Matrikel der Universität Heidelberg 1386–1662.* 3 vols. Heidelberg: C. Winter, 1884–93.

Tout, T. F. "Germany and the Empire." In *Cambridge Modern History,* edited by A. W. Ward, G. W. Prothero, and Stanley Leathes, vol. 1, *The Renaissance,* 288–328. Cambridge: Cambridge Univ. Press, 1903.

Tracy, James D. *The Politics of Erasmus: A Pacifist Intellectual and His Political Milieu.* Toronto: Univ. of Toronto Press, 1978.

Trausch, Jakob. "Straßburgische Chronik." In Jakob Trausch and Johann Wencker, *Les chroniques strasbourgeoises,* edited by Léon Dacheux. BSCMHA, 2d ser. 15 (1892): 3–207, nos. 2562–3237h.

Tribout de Morimbert, Henri. *La Réforme à Metz.* Vol. 1, *Le luthéranisme 1519–1552.* Annales de l'Est, no. 36. Nancy: Berger-Levrault, 1969.

Tyler, Royall. *The Emperor Charles the Fifth.* London: Allen & Unwin, 1956.

Ungerer, Edmund, ed. *Elsässische Hausaltertümer in Burg und Haus, Kloster und Kirche. Inventare vom Ausgang des Mittelalters bis zum dreißigjährigen Kriege aus Stadt und Bistum Straßburg.* 2 vols. QFKKEL, 2. Strasbourg: Karl J. Trübner, 1913–17.

Unruh, Georg Christoph von. "Die Wirksamkeit von Kaiser und Reich." In *Deutsche Verwaltungsgeschichte,* edited by Kurt G. A. Jeserich, Hans Pohl, and Georg-Christoph von Unruh, vol. 1:268–78. Stuttgart: Deutsche Verlagsanstalt, 1983.

Van Dülmen, Richard. *Reformation als Revolution: Soziale Bewegung und religiöser Radikalismus in der deutschen Reformation.* Munich: Deutscher Taschenbuch Verlag, 1977.

Van Durme, Maurice. *Antoon Perrenot, Bisschop van Utrecht, Kardinal van Granvella, Minister van Karel V en van Felips II (1517–1586).* Verhandelingen van de Koninklijke Vlaamse Academie voor Wetenschappen, Letteren en Schone Kunsten van Belgie, Klasse der Letteren, 15, pt. 8. Brussels: Palais der Academien, 1953.

Van Seggelen, A. "Erasme à Strasbourg." In *Erasme, l'Alsace, et son temps: Catalogue de l'exposition réalisée à la Bibliothèque nationale et universitaire de Strasbourg,* 21–24. PSSARE, collection "Recherches et Documents," 8. Strasbourg: Palais de l'Université, 1971.

Varrentrapp, Conrad. *Hermann von Wied und sein Reformationsversuch in Köln. Ein Beitrag zur deutschen Reformationsgeschichte.* Leipzig: Duncker & Humblot, 1878.

————, ed. "Zwei Briefe Wimpfelings." ZKiG 16 (1896): 286–93.

Vetter, Paul. *Die Religionsverhandlungen auf dem Reichstag zu Regensburg 1541.* Dissertation, Jena, 1889.

Vial, Eugène. "Jean Cleberger, marchand et banquier." *Revue d'histoire de Lyon* 11 (1912): 273–308.

Virck, Hans. "Lübeck und der Smalkaldische Bund im Jahre 1536." *Zeitschrift des Vereins für lübeckische Geschichte und Altertumskunde* 7 (1898): 23–51.

Virck, Hans, Otto Winckelmann, Harry Gerber, and Walter Friedensburg, eds. *Politische Correspondenz der Stadt Straßburg im Zeitalter der Reformation.* 5 vols. Strasbourg: Trübner, 1882–98; Heidelberg: Carl Winter, 1928–33.

Vögeli, Jörg. *Schriften zur Reformation in Konstanz 1519–1538.* Edited by Alfred Vögeli. 2 vols. in 3. SKRG, 39–41. Tübingen: Osiander; Basel: Basileia, 1970–73.

Vogelstein, Ingeborg. *Johann Sleidan's Commentaries: Vantage Point of a Second Generation Lutheran.* Lanham, Md.: University Press of America, 1986.

Vogler, Bernard. "Recrutement et carrière des pasteurs strasbourgeois aus XVIe siècle." RPHR 48 (1968): 151–74.

Vogler, Günter. "The Anabaptist Kingdom of Münster in the Tension between Anabaptism and Imperial Policy." In *Radical Tendencies in the Reformation: Di-*

vergent Perspectives, edited by Hans Hillerbrand, 99–116. SCSE, 9. Kirksville, Mo.: Sixteenth Century Journal Publishers, 1988.

―――. "Der deutsche Bauernkrieg und die Verhandlungen des Reichstags zu Speyer 1526." *ZfG* 23 (1975): 1396–1410.

―――. "Imperial City Nuremberg, 1524–1525: The Reform Movement in Transition." In *The German People and the Reformation*, edited by R. Po-chia Hsia, 33–49. Ithaca: Cornell Univ. Press, 1988.

Vogt, Wilhelm, ed. "Die Correspondenz des schwäbischen Bundeshauptmanns Ulrich Arzt von Augsburg a. d. J. 1524 und 1525." *Zeitschrift des Historischen Vereins für Schwaben und Neuburg* 6 (1879): 281–404; 7 (1880): 233–380; 9 (1882): 1–62; 10 (1883): 1–298.

Voigt, Johannes, ed. *Briefwechsel der berümtesten Gelehrten des Zeitalters der Reformation mit Herzog Albrecht von Preußen.* Königsberg: Borntrager, 1841.

Volk, Julius. "Zur Frage der Reichspolitik gegenüber dem Bauernkrieg." In *Staat und Persönlichkeit: Erich Brandenburg zum 60. Geburtstag dargebracht*, edited by Alfred Doren, 61–90. Leipzig: Dietrich'sche Verlagshandlung, 1928.

Wackernagel, Rudolf. *Geschichte der Stadt Basel.* 3 vols. in 4. Basel: Helbing & Lichtenhahn, 1907–24. Reprint. Basel: Helbing & Lichtenhahn, 1968.

Wagner, Johannes Volker. *Graf Wilhelm von Fürstenberg und die politisch-geistigen Mächte seiner Zeit, 1495–1547.* Pariser Historische Studien, 4. Stuttgart: Anton Hirsemann, 1966.

Waldeck, Oskar. "Die Publizistik des Smalkaldischen Krieges." *ARG* 7 (1909/10): 1–55; 8 (1910/11): 44–133.

Walder, Ernst. "Reformation und moderner Staat." In *450 Jahre Berner Reformation: Beiträge zur Geschichte der Berner Reformation und zu Niklaus Manuel*, edited by the Historischer Verein des Kantons Bern, 441–583. Bern: Historischer Verein des Kantons Bern, 1980.

Walter, Robert, ed. *Beatus Rhenanus, citoyen de Sélestat, ami d'Érasme. Anthologie de sa correspondance.* PSSARE, Collection "Grandes Publications," 27. Strasbourg: Oberlin, 1986.

Walther, Heinrich. "Bernhard Besserer und die Politik der Reichsstadt Ulm während der Reformationszeit." *Ulm und Oberschwaben* 27 (1930): 1–69.

Wartenberg, Günther. *Landesherrschaft und Reformation: Moritz von Sachsen und die albertinische Kirchenpolitik bis 1546.* Weimar: Hermann Böhlaus Nachfolger, 1988.

―――. "Die Politik des Kurfürsten Moritz von Sachsen gegenüber Frankreich zwischen 1548 und 1550." In *Deutschland und Frankreich in der frühen Neuzeit: Festschrift für Hermann Weber zum 65. Geburtstag*, edited by Heinz Duchhardt and Eberhard Schmitt, 71–102. Munich: R. Oldenbourg, 1987.

―――. "Zur Politik des Herzogs und Kurfürsten Moritz von Sachsen (1541–1553)." *Sächsische Heimatstimmen*, no. 4 (1987): 158–59.

Wattenbach, Wilhelm, ed. "Jacob Wimpfelings poetischer Dialog über Peter von Hagenbachs Tod." *ZGO* 22 (1869): 390–97.

Weber, Hermann. "Le traité de Chambord (1552)." In *Charles-Quint, le Rhin et la France. Droit savant et Droit pénal à l'époque de Charles-Quint*, 81–94. PSSARE, Collection "Recherches et Documents," 17. Strasbourg: Istra, 1973.

Weber, Wolfgang. *Priester der Clio. Historisch- sozialwissenschaftliche Studien zur Herkunft und Karriere deutscher Historiker und zur Geschichte der Geschichtswissenschaft 1800–1970.* Europäische Hochschulschriften, ser. 3, 216. Frankfurt am Main, Bern, and New York: Peter Lang, 1984.

Wehrmann, M., ed. "Vom Vorabend des Smalkaldischen Krieges. Zwei Berichte aus dem Juli 1546." *ARG* 2 (1905): 190–200.

Weiss, Charles, ed. *Papiers d'état du Cardinal de Granvelle d'après les manuscrits de la bibliothèque de Besançon*. 9 vols. Collection de documents inédits sur l'histoire de France, ser. 1, no. 19. Paris: Imprimerie royale, 1841–52.

Wencker, Jacob. *Collecta archivi et cancellarie iura*. Strasbourg: Treuttel & Würtz, 1715.

Wencker, Johann. *Supplément à la chronique de Wencker*. Edited by Léon Dacheux. BSCMHA, 2d ser. 15 (1892).

Wendel, François. *L'Église de Strasbourg, sa constitution et son organisation, 1532–1535*. Études d'histoire et de philosophie religieuses, 38. Paris: Presses Universitaires de France, 1942.

Weyrauch, Erdmann. *Konfessionelle Krise und soziale Stabilität: Das Interim in Straßburg (1548–1562)*. SFN, 7. Stuttgart: Klett-Cotta, 1978.

———. "Strasbourg et la Réforme en Allemagne du Sud." In *Strasbourg au coeur religieux du XVIe siècle*, edited by Georges Livet, Marc Lienhard, and Jean Rott, 347–68. PSSARE, 12. Strasbourg: Librairie Istra, 1978.

White, Hayden. *Metahistory: The Historical Imagination in Nineteenth-Century Europe*. Baltimore: Johns Hopkins University Press, 1973.

Wiesflecker, Hermann. *Kaiser Maximilian I.: Das Reich, Österreich und Europa an der Wende zur Neuzeit*. 5 vols. Munich: R. Oldenbourg, 1971–86.

Wille, Jakob, ed. "Briefe Jakob Sturms, Stettmeister von Straßburg." ZGO 33 (1880): 101–15.

———. *Philipp der Großmüthige von Hessen und die Restitution Ulrichs von Wirtemberg 1526–1535*. Tübingen: Laupp, 1882.

Williams, George H. *The Radical Reformation*. Philadelphia: Westminster Press, 1962.

Willoweit, Dietmar. "Das landesherrliche Kirchenregiment." In *Deutsche Verwaltungsgeschichte*, edited by Kurt G. A. Jeserich, Hans Pohl, and Georg-Christoph von Unruh, vol. 1, *Vom Spätmittelalter bis zum Ende des Reiches*, 360–69. Stuttgart: Deutsche Verlags-Anstalt, 1983.

Wimpheling, Jacob. *Apologia pro respublica christiana*. Pforzheim: Thomas Anshelm, 1506.

———. *Basilii magni de legendis antiquorum libris opusculum divinum*. Strasbourg: Matthias Hupfuff, 1507.

———. *Declamatio Philippi Beroaldi de tribus fratribus, ebrioso, scortatore et lusore. Germania Jacobi Wimpffelingi ad Rempublicam Argentinensem. Ad universitatem heydelbergensem Oratio Ja. Wimpfe. S. de annuntiatione angelica*. Strasbourg: Johannes Prüß, 1501.

———. *Divus Bernardus in symbolum apostolicum. Idem in orationem dominicam. Idem de fide christiana. Thomas Wolphius iunior in Psalmum benedicite*. Strasbourg: Matthias Schürer, 1507.

———. *Elegantiae maiores. Rhetorica eiusdem pueris utilissima. Multa invenies hic addita aliorum impressioni, multa castigata, et in ordinem longe faciliorem redacta*. N.p., [ca. 1493].

———. *Epistola excusatoria ad Suevos*. Strasbourg: Matthias Hupfuff, 1506.

———. *Epithoma Germanorum*. In *Hic subnota continentur: Vita M. Catonis, Sextus Arelius de vitis Caesarum, Benvenutus de eadem re, Philippi Beroaldi et Thomae Wolphii iunioris disceptatio de nomine imperatorio, Epithoma rerum Germanicarum usque ad nostra tempora*. Strasbourg: Johannes Prüß, 1505.

———. "Germania." In *Wimpfeling und Murner im Kampf um die ältere Geschichte des Elsasses. Ein Beitrag zur Charakteristik des deutschen Frühhumanismus*, edited by Emil von Borries. SWIEL. Heidelberg: Wissenschaftliches Institut der Elsaß-Lothringer im Reich, 1926.

———. *Guilhermus episcopus Parisiensis De collationibus et pluralitate ecclesiasticorum beneficiorum. Albertus magnus De adherendo soli deo. Sanctus Bonaventura ad fratres mendicantes, quales esse debeant erga praelatos et ecclesiarum rectores*. Strasbourg: Johannes Knobloch, 1507.

————. *De integritate libellus.* Strasbourg: Johannes Knobloch, 1505.

————. *De integritate libellus.* Strasbourg: Johannes Knobloch, 1506.

————. *Isidoneus germanicus ad R. D. Georgium de Gemmingen Spirensem prepositum Jacobi Vymphelingi Slestatini.* [Speyer: K. Hist, 1497].

————. *Opera Selecta.* Munich: Wilhelm Fink Verlag.

Vol. 1, *Jakob Wimpfelings Adolescentia,* edited by Otto Herding. 1965.

Vol. 2, *Jakob Wimpfeling/Beatus Rhenanus. Das Leben des Johannes Geiler von Kaysersberg,* edited by Otto Herding and Dieter Mertens. 1970.

Vol. 3, *Briefwechsel,* edited by Otto Herding and Dieter Mertens. 1990.

Winckelmann, Eduard, ed. *Urkundenbuch der Universität Heidelberg.* 2 vols. Heidelberg: Gustav Winter, 1886.

Winckelmann, Otto. "Der Anteil der deutschen Protestanten an den kirchlichen Reformbestrebungen in Metz bis 1543." *Jahrbuch der Gesellschaft für lothringische Geschichte und Altertumskunde* 9 (1897): 202–36.

————. *Das Fürsorgewesen der Stadt Straßburg vor und nach der Reformation bis zum Ausgang des sechzehnten Jahrhunderts: Ein Beitrag zur deutschen Kultur- und Wirtschaftsgeschichte.* 2 vols. QFRG, 5. Leipzig: M. Heinsius Nachfolger, 1922. Reprint. New York: Johnson Reprint Corporation, 1971.

————. *Der Schmalkaldische Bund 1530–1532 und der Nürnberger Religionsfriede.* Strasbourg: J. H. Ed. Heitz, 1892.

————, ed. "Straßburger Frauenbriefe des 16. Jahrhunderts." *Archiv für Kulturgeschichte* 2 (1904): 172–95.

————. "Straßburgs Verfassung und Verwaltung im 16. Jahrhundert." *ZGO* 57 (1905): 493–537, 600–639.

————. "Über die Bedeutung der Verträge von Kadan und Wien (1534–1535) für die deutschen Protestanten." *ZKiG* 11 (1890): 212–52.

Winterberg, Hans. *Die Schüler von Ulrich Zasius.* VKLBW, ser. B 18. Stuttgart: W. Kohlhammer, 1961.

Wittmer, Charles, and J. Charles Meyer, eds. *Le Livre de Bourgeoisie de la Ville de Strasbourg 1440–1530.* 3 vols. Strasbourg: Mairie de la Ville, 1948–55.

Wolfram, Herwig. "Gegenstände des Briefwechsels zwischen Ferdinand I. und seinen Geschwistern Karl V. und Maria von Ungarn." In *Beiträge zur neueren Geschichte Österreichs,* edited by Heinrich Fichtenau and Erich Zöller, 84–101. Veröffentlichungen des Instituts für Österreichische Geschichtsforschung, 20. Vienna, Graz, and Cologne: Böhlau, 1974.

Wolgast, Eike. *Die Wittenberger Theologie und die Politik der evangelischen Stände: Studien zu Luthers Gutachten in politischen Fragen.* QFRG, 47. Gütersloh: Gerd Mohn, 1977.

Wollbrett, Alphonse. "Notes sur le Duc Antoine de Lorraine vers 1525." In *La Guerre des Paysans 1525,* edited by Alphonse Wollbrett, 103–9. Saverne: Société d'Histoire et d'Archéologie de Saverne et Environs, 1975.

————. "Saverne-Lupstein dans la tourmente." In *La Guerre des Paysans 1525,* edited by Alphonse Wollbrett, 55–66. Saverne: Société d'Histoire et d'Archéologie de Saverne et Environs, 1975.

————. "Scherwiller-Châtenois et le Valle de Villé." In *La Guerre des Paysans 1525,* 89–92. Saverne: Société d'Histoire et d'Archéologie de Saverne et Environs, 1975.

Wunder, Gerd, ed. "Ein Verzeichnis des Straßburger Landgebiets aus dem Jahre 1516." *ZGO* 114 (1966): 61–65.

Yoder, John H. "'Les frères suisses.'" In *Strasbourg au coeur religieux du XVIe siècle,* edited by Georges Livet, Marc Lienhard, and Jean Rott, 491–99. PSSARE, 12. Strasbourg: Librairie Istra, 1978.

Zeller, Gaston. *La réunion de Metz à la France (1552–1648).* 2 vols. Publications de la Faculté des Lettres de l'Université de Strasbourg, 35–36. Paris: Société d'Édition "Les Belles Lettres," 1926.

————. "Valerand Poullain." *RA* 81 (1934): 339–51.

Ziegelbauer, Max. *Johannes Eck, Mann der Kirche im Zeitalter der Glaubensspaltung.* St. Ottilien: EOS Verlag, 1987.

Ziehen, Eduard. "'Frankfurter Anstand' und deutsch- evangelischer Reichsbund von Smalkalden 1539." *ZKiG* 59 (1940): 342–51.

Zophy, Jonathan W. *Patriarchal Politics and Christoph Kress (1484–1535) of Nuremberg.* Lewiston, N.Y.: Edward Mellen, 1992.

Zwingli, Huldrych. *Huldreich Zwinglis sämtliche Werke.* Edited by Emil Egli, Georg Finsler, Walther Köhler, and Oskar Farner. 24 vols. *Corpus Reformatorum,* 88– 101. Berlin: Schwetschke; Zurich: Verlag Berichthaus, 1905–91.

Index

Philip I (1515–60), duke of Pomerania-
Wolgast, 147, 190n.12, 191n.37,
319n.22
Philip II (1527–98), king of Spain
(r. 1556–98), 362, 363
Pico della Mirandola, Gianfrancesco
(1469–1533), humanist, 26
Pistoris, Johann, theologian, 39, 223
Pistoris, Simon (1489–1562), Saxon
jurist, 39
Platter, Thomas (Z), 116
Poland, kingdom: Smalkaldic League, 151
Polemics, 166
Pomerania, duchy, 173. *See also* Barnim
IX, duke of Pomerania-Stettin; Philip I,
duke of Pomerania-Wolgast
Poullain, Valérand (d. 1558), nobleman,
339, 351n.66
Prechter family (S), 340
Probst, Rudolph, 344
Provence, 150
Pruckner, Nikolaus, clergyman, 284n.53

Rabus, Ludwig (1524–92), clergyman (S),
338
Rambouillet, castle, 309
Ranke, Leopold von (1795–1886), 3–5, 7
Rastatt (Baden), 362
Ravensburg, free city: Smalkaldic War, 298
Rebstock family (S), 43n.3
Reformation: cities, 6; ecclesiastical
property, 162–70, 174; France, 158;
godly law, 164; North Germany,
252–54; territorial church, 170–72; free
cities, 6; communal, 7; historiography,
2–8; printing, 33
Reformation of Emperor Sigismund, 25
Regensburg Book, 210, 218, 223, 225,
239n.32
Regensburg, free city, 16, 236
Rehlinger, Wolfgang (d. 1557), merchant
and burgomaster (A), 88, 244n.121,
252, 307, 309–10, 324n.115, 340
Reinbolt, Matthis, electoral Saxon agent,
80
Renchen, Treaty of (1525), 42
Reuchlin, Johannes (1455–1522),
humanist, Pforzheim, 26, 29
Reutlingen, 150; Smalkaldic League,
190n.25, 191n.46
Rhenanus, Beatus (1485–1547), humanist,
Sélestat, 28

Rhine, river, 16; Lower Rhine, 16; Upper
Rhine, 12, 15–16, 124
Richard von Greiffenklau (1467–1531),
archbishop and elector of Trier
(r. 1512–31), 232
Ringmann ("Philesius"), Matthias
(1482–1511), called "Philesius,"
schoolmaster, St.-Dié, 27
Ritter, Gerhard, 5
Robespierre, Maximilien (1758–94), 7
Rodach meeting (June 1529), 70
Röder von Diersburg, Egenolf
(1475–1550), stettmeister (S), 73,
93n.92, 168, 339, 365
Rohrbach, Jäcklein, 40
Roman law, 167
Roman months. *See* Imperial taxation,
matricular levy
Rotwil, Hans Erhart von (d. ca. 1531),
magistrate (S), 91n.47
Roussel, Androuin, 176
Rublack, Hans-Christoph, 7
Rumler, Caspar (1563), magistrate (S),
352n.82
Rupert (1506–44), Count Palatine of
Zweibrücken, 190n.12
Rural revolts. *See Bundschuh*; Peasants'
War

Saarbrücken, 361
Sacramentarianism, 59, 62, 69–70, 73–75,
80, 85
Sailer, Gereon (d. 1563), city secretary
(A), 88, 219, 234, 252, 287n.117
Saint-Nicolas-de-Port, 361
Sale, Margarete von der, Hessian
noblewoman, 219, 261
Sastrow, Bartholomäus (1520–1603),
burgomaster of Stralsund, 330
Saverne, 40; Battle of (17 May 1525), 41
Savoy. *See* Emmanuel Philibert, duke of
Savoy
Saxony, duchy and electorate (Albertine).
See George, duke of Saxony; Moritz,
duke and elector of Saxony
Saxony, electorate and duchy (Ernestine):
ecclesiastical property, 171, 173;
restitution suits, 197n.150. *See also*
John, elector of Saxony; John Frederick,
elector of Saxony; Wettin dynasty
Schaller, Caspar, city secretary (B), 66,
99n.211

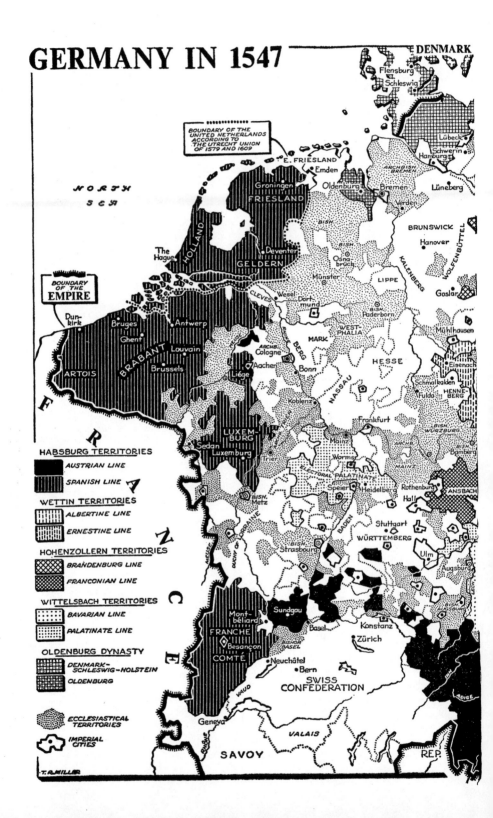

GERMANY IN 1547

BOUNDARY OF THE
UNITED NETHERLANDS
ACCORDING TO
THE UTRECHT UNION
OF 1579 AND 1609

BOUNDARY
OF THE
EMPIRE

DENMARK

Flensburg
Schleswig

Lübeck
Schwerin
Hamburg

NORTH
SEA

E. FRIESLAND
Emden

ARCHBISH.
BREMEN

Groningen
FRIESLAND

Oldenburg

Bremen

Lüneberg

Verden

BRUNSWICK

HOLLAND

The
Hague

Deventer

GELDERN

BISH.
Osna-
brück

Münster

Hanover

WOLFENBÜTTEL

KALENBERG

LIPPE

Goslar

Dunkirk

Bruges
Ghent

Antwerp

CLEVES

Wesel

Dort-
mund

BERG

BISH.
Paderborn

WEST-
PHALIA

Mühlhausen

BRABANT

Louvain

Brussels

Liége

ARCHB:
Cologne

Aachen

Bonn

MARK

NASSAU

HESSE

Eisenach

Schmalkalden

HENNE-
BERG

Fulda

ARTOIS

F
R
A
N
C
E

Koblenz

Frankfurt

BISH.
WÜRZBURG

LUXEM-
BURG

Sedan
Luxemburg

Trier

Mainz

ARCHB.
MAINZ

BISH.
Bamberg

Worms

Metz

BISH.
Metz

ELECTORAL PALATINATE

Speier
Heidelberg

Rothenburg

Hall

ANSBACH

DUCHY OF LORRAINE

Strasbourg

Stuttgart

WÜRTTEMBERG

BADEN

BISH.
STRASBOURG

Ulm

Augsburg

Mont-
béliard

FRANCHE

COMTÉ

Besançon

Neuchâtel

Bern

Sundgau

Basel

BISH.
BASEL

Konstanz

Zürich

BISH.
AUGSBURG

SWISS
CONFEDERATION

VAUD

Geneva

VALAIS

ADIGE

SAVOY

REP.

HABSBURG TERRITORIES

AUSTRIAN LINE

SPANISH LINE

WETTIN TERRITORIES

ALBERTINE LINE

ERNESTINE LINE

HOHENZOLLERN TERRITORIES

BRANDENBURG LINE

FRANCONIAN LINE

WITTELSBACH TERRITORIES

BAVARIAN LINE

PALATINATE LINE

OLDENBURG DYNASTY

DENMARK–
SCHLESWIG–HOLSTEIN

OLDENBURG

ECCLESIASTICAL
TERRITORIES

IMPERIAL
CITIES

T. R. MILLER